THE
POISON KING

ADRIENNE MAYOR

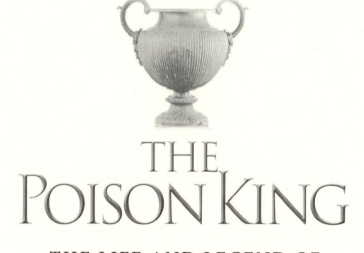

THE
POISON KING

THE LIFE AND LEGEND OF
MITHRADATES
ROME'S DEADLIEST ENEMY

PRINCETON UNIVERSITY PRESS

PRINCETON AND OXFORD

Library of Congress Cataloging-in-Publication Data
Mayor, Adrienne, 1946–
The Poison King : the life and legend of Mithradates,
Rome's deadliest enemy / Adrienne Mayor.
p. cm.
Includes bibliographical references and index.
ISBN 978-0-691-12683-8 (hardcover : alk. paper) 1. Mithridates VI Eupator, King of
Pontus, ca. 132–63 B.C. 2. Pontus—Kings and rulers—Biography. 3. Pontus—History.
4. Rome—History—Mithridatic Wars, 88–63 B.C. 5. Poisoning—Political aspects—
Rome—History. 6. Mediterranean Region—History, Military. 7. Black Sea Region—
History, Military. I. Title.
DS156.P8M39 2009
939'.33—dc22   2009015050

British Library Cataloging-in-Publication Data is available
This book has been composed in Minion Typeface
Printed on acid-free paper. ∞
press.princeton.edu

Printed in the United States of America

3   5   7   9   10   8   6   4

for Gerry

1941–2006

Que les Romains, pressés de l'un à l'autre bout,

Doutent où vous serez, et vous trouvent partout.

RACINE, *Mithridate*, 1673

❧ CONTENTS ❧

⚔ ILLUSTRATIONS ⚔

MAPS

⊰ DRAMATIS PERSONAE ⊱

Major figures in Mithradates' story
(other proper names are listed in the index)

ADOBOGIONA: Noble Galatian woman, rescued from poison banquet to become one of Mithradates' concubines.

AQUILLIUS: Rogue Roman official whose avarice led him to invade Mithradates' kingdom, beginning the First Mithradatic War; his greed was punished with molten gold.

ARCATHIUS: Mithradates' son by Laodice, brilliant cavalry commander, led vast barbarian army to liberate Greece in the First Mithradatic War.

ARCHELAUS: Tough Greek commander, Mithradates' star general in the liberation of Greece. Negotiated peace with Sulla, later joined Lucullus.

ARIATHES VI: Weak boy-king of Cappadocia controlled by his wife, Mithradates' sister, Laodice the Elder; he lost his life when he asserted himself.

ARIATHES VII: Mithradates' nephew and puppet ruler of Cappadocia. His defiance of his uncle cost him his life.

ARIATHES VIII: Doomed young pawn, set up as new king of Cappadocia by Nicomedes III.

ARIATHES IX: Mithradates' bastard son, established as king of Cappadocia.

ARISTONICUS: Heroic young rebel of Pergamon, led Anatolian revolt of the Sun Citizens against Roman rule when Mithradates was a boy.

ATHENION: Greek philosopher sent by Athenians to request Mithradates' liberation of Greece from Rome; elected commander in Athens to resist Sulla's siege.

ATTALUS III: Last king of Pergamon, eccentric recluse devoted to studying pharmacology. His will bequeathing his kingdom to Rome was contested by his son Aristonicus.

BACCHIDES: One of Mithradates' most trusted eunuch-advisers, assigned to save the royal harem from a fate worse than death at Roman hands.

BERENICE: Young woman from Chios whom Mithradates took into his harem, instead of condemning her with the rest of her people to slavery.

BITUITUS: Mithradates' faithful bodyguard, cavalry officer from Gaul; he remained with Mithradates until the very end.

CALLISTRATUS: Mithradates' secretary in charge of the king's papers, which may have included the formula for the *Mithridatium*; murdered by greedy Roman soldiers.

CASSIUS: Rogue Roman general who, along with Aquillius, Oppius, and Nicomedes IV, staged the disastrous, unauthorized invasion of Mithradates' kingdom.

CHAEREMON: Wealthy citizen of Nysa who aided the Romans; Mithradates offered a reward for his head.

CLEOPATRA THE ELDER: Mithradates' favorite daughter; at age sixteen she married Tigranes the Great and became queen of Armenia.

CYRUS THE GREAT: Founder of the vast Persian Empire; like Mithradates he fled as a youth to avoid assassination; served as a model for young Mithradates.

DAMOGORAS: Skilled Rhodian admiral allied with Rome, bested Mithradates in naval battle for Rhodes.

DARIUS I: Great Achaemenid conqueror of Persia; bestowed Mithradates' ancestral lands.

DARIUS III: Noble Persian emperor vanquished by Alexander the Great; Alexander's respect for Darius influenced Mithradates' vision of a new Greco-Persian golden age.

DORYLAUS: Orphaned boy of aristocratic Pontic family, raised as brother to Mithradates in the royal palace; friend and loyal commander in the Mithradatic Wars.

DRYPETINA: Devoted daughter of Mithradates; afflicted with double teeth.

FIMBRIA: Brutal Roman officer, overthrew his superior, Flaccus, and led his unruly legionnaires to ravage Anatolia; their lust for plunder undermined Lucullus's authority.

GORDIUS: Noble Cappadocian, Mithradates' friend, henchman, and special envoy.

HERMAEUS: Zoroastrian Magus, accompanied Mithradates to Kabeira, during war with Lucullus.

HYPSICRATEA: Valiant Amazon horsewoman-warrior from Caucasia; served as Mithradates' groom; she became his companion in battle and last true love.

KRATEUAS OF PERGAMON: Influential Greek herbalist, father of botanical illustration; Mithradates' fellow experimenter with antidotes and poisons.

LAODICE, QUEEN OF PONTUS: Mithradates' murderous mother, suspected of poisoning his father. Her attempts to do away with young Mithradates were later avenged.

LAODICE THE ELDER: Mithradates' oldest sister, regent of Cappadocia; thwarted her brother by marrying his enemy, Nicomedes III of Bithynia.

LAODICE THE YOUNGER: Mithradates' younger sister and his first wife; treacherous like her mother, Queen Laodice, she plotted against Mithradates.

LUCULLUS: Dogged, capable Roman general, Sulla's protégé; lost control of his troops and failed to destroy Mithradates and Tigranes in the Third Mithradatic War.

MACHARES: Mithradates' son by Laodice, viceroy of his father's Bosporan Kingdom in the Crimea; went over to Lucullus and paid with his life.

MARIUS: Great Roman populist leader, enemy of Sulla in Rome's Civil War; met Mithradates and vied for command of the First Mithradatic War.

METRODORUS THE ROME-HATER: Philosopher-statesman, invented memory and rhetorical techniques; Mithradates' speech writer and envoy.

METROPHANES: Mithradates' loyal Greek general throughout the Mithradatic Wars.

MITHRADATES CHRESTUS (The Good): Younger brother of Mithradates, lapdog of Queen Laodice. He did not live long.

MITHRADATES V EUERGETES: King of Pontus, Mithradates' father, philhellene of Persian ancestry; assassinated by poison when Mithradates was a boy.

MONIME: Intelligent Macedonian beauty from Stratonicea; Mithradates found her irresistible and agreed to her demand for the title of queen.

MURENA: Sulla's ambitious lieutenant; rashly began and lost the Second Mithradatic War.

NEOPTOLEMUS: Mithradates' Greek commander in Scythian, Greek, and Anatolian campaigns.

NICOMEDES III: Crafty king of Bithynia, allied briefly with Mithradates against Rome, then opposed Mithradates over Cappadocia.

NICOMEDES IV: Weak king of Bithynia; compelled by Roman legate Aquillius to invade Mithradates' kingdom without provocation, thus beginning the Mithradatic Wars.

NYSSA, ROXANA, and STATIRA: Mithradates' wretched younger sisters, imprisoned in a tower for life, to prevent their marriage and rival offspring.

OPPIUS: Rogue Roman general who, with Aquillius, Cassius, and Nicomedes IV, staged the disastrous invasion of Mithradates' kingdom.

PAPIAS: Mithradates' personal physician, worked closely with the botanist Krateuas.

PELOPIDAS: Greek philosopher-orator-ambassador in Mithradates' entourage.

PHARNACES: Mithradates' son and heir by Laodice; led a revolt against his father in the Bosporan Kingdom; made a deal with Pompey; ultimately crushed by Julius Caesar.

POMPEY THE GREAT: Roman general seeking glory; defeated Spartacus and Sertorius; took over Lucullus's failed command in the final Mithradatic War and brought it to a close.

SELEUCUS: Syrian pirate admiral of Cilicia, trusted friend of Mithradates.

SERTORIUS: Rebel Roman governor of Spain, commanded insurgent army of native Spaniards and Marius's exiled Populars; allied with Mithradates against Rome.

SPARTACUS: Thracian gladiator, led massive slave insurrection in Italy; may have planned to ally with Mithradates, who was encouraged by his revolt and saddened by his death.

STRATONICE: Harpist in Mithradates' court; became his lover and lady of Kabeira.

SULLA: Ruthless Roman patrician commander dispatched to avenge Mithradates' massacre of Romans and to recover Greece; destroyed Athens and won the First Mithradatic War.

TIGRANES II THE GREAT: Proud, inflexible Armenian monarch, amassed a vast Middle Eastern empire; Mithradates' close friend, son-in-law, and trusted ally.

XERXES: Great Persian king, fought Greeks at Thermopylae and Salamis; admired by Mithradates.

XIPHARES: Mithradates' son with Stratonice; he was killed to punish his mother.

⇐ TIME LINE ⇒

Some years are approximate

486 BC	Death of Darius I of Persia
323 BC	Death of Alexander the Great
202 BC	Hannibal defeated by Rome
190 BC	Antiochus the Great defeated by Rome
146 BC	Roman conquest of Greece, Corinth destroyed
135 BC	Spectacular comet coincides with conception/birth of Mithradates
134 BC	Probable birth year of Mithradates
133 BC	Attalus III of Pergamon wills his kingdom to Rome
133–129 BC	Aristonicus leads Anatolian Sun Citizens in revolt against Roman rule
120 BC	Mithradates V Euergetes assassinated by poison, second comet appearance; Mithradates VI crowned king of Pontus
119/118 BC	Mithradates goes into hiding to escape murderous plots of his mother
115/114 BC	Mithradates returns to Pontus, hailed as king; marries his sister Laodice, brings northern Black Sea and Scythia into realm
112–106 BC	Jugurthine War, Rome defeats Jugurtha
108 BC	Mithradates' extended reconnaissance mission in Anatolia
107–94 BC	Mithradates adds Colchis, western Armenia to Black Sea Empire, intervenes in Paphlagonia, Cappadocia, Galatia
96/94 BC	Mithradates forms alliance with his son-in-law, Tigranes of Armenia
91–89 BC	Social War, Italians revolt against Rome
89–85 BC	First Mithradatic War
89 BC	Nicomedes VI attacks Pontus at Rome's instigation. Mithradates sweeps to victory, liberating Anatolia, hailed as savior. Makes Monime his queen, Pergamon center of new empire

88–30 BC	Civil Wars in Rome
88 BC	Mithradates orders massacre of 80,000 Romans and Italians in Anatolia, executes the Roman legate Aquillius, who began the war in 89 BC
87 BC	Halley's Comet appears
88–85 BC	Mithradates' armies liberate and occupy Greece, Mithradates fails to take Rhodes. Sulla arrives to avenge the massacre and recover Greece
85 BC	First Mithradatic War ends in Rome's favor, Peace of Dardanus
83/81 BC	Sulla's lieutenant Murena attacks Mithradates, starting Second Mithradatic War; Mithradates is victorious
75 BC	Mithradates and Sertorius ally to make joint war on Rome
75/74 BC	Rome's puppet Nicomedes IV dies, wills Bithynia to Rome, igniting Third Mithradatic War
73–71 BC	Spartacus's gladiator-slave revolt in Italy
73–63 BC	Third Mithradatic War
73–70 BC	Lucullus is sent to destroy Mithradates. Meteorite interrupts battle in Bithynia; Mithradates besieges Cyzicus but Lucullus is victorious; Kabeira falls. Mithradates flees to Tigranes' Armenia, rebuilds army
69–68 BC	Lucullus crosses Euphrates, wins major victory over Tigranes and Mithradates, who escape. Lucullus loses control of his mutinous army
67 BC	Mithradates marches on Pontus, recovers his kingdom in major battle; meanwhile Pompey clears pirates from Mediterranean
66 BC	Pompey arrives in Pontus to replace Lucullus, deals Mithradates crushing blow in surprise moonlight battle, but Mithradates escapes with fugitive army into Colchis
65/64 BC	Mithradates evades Pompey, escaping over Caucasus Mountains to his Bosporan Kingdom, plans to invade Italy by land
63 BC	Earthquake jolts Bosporus. Mithradates' son Pharnaces stages coup. Mithradates commits suicide. Pompey declares victory, ending Mithradatic Wars
47 BC	Pharnaces tries to recover father's lost kingdom, invades Pontus. Crushed in short, brutal battle by Julius Caesar, who boasts *Veni Vidi Vici*

⊰ ACKNOWLEDGMENTS ⊱

I AM INDEBTED to my excellent editor at Princeton University Press, Rob Tempio, and the anonymous readers who offered valuable suggestions for improving the manuscript. I'm grateful for the early encouragement from Sam Elworthy, Kirsten Manges, Sam Popkin, Susan Shirk, and the LPG writers group of Princeton. Heartfelt gratitude goes to my agent Sandy Dijkstra and everyone at the agency. Valuable insights were offered at various stages by Murat Arslan, Glen Bowersock, David Braund, Deniz Burcu Erciyas, Tom Habinek, Toni Hayes, Bruce Hitchner, Jakob Munk Høtje, Henryk Jaronowski, Robert Keohane, John Ma, Brian McGing, Robert Proctor, John Ramsey, Walter Scheidel, John Strisino, Mehmet Tezcan, and Philip Wexler. I thank Jeffrey Bauman for helping to create the time line and dramatis personae, and Luca Grillo for help with translations. I'm grateful for Lauren Lepow's fine editorial guidance, Dimitri Karetnikov's eye for illustrations, Frank Mahood's pleasing text design and layout, and the proofreading wizardry of Barbara Mayor.

In 2008, a group dedicated to "our king" Mithradates, "the second Aleksandros of the World," was established on the Internet networking site Facebook, by Greek and Turkish people of Pontus. Mithradates has a growing presence on Facebook; as of this writing the group has more than four hundred international members. I thank the many friends of Mithradates Eupator on Facebook for unique perspectives and support.

Special thanks go to Peter van Alfen and Elena Stolyarik of the American Numismatic Society, and Dr. George Keremediev of the American Computer Museum, Bozeman, Montana. Artist Rubik Kocharian contributed his evocative painting of Mithradates and Tigranes the Great. Jakob Munk Høtje and Dick Osseman allowed me to use their photographs of Mithradatic archaeology in Turkey. My talented sister Michele Angel created the maps and two imaginative illustrations. Over the years, Christopher Duffin has provided photographs and literary evidence for *Mithridatium* and theriacs in medieval and early modern times. Hans Heiner Buhr of Tbilisi, Republic of Georgia, shared his photographs, paintings, and personal knowledge of the Caucasus Mountains. I'm grateful for thoughtful comments on early drafts by Ted Champlin, Ian Morris, Severo Perez, and Elaine Wise. I've profited from conversations with Kris Ellingsen, Deborah Gordon, and Barry Strauss, and from online research by N. S. Gill, K. Kris Hirst, David Meadows, and Tim Spalding. This book is dedicated to the memory of my dear friend Gerald Charles Olson. A man of bold intelligence, curiosity, and resilience, he would have enjoyed Mithradates' amazing tale. To three friends who read the entire manuscript and offered wise comments, my deep gratitude: Michelle Maskiell, Josh Ober, and Marcia Ober.

For research support, thanks go to Stephen Macedo and the Princeton University Center for Human Values; Denis Feeney and the Princeton Classics Department; and Anthony Grafton and the Princeton Humanities Council Old Dominion Fellows of 2005–6. Richard Martin and the Stanford Classics Department, and the History and Philosophy of Science and Technology Program, Stanford, have given me my first academic home. It was Ted Champlin of Princeton who first welcomed me as an independent scholar; I'm grateful for his friendship. I want to express my gratitude to Montana State University for the gift of an honorary doctorate in May 2007.

For Josiah, O Best Beloved, words are not enough—but a nomad's saying about friendship captures what I want to say: "Because he shared my burden when it threatened to slow my pace and kept by my side when we traveled lightly."

THE
POISON KING

Long ago and far away, in a little kingdom by the sea, a dazzling comet in the East foretold the birth of a remarkable Prince who would dare to make war on the mightiest empire. As an infant in his cradle, he was marked for greatness by lightning. While he was still a boy, enemies in the castle poisoned his father, the King. His own mother, the Queen, tried to do away with the Prince. But he escaped and lived like Robin Hood in the wilderness for seven years. He grew strong and brave and learned the secrets of poisons and antidotes. The Prince returned to his kingdom and killed the wicked Queen. He became a beloved King, ruling over many nations. When the powerful Empire across the sea invaded his realm, people from many lands joined his grand war. The battles against the Empire lasted his whole lifetime. Many beautiful queens sat by his side, but the King found true love with a woman as valiant in battle as he. When the King died, his passing was echoed by a terrible earthquake. For thousands of years afterward, the Great King's legendary deeds were remembered and retold.

I T SOUNDS like a fairy tale.[1] But add the documented facts and it's history. In about 120 BC, Mithradates VI Eupator the Great, king of Pontus, inherited a small but wealthy kingdom on the Black Sea (northeastern Turkey). Mithradates (Mithra-DAY-tees) is a Persian name meaning "sent by Mithra," the ancient Iranian Sun god. Two variant spellings were used in antiquity—Greek inscriptions favored *Mithradates*; the Romans preferred *Mithridates*. As a descendant of Persian royalty and of Alexander the Great, Mithradates saw himself bridging East and West and as the defender of the East against Roman domination. A complex leader of superb intelligence and fierce ambition, Mithradates boldly challenged the late Roman Republic, first with a shocking massacre and then in a series of wars that lasted nearly forty years.[2]

Poisoning was a traditional political weapon. Mithradates' father was murdered with poison, and Mithradates foiled several poison plots against himself. As a child, he dreamed of making himself immune to poisons. After hundreds of experiments, Mithradates unlocked the pharmacological paradox still studied today: poisons can be beneficial as well as lethal. Many believed that his special antidote was the reason for his celebrated vigor and longevity. After his death, Mithradates' trademarked elixir was imbibed by Roman emperors, Chinese mandarins, and European kings and queens, inspiring a flow of scientific treatises on the Poison King's mastery of toxicology. This is the first book to explain the inspiration and scientific principles underlying Mithradates' antidote.

Mithradates was an erudite patron of the arts and sciences. His military engineers built the first water-powered mill and technologically advanced siege engines. The cryptic Antikythera mechanism, the world's first computer, may have been one of Mithradates' prized possessions.

Recruiting vast, ethnically diverse armies from far-flung lands, Mithradates envisioned a powerful Black Sea Empire to rival Rome's might. He won magnificent victories and suffered devastating defeats in some of the most spectacular battles in antiquity. Luring the Romans deeper into hostile lands, Mithradates forced them to conquer and occupy the rich territory that they had intended only to plunder. Rome's best generals won battle after battle but were never able to lay their hands on the last "untamed" monarch to defy the Roman juggernaut. His followers revered him as the long-awaited savior of the East. The Romans called him the Eastern Hannibal.

Mithradates became a legend in his own time. After the long Mithradatic Wars, even the Romans developed a grudging admiration for their most relentless enemy. Mithradates enjoyed a colorful afterlife in art, music, and literature (see appendix 2). Medieval artists illustrated harrowing scenes from his reign, portraying him as a noble "Dark Knight" battling cruel Roman tyrants. Machiavelli praised him as a valiant hero; his reign fascinated Louis XIV. Immortalized in a tragedy by the great French playwright Racine, Mithradates and his doomed harem also inspired the fourteen-year-old Mozart to write his first opera. Poets celebrated the King of Poison: "I tell the tale that I heard told. Mithridates, he died old."[3] But even the details about Mithradates' last hours, death, and burial are shrouded in mystery.

For two millennia, Mithradates' extraordinary military and scientific achievements made him a household name, a major figure in the Roman Republic's all-star cast of characters, alongside Hannibal, Spartacus, Cleopatra, and Julius Caesar. Over the past half century, however, Mithradates' name and deeds began to fade from popular memory. Of all the nations that "came into mortal conflict with Rome," mourned one writer, "none is more utterly forgotten than the kingdom of Pontus. Her landmarks are uprooted, her temples fallen, and of her mightiest ruler there remain but distorted legends."[4]

But there are signs that Mithradates' star is rising again, as historians and archaeologists reconsider ancient struggles against imperialism, and as scientists revive the old dream of a universal antidote to toxic weapons. New crises ignite in many of the strategic lands where Mithradates once ruled, fought, and won allies, a list familiar from today's headlines: Greece, Turkey, Armenia, Ukraine, Russia, Crimea, Georgia, Chechnya, Azerbaijan, Syria, Kurdistan, Iran, Iraq. While researching Mithradates' astonishing feat of crossing the Caucasus Mountains to make his last stand in the Crimea, I pored over maps of this little-known yet historically important corner of the world. In August 2008, the Caucasus burst onto the world stage, as the Russian army attacked Georgia (ancient Colchis)—an independent former Soviet republic—over the contested regions of South Ossetia and Abkhazia. Invaders and refugees streamed over the very same rugged mountain pass traveled by Mithradates' fugitive army two thousand years ago.

Mithradates' name may be unfamiliar in the West today, but his reputation as a defender against imperialism was not forgotten in the East. "Everyone knows the history of the struggle between Rome and Mithridates," declared the great Russian historian Mikhail Rostovtzeff, and "everyone remembers that Mithradates made his last stand" in south Russia. In some former republics of the Soviet Union, Mithradates is still a local icon. For example, a Georgian biography of Mit'ridat appeared in 1965, and Russian novels about Tsar Mitridate Yevpatorus came out in 1993 and 2004. Between wars, sporadic scholarly and archaeological research takes place in Mithradates' Black Sea Empire. Considering the recent spate of political poisonings in Ukraine and Russia, there is black humor in the name of a bar in the king's old city of Pantikapaion (modern Kerch), daring you to order a drink in Mithradates' Place.[5]

In lands once allied with or ruled by Mithradates, he is recalled as a charismatic leader who resisted Western encroachment. In Armenia and Kurdistan, for example, many consider Mithradates (Mehrdad, Mirdad, Mhrtat) a national hero.[6] After a long period of ignoring Mithradates, Turkey is beginning to take an interest in the first ruler to unite and defend the diverse peoples of Anatolia against foreign invaders. In 2007, historian Murat Arslan published his dissertation *Mithradates VI Eupator, Roma'nin Büyük Düsmani* ("Rome's Great Enemy"), on the "ancient Anatolian hero, little known and neglected until today." Arslan likens Mithradates, in his defense of Anatolia against the Romans, to Alexander the Great saving Asia from the Persian Empire. The leading Turkish historian Sencer Sahin compares Mithradates to the Turkish national hero Atatürk, who successfully fought foreign invaders.[7]

ANCIENT SOURCES FOR MITHRADATES' LIFE

Nearly everything we know of Mithradates was written from his enemies' perspective, by the inheritors of Roman imperial culture who looked through a Roman lens eastward toward the expanding frontiers of the empire. The extant (and missing) ancient sources for Mithradates' life and times have been comprehensively evaluated by modern historians of the Roman world.[8] Of the fifty or so ancient texts that contributed details of Mithradates' life, our chief sources are Justin's summary of a lost history by Pompeius Trogus; Appian's *Mithradatic Wars*; Cassius Dio's history of Rome; Strabo's *Geography*; Memnon's fragmentary history of Heraclea on the Black Sea; Cicero's speeches; and Plutarch's lives of the Roman generals (Sulla, Lucullus, Pompey) who fought the Mithradatic Wars. Important material also appears in Pliny's *Natural History*, fragments of Sallust and Livy, and Diodorus of Sicily, Ammianus Marcellinus, Galen, and other Latin and Greek authors.

These ancient writers were able to consult the works of many other historians and a host of records, archives, living memories, and oral folklore, all irretrievable. Because the surviving texts were written from the vantage point of the victorious Roman Empire, outright and subtle biases were inevitable. To tell Mithradates' story from his own perspective, one would need to stand on the shores of the Black Sea and look, not just west toward Rome and Greece, but outward in all directions from Mithradates' kingdom and the allied lands that resisted Rome, lands with their own vital cultures and empires. This book takes up the challenge of trying to write from outside a Roman point of reference, to evoke a time before the imposing edifice of the triumphant Roman Empire.

As is often pointed out, certain foes of the Romans ended up more famous than their conquerors. Rome's fascination with its dangerous enemies, and admiration for their courage and ideals, produced a wealth of biographical material. Some Roman writers (Cicero, Tacitus, and Diodorus) were sharply critical of Rome's harsh imperialism and avarice. At least three sources (Strabo, Plutarch, and Trogus) had personal links to the Mithradatic Wars. They understood animosity toward the late Roman Republic and treated some aspects of Mithradates' life favorably. Regrettably, we cannot consult the lost accounts by Mithradates' contemporaries who were personally involved in the wars, such as Rutilius Rufus, Lucius Cornelius Sisenna, Lenaeus, Metrodorus, and Hypsicrates.[9]

Intriguing clues in ancient and medieval texts are now all that remain of a rich store of lively anecdotes that once circulated orally about Mithradates. Every scrap in the literary record is valuable—along with artistic, numismatic, epigraphical, and archaeological evidence, much of it only recently come to light. A surprising amount of material about Mithradates and his times can be pieced together, to form a flickering picture of his upbringing and education, influences and heroes, speeches and appeal to followers, military strategies, scientific experiments and leisure pursuits, love affairs, hopes and doubts, motivations, and his complex psychology—even the king's moods, jokes, and dreams were recorded.

HISTORICAL METHODS

The incomplete nature of the ancient record sometimes forces historians into the realm of guesswork. In such cases, the approach followed by the great detective Sherlock Holmes is appropriate. When compelled to rely on "guesswork," Holmes explained his method thus: We must "balance probabilities and choose the most likely. It is the scientific use of the imagination, but we have always some material basis on which to work."[10]

In piecing together a coherent historical narrative from "broken shards," to reconstruct missing elements that were taken for granted but not described in the ancient record, historians of antiquity draw on classical and modern knowledge to fill in background details of economy, cultural influences, climate, geography, topography, natural history, political alliances, and so on. Historical reconstruction is essential in retrieving a fully realized life of any ancient figure. In the endeavor to balance fidelity to history with fidelity to an individual from the past, however, character and motivations "cannot be completely and authentically represented or expressed in the domain of history" alone. To be faithful to Mithradates, the historical person we can never really know, one can apply "the scientific use of the imagination" to fill in the spaces between surviving accounts and contextual facts. This is especially apposite for Mithradates, a unique, atypical Hellenistic ruler.[11]

In recent years, historians have also introduced counterfactual, "virtual," or "what if" thought experiments as tools for understanding the meaning and ramifications of historical events, imagining alternative outcomes and filling in gaps. These techniques are not a modern invention. As early as the fifth century BC, for example, the Greek historian Herodotus and the playwright Euripides recounted alternative versions of the story of Helen of Troy, in which Helen never went to Troy but spent the entire war in Egypt. The Roman historian Livy asked what would have happened had Alexander the Great lived to invade Italy (Livy argued that Rome would have defeated him).[12]

John Lewis Gaddis's *Landscape of History* (2002) was influential in helping me map uncharted areas of Mithradates' life while maintaining historical fidelity. Gaddis also explains how scenario building allows historians to use their imaginations to revisit and replay the past, by asking in a disciplined way what might have happened under specific conditions.[13]

To narrate (and in a few cases to dramatize) Mithradates' story, I sometimes flesh out missing elements in the historical record, drawing on known facts, literary and archaeological evidence, comparable events, and probabilities. In these instances, I follow the widely accepted rules for disciplined alternative history, established in Niall Ferguson's *Virtual History* (2000): the details must be probable or plausible for Mithradates' time and place, and they must match contemporary experiences, derived from ancient literature, art, and history and/or archaeology. Phrases like "might have," "could have," and "perhaps" signal these passages, but I also clearly identify, in text or endnotes, all instances of my filling in gaps or dead ends, adding historically appropriate details, reconciling contradictory accounts, or proposing logical scenarios for how events could have unfolded. In proposing scenarios, I adhere to the known historical landmarks and "conditions of possibility" in the ancient sources. This approach differs significantly from historical fiction, in which novelists are free to contradict known facts and create new characters and conditions.[14]

MODERN VIEWS OF MITHRADATES AND HIS BLACK SEA EMPIRE

Despite his extraordinary achievements and role in the downfall of the Roman Republic, Mithradates has received remarkably little scholarly or popular attention. Théodore Reinach's magisterial *Mithridate Eupator, roi du Pont*, in French (1890) and German (1895), remains a great authority on Mithradates, despite its *Belle Epoch* outlook. Since Reinach, a great deal of new material—scientific studies, historical analyses, and archaeological evidence—has come to light to explain Mithradates' toxicological research, his rich afterlife, his Black Sea context, and his ambitions and accomplishments. *The Poison King* is the first full-scale biography of Mithradates, from birth to death and beyond, in well over a century.

The first work exclusively about Mithradates in English was a popular biography by the historical novelist Alfred Duggan: *He Died Old: Mithradates Eupator, King of Pontus* (1958). Duggan's references to "cringing Asiatics" and "red Indians" date the book drastically. A stereotyped image of Mithradates as a cruel, decadent "oriental sultan," an "Asiatic" enemy of culture and civilization, originated in the 1850s with the great Roman historian Theodor Mommsen. Lâtife Summerer's survey of Mithradates' reception in Europe draws attention to the racist assumptions of Mommsen, who compared Mithradates to Ottoman despots, and of Hermann Bengston, writing a century later, who declared that the massacre of 88 BC "could only be conceived in the brain of an Asiatic barbarian." As Summerer notes, Reinach, who praised Mithradates' intellect, claimed that his portraits revealed the "broad nostrils, thick lips, and fleshy chin of a self-indulgent oriental sultan," in contrast to the perfect profiles of classical Greeks. Mommsen's stereotype persists in, for example, Colleen McCullough's novel *The Grass Crown* (1991).

Michael Curtis Ford's 2004 novel *The Last King*, told from the point of view of Mithradates' son, portrays the king as a brilliant Greek commander. Mithradates makes an appearance as "an ambitious despot" from the East, "power hungry and ruthless," in Tom Holland's *Rubicon* (2003), and a military history by Philip Matyszak depicts Mithradates as savage and vindictive, "almost a monster," but magnificent in defeat.[15]

European scholars after Reinach have focused on specific aspects of Mithradates' reign. Brian McGing analyzes his propaganda and diplomacy in *The Foreign Policy of Mithridates VI Eupator* (1986). The campaigns against Mithradates from the Roman perspective are covered in the *Cambridge Ancient History,* volume 9 (Crook et al. 1994). Luis Ballesteros Pastor's *Mitridates Eupator, rey del Ponto* (1996) assessed Mithradates' conflicts with Rome as an independent Hellenistic monarch, and Attilio Mastrocinque's *Studi sulle guerre Mitridatiche* (1999) considered how ancient biases influenced modern views of the king.

The lands around the Black Sea are beginning to attract scholarly attention in their own right. Stephen Mitchell's two-volume *Anatolia*

(1993–95) was the first comprehensive study devoted to ancient Asia Minor. The Black Sea Trade Project (1996) of the University of Pennsylvania Museum of Archaeology and Anthropology used advanced archaeological techniques to explore ancient Sinope, the capital of Mithradates' kingdom. In 2006, archaeologist Gocha Tsetskhladze founded the interdisciplinary journal *Ancient West & East*. The Chinese Academy of Social Sciences Institute of History sponsors scholarship about Eurasia, defined as stretching from the Yellow Sea to the Danube. Deniz Burcu Erciyas (2006) surveyed Mithradatid archaeology around the Black Sea; Susan Alcock's "archaeology of memory" is uncovering the impact of Roman imperialism in Armenia; and a study of the impact of the Mithradatic Wars on civilians, by Toni Ñaco del Hoyo and colleagues, appeared in 2009. The Danish Centre for Black Sea Studies (founded in 2002) hosted an international conference of leading Mithradates scholars in 2007: the superb collection of papers, *Mithridates VI and the Pontic Kingdom,* was also published in 2009.[16]

For many readers, Mithradates' story may bring to mind current events in the Middle East, Transcaucasia, and former Soviet republics around the Black Sea. As a classical folklorist and a historian of ancient science, I first became fascinated by Mithradates' life and legend while researching unconventional warfare and the use of poisons in antiquity.[17] My initial research began in the shadow of the terrorist attack of September 11, 2001, on New York City and the Pentagon, masterminded by the charismatic Islamic leader Osama bin Laden, who eluded capture by disappearing into the mountains between Afghanistan and Pakistan. I began writing during the "war on terror" and invasion of Iraq in 2003, which President George W. Bush justified by a spurious *casus belli*, claiming that Saddam Hussein of Iraq not only possessed weapons of mass destruction but was protecting the terrorists responsible for 9/11. As of this writing, spring 2009, U.S. military forces have been unable to capture or kill Osama bin Laden and are still engaged in wars in Iraq and Afghanistan. Some parallels with Rome's decades-long failed mission to capture Mithradates have already been drawn by others.

Mithradates' blows against a Western superpower two thousand years ago have begun to recapture the attention of Western commentators and the supporters of Islamic insurgencies. As it has for two millennia, Mithradates' name continues to strike discordant notes. Italian journalists compared Osama bin Laden to Mithradates in 2003. In 2007, a classicist and conservative commentator, E. Christian Kopff, remarked that

"Rome suffered its own version of 9/11 in 88 BC," when Mithradates "massacred 80,000 Roman and Italian businessmen and traders and their families." Even though many Roman generals defeated Mithradates in battles, he "remained at large, a hero in the Near East," posing a threat to Rome's national interest as long as he lived.[18]

"The story of Rome and Mithridates is worth pondering today," notes Robert W. Merry, an expert on international economics. "Imperial expansion always breeds the likes of Mithridates in the far-flung reaches of the imperial domain." It was the decades of inconclusive wars in the Near East to crush Mithradates and his followers, remarked Merry, that ushered in the "internal chaos and violence" which would end the four-hundred-year-old Roman Republic.[19]

Islamicists and their sympathizers often cast their resistance to Western superpowers in terms of resistance to "Rumieh," the Arabic name for ancient Rome. The former Indian ambassador to Turkey, Azerbaijan, and Jordan, K. Gajendra Singh, sees "echoes of Mithradates" in the Iraq War. He maintains that Western hegemony in the Middle East began when the Roman army first invaded Anatolia. Since then, says Singh, the West has "demonized Mithradates VI of Pontus for standing up to Rome." In Singh's view, the West exploits Mideast oil resources "with the connivance of client rulers" just as the Roman Empire "ruthlessly exploited and taxed their subjects in Asia."[20]

Striking parallels between current world crises and the Mithradatic Wars arose during the completion of this book. The resurgence of piracy on the high seas, as Somalian pirates captured international oil tankers and held them for ransom, recalls the powerful pirate fleets of the first century BC, allies of Mithradates. Piracy thrives when authority is disputed and superpowers are distracted. Rome, contending with civil uprisings and provincial revolts as well as with Mithradates' challenges, was severely hindered by the pirates infesting the Black Sea and Mediterranean.

The global economic collapse of 2008/9 bears striking similarities to the financial catastrophe that Rome suffered when Mithradates invaded Rome's Province of Asia and wiped out the Roman presence there in 88 BC. As the great statesman Cicero explained, when so many thousands of "investors lost large fortunes, there was a collapse of credit at Rome, because repayments were interrupted. It is impossible for many individuals in a single state to lose their property and fortunes without involving still greater numbers in their ruin."[21]

MITHRADATES' SIDE OF THE STORY

Extreme, charismatic personalities have always attracted popular fascination. In explaining the magnetism of the "Bad Men of antiquity" (and
modernity), Edward Champlin, biographer of two Roman emperors
with notoriously negative press, Nero and Tiberius, cites a fundamental
truth: those considered heroes are not always good human beings. [22]
Many revered historical figures perpetrated deplorable acts. And even
ultimate failure need not tarnish heroic status; nobility in defeat can win
glory.

Combining the history of science, military history, and biography, I
tell a tale of genius, charisma, and idealism ultimately destroyed by a
powerful empire that could tolerate no rival. Capable of savage acts as
well as gallant compassion, Mithradates embodied paradox. He was a
Persian monarch who idealized democratic Greece and despised the
Romans as uncivilized barbarians. The typical view of classical antiquity
pits the civilized West (Greece, Rome) against the barbarian East (Persia).[23] Mithradates' dream was to unite the great cultures of Greece and
the East to resist the seemingly unstoppable tide of the Roman Empire.
In this romantic goal—and against impossible odds—Mithradates carried forward Alexander's vision of a new, diverse Greco-Asian empire for
more than half a century.

My goal is to render a three-dimensional, holistic portrait of Mithradates and his world, and to try to explain his complex legacy. An articulate and erudite philhellene, admirer of Alexander the Great, and proud
heir of Cyrus and Darius of Persia, he was a courageous warrior, brilliant
strategist, devious poisoner, daring gambler, scientific researcher, avid
lover, unpredictable parent, connoisseur of art and theater, escape artist,
sometime terrorist, and relentless nemesis of the Roman Empire. Mithradates' vital afterlife in art, music, literature, and science is an important
part of the story. This is the first biography to take account of the popular
lore that surrounded Mithradates from his birth to the present day. To
illuminate his life and the legend, I've drawn on the widest possible range
of sources, from antiquity to international modern scholarship, and from
the most recent numismatic, archaeological, epigraphical, and pharmacological discoveries to medieval chronicles, Gothic folklore, European
tragedies, operas, modern fiction, and poetry.

Like the paradoxical toxins and antidotes he sought to control, Mithradates was a double-edged sword: corrosive of the predatory Roman Re-

public and protector of Rome's intended prey. In the end, the Romans emerged victorious. Yet Mithradates proved to the world that the new Roman Empire was not invincible. He forced the Romans to conquer and occupy the Mideast, a perpetual trouble spot for them. His popular cause led Rome to rethink its imperial policies. The long pursuit of this formidable enemy coincided with the death of the old Roman ideals of honor and freedom. Mithradates helped define for the ancients the limits of violent resistance and prepared the way for new methods of grappling with tyranny in the transition from Republic to Empire, from BC to AD.

Mithradates' story is well worth our attention. Modern parallels may sharpen our interest. But as the curious reader delves deeper into the ancient narratives, one is swept away by the sheer audacity, the epic defiance, the chiaroscuro effect of treachery and revenge set against compassion and idealism, the noble dreams and dreadful nightmares, and the tantalizing unsolved mysteries. Mithradates' incredible saga is a rollicking good story.

1

Kill Them All, and Let the Gods
Sort Them Out

Iν SPRING of 88 BC, in dozens of cities across Anatolia (Asia Minor, modern Turkey), sworn enemies of Rome joined a secret plot. On an appointed day in one month's time, they vowed to kill every Roman man, woman, and child in their territories.

The conspiracy was masterminded by King Mithradates the Great, who communicated secretly with numerous local leaders in Rome's new Province of Asia. ("Asia" at this time referred to lands from the eastern Aegean to India; Rome's Province of Asia encompassed western Turkey.) How Mithradates kept the plot secret remains one of the great intelligence mysteries of antiquity. The conspirators promised to round up and slay all the Romans and Italians living in their towns, including women and children and slaves of Italian descent. They agreed to confiscate the Romans' property and throw the bodies out to the dogs and crows. Anyone who tried to warn or protect Romans or bury their bodies was to be harshly punished. Slaves who spoke languages other than Latin would be spared, and those who joined in the killing of their masters would be rewarded. People who murdered Roman moneylenders would have their debts canceled. Bounties were offered to informers and killers of Romans in hiding.[1]

The deadly plot worked perfectly. According to several ancient historians, at least 80,000—perhaps as many as 150,000—Roman and Italian residents of Anatolia and Aegean islands were massacred on that day. The figures are shocking—perhaps exaggerated—but not unrealistic. Exact population figures for the first century BC are not known. But great numbers of Italian merchants and new Roman citizens had swarmed to recently conquered lands as Rome expanded its empire in the late Republic. Details of the bloody attack were recorded by the Roman historian

FIG. 1.1. Mithradates the Great, silver tetradrachm, 86–85 BC. Bibliothèque National de France.

Appian, whose figures were based in part on the memoirs of Cornelius Sulla, the Roman general dispatched by the Senate to avenge the killings. Other details emerged from accounts of eyewitnesses and survivors, such as P. Rutilius Rufus, a Roman official who escaped and wrote a history of the attack and its aftermath. More facts came from enemy combatants and communiqués captured by Sulla in the war that erupted after the massacre. Ancient statistics often represent guesswork or exaggeration. Even if the lower death toll of 80,000 was inflated, as some scholars believe, and if we reduce the count of the dead by half, the slaughter of unsuspecting innocents was staggering. The extent of the massacre is not in doubt: modern historians agree with the ancient sources that virtually all Roman and Italian residents of Provincia Asia were wiped out.[2]

The plan was meticulously synchronized, and it was carried out with ferocity. As the fateful day dawned, mobs tore down Roman statues and inscriptions that had been erected in their public squares. We have vivid accounts of what happened next from five of the numerous cities where Romans were slain.

Pergamon, a prosperous city in western Anatolia, was fabled to have been founded by Hercules' son. Like many Hellenistic cities populated by Greeks who intermarried with indigenous people, Pergamon after Alexander the Great's death (323 BC) had evolved a hybrid of democracy and Persian-influenced monarchy. The cultural center of Asia Minor, Pergamon boasted a vast library of 200,000 scrolls, a spectacular 10,000-seat theater, and a monumental Great Altar decorated with sculptures

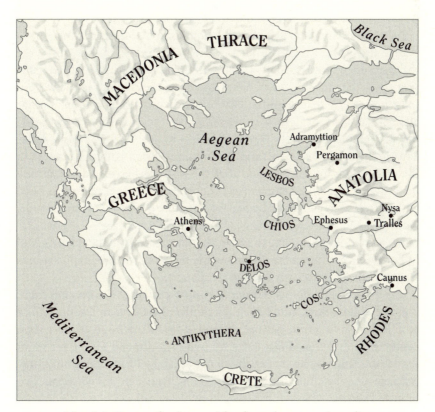

MAP 1.1. Greece, the Aegean Islands, and western Anatolia.
Map by Michele Angel.

of the Olympian gods defeating the Giants. People came from all around the Mediterranean seeking cures at the famous Temple of Asclepius, god of medicine. The Romans had chosen Pergamon to be the capital of their new province. But by 88 BC, most of western Asia was allied with King Mithradates, who had taken over the royal palace in Pergamon for his own headquarters.[3]

When the violence began that day in Pergamon, thousands of terrified Roman families fled out of the city gates to the Temple of Asclepius. By ancient Greek custom, all temples were sacred, inviolable spaces, havens from war and violence, under the protection of the gods. Under the right of asylum (*asylia*), anyone—citizen, foreigner, slave, innocent or guilty—could find refuge inside a temple. Pursuers usually dared not commit the sacrilege of murder before the gods. But on this day, there was no mercy for the people crowding around the statues of the healing god. The Pergamenes burst into the sanctuary and shot down the trapped men, women, and children in cold blood, at close range with arrows.

Meanwhile, as night fell in *Adramyttion,* a shipbuilding port, the townspeople drove the Roman settlers down to the seashore. The desperate throng plunged into the dark water. The killers waded in after them, cutting down the men and women and drowning the children in the waves.

In *Ephesus,* a cosmopolitan city of nearly a quarter million, similar atrocities defiled the Temple of Artemis. The Ephesians took great pride in their temple, one of the Seven Wonders of the Ancient World. Amazons had worshipped here, and the fabulously rich King Croesus built the original temple. It was said that the goddess herself had magically lifted the colossal lintel stone over the entrance. The sanctuary was filled with priceless treasures dedicated to Artemis, protector of supplicants. Known as Diana to the Romans, Cybele or Anahit in the Near East, Artemis was honored by Greeks and barbarians alike. When Paul preached in Ephesus a century after the massacre, he acknowledged that Artemis was still "the goddess worshipped by all Asia."[4]

The Temple of Artemis claimed the most ancient tradition of asylum. The Ephesians liked to tell how Alexander the Great had visited their temple and, in a grand gesture, extended its radius of protection. Two centuries later, King Mithradates himself had climbed onto the roof of the temple and declared that the new boundary of asylum would now reach as far as he could shoot an arrow (his arrow flew a *stade*, about two hundred yards).

Everyone in the Greek world understood that murder in a sacred place was taboo. In fact, the citizens of at least one community allied with

FIG. 1.2. Temple of Artemis, Ephesus, site of massacre of Romans, ordered by
Mithradates in 88 BC. Andre Castaigne, 1897.

Mithradates, the island of Cos, spared the Roman families who huddled
inside the temple on the day of the massacre. When townspeople began
smashing statues in Ephesus, the Romans naturally fled to the great

Temple of Artemis. But the Ephesians violated the hallowed tradition of sanctuary. Charging through the temple's carved cypress doors, they chopped down the suppliants as they clung to statues of the goddess.[5]

Farther south, in the port of *Caunus*, the bloodbath continued. Famed for delicious figs, Caunus was also notorious for its unhealthy salt marshes. At the time of the massacre, Caunus's main exports were salt and slaves for the Romans. The town had long been the butt of jokes about the greenish skin of the malaria-ridden populace, whose summer fevers were attributed to their eating too many of the famous figs. The city's dismal reputation continued into the Byzantine era. "Those wretched Caunians!" railed an early Christian orator. "When did they ever produce a worthwhile citizen? All their misfortunes are due to their extreme folly and rascality."

In 167 BC, the Romans had "liberated" Caunus from the powerful island of Rhodes. Yet in 88 BC, the citizens of Caunus were especially savage. On the day of the attack, the resident Italians clustered around a Roman statue of Vesta, the goddess who protected families and guaranteed Rome's survival. The Caunians pursued them, grabbed the children and killed them in front of their parents, then slaughtered the screaming women. They cut down the men last, heaping their bodies atop their families.

Tralles, a wealthy trading town known for fields of colorful snapdragons and heliotrope, had long resisted Rome. In retaliation, the Roman Senate had taken away the city's privilege of minting coins. When the citizens received Mithradates' secret missive, they dithered, worried about bloodguilt. The assembly voted to hire someone else to do the dirty work, a thug named Theophilus from Paphlagonia, a region famed for fine horses but stereotyped as the home of truculent, superstitious rubes. On the appointed day, Theophilus and his gang rode into Tralles, wearing wicker helmets and high leather boots, armed with scimitars. They herded the Italians inside the Temple of Concord, built by the Romans themselves and dedicated to peace. Survivors were haunted by the image of the attackers slashing at the victims' hands, which were left clutching the sacred statues.[6]

Similar scenes took place in many other towns allied with Mithradates. We know, for example, that Romans were killed on the island of Chios, because Mithradates later accused the Chians of not sharing confiscated Roman property with him. At Nysa, east of Tralles, ancient inscriptions indicate that resident Italians were murdered in the Temple of Zeus.[7]

"Such was the awful fate that befell the Romans and Italians of Asia," wrote the historian Appian, "men, women, and children, their freedmen and slaves of Italian origin." Five hundred years later, the butchery was still an icon of horror. At the twilight of the Roman Empire, as Vandals and Goths swept across North Africa, Saint Augustine (b. AD 354 in what is now Algeria) described the terrible catastrophes that the Romans had suffered when they were still pagans. He recalled that "disastrous day when Mithradates, king of Asia, ordered that all Roman citizens residing anywhere in Asia—where great numbers were engaged in business—should be put to death." "Imagine the miserable spectacle," continued Augustine, "as each person was suddenly and treacherously murdered wherever he or she happened to be, in bed or at table, in the fields or in the streets, in markets or in temples! Think of the tears and groans of the dying." Indeed, Augustine exclaimed, "we should even pity the executioners themselves, for just as the slain were pierced in body, the killers were wounded in spirit. What cruel necessity," he asked, "compelled these ordinary people to suddenly change from bland neighbors into ruthless murderers?"[8]

Who were the killers? Historians had long assumed that the lowest "rabble" must have carried out the slaughter. But a close reading of the ancient sources now leads scholars to conclude that ordinary people of all classes, ethnic groups, and walks of life participated in the popular coalition to wipe out Romans. The killers were indigenous Anatolians, Greeks, and Jews reacting to Rome's harsh rule and corrupt system of taxation, which threw individuals and entire cities into deep debt. In 88 BC, Mithradates' opposition to Rome appealed to wealthy and poor alike. Even if the death toll was lower than the 80,000 to 150,000 reported in antiquity, the massacre's message was stark. As Appian wrote in his account of the Mithradatic Wars, the atrocities made it very plain how deeply the Roman Republic was detested for its rapacious policies. Contemporary Romans acknowledged the reasons for the attack. In Asia, warned the great statesman Cicero, "the Roman name is held in loathing, and Roman tributes, tithes, and taxes are instruments of death."[9]

The Italian settlers, with their households and slaves, "wove themselves into the fabric of these Anatolian cities, achieving economic power and political position." By 88 BC, a large population of Roman merchants, moneylenders, tax collectors, slave traders, entrepreneurs, shopkeepers, and others lived among the Greco-Asians as neighbors. Many of the new settlers had acquired their land from native people bankrupted by Roman taxation. The Romans spoke Latin or Italian dialects among themselves but bargained in Greek in the marketplace. They bet on the cockfights, prayed in the temples, and laughed and cried in the theater. Yet they did not blend in. Their clothing and customs were different. Everyone knew who the Romans were. As historian Susan Alcock points out: "They knew where they lived. And they displayed every sign of hating their guts."[10]

Slavery was salt in the wound. Although many Greeks kept slaves, the massive Roman demand for slave labor clashed with the inclusive melding of democratic traditions and indigenous monarchies of Anatolia. Slavery was forbidden by ancient Persian law and religion. The Romans preferred to enslave non-Italians, especially people from the Near East. There was a seemingly endless supply of prisoners of war from the empire's advancing frontiers, and pirates prowled the Black Sea and eastern Aegean seeking human booty to sell to the masters of the Mediterranean world. It was said that as many as ten thousand captive people from around the Black Sea and the Near East might be traded in one day at the great Roman slave market on the once-sacred island of Delos. Crushing taxes were another form of servitude, forcing even the wealthy into debt and compelling some families to sell their children into slavery. A typical elite Roman owned several hundred slaves; a craftsman two or three. According to the latest estimates, there were roughly 1.5 million slaves in Italy at this time. The ratio of slaves was higher in the Roman Province of Asia. In Pergamon, for example, slaves made up about one-third of the population.[11]

Most of those held in bondage spoke non-Italian tongues, but even without the marker of language it was easy to recognize slaves. Many had Latin words crudely tattooed across their foreheads identifying them as Roman property. Slaves (and salt) were commodities subject to Roman duty taxes. According to a legal inscription of this period found in Ephesus, imported slaves were to be tattooed with the words "tax paid." (During the later Empire, "Stop me, I'm a runaway" was another motto that Roman masters etched on the brows of slaves.)[12]

A few years before the massacre, the Romans had punished the Ephesians for protecting a fugitive slave who had taken refuge in the Temple of Artemis. The Ephesians (who believed they were the descendants of one thousand runaway Greek slaves) had prevented a Roman official from entering the temple to retrieve his property, perhaps a local man enslaved for debt. In the inscribed records of cures that people sought at temples of Asclepius, archaeologists have found the names of slaves who prayed to the healing god to remove their forehead tattoos. Runaways often wore pirate-style bandanas to hide the marks of their bondage;

others attempted to remove the tattoos with caustic salves. After the massacre, about six thousand liberated slaves joined Mithradates' cause, swelling his army with highly motivated fighting men filled with hatred for Romans.[13]

As word of the attacks of 88 BC spread, mercenary soldiers commanded by Roman officers in the East deserted en masse. The Roman navy, manned by Greek sailors stationed in the Black Sea, went over to Mithradates, bringing hundreds of warships to his cause. And the complicity of each murderous city—the entire populace—was now sealed in blood. Mithradates' master plan ensured what scholars of international relations call "credible commitment." In diplomatic stare-downs and in warfare, one side can reinforce its strategic position by deliberately cutting off its own options, thereby making its threats more believable. All Roman Asia was now credibly committed to war on Rome.

Back in Italy, the reaction was shock, outrage, fear. Mithradates' timing was unerring. Violent civil war was erupting in Italy; the Roman losses in Asia precipitated a massive financial crisis in Rome. A series of awful portents had terrified the city. Out of a clear blue sky, a celestial trumpet blared out a long, mournful note. Etruscan soothsayers (traditional interpreters of divine messages) declared that it heralded the end of an age and the advent of a new world order. Halley's Comet (as we now call it) appeared, another dreadful portent. The Senate declared Mithradates Rome's most dangerous enemy and dispatched the ruthless general Sulla on a search-and-destroy mission.[14]

The massacre of 88 BC was unique, even in that blood-soaked era. It did not occur in towns at war, nor was it a rampage by soldiers in the aftershock of battle. In no other episode in antiquity was ordinary people's killing of so many specifically targeted civilians so painstakingly planned in advance. No other ancient terror attack featured simultaneous strikes in so many cities.[15] The indigenous revolt in Roman Britain led by the warrior queen Boudicca is sometimes compared to the massacre of 88 BC. Her uprising in AD 59 culminated in the slaughter of about seventy thousand Romans and British sympathizers, but those killings were spontaneous, not planned and methodical. (See box 1.1 to compare mass killings and deaths in natural disasters in antiquity and modern times.)[16]

Genocide is a charged concept, but it seems fair to cast the carnage of 88 BC as genocidal. Genocide, defined by the United Nations in 1948, specifies killing or maiming with intent to destroy, in whole or in part, a national, ethnic, racial, or religious group. Mithradates' intent to exterminate Romans living in Anatolia was explicitly based on language and

BOX 1.1

COMPARISON OF ESTIMATED DEATH TOLLS OF SOME NATURAL DISASTERS
AND MASS KILLINGS, ANTIQUITY TO PRESENT

Plague at Athens, beginning of Peloponnesian War, 430–428 BC: about 75,000 dead

Boudicca's revolt in Roman Britain, AD 59: about 70,000 dead

Nazi Germany's genocide against European Jews, 1940–45: 6,000,000 dead

U.S. atom bombs dropped on Japan, 1945: 80,000 killed by initial blast at Hiroshima; 40,000 killed by initial blast in Nagasaki (death tolls doubled in ensuring months)

Pol Pot's Khmer Rouge death toll, Cambodia, 1976–79: 750,000 to 1.7 million dead

Saddam Hussein's attacks on Kurdish villages, northern Iraq, 1988: about 50,000 dead

Serbian slaughter of Muslims in Bosnia, July 1995: about 8,000 dead

Hutu massacre of Tutsi, Rwanda, 1994: 800,000 dead in 100 days, about 8,000 per day

Al Qaeda attack on World Trade Center, New York City, and Pentagon, Washington, DC, September 11, 2001: nearly 3,000 dead

Tsunami, Indian Ocean, December 2004: 174,000 dead

Earthquake, Pakistan and India, October 8, 2005: 73,000 dead

Cyclone Nargis and floods, Burma/Myanmar, May 2008: about 100,000 dead or missing

Earthquake and aftershocks, China, May–June 2008: more than 68,000 dead

ethnic origin. His goal was the elimination of an enemy by destroying the entire Italian-speaking population in Asia Minor.[17]

Was the massacre an act of terrorism, as we understand it today? Terrorism is another highly controversial concept, but most would agree that terrorism is a deplorable tactic, usually defined as the use of violence against innocents in order to inspire fear in the service of a political goal. In 88 BC, unsuspecting Roman noncombatants were systematically killed, and the perpetrators' intention was to convince Rome to alter its foreign policy and withdraw from Asia. Of course, the Romans also carried out acts of terrorism at home and abroad. As historian Gregory Bolich pointed out in a recent article on terrorism in antiquity, "Whenever Romans indulged in state-sponsored terrorism, subjugated people responded in kind." Those who resort to terrorism always believe that their ideals and objectives justify it, notes Bolich, and it is the victims who ultimately decide what qualifies as terrorism.[18]

But the official definition of terrorism is debated. It is often said that one nation's terrorists may be another nation's freedom fighters, and that "war is terror within bounds" whereas terrorism exceeds the horrors expected in warfare. Some maintain today that state-sponsored mass killings of civilians are not technically acts of terrorism. Even the United Nations has been unable to come up with a definition accepted by all members. According to the UN draft of 2005, "the targeting and deliberate killing of civilians and noncombatants cannot be justified or legitimized by any cause or grievance," and any such action to "intimidate a population or to compel a government [to act] cannot be justified on any ground." But, notably, the phrase that originally concluded this sentence— "and constitutes an act of terrorism"—was deleted in the final version.[19]

It is challenging to try to apply concepts drawn from modern international law to the past without being anachronistic, cautions R. Bruce Hitchner, historian of Rome and director of the Dayton Peace Accords Project. Hitchner points out that the Romans themselves and other peoples in antiquity regularly carried out activities in war and peace that clearly fall into the categories of genocide, terrorism, and crimes against humanity. Ancient societies as a whole were fundamentally violent, he notes, and the first century BC was fraught with private, collective, and state-sponsored acts of terror. "It's high time we acknowledge the darker side of antiquity." Hitchner's conclusion: "The massacre of 88 BC certainly looks like terrorism, genocide, *and* a crime against humanity."[20]

In terms of scale and cold-blooded premeditation, the black day in 88 BC was the most horrendous and most successful single act of terror in ancient history (more details of this event are given in chapter 8). Yet most modern Roman historians tend to gloss over this "disquieting episode." This tendency reflects a kind of "scholarly amnesia," in Susan Alcock's words—an attempt to smooth over the violence of Rome's annexation of the East by focusing instead on the peaceful "high culture" and consensus that emerged in the later Empire. But instead of conveniently forgetting the massacre of 88 BC, suggests Alcock, historians should probe the complex "back story" to understand the cultural collisions that helped to create Mithradates' world.[21]

It is disappointing that historians have not given this "extraordinary event in antiquity" the discussion it deserves, agrees Deniz Burcu Erciyas, a young Turkish historian. "Until today," notes Erciyas, "very few events have surpassed this level of genocide." Certainly, in our own era, when mass killings and terrorism have become all too familiar, it seems worth paying attention to a historic attack of such scale and savagery in the ancient Near East, a moment in which aggrieved, diverse populations came together to strike a vicious blow against the dominant imperial power.[22]

After the massacre, Mithradates' armies marched into Greece, freeing the mainland Greeks from Roman domination. Hailed as a liberator whose birth had been foretold by ancient oracles, the brilliant strategist became the most powerful ruler in western Asia, annexing territories and winning the loyalty of zealous followers from the Black Sea to ancient Iraq. Thus the Romans—wracked by bloody civil conflict and slave uprisings in Italy—were drawn into a long war in the Mideast, costing countless lives, draining treasuries, and gnawing at Rome's image of invincibility.

Rome's best generals, from Sulla and Lucullus to Pompey the Great, would attempt to destroy Mithradates, but he eluded capture. Each time the Romans had him in their grasp, he slipped away to plan new attacks with his seemingly inexhaustible armies. The most dangerous threat to Rome since Hannibal, Mithradates won stunning victories in some of the most spectacular battles in antiquity.[23] Yet he also suffered staggering defeats that reduced his army to a few ragtag survivors. The charismatic ruler's uncanny ability to surge back stronger after each setback unnerved the Romans. Mithradates' tactics were often underhanded, diabolical, devastating. Yet he also pursued some noble ideals: Mithradates freed thousands of slaves, pardoned prisoners of war, granted wide democratic voting rights, and shared his royal treasure with his followers. Contradictions like these helped to create the king's legendary aura.

Mithradates' dual image as a tragic hero confronting the juggernaut of empire and as an icon of cruelty persisted throughout the Middle Ages into modern times in Europe and the Middle East. Even though Mithradates' Greco-Persian heritage and appeal combined Eastern and Western traditions, his lifelong conflict with Rome seemed to epitomize for many a collision of East and West. For the Romans, Mithradates' Greekness made him culturally superior, but his Persian-Anatolian heritage made him an inferior barbarian. Cicero, who lived through the Mithradatic Wars, demonstrates the Roman ambivalence toward the man who perpetrated "the miserable and inhuman massacre of all the Roman citizens, in so many cities, at one and the same moment," with the intention of erasing "all memory of the Roman name and every trace of its empire." They called this Mithradates a god, continued Cicero; they called

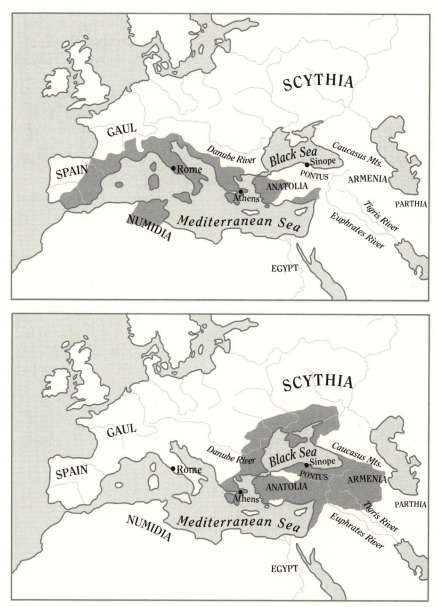

MAP 1.2. (Top) the extent of the Roman Republic's rule, in about 100 BC. (Bottom) Mithradates' ideal "Black Sea Empire." The shading indicates the furthest extent of Mithradates' fluctuating power and influence during the Mithradatic Wars, including his kingdoms, his conquests, and his core allies—lands from which he could recruit armies. Maps by Michele Angel.

him their Good Father and the Savior of Asia; they called him Liberator. Yet after Mithradates' death, Cicero himself called Mithradates the "greatest monarch since Alexander" and the most formidable opponent Rome had ever encountered. For generations after his passing, Mithradates could not be spoken of without "anxiety mixed with admiration," as the Roman writer Velleius Paterculus commented in AD 30. Mithradates, he declared, possessed exceptional bravery and a great spirit, but in his hatred for Rome, he was another Hannibal.[24]

Mithradates remains an ambiguous figure for many today: hero and model to some, perpetrator of monstrous crimes against humanity according to others. How did this one individual mobilize such virulent animosity against the mighty empire? Who was this man—and why did he harbor such murderous hatred toward Rome?

2

A Savior Is Born in a Castle by the Sea

THE STAR appeared in the East, so brilliant that it seemed to rival the sun and set the night sky aflame. The luminous tail curved across a quarter of the heavens, as long as the Milky Way. The year was 135 BC.

Across Anatolia, and from the Caucasus to Persia, the comet was greeted with rejoicing. According to well-known prophecies, a bright new light in the sky would announce the coming of a savior-king, a messiah or great leader who would triumph over enemies. Four generations later, another marvelous star in the East would lead the Magi to the little town of Bethlehem to honor the humble birth of another savior. But before the Star of Bethlehem there was the Star of Sinope. The comet of 135 BC coincided with the birth of Mithradates VI Eupator Dionysus, in Sinope, capital of Pontus on the Black Sea.

The infant's family name, Mithradates (Old Persian *Mithradatha*, "sent by Mithra"), commemorated the ancient Iranian (Persian) god of Sun, Light, and Truth. In ancient Persian traditions, a great fire or light from the heavens had accompanied Mithra's birth. According to the Roman historian Justin, two heavenly portents foretold the future greatness of the newborn prince of Pontus. "In the year that Mithradates was begotten, and again when he first began to rule, comets blazed forth with such splendor that the whole sky seemed to be on fire."[1]

Justin's account of the two comets was based on a now-lost history by Pompeius Trogus. Trogus drew on eyewitness reports of his uncle, a cavalry officer from the Vocontian tribe of Gaul who fought in the Mithradatic Wars. The ancient sources for the life of Mithradates are fragmentary. Except for some of the king's speeches, remarks, inscriptions, and correspondence, what survives of Mithradates' story was written from the standpoint of imperial Rome, the ultimate victor after his death in 63 BC.

Much of the legendary and popular lore surrounding Mithradates' birth and early years was subject to ancient spin and counterspin. But contemporary and later Greek and Roman authors preserved what was known about Mithradates' life and described the historical events before, during, and after his long reign. If we combine what has come down to us from antiquity with what is known about royal Persian, Anatolian, and Macedonian-Greek customs in the Hellenistic age—the era after the conquests of Alexander the Great—we can piece together a realistic picture of Mithradates' birth, childhood, education, and early reign. And we can try to understand his appeal to followers.

Were the comets simply grandiose propaganda, invented by Mithradates' supporters after the great king's death? Were they just another fantastic tale "concocted in antiquity to add luster to Mithradates' reputation"? This has been the generally accepted opinion of modern historians. The view was first advanced in 1890 by Théodore Reinach, the great authority on the king of Pontus, who was unaware that European astronomers had recognized the reality of the two comets as early as 1783. Most classical historians continue to view the story of the comets as a politically motivated "myth" based on ancient Iranian (Persian) legends. To learn the truth, we need to look beyond classical scholarship.[2]

In fact, the comets were not simply a fiction created to glorify the memory of Mithradates. Two spectacular comets really did appear exactly as described by Justin. Proof comes from the other side of the world. In China, royal astronomers of the Han dynasty observed this same pair of distinctive comets. Archaeologists have discovered their remarkably detailed astronomical records and drawings on ancient silk manuscripts in Han tombs.

The Han records reported that two extremely rare "war banner"–type stars appeared for about two months in late summer and fall of 135 BC and again in 119 BC. Trailing fiery tails like battle pennants, the pair of comets caused great excitement in China. According to the Han soothsayers, "war banner" comets predicted massacres, terrible wars, and the rise of a great conqueror. The Chinese astronomers' descriptions and diagrams match the unique features of the comets described by Justin. Extraordinarily brilliant, with very long, curving dust tails filling much of the sky, each comet took four hours to rise and set, and was visible for seventy days.[3]

John T. Ramsey, a historian who studies ancient observations of celestial events, recently reexamined these independent Chinese observations of the comets to determine the years of Mithradates' birth and the beginning of his reign. Ancient Greek and Latin sources are inconsistent about the chronology of this period; the only secure date is the year of Mithradates' death in 63 BC. Ramsey's comparison of the Roman and Chinese astronomical details indicates that Mithradates was probably born in the spring of 134 BC (conceived in summer or autumn of 135) and was crowned king in about 119, when he was fourteen or fifteen. At least two Roman sources agree with the birthdate of 135/134.[4]

The comets also solve a numismatic mystery. A series of tiny, small-denomination coins was issued in the early years of Mithradates' reign. These little bronze "pennies," with a star and the winged horse Pegasus on one side and a comet on the other, circulated in outlying territories of Mithradates' kingdom. They were intended for ordinary people around the eastern Black Sea—Colchis (modern Republic of Georgia) and Crimea (Ukraine)—who would use them to buy food and other necessities.

The comet on these coins puzzled classical numismatists. At the time of Mithradates' birth, Greeks and Romans dreaded comets as portents of doom. The word "disaster" comes from the Latin for "dire star" or comet—comets were traditional harbingers of war or the violent over-

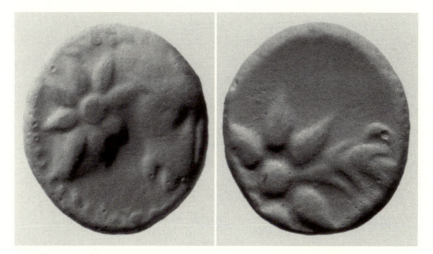

FIG. 2.1. Comet coin. Small bronze coin minted early in Mithradates' reign, showing star on neck of Pegasus (left). The reverse (right) depicts the comet of 135 BC, taken as a sign of the birth of a savior-king. Staatliche Museen, Berlin, photos by Roberta Dupuis-Devlin, courtesy of John T. Ramsey.

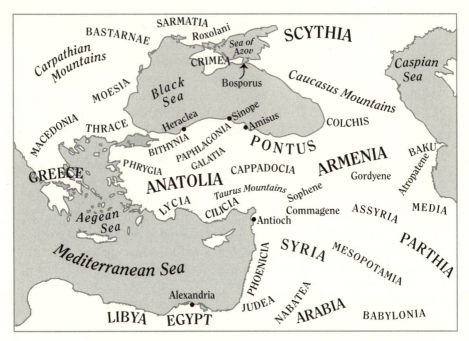

MAP 2.1. Eastern Mediterranean and Black Sea region: Mithradates' sphere of influence. Map by Michele Angel.

throw of rulers. Other coins of the Kingdom of Pontus usually displayed the king's portrait with a crescent-and-star symbol. As far as the classical historians knew, no ancient coins depicted objects of ill omen—and no other coins of this period featured a comet.[5] Why, the scholars wondered, would Mithradates risk minting coins stamped with such a sinister image?

It turns out, however, that Mithradates' comet coins were not unique—and comets were not a bad omen in his lands. Unknown to classical historians in the West, coins depicting a comet were also minted in Armenia during this period. In 2004, I came across a brief note in the journal *Astronomy & Geophysics* describing a comet image on silver and copper coins minted by the Armenian king Tigranes II between 83 and 69 BC. The Armenian coauthors, a physicist and a numismatist, were interested in identifying the comet, rather than its historical significance. Their note was unknown to Western historians of the Greco-Roman world, until I brought it to the attention of John Ramsey, who included this new evidence in his 2006–7 catalog of ancient comets.

The coins of Armenia ordinarily portrayed kings wearing a traditional tiara decorated with two eagles and an eight-rayed star. But these unusual coins show Tigranes II wearing a tiara decorated with a comet trailing a long, curved tail. The Armenian scholars speculated that the comet on the coin was one of the earliest artistic representations of Halley's Comet, which appeared in 87 BC, during Tigranes' reign.[6]

But who was Tigranes and why would he—of all ancient rulers of this time—also decide to place a comet on his coins? Of Persian-Alan ancestry, Tigranes the Great ruled the kingdom of Armenia. He was Mithradates' most trusted ally; his queen was Mithradates' favorite daughter. Tigranes extended his vast domains from the Caucasus Mountains to Mesopotamia. These two powerful monarchs were close friends, and as the story unfolds we'll learn of their daring exploits together during their campaigns against the Romans.

Looking at the evidence from a Persian-influenced—rather than Roman or Greek—point of view, we can solve the "mystery" of the remarkable comet coins issued by Tigranes and Mithradates. Comets terrified the Greco-Romans, but in the Near East, a great blaze of light in the sky was a hopeful sign of the rise of a powerful leader. When Halley's Comet appeared in 87 BC, the year after the great massacre of Romans by Mithradates' allies, it sent shivers of fear through Italy, where comets were evil

Fig. 2.2. Coin of Tigranes II of Armenia, large silver tetradrachm, 83–69 BC. Tigranes' tiara is decorated with a comet with a curved tail, associating him with the rare comets of 135 and 119 BC, emblems of Mithradates' cause. Courtesy Spink of London, drawing by Michele Angel.

omens. But in the Near East, the spectacular pair of comets of 135 and 119 BC had *already* been interpreted as favorable omens associated with Mithradates' birth and rise to power. So, when a third comet appeared in 87 BC, it would be seen as yet another guarantee of Mithradates' grand destiny. In the East, Halley's Comet seemed to signal divine approval of Mithradates' and Tigranes' victories thus far.

The comet on Tigranes' tiara has a prominent curve in its tail. This curve is a rare feature that was definitely present in the "war banner" comets of 135 and 119 BC. In contrast, Halley's Comet always has a straight tail. These facts suggest that Tigranes' tiara and his coins alluded to the two distinctive, curved-tail comets of 135 and 119 BC, linked to Mithradates, rather than to Halley's Comet. Tigranes' comet imagery not only confirms the positive meaning of comets in the East, but it may have been a public declaration of Tigranes' commitment to Mithradates' cause.[7]

Mithradates' comets of 135 and 119 BC appeared in the constellation Pegasus. This position in the sky helps explain why he chose the winged horse as his personal emblem. Pegasus was a symbol that bridged East and West, like Mithradates himself. In Greek myth, Pegasus carried the god Zeus's lightning, but the immortal flying horse originated in Mesopotamian mythology. Moreover, a comet in the horse constellation would have carried even deeper meaning for Mithradates and his Persian-influenced followers. The Sun god Mithra always recognized a new king by sending an omen via his sacred animal, the horse.[8]

The curved shape of the twin comets' tails held special significance too. In Anatolia, the new stars' crescent tails might have called to mind the crescent and star symbol of Pontus. But even more awe-inspiring was the resemblance to a distinctive weapon. In Mithradates' world, comets were associated with war because they looked like great swords suspended in the sky. The rare comets of 135 and 119 had curved tails, reminding the Chinese of war banners. In the Near East, however, the crescent shape called to mind a particular kind of sword, the sickle-shaped *harpe*, the Persian scimitar, the signature weapon of Mithra himself.[9]

The indigenous populations of Anatolia, Armenia, Media, Syria, Scythia, and other lands of the old Persian Empire—unlike the Romans who feared comets—interpreted comets as signs of hope, not grounds for despair. The comet coins of Mithradates and Tigranes promised that a great king had come to fulfill the ancient predictions about a new star in the East and salvation from tyranny. Viewed from this Eastern perspective, the comets point to a startling, overlooked fact. Some 130 years before the Star of Bethlehem led the Wise Men to assign the savior's role to another newborn, those hopes of salvation centered on Mithradates.

THE PROPHECIES

Mystical prophecies about the destruction of the world's last empire were already swirling long before Mithradates' birth. In antiquity, oracles, dreams, omens, and prodigies (wondrous, eerie events) were often interpreted to convey political messages, especially in times of crisis. As Rome's power and brutality increased, so did the sense of impending doom. Many oracles were read by Romans and non-Romans alike as warnings about the ultimate fate of the Republic. Some poetic visions evoked the imagery of the sacred symbol of Rome—the she-wolf that nursed the infant twin founders Romulus and Remus. Some warned that

FIG. 2.3. Wolf, the sacred symbol of Rome, nursing the twin founders of Rome, Romulus and Remus. Silver didrachm, Italy, 269–266 BC, 1944.100.15, bequest of E. T. Newell, Courtesy of the American Numismatic Society.

the offspring of a wild predator would someday tear their own mother-land to shreds.[10]

After the defeat of Rome's great enemy, Hannibal, in the Second Punic War (202 BC), the Romans took lands in Spain, North Africa, Greece, and the Near East. This early Roman expansion was not carried out according to an imperial master plan. Instead, the Senate conferred approval on ambitious commanders seeking personal glory and riches through foreign conquests. In conquered or threatened lands, the Romans were feared as bloodthirsty, driven by lust for gold and triumph. The historian Polybius described how Roman soldiers took special pride in a vicious way of war. Their orders, he claimed, were to systematically kill every living thing before beginning to loot. In the legions' wake, said Polybius, lay smoldering battlegrounds and devastated towns, streets and fields strewn with the bodies of men, women, and children put to the sword, and even dogs, sheep, and cows chopped to pieces.[11]

In the East, hopes for salvation grew. The most famous apocalyptic revelation was an ancient Iranian prophecy known as the Oracle of Hystaspes, a Persian-Babylonian sage. This oracle foretold the destruction of Rome by fire and sword and the coming of a savior-king from the East whose birth would be proclaimed by a brilliant light from heaven. Another prophecy, the Zoroastrian apocalyptic scripture of the third century BC called the Bahman Yasht, envisioned an avenging savior-prince who would be born under a shooting star: this prince would drive foreign tyrants out of Asia. An ancient oracle of Egypt promised that the gods would send a great king from the Orient. The Hebrew prediction (Daniel 2.7) of the downfall of the "last great empire" was written in 165 BC, just thirty years before Mithradates' birth. During Mithradates' reign, a handbook of Egyptian star omens was widely read: comets signified massive war losses for Rome in Asia.[12]

Macabre events seemed to confirm the oracles. A ghastly tale, recounted by a compiler of popular lore, began to circulate after 191 BC. In that year, the Romans defeated the Greco-Babylonian (Seleucid) king Antiochus III at Thermopylae in Greece. While the Roman victors were plundering the enemy corpses on the battlefield, a Syrian cavalry officer named Bouplagos rose up from the dead. Bleeding from twelve gruesome wounds, the ghost warned in a rasping whisper that Zeus would send a "bold-hearted tribe" to punish Rome. The Roman soldiers panicked, and their generals, "much shaken by this utterance," consulted the Oracle at Delphi. But the Delphic Oracle was ominous too, threatening awful punishment for Rome's outrages in Greece and Asia.

FIG. 2.4. The Wolf and the Head, seventeenth-century lead sculpture, Grove of the Wolf and the Head, Versailles. Réunion des Musées Nationaux/ Art Resource, NY.

The next day, the Roman general Publius fell into a frenzied trance, raving about horrible wars to come, gory atrocities, and "unspeakable desolation" for Rome. Terrified soldiers rushed to his tent—many died in the stampede. The Romans heard their trusted commander howl, *I see a great king from the land of the rising sun who shall recruit a mighty army of many nations to obliterate Rome!* Publius scrambled up a tree and declared that he himself would be devoured by a wolf, the sacred symbol of Rome. Aghast, the men watched as a wolf attacked and ate their esteemed general. Only his head remained—and it continued to predict doom. So the nightmarish story went, and as the tale spread, many believed. In years to come, many remembered.[13]

As Rome's predatory ambitions rose, dire omens proliferated: rains of blood, plagues, monstrous births, talking cows. The Sibylline Books, ancient texts written on palm leaves and stored in a stone chest beneath the Temple of Jupiter in Rome, had been consulted by priests during crises since Rome's foundation. These cryptic writings spoke of a "great conflagration from the sky falling to earth" and foretold terrible devastation and violent conflict for Rome.

The so-called Third Book of the Sibylline Oracles (different from the Roman Sibylline utterances) was another source of bad news for the Romans. Some of its passages were ancient, but others were apparently composed by anti-Roman Jews living in Anatolia during Rome's expansion (160–140 BC and 80–40 BC). The widely circulated Third Sibylline Book declared that Rome's impending corruption and ruin would come when a comet appeared as a "sign of the sword . . . and death" (Mithradates' comets resembled curved swords). *Then,* declared the oracle, *all the peoples of the East will rise up and unite, forcing Rome to pay back three times the riches it has plundered. They shall enslave twenty Romans for each Asian in servitude to Rome.*[14]

In 88 BC (the year of the massacre of Romans), the Greek philosopher Athenion met with Mithradates and brought back a message of hope to Athens. Rome's conquest of Greece (200 to 146 BC) had brought much suffering. In Epirus in 167 BC, for example, the Romans systematically enslaved the entire population. The destruction of Corinth in 146 was another tragedy never forgotten by the Greeks. Just before the massacre of 88 BC, Athenion delivered a rousing speech to the demoralized citizens of Athens: "Oracles everywhere promise that Mithradates—already hailed as a god in Asia—will be victorious!"[15]

These sensational events and portents from so many different sources, predicting the fall of an evil empire and the advent of a savior-king born under an Eastern star, became intertwined and loomed large in Mithradates' story during his lifetime. These oracles and the comets nourished the king's self-image and his official publicity. The prophecies helped create fertile ground for popular support of his campaign against the tyranny of Rome. Mithradates, "the oriental saviour king of oracles and prophecies," hoped that all people "would see in him the king from the east destined to bring about the destruction of Rome foretold in oracles."[16]

The widespread belief in the ancient Near East that heavenly fire or light would announce the birth of a redeemer helps explain another story told about Mithradates. When he was a baby, lightning struck his cradle. Mithradates was unharmed, but the lightning left a distinctive scar—in the shape of a diadem or crown—on his forehead. Some said the lightning strike inspired his nickname, Dionysus, after the Greek god of liberation, change, and new beginnings. Dionysus had been marked for greatness by Zeus's divine lightning while still in the womb. Mithradates used this name in his propaganda and placed Dionysus's image on his coins—an immediately recognizable symbol of opposition to Rome. The god's worship had been banned by the Roman Senate in 186 BC, because of Dionysus's association with slave revolts and foreign rebellions.[17]

In Greco-Roman popular lore, a nonfatal lightning strike promised great distinction and fame. Similar beliefs held in the East too. According to the writings of the Magi (Persian Zoroastrian priest-astronomers), the savior-king was to be distinguished by a special mark on his body. The Magi in his father's palace saw Mithradates' lightning scar as a sign of divine approval; the diadem shape meant the gods had "crowned" him at birth. Many figures in history, myth, and legend have been marked for eminence by a bolt of lightning, from King Darius I of Persia and Alexander of Macedon to Harry Potter of Hogwarts. Mithradates' lightning story is unverifiable, of course, but it's not impossible: two out of three people stuck by lightning do survive. What is significant is that all these accumulating omens, prophecies, oracles, mythic traditions, and extraordinary natural phenomena were coalescing around the time of Mithradates. He was uniquely placed to take advantage of these converging Eastern and Western beliefs.[18]

ROYAL BLOOD

Another Mithradatic claim long rejected as fable turns out to receive support in genealogical and historical evidence. Mithradates traced his father's bloodline to Persian kings and his mother's family to Alexander the Great. He also declared that his ancestral lands had been bestowed by Darius I, the great Achaemenid ruler who had consolidated the vast Persian Empire (d. 486 BC). It has been widely assumed by modern scholars that propagandists invented this noble ancestry for Mithradates.

Macedonian and Persian family trees are tangled, and further complicated by the ancient practice of reusing the same royal names over many generations. (Luckily, nicknames were common, and sometimes people had more than one, like Mithradates Eupator Dionysus). Two classical historians recently reevaluated the evidence in the ancient sources pertaining to Mithradates' heritage. Their investigation reveals that Mithradates' paternal line was in all probability related by blood to Darius I, who had married two daughters and a granddaughter of Cyrus *Vazraka*, "the Great," founder of the Persian Empire. So Mithradates' claim to descend from Cyrus and Darius was not mere propaganda. Darius had granted a fiefdom to Mithradates' ancestors, which became a powerful satrapy (provincial governorship) centered in the ancient Greek city of Sinope, in Pontus on the Black Sea.

What about the Alexandrian lineage? Mithradates was related to Barsiné, a Persian princess captured by Alexander after the Battle of Issus in 333 BC. Barsiné had a son with Alexander and resided in Pergamon, where she maintained ties with Mithradates' family. Mithradates' mother, Laodice, a princess from Antioch (Syria), was a descendant of Alexander's Macedonian general Seleucus Nicator, the founder of the new Macedonian-Persian Empire, stretching from Anatolia and central Asia to Babylonia and Iran.[19]

It was Alexander's dream to meld Greek and Persian bloodlines and cultures as the foundation for a magnificent hybrid civilization. After

Alexander's conquest of Persia, marriage alliances were carried out on a grand scale among Macedonian and Persian aristocrats. Laodice's kinship to Alexander is plausible, since Macedonian nobles shared bloodlines, but impossible to prove or disprove. Modern DNA studies show that the genetic material of powerful rulers, such as Genghis Khan, was generously dispersed in numerous unofficial offspring. This common practice, along with the custom of large harems for Macedonian and Persian royalty, gives further support to Mithradates' claim to be the heir—by blood, land, and ideals—of the greatest rulers of Greece and Persia.

As with the comets and oracles, what really matters is that Mithradates' illustrious ancestry was unquestioned in antiquity. Mithradates himself, his supporters, and his enemies all saw him as the living embodiment of Alexander's vision of Persian-Greek fusion.

Until the end of his life, Mithradates cherished a cloak believed to have belonged to Alexander. How could Mithradates have obtained such a relic? Was the robe handed down in his mother's noble Macedonian family? Or did Barsiné present her lover's mantle to Mithradates' relatives in Pergamon? The ancient historian Appian inadvertently provides a clue. Appian says that after Mithradates' death in 63 BC, the Romans discovered Alexander's cloak in Mithradates' castle, among the treasures that Mithradates had received from Cleopatra III, wife of Ptolemy VIII of Egypt. During a succession crisis in Egypt, this queen had stored her treasures for safekeeping on the island of Cos. Some years later in 88 BC, the year of the great massacre of the Romans, Cos turned over these treasures to Mithradates. But how could a mantle belonging to Alexander the Great come to be among Cleopatra III's treasures?

Genealogical detective work provides an answer. Cleopatra, her husband, and her father were all direct descendants of Alexander's best friend and general, Ptolemy. When Alexander died in 323 BC in Babylon, Ptolemy hijacked the corpse—and presumably his cloak—to Egypt, in order to support his claim to be Alexander's successor. Cleopatra's husband may well have inherited this precious relic from his Macedonian ancestors.[20]

Again, however, the robe's true provenance is irrelevant. Everyone, including the Romans, believed that Mithradates had inherited Alexander's mantle, and that it was an authentic physical link to Alexander. To wear Alexander's cloak was not merely symbolic for Mithradates. In ancient Persian court rituals, the robe or *khilat* of a venerated person or ruler was thought to transmit the owner's personal qualities and authority. Cyrus the Great presented his fine purple robe to his most beloved friend; Darius III dreamed that Alexander wore his royal robe; numerous other examples of the ritual (*dorophorike* in ancient Greek) appear in Old Testament and other Near Eastern writings. This ancient concept is the basis of well-known legends about Saint Paul's cloak and the robe worn by Jesus. The idea lives on today in our phrases "to assume the mantle" and "to vest power," and in the desire to possess clothing worn by cult figures. Two striking modern examples occurred in 2006. In Lebanon, Shi'ite Muslims flocked to see the *abaya* or robe worn by the Hezbollah leader Nasrallah, displayed in several cities. Meanwhile in the United States, the fabulous gold lamé cape worn by Elvis Presley ("The King") received high bids in a celebrity auction (Presley's cape was decorated with a sequined *comet* design).[21]

By Mithradates' time, Alexander's life had achieved cult status, and—as we shall see—Mithradates shared many notable commonalities with his idol. Some resemblances were real, others were embroidered with legend, but Mithradates' followers saw every parallel as proof of his glorious destiny.[22]

THE MYTHIC HERO SCRIPT

Precious little is known about Mithradates' youth. Curiously, however, an obscure childhood is typical of larger-than-life individuals whose exploits become legendary. What we do know about Mithradates' early years comes from a few passages in Justin and passing remarks by other ancient historians. Some of the episodes in these accounts sound like the stuff of fairy tales. This has led modern historians to reject several events in Mithradates' life as propaganda fabricated after the fact by his supporters.[23]

Some suspicion is justified. Mithradates was keenly aware of his public image, and some loyalists were experts in manipulating public relations. Yet many unusual details in the king's life are accepted as true, supported by historical and archaeological evidence. Some incidents are likely or plausible. Other anecdotes seem extraordinary—yet none are impossible. But the meaning of Mithradates' compelling life story goes beyond political propaganda. What is truly striking is that his biography parallels a standard sequence of incidents typically found in the life stories of mythic heroes across different times and cultures.

The universal pattern of "hero-defining" attributes of legendary and historical personages was first recognized by psychologist Otto Rank and comparative myth scholar Fitzroy Raglan. Their model has been refined and applied to dozens of heroic figures in myth, history, and popular culture around the world, from antiquity to the present. Appendix 1 lists the twenty-three features that distinguish mythic heroes. There are variations in how different scholars interpret key events in individual lives, but folklorists have calculated the mythic-hero scores of, for example, Moses, Oedipus, and Cyrus the Great (20–23 points); Jesus, Muhammad, Hercules, and King Arthur (18–20); Alexander the Great, Buddha, Joan of Arc, and Robin Hood (13–16); Harry Potter (14); Spartacus (12); and John F. Kennedy (5).[24]

Since antiquity, Mithradates has been admired by many as a champion of anti-imperialism, despite his eventual defeat. But modern Western historians tend to cast Mithradates as Rome's evil "Oriental" nemesis, rather than a heroic figure. Perhaps that's why no one has ever thought to calculate Mithradates' rating on the archetypal hero index. How does his story measure up by the established criteria for immortal legend?

The points add up quickly. Prophecies predicted Mithradates' birth and rise to power. His father, King Mithradates V, and his mother, Laodice, a princess, may have been related through intertwined Persian-Macedonian family trees. Conceived under the rare comet of 135 BC, the infant Mithradates survived a lightning strike. He was associated with the gods Mithra and Dionysus, and—like Alexander the Great—he claimed Hercules as a divine ancestor. As a youngster, Mithradates eluded murder plots by his guardians, by experimenting with antidotes, ultimately inventing a secret potion that protected against all poisons. As a teenager, Mithradates disappeared. For seven years no one knew whether the crown prince of Pontus was dead or alive. As the following pages will reveal, by the time he was a young man, Mithradates had already tallied an impressive score of 10 on the mythic hero scale. Without giving away what transpires, over his long and dramatic lifetime Mithradates fulfilled *all* the remaining requirements of the mythic hero index, for a perfect score of 23 (see appendix 1).

Historical personages for whom there are complete written records normally rate 5–10 points. Mithradates' high score indicates that many aspects of his life were preserved orally, in popular lore. Some events (comets and prophecies, ancestry, toxicological experiments, horsemanship) are documented, while other stories coalesced around grains of truth, or were exaggerated or made up—although nothing reported in the sources is beyond belief. Mithradates was brilliant at presenting himself as the savior of Greek and Persian civilization and the scourge of Rome. Undoubtedly he encouraged favorable interpretations of oracles and omens, assassination attempts, narrow escapes, notable feats, gallant deeds, and other actual events to his advantage. But much of what historians assume were deliberate falsehoods dreamed up as propaganda were more likely the result of a gradual, natural process. In the "Snowball Effect" of oral tradition, the actual facts of Mithradates' life mingled with probable and then with plausible events. Between romance and reality, propaganda and plausibility, lies the real story. As we consider what seem like improbable events in Mithradates' story, it's worth keeping in mind that, in scientific probability/possibility theory, probability applies only to the future, not to past events. Even if something reported in the past had small odds of occurring, that doesn't mean it didn't happen. Over time, of course, Mithradates' story accumulated more and more narrative details that conformed to the heroic archetype. Mithradates' high score is the result of the accretion of mythic motifs in oral tradition around actual events; contemporary public relations; and a genuinely remarkable life.[25]

One senses that Mithradates himself understood the mythic hero script and endeavored to live it out. The circumstances of his birth and many other events were beyond his control, of course, yet from a very early age it seems that Mithradates self-consciously cast himself as the hero of his own epic saga. As a child, Mithradates heard the oracles surrounding his birth and absorbed the life stories of illustrious ancestors and other role models from myth and history. Hidden under his curly bangs was the special lightning scar shaped like a diadem. It would be no wonder if Mithradates came to think of himself as a mythic hero and resolved to behave like one. Most of the crucial elements of the heroic plotline were readily available to him, two millennia before modern myth scholars recognized the Persian king Cyrus the Great as the epitome of the historical hero. Another real-life idol, Alexander, followed the heroic pattern, which is also prominent in the myths of the divine Mithra, Dionysus, and Hercules.[26]

Folklorists have a word to describe the way real-life actions can be guided by legends: *ostension*. Ostension explains how widely known myths and legends sometimes shape ordinary people's behavior patterns, leading them to enact or perform certain elements from mythic narratives, thereby translating fiction into fact. Events inspire stories and stories influence events.[27] The concept of ostension is another reason why some episodes in Mithradates' life story appear to mirror Greek myths and theater. If Mithradates was guided by something like a mythic hero script, that helps explain his phenomenal self-confidence and ability to surge back after crushing losses. Mithradates' belief that he was a hero in the classical mold, marked from birth for a glorious destiny, was a wellspring of his perseverance and resourcefulness in times of crisis. He was determined to be remembered for all time.

Mithradates was not introduced to his father until he was five years old (a Persian custom intended to protect the king from grief should his son die in infancy). Until then, the little prince lived with his mother, Queen Laodice, and concubines and children in the harem. Mithradates listened to exciting myths and legends recounted by the women and their guardians and confidants, the eunuchs—castrated males who served as trusted attendants, generals, and powerful advisers in Persian-influenced courts. Notably, of the many names of eunuchs that have survived from antiquity, half are from Mithradates' reign, a fact that reminds us of the constant court intrigues in this era.[28] Indeed, palace conspirators would plot to do away with the young ruler after the untimely death of his father. But that was still in the future. While the old king still lived, he oversaw his heir's education. As soon as the boy celebrated his fifth birthday, tutors began his immersion in classical Greek lessons and the Persian essentials of kingship.

3

Education of a Young Hero

THEY mounted the boy on the wide back of the high-strung stallion. Whirling and bucking, the horse galloped away with the little rider gripping the reins and his child-size javelin. The prince was only ten, but husky and tall for his age. He'd been riding horses since age five. But this steed, fresh from the high pastures of Cappadocia, was not yet broken. As the horse raced across the field, Mithradates seemed in peril of being thrown—but somehow he hung

FIG. 3.1. Small boy on a high-spirited horse, life-size Hellenistic bronze sculpture from time of Mithradates, ca. 150–125 BC. National Archaeological Museum, Athens, Greece. Vanni/Art Resource, NY.

on. He managed to control the horse and hurl his spear with force and skill surprising in someone so young.

Some in the palace suspected that the young prince had survived a plot to arrange a fatal riding accident. Perhaps they thanked Pegasus, the boy's protector. Others may have recalled that the god Mithra always showed favor to a new ruler by sending a horse omen. Some Greek grooms might have whispered that malevolent ghosts, *taraxippoi* ("horse-frighteners," the spirits of dead charioteers), spooked the animal. Everyone was reminded of the young Alexander the Great, who had impressed his elders by taming a wild horse.[1]

Aside from Justin's vignette of the close call with the bucking horse, most of Mithradates' childhood is a blank. Ancient writers described the adult Mithradates' extraordinary size, strength, and stamina; his gargantuan appetites, earthy humor, and sexual preferences. All agree that he was a brilliant military strategist, fluent in many languages, a courageous fighter, and a gifted toxicologist. A cultured patron of music and the arts, the king loved spectacle and grandiose gestures. There is ample evidence of Mithradates' implacable hatred of Rome, pride in his Persian-Greek ancestry, and his imitation of Alexander the Great. His noble ideals and charismatic—and often paranoid—personality are well attested, as are the striking contradictions in his character. As king, Mithradates could be merciful or ruthless, chivalrous yet cruel. By filling in the gaps and fleshing out scenes in the incomplete ancient accounts with known facts and evidence about Mithradates' time and place, and by working back from what what we know about the man, we can imagine the boy.[2]

This approach raises new questions about Mithradates. What shaped his character and public persona? Who—besides Alexander and Cyrus the Great—were his models? Which mythic, historic, and current events made strong impressions? Why such deep animosity toward Rome? What were his ultimate goals? What inspired his scientific pursuits? What was the origin of his search for the perfect antidote? First, let's set the scene in Sinope, where young Mithradates received his education, then consider some likely influences during his formative years.

PONTUS, CULTURAL CROSSROADS

Mithradates' father, Mithradates V Euergetes ("Benefactor"), inherited the wealthy Kingdom of Pontus in about 150 BC. Euergetes expanded Pontus's influence, annexing land and making advantageous marriage alliances. He and Queen Laodice had seven children. Continuing the tradition that frustrates historians, the royal pair named both sons Mithradates and called their first two daughters Laodice. The boys had nicknames: our Mithradates was dubbed Dionysus as a boy and later added Eupator ("Good Father"). His younger brother was Mithradates Chrestus ("the Good"). Their three younger sisters were Nyssa, Roxana, and Statira.

To gain control of Cappadocia, the kingdom south of Pontus, Euergetes married his eldest daughter Laodice (Mithradates' older sister) to the boy-king Ariathes VI, whose mother had placed him on the throne after poisoning his five brothers. Poisoning was a typical form of royal succession in this era. Not long after the self-assured Laodice—a few years older than her husband—arrived in Cappadocia, her wicked mother-in-law was conveniently murdered.[3]

Mithradates Eupator's best friend was Dorylaus, raised in the palace as a brother. Dorylaus was the orphaned nephew of General Dorylaus, best friend and military adviser of Mithradates' father. Dorylaus's family was related to the historian Strabo, who was born in Amasia, Pontus, in 63 BC (the year of Mithradates' death). Strabo wrote extensively and nostalgically about his homeland and the surrounding countries. He described Sinope's impressive fortifications, beautiful gardens, old peach and olive orchards, handsome marble buildings, fine temples, lively market, and new gymnasium. Strabo's narrative also tells us about the kind of education an aristocratic boy received in Pontus.

Strabo recounted how his own family had been sundered by the Mithradatic Wars. His mother was a great-granddaughter of General Dorylaus, and his mother's uncle, Moaphernes (a Persian name), was a friend of Mithradates. Strabo's great-uncles served Mithradates, and his paternal grandfather was one of his commanders, overseeing fortresses in Pontus. Near the end of the Mithradatic Wars, Strabo's grandfather turned the forts over to the Romans but never received the promised reward, something that still rankled Strabo.[4]

Other information links Strabo and Mithradates. Strabo's mother sent him to school in Nysa near Tralles, towns that had massacred Romans in 88 BC. Later Strabo studied with Tyrannio, a learned friend of Mithradates. Strabo mentions a relative named Theophilus. This name, in view of Strabo's pro-Mithradatic ties, led Strabo's modern biographer to wonder whether Strabo was related to Theophilus of Paphlagonia, hired by the people of Tralles to slaughter the Romans in 88 BC. That remains an intriguing guess, but Strabo, a native Pontian who has much to tell us about Mithradates' world, was typical of the multiethnic heritage and complicated politics of Anatolia in the first century BC.[5]

Native Anatolians, Greek colonists, Persians, and Alexander's Macedonians were powerful influences in Mithradates' homeland. Greek culture was strong in the large cities on the Aegean coast, but much less marked in the ports rimming the Black Sea. The great Russian historian M. Rostovtzeff characterized the Hellenic influence around the Black Sea as "a thin Greek shell around a hard native kernel." In the Anatolian heartland and Pontus, Persian-influenced and indigenous culture predominated.[6]

At the same time, Mithradates' father was a philhellene and Greek was the official language of his court. Ambassadors and eunuchs, peripatetic Greek philosophers and Black Sea pirates, polyglot traders and tattooed Thracians, snake charmers and grim Magi, learned doctors and shamans, soldiers and storytellers from many different lands rubbed shoulders in the palace of Sinope. Surrounded by so many diverse ethnicities, dialects, and backgrounds, Mithradates could practice his gift for languages at an early age. In this dynamic, cosmopolitan milieu, exciting tales of the Persian heroes Cyrus and Darius mingled naturally with the exploits of Alexander of Macedon and Hannibal of Carthage.[7]

In such a melting pot, religious beliefs and practices were eclectic and overlapping. Young Mithradates performed Greek rituals for the Olympian gods, but he also worshipped ancient Anatolian and Iranian deities. Mithradates' father was devoted to Apollo and Zeus, but as king he was also the high priest, or Magus, in the Zoroastrian worship of the Iranian Sun divinities Ahuramazda and Mithra. As a boy Mithradates observed his father saluting the rising sun and consulting the Magi about omens and dreams. When his father made fire offerings on mountaintop altars, young Mithradates learned the ritual duties he would inherit.

Much about ancient Persian religion remains a mystery, but historians agree that Truth was the highest ideal. Free will was a key moral concept. Sun and Light were revered. Fire was sacred. The respect and awe accorded to fire was a natural impulse in the petroleum-rich deserts of Mesopotamia and the oil deposits of the Crimea, and in Baku by the Caspian Sea. These were places where fountains of volatile naphtha and lakes of asphalt combusted spontaneously and burned eternally with super-hot, blue-orange flames unquenched by water. Such sacred fiery substances—common in Mithradates' lands but unfamiliar to the Romans—would prove valuable in battle.

Herodotus, Xenophon, Strabo, and other Greek historians described the Persians' dualistic worldview, in which Light and Truth (*Arta* in Old

Iranian) eternally battle the evil forces of Darkness and Lies (*Druj*). Dishonesty was reprehensible. Debt was a morally deplorable condition, because indebted people were susceptible to deceit and enslavement. Debtors and slaves were unable to exercise free will, unable to chose to struggle against Darkness. These beliefs help explain why the hatred of Romans was so profound in the Persian-influenced Province of Asia. Under Rome's rapacious and corrupt taxation policies, moneylenders charged exorbitant interest rates and confiscated all of an indebted man's possessions when he defaulted; then he was enslaved and sold to Roman masters. Roman taxes plunged entire cities into overwhelming debt, forcing them to sell artworks and other treasures, their land, and their own people. Even the wealthiest kings succumbed to bankruptcy and blackmail. To oppose the Romans was to fight on the side of Truth and Light.[8]

School Days

Like Cyrus and Alexander, Mithradates was nurtured by a large circle of guardians, tutors, and trainers. His playmates were Dorylaus, Gaius (son of Hermaeus, also considered a stepbrother), and other boys from aristocratic Greek, Persian, Cappadocian, and indigenous Anatolian families. The boys' education was a blend of Greek and Persian culture and athletic training. Many of the teachers were Greeks versed in *paideia*, traditional Hellenic literature, classical art and music, mythology and history, with readings from Aristotle, Plato, Thucydides, Xenophon, and Herodotus. The boys memorized Homer's *Iliad* and Greek poetry and plays. Alexander had loved to quote from the plays of Euripides. Mithradates' favorite drama might have been *The Persians*, written by Aeschylus after the Greeks defeated Xerxes at Salamis in 480 BC. Aeschylus painted the Persian soldiers and their weapons in luminous colors, and treated the Persian king sympathetically, as a valiant, noble despot who tragically underestimated the Greek love of liberty—a mistake King Mithradates would avoid.[9]

Mithradates' education included botanical medicine with Persian rhizotomists and Greek "root-cutters." The Magi were adepts in plant poisons and antidotes. Mithradates' own grandfather, King Pharnaces I, had discovered a plant, called *pharnaceon*, reputed to be a cure-all. Aristotle, Alexander's tutor, had inspired a love of natural history and medicine in his student. Mithradates, too, was fascinated by natural sciences and medicine—but with a twist. Mithradates' passion was poisons. He understood the duality of *pharmaka,* drugs derived from powerful plant, mineral, and animal substances. Paradoxically, these substances could be fatally toxic or they could serve as a health-giving tonic. Everything depended on the dosage. And for every poison, Nature provided an antidote—indeed, some poisons could be counteracted by other poisons.[10]

One ancient historian, Memnon, declared that Mithradates was a serial poisoner from childhood on.[11] This seems unlikely, although during his long reign Mithradates certainly did wield poison as a weapon. Memnon's rumor probably originated because of young Mithradates' experiments with poisons, based on the principles that toxins could be used for good or ill. It's likely that he began investigating easily available poisons as a boy. Pontus was blessed with an abundance of deadly natural resources. Children learned to identify common toxic plants, such as aconite (monkshood), hellebore, nightshade, yew, henbane, hemlock. A budding toxicologist could capture venomous spiders, wasps, and snakes, and carry out poison experiments on small animals.

The prince pursued harmless hobbies too, collecting beautiful agates, crystals, and minerals. As king, Mithradates wrote treatises on gemology and amber, and his famous collection of exquisitely carved agate goblets and cameo rings ended up in the hands of various extravagant Romans after his death, later finding their way into royal museums in Europe.

A Persian prince's upbringing was described in exciting detail by the Greek historians Herodotus and Xenophon, whose books Mithradates read. Both writers had traveled extensively in the old Persian Empire, and, like Aeschylus, they admired certain Persian customs and values taught at an early age, such as justice, gratitude, responsibility, and self-control. We can be sure that young Mithradates heard plenty of family lore from his relatives about the origins of his kingdom and his glorious forebears. But Mithradates could also pore over the lively accounts of his ancestors by Herodotus and Xenophon, to learn how to become a proper Greco-Persian monarch.

Xenophon's own story was thrilling: he had commanded ten thousand Greek mercenaries fighting for the Persian usurper Cyrus the Younger's lost cause in Mesopotamia, in about 400 BC. Xenophon's memoir, *The March of the Ten Thousand,* told of the long, arduous trek home by way of Pontus. Xenophon's vast army had camped right outside the stone walls of Sinope—Mithradates' own hometown had provided Xenophon's soldiers with food and supplies.[12]

Xenophon's historical romance, *The Education of Cyrus,* brims with stirring tales about the boyhood, military career, and chivalry of the elder Cyrus, founder of the Persian Empire in about 550 BC. Xenophon recounts how Cyrus the Great became a good and enlightened king, commited to Truth and Light, ruling myriad independent tribes from Parthia to the Black Sea with their consent. Cyrus's respect for Truth also encompassed justice, mercy, and generosity. Xenophon reveals the secret of the great ruler's power, a question of interest to Mithradates. It was Cyrus's ability to inspire awe and fear while winning the loyalty and affection of his followers. Persians believed that the best king was a strong-willed, benevolent father to his people. Notably, Mithradates later chose the nickname Eupator ("Good Father").[13]

Xenophon tells how Cyrus, an expert charioteer, redesigned the archaic chariot for war. He gave it stronger, longer axles and a high, bronze-armored turret to protect the driver, and armored the driver and four horses in chain mail. Then Cyrus added a fiendish flourish: sharp curved blades extending about three feet out from the wheels. Cyrus's retooling transformed the chariot from a fancy, flimsy taxicab into a monstrous threshing machine that could churn through enemy lines. Some of Xenophon's most riveting passages describe the horrible effects of Cyrus's three hundred scythed chariots.[14]

Mithradates himself became a champion at racing chariots, a dangerous contest inaugurated by Cyrus. The little prince probably began driving chariots at eight or nine. Controlling a team of two or four horses for up to twelve laps around a crowded race course with hairpin curves—and no rules—demands extraordinary skill and strength. As an adult, Mithradates won chariot races in games around the Aegean and Anato-

FIG. 3.2. *A Chariot Race*, Alexander Wagner, 1898. Manchester Art Gallery.

lia. His size, strength—and daring—allowed him to take this high-risk sport to unheard-of extremes. Cyrus had driven eight horses abreast. Mithradates topped him, winning fame for driving chariots with ten racing steeds! The more horses, of course, the greater the thrills and spills. This exploit later inspired the young Roman emperor Nero to pen a poem criticizing Mithradates' hubris (by Nero's day, the number of Mithradates' chariot horses had been exaggerated to sixteen). Later, competing at the Olympic Games in Greece, Nero attempted to match Mithradates' amazing feat. The emperor crashed and nearly died.[15]

Since the time of Cyrus, aristocratic Persian boys were taught the three pillars of a noble education: Ride, Shoot, and Tell the Truth.[16] Boys began riding soon after learning to walk. As we saw, conspirators inside the court tried to arrange riding accidents to do away with the rightful heir of Pontus. There were also attempts to poison him. Many—including Mithradates—believed that his mother, Queen Laodice, was involved. There is no reason to doubt these ancient suspicions. Such schemes were common in the treacherous world Mithradates inhabited.

Perhaps because of the dangerous steeds he was given to ride, Mithradates became an expert horseman of legendary endurance. Learning to shoot meant expertise with the bow and arrow and hurling javelins from a galloping horse, crucial skills in hunting and warfare. Mithradates and his friends lived like boot camp recruits, taking turns guarding the citadel of Sinope, practicing hand-to-hand combat with the Persian *harpe*, saber, and spear. They ate spartan meals of bread, watercress, and water. They were taken on short excursions into the countryside to hunt rabbits and other small game. Within his father's game park, they practiced stalking stags and old lions, perhaps boars and bears. Mithradates loved the hunt—the boys were impatient for the time when, like Cyrus, Xerxes, Darius, and Alexander, they would venture into the mountains after real wild animals. Vigorous athletic and military training was part of Greek education, too, and historians tell us that Mithradates, an unusually tall and robust youth, excelled in wrestling, boxing, foot racing, swimming, wielding the dagger and sword, and traditional face-to-face hoplite combat with spear and shield.[17]

As future commander of Pontus's army, Mithradates needed to learn how to rule and protect his kingdom's wealth and independence. His father expected his son to know the history, geography, economy, natural resources, towns, roads, fortresses, and trade relations of Pontus and the neighboring lands.[18] Mithradates would inherit his father's foreign policy concerns, too, which included clashes with the powerful Scythian nomads

FIG. 3.3. Boys' wrestling lesson. Andre Castaigne, 1895.

of the northern Black Sea area and steppes. Intricate diplomacy maintained balance among the democratic Greek cities and indigenous monarchies of the East. The complex negotiations and shifting alliances of
this period are extremely difficult to follow in the fragmentary ancient
accounts and are much debated by modern historians. But the key issue
for an Anatolian monarch was how to handle Rome's burgeoning power
and imperial designs in the lands east of the Mediterranean.

During the final Punic War, Mithradates' father had aided Rome, sending troops to help defeat Carthage in 146 BC. When Mithradates was a

boy, his father sided with Rome again, helping to suppress a popular uprising in Anatolia. The Roman Senate recognized the Kingdom of Pontus as an official "Friend of Rome"—in other words, a client state they expected to control.[19]

In the lands influenced by the venerable civilizations of Greece and Persia, the ambitious, raw power of upstart Rome inspired contempt mixed with fear. Rome had a history of suddenly turning on its allies. As a child, Mithradates learned the names of the important clans in Rome: the Julii, Cornelii, Lucinii, Aquillii, and others. He was conversant in Roman history and myth. In later speeches he mocked Rome's legend of the wild wolf that had nursed the founder twins Romulus and Remus, and revealed his deep knowledge of Roman conquests and conflicts. Mithradates grew up very aware of Rome's great power. Negotiating with Romans was like walking a tightrope over a deep gorge, easy to fall off, impossible to sidestep. There were only two options, both risky: become Rome's "friend" or confront Rome head-on. For a savior-prince predestined for mythic glory, there was only one honorable path.

But perils lurked close to home too. Struggles over power, territories, and independence constantly arose among and within the Hellenistic monarchies, states with fluid borders and unstable ruling families left over from the old Persian and Macedonian empires. The courts seethed with conspiracies, intrigues, factions, betrayals, poisonings, and murders. At a tender age in Sinope, Mithradates understood that his most treacherous enemies might be his friends and family; even his own mother was suspect.

Pontus was rich. Its navy controlled the Black Sea trade. For as long as anyone could remember, swift pirate ships had plied the same waters. Large pirate fleets amassed wealth by supplying the sprawling Roman slave market on the island of Delos, unloading thousands of fresh captives every day. During Mithradates' childhood, he heard a lot of talk of piracy and certainly met pirate captains in his father's banquet halls. Pirates were raiding ship and shore with increasing boldness, even kidnapping Roman nobles for ransom. More than a thousand pirate vessels cruised the Black Sea and the Aegean during the first century BC. They considered themselves a sovereign nation of the high seas. Pontus had long benefited from lucrative arrangements with the pirates, ensuring safe harbors and markets where they could sell booty. His father's military adviser, the elder Dorylaus, recruited mercenaries and pirates in the Aegean and the Black Sea for Pontus. During his own wars on Rome, Mithradates would count the great pirate navies among his strongest allies.

Mithradates' access to money throughout his life has posed a perennial puzzle for historians: pirate plunder was surely one source.[20]

Another source of Pontus's wealth was the Black Sea's abundant tuna and mackerel. Tons of salted fish were exported each year to the Mediterranean. Peaches, apricots, figs, nuts, olives, and grain grew along Pontus's mild coast, watered by rivers from great mountain ranges. A system of roads linked the trading ports of Sinope and Amisus to Amasia and other inland towns. Thick forests provided pine for shipbuilding, walnut and maple for furniture, and game for meat, hides, and even *pharmaka*. Beavers, for example, were a prized Pontic product. Beaver testicles were valued for treating fever and boosting immunity and sexual vigor (castoreum, from the musk glands, contains salicylic acid, the active ingredient in aspirin, from willow bark, the beavers' chief food). Pontus also possessed plentiful gold, silver, copper, iron, rock salt, mercury, sulphur, and many other rare minerals used for pigments and medicine—or for poison.[21]

Pontus had long-standing ties with Pantikapaion (Kerch, Ukraine), a city and fortress on the Chersonese (Crimea) guarding the Cimmerian Bosporus (Kerch Straits) connecting the turbulent, deep Black Sea to the shallow Sea of Asov. Across the strait on the Taman Peninsula was the citadel of Phanagoria. These two wealthy ports controlled the crucial salt-fish trade and grain from the Scythian steppes, bound for Mediterranean markets. In this region today, archaeologists (and tomb robbers) excavate many *kurgans*, grave mounds from Mithradates' time. The magnificent gold jewelry, realistic golden death masks, weapons, fine pottery, exquisitely carved gems, and other grave goods give us a glimpse of the riches of these lands, which would later become part of Mithradates' expanded kingdom.[22]

Roiling pools of black oil, belching tar volcanoes, and fountains of ever-burning naphtha on both sides of the Cimmerian Bosporus had long inspired awe. Earthquakes periodically ravage this region. As a boy, Mithradates may have listened to the historian Theopompus of Sinope explain how the earth suddenly split open on the Taman Peninsula, spilling out the stupendous skeletons of monsters and giants (actually mastodon fossils). Instead of taking these sacred relics to be displayed in the temple, as cultured Greeks did, Theopompus said that the nomads simply heaved the fearsome bones into the Sea of Azov. A young prince in Sinope would be eager to see for himself the marvelous sights and curious peoples, the landscapes of legendary grandeur and exciting possibilities of the northern Black Sea.[23]

Any child growing up in Sinope heard anecdotes about the city's most famous citizen, Diogenes the Cynic (b. 403 BC). The eccentric philosopher, who called a capacious wine jug home and performed all bodily functions in public, was exiled from Sinope, but his unconventional ideas were very influential. Mithradates knew the famous story of Diogenes' meeting with Alexander, who admired the philosopher's way of life. Diogenes taught that wisdom flowed from decisive physical action. He advocated wandering the countryside with few possessions, living austerely off the land, and following a rigorous regimen of endurance training.

Was young Mithradates influenced by Diogenes? He grew up with Persian-Macedonian luxuries, elaborate carved couches and thrones under golden canopies, lavish banquets and expensive tapestries and artworks, servants to read aloud to him and to think up diversions, silver nails in his boots, myrrh-scented baths, and perhaps even golden sand imported from Egypt for his playground. As king, he accumulated and enjoyed untold riches. But he knew that the greatest military leaders, Cyrus, Alexander, and Hannibal, were tough warriors who scorned the soft court life. Like them, young Mithradates looked after his own armor, weapons, and horses, and reveled in the outdoor life and hardship that were part of his own education. And as we shall see, young Mithradates would eschew luxury and live for several years much like Diogenes, sleep-

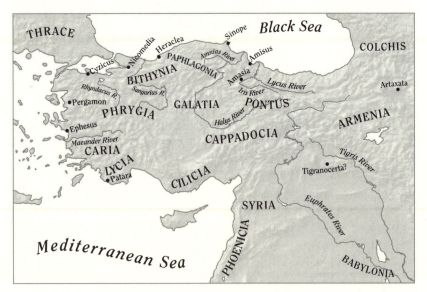

MAP 3.1. Anatolia, Armenia, Mesopotamia, and the Near East. Map by
Michele Angel.

FIG. 3.4. The *Argo* sailing toward the rising sun and Colchis, on the Black Sea. German artist unknown.

ing under the stars, rambling in the mountains, and devising his own bodybuilding program.[24]

But before he set out on that adventure, Mithradates was schooled in history and geography. Sinope traded with Greek and barbarian outposts all around the Black Sea. Beyond the mouth of the Danube ranged seminomadic warrior tribes of Moesia and Thrace. Neighboring Bithynia was the traditional gateway between Asia and Europe, and inland lay Galatia (settled by Gauls in the third century BC) and rough Paphlagonia. Far south rose the snow-capped Taurus Range of Cappadocia (Persian *Katpatuka*, "land of fine horses"). To the east lay the rich mountain kingdom of Armenia, named after one of Jason's Argonauts. Hannibal had designed Armenia's heavily fortified royal capital, Artaxata (*Artashat*, "Joy of Truth"), after he lost the Second Punic War to the Romans (at Zama, 202 BC). Even Hannibal had spent time in Mithradates' homeland.[25]

Hannibal in Anatolia

Young Mithradates probably memorized Hannibal's adventures down to the last detail, taking in every success and setback in the Carthaginian's relentless wars against Rome. Mithradates knew that, as a little boy, Hannibal had taken a sacred oath to never cease fighting the detested Romans. Hannibal kept his vow until his death at age seventy, in 182 BC, about fifty years before Mithradates' birth.

FIG. 3.5. Hannibal drinking poison to avoid capture by the Romans. Boccaccio, *Des cas des nobles homes et femmes maleureux,* ca. 1470–83, British Library. HIP/Art Resource, NY.

After Rome had devastated the Carthaginian army, Hannibal was forced to flee North Africa (195 BC). He spent the rest of his life in Anatolia, advising other enemies of Rome. He convinced King Antiochus III of Syria to make war on Rome by invading Greece. But Hannibal and Antiochus suffered a disastrous defeat at Thermopylae (191 BC). That battle held special meaning for Mithradates, because of the notorious prophecies of the Syrian ghost who rose from the dead and the raving Roman general, predicting that a savior-king would rise in the East to punish Rome.

After another decisive defeat of Antiochus by the Romans at Magnesia (south of Pergamon) in 189 BC, Hannibal was welcomed to Bithynia by King Prusias. With his new ally, Hannibal continued to wage war on Rome and its client kings. In a naval battle, Hannibal was outnumbered by Rome's client, King Eumenes II of Pergamon. Young Mithradates, with his interest in poison snakes and cunning tactics, would have appreciated Hannibal's ploy. He sent his sailors ashore to collect venomous vipers, which they stuffed into clay jars. Hannibal won the day by catapulting the writhing snakes onto the decks of Eumenes' ships.

The old general's last hours were dramatic and uncompromising. In the end, King Prusias betrayed Hannibal to the Romans. As the Romans closed in, Hannibal—one-eyed since crossing the frozen Alps—holed up in his castle in Bithynia, fitted with secret doors on every side. But escape was impossible now. An ugly death at Roman hands loomed. Hannibal took control of his fate. He slipped off the golden ring he always wore, pried open the hidden compartment, and swallowed the dram of deadly poison. With that last defiant act, Rome's first great enemy entered the realm of legend.[26]

THE POISON GARDENS OF MAD KING ATTALUS

More recent resistance to Rome also fired young Mithradates' imagination. The revolt of several Anatolian cities against Roman rule, while Mithradates was a boy, was a raw memory of imperial might. The insurrection was led by an idealistic young rebel named Aristonicus, a son of King Eumenes II of Pergamon and a harpist's daughter from Ephesus. Aristonicus was the younger stepbrother of Attalus III, who succeeded Eumenes. King Attalus was peculiar, paranoid, reclusive. He was called crazy for preferring science to governing, and he had no heirs. As a boy, Mithradates heard rumors accusing Attalus of poisoning enemies and relatives. Withdrawing from court life, letting his hair and beard grow long and scraggly, Attalus set aside his crown and took to wearing simple garments. He spent his days tending his gardens, studying botany, pharmacology, and metallurgy. He died suddenly of sunstroke in 133 BC.

But was Attalus really insane, as portrayed by Justin and other historians? A revised view was proposed in 1988 by Kent Rigsby. Rigsby reasoned that the king's reputation for murder and madness was distorted by those who wanted to make Attalus seem unfit to name his successor. Pointing out that scientific and philosophical pursuits were typical of sophisticated Hellenistic monarchs, Rigsby suggested that "in reality, Attalus was a scientist and scholar." The king may have been eccentric, but his activities represent serious scientific research. Pergamon, with its great library, active scientific community, and the healing temple of Asclepius, was the center of medical learning.

But the remarkable significance of Attalus's research has been overlooked by Rigsby and other historians. Justin's most damning example of Attalus's madness was his obsession with "digging and sowing in his garden" and his bizarre practice of concocting "mixtures of healthful and beneficial plants, drenched with the juices of poisonous ones," which he presented as "special gifts to his friends." The historian Plutarch tells us that Attalus cultivated toxic plants such as "henbane, hellebore, hemlock, aconite [monkshood], and belladonna in his royal gardens and became an expert in their juices and fruits." Galen, the celebrated physician from Pergamon (b. AD 129), added that Attalus also experimented with antidotes against the venoms of spiders, scorpions, toxic sea slugs, and snakes. Galen praised the king for testing his mixtures only on condemned criminals.[27]

Can it be a coincidence that the youthful Mithradates engaged in the very same sort of activities and experiments as had mad King Attalus? We know that Mithradates created his renowned "universal antidote," the *Mithridatium*, by mixing tiny doses of deadly poisons with antidotes. Mithradates—who would achieve lasting fame as the world's first experimental toxicologist—may well have been inspired at a young age by his grandfather Pharnaces' discovery of a panacea and by the unusual research first begun by the last king of Pergamon, "mad" Attalus.

Attalus's sudden death in 133 BC, about a year after Mithradates' birth, set in motion the chain of events that would eventually lead to Mithradates' wars on Rome. Attalus's will shocked everyone: he bequeathed his kingdom to Rome. This unexpected inheritance became the basis for Rome's vast and lucrative "Province of Asia."

Was Attalus's will a Roman forgery, as Mithradates would later claim? What ruler in his right mind would will his kingdom to Rome? Attalus's stepbrother Aristonicus immediately organized a popular rebellion, to claim the throne and keep the Romans from annexing the kingdom.

ARISTONICUS AND THE CITIZENS OF THE SUN

Aristonicus established rebel headquarters at Leucae, founded by a Persian rebel leader in the fourth century BC. Attalus's navy quickly joined Aristonicus. Pro-Roman officials in Pergamon attempted to appease the population by granting citizenship to foreigners, mercenaries, and freedmen, but numerous cities joined Aristonicus, including Colophon, Myndos, Tralles, Nysa, Phocaea, Thyateira, Stratonicea in Mysia, Apollonia, and the island of Samos. The Stoic philosopher Blossius, a supporter of democratic principles and an exile from Rome, also supported Aristonicus's cause.[28]

The city of Ephesus, allied with Rome at the time, sent a fleet against Aristonicus at Cyme. He lost the battle and fled far inland. All seemed lost. But now the story of Aristonicus's revolt gains real momentum, with much to enthrall young Mithradates. The rebel leader eluded capture, traveling to his base of support in the Persian-influenced central Anatolian highlands. Here Aristonicus established a utopian city-state, called Heliopolis, "City of the Sun." The citizens were free and equal, and Aristonicus promised to liberate all slaves and cancel debts, eradicating evils that were particularly identified with Rome. He assembled a great army of Heliopolitae, "Citizens of the Sun," indigenous Anatolians and descendants of Alexander's Macedonians, poor and middle classes, debtors and slaves. From his new stronghold, Aristonicus issued coins asserting his royal claim. All these developments greatly alarmed the Romans, already beset by slave revolts and indigenous uprisings in Italy.

Most modern pro-Roman historians downplay the revolutionary nature of Aristonicus's insurrection, suggesting that his motive for mobilizing "resourceless people" and slaves was nothing but "desperation" after the naval defeat. They point out that Aristonicus defended monarchy. But in Anatolia, independent "democratic monarchy" was a traditional, popular, anti-Roman concept. Aristonicus's ideology and his campaign— the first popular Anatolian uprising against Roman domination—might well have been a model for Mithradates' own war on Rome, his appeal to followers, and his policies of erasing debts and freeing slaves. The tale of the young rebel from Anatolia ("land of the rising sun") battling over-whelming odds and Roman treachery would have appealed to Mithradates, who was a boy when the uprising was quelled. Later, Mithradates' own campaigns against Rome could be seen as keeping the faith of Aristonicus's insurgency, as well as Hannibal's boyhood vow. As we shall see, Mithradates frequently alluded to Aristonicus's revolt in his speeches.[29]

The names chosen by Aristonicus for Heliopolis and its "Citizens of the Sun" receive scant comment from Roman historians, and contemporary Romans apparently missed the significance too. But these names radiated mystical and political symbolism in Greco-Persian lands. Notably, a Zoroastrian tribe of Armenia called themselves by a similar name, Arevordik ("Children of the Sun"), and prided themselves on never submitting to tyrants. For Mithradates, and for Aristonicus's followers, "citizens" and "polis" reflected Greek democratic traditions. "Of the Sun" evoked the ancient Persian god Mithra, Mithradates' namesake. The name "Citizens of the Sun" announced that Aristonicus and his army were fighting on the side of Light and Truth against the forces of Darkness.

Mithradates' father, and the rulers of Bithynia, Cappadocia, Ephesus, and Paphlagonia, were nervous about Rome's reaction. They agreed to send troops against Aristonicus. But the Citizens of the Sun persevered. It appeared that Aristonicus would be acclaimed king of Pergamon and Greater Phrygia. The Roman Senate dispatched its own legions in 131 BC, commanded by P. Licinius Crassus. But Crassus was bent on plundering Attalus's palace instead of leading a campaign. His disorganized army was routed in a battle near Leucae. Crassus, surrounded by a hostile mob, poked a Thracian in the eye with his whip. The enraged barbarian stabbed Crassus to death. The Roman's head was presented to Aristonicus.

The Citizens of the Sun won more victories. Rome sent M. Perperna to put down the spreading insurgency. Perperna, fresh from suppressing a slave revolt in Sicily, captured Aristonicus alive. Although Perperna suddenly died (reportedly of disease), Aristonicus was sent in chains to Rome, along with Attalus's fabulous treasures from Pergamon. The rebel leader was cast into the Tullianum, a stone dungeon twelve feet deep, described by the historian Sallust as "repugnant and fearsome from neglect, darkness, and stench." The state executioner strangled Aristonicus in his cell in 129 BC.

In Cyme, where Aristonicus's navy had been defeated, it was said that the statue of Apollo wept. Inspired by their leader's martyrdom and Rome's ineffective campaign—and perhaps seeing Perperna's sudden death as a good omen—the Citizens of the Sun continued to resist. The Senate dispatched the ambitious consul Manius Aquillius to crush the insurrection and establish Roman provincial government in Pergamon. It must have impressed Mithradates that the cities loyal to Aristonicus still held fast, protecting the Sun Citizens inside their fortified walls.

Aquillius faced a series of long-drawn-out sieges before he could occupy the land and set up the new government. To bring the war to a quick end, Aquillius resorted to a ruthless solution. He ordered his men to pour poison into the water supplies of the besieged cities. This biological weapon killed soldiers and noncombatants alike, and Aquillius's army easily overran the cities. Even in Rome, however, some critics deplored such a barbarous tactic, declaring that Aquillius's expedient victory dishonored old Roman military values.[30]

Aquillius took over Pergamon and levied heavy taxes for personal profit. Aristonicus's rebellion was over, and Rome's allies were rewarded. Mithradates' father received Greater Phrygia in thanks. But popular outrage was visceral in the territories coveted by Rome. Aquillius's vicious victory through poison and his suffocating taxation intensified the loathing for Rome. Cities that had supported Aristonicus's revolt were severely punished. Yet even the official "friends" of Rome experienced anxiety rather than security. Everyone was beginning to realize that Rome had a nasty habit of attacking former clients.

During his childhood, Mithradates would have heard many details of Aristonicus's Anatolian uprising that are lost to us. He may have known, for example, whether Aristonicus, grandson of a harpist, had been named after Alexander's brave harpist friend Aristonicus who died gloriously in battle. Mithradates also would have learned which poison Aquillius had used to taint the wells. Hellebore, a common plant with a notorious military history, was probably the agent of death. Mithradates, who studied toxic plants and warfare, could recall the infamous story of a similar siege situation, some five hundred years earlier in Greece. The victorious generals—aided by a corrupt doctor—had annihilated the townspeople by poisoning the water supply with crushed hellebore.[31]

MEDEA'S MAGIC POTIONS

Wedged between Armenia and the sheer cliffs where the Caucasus Mountains plunged into the eastern Black Sea lay fabled Colchis (Georgia), a harsh land rich in gold and exotic minerals and plants. In Greek myth,

Zeus had chained Prometheus, the rebel Titan who brought fire to mortals, on the highest peak in the Caucasus, sending an eagle to tear out his liver for eternity. Mithradates and his friends heard exciting myths set in their own native lands. In the epic poem about Jason and the Argonauts and their quest for the Golden Fleece, the *Argo* sailed east toward the "Sun's golden treasure house," along the southern shore of the Black Sea, stopping for adventures and founding towns.[32] In Sinope, Mithradates might have played near the marble statue of his city's founder, the Argonaut Autolycus.

The Argonauts had marveled at Pontus's iron mines and its weird towers of salt on the Halys River. Pressing on to Themiscrya, the great Amazon stronghold on the Thermodon River, the Argonauts sailed to far Colchis under the forbidding Caucasus Mountains. There Jason fell in love with Medea, the beautiful barbarian sorceress.

FIG. 3.6. Medea in her Chariot of the Sun. The sorceress of Colchis wears a mantle and a Persian-Phrygian cap, like those worn by Zoroastrian Magi and Amazons. Detail, Lucanian calyx-crater ca. 400 BC. Cleveland Museum of Art, Leonard C. Hanna Jr. Fund 1991.1.

Mistress of poisons and magic, granddaughter of the Sun god, Medea could tame mysterious fire from the black oil pools of Baku on the Caspian Sea, to create unquenchable flames. Her potions bestowed superhuman strength or deathlike sleep and made one invulnerable to fire or sword. Medea knew the secrets of deadly dragon's blood and all the antidotes for serpent venom. It is easy to picture young Mithradates, future toxicologist, enthralled by the description of Medea alighting from her Sun-chariot to gather *pharmaka*.

In the gloom of night, clothed in black, murmuring eerie incantations, Medea climbed higher and higher into the Caucasus Mountains. There, springing from the ichor that had flowed out of Prometheus's side, a flower the color of saffron bloomed on tall twin stalks. From the fleshy root, blood-red sap oozed. This crimson liquid Medea captured in a pure white shell from the Caspian Sea.[33]

THE MIGHTY HERCULES

In young Mithradates' eclectic pantheon of mythic role models, the Persian sorceress Medea was joined by Hercules, the Greek superhero who rescued Prometheus from his torture. In the course of his adventures, Hercules had traveled across the towering Caucasus Mountains into Scythia, where he won a duel with Hippolyte, queen of the Amazons. The natives of the city of Pergamon believed they were the descendants of Hercules' son Telephus. Like Alexander, Mithradates also claimed descent from Hercules. Three remarkable marble statues show how deeply Mithradates identified with Hercules. The first, a sculpture in Pergamon —probably created in 88–85 BC when Mithradates established royal headquarters there—depicts a fatherly Hercules wearing his signature lionskin cape, holding his infant son Telephus. Recent analysis of portraiture in contemporary coins and sculpure suggests that the model for the little boy was none other than Mithradates!

The child's profile and hairstyle strongly resemble portraits of the adult Mithradates on his early silver coins. The pudgy face was not meant to be a good likeness of Mithradates as a toddler. But the similarity to Mithradates' coin portraits—and the message—would have been immediately recognized by everyone. The likeness was so obvious that, after his defeat of Mithradates in 63 BC, the Roman general Pompey seized this statue of Baby Mithradates to show off in Rome.[34]

FIG. 3.7. Hercules and his son Telephus, Pergamon. The boy was intended to resemble Mithradates, who claimed Hercules as a forefather. Chiaramonti Museum, Vatican. Scala/Art Resource, NY.

Another statue group, discovered in 1925 at the Great Altar of Pergamon, shows a youthful Hercules freeing Prometheus. The young man in the lionskin is a lifelike portrait of Mithradates on the verge of manhood. It is similar to another well-known portrait statue in the Louvre that is securely identified as the adult Mithradates, also wearing Hercules' lionskin (fig 6.1). The image of Mithradates as Hercules liberating the chained Titan had great symbolic value for Greeks and the people of the East, because it depicted the king as a savior-liberator.

FIG. 3.8. Young Mithradates as Hercules freeing Prometheus, marble sculpture group, Pergamon. Berlin, Bildarchiv Preussischer Kulturbesitz/Art Resource, NY.

ALEXANDER AND DARIUS

Portraits on coins show that Mithradates copied Alexander's flamboyant shoulder-length hairstyle. Alexander's charisma, military genius, grand dreams—and tragic death just before his thirty-third birthday—had made him a cult figure, not just for Greco-Persians like Mithradates, but for many Romans too. Even as a child, Mithradates discovered much in Alexander's life story that matched his own, and much to emulate. To portray Mithradates as the new Alexander, the antithesis of uncivilized Rome, Mithradates and his circle loved to draw comparisons between the two. Incidents like Mithradates' taming of the wild stallion, described above, fostered popular associations between the beloved Alexander and the prince of Pontus.[35]

Like Alexander, Mithradates had a magnetic personality. Did young Mithradates consciously mirror his hero's well-known mannerisms? Alexander had a habit of tilting his head to the left; some sculpted portraits of the youthful Mithradates not only resemble Alexander but also show his head inclined leftward. Alexander was also said to have a "certain melting look in his eyes." We can imagine young Mithradates perfecting his version of Alexander's "melting gaze" on his friends Dorylaus and Gaius, his little sisters, and other children in Sinope. Alexander's companions had even claimed that his body and clothing exuded a pleasant, sweet fragrance. That, too, was something Mithradates could achieve, with myrrh and other perfumes used by men and women in Persian-influenced courts.[36]

Mithradates could probably recite the life story of Alexander (b. 356 BC), who set out at about age twenty-two to conquer the most powerful empire in the world. The Persian Empire under Darius III ranged over three continents and ruled about 25 million diverse people. But by the time Alexander died (in 323 BC, almost two hundred years before Mithradates' birth), Darius's empire had been incorporated into the new Macedonian Empire, stretching from Greece and Anatolia to Egypt and all the way to the Himalayas.

The mesmerizing story of Alexander and Darius III held many lessons for Mithradates. The Macedonians were outnumbered two to one, yet Alexander overwhelmed Darius's army at Issus (333 BC). Darius made a daring escape in his chariot and recruited 200,000 more warriors from the fringes of his empire, backed by armored cavalry, ranks of dread scythed chariots, and war elephants. The two armies met again at Gaugamela (331 BC). But Alexander's brilliant maneuvers again decimated the Persians. This time, Darius was able to slip away on horseback. At his defeat, Darius had expressed admiration for Alexander, even approving him as his successor to rule the Persian Empire. Fleeing to the far eastern reaches of his empire, Darius was murdered by his closest generals. Mithradates knew that Alexander famously wept over Darius's corpse and buried him with great honors at Persepolis. Rejecting the traditional Greek hatred of barbarians (non-Greeks), Alexander welcomed his new subjects into his inner circle. Their mutual esteem and courtly gestures made Darius and Alexander into perfectly matched noble adversaries, like brave knights in a medieval tale of chivalry. Mithradates took great pride in his connections to both commanders and embraced a visionary dream of fusing Persia and Greece to overcome Rome, the barbarous empire of the West.

After his conquest of the Persian Empire, Alexander had adopted Persian customs and Persian dress. The ancient historians tell us that Mithradates wore old-fashioned Persian costumes. This seemingly eccentric habit was a way of honoring—and calling attention to—his Persian heritage and another way to imitate Alexander too. We know that Mithradates inherited antique furniture and other treasures from Darius I. On rainy days in the palace at Sinope, the boy could visit the storerooms and open cedar treasure chests filled with Persian tiaras, golden earrings, bracelets, and necklaces, rings and carved gems; jars redolent of exotic perfumes, and vintage finery, long white robes edged with purple and embroidered with gilded hawks and lions.

Mithradates knew that Alexander had taken care not to dress in the extravagant fashion (ridiculed by the plainly dressed Greeks) of the Medes, the ancient kinsmen of Persian kings. Nor did Alexander chose to wear the full royal Persian costume, a fancy long robe over trousers and turned-up slippers, topped with a tiara. Instead, Alexander combined Greek and Persian styles into a modest but elegant fashion statement: a simple, short, pure white tunic belted with a Persian sash that held his dagger, and sandals, no trousers or crown (the Macedonians considered the Persian tiara and trousers outlandish). Some of Alexander's armor included antique pieces.

Young Mithradates also designed his own dashing, hybrid ensemble, probably after experimenting as a boy. Like Alexander, he wore a simple diadem (a purple and white ribbon tied around his head) and a brilliant white tunic, modestly embroidered with purple hems. The tunic was belted with a Persian-style, jewel-encrusted sash to hold the golden scabbard of his dagger against his thigh. Old-fashioned Persian trousers and leather boots with turned-up toes completed the king's outfit.[37]

THE KING IS DEAD, LONG LIVE THE KING

During his boyhood in Sinope, mythic deeds, historical models both good and bad, and his scientific poison projects occupied Mithradates' thoughts. He spent his days collecting rocks and reptiles, riding and hunting with his friends, reading and daydreaming. It must have seemed a happy and idyllic time, with only fleeting clouds.

Mithradates' father held many feasts for courtiers and honored guests, with enthusiastic drinking, slabs of venison and lamb and Black Sea tuna, bread and olives, cherries and peaches. In 120 or 119 BC, Mithradates celebrated his birthday, his fourteenth or fifteenth. According to Persian custom, a birthday called for a banquet of special magnificence. A whole ox, camel, or donkey was roasted inside a giant brick oven. Each course was served separately, along with a great deal of wine. A flight of many different honeyed sweets followed, while conjurers from Parthia,

Indian snake charmers, Syrian tumblers and dancers entertained, and harpists and drummers filled the great hall with music.[38]

At one of his lavish banquets, Mithradates' father suddenly clutched his throat. Lurching out of his chair, he fell dead, his heavy silver cup rolling silently across the thick carpet. In that one moment, Mithradates' whole world was thrown into tumult.

Mithradates V Euergetes was assassinated in about 120 BC in Sinope, poisoned by persons unknown. The deed was done while the king's friend, General Dorylaus, was away in Crete, recruiting for Pontus's army. When he received the news of the murder, it was too dangerous to return. He remained in Crete.[39]

Paranoia suddenly replaced Mithradates' vague mistrust of his mother. Was he next? Who could be trusted? He turned to his closest companions and best friend, young Dorylaus. Perhaps he also found support among some teachers and courtiers. Comparisons to the assassination of Alexander's father, Philip of Macedon, were inevitable, and the parallels must have been chilling for Mithradates. Philip was murdered at a wedding banquet. Alexander had blamed his father's great enemies, the Persians, but many suspected his mother Olympias. Characterized by ancient historians as a jealous, murderous witch, Olympias terrified men with the huge, tame snakes she bred for Dionysian orgies. Mithradates had heard the ghastly stories about what happened after Philip's violent death. Olympias had burned Alexander's infant half brother to death and poisoned Alexander's other half brother with drugs that destroyed his mind.[40]

In Sinope, some worried that Romans might have been behind the assassination of Mithradates' father, but the ancient evidence points to a palace coup. Was Mithradates' own mother, Queen Laodice, really a wicked witch, as Olympias was reputed to have been? To modern readers, the idea of murderous mothers seems like a Grimms' fairy tale, but Mithradates knew of many ambitious queens in neighboring kingdoms who seized power through intrigue, murder, and poison. The mother of Prince Ariathes of Cappadocia, for example, had poisoned Ariathes' five younger brothers one by one. Mithradates noticed that his mother doted on his little brother Mithradates the Good. The murder of Mithradates' father supports Justin's statement that there were plots to do away with Mithradates himself. As modern historians point out, Mithradates' life really was in danger: the unknown murderers of his father were embedded in the palace among his guardians and tutors. It is easy to believe that Queen Laodice was complicit.[41]

After his father was buried in the royal mausoleum at Amasia (the old Pontic capital), young Mithradates was crowned king of Pontus, in 120 or 119 BC. His father's will apparently left the kingdom to the joint rule of Queen Laodice, Mithradates, and his brother Mithradates the Good. Since both princes were underage, Laodice retained all power as regent, and she favored her younger, more malleable son. Laodice's love of luxury made her a compliant client of Rome. Over the next few years, she accepted their bribes, and her extravagance pushed Pontus into debt.

In 119 BC, a marvelous omen suddenly appeared in the sky. The spectacular comet with the long scimitar tail, observed before Mithradates' birth, returned, just as he was crowned king. The Magi and people in Persian-influenced lands rejoiced: this heavenly sign affirmed that Mithradates was indeed the savior-king sent by Mithra, the great leader who would rescue the East from Rome, as promised by the comet of 135 BC and widely known prophecies. The rare coins depicting a comet may have been minted just after his coronation (see fig. 2.1).

But Mithradates knew he had to devise a survival plan, or he would never live to fulfill his destiny. He began carrying his dagger with him at all times. At night he kept the blade under his pillow, just as Alexander had done.[42]

THE POISON PRINCE

What was the poison that killed his father? This compelling question recalled other unsolved royal deaths, like that of Alexander. Alexander's companions believed that he had been murdered with a nameless poison, a mysterious substance of curious lore, an ice-cold "dew" collected from the mossy rocks where the River Styx cascaded over a high cliff in Greece. The "dew" was so corrosive that it dissolved metal and could be stored only in the hoof of a mule. Modern toxicologists have been unable to identify this poison. The ancient descriptions point to an acidic substance: a likely culprit may be a recently discovered, naturally occurring, extremely toxic acidic bacteria found in calcium carbonate crusts that leach out from limestone bedrock.[43]

But Mithradates had to consider more easily available possibilities closer to home. Was his father the victim of some noxious plant? They were myriad: henbane, yew, deadly nightshade, hemlock, mandrake, monkshood, hellebore, poppies, mushrooms, oleander. . . .

Mithradates had dabbled in toxic experiments as a boy, goaded by fears of poisoning. But now it was a matter of life and death. According to Justin, when his enemies' attempts on his life "failed because of the boy's superior strength and skill, they tried to kill him with poison." He began urgent investigations of *pharmaka*, secretly testing them on others and himself. For models young Mithradates could look to the mythical sorceress Medea, but also to his grandfather's panacea, to Attalus's misunderstood toxicological research in Pergamon, and to Alexander's bold —nearly fatal—scientific experiments in Babylonia and India with naphtha and powerful potions. Alexander had prescribed drugs and antidotes for his companions and himself. In India, for example, Alexander's men were dying gruesome deaths after being attacked with swords dipped in snake venom. Alexander dreamed of the plant that could save them, and consulted with Hindu doctors about antidotes for snakebite. Another time, Alexander was courageous enough to drink down a beaker of medicine that knocked him unconscious, almost killing him. Now Mithradates, too, would dare to search for the perfect formula to neutralize all poisons.[44]

Toxic natural resources abounded in the Black Sea region. The nomads of Scythia dipped their arrows in a sophisticated concoction of viper venom and other pathogens; their shamans were experts in antidotes based on venom. In Armenia's remote lakes lurked venomous fish, and Pontus boasted its own poisons. Wild honey, distilled by bees from the nectar of poisonous rhododendrons and oleander so profuse on the coast, could kill a man. Even the flesh of Pontic ducks was poisonous. The ducks thrived on hellebore and other baneful plants, and the bees enjoyed a strange immunity to poison. Did these mysterious facts inspire Mithradates to search for ways to inure himself to poisons?[45]

Nefarious, rare minerals were mined in Pontus. Sinope was the center for processing and exporting Sinopic red earth, realgar, orpiment, and other glittering dark red and yellow crystals surrounded by magical and ominous folklore. Known by many different names, these minerals occurred in association with quicksilver (mercury), lead, sulphur, iron ore, cobalt, nickel, and gold. The mines exhaled vapors so noxious that they were said to be worked only by slaves who had been sentenced to death for terrible crimes. One of the most infamous of the mines was Sandarakurgion Dag (Mount Realgar), described by the geographer Strabo. On the Halys River near Pimolisa, gangs of two hundred slaves labored to hollow out the entire mountain. Strabo notes that Mount Realgar Mine was finally abandoned as unprofitable, because it was too expensive to continually replace the slaves as they dropped dead from the toxic fumes.[46]

Fig. 3.9. Mine slaves, like those who worked in toxic Mount Realgar.

The various ancient words for groups of related compounds make them difficult to sort out and identify today. *Cinnabar, zinjifrah, vermilion, Sinopic red earth, ruby sulphur, miltos sinopike, sinople, orpiment, oker, sandaracha, sandyx, lithargyron, zamikh, arsenicum, arhenicum, zirnikhi, sindura, minium, Armenian calche, realgar, dragon's blood:* all were ancient names for the many forms of toxic ores containing mercury, sulphur, and/or arsenic. Sinopic red earth was used to waterproof ships; many of these costly substances were prized as brilliant pigments, varnishes, and textile dyes; they were also important in alchemy and medicine.[47]

But Mithradates investigated their more sinister qualities. Arsenic—from the Persian word *zamikh* ("yellow orpiment," Arabic, *al-zarnikhi*)—was a deadly, odorless, tasteless poison undetectable in food or drink—the ideal toxin for murder. The poison that someone slipped into his father's meat or wine was most likely pure arsenic, produced by heating realgar (Arabic, *rhaj al ghar*, "powder of the mine"), red arsenic sulfate.

Mithradates discovered a curious phenomenon. By ingesting minuscule amounts of arsenic each day, he learned that one could build up an immunity to larger doses that would otherwise be fatal. Perhaps he achieved tolerance to arsenic at an early age, since, as Justin states, the conspirators in the palace failed in their attempts to poison him while he was a boy. He took other precautions, too, like those suggested by the

Roman satirist Juvenal: "Trust none of the dishes at dinner, those sweets are black with the poison your mother put in them, whatever she offers you, make sure another samples it first. Let your tutor test each cup you are poured!"[48]

Mithradates supplemented his clandestine study of toxicology by stepping up his physical training. Hunting was a perfect excuse for spending time away from the castle. Meanwhile he planned his next move. From his reading of Xenophon's books, his grounding in myth and history, Mithradates would have known exactly what was required of a young hero whose life was in danger. One day, armed with his bow, dagger, and javelin, the intrepid prince rode out of Sinope's gates with his most loyal companions. They did not return.

4

The Lost Boys

D<small>READING</small> that his enemies in the palace would succeed with the sword what they had failed to accomplish with poison," Mithradates was compelled to protect himself.[1] There were only two choices. Young Mithradates could remain in Sinope dominated by his treacherous mother, hoping to survive until he was old enough to wrest power away from her. Or he could take decisive action, the sort of path advocated by Sinope's philosopher, Diogenes. Mithradates' destiny, promised by oracles and comets, demanded that he seize the second option.

In devising a plan, Mithradates could consider the experiences of Cyrus of Persia, Alexander, and Mithradates I, the founder of the Pontic Kingdom. Each had left home and family for a period of time before assuming power. While in exile, these leaders gained wisdom, faithful followers, political clout, and popular favor. The rebel leader Aristonicus had also found refuge and support in the Anatolian heartland.

Listening to Persian tales of his ancestors and reading Xenophon's writings, Mithradates could identify with Cyrus the Great, whose enemies had tried to kill him as an infant. At age thirteen, Cyrus left the royal palace at Susa and lived in Media, eventually returning to become ruler of all Persia. In action-packed descriptions of Cyrus's big-game hunts and other adventures, Xenophon told how the future king of Persia and his friends learned self-reliance and decision making through daring exploits together in the Iranian highlands. In Xenophon's *On Hunting*, written for young Greek noblemen, a boy could find exciting anecdotes and practical advice. The experience of hunting together instilled virtue, leadership, and military prowess in adolescent aristocrats. Xenophon not only detailed all the proper clothing, equipment, and methods for chasing game, but the great Greek general declared that excellence in the hunt naturally produced heroic warriors and commanders.

Fig. 4.1. Youthful Mithradates, marble head (3 inches high) from miniature statue, discovered in 1992 in the temple on the acropolis of Pantikapaion. Zin'ko 2004 and Kerch Museum, "Ancient Sculptures," Kiev, 2004. Photo courtesy of Jakob Munk Højte.

Mithradates' hero Alexander had loved to hunt with his friends—they relaxed by chasing rabbits and weasels and proved their manhood by killing lions and bears. A headstrong, reckless teenager, Alexander was famous for risking danger in both hunting and war. Mithradates surely envied Alexander's opportunity to go on his own authority to battle at age sixteen, while his father was away. Later, during a family crisis, Alexander summoned his companions and rode off to the wilds of Illyria, in the far west of the Macedonian Empire. There Alexander and his friends lived on their own by hunting. When Alexander's father was murdered, Alexander had to act quickly to win the trust of the Macedonian army. Ideas for a similar venture, one that would combine hunting with statecraft, began to take form in Mithradates' mind.[2]

According to Justin, Mithradates came up with "a bold plan that called for great resourcefulness and perseverance." Justin's account is terse but revealing: beginning in childhood, Mithradates was fixated on survival. On guard against plots, especially poisoning, he fortified himself with antidotes and athletics. After his father's death, Justin says, Mithradates and some companions disappeared from Sinope. For seven years, they never slept under a roof and survived by hunting, bivouacking in the mountains. The young king built endurance by chasing wild beasts on foot and outrunning them when they turned to attack him. Sometimes, like the Greek superhero Hercules, Mithradates even dared to pit his might against dangerous wild animals by wrestling and killing them bare-handed.[3]

Justin is describing exactly the kind of Greco-Persian aristocratic "boy scout" activities encouraged by Xenophon. By these methods, says Justin, Mithradates not only evaded the attempts on his life, but also developed great strength and passed amazing tests of stamina and courage. After seven years away, Justin writes in his concise style, Mithradates returned to Sinope, dealt with his enemies, and began his reign.

Regrettably, the laconic Justin is our only surviving source for this important period, the time after the assassination of Mithradates' father in about 120 BC until the beginning of Mithradates' independent reign in about 115 BC. Because Justin was condensing the lost work of another historian, Trogus, his version omits, conflates, or repeats some events. If only we had Trogus's original full accounts! Some modern historians, faced with inexact dates, reject Justin's chronology altogether, pointing out that statues and inscriptions honoring Mithradates and his younger brother were erected in Delos in 116/115 BC, five years after their father's murder, while Mithradates was supposed to be away from Sinope. But Queen Laodice could easily have erected statues and inscriptions on behalf of the young coheirs, during Mithradates' absence. Indeed, this would have been a wise propaganda move to counter rumors that the missing prince had been done away with. In response, Mithradates' supporters might have issued coins featuring his birth comet while he was in exile, as a way to advertise the young king's destiny and prepare for his eventual return. Both factions had good reasons to publicize his image while Mithradates was absent.[4]

It is true that Justin's "seven years" is a suspiciously mythic number: seven often stands for "several years" in folklore contexts. Stripped of the folkloric flourishes, however, Justin's account is neither sensational nor illogical. There is nothing incredible about the idea that Mithradates disappeared after his father's murder. He faced real peril in Sinope: there are many examples of murdered royal children in this era. There is no reason to doubt that the crown prince departed with some companions in the manner described by Justin (and perhaps detailed by Trogus). We cannot know exactly how long Mithradates was actually away, but four or five years is a reasonable interval.[5]

How did Mithradates organize his escape? What happened during the most mysterious period of Mithradates' life, the years between his father's murder and the day that Mithradates returned to power? What follows is a plausible scenario for how Mithradates' self-imposed exile might have unfolded, based on known facts and informed speculation.

The Plan

The journey was not a spontaneous lark but would have required months of meticulous planning. A secretive, creative, and daring youngster, sure of his place in history, Mithradates thought up a strategy that recapitulated episodes from the lives of his heroes and incorporated his love of the hunt. The royal heir of Pontus was surrounded by close friends his own age and a little older, including some noblemen in their twenties. This circle of comrades replicated the elite retinues that had surrounded Alexander and Cyrus.

Mithradates' best friend Dorylaus helped with logistics. His life was threatened too. As the nephew of the murdered king's general Dorylaus, young Dorylaus would have been targeted by the conspirators in the palace. We can imagine the two boys whispering late into the night, deciding who among their schoolmates could be trusted to accompany them. Mithradates' spoiled little brother, Mithradates the Good, was not included. From inscriptions on portrait busts found in Delos, we have the names of some of Mithradates' closest associates in his early reign. Some may have been members of his youthful entourage, such as Gaius son of Hermaeus, and Diophantus son of Mithares, and Gordius, the Cappadocian who became Mithradates' special envoy.

The runaways expected to keep on the move for some years, until they felt strong enough to seize victory. Too large a group might attract attention. A group of eight or ten could efficiently hunt and provide for themselves. Mithradates must have radiated confidence and intellect by age fourteen or fifteen, to have such devoted companions who agreed to follow him in exile. Impelled by friendship and adventure, they could also hope for great rewards. They knew that Alexander's companions had inherited his kingdom. The incentive for Mithradates and Dorylaus was powerful: they were running for their lives.

Now, with the plan roughly plotted out, Mithradates talked incessantly about hunting; Justin tells us he "feigned a great passion for the hunt" before he disappeared. His band stayed away longer on each outing, without drawing suspicion. Maybe the group cached provisions and coins in secure outposts during forays before the big day. The young king could requisition extra horses from the royal stable for an extended hunting trip. After all, hunting was his favorite activity, an obsession really. I imagine that Mithradates and his friends were prepared to depart by 118/117 BC. Mithradates could portray the expedition as a special occasion to celebrate his sixteenth birthday and his first year as the boy-king of Pontus.

As Mithradates and his companions rode out after his birthday banquet that spring, each wore practical hunting attire of subdued colors, as recommended by Xenophon—no bright white or purple! The young men wore dun-colored tunics, hats, short woolen cloaks, and high leather boots; some wore Persian trousers, like Mithradates. Their leader was distinguished by his simple diadem and a heavy gold signet ring with the royal seal of Pontus. Each boy took a pair of javelins, staff and cudgel, bow and arrows, sword and dagger. Favorite hounds trotted alongside the pack horses loaded with bedding, nets for big game, cups and utensils, personal items such as musical instruments, gaming pieces, fishing hooks and line, and best-loved books. Each adventurer carried a leather pouch bulging with coins for necessities and food, and to reward citizens of Pontus. Money would also be needed for temple dedications.[6]

Mithradates could procure a map of Pontus, and information about mountain ranges, rivers, and springs; towns and villages, fortifications, temple precincts; royal highways, minor roads, and trails over mountain passes.[7] The group had long ago scouted out their first campsite, a full day's ride away. The boys bid casual farewells to families and friends, acting as though they would soon return, but knowing they would not see them again for several years—if ever.

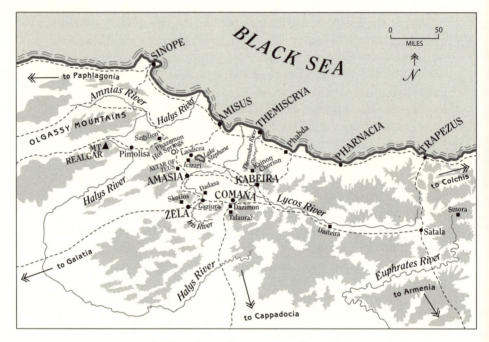

MAP 4.1. The Kingdom of Pontus. Map by Michele Angel.

OUTWARD BOUND

At sunrise, the band set out south from Sinope's gates, taking the middle fork over the hills to the Amnias River valley. The west fork headed along the rocky coast to the tiny coves of Paphlagonia; the east route followed the coast to Amisus. The mountains and valleys of Anatolia run east-west. Crossing the foothills, the hunting party forded the Amnias and turned their horses southeast on the old Persian road along the Halys River. On the riders' right rose heavily forested mountains with good campsites, pure water, and excellent hunting. But they would not linger within reach of Sinope. Crossing the stone bridge over the Halys, the riders continued past small villages along the ancient road. The first nights were filled with excitement tinged with anxiety at the enormity of their mission.

The conversation might have turned to poisons as the group bypassed the road to the fortress guarding Mount Realgar Mine, where slaves dropped dead from inhaling the grievous fumes of Sinopic red earth. This deadly substance—arsenic—was probably what killed their king, Euergetes. Mithradates intended to continue his toxicological studies, looking forward to testing new *pharmaka* in the field. To live long enough to attain all the ambitious goals he had set for himself, he needed to perfect his antidote.

But first, keeping in mind Alexander's first move after the assassination of his father, Mithradates understood how vital it was to win the trust of his father's military commanders in the kingdom. Many might regard him as the puppet of his powerful mother, unlikely to live to celebrate his twentieth birthday. He had to send a strong signal to Pontus's armies to assure them that Mithradates VI Eupator was now their leader in fact as well as name. He must convince them that he had a real strategy for regaining power in Sinope. They needed to know that Mithradates would bring glory to the kingdom and wealth and victory to its warriors.

In the first century BC, Pontus and the other eastern territories of Anatolia resembled a medieval feudal landscape. A system of roads connected major cities; minor routes linked villages, temple lands, and hereditary estates; and there were many horse trails and footpaths. Castles and strongholds guarded strategic locales. Mithradates' logical first goal would have been the citadel of Amasia, about 150 miles from Sinope.

At the next major crossroads, Mithradates' party reached the Iris River and a well-known spa called Phazemon, where the travelers made dedications to the healing god Asclepius and to the lovely nymphs who were said to frolic in the warm springs. Refreshed after relaxing in the medicinal baths, the young riders continued to Amasia. There was no reason to avoid the main roads; they were not yet missed in Sinope. Near Amasia, they ascended the hilltop Temple of Zeus Stratios (leader of armies), where Mithradates had often watched his father perform fire sacrifices at the high altar (Mithradatids worshipped Zeus as a form of Ahuramazda/ Mithra). Perhaps Mithradates himself now performed the ceremony for the first time. The ruins of this altar, with inscriptions dedicated to Zeus, are still visible today.[8]

Queen Laodice's power lay within the palace at Sinope and perhaps extended to a few nearby towns. Mithradates' father's friends and troops still controlled the fortifications of Pontus; they would welcome Mithradates and his companions. The citizens of the *chora* (countryside) were faithful to the murdered king and his son, and Amasia was the home of Dorylaus's family. The historian Strabo lavished praise on the beauty and strategic position of his native Amasia, the former capital (the royal residence was moved to Sinope in about 183 BC). The fertile valleys of the *chora* were famous for fruit and grain, and rich silver mines lay to the northwest.

Amasia was guarded by an impregnable fortress perched on twin peaks connected by a natural rock bridge. Subterranean staircases and several secret reservoirs enabled the fort to withstand long sieges (these features can be seen today in the ruins at Amasia). When Mithradates and his company arrived, the soldiers showed the king these secret passages and water tanks, and outlying watchtowers that communicated with Fortress Amasia. This was just the sort of valuable knowledge Mithradates needed to have as commander of Pontus's armies.[9]

Writing a few decades after the death of Mithradates, Strabo visited all of the old Mithradatic strongholds. He climbed up to the ancient stone tower at Sagylion in the *chora* of Amasia, overlooking the hot springs. This tower, noted Strabo, contained yet another large reservoir, once "very useful to the kings of Pontus." By Strabo's day, however, all of Mithradates' secret cisterns were bone dry, choked with huge boulders on the orders of Pompey the Great after the end of the Mithradatic Wars.[10]

But on that fresh spring day in 117 BC, the fragrance of apple blossoms on the breeze, Mithradates and his friends ascended Sagylion Tower and Amasia's walls to inspect the fortifications and admire the

FIG. 4.2. Amasia, former capital of Pontus. Ruins of the Mithradatic fortress are visible atop the peaks, high above the Iris River. Engraving, Taylor, 1884, courtesy of F. Dechow.

FIG. 4.3. Ruins of Amasia's fortifications on the peaks above the Iris River.
Photo courtesy of Dick Osseman, 2007.

view. From the bracing heights north of Amasia, they could gaze down
on the treeless plain around Lake Stephane some miles away. By the lake,
one could make out Laodicea, founded by Mithradates' mother after his
father's murder. She had accepted Roman loans—money from slavery
and taxes bled from Anatolia—to build an extravagant lakeside villa and
Castle Icizari on a limestone bluff. As he surveyed the scene, Mithradates
could not suppress a grin. His mother had located her castle based on
proximity to the hot springs and the pretty lake. She was thinking of ease
of travel and entertaining, instead of a defensible location.

After the end of the Mithradatic Wars, Strabo visited Lake Stephane,
reporting it to be jumping with fat fish. But Strabo found Laodice's fine
palace a pile of rubble, overgrown with vines, surrounded by fields of
grain. Her castle was deserted, but still standing. Today one can still see
Castle Icizari (Kizari) near the village that retains her name in Turkish,
Ladik. Archaeologists have discovered bronze coins here, engraved with
Laodice's name, issued during Mithradates' absence. These finds and
other coins stamped with her name and portrait, along with the star-
and-crescent emblem of Pontus, indicate that Laodice considered her-

self the legitimate sovereign of Pontus. Some historians suggest that she intended Laodicea to be the new capital of Pontus.[11]

Mithradates avoided this region controlled by his mother. But the rest of Pontus was dotted with hundreds of other strongholds, fortresses, towers, and guard stations manned by loyalists and "nobles of ancient Persian stock ruling their secluded fiefs from craggy castles deep in the forest."[12] They would welcome Mithradates as their chieftain and supply provisions and new horses. Mithradates meant to visit as many fortifications as possible, to win support throughout his kingdom. It was also imperative to claim Mithradatic treasures and arrange to safeguard the gold and silver that his father had stored in these isolated castles over the years. Gaining the trust of the garrison at Amasia, Mithradates would receive travel information and more detailed military briefings about secret treasuries, armories, and lesser-known routes over the mountains.

If reports of the Romans' activities reached Amasia, he must have agonized over their imperial designs on western Anatolia and his mother's acquiescence. Laodice allowed the Romans to take away Greater Phrygia, which the Roman Senate had presented to his father after the rebellion of Aristonicus and the Sun Citizens. In about 116 BC, while Mithradates was in exile, a party of ten Roman officials arrived in Sinope to arrange the takeover of this new province. Queen Laodice withdrew the Pontic army from Phrygia and disbanded the kingdom's forces. She also advised her daughter, Laodice the Elder, queen of Cappadocia, to ally with Rome. His mother was selling out the great accomplishments of the reign of Mithradates' father.[13]

One important key to winning the Pontic armies' loyalty was to demonstrate continuity of the royal line. Alexander, for example, had visited the tomb of Cyrus the Great as a way of portraying himself as the next true king of Persia. Mithradates' emotions must have intensified when he and his friends paid their respects at the mausoleum of his royal ancestors in Amasia. Five elaborate sepulchers of the kings of Pontus were carved into the cliffs high above the river, in accordance with ancient Iranian and Anatolian funeral customs. This magnificent necropolis and the handsome walls of the fortress on the acropolis of Amasia are the most impressive archaeological remains in all Pontus. In 2002, archaeologists discovered internal staircases and tunnels connecting the tombs with the castle above. An inscription identifies the resting place of Mithradates' grandfather Pharnaces I. Each tomb had a terrace planted with wildflowers. In Zoroastrian belief, the king's personal fire was extinguished upon death, but his *xvarnah* (spirit) might still cling to the bones interred

FIG. 4.4. Rock-cut tombs of Mithradatid kings at Amasia. (Top) tombs of
Mithradates I and II and Ariobarzanes; (bottom) tombs of Mithradates III
and Pharnaces I. Mithradates V Euergetes and Mithradates VI Eupator were
buried here too. The Persian-style tombs were accessible by long ladders
or by rock-hewn tunnels from the acropolis fortifications.
Photos courtesy of Jakob Munk Høtje.

in the tomb. If Mithradates' ancestors' spirits remained nearby, surely they smiled on the boy's daring plans to escape assassination and avenge his father's murder.[14]

A warm welcome at Amasia bolstered Mithradates' confidence and his companions' enthusiasm for their great adventure. Vowing to return one day when Amasia's famed golden apples were ripe, Mithradates traveled southward along the Iris River, stopping at another of his father's fortresses, Dadasa, on a high bluff above the village of Gaziura. From Gaziura, a road led west toward Zela, defended by another fortress, Skotios. There was a large temple-domain at Zela, founded centuries earlier by Scythian nomads, sacred to the Persian goddess Anahit. If the boys from Sinope were lucky enough to arrive during her annual festival, they would have joined crowds of intoxicated men and women dressed in Scythian costumes—leggings knitted in zigzig patterns, leather tunics, and pointed, tassled caps—and, in Strabo's words, "reveling wantonly."

After Zela, the boys returned to the easterly route, crossing the bridge over the Iris to visit more castles at Dazimon and Talaura. From here they may have made a foray south to the Halys River, on the road to Cappadocia. With each face-to-face consultation with his father's commanders, Mithradates received pledges of their support and ensured that he controlled his inheritance. The coin and treasure hoards hidden in each of these forts would be of great importance to Mithradates in the wars to come.[15]

THE TURRET-FOLK

As the leaves began to turn red and gold, Mithradates led the group north, toward the mild sea coast, a good place to spend their first winter. The route went by way of Kabeira, a fortified palace of the ancient kings of Pontus. Strategically placed on the Lycos River, the defensible location and wild beauty of Kabeira made a very strong impression on young Mithradates. Strabo noted that it was encircled by heavily wooded mountains, with plenty of game.

One of the most impressive features near Kabeira was a year-round natural spring on a high crag above the river, some miles to the northwest. The spring gushed forth in a powerful waterfall that cascaded down the sheer rock face into the deep ravine below. Besides the fortified royal residence, Kabeira maintained a large sanctuary dedicated to the Anatolian moon god Men and the moon goddess Selene. At the temple, founded by Pharnaces I, the kings of Pontus traditionally swore their sacred oaths, invoking Men to bestow health, safety, and prosperity. The boys of Sinope admired the image of the god holding his javelin, astride his horse, with the crescent moon over his shoulder.[16]

From Kabeira, Mithradates might have decided to take the little-used winding trail over the mountains to the Black Sea. Strabo describes this region's herds of gazelle and grain fields, and grapes, pears, apples, and nuts in such abundance that one could gather food all year long. Strabo even mentions the deep carpets of fallen leaves, for cushioning wayfarers' beds. Continuing to follow the narrow seashore road toward the sunrise, the riders from Sinope were retracing the route traveled by Xenophon and his ten thousand Greek mercenaries, and by Jason and the Argonauts. Exporing the rocky coast, the group discovered hidden coves frequented by pirates plying the Black Sea. The road petered out into a rough track in the remote *chora* of Trapezus, a town with an excellent harbor. From Trapezus, a route headed south over the Zigana Pass into the upper Euphrates River valley and Armenia. To the northeast lay Colchis, "legendary land of gold, poisons and witchcraft." In the distance were the forbidding Caucasus Mountains, and beyond that, the boundless steppes of Scythia.[17]

As their horses picked their way along the coastal path, Mithradates called in at the forts of Side, Phabda, Chabaca, and Pharnacia. Villagers here made their living mining silver and zinc and fishing for tuna. Each hamlet was deeply honored to be visited by the young king of Pontus; they greeted the royal hunting party with fish, bread, and wine. Three hundred years earlier, Xenophon and his army had enjoyed similar hospitality from the villagers' ancestors. When Mithradates and his friends arrived at Trapezus, they would have recalled how Xenophon's homesick soldiers had shouted for joy upon finally coming in view of the Black Sea here.

During their travels, Mithradates was becoming familiar with his future subjects and his kingdom's natural resources and geography, its fertile valleys, harbors, and strongholds in majestic mountains. He and his young friends embraced the risks and hardships, always vigilant for sudden storms in the mountains, several species of venomous snakes, and fierce wolves, boars, and bears. Another danger came from isolated peoples and their deadly flora. In the mountains of Pontus and Armenia, pocked with silver, zinc, tin, and iron mines, dwelled many "strange, primitive tribes," the Paryadres, Sanni, Byzeres, Cercitae, and Mosynoeci, to name only a few listed by Strabo. Mithradates, with his knack for languages, was quite eager to meet these exotic groups and see whether he could communicate with them. The shamans must know rare toxins and arcane antidotes. Would the archers reveal secret recipes for poison arrows? Toxic hellebore, belladonna, and blue monkshood flourished in the meadows and mountainsides. The travelers had to make sure their horses did not eat these lethal plants. Mithradates carefully collected specimens, keeping notes on their properties and antidotes.

The boys had probably already experimented with hellebore-tipped arrows, used by the Gauls and others for hunting rabbits. The technique worked well, as long as one quickly cut away the tainted flesh around the wound. The Gauls carried antidotes with them, in case of self-injury with an arrow, as did the Scythians. One day, Mithradates could hope to meet the Soanes, a tribe of remote Colchis famous for their arrow drug. Strabo remarked that the stench of a Soane arrow whizzing past one's head was noxious enough to kill a man!

The Mosynoeci ("Turret-Folk") were the "worst of the savage mountain tribes," in Strabo's opinion. Subsisting on chestnuts, pickled fish, and the flesh of wild animals, the Turret-Folk carved dugout canoes, wielded iron battle-axes and spears, and constructed tree houses on scaffolds in the dense rhododendron forests on the mountainsides above the sea. Xenophon, who had led his Ten Thousand through their territory, reported that the tribe elected a "king" to dispense justice. This king was kept captive on the highest scaffold. If his judgments failed to please, the people starved him to death. The Turret-Folk, observed Xenophon, relished having sex in public, and the pale skin of the men and women—and even the children—was heavily tattooed, "covered with colorful patterns of all sorts of beautiful flowers." The Turret-Folk were hostile to strangers, notorious for attacking unsuspecting wayfarers by leaping down on them like killer apes from their *mosyni*, "turrets." This must be how Mithradates and his friends first made their acquaintance. Somehow Mithradates won this warlike group over: the Turret-Folk would prove to be an important ally in the last Mithradatic War.[18]

When spring arrived, the lost boys from Sinope led their horses up the switchbacks into the mountains and disappeared into the cool, high forests where the last snowflakes sifted down from the evergreen boughs. Whooping with exhilaration, the young men celebrated the first anniversary of their freedom to live by their own wits, like Robin Hood and his Merry Band in Sherwood Forest. They looked forward to seasons to come, dodging any authorities with ties to the traitors back in Sinope, plotting their triumphal return.

Munching almonds, pistachios, chestnuts, and dried figs collected at the lower elevations, and copying wise old Diogenes' austere regime of foraging, the boys gathered tender green shoots through spring and into summer. Remembering how young Cyrus exhorted his companions centuries before in Persia, Mithradates declared that pure, icy water from melted snow was perfect for slaking thirst, and that the earth herself provided the finest bed. Golden pears, *dziran* (apricots), and plums ripened through the months. As summer faded, the youths gorged on the wild cherries native to Pontus and the steppes and dried some for provisions. Mithradates' band may even have met some rustic folk who taught them how to curdle mare's milk with cherry juice, to make the refreshing fermented drink enjoyed by Scythian nomads. The fruit seemed to ease the strains of their vigorous outdoor life—and indeed, cherry juice has been shown to soothe aching muscles.

Weeks passed, months, then years. Mithradates' party hunted hares, gazelles, wild goats, and deer, draping trophies of their kills on tree branches as dedications to the local gods. Fishing in pristine lakes and streams added variety. Some of the older boys showed off by making artificial flies, tying feathers artfully to the fish hooks, a new technique invented in Greece a century earlier. One day the hunters killed a Pontic beaver and dared each other to eat the testicles, reputed to fortify one's manhood. Everyone kept on the lookout for ferocious lions and bears that still roamed here, just as in the glorious days of Hercules.[19]

PERILOUS PASTIMES

As the boys gained confidence and skill, they sought more dangerous game. The most experienced hunters boasted of facing down fierce wild boars. Hunting boar was the essential test of manhood in Alexander's Macedonia: only those who had personally killed a boar with a spear (without a net) were considered worthy. Recalling the great boar hunts of the Greek heroes of myth (and one heroine, Atalanta), the boys wondered, Was it really true that the more enraged the boar, the more fiery the tusks? Old hunters claimed that the red-hot tusks could singe the fur of the hunting hounds.

Xenophon explained the method of hunting boar. Wielding nine-foot war spears with fifteen-inch blades, fitted with a crosspiece to prevent the beast from running up the lance, Mithradates and his friends, yelling with excitement, pursue the beast until it is cornered. Warily, the muscular

FIG. 4.5. Young men hunting boar, mosaic, Piazza Armerina, Sicily.
Scala/Art Resource, NY.

and brave prince approaches. If he misses his mark, the desperate animal
will charge and gore the boys and dogs. Mithradates dispatches the boar
with a well-aimed thrust, and his friends dine royally that night.[20]

One early spring near Trapezus, after dropping in on their new friends
the Turret-Folk, the explorers ride through lush stands of magenta, pink,
and white rhododendron blossoms. They have learned that the poison
sap of these flowers makes arrows lethal. Along the winding trail in the
forest, they notice a number of wild beehives, the waxy combs dripping
tempting honey. Mithradates, his mind buzzing with his toxicology
experiments, recalls the warnings of the Turret-Folk to avoid eating any
honey in these beautiful forests. What a delicious paradox: a sweet poison! Suddenly he understands why Xenophon's entire Greek army had
mysteriously collapsed, unable to rise for three days after sampling the
wild honey of Trapezus. Xenophon wrote that he was mystified to see all
his men strewn on the ground, totally defenseless in unfamiliar territory.

Mithradates regales his friends with Xenophon's lurid description of
the powerful effects of rhododendron nectar.[21] Curious, the boys inves-

tigate: the honey is thin and runny, reddish and slightly bitter, nothing like the golden honey cakes served at their birthday banquets back home. A dab of the dark stuff tickles their palms. The tongue tingles after a tiny taste. Mithradates challenges his companions to a devilish contest. He'll be the judge. Who can eat the most honey without slurring his words, stumbling around like a drunkard, shitting his trousers, or finally passing out cold?

No doubt there were many other competitions, as Mithradates coolly expanded his scientific knowledge of poisons and antidotes and as the young men tested themselves. They were absorbing lessons in loyalty, teamwork, trust, and leadership, and gaining practical knowledge. How far could one shoot an arrow or throw a javelin? How many stades (8 stades = about 1 mile) could one ride in a day? Who could tolerate the most hornet stings? What is the best treatment for snakebite? Just how fast could one run when chased by an angry bear? Contests showed who was best at reciting Homeric verses, quoting poety, wrestling, mock combat, swimming. The boys challenged each other to footraces, horse races, and countless other daredevil games.

THE TEMPLE OF LOVE

This was a pack of energetic, athletic teenage boys, reveling in their freedom, seeking experience and adventure. What were their sex lives like during those years alone together? Some of the youths in the group paired off as lovers, in the traditional aristocratic Greek style. Others enjoyed bisexual encounters, paralleling the well-known inclinations of Alexander the Great and his Macedonian companions, as well as many leading Roman aristocrats of Mithradates' day. That was not the traditional Persian way, however, according to the Greek historian Herodotus—he claimed that the Persians had learned from the Greeks to accept homosexuality. Roman historians remarked—with surprise, given his Greek tutors—that Mithradates was attracted only to women, never to boys or men. Others in his circle probably shared this interesting quirk.[22] But where would young Mithradates and his friends find willing girls in rural Pontus?

At his father's banquets, Mithradates, Dorylaus, Gaius, and their schoolmates had overheard the men bragging about their sexual exploits in certain notorious temple sanctuaries in Anatolia. Devoted to the cults of Near Eastern goddesses of love (Mylitta, Ma, Enyo, Anahit, and Bellona), these

rich temple complexes maintained vast holdings of sacred
land and employed thousands of
priests, priestesses, and workers.
In Pontus, the high priest was very
powerful; his only superior was
the king who appointed him. The
temples' great wealth came from
sacred prostitutes, a well-known
but little-understood ancient practice. In Pontus, Cappadocia, Armenia, Babylon, Lydia, and some
other ancient cultures, it was the
custom for young women to have
sex with strangers in the temple
before they married. They donated
the silver they earned to the goddess.

The most renowned of these
temples of love were Comana Cappadocia and Comana Pontica. The
historian Diodorus described a
visit to Comana Pontica as a relaxing and entertaining romp, rather
than a solemn religious ritual.
While still in Sinope, Mithradates
and the boys dreamed of one day
visiting these pleasure gardens,
imagining themselves welcomed
by bevies of beautiful girls dedicated to enjoying sacred sex with
strangers who happened by. In the
flowery words of the Epicurean
philosopher Lucretius, a contemporary of Mithradates who wrote
of love and lust, *The dreams of
young boys on the verge of man-
hood are often invaded by images of alluring, delightful women, and the
boys' bodies discharge fluids while fast asleep—even the costly splendors of
oriental coverlets do not escape a soaking.*[23]

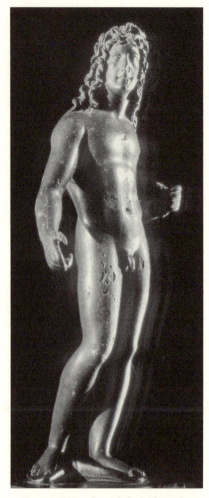

Fig. 4.6. Youth with long hair, late
Hellenistic bronze statue from
Pontus, identified as Mithradates.
Note similarity of head and leonine
hairstyle in the Hellenistic coin
portrait of Alexander in fig 5.2.
Sothebys, Werner Forman/Art
Resource, NY.

Now the youths had the opportunity to make those dreams come true! The head priest at Comana Pontica, in the picturesque Iris River valley, had been appointed by Mithradates' father. Second only to the king, the priest was in a position to know many secrets and to give and receive many favors. Here was a unique chance for Mithradates to mix business with pleasure. This most trusted person, a relative or close friend of the murdered king, would receive Mithradates as his new monarch. So, driven by what Lucretius called the "tyranny of lust" that comes with an "adolescent's ripening years and strengthening loins," Mithradates and his friends, we may reasonably assume, visited the gardens of Comana more than once in the years they were out on their own.

What happened in Comana stayed in Comana. But a translation of Lucretius's discreet, scientific Latin description of the ideal sexual encounter gives a sense of Mithradates' interludes in Comana: *Both men's and women's yearning for bliss comes in irresistible waves. . . . Body clings greedily to body, eager limbs entwine, moist lips are pressed against lips in fierce kisses, breaths are drawn through clenched teeth, and it is seed-time in the fields of Venus.* Several ancient writers describe the customs at these temples. It seems that the young women could refuse offers and choose partners based on their own taste, beckoning to those whose status and physical appeal most matched their own. We can imagine that Mithradates' young aristocrats were embraced as handsome, rich "strangers" known to be very generous with silver coins.[24]

Shared experiences at Comana strengthened the bond between Mithradates and his friend Dorylaus. At some point, Mithradates promised Dorylaus that as soon as he regained control of his kingdom, he would appoint him high priest of the Temple of Love.

RUSTIC LESSONS

Living close to nature, observing plants, animals, insects, birds, and reptiles, appealed to Mithradates. Like Alexander, he was keenly interested in natural history and possessed an experimental turn of mind. A discovery, while gathering firewood, of a salamander under a rotting tree, for example, might end badly for the amphibian. What boy could resist testing the folk beliefs surrounding salamanders? Were they really impervious to fire? Dried "salamander" skins were used in antiquity to store precious royal possessions. Traders in Sinope displayed sheets of the gray, fibrous "wool" shed by giant salamanders in remote India (in

fact, natural asbestos from Tajikistan). The salamander's reputed in-
vulnerability to burning would fascinate a young man preoccupied with
acquiring personal immunity to poisons and making himself invincible.
Mithradates recalled the assertion by Alexander's tutor, Aristotle, that
salamanders could not only walk through fire but could actually extin-
guish flames. If Mithradates experimented with a salamander in the fire,
he probably proved Aristotle mistaken. The boys may have tested other
folklore about salamanders—they were toxic, yet their flesh mixed with
honey was supposed to be an aphrodisiac.[25]

Conversation around the campfire often turned to military history and
tactics. What substances, for instance, would best protect wooden siege
machines, stone walls, and palisades from flaming arrows or burning
naphtha? Some military experts recommended dousing walls and siege
engines in sour wine (vinegar) as a defense against fire. Vinegar is a real
fire retardant. But Mithradates, recalling Hannibal's campaigns against
the Romans, would have pointed out that vinegar-drenched stones had a
tendency to crack and crumble if they overheated in a fire attack. Everyone agreed that alum, if one could import enough of this rare mineral
from Egypt or Syria, was the superior fire retardant for military defense.

During the years away from Sinope, Mithradates and his friends could
continue their interrupted education by reciting epic poetry, discussing
history, debating philosophy, and reading books. The new technique
of binding vellum (sheepskin) parchment into a book form had been
invented in Pergamon about fifty years earlier, to replace Egyptian papyrus scrolls. This technology allowed the young aristocrats to carry durable, compact editions of their favorite works. Vellum books also enabled
Mithradates to keep written records of his scientific investigations through
all his travels and campaigns.[26]

Mithradates knew that Alexander had cherished his copy of Homer's
Iliad, annotated by his teacher Aristotle. Even on war campaigns, Alexander kept this scroll beside his dagger under his bed. After he defeated
Darius III, Alexander stored his *Iliad* in a richly wrought casket, one of
the Persian monarch's most precious treasures. It's not unthinkable that
the prince of Pontus copied Alexander and kept his own book of Homer
in a similar bejeweled casket, perhaps discovered among the heirlooms
of Darius I.[27]

In Homer's epic about the first "world war" between Europe and Asia,
Mithradates found engrossing descriptions of the Trojans, who defended
Anatolia against the Greek aggressors. From Mithradates' perspective,
to resist the invaders from the West, who came to Asia to plunder and

loot under the pretext of retrieving a king's stolen wife, seemed just and righteous. Imagine Mithradates' scorn when he learned from his tutors in Sinope that the uncouth Romans actually believed that they were descended from the magnificent Trojans of Anatolia.

Like his Persian ancestors, who had their own translations of the *Iliad*, Mithradates appreciated the epic from the point of view of the Trojan king Priam. He knew that Xerxes made a special trip to Troy (480 BC). Xerxes had climbed the stone stairway of the highest tower of Priam's citadel, and his Magi had sacrificed one thousand cattle to the spirits of the Trojan heroes. Alexander had visted Troy, too, and poured a libation to the Greek champion Achilles. Mithradates hoped to see Troy one day, to marvel at the oversized bronze weapons of the Trojan hero Hector and the harp plucked by Paris. A royal visitor might try on Ajax's huge bronze helmet, even touch the enormous bones of the ancient warriors.

Like Xerxes, Mithradates would imagine King Priam in his tower, surveying the polyglot legions of Persia's allies from around the Black Sea and beyond. Priam's armies massed on the plain below Mount Ida, at the grave mound of the Amazon queen Myriné. The homelands of Priam's allies were at the edge of the world for the ancient Greeks, who called them barbarians. But their names, recited by Homer, would have rung wonderfully familiar to Mithradates. There were Paphlagonians from wild-horse country and Scythian nomad-archers, quivers bristling with poison arrows, riding sturdy steppe ponies. Expert bowmen came from Pontus, joined by Bithynian and Lydian knights resplendent in golden armor. Mystic seers from the eastern hinterlands mingled with bronze-clad warriors of Caria where bird augurs told the future. Battalions from cave-riddled Cappadocia and silver-rich Mysia, even far Armenia sent warriors to help defend Troy. Finally, a contingent of Amazons rode in, led by their beautiful warrior queen, Penthesilea. She would fight the mighty Achilles himself. As the Amazons joined the masses of far-flung tribes gathering on the Trojan plain, amid swirling dust and clanging spears and dancing horses, "there arose the tremendous din of myriad tongues." Yet the Trojans united all these scattered tribes in one cause, to defend Anatolia.[28]

Mithradates' own lands were replete with romantic Amazon lore. Amazon grave mounds marked the countryside; Amazons were believed to have founded many Anatolian cities, including Sinope, Amasia, Amastris, and Themiscrya in Pontus, and Ephesus, Mytilene on Lesbos, Smyrna, Priene, Cyme, Pitane, Magnesia, Thyatira, Amazonion, and Myrina. The greatest Greek heroes of myth had fought and loved warrior women from the East. Even Cyrus and Alexander had encountered strong-willed Amazon queens. Mithradates would have known all these tales by heart. Such independent women were foreign to the ancient Greeks, but in Mithradates' world, queens were powerful rulers, like his mother and sister. Fierce women warriors were not imaginary, but real. Among the war-loving Sarmatians, Alans, Scythians, Sirginni, Massagetae, and other nomads around the Black Sea, men and women dueled before marrying, and the women rode into battle with the men. As they traveled deeper into Eastern lands, Mithradates and his friends teased each other with the possibility of meeting a party of young, independent horsewomen. Perhaps they would agree to go on together as a tribe of equals, like the romantic story of the young Scythian hunters and the Amazon warriors who joined forces and became the Sarmatians, recounted by Herodotus and Justin.[29]

Priam's legendary army was surpassed by that of Xerxes. Herodotus, born in Caria under Persian rule, conjured up colorful panoramas of Xerxes' millions of troops mustered from the corners of the Persian Empire. In the exotic pageantry of Xerxes' multitudes massed on the plain, each contingent displayed the distinctive armor and weapons of their homelands. Brandishing scimitars, lances, swords, poison darts, quivers fashioned from the tanned skins of human foes, they rode scythed chariots, cavalry horses, and war camels.[30] King Darius had commanded equally diverse and vast hosts of Persians and allies to fight Alexander. And like King Priam in the *Iliad* and the great Persian rulers, Alexander also recruited multiethnic warriors from remote, mysterious places, as far away as Afghanistan and India. Reading about these diverse armies in myth and history, the youthful Mithradates could glimpse his own polyglot armies of the future, recruited from the same marvelous lands described by Homer, Herodotus, and Xenophon.

HOMEWARD BOUND

Occasional news of the Romans reached the hinterlands, and Mithradates was creating his own information network. He knew that Roman slave traders and tax collectors were preying on western Anatolia, and heard reports of his mother's collusion with the Romans. As they increased the distance between themselves and Sinope, Mithradates and his band could reveal their true identities. Rumors of Mithradates sightings probably filtered back to his mother and her faction, even to the

Romans in Pergamon. Mithradates probably intended for some news to get back to supporters in Sinope, to counter any attempt by his mother to spread rumors that he was dead. Popular tales of his exploits enhanced his reputation, while his band remained elusive, always on the move.

People in the East remembered the two spectacular comets and the Magi's ancient prophecies. Men and women handled the small-denomination coins stamped with Mithradates' name and his comet whenever they went to market. They were thrilled to meet the exiled king in person or to hear exciting rumors that he and his band of young knights were traveling around the Kingdom of Pontus, gathering strength. Stories probably circulated about the handsome young king's adventures, with romantic details about his feats and sayings. Pontus awaited the day when Mithradates VI Eupator, the savior-king, would emerge from hiding and begin his reign, like the divine hero Mithra emerging from the dark cave in a burst of brilliant light.

Reflecting on all he has learned in the years away from Sinope, Mithradates —perhaps eighteen or twenty now—feels pride mixed with restlessness. Alexander, he knows, took over the Macedonian throne at age twenty. The future of Mithradates' kingdom obsesses him; he is weary of brooding on his father's assassination and the queen's treachery. Is his young brother still a passive creature controlled by his calculating mother? Have his sisters fallen under her spell too? His outrage at the Roman depredations in Anatolia inflames his idealistic commitment to what is true and bright. Mithradates feels strong, invincible, impatient for action. His friends agree: it is time to seize power, time to punish the wicked, time to fulfill the oracles sent by the gods.

5

Return of the King

AS Mithradates and his friends ride toward Sinope, they reap the rewards of their years in the countryside. A self-assured young man now, Mithradates has cultivated the trust of the commanders of forts, local leaders, and the people of Pontus, as well as warlike groups in the hinterlands.

The ancient sources say only that Mithradates returned to Sinope and took back his throne, leaving us to imagine how these events actually came to pass. As Mithradates headed home, in about 115/114 BC, garrison soldiers and armed bands probably joined his original company, fired by the young king's mission to avenge his father's murder. Made up of people from all ranks of society and from all corners of Pontus, this modest militia foreshadowed the large armies that the king would summon in the coming wars with Rome. This was the first demonstration of Mithradates' remarkable appeal to elites and ordinary folk of diverse backgrounds.

Rumors (or secret messages) may have prepared some for the return of the beloved prince. Then, one morning, Mithradates' noble companions ride into Sinope, led by Dorylaus. The young men radiate confidance. Excitement surges through the crowd as the citizens recognize the long-lost boys of prominent families. Anticipation mounts as lookouts on the ramparts sight an army approaching. Mithradates, mounted on a fine horse, finally appears inside the gates of his city.

The citizens behold their prince, tall and muscular, his handsome face framed by dark hair like a lion's mane in the style of the great Alexander. Mithradates' imposing height, powerful physique, and self-assurance were impressive. His complexion may have been noticeably pale, from minute doses of arsenic.[1] A luminous, translucent quality would set him apart from his companions, suntanned from years living outdoors. For those who recalled the oracles, the divine lightning, and the bright comets, the

FIG. 5.1. Mithradates VI Eupator, large marble head (95 cm, ca. 3 feet high), found in Inopus spring near the Mithradates Monument, Delos. Louvre, Erich Lessing/Art Resource, NY.

sudden reappearance of Mithradates would evoke the idea of the long-awaited savior-king emerging in an aura of light.

It was a bloodless coup, with little resistance from his mother and her coterie. Queen Laodice died mysteriously while confined in prison; Mithradates the Good did not survive her. Some sources state that Mithradates killed his mother and his brother. Modern historians strug-

FIG. 5.2. (Left) Hellenistic bust of Alexander. Many similar copies were made from Alexander's death in 323 BC through the time of Mithradates, as well as coin portraits. (Right) leonine portrait of Alexander on silver tetradrachm, Macedonia, 90–75 BC, issued during Mithradates' reign. Note strong resemblance to bronze statue said to be Mithradates from the same era, fig 4.6. Bust, Alexandria, Egypt, British Museum, GR 1872.5–15.1, photo by Andrew Dunn, www.andrewdunnphoto.com, wikicommons cc-by-sa-2.0. Coin courtesy of Joseph Sermarini, Forum Ancient Coins, www.forumancient coins.com.

gle to sort out the "impossibly compressed" and tangled chronology of Mithradates' early career.[2] Exactly how did he assume power, neutralize his adversaries, and select a wife? Here is a plausible scenario of Mithradates' revenge and first marriage, taking into account what is known from ancient sources and filling in missing details with reasonable conjecture.

Mithradates, we can assume, had already begun to organize the web of informants that we know he relied on as king. These sources kept him apprised of the whereabouts of his mother and her retinue, and any roving Roman officials. His goal was to orchestrate a seamless assumption of power. The logical approach would have been to time his surprise return to Sinope to coincide with Queen Laodice's absence.

The queen often stayed in her new capital, Laodicea—entertaining guests at her palatial villa at Lake Stephane and luxuriating in the hot baths. Let us guess that the pampered princeling Mithradates the Good would be at his mother's side, while Mithradates' little sisters, Nyssa, Roxana, and Statira, remained in the nursery at Sinope, guarded by eunuchs. While Laodice idled at her retreat, no Romans would visit Sinope. Courtiers loyal to his mother would be left in charge there, with his teenage sister, Princess Laodice the Younger. Was she still as clever and pretty as Mithradates remembered?

In the season of ripening apples, Mithradates gives the order to march to Sinope. At Amasia, he dispatches an armed contingent to Laodicea. Security at Laodice's villa was lax; Mithradates already knew that the place was not easily defended. In the carefully planned velvet coup, his men overcome the queen's guards and occupy Castle Icizari and her villa. Laodice and her young son are locked inside. After all, upon his return to the throne, it is perfectly proper for King Mithradates to ensure the "security" of his mother, younger brother, and their friends. Now Queen Laodice and her circle are prisoners in their gilded palace, while Mithradates makes his triumphal reentry into Sinope.

Confining the queen at her villa was more subtle than publicly throwing her into the dungeon at Sinope. But it would be dangerous to let his treacherous mother, his feckless coheir, and other enemies live on while Mithradates established his new government. After he dismissed his mother's cooks and royal tasters, the way was clear for Mithradates to plan a last lavish banquet at her villa. We can imagine him overseeing the preparation of extravagant dishes, the most luscious fruits, the most expensive wines—and for dessert, her favorite honey cakes.

Arsenic—poison of kings and king of poisons—was almost certainly the secret ingredient. Colorless, odorless, flavorless, arsenic could be added to any drink or dish. Mithradates knew that just sixty parts per million (ppm), or less than a tenth of an ounce, would be deadly in a goblet of rose-perfumed water or red wine. But why not allow his mother's guests to enjoy their sumptuous last supper without interruption? Mithradates, recalling the paradox of poisonous honey, savors the irony of creating a bittersweet treat. He stirs the arsenic powder into a pot of honey and drizzles it over the syrupy-sweet cakes.

After dessert, the guests withdraw to admire the sunset. Within half an hour, the queen and her son sense a faint, metallic taste on their tongues. Beads of sweat glisten on their clammy brows as they become aware of impending nausea and stomach cramps. Saliva fills their mouths, but it is impossible to swallow. Their eyes take on an uncanny reddish sparkle. Suddenly the royal pair begin clawing at their throats, drooling and moaning. After an hour or so of vomiting and diarrhea, Mithradates' mother and his only rival are writhing in convulsions. Shock follows. By midnight, both are dead.

THE KING TAKES A WIFE

At the royal funeral for the queen and his brother, Mithradates observes the beauty and composure of his sister, Laodice the Younger. They are practically strangers; she was a spoiled little girl in the nursery when he last saw her: now she is sixteen or seventeen. To continue our plausible scenario, let us imagine Laodice fawning over her older brother Mithradates, so handsome and strong and bold. Life was so insipid and her mother's rule so vexing while he was away. How she missed him all these years!

Laodice teases: Who will her brother take as a bride? King Mithradates VI Dionysus Eupator must have a proper queen, not just a harem of frivolous beauties. Mithradates agrees. The new sovereign of Pontus must select a worthy wife. She will be the mother of his legitimate sons, ensuring his succession. The royal spouse must be perfect, and her bloodline should complement Mithradates' illustrious Greco-Persian heritage. Who could possibly fulfill that role? At last, Mithradates announces his decision. The king of Pontus will marry his own sister, Princess Laodice the Younger.

It was an unexpected choice, but probably no one was shocked. Egyptian pharaohs and the Macedonian rulers of Egypt routinely practiced incestuous marriage; two kings of Egypt married their sisters during Mithradates' reign. Mithradates was aware of many such pairings in other Hellenistic courts; for example, Mithradates' great-uncle, Mithradates IV (160–150 BC), had married his sister, also named Laodice, and Antiochus I of Syria had married his stepmother (280 BC). In Armenia, Tigranes IV married his half sister Erato (6 BC). Marriage between royal half siblings was common in ancient Greece, too, and full-sibling royal marriage (*hvaetvodatha*) was an ancient Zoroastrian practice. Marrying relatives was accepted as a way to preserve the purity of the royal blood. Mithradates' choice may also have reflected his knowledge of the "mythic hero" script. After defeating a powerful enemy, a traditional hero marries a princess, often the daughter of his enemy or his predecessor. Princess Laodice was all three.[3]

So, not long after he reclaimed his crown, when he was about twenty-one, Mithradates wed his own sister. But Mithradates carried the logic of sibling marriage to an eccentric—and egocentric—degree. If no other family was grand enough to marry into such a distinguished royal line, then who was worthy to marry his other sisters? Only Mithradates. And what if Laodice the Younger did not give him sons?

To control the genetic legacy of his family and in case he might need to marry another sister later, Mithradates, the ancient sources state, decided to keep his younger sisters—Nyssa, Roxana, and Statira—virgins forever. They would never produce troublesome pretenders. Spinsterhood was almost unheard-of in antiquity, except for virgin priestesses. Like Rapunzel in her tower, the three sisters were totally secluded under guard for life, but no fairy-tale prince ever rescued them. This decision to lock away his young sisters is one of the earliest indicators of Mithradates' cruel, calculating side. As we shall see, all of Mithradates' siblings met wretched fates, victims of their brother's extraordinary pride and paranoia.

QUIRKS OF THE KING

There were other eccentricities. Mithradates' childish obsessions with invincibility matured and intensified. Like mad King Attalus of Pergamon, Mithradates cultivated poison gardens of blue monkshood, polemonia ("plant of a thousand powers"), deadly nightshade, henbane, and the like, with his Greek "root-cutter" Krateuas, also of Pergamon. The first ethnobotanist and the father of botanical illustration, the Poison King's fellow experimenter, Krateuas wrote two influential treatises that were among the king's treasures brought to Rome after Mithradates' death. The natural historian Pliny the Elder (AD 23–79) described these books, now lost. One was the first to include realistic colored paintings of hundreds of medicinal plants; the other was a detailed pharmacology manual. Mithradates "was the first to discover several different antidotes to poisons," noted Pliny, and "some of these plants even bear Mithradates' name." Krateuas named several plants after his patron—for example, pink Mithridatia (liliaceous *Erythronium*) and feathery-leaved *Eupatorium*.[4]

Krateuas collaborated with the royal physician Papias and a team of healers. The ancient authors say Mithradates was always accompanied by a group of shamans from a Scythian tribe north of the Sea of Azov, called the Agari. Many in the court must have found these shamans frightening, but the weird snake charmers knew how to transform viper venom into medicine (a feat only recently discovered by modern medicine). They could also have known the secrets of poisonous agaric mushrooms, named for the Agari region in Scythia.[5]

Mithradates tended flocks of Pontic ducks, feeding them the baneful plants they preferred and harvesting their eggs, blood, and flesh for his experiments. Hoping to exploit their "ability to live on poisons," Mithradates "mixed the blood of the Pontic ducks into his antidotes," wrote Pliny.[6] It's likely that Mithradates' medicinal gardens were in secret locations at several royal residences. In his laboratories, under heavy guard, the Poison King would have stocked a variety of deadly minerals and biotoxins—arrow drugs, crystallized snake venoms, stingray spines and jellyfish, scorpions from Mesopotamia and Libya, poison fish from Armenia, poisonous plants and toadstools, rhododendron honey, realgar and other toxic pigments—along with alexipharmic antidotes from near and far.

These royal treasures seem very different from the tributes collected by Mithradates' royal ancestors. They prized such things as water from the Danube and sand from Egypt, to advertise the vast reach of their kingdoms. But Persian kings also kept exotic poisons in their treasuries. The Roman natural historian Aelian described dreadful—and rare—natural biotoxins that could be obtained from India. One poison, derived from Purple Snake (*Azemiops*) venom, was so lethal that a drop the size of a sesame seed would kill.

The most prized Indian poison was the mysterious *dikairon*, said to be excreted by a tiny orange "bird" that nested in the Himalayas. A few grains of *dikairon*, it was said, would bring a dreamy death in a few hours, ideal for suicide. I have suggested elsewhere that *dikairon* might have been *pederin*, exuded by large orange blister beetles of Asia, often found in bird nests. It is one of the most powerful biotoxins known to modern science, more potent than cobra venom. According to Aelian, this precious substance was "given exclusively by the kings of India to the kings of Persia." Mithradates may have acquired some for his own pharmacy.[7]

Mithradates collected scientific treatises on *pharmaka* and corresponded with scholars about poisons and antidotes. His linguistic talents meant he could decipher scientific texts in many languages, from Old Persian to Sanskrit. It is quite possible that Mithradates obtained copies of ancient Hindu texts, such as the *Arthashastra* by Kautilya, adviser to King Chandragupta in the time of Alexander. This manual spelled out numerous recipes for creating poisons and antidotes. Another Hindu treatise, the *Laws of Manu* (500 BC), not only advised maharajas to employ tasters, but also counseled them to "mix all their food with medicines that are antidotes against poisons."[8] Was it this ancient Indian concept that led King Attalus—and Mithradates—to "mix tiny amounts of poisons with remedies" to protect themselves and their friends? We'll never know, but it was Mithradates who gained notoriety for applying scientific methodology to this ancient principle. Experimenting tirelessly to perfect his universal antidote, Mithradates started each day by ingesting the best concoction he and his doctors had devised so far (see plate 4).

Another eccentricity was Mithradates' appearance. One of the few Hellenistic kings to wear his hair long, Mithradates sported a curly mane that recalled Alexander's. It was also a strong political statement. Long hair for men in this era was distinctly un-Roman, a "barbarian" attri-

FIG. 5.3. Mithradates' Persian-style garments may have been similar those of his contemporary Antiochus I of Commagene (69–43 BC) (left) on tomb at Nemrud Dagh (modern Turkey), wearing Greek and Persian clothing—Persian tiara and crown, Greek cloak, Persian riding tunic studded with stars, Persian trousers. He accepts the symbol of sovereignty from the Sun god Mithra-Ahuramazda holding a Zoroastrian *barsom*, a wand of myrtle twigs, wearing the traditional Phrygian-Persian cap decorated with stars (this "liberty cap" became a symbol of freedom in the Roman era). (Right) King Darius I, sixth-century BC, in Persian *khilat* or robe of honor embroidered with medallions, trousers, and a tiara-crown. Dover.

bute.[9] The king maintained his youthful habit of wearing old-fashioned royal Persian costume—long-sleeved tunic of white linen edged in purple over trousers gathered at the ankle. Mithradates was a connoisseur of agate rings, and his simple diadem of purple and white ribbon may have been complemented with golden earrings. And everyone understood that Mithradates was always armed, even inside the palace at banquets. No one could ignore his impressive dagger, lying along his thigh at all times.

Mithradates would have favored a curved Persian-style dagger or short sword (*acinaces*; Old Persian, *akinaka*; Latin, *sica*) like those of his Iranian ancestors. Xenophon described the short dagger carried by Cyrus the Great. By Mithradates' day, the *sica*, scimitar, had become associated with pirates and bandits (dubbed *sicarii* by the Romans). A crescent blade still carries a swashbuckling cachet today. Mithradates' dagger was probably about sixteen inches long, keenly sharp on both edges, with a short cross-guard and a hilt encrusted with jewels. Recalling the ring with the secret poison that saved Hannibal from Roman captivity and execution, Mithradates had his sword maker customize his dagger. We are told that the hilt had a removable pommel and a hollow compartment for poison. The ornate scabbard hung from a richly decorated belt, at Mithradates' right hip. This was a thrusting, stabbing blade that could be drawn blade-down in a surprise attack. It was widely known that the great Alexander had murdered two enemies bare-handed with a similar dagger.[10]

The king wore his dagger while dining with friends, and the cold blade rested under the silk cushions whenever he slept or took pleasure in bed with Laodice or one of his lovers. He owned other personal weaponry, too, of course: wicked short knives that could be concealed on his body, javelins for hunting and war, and his bow and arrows. Everyone noticed that Mithradates' bow and quiver were always hanging where he could see and reach them.

These precautions, like the phobia about poisoning, reflected a justifiable need for self-defense since childhood. Popular stories exaggerated Mithradates' reputation for hypervigilance. One tale claimed that he was so paranoid that he devised a bizarre zoological alarm system to protect himself while asleep. The king's slumber was guarded by a stag, a horse, and a bull. Staked around his tent on campaigns, these animal bodyguards were trained to detect the breathing of anyone who approached and alerted him with a clamorous alarm—bleating, whinnying, and

bellowing. The image is amusing, yet not inconceivable when one remembers that a gaggle of noisy geese guarded the Capitol in Rome.[11]

When he was a baby, lightning had burned Mithradates' cradle, scar-
ring his forehead. Early in his reign, he survived another lightning strike.
This time it struck his quiver, hanging beside his bed, burning up the
arrows. The royal seers were summoned. According to Plutarch, they pro-
nounced this an excellent omen, foretelling that his archers would win
important victories.[12]

PRIORITIES

In exile, Mithradates had pondered strategies as ruler of Pontus. The first
priority was to reverse the damages done by his mother to Pontus's military strength and economic independence. The next step was to restore
and extend the territory and status that his father had gained. He had
to avoid becoming a Roman satellite. The Senate's removal of Greater
Phrygia from Pontic control (116 BC) had enraged Mithradates. How
dare they take what belonged to Pontus, an official Friend of Rome?

Through cunning diplomacy, intrigue, and judiciously applied military might, Mithradates planned to solidify alliances and expand his
influence in the entire Black Sea region. Roman foreign policy was unstable, with civil unrest and slave revolts in Italy and crises in Germany,
Spain, and North Africa, all demanding military commitments. Mithradates intended to make his Kingdom of Greater Pontus powerful enough
to stand up to the aggressive, treacherous Romans. But it had to happen
without attracting their attention.

Could he convince Rome to share power, to be content with hegemony in the West, while he, the divinely anointed King Mithradates,
ruled the East? Other powerful leaders before Mithradates—Hannibal,
Antiochus the Great, Jugurtha—had attempted to negotiate or grapple
with Rome as equals, or at least to achieve a kind of equilibrium, but
Rome could tolerate no other superpowers. Yet, as he observed the crises
engulfing the Republic from his vantage point in Pontus, Mithradates
hoped to convince the Romans that it was in their best interest to withdraw from Anatolia, to confine their empire to what they already possessed in the western Mediterranean, Europe, and North Africa, while
he—the rightful inheritor of the great Macedonian-Persian kingdom,
ruled Greece, the Black Sea, and the Near East.

Mithradates' early reign was marked by a series of rapid and brilliant conquests. The precise chronology is debated, but within the first two decades Mithradates tripled the territory of Pontus, winning important resources and allies. He tamed the "wild" Scythians and intervened to control or ally with neighboring kingdoms around the Black Sea. The ancient sources offer some historical landmarks, but it is up to us to guess how these events unfolded. How, for example, did Mithradates manage to deflect Rome's disapproval of his actions, turning their reactions to his own advantage? How was he able to entice the Romans to play the aggressor, while he accrued power and attracted followers? What were his long-range plans? How would he orchestrate the unavoidable show-down with Rome?

First, Mithradates needed to learn everything he could about the Republic's recent history and current situation. Who were the most powerful men in Rome, the rising stars? How much manpower could Rome afford to post to the Asian Province? What weaknesses could be exploited? Upon his arrival in Sinope, we know that Mithradates recalled his father's advisers and gathered informants to help him assess the situation across the Mediterranean. His most trusted adviser was his boyhood companion, Dorylaus. As the highest-ranking military officer and chief of the royal bodyguards, Dorylaus was a key member of the "King's Friends," an inner circle of Greeks, Anatolians, Persians, and foreign allies from all social ranks. Dorylaus was now also high priest of the Temple of Love at Comana Pontica, a lucrative, luxurious posting that automatically made him second in command.

A mutilated portrait of Dorylaus, inscribed with his name and titles, was discovered by French archaeologists in the 1930s. It was one of twelve marble busts of the King's Friends displayed in the Mithradates Monument on the island of Delos. A statue of Mithradates undoubtedly stood in the center. In the eighteenth century, a badly damaged marble head and torso from a larger-than-life statue, made in about 100 BC, had been found in the Inopus streambed beside the Mithradates Monument. The identity of the idealized king, wearing a metal diadem and draped in a cloak, was debated. The statue is now thought to portray Mithradates; the features strongly resemble his portraits on coins of this period (see fig. 5.1).[13]

From the inscriptions inside the monument, archaeologists identified ten of the twelve friends and allies that Mithradates wished to publicize. The frieze of busts is unique because it was the first public monument from antiquity to depict Greeks and Persians (as well as Syrians and

Parthians) as colleagues, and it proves that Mithradates was allied with Syria and Parthia at an early date. The labeled portraits—which might have been realistically painted—were Dorylaus; Gaius son of Hermaeus; Mithradates' private secretary, son of Antipater (name defaced); Papias son of Menophilus (Mithradates' physician); Asclepiodorus of Delos (father of a priest); Diophantus (Mithradates' general who subdued Scythia); two unnamed officials from the Arsacid Kingdom of Parthia; King Ariathes VII of Cappadocia (Mithradates' young nephew, son of his older sister Laodice); and King Antiochus VIII Grypos ("Hook-Nose"), the last Seleucid king of Syria. Grypos, a fascinating figure, and Mithradates had much in common. Grypos, too, had mastered poisons at a young age, after his older brother was poisoned by his scheming mother. Around the time that Mithradates was evading his own mother's plots (about 125 BC), Grypos was reclaiming his throne by tricking his mother into drinking a goblet of poison that she had prepared for him.[14]

The Mithradates Monument, dedicated in 102/101 BC, on behalf of the Roman People, Delos, and the Athenians, shows how popular Mithradates was in Greece. He was also considered a Friend of Rome: the monument included a statue of Mithradates dressed—improbably—as a Roman legionary. The head is missing, but the inscription identifies it as Mithradates. The statue may have been a mass-produced body in legionnaire garb topped with a head of Mithradates, a common expedient in an era when the fortunes of Rome's "friends" fluctuated wildly.[15]

MEANWHILE IN ROME

The chaotic, blood-soaked events in the last decades of the Roman Republic, before, during, and after the Mithradatic Wars, have been extensively described by modern historians, based on multiple histories and commentaries by ancient Roman authors. Since we are in Pontus with Mithradates, looking through his eyes, relying on his spies, informants, and advisers, and their interpretations of events, this section considers what he could have known about Roman history and current events, and identifies significant individuals destined to tangle with Mithradates.[16]

Among Greek and Persian-influenced cultures, Rome was viewed as a brash, uncivilized newcomer, dangerous and powerful but with an impoverished cultural history—even their language seemed crude and rigid compared to Greek. And Rome's worst enemies could not have invented a more negative origin story. Mithradates understood how easy it was to turn their sacred myth about the fierce *lupa*, she-wolf, who nurtured Romulus and Remus, into lurid propaganda against the Romans. According to the Romans' own myth, the she-wolf's children were murderers: Romulus killed his own brother, and the first Romans were violent fugitives and rapists. Anyone who knew Latin could joke that *lupa* was slang for "whore."

In antiquity, wolves were feared as bloodthirsty marauders, killers of flocks. Rome's opponents in Italy and the provinces often cited the old proverb "You Romans send as guardians of your flocks, not dogs or shepherds, but wolves." As early as the fifth century BC, indigenous Italians had likened the Romans to crazed wolves. Later in his reign, Mithradates would ally with Italian rebels, who declared war on the Roman Wolf, vowing to destroy its "lair," the city of Rome. The rebels issued coins showing the Italian Bull goring the Roman Wolf. Archaeologists have also discovered gold Italian coins similar to Mithradates' Pontic coins, showing Dionysus, an allusion to Mithradates' nickname and a symbol of rebellion against Rome.[17]

Mithradates studied Roman history, from a Greek and Anatolian perspective, of course. These views can be glimpsed in the writings of Strabo, a native of Pontus. Strabo pointed out that the Romans had "enlarged their own country by the dismemberment of that of others," a policy that led to frequent revolts. Ancient Greek historians and philosophers hostile to Rome argued that if Alexander had lived, there would be no Roman Empire, a view that surely influenced Mithradates. He attracted many philosophers and statesmen to his entourage, among them Pelopidas, Xenocles, Diodorus of Adramyttion, and Metrodorus of Scepsis (near ancient Troy). An inventor of memory devices and a dazzling new rhetorical style, Metrodorus's acid criticism of Rome earned him the nickname Misorhomaios, "Rome-Hater." Mithradates bestowed exceptional honors on Metrodorus, even referring to him as "father." Metrodorus was appointed as a kind of "supreme court" judge whose decisions were independent of the king. Mithradates' speeches include many touches that suggest the hand of Metrodorus the Rome-Hater.[18]

Mithradates learned how Rome's monarchy had been replaced by a republic, governed by patricians, aristocratic clans who had received special political powers under the old kings. In the early Republic, the poor citizens had suffered great debt, loss of land, and food shortages. The poor plebeians, plebs, had banded together in the fifth century BC and created their own organization, a kind of parallel state, electing tribunes to improve their circumstances. The plebs gained some debt relief and land grants in newly acquired territories. As they won more political power, some ambitious, rich citizens joined forces with them. The exclusive privileges of the old noble families began to decline, precipitating direct conflict between patricians and plebs. This "struggle of the orders" brought about the rise of a new elite, made up of old families and wealthy allies of the plebs. This new elite ruled Rome through its domination of the Senate. Mithradates' actions and speeches reveal that he had an excellent understanding of how the government by the Senate and "People of Rome" functioned.

After the indigenous people of Italy were subdued, Rome had embarked on overseas adventures. Rome's challenge to the great Carthaginian Empire in North Africa for control of Sicily began the Punic Wars, 264–146 BC. Hannibal invaded Italy in the Second Punic War, but his splendid victories came to naught. Hannibal was defeated in 202 BC, but, as Mithradates and his allies knew, the Carthaginian kept up the fight in Anatolia until his death in Bithynia. Ever after, Rome feared that another powerful enemy of Hannibal's caliber might arise. Mithradates recognized that this anxiety kept them intolerant of independent-minded monarchs.

After the defeat of Hannibal, Rome's image was admired—until they began a series of ferocious wars to conquer Greece, Spain, and Gaul. The violent Roman culture of war and strife had bred generations of steadfast men and women of great physical and moral courage. Many in the ancient world respected the traditional Roman values and were impressed by rousing narratives describing unwavering loyalty, patriotism, and integrity.[19] Mithradates and his allies knew the life stories of Rome's greatest military leaders, such as Scipio Africanus, as well as they knew the stories of the Romans' noble enemies, like Hannibal and Jugurtha.

Tales of valor and glory continued to coalesce around Roman war heroes and their powerful opponents. But more and more accounts of Roman atrocities and savage behavior began to circulate as the old Roman order began to morph into a relentless engine of imperial expansion and resource extraction. Well before Mithradates assumed his throne, events in Rome seemed to overflow with every human passion, virtue, and vice. There were mountains and valleys of emotion, volcanic rage and cruelty, springs of mercy, abysses of terror. Mithradates appreciated that some Roman statesmen deplored the corruption of the traditional Latin virtues —austerity, bravery, justice, piety, mercy, and moral rigor.

By the beginning of the first century BC, people from the Senate House in Rome to far-flung marketplaces across the Mediterranean were discussing frightening portents casting shadows over the empire and its ruthless—and superstitious—leaders driven by lust for power. For every glorious battle and triumph, it seemed that some Roman commander sat brooding amid the ruins of another great city and wept over the desolation his army had wrought—or over his own shattered ambitions.

By the time Mithradates assumed his throne, Rome had transformed itself into a war machine, oiled with blood and plunder, ravenous for more slaves, more land, more riches: too much was not enough. By the first century BC, Rome had become a predator driven to survive by attacking and devouring. Plebs, patricians, new citizens, tax collectors, warlords, all had grown fat on the prey gobbled up by the beast of war. Each victory sharpened the appetite and the killer instincts of the predator. For Mithradates and other outside observers, Rome was a wolf that must kill to live and lives to kill. Recently, this same lupine image was used by modern historians to explain Rome's success, likening the late Republic and Empire to a voracious predator for whom there can be no rest, no turning back. The scholars point out that, compelled by the logic of the predatory imperial state, it was impossible for Rome to stop attacking and consuming in every direction.[20]

In the decades just before Mithradates' reign, the Great Wolf's attention swung toward Greece and the eastern Mediterranean. Conquests in Macedonia and Greece drew Rome to invade Asia Minor, in 191–188 BC, with the ultimate defeat of King Antiochus the Great of Syria at Magnesia. Uprisings in freedom-loving Greece were savagely crushed in the 140s. The Roman army's destruction of Corinth in 146 BC by fire, with unprecedented looting and the methodical slaughter of the populace, was a horrific event.[21] In Mithradates' day, it was still a searing, living memory. In that same year, Roman legions had utterly destroyed Carthage and sold the Carthaginians into slavery, ending the Third Punic War. Greece and North Africa became Roman provinces. In 133 BC, Rome inherited Phrygia, bestowed by Attalus's dubious last will and testament.

Rome's conquests delivered great wealth from plunder and taxes and a glut of human captives. But the chasm widened between rich and poor, especially in Italy, as the rich grabbed more and more land holdings, monopolized resources, raked in lucrative investments in the provinces, and choked newly conquered territories with taxation and debt.[22] In 133 BC, murderous political violence broke out in Rome over land distribution and the unfair burdens of hard fighting in Spain, opening the floodgates of unrelenting civil wars. The next year, in 132, a massive slave revolt had to be crushed in Sicily. That same year Aristonicus's Sun Citizens rebelled in Anatolia: his cities were finally broken in 128 BC.

News of Italy's current civil uprisings and overseas wars reached Mithradates in Sinope via travelers, traders, Roman exiles, Greek and Celtic refugees, spies, ambassadors, and pirates. Mithradates followed the careers of the main players and studied the characters, words, and deeds of the leaders emerging in the tumultuous period of the late Roman Republic. These were men like the bitter rivals Marius and Sulla; the courageous cavalry officer Sertorius who would lead a rebellion in Spain; the merciless Manius Aquillius, poisoner of cities; and Lucullus, Sulla's resourceful young lieutenant.

KING JUGURTHA'S DOWNFALL

Of particular interest to Mithradates was Rome's long war with King Jugurtha of Numidia, once a trusted ally. Jugurtha's kingdom, inhabited by Berber nomads, lay between the Roman province that had once been Carthage and the kingdom of the nomadic Moors (Mauretania). Numidia provided the lions, leopards, and bears for circuses in Rome. Jugurtha had originally hoped to coexist with Rome but found all his diplomatic efforts blocked. After a series of vacillating decisions and conflicting diplomatic signals, and in the wake of poor military leadership, Rome declared war on Jugurtha in 112 BC.

Mithradates surely observed the progress of the Jugurthine War, and what it might mean for his own confrontations with Rome. North Africa's flora, fauna, and medical knowledge were also of great interest. There were reports of a mysterious tribe, the Psylli, immune to poisonous serpents and scorpions. According to the Romans, the Psylli were so "habituated to snake bites that their saliva was an effective antivenin" (antivenin is derived from human antibodies to live snake venom). Mithradates would have been fascinated to learn that Roman army doctors collected the saliva of Psylli nomads to counteract snakebites suffered by legionaries on the African campaigns. Roman writers railed against Psylli and other "professional poisoners" who set up shops in Rome around this time. Mithradates may have invited some Psylli to join his medical team.[23]

The Roman campaigns against Jugurtha held practical military lessons for Mithradates. A series of incompetent Roman generals managed to win numerous battles, but could never deliver victory, in a war of dubious motivation. During a lull in the war, the Numidian population of Vaga set upon a Roman garrison during a festival. In a massacre with similarities to the large-scale one Mithradates would order in 88 BC, they slaughtered the unarmed soldiers and their women and children.

In about 107 BC, five years into the war, Marius took the Roman command. Vowing to overcome the Numidians, he reorganized the legions to include proletarian soldiers. But victory still eluded Marius. Whenever Jugurtha and his son-in-law, King Bocchus of Mauretania, appeared to be pressed to the wall, they slipped away into the hinterlands and recruited fresh warriors among the nomads. Mithradates might possess a similar advantage, if Pontus could control or ally with the nomadic groups around the Black Sea and beyond Armenia. Indeed, in the coming wars with Rome, Mithradates and his son-in-law Tigranes of Armenia would elude Roman pursuers by melting back into uncharted nomad territory, where they raised fresh armies.

Finally, Marius's lieutenant, Sulla, bribed Bocchus to betray his kinsman Jugurtha. Shrewd, calculating Sulla promised Bocchus part of Numidia and the dubious status of "Friend of the Roman People." Bocchus turned over Jugurtha. Marius celebrated a Triumph, dragging the mighty King Jugurtha bound in chains through the streets of Rome. Marius's procession displayed incredible booty: 3,000 pounds of gold, 6,000 pounds of silver, and 300,000 drachmas.

After the procession, following Roman custom, Marius's thugs stripped off Jugurtha's royal robes. In the struggle to seize his golden earring, they tore off his earlobe. The king of Numidia was thrown down into the Tullianum, the same dark dungeon where Aristonicus, leader of the Sun Citizens, had been strangled. That was a fate Mithradates intended to avoid. The once-proud Jugurtha went mad and starved to death in 106 BC. That same year saw the birth of a Roman boy who would become Sulla's protégé, nicknamed the "Bloodthirsty Teenager," later known as Pompey the Great.[24]

To Marius's disgust, his rival Sulla seized credit for the victory. Sulla loved to show off a gold signet ring with a carved gem depicting himself accepting Jugurtha's surrender. Coins were issued showing Sulla on a throne above Jugurtha bound in chains. The Senate even approved a marble statue group showing Jugurtha kneeling before Sulla. According to the historian Plutarch, this final insult "almost drove Marius insane with rage." During the first rounds of the battle to the death between Marius and Sulla, Marius himself visited Mithradates in 99 BC. Mithradates could have heard details of the Jugurthine War then and probably learned more about Sulla too.[25]

Mithradates watched Roman manpower stretching to the breaking point, despite the innovations of Marius to recruit poor men into the army. Marius's military reforms inadvertently ushered in the rise of private armies made up of battle-hardened plebeian veterans wholly dependent on spoils and loyal only to their commanders. Such commanders could be played off against one another, as one hungry predator might attack a rival. The events shaking Rome's foundations just before and during Mithradates' early reign seemed to suggest that the awesome machine was juddering. Perhaps the Great Wolf was not so invincible after all.

THE REIGN BEGINS

The Pontic army had dwindled under his mother's rule. To avoid becoming a passive client of Rome, Pontus needed a strong army. Mithradates started modestly, recruiting an army of 6,000 Greek mercenaries, about the equivalent of a Roman legion. This force of traditional Greek hoplites, armed with shields and spears, was trained to fight in very close formation. Roman military organization, in this period, was based on legions (about 5,000 men), each legion made up of ten cohorts of about 480 soldiers in three ranks, armed with light javelins and wicked machetes, supported by about 300 cavalry.[26]

In Pontus, Mithradates paid assiduous attention to training cavalry and war chariot drivers. He recruited experienced Greek seamen from around the Black Sea, organizing a large, efficient navy. The Romans had manned a big navy during the Punic Wars, but they had allowed it to decline. Mithradates' ships now dominated the Black Sea, and the roaming pirate fleets were his allies. Early in his reign, Mithradates annexed Trapezus in eastern Pontus. Its hidden pirate coves made Trapezus the perfect home base for his navy. These early activities marked the beginning of Mithradates' grand plan for a Black Sea Empire.

MITHRADATES' FAMILY

Meanwhile Mithradates attended to domestic responsibilities. If he followed traditional Persian custom, his honeymoon began on the first night of spring and he fasted that day, eating nothing but an apple and a dish of camel marrow. Roughly a year later, in about 113 BC, Mithradates and his sister Laodice had their first son. Predictably, they named him Mithradates. Laodice had two more sons with Mithradates, named Arcathius (Greek, "ruler") and Machares ("warrior"). In 110, a daughter was born. Instead of naming her Laodice, as might be expected, Mithradates chose a traditional Macedonian name, Cleopatra.

Mithradates enjoyed sex with many women who caught his eye. The names of several of Mithradates' lovers were recorded: besides Laodice, there were Adobogiona (Galatian), Monime (from a Milesian family settled in Stratonicea), Berenice (Chios), Stratonice (Pontus), and Hypsicratea (Caucasia). Mithradates fathered numerous offspring. I found the names of nineteen children born to women other than Laodice in the ancient sources, bringing the total number of Mithradates' known, named progeny to twenty-three.

The boys born to concubines were named after illustrious Persians: Cyrus, Xerxes, Darius, Artaphernes (one of Darius III's generals), Oxathres (a brother of Darius who became Alexander's general), Pharnaces (Mithradates' grandfather), and Xiphares. Other sons mentioned in the ancient sources were Mithradates of Pergamon, Phoenix (son of a Phoenician or Syrian concubine), and Exipodras. A man named Archelaus was raised as the son of Mithradates' general Archelaus, but he claimed that his real father was Mithradates. That is not implausible—but he might have been a maternal grandson of Mithradates, who may well have married one of his daughters to his favorite general.

Mithradates' daughter Adobogiona's name was Galatian; other girls' names were Greek: Nyssa, Eupatra, Athenais, and Cleopatra the Younger. He called his most devoted daughter Drypetina, the diminutive form of the name of Darius's daughter Drypetis. The king's last two daughters received Persian names, Mithradatis and Orsabaris (from *berez*, "brilliant Venus"). All of Mithradates' children were said to be extraordinarily attractive, with one exception. Poor Drypetina's appearance was marred by an accident of nature: her baby teeth never fell out, so she had a double set of teeth.[27]

CASTLES, GOLD, ALLIES

Mithradates initiated an intensive—and expensive—fortress-building program. He constructed seventy-five castles in Pontus and his eastern lands during his long rule. That's more than one castle a year. Each new stronghold contained hidden cisterns, weapons caches, trapdoors and stone steps to an underground treasury carved out of bedrock, like the older castles of Pontus and Armenia. In these secret vaults were stacked bronze caskets bound with iron, filled with gold and silver, highly strategic in the coming campaigns. The construction projects were signs of Mithradates' foresight and obsession with security, but they also indicate his ready supply of money.[28]

What was the source of Mithradates' seemingly unlimited stores of gold? The question must have puzzled the Romans and his neighbors as much as it nags modern historians. We know that Pontus's prosperity came from trade and rich natural resources, gold, silver, iron, and precious minerals. Mithradates' affluent forefathers had hidden away coin hoards in castles throughout the realm (unavailable to Queen Laodice as regent). How Mithradates the Great became so *very* rich remains a mystery. Somehow he was never short of cash, throughout the long wars with Rome. Not only could the king raise an army on short notice, but he always had plenty to pay his soldiers well.

Mithradates drew substantial revenues from tributes and his control of Black Sea trade in grain, salt fish, wine, olive oil, honey, wax, gold, iron, minerals, dyes and pigments, leather, furs, wool, linen, and other goods. His tax policies must have been wisely calculated to enable him to profit from commerce without suppressing it, a policy that would have differed radically from Rome's at that time.

Mithradates' Scythian allies controlled rich gold fields. The nomads also looted *kurgans*, grave mounds, that dot the steppes around the Sea of Azov and the Black Sea. Modern archaeologists have discovered that many of the elaborate graves had been plundered in antiquity—some even contain the skeletons of ancient would-be robbers. The evidence suggests that successive waves of nomads dug for treasure in the *kurgans* of newly conquered lands.[29] Some of this gold may have found its way to Pontus as tribute and in trade agreements.

Mithradates also profited from overland trade with India and China. The Silk Route had opened during Mithradates' childhood; the first camel caravans arrived in Parthia bearing Chinese silk in exchange for fine Parthian horses in 106 BC. As Chinese armies pressed westward into the Tarim Basin, and as Parthia began to clash with its neighbors in the Middle East, caravans shifted from the southern to northern routes through Colchis and Pontus to the Black Sea. Again, Mithradates would have encouraged this trade without overtaxing it.[30]

Yet another stream of wealth may have been related to the extensive black market in slaves and plunder carried on by pirates based in Crete, Cilicia on the coast of Syria, and the Black Sea. Piracy in the first century BC was not small-scale thievery and robbing ships at sea. This vast shadow navy constituted a political power in its own right, a terroristic paramilitary force, controlling the sea-lanes of the eastern Mediterranean and the Black Sea. Pirate harbors in Crete and Cilicia were protected by invincible fortresses. The corsairs not only looted ships' cargoes and held rich passengers for ransom; they made bold raids inland to capture droves of slaves, and they even besieged walled cities. Pirates offered mercenary services to warring parties during the late Hellenistic period. As a matter of war strategy and for profit, Mithradates continued and built upon his father's lucrative relations with the pirate admirals.[31]

Mithradates also maintained his father's friendships and lucrative trade links with Athens and the Greek islands. He cultivated the Greek and Persian-influenced cities of western Anatolia, and established amicable terms with Armenia, Syria, Media, Parthia, and Egypt.[32]

If Mithradates could also befriend the Scythians, annex lands around the Black Sea, secure good relations with independent Greek and indigenous ports, and ensure a peaceful trade climate, the entire Black Sea could become Mithradates' own personal lake. Everyone would profit, especially Pontus. Before Mithradates, the Greeks and Romans held a negative notion of the Black Sea. They compared its shape to a fearsome Scythian bow, with its distinctive double curve—a particularly ominous image, since Scythian archers were dreaded for their unholy skill at shooting poison arrows. Before Mithradates, the Black Sea was seen as an obstacle instead of an opportunity. His decision to control and develop the entire Black Sea region was a creative, brilliant new strategy.[33]

BLACK SEA EMPIRE

The Greek cities on the north coast of the Black Sea were in constant conflict with the steppe nomads. They paid tributes to buy protection from one tribe of Scythians, Sarmatians, Tauri, Thracians, Roxolani, or others (commonly referred to collectively as "Scythians"), only to see them superseded by another, stronger group, which demanded yet another ransom.[34] Early in his reign, Mithradates received an embassy from the strategic Kingdom of Cimmerian Bosporus (Crimea). King Parisades asked Mithradates to intervene to protect the northern Black Sea from the marauders. Seizing the opportunity, Mithradates immediately sent his army and navy, led by his Greek general Diophantus and admiral Neoptolemus.

After an arduous campaign, Diophantus was eventually victorious. In the end the nomads agreed to be independent allies of Mithradates, promising tribute, mutual protection, and aid. Scythian and other nomad warriors often enlisted as mercenaries in armies of foreign leaders they respected. An intelligent commander with great diplomatic skills, Diophantus negotiated a peace with the Scythians, the Sarmatians, and the Bosporan Kingdom, all to Mithradates' advantage.

In 1878, near Pantikapaion, Russian archaeologists discovered a long inscription on a statue of Diophantus. It is a detailed summary of the Scythian campaign, naming the fortresses erected for Mithradates, and hailing Diophantus as the "first foreign invader to subdue the Scythians," praising the commander's courage, wisdom, and kindness. Another honorific inscription (published in 1982) graced a statue of Mithradates himself here. This inscription is highly significant because it refers to Mithradates as the "King of Kings." This was a coveted ancient Iranian title (Persian, *Shahanshah*) that could be held by only one supreme Near Eastern ruler at a time.[35]

Mithradates' own forceful personality, illustrious ancestry, and generous terms of diplomacy, along with his horsemanship, prowess with bow and arrow, knowledge of the nomads' dialects, and respect for their culture, impressed the Scythians and other northern tribes.[36] Mithradates betrothed some of his daughters to the nomad chieftains and promised glory and riches to the groups who joined him.

No one had ever really vanquished the fiercely independent nomads. Mithradates was extremely proud of his success in the north. He liked to point out that his new allies, the expert mounted archers of central Asia, had bested the armies of Cyrus, Darius, and Alexander. Pontus's new, powerful influence in this northern region apparently passed under the Roman radar. Even if the Senate took notice, it would have approved stability that ensured grain, salt fish, and other goods bound for Italy in exchange for olive oil and wine. Diophantus's pacification and reorganization of the northern Black Sea region was a remarkably successful military and diplomatic mission. Mithradates now enjoyed almost inexhaustible supplies of men, grain, gold, and raw materials.

By 106 BC, Mithradates had absorbed the Crimea and the Taman Peninsula into the Kingdom of the Bosporus. The fortresses of this strategic region and the wealthy cities of Phanagoria and Pantikapaion became his royal residences. The bulk of Mithradates' agate and gem collection

probably came from this region, which was also known for pomegran-
ates, figs, apples, and pears. It is interesting to learn from Pliny that Mithradates sent gardeners to transplant and cultivate laurel (bay trees) and
myrtle in the Crimea. These two sacred plants, native to the Mediterranean, were important in Greek mythology, medicine, and religious
rituals signifying victory. Despite the botanists' best efforts, however, the
plants failed to thrive in the north.[37]

After three seasons of ferocious fighting, Colchis, a strategic land on
the remote eastern Black Sea, also pledged allegiance to Mithradates. He
annexed the rugged western part of Armenia as well, forging good relations with independent Anatolian and Persian chieftains there. On the
western Black Sea, Mithradates allied with the war-loving Thracians
and the powerful Iranian-influenced Bastarnae and Roxolani, again after
tough fighting. The Germanic Gauls (Celts) who strongly resisted Roman

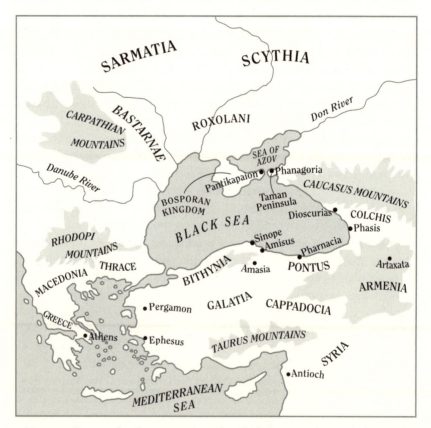

MAP 5.1. Eurasia; lands surrounding the Black Sea. Map by Michele Angel.

military advances also supported Mithradates. The king now ruled or was allied with all the lands around the Black Sea, except for northwest Anatolia and the mountainous coast north of Colchis.[38]

Mithradates' grand strategy for the Black Sea was coming into being (see maps 1.2 and 5.1). The idea was to secure a coprosperity trade zone and tax it fairly. The plan would benefit everyone, including the Scythians, who were beginning to settle into towns, and even the Romans, who depended on grain from the steppes. Mithradates could recruit Black Sea pirate sailors to join his legitimate navy for regular pay, and reward others to prey on the rich ships of holdout states that declined to join his coprosperity plan. Mithradates, as organizer, enforcer, and duty collector of this Black Sea Empire, would profit greatly, of course. But he could promise that everyone else would grow rich too. Indeed, the immense and surprising wealth that archaeologists are uncovering in the northern Black Sea region—not just in urban areas but in the *chora*—reveals the great success of Mithradates' concept.[39]

Mithradates' farsighted vision offered a positive alternative to Rome's rapacious greed and violent resource extraction in its early period of conquest. Instead of continual war, Mithradates offered peace. Instead of imposing bloodsucking taxes and debt, Mithradates would tax moderately and reinvest taxes in military measures to ensure security. Mithradates stood for a new vision of mutual prosperity, while the Romans of the late Republic pursued corruption, selfish profit, and plunder. It is easy to see the strong attraction of such a strategy and the deep loyalty it could generate. Mithradates' Black Sea would become the central pivot, the benevolent middleman in a grand Eurasian trading community. As long as Mithradates Eupator (the "Good Father") ruled, all could expect to live long and prosper.

But what about his neighbors, Cappadocia, Bithynia, Paphlagonia, Galatia? Mithradates' intrigues in the Roman-controlled sphere west of Pontus would require stealth and delicacy. Phrygia and western Anatolia presented even more problems. The heart of Provincia Asia was occupied by Roman troops, colonial administrators, tax farmers, and tens of thousands of Roman settlers. Mithradates needed the most up-to-date information about these lands.

Despite his successes in empire building, Mithradates was beginning to feel restless. He missed the invigorating outdoor life he had enjoyed with his companions in exile. Justin commented, "Mithradates would rather spend his time in the open plains and mountains instead of at the dinner-table." He longed to be "training with his brothers-in-arms in the field, instead of relaxing at court with his cronies. He preferred to compete in foot-races and horse-racing and tournaments of strength" than to make small talk with Queen Laodice and the courtiers.[40] How could he recapture the exhilaration of his youthful rambles in Pontus and further his long-term goals at the same time?

The Fact-Finding Mission

Justin tells us that Mithradates set off again from Sinope with close friends, this time on an extensive reconnaissance expedition. The timing of this grand tour is not certain, but it may have been around 110/108 BC. Traveling incognito, the group roamed Galatia, Paphlagonia, Cappadocia, and Bithynia, gathering information for future campaigns. "No one was aware of their presence," writes Justin. What better way to gain deep knowledge of Pontus's neighbors, lands that the king intended to absorb into his kingdom? Mithradates was always thinking ahead, like his heroes Cyrus and Alexander.[41]

Mithradates reconnoitered Anatolia's cities and scouted defenses. Exercising his remarkable memory, he took note of the natural resources, roads, people, and terrain. In Bithynia especially, says Justin, Mithradates "boldly surveyed all the areas that would favor his victory there, already imagining himself master of Asia." As Reinach pointed out, this intelligence-gathering trip surely reinforced the ambitions of the young king.[42] Wherever the royal band did identify themselves, in Greek and indigenous towns and villages, they were greeted enthusiastically. The oracles surrounding Mithradates' birth were not forgotten among anti-Romans; his conquests of Persian-influenced lands around the Black Sea had made him "King of Kings." It was valuable for Mithradates to hear local complaints about Roman settlers, and to learn where he could rally support and recruit soldiers.

The royal companions probably engaged in contests of skill and stamina on the road. If Mithradates and his band attempted to match Alexander's endurance in riding and marching long distances, for example, they would have to have made successive marches of 400 stades (a total of about 150 miles). Mithradates was a strong horseman: ancient writers say that he was able to ride about 1,000 stades (110–25 miles) in a single day with fresh horses.[43]

They visited isolated fortresses in Bithynia, Galatia, and Paphlagonia. In Paphlagonia, Mithradates surely visited Cimiata, the fort built by

Mithradates I of Pontus. Not far from here, near Pimolisa, lay the gloomy, deep caverns of Mount Realgar Mine, with its deadly mother lodes of arsenic-laden minerals. Mithradatic strongholds also existed in Cappadocia; in Galatia lay the hidden castles Blucium and Peium, where great treasures were stored. These places were dominated by powerful local outlaws and chieftains—people who could be of great value in the coming war.[44]

The group may have visited historical sites of special interest to Mithradates, such as Troy, site of the legendary war between the Greeks and Priam's vast armies of Trojans and barbarians. In Lydia, Mithradates could hang a pendant or bracelet on the ancient plane tree revered by Xerxes in 480 BC. The Persian monarch had honored the venerable tree with expensive ornaments, golden necklaces, copper bracelets, and even a fine embroidered robe. Ever since, travelers draped their own offerings on the branches. Gordium in Phrygia was another venerated landmark: here the brash young Alexander had slashed his sword through the Gordian Knot.[45]

We know that Mithradates made pilgrimages to places where Alexander stopped. At Ephesus, for example, where Mithradates enlarged the sanctuary by shooting an arrow as Alexander had done, he sought out an inn honored by the Macedonian's presence. In Priene, one could visit another house where Alexander had stayed. Bedding down where Alexander once slept, Mithradates—like many an ambitious conqueror since—must have compared his own accomplishments to those of his hero, who had died knowing he was master of the world at age thirty-two.

On this grand tour, Mithradates called in at Cyzicus and Heraclea, two independent, strongly fortified Greek cities that would later defy him. Mithradates also visited Pergamon, the capital of the Romans' Asian Province; here he heard many complaints of corrupt government and gross overtaxation. Cilicia, with its harsh landscape and rocky coast, was another important stop. This was the headquarters of the dashing Syrian pirate admiral Seleucus, a good friend of Pontus.

We also hear that Mithradates sailed to the island of Rhodes, a powerful independent Greek city-state with its own navy. The island was celebrated for withstanding a great seige in 305/304 BC, by Demetrius Poliorcetes of Macedonia, who had failed on a magnificent scale. He left behind his gigantic seige towers, which Rhodians used to create a huge statue of the Sun god Helios, the Colossus of Rhodes, one of the Seven Wonders of the Ancient World. The Colossus had toppled in the earthquake of 222 BC. Mithradates and his men could marvel at the enormous bronze limbs still scattered around the harbor, keeping an eye out for the island's poisonous vipers and giant lizards. The mission in Rhodes was mainly political. Might Rhodes, an ally of Rome that controlled part of Lycia, agree to become a friend of Pontus? Mithradates bestowed generous gifts to the city, and the Rhodians erected a marble statue of Mithradates in their *agora*, marketplace.

Next Mithradates sailed to the little island of Delos. Italian merchants dominated wealthy Delos, which the Romans had turned into a vast slave depot. The small Greek community there welcomed Mithradates as a patron of the island and friend of Athens. Mithradates gave votive tablets to the Temple of Asclepius and to Zeus on Mount Kynthos, and he inscribed two tablets in the Temple of Serapis, the Egyptian god of healing and dream interpretation. This commercial nexus of the Aegean was crucial for winning Greek support and gathering news from Italy.[46]

While he was away, Mithradates had left his wife, Queen Laodice, his eunuchs, and some of the King's Friends in charge. Even though it was always dangerous for a ruler to leave home, for security reasons Mithradates did not advise anyone of his travel plans or when to expect his return. Mithradates and his companions were gone so long—at least a year, maybe longer—that it was believed that they had perished.[47] Embracing the role of the tragically widowed queen of Pontus, anticipating ruling the kingdom as her mother had done after her father's murder, Laodice publicly mourned the death of her brother-husband. The grieving young widow consoled herself by having love affairs with Mithradates' friends in Sinope.

6

Storm Clouds

ONE DAY, without warning, Mithradates and his companions suddenly reappeared at the gates of Sinope—to the shock and distress of Laodice and her lovers. But the citizens of Pontus joyfully welcomed their king home after such a long absence. Except for a few significant details, we are left in the dark about Mithradates' homecoming. Here is a reconstruction of how things may have gone, based on the facts recorded by Justin.[1]

THE HONEYMOON'S OVER

Someone, neglecting to do the arithmetic, tactlessly congratulated the king on the birth of another son by Queen Laodice during his absence. He had been gone too long for the child to be his. Hiding his rage, Mithradates embraces his wife and then visits the harem nursery to count his children. Festive banquets are being prepared to welcome him. Making the rounds of the palace, the king calls in at the royal kitchens to check on preparations, chatting amiably with the cooks, maids, and serving women. All are flushed with excitement at the return of their king.

But two of the serving women seem uneasy. Mithradates draws them aside, escorting them to a shady portico, out of sight and hearing of the others. We know that the women informed on Laodice. Let us suppose they were flaxen-haired Gauls from the Danube tribes, whose goodwill Mithradates cultivated. The maids' pale eyes widen when the king speaks in their dialect. He explains that he has been learning it from his friend and bodyguard, Bituitus, a strapping chieftain of the Allobroges, whose land had been annexed by Rome.

Mithradates' penetrating stare and questions elicit the women's terrible secret. Words tumble out, confirming his suspicions. Queen Laodice

Fɪɢ. 6.1. Mithradates as Hercules, wearing a lionskin cap. Marble, 13 inches high. Alexander the Great was often depicted in the same manner. Louvre. Réunion des Musées Nationaux/Art Resource, NY.

had became pregnant by one of his "friends." Laodice "thought she could conceal her unfaithfulness by an even greater crime." The servants warned Mithradates that his sister and wife, the mother of his heirs, was planning to slip poison into his food at the feast. They also named the queen's coconspirators.[2]

Cursing his dead mother for raising such a treacherous daughter, Mithradates immediately executed Laodice and her collaborators. Was Laodice trying to replicate her mother's scheme, to take over the kingdom and rule as regent of a young crown prince? We are not told how Laodice was killed. When it was necessary to do away with someone, Mithradates almost always chose indirect means, usually poison (with

FIG. 6.2. (Left) Mithradates poisons Laodice, his wife/sister; (right) Mithradates wins a duel. *Tresor des Histoires/Mithridate fait boire du poison/* MS 5077 res, folio 194v. and *Cas des nobles hommes et femmes/Mithridate, Roi,* MS 5193, folio 241v, Bibliothèque Nationale de France.

the exception of two spectacular public murders, described later). Perhaps, in cold scientific mode, the king and his botanist Krateuas used this opportunity to test and compare some quick-acting poisons on Laodice and her cohorts. The bastard boy was allowed to live; perhaps he would come in handy someday.[3]

After the execution, we learn that Mithradates vowed never to marry again. Queens—especially queens named Laodice—spelled trouble. He had three legitimate male heirs now and a large harem filled with lovely, replaceable courtesans with no claims on him. Why should he ever take another official wife?

After Laodice's betrayal, the king threw himself into athletic training and building up his army and treasury. In his early thirties now, Mithradates was fit and competitive; he enjoyed wrestling and boxing tournaments, javelin throwing, martial arts contests, hand-to-hand duels, weight lifting, and other tests of strength. He competed in horse and chariot races around Anatolia and the Aegean; marble inscriptions from Chios and Rhodes name Mithradates as victor in equestrian events.[4] In Sinope, there were banquets with raucous entertainments by jesters, acrobats, Median fire jugglers, snake handlers, magicians, and contortionists. Mithradates appreciated refined cultural entertainments too. His

FIG. 6.3. Inscription found on the island of Chios listing victors in equestrian and chariot events. Mithradates' name appears four times.

court attracted the best musicians, actors, and poets to declaim Homeric verses.

A well-known "inconvenience of greatness" is that toadies are drawn to power as iron filings cling to a lodestone. Mithradates was surrounded by opportunists and flatterers. One man in particular, a conjurer named Sosipater, has come down in history as the most shameless sycophant in Mithradates' court. During times when the king was beset by doubts and suspicion, sycophants swooped in, accusing others of plotting against the king. Plutarch, who wrote an essay on how to distinguish friends from flatterers, remarked that some of Mithradates' courtiers were so keen to curry favor that they would offer themselves as guinea pigs for his medical experiments.[5]

Mithradates sponsored drinking contests in Sinope, offering a fabulous prize—one talent of silver—to the winner. A popular athlete from Cyzicus, Kalomodrys, nearly matched Mithradates' capacity for wine. The king himself usually won, gallantly awarding the honors to the runner-up. There were gargantuan eating competitions too. But no one could surpass Mithradates in his ability to devour platter after platter loaded with slabs of meat and bread. Mithradates even earned a place (number eight) in antiquity's Top Twelve Gluttons of All Time! Half of the men on the list hailed from Anatolia, where eating and drinking vast quantities was a folk tradition demonstrating wealth and manly vigor. Mithradates' massive physique and energy may have accounted for a huge appetite, but his capacity also harked back to his ancestors. Darius I boasted of his ability to hold his liquor as one of his great achievements. And people still shook their heads in awe over Alexander's ability to imbibe two dozen toasts to his companions' health in one night—and his vicious two-day hangovers after rowdy drinking bouts with his hard-living Macedonians.[6]

When he was not chariot racing, or showing off his superior strength and cast-iron constitution, Mithradates was recruiting soldiers for Pontus's expanding army. A serious scholar of military history, he studied the strategies and tactics of famous commanders. Mithradates and his engineers attached scythe blades to his war chariot axles, a long-forgotten innovation of Cyrus the Great. To toughen his infantrymen, cavalry soldiers, and chariot drivers, Mithradates ordered all to participate with him in rigorous daily calisthenics and field exercises. "Like King Mithradates himself," wrote Justin, "his army became inured to hardship and invincible. Soon, he had created an unbeatable military force." Mithradates had gathered the intelligence he needed about his neighbors, and a large, capable army stood ready. It was time to complete his Black Sea Empire by taking over Cappadocia, Bithynia, and Paphlagonia. But this would entail direct confrontation with Rome.[7]

BITHYNIA

Sometime in 108–104 BC, Mithradates made an alliance with the crafty King Nicomedes III of Bithynia. Nicomedes, like his father, had been an ally of Rome. But, after Bithynia had helped to suppress Aristonicus's revolt, its request for part of Phrygia was denied in favor of Mithradates' father. So Nicomedes III had good reasons to resent Pontus, and he was adept at treading the diplomatic tightrope with Rome.

FIG. 6.4. Mithradates' nemesis Nicomedes of Bithynia (similar portraits were used for Nicomedes III and IV). 1944.100.41904, bequest of E. T. Newell, courtesy of the American Numismatic Society.

When the Roman commander Gaius Marius requested troops from Bithynia to help subdue Germany, Nicomedes' bold retort had made a good impression on Mithradates. Nicomedes declared that he had no army to send because all of Bithynia's free men had fallen into debt and were sold into slavery by greedy Roman tax collectors. This reply had forced the Senate to pass a law forbidding the enslavement of the free citizens of Rome's allies.

Mithradates' alliance with Nicomedes was well timed: Roman armies were spread thin, embroiled in war with King Jugurtha of Numidia and staving off the Germanic tribes. Mithradates and Nicomedes agreed to invade weak Paphlagonia. All went smoothly. But when the news reached Rome, the Senate sent ambassadors demanding the restoration of Paphlagonia's king. In a defiant retort, Mithradates asserted that

Paphlagonia had actually belonged to his father by inheritance. I'm surprised, Mithradates claimed, that Rome would question this now, since they had never doubted my father's right to Paphlagonia before. Taken aback by this arrogant response, the ambassadors failed to call Mithradates' bluff, and turned to Nicomedes.

Nicomedes took a sneakier tack. He contritely promised to restore Paphlagonia to its rightful ruler. Then he renamed one of his own sons with the traditional name of ancient Paphlagonian kings: Pylaemenes. Nicomedes boldly installed this pseudo-Pylaemenes on the throne. The Romans were tricked into approving this new king. When they finally figured out the ruse, the embarrassed Roman dignitaries hurried home. Nicomedes III emerged as the real ruler of Paphlagonia.

Mithradates, impressed by Nicomedes' slick trick, responded by seizing part of Galatia. He built a major fortress there, Mithradateion. Meanwhile, he considered his options in Cappadocia.[8]

Murder in Cappadocia

Cappadocia was ruled by Mithradates' older sister Laodice, through her husband, King Ariathes VI. They had two sons (confusingly, both boys were also named Ariathes, reflecting their Persian blood). According to the historian Appian, the original kings of Cappadocia and Pontus had shared a royal bloodline, and Mithradates the First had possessed both Galatia and Cappadocia. This history had justified Mithradates' father's indirect control of Galatia and Cappadocia, and Mithradates intended to do the same.

Gordius, a Cappadocian noble in Laodice's court, was Mithradates' good friend. Presumably, it was Gordius who informed Mithradates that Laodice's young husband was beginning to assert himself. An independent-minded Ariathes was troublesome for both Laodice and Mithradates. Mithradates gave Gordius orders to eliminate King Ariathes VI. We are not told the means, but poison comes to mind. This favor made Mithradates' older sister Laodice the regent for her firstborn son, Ariathes VII, Mithradates' nephew. With this move, Mithradates expected to manipulate Cappadocia—provided his sister cooperated with him.[9]

But the ploy backfired. After Gordius's murder of Ariathes VI, the devious Nicomedes III of Bithynia saw an opening. Without informing Mithradates, his ally, Nicomedes suddenly invaded Cappadocia (ca. 103/ 102 BC). Taken by surprise, Mithradates rushed with his army to rescue his sister. But when he arrived, he discovered that the resourceful widow Laodice had agreed to marry Nicomedes. His sister in bed with that odious backstabber! It occurred to Mithradates that she had probably invited Nicomedes to "invade." This unexpected alliance meant that she and Nicomedes would manage Cappadocia together, through her pliable son Ariathes VII.

Mithradates quickly shifted gears. He proceeded with the rescue mission to place his nephew Ariathes on the Cappadocian throne. In the battle, Mithradates overcame Nicomedes' army and sent him and Laodice packing, back to Bithynia. Mithradates' nephew, Ariathes VII, became the new boy-king of Cappadocia. The young man's portrait was included in Mithradates' circle of friends in the Delos Monument. But the inexperienced young prince needed a handler, if Mithradates was to control Cappadocia indirectly, without arousing the Roman Senate. Uncle Mithradates suggested that his nephew invite Gordius—the murderer of the youth's own father—to be his adviser! Young Ariathes VII recognized the trap. If he accepted Gordius, he would become an expendable puppet. If he refused, Uncle Mithradates would have a pretext for war. Ariathes refused and resolutely led his army onto the battlefield.

Foiled again! Not only had the boy inherited Laodicean defiance from his mother and grandmother, but Mithradates' spies reported that Nicomedes was sending support. His scheme thwarted, Mithradates now faced a dubious outcome in battle with a stubborn teenager. Exasperated, Mithradates drew up his formidable army: 80,000 infantrymen, 10,000 cavalry, and 600 scythed chariots. These numbers are likely somewhat exaggerated; still, Mithradates' impressive forces demonstrate his wealth and popularity. But how he hated to waste his army to achieve what should have been a bloodless takeover. Mithradates prepared another decisive plan of action.

He sent for his eight-year-old stepson, his dead wife Laodice's bastard. What happened next was reported by Justin in graphic detail, perhaps because there were so many witnesses. Relying on Justin's vivid account, we need only fill in a few minor details and the scene takes on a cinematic quality.[10]

At sunrise, the two armies marched out on the battleground. We hear the clink of weapons being readied and war banners snapping in the wind. Suddenly, King Mithradates strides out to a hillock between the armies, visible to all. He calls for a meeting on the middle ground with his nephew. Mithradates ostentatiously lays down his bow and arrows, his javelins, and unbuckles his sword. Ariathes, suspicious, sends a guard over to search his uncle for concealed weapons. The soldier nervously begins to pat down Mithradates from his powerful shoulders to his leather boots. As the man's hands grope Mithradates' trousers "somewhat too attentively," the king interrupts with a crude joke: "Watch out! You might find a weapon quite different from what you are seeking!" The guard backs off, flummoxed.

Ariathes approaches the grassy knoll between the armies where Mithradates stands alone, smiling pleasantly. The supporters and soldiers in the front ranks on each side look on, tense, silent. Mithradates takes his nephew's arm, asking him for a private word. As they turn to walk together, Mithradates quickly reaches into his trousers and pulls out a stiletto concealed alongside his penis. With one brutal stroke, the blade slices the young man's throat.

Mithradates reaches down to pick up his dead nephew's crown from the dust. Walking in a stately fashion over to the terrified young boy on the sidelines, he places the crown with a flourish on his head and shouts out his new name: *All hail Ariathes, King of Cappadocia!* On cue, grim Gordius steps forward and leads the dazed new ruler of Cappadocia away. Shocked at the pantomime of violent succession they have just witnessed, and now with no king to fight for, the real Ariathes' commanders and men fell into confusion and impotence. In only one other instance would Mithradates violently kill a man in public for the shock value.

Gordius's rule, with Mithradates' stepson Ariathes, was popular in Cappadocia. But a few years later, in about 96 BC, Nicomedes III staged a revolt. He had sent for the younger brother of the murdered king. This hapless pawn was hailed as Ariathes VIII. Mithradates dispatched his army and quelled the rebellion. What happened to Ariathes VIII? The story was that the boy died of "a disease brought on by grief." Mithradates' bastard son, now dubbed Ariathes IX, continued to rule with Gordius as the true power behind the throne.[11]

Meanwhile, Mithradates opened lines of communication with the anti-Roman rebels in Italy, courted the Danube Gauls, and showered the northern nomads with largesse. He was a beloved patron of the Greeks and sent embassies to North Africa, Egypt, and Parthia. He also dispatched envoys bearing gifts to Rome. The historian Diodorus characterized these as "large sums of money with which to bribe the Senate." At any rate, his envoys, philosopher-statesmen from Anatolia, were gravely insulted by officials in Rome—a capital offense in Roman diplomacy, as Mithradates knew. His ambassadors immediately pressed charges in a public trial.[12]

Mithradates was consolidating his holdings and expanding his influence, although both Nicomedes III's cleverness and Roman retaliation would soon test the solidarity of his empire. Not long after murdering his nephew Ariathes, Mithradates had a chance to meet one of the most famous representatives of Roman power in person.

A Parley with Marius

In about 99/98 BC, Gaius Marius, the great plebeian war hero struggling to maintain his power in Rome, arrived in Anatolia. His Popular faction had just lost an election amid a murderous uprising inside the city. Old clan feuds were erupting into violence; it was the beginning of the bloody civil wars that would consume Rome for the next two generations. Leaving his loyal army of veterans behind, Marius sailed to Cappadocia and Galatia.

Marius, about fifty-eight, more than twenty years older than Mithradates, was a tough, courageous leader, beloved by his soldiers. He dug trenches, ate rations, and slept on the ground like them. Marius had served with distinction in Spain and Africa, and in Germany his legions had slaughtered more than 300,000 and enslaved more than 150,000 people. In physical strength, military skill, and ruthlessness, Marius was a Roman whom Mithradates could admire and learn from.

Mithradates would have been eager to hear Marius's version of the capture of Jugurtha, rebel king of Numidia. There were reports that the ambitious patrician officer Lucius Cornelius Sulla was taking all the credit for Marius's victory in North Africa. Sulla was now in Rome with his own army, poised to seize total power. Civil war between these two bitter foes—the older Marius and his one-time protégé Sulla—loomed. The two enemies were vying to win command of the army that the Senate would soon have to send to subdue Mithradates. Would it be Marius or Sulla who would become his greatest challenge?

Marius claimed he had come to fulfill a sacred vow, to consult the oracle of the great Anatolian mother goddess Cybele in her sanctuary at Pessinus. Like most great Roman and other leaders of his day, Marius was not only personally superstitious; he also grasped the value of religion in politics. As a boy, Marius had rescued some baby eaglets; his soothsayers interpreted this as a sign that he would achieve supreme authority in Rome. In Libya, an omen of two scorpions fighting had allowed him to escape death. Marius was always accompanied by a covey

Fig. 6.5. *Marius Meditates on the Ruins of Carthage*, J. Vanderlyn,
engraving, 1842.

of Etruscan augurs who interpreted portents, and he was not above
creating his own positive omens on campaigns. In Germany, for example, his soldiers captured a pair of vultures, fed them well, and then fitted
them with bronze collars. The tame raptors could always be seen soaring

above Marius's armies. The idea that Marius's vultures would soon feast on dead Germans made his men confident of victory.

In the turbulent years just before Marius's trip, frightening omens of flaming spears and shields in the heavens were observed over Italy. In 104 BC, Roman seers reported that "weapons in the sky had suddenly rushed together from east and west, and those from the east overcame those of the west." During his meeting with Marius, Mithradates may have conversed in Aramaic about these omens with Marius's Syrian prophetess, Martha. She had been discovered at the gladiatorial games in Rome, accurately predicting which men would be victors. Now Marius claimed that he "followed Martha's advice in all undertakings." She accompanied him everywhere, carried in a fancy litter by tall slaves from her own native Syria. Dressed in a crimson robe fastened with a golden brooch and waving a little spear decorated with ribbons, Martha directed Marius's theatrical religious sacrifices.[13]

If Mithradates was eager to learn about Marius, so, too, Marius sought to know more about the king of Pontus. From his seers and Martha of Syria, Marius was aware of the oracles surrounding Mithradates' birth. He wanted to meet this ambitious, popular ruler and gauge his character, figure out his intentions. For Marius had really come to investigate the Cappadocian situation. How imminent was war? How could Marius arrange to win glory in the conflict already brewing over Mithradates' growing power?

This was Mithradates' first face-to-face audience with a charismatic Roman warlord. Both leaders were consumed with curiosity yet eager to appear strong and confident.[14] Mithradates received Marius "with great attention and respect." With his ramrod posture, permanent scowl, and commanding voice, Marius was an imperious presence. His deep distrust of aristocratic luxury and erudition was well known; Mithradates could shift into a rustic, soldierly persona for the parley. Perhaps they met on the royal exercise grounds. Marius was proud of his expertise with weapons and his horsemanship; he exercised daily with much younger soldiers. Mithradates loved to show off as well—they were well matched, and in another life they might have been friends.

The tough old warrior's parting words to Mithradates are famous: "Either make yourself stronger than the Romans, or obey them!" Modern historians are divided on the subtle meaning of Marius's imperative. Was this a friendly warning? Was Marius daring Mithradates to take on Rome? Marius's stern sound bite was reported in Rome and enhanced his stature in the Senate.[15]

The face value of Marius's message was banal. "Overcome or surrender" could be standard advice for anyone, anytime. As both men well knew, "Be stronger or submit" also applied to Marius's own position vis-à-vis Rome and his enemy Sulla. Mithradates' calculated actions so far showed that he already intended to become so strong that he would never have to obey Rome. Sizing each other up, weighing the other's steel will, each man privately acknowledged the truth behind the cliché: there was no middle way for either man. But were they destined to be friends or foes? We cannot replay the body language, facial expressions, tone of voice, or gestures that must have conveyed so much at this meeting. I imagine that as the simple sentence was uttered, the two men locked eyes in perfect understanding.

FACE-OFF WITH ROME

Thanks to the interference of Nicomedes III, the Cappadocian circus began spinning out of Mithradates' control, inciting the anger of Rome, dashing Mithradates' preference for oblique action. When Laodice's younger son, Ariathes VIII, died of "grief" and Mithradates secured Cappadocia, Nicomedes feared that Mithradates would turn on Bithynia next. To incite the Romans against Mithradates, Nicomedes and Laodice found a handsome young man and slyly coached him to pretend to be a "lost third son" of the murdered King Ariathes VI, Laodice's previous husband. Laodice accompanied this new impostor to Rome and won an audience with the Senate, as queen of Bithynia and Cappadocia. Laodice swore that this youth was her son and the rightful heir of Cappadocia.

Mithradates immediately dispatched his aide Gordius to Rome. The regent of Cappadocia delivered a spirited countermessage to the Senate. This boy was an impostor! Gordius revealed that the youth was really the son of a supporter of the notorious enemy of Rome, the rebel Aristonicus. It is striking that Mithradates and Gordius raised the specter of the revolt of the Sun Citizens (133–129 BC). That popular Anatolian insurgency— some thirty years earlier—still had the power to alarm the Senate and to galvanize Mithradates' followers.

Gordius also tried to bribe Roman officials. The senators' response was measured. Both Nicomedes and Mithradates were ordered out of the kingdoms they had attempted to dominate. The Senate officially liberated Paphlagonia and commanded the Cappadocians to chose a new king, since their royal family was now extinct.

At this time, Sulla, the new praetor of Rome, was on his way to Cilicia with a legion (about five thousand men). His orders were to suppress the pirates there. But Sulla made a detour to Cappadocia. This was Mithradates' first indirect encounter with Sulla, who was a few years his senior. Sulla's army overcame the troops protecting Gordius and his young charge, commanded by Mithradates' general Archelaus. Gordius and young Ariathes IX had to return to Pontus, as Sulla personally crowned the new Cappadocian ruler, Ariobarzanes (ca. 95 BC). Sulla's threatening presence was matched by his words. He warned the "minor kings" of Anatolia to withdraw from their recent landgrabs or else.[16]

Mithradates observed with disgust the acquiescence of the Bithynian weasel, Nicomedes III. Nicomedes and Laodice were bankrupt: they clutched at an alliance with the Roman Republic as though it were a lifeline. Mithradates, hemmed in by Roman troops in western Anatolia, offered no resistance. He withdrew his armies and bided his time.

KING TIGRANES OF ARMENIA

Mithradates turned his attention east, to Armenia, far from Rome's notice. He needed a strong, reliable ally. For the time being, he wanted to avoid confrontations with Rome. In about 96 BC, Tigranes II of Armenia returned from the Parthian Empire (ancient Persia, modern Iran), where he had lived for the past thirty years, to assume his father's throne.

As a boy, Tigranes (Persian for the planet Mercury) was sent as a royal hostage to be raised in the Parthian court. In Ctesiphon, he was educated in Parthian culture, a melding of nomadic and ancient Iranian traditions. Persian influence was very strong in Armenia, and Tigranes' mother was an Alan princess from beyond the Caucasus. Like royal marriage alliances of this period, the practice of sending a prince as a hostage was a way to ensure civil relations between distrustful allies. (Other examples were Philip of Macedon, educated in Thebes, and Cyrus the Great, raised in Media.) When Tigranes' father died, the Parthians allowed Tigranes, at age forty-six, to don the Armenian royal tiara with the understanding that he would abide by Parthia's wishes, as his father had. But Tigranes harbored big ideas for building an Armenian empire.

In about 94 BC, Gordius rode to Tigranes' court in Artaxata as Mithradates' envoy. Tigranes' high ambitions were matched by keen intelligence. He would have been familiar with the oracles about Mithradates and the comets of 135 and 119 BC, and the Magi's blessing of the long-awaited "savior-king" of Pontus. He kept abreast of Mithradates' conquests. An alliance with this rising emperor of the Black Sea could be useful. Tigranes was in a position to protect—and also profit from—trade on the northern Silk Route from China to the Black Sea.[17] Tigranes listened to Mithradates' side of the story, as Gordius filled him in on the Romans' imperial machinations in western Anatolia.

Gordius had a proposition. He suggested that Tigranes attack weak Cappadocia and remove the Roman puppet Ariobarzanes. In exchange, King Mithradates of Pontus offered His Majesty the hand of his beloved daughter, Princess Cleopatra, age sixteen. The ancient writers agree that Mithradates cared deeply for all his daughters, and they returned his love. Indeed, his genuine attachment to them made his daughters all the more valuable in marriage alliances.

Tigranes agreed to the alliance. Armenia had fought against the Romans on the side of Antiochus the Great and had given refuge to Hannibal, who had designed Armenia's capital city. But Tigranes had lived most of his life in distant Parthia, far from Roman reach. According to Justin, Tigranes knew little of Rome and did not anticipate that the Romans would object so strongly to a regime change in Cappadocia. Tigranes presented Gordius with some fine Armenian steeds for his journey back to Cappadocia, to prepare the way for Tigranes' attack (see plate 5).[18]

Mithradates was about forty in 94 BC, a few years younger than his new son-in-law. After the royal wedding sealed their treaty, the two monarchs became friends and natural allies, respecting each other as equals. Both were strong-willed, rich, ambitious, energetic, and popular. Both loved to ride spirited horses and lived for the chase, savoring the spartan outdoor life as much as they basked in luxury at court. They hunted deer, boar, and lion together, staying at Tigranes' hunting lodges in his forest and mountain estates. Although both spoke Greek, Mithradates quickly picked up Parthian and Armenian. In court, the pair dressed in complementary traditional Persian-style garb, Tigranes in dark purple and a tiara, Mithradates in gleaming white with a simple purple diadem. As was his practice, Mithradates would have presented Tigranes with an agate ring bearing his portrait.

Traditionally, Armenian monarchs wore a distinctive tiara studded with stars, but Tigranes' was unique. His was decorated with a comet trailing a long curving tail, an image that appeared on some of Tigranes' coins (see fig. 2.2). Mithradates would have taken this comet design as a signal of Tigranes' allegiance to Pontus, as an allusion to the spectacular comets heralding the long-awaited savior. Mithradates considered himself the "King of Kings," *Shahanshah*, the ancient title for the most powerful ruler in Persian-influenced lands.[19]

But Armenia's first great king, Tigranes, had his own agenda. The older monarch did not see himself as doing Mithradates' bidding. Their mutual support furthered Tigranes' own goals of unifying and expanding his kingdom. Tigranes had already annexed part of Cappadocia and was extending south, taking over the weak kingdom of Syria. He also bit off a big chunk of territory from the Parthians, who were fighting nomadic invasions on their eastern frontier. In time, Tigranes' supreme armies would ravage Mesopotamia and occupy Syria, Phoenicia, and Cilicia. The Armenian conqueror rewarded cities that joined him, laid waste to those that resisted, and moved whole populations around as though they were game pieces. While Mithradates was engaged in the coming wars with Rome, Tigranes would begin building his fabulous new city, Tigranocerta. Intended to rival the magnificence of Susa and Babylon, the city was populated with the displaced citizens of towns that Tigranes leveled. Encouraged by his victories—and perhaps by the appearance of Halley's Comet later during his reign—Tigranes would even begin referring to himself as "King of Kings."

But when he first allied with Tigranes in 94 BC, Mithradates was unaware of his new son-in-law's grand plans. After Tigranes wed Cleopatra, the two friends struck another bargain. In their joint campaigns in Cappadocia and elsewhere, they agreed that Mithradates would take the cities and the land. All captives and treasure would belong to Tigranes. The arrangement indicates that Mithradates' flow of revenue was already copious and reliable. He returned to Sinope, having set things in motion to regain indirect control of Cappadocia. Tigranes' attack would be a way of testing the Roman resolve. Mithradates' preparations for war included very heavy coin minting in 93–89 BC, to pay for large armies and arms.[20]

The tangled situation in Anatolia became even more complex, and the chronology of events is hopelessly confused. We know that when Tigranes' army, led by generals Mithras and Bagoas, invaded Cappadocia (in about 93 BC), the new puppet king Ariobarzanes panicked. He fled, sailing to his protectors in Rome. According to plan, Tigranes then recalled Ariathes IX and Gordius from Pontus to rule Cappadocia on Mithradates' terms.

Tigranes had kept his part of the bargain. He had no interest in making war on Rome, and, anyway, Cappadocia was impoverished from years of despoiling armies. Tigranes took more captives than plunder. The Armenian army slipped away, back to Artaxata, to pursue Tigranes' own grand strategies.[21]

A TRAP FOR AQUILLIUS

Around this time, Mithradates learned that his old foe, Nicomedes III of Bithynia, had died. He was succeeded by his weak son, Nicomedes IV, a brutal tyrant. Mithradates' spies informed him that Nicomedes' half brother, Socrates the Good, had popular support. Mithradates sent an assassin named Alexander to murder Nicomedes IV, but the plot failed.[22]

Next, Mithradates gave Socrates command of a Pontic army. It seems that Mithradates also promised Socrates the hand of his daughter Orsabaris, a traditional way of sealing an alliance and maintaining indirect control of the throne (her name appears on Bithynian coins at this time). The Bithynian people welcomed Socrates as he marched across the countryside of Bithynia. But when Socrates approached the capital, Nicomedia, there was a stalemate, with Nicomedes IV barricaded inside his castle.

Meanwhile, to distract the Romans, Mithradates sent envoys to the tribes north and west of the Black Sea (Thracians, Cimmerians, Bastarnae, Sarmatians, Roxolani). Offering rewards, he urged them to attack the Roman garrison in Macedonia, northern Greece.[23]

Soon, however, the Roman Senate, having staved off the war with the Italians for a while by offering them citizenship, turned its attention back to Provincia Asia. Cappadocia and Bithynia were supposed to be passive client kingdoms. Now both were in crisis again, with the puppets Ariobarzanes and Nicomedes IV cowering in Rome, begging for aid. Troubled by the new developments, but unable to spare any more troops, the Senate dispatched Manius Aquillius to impose order in Anatolia. By senatorial decree, Aquillius's dual mission in 90 BC was to restore Nicomedes IV's rule in Bithynia and return Ariobarzanes to the Cappadocian throne. Both client kings understood that they ruled at Rome's pleasure. Aquillius would be backed up by Lucius Cassius, governor of Asia, and one Roman legion stationed in Pergamon.

Aquillius was an ill-considered choice for this sensitive diplomatic mission. He was the son of Manius Aquillius the elder—detested throughout Anatolia as the notorious Roman governor who had destroyed the Sun Citizens with poison. Infamous for his corrupt government in Pergamon, Aquillius senior had been tried in Rome for gross avarice, profiteering, and bribery, but escaped punishment. His son would not be so lucky. Aquillius junior—unaware of the ghastly fate in store for him—sailed to Bithynia, expecting to make a fortune as his father had, by raking in bribes and skimming exorbitant taxes.[24]

With his ally Tigranes of Armenia occupied in the east, and with the Senate sending threatening envoys like Sulla and Aquillius, Mithradates had to reframe his strategy and remain flexible, without losing face. Conveniently, Socrates the Good suddenly died of an unknown cause. Apparently he ate or drank something that disagreed with him, as did so many whose earthly existence had become inconvenient for the Poison King. Orsabaris returned home to Pontus, and Mithradates recalled the Pontic army. As a result, the military crisis in Bithynia sputtered out just as Aquillius and Cassius arrived with the Roman legion, reinforced with draftees from Phrygia and Galatia. Nicomedes IV scrambled back onto the throne of Bithynia.

But Nicomedes IV had been compelled to borrow heavily from Roman backers to finance his restoration. Not only had he mortgaged his kingdom to his financiers, but he had promised big payoffs to senators who returned him to power. Mired in blackmail and debt, stripped of free will, Nicomedes was—to put it in terms familiar to Mithradates and his Persian-influenced followers—sucked into the abyss, forced to do the bidding of the forces of Darkness and Deceit.

Aquillius and his gang of Roman legates paid a visit to Nicomedes in Bithynia. Aquillius reminded the client king of his overdue financial obligations. But Nicomedes complained that the Bithynian countryside had been plundered by Socrates' troops, sent by Mithradates. Bithynia's royal treasury was empty. How, Nicomedes whined, could he possibly pay off his debts?

Aquillius had a cunning plan. Bithynia was broke? Well, Pontus was rich. Mithradates had supported the pretender Socrates the Good, who tried to steal Nicomedes' crown. Roman informers reported that Mithradates' entire navy was in the northern Black Sea. Aquillius instructed Nicomedes to send his fleet to raid Mithradates' unprotected port cities. At the same time, Nicomedes' army should make incursions over the border, pillaging towns of western Pontus. While Nicomedes collected the money he owed, Aquillius promised that Cassius's Roman legion would defend Bithynia from retaliation. Nicomedes had no choice. He capitulated and followed Aquillius's orders. Nicomedes, who had come from a long line of collaborators, became Rome's creature for the rest of his days.[25]

And thus began the war with Rome that would last all of Mithradates' life.

In late 89 BC, Nicomedes IV sent his ships to assault Mithradates' ports as far east as Amastris, and he ordered his troops to attack western Pontus. Nicomedes did return with plenty of booty to repay his outstanding debts to the Roman senators, generals, and other creditors. Nicomedes' master, Aquillius, assumed the raids would teach the arrogant "minor king" Mithradates a lesson. But fear gripped Nicomedes' heart. For during all his incursions, his men had met no resistance at all. It was like raiding an unguarded candy store. Where were the local garrisons? This eerie silence from Mithradates could not bode well.

Mithradates was far from ignorant of Aquillius's provocations; his friends in Bithynia must have informed him of Aquillius's plan. Mithradates' army and navy, all his forces, were in readiness, but he held off. Instead, he sent his navy on exercises in the northern Black Sea. He dispatched messengers to Pontus's rich ports and the towns on the frontier to warn them of the coming attack and to inform them of his strategy. Accordingly, the populations of the places targeted by Nicomedes had withdrawn to safety, leaving behind enough valuables to be grabbed up by the Bithynians. No Pontic troops were in sight during the invasion.

Mithradates "wanted to have a good and sufficient cause for war," says Appian. He understood that the Romans distrusted and covertly sought to destroy the great Black Sea Empire he was creating. Nicomedes was a weakling, impelled by his Roman masters to attack Pontus. This confrontation had been building for a long time. Mithradates saw that Rome, preoccupied with the Social War in Italy, could not afford to send any more legions to Anatolia.[26] Nicomedes' invasion allowed Mithradates to set a trap. The Roman generals in Bithynia and their reluctant coalition had walked right in. Now, before all the world, Mithradates was the innocent, unsuspecting victim of an aggressive, unprovoked attack on Pontus, instigated by the rapacious Roman wolf.

Until now, Mithradates' policy had been to probe and test, goad and withdraw, constantly assessing Rome's reactions. He "orchestrated crises here and there, sowing confusion and ambiguity in Rome," remarks historian Brian McGing, "all the while observing carefully, making Pontus invincible and prepared for war, so that when the situation exploded, the chips would all fall to his advantage." Mithradates had already sent the eminent orator Xenocles of Adramyttion and other envoys to Rome, to plead Anatolia's complaints before the Senate. Until Aquillius and Nicomedes invaded Pontus, the king's actions had been patient and opportunistic.[27]

MITHRADATES MAKES HIS CASE

Now Mithradates seized the opportunity to make his case against Rome in a very public manner. He dispatched an eloquent Greek statesman named Pelopidas to a high-profile debate with Nicomedes' spokesmen, to be judged by Aquillius, Lucius Cassius, and Quintus Oppius at their camp in Bithynia. Appian, who had access to imperial archives and the memoirs of some who were present, recounts what was said by each party. One of Appian's sources was P. Rutilius Rufus, a former friend of Marius who later wrote a history of the Mithradatic Wars (now lost). An honorable and sympathetic provincial official in 105 BC, Rutilius had attempted to restrain ruthless tax collectors but was condemned in Rome for his efforts in 92 BC. After that, Rutilius remained in Anatolia, where he was a popular figure. Another source for these meetings was Lucius Cornelius Sisenna, a Roman soldier-historian of the Mithradatic Wars, whose multivolume chronicle is now lost but was consulted by surviving historians like Appian and Sallust.[28]

Modern historians accept the speeches recorded by Appian as accurate reflections of the grievances that Mithradates communicated to the Roman representatives, even if their actual words have been lost. Mithradates, master of propaganda, would have disseminated these speeches to friends and allies in Anatolia and Greece. Mithradates also intended to present his case before the Senate, so his arguments probably existed in written form, consulted by ancient historians.[29]

As an astute student of traditional Roman foreign policy, Mithradates assumed that the Senate would not approve of Aquillius's decision to start a war. Yet Mithradates had to prepare for every contingency, since it was becoming obvious that developments in Italy were undermining the Senate's power to control ambitious military commanders like Sulla, Marius, and Aquillius.

Pelopidas began by reminding the Romans that Mithradates' father had been an official Friend of Rome—and that Mithradates himself had maintained this peaceful friendship. In return, said Pelopidas, "Phrygia and Cappadocia were wrested away from Mithradates. Cappadocia had always belonged to Pontus. It was recovered by Mithradates' father, with no opposition from Rome." Pointing at Aquillius, Pelopidas said, "Your own Roman general, your father, Manius Aquillius, gave Phrygia to Pontus, as a reward for the victory over Aristonicus and the Sun Citizens."

Now, Pelopidas told the Romans, "you allow Nicomedes' navy to threaten the security of the Black Sea trade. You let Nicomedes overrun Pontus and carry off plunder—in quantities of which you are well aware." The clever juxtaposition of peaceful trade with illicit plunder cast the Romans as pirates, while depicting Mithradates as the peaceful protector of Black Sea commerce.

"My king was not unprepared to defend himself from these attacks," continued Pelopidas. But he "held back from war, so that you might be eye-witnesses to these events." Pelopidas concluded his speech simply, alluding to Rome's tendency to betray its allies. "Mithradates, Rome's friend and ally, calls upon you to defend us against the aggression of Nicomedes, or at least restrain him."

Nicomedes' ambassadors countered Pelopidas's plea. Mithradates had plotted against Nicomedes to place Socrates the Good on the throne by force of arms, they claimed. The late and lamented Socrates, once a peaceful prince, had fallen under Mithradates' evil influence. In fact, they declared, "All of Mithradates' plots are really aimed at you Romans!"

"All his actions are examples of Mithradates' arrogance and hostility, and his disobedience of your orders. Just look at his preparations for war! Mithradates stands in complete readiness for the great war he is planning." The Bithynians cataloged the vast armies under Mithradates' command. The Pontic army includes "a great force of allies, Thracians, Scythians, and all the other neighboring peoples, now that Mithradates has taken over the Crimea and northern Black Sea. Mithradates has even formed a marriage alliance with Armenia, and he is sending envoys to Egypt and Syria!" His navy already has three hundred warships, and he has even hired expert sailors from Phoenicia and Egypt. "Mithradates is not just gathering these forces to fight Nicomedes," they warned. "These preparations are aimed at Rome!"

Nicomedes' envoys outlined Mithradates' strategy. "He pretends to have an argument with Bithynia, but his real target is you! If you are wise," intoned the ambassadors, "you won't wait until he declares war on you. Look at his deeds, not his words. Bithynia is your true friend and ally; don't sacrifice us to this hypocrite who feigns friendship." Mithradates is not just our enemy, they thundered, Mithradates threatens Rome itself!

Pretending to be objective, the Romans allowed Pelopidas a rebuttal. "Well, if Nicomedes wants to complain about past events, we bow to Rome's judgment," drawled Pelopidas. "What we are concerned about are the wrongs that have just occurred, *right before your eyes*: the ravaging of Mithradates' territory, the interruption of trade in the Black Sea, the carrying away of vast plunder from Pontus." Pelopidas repeated his simple—and reasonable—request: "Again, we call upon you Romans! Either prevent such outrages or help Mithradates regain his losses from Bithynia. At the very least, stand aside and allow Mithradates to defend himself!"

The generals were already committed to Nicomedes IV. But Pelopidas's eloquent speech "put them to shame," reminding them that Pontus's old alliance with Rome was still in force, and that Aquillius's own father had given Phyrgia to Mithradates' father, and pointedly contrasting Roman violent disruption with Mithradates' protection of free trade. Indeed, Mithradates had complied and withdrawn his armies; he had done Rome no harm. The Senate had not commissioned Aquillius to make war on Mithradates. The generals were "at a loss for some time about what answer to make."

Finally, after a long consultation, they came up with this "artful response": "We would not wish Mithradates to suffer harm at the hands of Nicomedes. Nor can we allow Mithradates to make war on Nicomedes. It is not in Rome's best interest for Bithynia to be weakened."

Pelopidas reported back to Mithradates in Sinope. The Romans' brusque denial of justice, in such a public manner, gave Mithradates no other option.[30] He immediately called for his stepson Ariathes IX, invested him with a large army, and sent him to take Cappadocia. Ariathes drove Ariobarzanes back to Rome and regained Cappadocia's throne.

Then Mithradates dispatched Pelopidas back to the Roman camp on a very important mission. Appian reported the speeches at these meetings, too, with details that convey the gist of Pelopidas's orations and demonstrate Mithradates' genius for diplomacy and propaganda. The speeches show how cleverly Mithradates must have built his case against the Romans in Anatolia, revealing Aquillius as the aggressor driven by pure greed, thereby justifying Mithradates' defensive reaction.

"O Romans, how patiently King Mithradates has borne the wrongs done to him," began Pelopidas. His heavy gold and agate ring with the portrait of his king glinted as he gestured. "Not only did you deprive Pontus of Phrygia and Cappadocia. You stood by and watched while Nicomedes invaded Mithradates' sovereign territory. We appealed to your friendship, but instead you treated Nicomedes as the victim and Mithradates as the accused."

The next portion reflects Mithradates' excellent understanding of Roman constitutional law. "You will be held accountable to the Roman Republic for what has just taken place in Cappadocia!" Pelopidas warned Aquillius not to start such a major war without an official senatorial decree. If you do, "you generals will be called to defend your actions in Rome when Mithradates lodges a formal complaint against you before the Senate."

Then the ambassador described exactly what the Romans would be up against, should they make war on the most powerful ruler in the East. "Bear this in mind, Romans. My king Mithradates rules his ancestral domain of Pontus. He also rules many neighboring lands: the Colchians, a very warlike people; all the Greeks around the Black Sea; and all the barbarian tribes beyond. Mithradates has allies ready to obey his every command: Scythians, Taurians, Bastarnae, Thracians, Sarmatians, and all those tribes in the regions of the Don, the Danube, and the Sea of Asov! King Tigranes of Armenia is Mithradates' son-in-law and he counts King Arsaces of Parthia as his ally. My king already has a large number of ships, and many more are being built as we speak. We possess war materiel of every kind in abundance."

Pelopidas predicted that the rulers of Egypt and Syria would rush to Mithradates' aid. Then he raised a chilling image sure to alarm the Senate: "Your newly acquired provinces in Asia, in Greece, in Africa, and in Italy itself will come to our side. Your Italian colonies are waging a relentless war against you right now, because they cannot endure your greed. You can't even subdue your colonies in Italy, yet you attack Mithradates and set Nicomedes on him! You treat us like an enemy, yet you still pretend to be our friend!"

Mithradates had instructed his ambassador to conclude by presenting the Roman generals with an insult wrapped in a threat wrapped in an ultimatum. If they accepted his request for justice, Mithradates would win; if they fell for the bait, he was prepared for war. "Come now, choose!" exclaimed Pelopidas. "Restrain Nicomedes from harming Pontus, your old ally. If you do this, King Mithradates promises to help you put down that troublesome rebellion in Italy. Either throw off the deceitful mask of friendship—or let us go together to Rome and settle the dispute there."

The Roman generals reacted as Mithradates expected. Aquillius ordered Mithradates to stay out of Bithynia and announced that they would restore Ariobarzanes to Cappadocia's by now rather rickety throne.

Roman centurions then forcibly escorted Pelopidas to the border of Pontus, for fear that he would be able to rally the Bithynian countryside to Mithradates' cause. This detail suggests that popular hostility to Rome and support for Mithradates must have been palpable.

"Without waiting to hear what the People of Rome and the Senate would decide about such a great war," writes Appian, Aquillius immediately prepared to invade Pontus. Mithradates had goaded him into starting a major war with a Friend of Rome without senatorial approval. Aquillius's decision was a sharp break from traditional Roman foreign policy at the end of the Republic. Powerful, rogue commanders could now make war for their own gain, as the Senate's power waned.[31]

Aquillius ordered ships to block the entrance to the Black Sea. According to Appian's figures, the invasion force totaled 176,000 men (12,000 were Roman legionnaires). The three commanders took up positions in early 89 BC. Aquillius's 40,000 massed on the border of Pontus south of the Olgassy Mountains. Cassius's 40,000 marched to the frontier of Bithynia and Galatia, Oppius's 40,000 held the route through Cappadocia. Aquillius instructed Nicomedes IV that his 56,000 Bithynians would lead the invasion of Pontus.[32]

Mithradates was more than ready for them.

7

Victory

Aquillius ordered Nicomedes IV to lead his army into Pontus, ravaging the countryside as they advanced. They were unaware that Mithradates could call on an overwhelming force, far beyond what the Romans could have anticipated. According to Appian, Mithradates commanded 250,000 soldiers and 50,000 cavalry (including all the reserves and commitments that Mithradates could count on from allies around the Black Sea and Armenia). According to Memnon, Mithradates had 190,000 infantry, 10,000 cavalry.[1]

Mithradates, in his mid-forties, had little combat experience. For this first crucial battle of his career, Appian says that Mithradates personally took charge of the troops massed at Sinope, placing Dorylaus at the head of the Greek phalanx. The fabulous wealth of Pontus was on display in the ranks of hoplites with beautifully wrought bronze helmets and breastplates, gilded spears, and shields flashing with jewels. There were bowmen, slingers, and peltasts (fighters armed with light swords and javelins), noble Persian-Cappadocian knights, and Scythian and Sarmatian archers mounted on tough steppe ponies adorned with golden trappings. His ally Tigranes had contributed 10,000 Armenian cavalry riding large Parthian steeds. Mithradates' 300 warships and 100 pirate biremes displayed magnificent prows and luxurious decor. No expense was spared: the pageantry impressed his own soldiers and sailors as well as the populace, and it intimidated the enemy.[2]

As supreme commander, Mithradates took a strong hand in planning strategy. He found a vantage point from which to direct the action and dispatch more troops as needed. Among his experienced field generals were the brothers Archelaus (who had skirmished with Sulla) and Neoptolemus, who had helped subdue Scythia.

In a rare gesture of trust, Mithradates appointed his son Arcathius, a young man of twenty, to lead the prized Armenian cavalry. Hellenistic kings were usually loath to allow blood relatives to command forces that could be turned against them. Historians ask, Why would Mithradates, whose paranoia was notorious, give this important command to his son? I think the answer lies in Mithradates' admiration for Alexander. Philip of Macedon had famously placed his eighteen-year-old son Alexander in charge of the cavalry at the important battle of Chaeronea in 338 BC. Alexander's audacious maneuvers had turned out to be the key to Philip's great victory. Now in 89 BC, while Mithradates assumed the commanding role of a Xerxes or Darius the master strategist, observing the battle from a high vantage point, he cast his son in the role of young Alexander.

At the Amnias River, Mithradates' generals brought out only a small force, 40,000 light infantry and Arcathius's 10,000 Armenian cavalry, greatly outnumbered by the Bithynian-Roman coalition.[3] But hidden behind the ranks of men and horses, a deadly surprise awaited the invaders: Mithradates' 130 war chariots equipped with whirling scythes.

Chariots, known to Greek traditionalists from the epic poems of Homer, had enjoyed renewed popularity after the Romans conquered Greece. But these days chariots were used only for racing or parades, not war. In the circus in Rome, fancy chariots were drawn by prancing show horses, even by ostriches and tigers. War chariots with rotating, sickle-shaped blades projecting from the axles were an archaic weapon of the distant past, perfected by Mithradates' ancestor Cyrus the Great.

An aficionado of chariot warfare as well as of racing, Mithradates was aware that these Persian terror machines hadn't dominated a battlefield since Alexander fought Darius III in the fourth century BC. Mithradates would have studied the battle at Gaugamela, in 331 BC, when Alexander defeated Darius. In that case, Alexander's troops had been well prepared for Darius's death machines. The Macedonians simply opened their lines to let the scythed chariots pass by and then attacked them from the rear.[4]

Alexander's surprise tactic had essentially ended the era of chariot warfare. On this day in 89 BC, however—more than two hundred years later—Mithradates was counting on his contemporaries' having forgotten Alexander's evasive maneuver.

The Mithradatic Wars Begin, 89 BC

As Nicomedes' great army approached across the plain, Mithradates' general Neoptolemus sent his men out to seize a rocky hill. The battle began. Bithynian skirmishers swarmed the hill, and Neoptolemus quickly advanced with more men, yelling for Arcathius to bring up his cavalry. Arcathius's Armenian horsemen charged into Nicomedes' phalanx, a risky decision that could have resulted in heavy casualties. The move seems to mimic young Alexander's feat at Chaeronea. Was he attempting to replicate Alexander's coup, using cavalry as a shock weapon to charge head-on instead of harassing the enemy's flanks? The tactic worked: Arcathius's cavalry charge bought more time for Neoptolemus's phalanx to engage the startled enemy.

As Arcathius chased the enemy cavalry off the field, bloody fighting erupted behind him. Would Nicomedes' superior numbers prevail? Neoptolemus's men were falling back. Archelaus rushed to his brother's rescue, leading a wedge of soldiers in from the right, forcing the Bithynians to turn and fight off the fresh troops. Cleverly, Archelaus yielded ground to them little by little, drawing the Bithynians away from his brother's men, giving them the chance to rally.

Nicomedes' Bithynian phalanx was now bunched up, the men standing back-to-back, straining to defend themselves on two fronts of the brother-generals' assaults. Peering through the dust swirling over the fight, Craterus, Mithradates' chariot master, grinned. The beleaguered phalanx presented his ideal target. Receiving the gleeful signal from his commander in chief, Craterus unleashed his chariots. The drivers whipped their powerful horses into a full-speed gallop. Suddenly 130 war chariots surged out and bore down like guided missiles on Nicomedes' men. The vicious blades, spinning at a velocity three times the speed of the wheels, churned through the densely packed enemy. The shock was overwhelming, the carnage terrible.

At the time of this battle, the natural philosopher Lucretius (100–55 BC) was a boy in Italy. Lucretius later wrote a hair-raising description of a scythed chariot attack. His introductory phrase, "They say," suggests that this scene was based on the memories of survivors or witnesses.[5]

They say the scythed chariots, ravenous for slaughter, sheared off limbs so suddenly that legs and arms fell writhing on the ground before a man even felt any pain. In the ardor of battle, one soldier continued to fight, not realizing that his left arm and shield had been carried off

Fig. 7.1. Scythed chariot attack. Andre Castaigne, 1899.

in the wheel. Meanwhile his companion attempted to rise on one leg, while his other lay twitching its toes in a pool of blood.

Nicomedes' soldiers, wrote Appian, were "aghast to see their mangled comrades sliced in two and still breathing, hanging on the scythes. . . . Overcome by the hideousness of the slaughter, the ranks scattered in confusion." Nicomedes narrowly escaped: he and his Roman entourage fled to Aquillius's camp on the border, the same direction taken by his cavalry. Abandoned by their king, some of Nicomedes' soldiers still fought valiantly, wading through the bodies of dismembered comrades. But they were soon surrounded and overcome.[6]

Half of Nicomedes' forces were dead. The survivors surrendered that night. Mithradates' jubilant army overran the abandoned camp and captured the entire train of supplies. The Pontic generals were delighted to discover that the terror-stricken Nicomedes had left behind his war chest, filled with silver and gold—treasure drained, as they knew, from Anatolia. Thousands of prisoners were marched to Sinope.

Mithradates came out to receive the prisoners. Glowing with victory, the king addressed them. One can imagine Mithradates boasting that a modest number of righteous soldiers fighting on the side of Truth and

FIG. 7.2. Mithridates VI Eupator, silver tetradrachm, Ephesus mint, 88/87 BC. The reverse shows Pegasus and the Pontic star and crescent. 1967.152.392, bequest of A. M. Newell, courtesy of the American Numismatic Society.

Light, and led by superior Greek generals, had overcome a much larger invading army. He could point out that most of his vast troops had not even engaged in the fight. The losers may have fought courageously, but they had been misled by the forces of Darkness. Gesturing at the wagons of abandoned supplies he'd captured from Nicomedes, Mithradates made a surprising announcement. All the captives were free to go. His men divided up the supplies, handing out Nicomedes' provisions, food, clothing, and coins to each enemy soldier for his journey home.

This benevolent act, and others like it, broadcast by word of mouth, gave Mithradates a reputation for clemency toward his enemies. *Philanthropia*, mercy toward captured foes, was a Greek ideal embraced by Hellenistic monarchs. Like them, Mithradates admired Alexander's reputation for being as "gentle after victory as he is terrible in battle."[7] Is this when Mithradates began referring to himself as Eupator, the "Good Father"?

Many survivors of the disastrous Roman-Bithynian invasion of Pontus were mercenaries and draftees from Galatia and Phrygia. With no incentive to return to Bithynia or help the losers Nicomedes and Aquillius, they joined the Pontic army. Bithynia and Paphlagonia fell to Mithradates' control. News of his spectacular victory and his magnanimous freeing of prisoners of war spread over the land, convincing many cities to take up his cause, eager to welcome Mithradates "as god and savior." Ancient writers tell how the populace of many Anatolian cities dressed in white garments and flocked to greet Mithradates, requesting his help against the Romans and acclaiming him with divine titles.[8]

MEANWHILE IN THE ROMAN CAMPS

Nicomedes had scurried away to Aquillius's encampment, where he had to explain to his masters how he lost so many men, all his supplies, and his war chest. Appian says that Aquillius and the Roman generals were horrified by the fiasco. Too late they realized that they had heedlessly "kindled a great strife without good judgment." But even more alarming, they had lost a war they had begun without any public decree from the People of Rome. They were now nothing but rogue enemy combatants trapped in hostile territory, with no backing from the Senate.

An exultant Mithradates rode out from Sinope on his finest horse, with an advance guard of 100 Sarmatians. The party ascended Mount Scoroba in the Olgassy Mountains. From these lofty peaks rising above dense pine forests they could look down toward Aquillius's vulnerable camp. There were numerous native sanctuaries in these mountains: it is likely that Mithradates performed a sacred fire ceremony here to thank the gods Ahuramazda, Mithra, and Zeus the Warrior for his great victory.

On the ascent of Mount Scoroba, Mithradates' 100 Sarmatians surprised 800 of Nicomedes' cavalrymen trying to reach Aquillius's camp. Even though they outnumbered the Sarmatian horseman 8 to 1, the Bithynians fled in terror from the nomads. The Sarmatians captured most of them and brought them to Mithradates. The king gave these men supplies and released them. Like their compatriots, they, too, joined the Pontic cavalry.

Down in Aquillius's camp, Nicomedes had a frightening premonition. In the middle of the night, he fled again, to the camp of Cassius. Aquillius, in fear of Mithradates' rapid advance, ordered his 40,000 soldiers and 4,000 cavalry to retreat. He hoped to reach the stronghold of Protopachion (eastern Bithynia). But Mithradates' army, led by Neoptolemus and Nemanes (an Armenian commander sent by Tigranes) overtook him that same day. This battle went very badly for Aquillius: nearly 10,000 of his men lay dead on the field. Neoptolemus captured Aquillius's camp and brought 300 prisoners to Mithradates. Following his well-established practice of *philanthropia*, he treated them kindly and set them free. The 300 joined the good fight.[9]

But Aquillius had escaped, taking plenty of money with him. He reached the banks of the Sangarius and crossed the dark, swirling river by night. Then he headed southwest toward Pergamon, where he had once been the administrator of Rome's Asian Province.

Meanwhile, Cassius and Nicomedes retreated southwest to a strong-hold called the Lion's Head, near Nysa on the Maeander River, east of Tralles. These sophisticated, wealthy towns had supported Aristonicus's Sun Citizens' revolt in 133–129 BC. But a pro-Roman citizen of Nysa named Chaeremon supplied Cassius's men with 60,000 bushels of grain at the Lion's Head. Archaeologists have discovered an inscription at Nysa from Cassius thanking Chaeremon for his support.[10]

Originally Cassius had about 40,000 men, but most of them had peeled off to join Mithradates. Panicked by Mithradates' relentless approach, Cassius tried to levy raw recruits from the countryside. His centurions drafted a mob of farmers, shopkeepers, "artisans, and rustics." These people were hostile to the Romans and sympathetic to Mithradates. Appian says that Cassius attempted to train these "unwarlike men" but had to give up in frustration. Cassius moved farther east to Apamea, a pros-perous trading center. A long-established Jewish community, this town also sided with Mithradates. A severe earthquake struck Apamea just as Cassius arrived. Forced to flee again, Cassius now gave up any idea of fighting and simply hoped to reach Rhodes, the independent island allied with Rome.

Mithradates and his army soon arrived in Apamea, hot on Cassius's trail. After viewing the earthquake damage, Mithradates donated one hundred talents to repair the buildings. He was well aware that Alexander had once been very generous in repairing quake-damaged Apamea.[11]

Sweeping Victories in Anatolia

As he took control of his new domains, Mithradates named governors to administer the territories. His administrative style was practical and flexi-ble. Some lands (Colchis, the Bosporus) were designated vice-kingdoms; others he considered vassal-kingdoms (for example, Cappadocia under his son Ariathes and possibly even Armenia under Tigranes). Still other areas were administered by military leaders or governors. In a striking move, harking back to his Persian origins, Mithradates revived the ancient Persian title for his governors in Greater Phrygia: he called them *satraps*.

With Mithradates closing in, the Roman sympathizer Chaeremon of Nysa had to run for his life. With his sons, Chaeremon fled to Tralles, making for Ephesus. They were joined by many other fugitives. Mithradates' victories were sweeping all before him. There was an exodus of inland Roman settlers moving toward the large coastal cities, where they sought refuge among the larger Italian populations, hoping to escape to Italy or safe islands. The road to Tralles, winding across deep gorges and stinking, yellow-orange streams, was lined with tombs. The fugitives passed through an ominous landscape of caves sacred to Pluto, god of the Underworld. The caverns emitted clouds of sulphurous gases, deadly to birds and animals, avoided by all except the strange eunuch priests of Cybele.[12]

Mithradates, arriving in Nysa, was enraged to find Cassius's monument in the city square thanking Chaeremon for his aid. Spies informed Mithradates that the traitor had fled with streams of Romans and sympathizers toward the coast. Two remarkable inscriptions, urgent public proclamations from Mithradates to his satrap in Nysa, were discovered in the late 1800s. These ancient "Wanted Dead or Alive" posters, disseminated throughout the land, contain crucial information about Mithradates' plans, his intelligence operations, political rhetoric, and administrative style—and his vengeful compulsion to destroy all Romans and their local supporters.[13]

The first letter reads:

King Mithradates to the Satrap Leonippus, Greeting
Whereas Chaeremon, a man most hateful and most hostile to our state, has always consorted with our most detested enemies, and now—learning of my approach—has removed his sons Pythodorus and Pythion to a place of safety and has himself fled, Proclaim that if anyone captures Chaeremon or Pythodorus or Pythion alive, he will receive 40 talents, and if anyone brings me the head of any of these three, he will receive 20 talents.

Mithradates soon received an update from his spies. Now he knew that Chaeremon had reached Ephesus and had sent his sons with Cassius on to Rhodes. The king dictated another public decree to his satrap:

> Chaeremon has arranged the escape of the fugitive Romans with his sons to Rhodes. Now—learning of my approach—he has taken refuge in the Temple of Artemis in Ephesus. From there, he continues to communicate with the Romans, the common enemy of mankind. His confidence in the face of the crimes he has committed could be the starting point of a movement against us. Consider how you may by any means bring Chaeremon to us, or how he may be arrested and imprisoned until I am free of the enemy.

Clearly, Mithradates saw Chaeremon and other Roman collaborators in Anatolia as a threat as dangerous as the Romans themselves. They must not be allowed to survive and connive with Romans to create a resistance movement. The counterinsurgents had to be rooted out with the help of the Anatolian populace. Mithradates' phrase, "Romans, the common enemy of mankind," stands out as a powerful play on words. According to the Romans' own, widely known propaganda, Rome called itself the "common benefactor (or savior) of mankind." Mithradates' clever rewording twists Rome's self-image into a parody that resonated with anti-Romans throughout the land.[14]

Mithradates' agents were also searching for Aquillius and Nicomedes. Nicomedes was hurrying toward Pergamon, hoping to catch up with Aquillius. But Aquillius was already heading for Rhodes, desperate to meet up with Cassius and escape to Rome.

What about Oppius, the third Roman general in this unauthorized war? Oppius had camped in Cappadocia with forty thousand men, most of whom deserted after the defeat of Nicomedes. Oppius now made his way with the remnant to Laodicea on the Lycus River and appealed to the prosperous city of Aphrodisias for reinforcements. In 1982, archaeologists found two inscriptions showing that Oppius received that aid. Meanwhile, Mithradates led his triumphant armies across Phrygia, demolishing Rome's hold on Provincia Asia.[15]

When Mithradates routed the Roman coalition, he received an exuberant welcome in Bithynia, Galatia, Cappadocia, and Phrygia. On the march, he confiscated great quantities of gold and silver, which had been amassed by former kings, and he took possession of a great deal of military equipment. The location of these treasures must have been surveyed during Mithradates' early reign. Directing his generals to secure southwestern Asia Minor, Mithradates himself led the advance through Phrygia, his ranks swelling with followers as town after town pledged allegiance to the savior-king. He was being hailed as a liberator in the very land

FIG. 7.3. Captive Roman general (right) forced to serve Mithradates (left). *Faits et dits memorables*, Français 289, folio 482, Bibliothèque National de France.

where Aristonicus had based his Sun Citizens' revolt of 133–129 BC. Ever mindful of auspicious events, Mithradates went out of his way to pitch his tent near the old inn once occupied by Alexander the Great, a place he'd visited on his fact-finding mission.[16] That early reconnaissance was paying off a thousandfold now.

Because it was occupied by Oppius and his men, Laodicea on the Lycus—famed for black sheep—was the first place to resist Mithradates. Mithradates surrounded the town and sent a messenger. "Laodiceans," proclaimed the herald, "King Mithradates promises that none of you will be harmed if you turn over the Roman general Oppius!"

The Laodiceans allowed Oppius's soldiers to depart; many joined Mithradates. Then, as a mocking crowd gathered, the Laodiceans prodded Oppius's *lictors* (color guard), wearing red tunics and carrying his legion standards, out the city gate, and then Oppius himself. Oppius would spend the next few years as a kind of pet captive in Mithradates' retinue. The king never harmed Oppius but enjoyed exhibiting the tame Roman general as his personal servant in each city he visited.[17]

New World Order

Aphrodisias joined Mithradates' cause. An inscription describes how the city had previously sent envoys to Rome to plead for relief from corrupt tax farmers before the Senate on behalf of all the Greek cities in Asia Minor.[18] Some pockets of resistance still remained, especially in Lycia, allied with Rhodes: Patara, Telmessus, Apollonis, Termessus, Stratonicea, Magnesia on the Maeander, and Tabae were still holding out. Mithradates sent troops to beseige them, commanded by Pelopidas, the ambassador who had confronted Aquillius and the Roman generals in their camp before the war. Other cities—Tralles, Pergamon, Adramyttion, Caunus, Cnidus, Mytilene, Miletus, Erythrae, Smyrna, Iasus, Ceramus, Magnesia near Sipylus, Arycanda, Ephesus, and the islands of Cos, Lesbos, Samos, and Chios—all willingly went over to Mithradates. Rhodes was the only hope now for Cassius and Aquillius.

When the news of Mithradates' great victories reached the Roman fleet blocking the entrance to the Black Sea, the Greek sailors began shouting with joy. They took over the ships for Mithradates, who now controlled the entire Black Sea as well as the Aegean. Mithradates established his new headquarters in the magnificent palace of King Attalus III on the fortified acropolis of Pergamon, former capital of Rome's Asian Province. In the palace, anything that remained of Attalus's old botanical gardens and toxicological notes and specimens would have intrigued Mithradates and his medical team. The king bestowed the name of his childhood companion Dorylaus on a city in Phrygia, Dorylaion. Mithradates began minting beautiful silver tetradrachms with his portrait in Pergamon, and the city of Smyrna also stamped bronze coins with his likeness. Other cities, including Ephesus, Miletus, Tralles, and Erythrae, issued new gold staters to trumpet their independence from Rome.[19]

Hearing of his victory, the desperate Italian rebels, fighting for their lives in Italy, sent envoys to Mithradates. The leader of the Marsi, Silo, begged Mithradates to join forces. In response to the requests to send an army to Italy to help overthrow the Romans, Mithradates "promised that he would lead his armies to Italy after he had brought Asia under his sway." Archaeologists have discovered special-issue gold and silver coins with images of Dionysus (god of liberation) and Mithradatic devices commemorating the communications between Mithradates and the insurgents in Italy from this time.[20]

Mithradates' first acts as the savior of Anatolia were social reforms aimed at redressing complaints against the Romans and their supporters. In what the historian Luis Ballesteros Pastor calls the "Mithridatic Revolution," Mithradates relieved public and private debts, canceling loans owed to Roman and Italian creditors, winning support from the middle and lower classes. Mithradates also granted everyone exemptions from taxes for five years, which pleased the wealthy. These radical acts underline Mithradates' own great wealth, now enhanced by the treasuries he had recently confiscated. But one could also say that Mithradates' new order championed a hybrid sort of government, a benign Persian-influenced monarchy enlightened by Greek democratic traditions, offering a real alternative to Rome's oppressive administration of its provinces during the late Republic. The oligarchies controlled by the Roman consuls were broken up in Anatolia, and in the next year Mithradates would order his cities to grant broad citizenship and civic rights.[21]

Thinking ahead, Mithradates must have been contemplating his options for dealing with the large numbers of Roman residents that still remained in Anatolia. He could not risk the emergence of a Roman resistance movement abetted by local sympathizers like Chaeremon. If he could take over the Aegean and Greece, Rome would be forced to withdraw from the eastern Mediterranean. The Adriatic Sea would become the new boundary between East and West, between Mithradates' dominions and Rome's. If the fighting continued, mainland Greece was the traditional battlefield for struggles pitting Eastern against Western powers. Mithradates sent envoys to Athens to broadcast the good news and to let them know he planned to liberate Greece.[22]

It may have been at this time that Mithradates bestowed gifts of his magnificent armor to the cities of Nemea and Delphi in Greece. According to ancient writers, a sense of Mithradates' extraordinary size could be gauged from his helmets, breastplates, greaves, and weapons. The armor, which glittered with precious metals and gems, was impressively large— probably deliberately oversized. Mithradates may have admired the enormous armor of the mythic heroes of the Trojan War displayed at Troy, and he certainly knew the famous story of Alexander's psychological warfare tricks in India. Alexander ordered his blacksmiths to forge several pieces of huge armor and weapons, which he left along with gigantic horse equipment at his camp, in order to frighten the Indian armies into submission.[23]

Historians ancient and modern have marveled at Mithradates' extraordinary success in the First Mithradatic War. In less than a year he had gone from a minor king of a rich little realm on the Black Sea to one of the most powerful rulers in the ancient world. In 89 BC, Mithradates gave a public speech recounting his spectacular victories, castigating the Romans, and exhorting his followers to continue the fight. Pelopidas, Xenocles, Metrodorus the Roman Hater, and other philosopher-statesmen probably helped prepare Mithradates' text. Dressed in his finest Persian robe and trousers, wearing rings of agate (thought to make one's speech convincing), Mithradates would have delivered this oration in the great Theater of Pergamon. Outdoor amphitheaters were often used for political gatherings; Pergamon's held ten thousand people.

The speech has been preserved by ancient historians. Probably many different versions of this crucial oral presentation—essentially a policy statement and declaration of war—circulated orally and in writing among Mithradates' enemies as well as his followers. Mithradates, maestro of public relations, would certainly have distributed copies to his allies. In a departure from his usual brevity, the historian Justin stated, "I consider this speech worthy of including in entirety in my abridged version of Trogus's history, just as it was originally written." Justin sought out a full copy of the speech that he considered original and verbatim. Modern historians have pointed out what they see as exaggerations and distortions for propaganda and rhetorical effects, but these might also confirm that Justin's version reflects parts of Mithradates' actual speech. There are some obvious signs of later additions by hostile writers: for example, it seems unlikely that Mithradates would publicly brag that he had murdered Socrates the Good of Bithynia and his nephew King Ariathes of Cappadocia.

Whether or not the version Justin published is the word-for-word speech delivered by Mithradates that day in Pergamon, it is an accurate summary of Mithradates' program, his foreign policy, and his rationale for war with Rome. It offers the best insights we can have into Mithradates' vision of himself as the inheritor and unifier of Greek and Persian cultures—the ideal alternative to Rome—and it explains his compelling appeal to so many diverse groups outside Rome.[24]

DECLARATION OF WAR

Mithradates' speech is quite long. Here is the essential substance, combining paraphrase with direct quotations from Justin's version.

> It would have been desirable [began Mithradates] to have had the opportunity to decide whether to be at war or at peace with the Romans. But even the weakest person must defend himself and retaliate when attacked. Now it is obvious the Romans were not simply hostile. They have begun a great war and now they must pay the consequences.
>
> I am confident of victory. You know as well as I do that the Romans can be beaten. We have already defeated Aquillius and Nicomedes and driven the Romans out of Cappadocia. The Romans are not invincible: The Samnites of Italy have defeated Roman armies. King Pyrrhus of Epirus won three battles against them. Hannibal was victorious in Italy for more than sixteen years—and it was not Roman military strength that defeated Hannibal in the end, but the bitter rivalries of his own people.
>
> The Romans have enemies everywhere. In Anatolia, the Romans have hammered deep hatred into our peoples, by their corrupt government, rapacious tax-collecting, and public auctions of our property. Ever since Rome was founded, the native Italians have carried on perpetual wars with Rome, fighting for independence. The Gauls— famed for their spirit and valor—invaded Italy and took over many Roman cities. The Romans are terrified of the Gauls and pay them ransom, but we can count the Gauls as our friends. Italy is being overrun by many thousands of these courageous peoples. Right now the Teutones and Cimbri are assailing Rome like a whirlwind!

Mithradates' intelligence sources were formidable; his spies and friends in Italy and the provinces kept him very well informed. In the next portion of the speech he revealed what he had learned about Rome's struggles with Italian tribes and the impending civil war.[25]

> At this very moment, all of Italy has risen up in war, following the lead of the Marsi and the Samnites. These peoples are demanding not just independence, but also a share in the government and the rights of citizenship. At the same time, Rome is also torn by internal strife among its leading men. This conflict is just as bloody as the war with the Italians, and much more dangerous for Rome's survival.
>
> Even if the Romans could pursue individual wars against each of

these enemies, this collective assault will overwhelm them. How [asked Mithradates] can they imagine they could have their hands free for a war with us? We must fight the Romans sooner or later. Let us seize this chance and swiftly build up our strength. The Romans have their hands full of trouble—now is the time!

Here Mithradates set out his grievances against Rome.

The Romans started a war against me when I was just a child, from the moment they took away Greater Phrygia, which they had granted to my father. This land already belonged to my great-grandfather Mithradates II, who received it as dowry when he married the sister of Seleucus II. Ordering me to leave Paphlagonia was another act of war! My father had inherited Paphlagonia peacefully.

I complied with all these harsh Roman decrees. I relinquished Phrygia and Paphlagonia. I removed my son from Cappadocia, even though I had won it fairly and the Cappadocians requested my friend Gordius as their king. I even killed Socrates the Good when the Senate wanted to take over Bithynia. But did any of this mollify the Romans? No. They became more oppressive every day.

The Romans sent Nicomedes of Bithynia—the son of a vulgar dancing girl!—to attack Pontus. When I tried to defend my kingdom, they made war on me.

But I'm not the only victim of the Romans, continued Mithradates.

The Romans hate the power and majesty of great kings of great lands. They cheated my grandfather, King Pharnaces I, who should have inherited Pergamon. They even mistreat their allies. After King Eumenes II of Pergamon helped the Romans crush King Antiochus the Great, the Gauls, and the Macedonians, the Romans declared Eumenes an enemy and destroyed his son, Aristonicus. No one rendered the Romans greater service than the African King Masinissa of Numidia, who helped Rome defeat Hannibal. Yet they turned on his grandson Jugurtha, and viciously paraded him as a slave in chains before throwing him in prison to die.

Why do the Romans hate great and good kings? Is it because their own history is filled with a string of shameful kings? Lowly Latin sheepherders, Sabine soothsayers, exiles from Corinth, slaves from Etruria—these were the Roman royalty.

The Romans are so proud of their founders, Romulus and Remus. By the Romans' own account, their founders were suckled at a she-wolf's teats! That explains why the entire Roman population has the temperament of wolves! Like wolves, the Romans have an insatiable thirst for blood and a ravenous hunger for power and riches.

My pedigree is superior to that motley Roman rabble, boasted Mithradates.

My family can be traced back on my father's side to Cyrus and Darius, the founders of the Persian Empire. On my mother's side, I am related to Alexander the Great and Seleucus Nicator, founders of the Macedonian Empire. Moreover, not one of the peoples in my new kingdom has ever fallen under foreign domination or been ruled by foreign kings. Even Alexander the Great never ruled Pontus, Cappadocia, Paphlagonia, Bithynia, or Armenia—not to mention Scythia!

Before me, only two other kings, Darius and Philip, had ventured to even enter Scythia, much less subdue it. Any campaign beyond the Black Sea means extreme hardship and great risk. Not only are the nomads fierce and courageous, but they have no towns or property and their land is protected by desert wastes and freezing mountains. Those great kings barely escaped alive from Scythia! When I went to Scythia, I was just a raw novice at war. Yet now, I draw most of my strength against the Romans from my allies in Scythia!

Our war against the Romans on our own land is entirely different. Our climate is mild. No soil is more fertile than ours, no land has as many important cities. If we take courage and pursue this war, I promise you we'll spend more time celebrating than fighting, more time counting our riches, than going on campaign. Think of the wealth of Phrygia, Lydia, Ionia! We don't even have to storm these lands; all we have to do is occupy them!

I've already recovered all of Pontus, Cappadocia, Paphlagonia, and the Bosporus, my rightful dominions. I'm the only man in the world to have subdued fierce Colchis and Scythia. My soldiers and my enemies can testify to my fairness and generosity.

All Asia has been awaiting me, declared Mithradates. Just imagine what a great army we can achieve if you follow me to glory!

After arousing the fervor of his followers by word and deed, Mithradates, savior-king of Asia, plunged into the thick of his lifelong struggle against Rome. The primary objectives now were to consolidate his power in southern Anatolia, demonstrate naval supremacy in the Aegean, expel the Romans from the East, and liberate Greece. If the Senate chose to send either Sulla or Marius to oppose him, he wanted to have the best advantage. It would be better to defeat the Romans later, in Greece, than to have to fight them in the lands he now occupied. So, with the Anatolian coast and the entrance to the Aegean in his control, Mithradates called on pirate fleets and other allied ships to join the Pontic armada sailing out from the Black Sea to the Aegean to take Rhodes. That island was also the destination of Aquillius and Cassius.

Loot and Love

Mithradates continued to march across southern Anatolia, accompanied by a retinue of speechwriters, eunuchs, doctors, bodyguards, and troops. The citizens of Ephesus celebrated Mithradates' arrival by toppling statues erected by the Romans in their city. Mithradates sailed over to the island of Cos where he was received with jubilation. The people of Cos turned over a vast hoard of money and treasures that had been placed in the Temple of Asclepius for safekeeping by the queen-regent of Egypt, Cleopatra III (wife of Ptolemy VIII, descendant of the best friend of Alexander the Great). One of the treasures was her grandson, the young son of the reigning ruler, Alexander, in Egypt. Malleable royal heirs could come in handy: Mithradates took the boy into his court and raised him with his other sons.

Cleopatra's treasure included splendid works of art, statuary, paintings, vases, faience, gems, jewelry, royal costumes, and coffers of gold and silver coins. This caravan of valuables was sent under heavy guard to Pontus. One very special item, stored in a cedar chest and carefully labeled, was the vintage cloak of faded purple that had adorned the shoulders of the great Alexander. Mithradates' possession of this priceless heirloom reassured the king and his followers that he was the true inheritor of Alexander's legacy, the one who could liberate Greece from the Roman yoke.

Mithradates also carried away a large hoard of money, eight hundred talents, from Cos. According to the Jewish historian Josephus, the money was intended for the Temple in Jerusalem, deposited on Cos by Jews of Anatolia for safekeeping.[26]

Next, Mithradates took Stratonicea, where Macedonian and indigenous traditions mingled: the city had supported Aristonicus's revolt. It was in Stratonicea (according to Appian, or perhaps in Miletus, as Plutarch wrote), that a self-possessed young Macedonian woman caught

FIG. 7.4. Mithradates and Monime, who negotiated for the title of queen. Illustration for Racine's play *Mithridate*, artist unknown.

Mithradates' eye. The daughter of Philopoemen, a prominent citizen, Monime was a beauty "much talked about among the Greeks." Plutarch recounted the fascinating story of her courtship. The fate of Mithradates' first wife, his sister Laodice, was common knowledge, and so was the king's resistance to making any woman his official queen after Laodice's treachery. Mithradates was strongly drawn to Monime. Thinking he would make her the jewel of his harem, he began negotiations with her father.

But Monime herself rejected Mithradates' offer of fifteen hundred gold pieces. She held out for more. Monime demanded a marriage contract and insisted that Mithradates give her the royal diadem and title of queen. Mithradates found Monime irresistible. Raised among strong, willful women, and as a gambler extraordinaire, Mithradates was attracted to powerful personalities whose intelligence complemented his own. For the past dozen years, the king's only female companionship had been casual trysts in his harem. As Monime knew, victory is an aphrodisiac. Mithradates, reveling in his great good fortune and feeling expansive, agreed to her conditions. The royal scribes prepared the marriage contract, and the gold was turned over to Philopoemen. Mithradates appointed Monime's father as his overseer in Ephesus. After the king tied the purple and gold ribbon around the head of his new queen, the pair withdrew to the private rooms of the palace in Pergamon to become better acquainted.[27]

MEANWHILE IN ROME

Alarming news reached Rome, telling of the unauthorized attack on Pontus by Nicomedes IV, instigated by Aquillius. The senators heard messengers recount details of the ignominious defeat, the flight of the three Roman generals, followed by Mithradates' triumphant sweep through the Province of Asia. The loss of Roman honor and possessions demanded a quick and decisive response. The Senate declared war (after the fact!) on King Mithradates VI Eupator. The two rival consuls, Marius and Sulla, cast lots to see who would win the command of this long-expected Mithradatic War. The gods did not favor Marius. It was Sulla who won the coveted generalship.

But the city of Rome was torn by civil strife and murder, and almost all Italy was in open rebellion. Rome's available troops were already fighting on many fronts; how could the Senate spare legions to send across the Mediterranean? Sulla was too embroiled in the civil war against Marius and his allies to depart for Asia. Mithradates' excellent intelligence sources had again given him impeccable timing. Rome's delayed military response would allow him time to build more ships and naval seige engines to attack Rhodes, while Mithradates' armies marched to liberate Greece.

The crisis atmosphere in Rome was compounded by a hard economic reality. There was no money to finance Sulla's legions. The senators voted to take an unheard-of emergency measure. "So limited were their means at the time, and so unlimited were their ambitions," wrote Justin, that the Senate seized the ancient treasures of Rome's legendary King Numa, the successor of the founder, Romulus. King Numa had set aside his special treasure six hundred years earlier with instructions that it was to be used only for holy sacrifices to the gods. While Mithradates was in his counting house happily counting out his gold, the Senate's agents were desperately selling Rome's most sacred treasure to the highest bidders. Appian commented that the market price of Numa's legacy came to only nine thousand pounds of gold. "This was all Rome had to spend on so great a war."[28]

Rhodes, meanwhile, was Mithradates' immediate target. The island prepared for war, calling on Telmessus and its other allies in Lycia for aid.

AQUILLIUS CAPTURED

Aquillius had managed to reach the coast across from Lesbos. Oppius, he had heard, was Mithradates' sorry captive; Nicomedes IV was sailing to Rome; Cassius's whereabouts were unknown. Aquillius commandeered a boat to take him to Mytilene on Lesbos. There he hoped to arrange passage back to Italy. According to the historian Diodorus, Aquillius found refuge with a local doctor. But the citizens of Mytilene sided with Mithradates. They sent a posse of "their most valiant young men to the house where Aquillius was staying. They seized Aquillius, put him in fetters," and rowed him back to the mainland, where they turned him over to Mithradates' men. The soldiers set the prize prisoner on a donkey and paraded him before jeering crowds. All along the road to Pergamon, the soldiers forced the captive to repeat his name—Manius Aquillius—and confess his crimes against the people of Anatolia.[29]

Fig. 7.5. Road to Pergamon, the acropolis and Mithradates' palace in the distance. Steel engraving, T. Allom, 1840, courtesy of F. Dechow.

All recognized the man's name on the way to Pergamon. Fearful Romans in the area kept a low profile and stayed home. Everyone else spit on the memory of the captive's notorious father, the elder Manius Aquillius, former Roman governor of Pergamon, erstwhile capital of Rome's Asian Province. Deeply hated for crushing taxes, he had hatched schemes so egregious that he'd been prosecuted for extortion, yet acquitted. All remembered how Aquillius senior had poisoned innocent men, women, and children trapped in the cities that supported the Sun Citizens' rebellion.

Exploitation by tax profiteers like Aquillius and his son had kept resentment boiling in Anatolia, which the Romans viewed as an El Dorado overflowing with gold and natural resources theirs for the plundering. When Mithradates was a youth in exile, the elder Aquillius had interfered in his mother's realm of Pontus, draining its treasury with high-interest loans. Officially, provincial tax rates were supposed to be set in

Rome, but the office of tax collector was sold to the highest bidder, who then squeezed as much as he could for personal profit while the Roman courts of justice turned a blind eye. Aquillius the younger had headed the provincial commission in Asia, and, like his father, he was guilty of levying corrupt taxes and bribery. And now, as everyone knew, Aquillius's arrogant son had blackmailed and ordered the king of Bithynia, Nicomedes IV, to invade Pontus, out of pure greed.[30]

Jubilation and revenge inflamed the Greeks and Anatolians who turned out to castigate the shackled Roman on his humble mount. As humiliating as the procession was, Aquillius dreaded his meeting with King Mithradates more. The tables were turned, the Romans were on the run, and Mithradates ruled Asia.

The man on the donkey could not imagine what awaited him in Pergamon.

(*top*) Plate 1. Mithradates testing poisons on a condemned criminal. The doctors Papias and Krateuas (right) display monkshood (*Aconitum apellus*), ginger (*Zingiber officinale*), and gentian (Gentiana lutea). "The Royal Toxicologist," by Robert Thom, History of Pharmacy, Pfizer. American Pharmacists Association Foundation.

(*bottom*) Plate 2. Mithradates and Hypsicratea, riding to battle. "Hypsicratea, concubine of Mithradates, follows her mate to battle," by Antoine Paillet, 1672. Chateau de Versailles. Réunion des Musées Nationaux/Art Resource, NY.

PLATE 3. Scenes from Mithradates' life story, depicted within the castle, beginning with poisoning his mother and brother (far left); Mithradates besieged (center); his death (right); and ending with the rebellion of Pharnaces (foreground). Medieval manuscript illustration. *Miroir historial; speculum historiale/ Mithridate*, Français 50, folio 172, Bibliothèque National de France.

PLATE 4. Mithradates (left) takes the antidote, offered by his herbalist Krateuas (right).
This elaborate gold and terracotta *Mithridatium* jar, decorated with scenes from
Mithradates' life, is one of a pair of sixteenth-century drug jars with glazed, watertight
interiors. These jars would have been prominently displayed by the owner or apothecary.

PLATE 5. Mithradates the Great in lionskin cap (right) and Tigranes in tiara (left) seal their alliance in Tigranes' palace in Artaxata, Armenia. Painting by Rubik Kocharian, 2008, portrays the friends clasping hands, dressed in costumes like those in contemporary images of Persian-influenced Hellenistic kings.

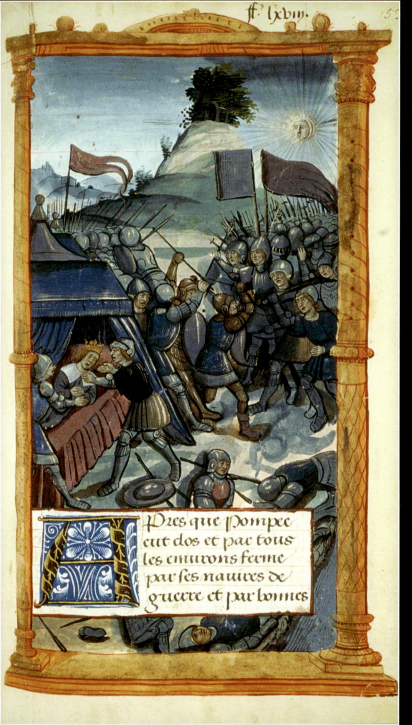

PLATE 6.
Moonlight
Battle.
Mithradates
awakened by
friends (left)
as Pompey
attacks by the
full moon.
*Plutarch's Life
of Pompey*,
ca. 1500,
presented
to Louis XII
of France.
Koninklijke
Bibliotheek,
The Hague.

PLATE 9. Pompey turns away from the corpse of Mithradates, while men fight over his crown and scabbard. *Plutarch's Life of Pompey*, ca. 1500, presented to Louis XII of France. Koninklijke Bibliotheek, The Hague.

(*OPPOSITE PAGE TOP*) PLATE 7. Caucasus Mountains, between the Black Sea and the Caspian Sea. Mithradates probably crossed the Daryal Pass in the center of the range. NASA Visible Earth satellite image, www.visibleearth.nasa.gov.

(*OPPOSITE PAGE BOTTOM*) PLATE 8. Mithradates (incognito) and Hypsicratea, departing. *Des dames de renom, De mulierbus claris/Hypsicratea*, Français 599, folio 67, Bibliothèque National de France.

PLATE 10. Horseman on the steppes. Photo by David Edwards/National Geographic.

Terror

I N THE PALACE at Pergamon, Mithradates was enjoying two honeymoons, one political and the other personal. Between romantic interludes with his new love Monime, the king reveled in his victories and devised a public punishment for Aquillius. The Roman deserved to die for invading Pontus and preying on Anatolia. The king's heralds summoned the populace to the Theater of Dionysus, perched on a steep hillside of the Acropolis, where Mithradates had recently delivered his speech declaring war on Rome.

The crowd watches as a super-hot bonfire is stoked in the center of the theater. Next, a "giant" figure well known in Pergamon, a freakishly tall soldier called Bastarna (from the Bastarnae of Carpathia), appears, riding a huge horse at a stately pace around the fire, dragging a long chain. At the end of the chain stumbles Aquillius. Suspense builds, and a dramatic recitation of the prisoner's crimes incites the audience.

Next, with exaggerated ceremony, heaps of gold coins from Mithradates' treasury are trundled out. The glittering coins ring out as men laboriously tip them into a large stone crucible suspended over the fire. Within a few minutes, the coins are melted down. A glimmer of what is in store begins to dawn on the crowd and Aquillius. Then his captors force his jaws open and pour the molten gold down the greedy Roman's throat. A diabolical last meal for a glutton for gold.[1]

In its shocking visual impact, the dramatically staged execution of Aquillius recalls Mithradates' public stabbing of his nephew Ariathes in full view of the opposing armies in Cappadocia. A generation later, in 53 BC, the king of Parthia copied Mithradates and poured gold down the throat of another rich Roman invader loathed for his greed, M. Licinius Crassus. The raw symbolism of death by molten gold catapulted this atrocity into a byword for cruel—if poetically just—revenge in the Middle Ages and beyond. The image of angry, colonized people forcing the

FIG. 8.1. The horrific execution by molten gold—just deserts for
greedy Romans —became an icon of poetic justice after 88 BC, when Mithradates ordered the death of Aquillius. This image shows the execution of M.
Licinius Crassus by the Parthian king, in imitation of Mithradates' execution
of Aquillius a few years earlier. Pierre Coustau, *Pegma*, 1555, Glasgow
University Library, Special Collections.

imperialist to have his fill of gold was still deeply seared into the popular
consciousness some fifteen hundred years later. European historians and
artists appropriated the same scene to imagine how Moctezuma, the last
king of the Aztecs, punished the Spanish conquistadors' insatiable lust
for the yellow metal.[2]

In 88 BC, however, Mithradates' vicious execution of one detested
Roman was soon overshadowed by an even more horrific event: the cold-
blooded massacre of tens of thousands of Italian-speaking residents in
Provincia Asia.

DEATH TO THE ROMANS

After Mithradates shattered the Roman coalition armies and began his
sweep down through central Anatolia, Romans and their sympathizers
fled before him to the coast. Among them were Chaeremon of Nysa and

his family and the Roman general Cassius. Mithradates' decrees offering rewards for Chaeremon cast new light on the situation in the Roman province, not fully explained in the ancient texts. The inscriptions tell us that Italian refugees—bringing their households and slaves—were flowing into Ephesus, Adramyttion, Caunus, and other major cities near the coast.

So, in the months before the massacre of 88, great numbers of Romans and Italians were already camping out in temple sanctuaries for safety. Soldiers from the defeated Roman legions also joined this stream of refugees. This means that the Latin-speaking populations of these cities soared in the months before the order to kill them was actually carried out. By converging in a few major cities, the desperate fugitives became even more vulnerable. This mass exodus helps account for the terrible success of Mithradates' order, which effectively wiped out the Roman presence in Asia Minor.

The adventures of one Roman who survived are hinted at in the ancient sources. It was rumored in Rome that the former provincial officer, Rutilius Rufus, had escaped death during the massacre because he disguised himself in Greek clothes. Some Italians did avoid the fate of their countrymen by wearing distinctive Greek clothing, but it is more likely that Rutilius Rufus was spared because he was so respected in Anatolia for trying to protect the province from ruthless tax collectors. It was well known that the Roman Senate had punished Rutilius for his leniency, convicting him on trumped-up charges. In 92 BC, he had settled in Smyrna, north of Ephesus, where he was welcomed by the populace with honors and flowers.

It seems that friends in Smyrna warned Rutilius about the massacre and arranged for his safe passage to Mytilene, Lesbos, the same island where Aquillius was captured. Italian scholar Attilio Mastrocinque recently suggested that Rutilius may have played a role in turning Aquillius over to Mithradates. The ancient historian Theophanes of Mytilene had even spread a story implicating Rutilius in the planning of the massacre of 88 BC. In any event, we know that Rutilius survived to write an influential memoir about the Mithradatic Wars. Sadly, Rutilius's *Memoriae* no longer exists, like so much of the literature of the ancient world.[3]

Appian reported that a few Italian refugees gathered on Rhodes. Among them were Cassius, Aquillius's cocommander in the fiasco, and the sons of Chaeremon of Nysa. His sons survived, but Chaeremon remained in Ephesus and was believed to have died with the other Romans inside the temple. The stories of why Rutilius lived and why Chaeremon chose to stay behind are just two of the thousands of personal tales of heroism and cowardice, survival and slaughter, now lost to history.

The awful events that day in Ephesus, Pergamon, Adramyttion, Caunus, Tralles, and other cities were recounted in chapter 1. Other pro-Mithradatic cities where massacres occurred include Nysa, Apamea, Cnidus, Miletus, Smyrna, Erythrae, and the Aegean islands of Cos, Lesbos, and Chios. We know they were regarded as complicit, because these places were singled out for severe punishment by Sulla, the Roman general who came to avenge the massacre.[4]

The massacre raises a host of questions. How was it coordinated? When exactly did it occur? Where was Mithradates? How could he be so certain that so many people would carry out the command? We've already seen how deep resentment arose over harsh Roman occupation, taxation, and slavery in the Greek world and Anatolia. Mithradates' victories had the hated Romans on the run. But the savagery of the attacks in 88 BC tells us that Italian settlers were loathed to an extraordinary degree, by all classes of society. The reasons are multilayered.

The Roman historian J.P.V.D. Balsdon documented Rome's "good and bad press" gleaned from ancient authors. Many observers admired traditional Roman culture and battle prowess, courage, and virtue, but Balsdon notes that Romans of this era were also widely disliked for their "insensitivity and offensiveness abroad." Marcus Cornelius Fronto, a prominent Libyan-Italian orator (b. AD 95 in Carthage), wrote that the "Romans lack warmth; they are a cold people." Diodorus of Sicily, a Greek historian who wrote just after the Mithradatic Wars, remarked that "in days of old, the Romans adhered to the best laws and customs [and] over time they acquired the greatest and most splendid empire known to history. But . . . the ancient practices gave way to pernicious tendencies." Relations between Roman officials and the colonies tended to be poisoned by "mutual suspicion and power imbalance," even among local elites. Arrogance and superiority led to a stereotype of the "Ugly Roman" businessman aggressively seeking profit and power, bankrupting and enslaving local families.

Typical Roman views of the indigenous people of the Near East were stereotyped too. Romans considered Anatolians stupid and inferior, natural slaves. The physical attributes of enslaved populations were crassly compared. For example, Romans claimed that Syrians, Jews, and Greeks of Asia Minor were naturally submissive. They purchased Bithynians and Syrians for bearing litters because of their height; Gauls were said to be better than Spaniards for tending herds, and so on. Romans tossed off insulting proverbs and odious ethnic slurs, such as "Carians are only useful for testing poisons" and "All Phrygians improve with beating."[5]

Mithradates' personal and political motives for the massacre were even more complex. It's interesting to speculate whether he knew of the similar massacre of Romans in Numidia during the Jugurthine War. In Vaga during a festival, ordinary folk and nobles together had carried out the premeditated slaughter of Roman soldiers and their families garrisoned in the town (108 BC). Marius, a veteran of the Jugurthine War, may have described this massacre to Mithradates at their meeting, but Mithradates could have heard it from any number of other sources. Did the slaughter at Vaga and similar reprisals against Roman immigrants and traders during Jugurtha's war serve as a model for the massacre of 88 BC? If so, did Mithradates anticipate a harsh Roman response to his own plan? After Vaga, the avenging Roman general Metellus ordered his soldiers to chop all the inhabitants into little pieces. Mithradates had to know that Rome would seek revenge for his order, but he must have believed that troubles at home in Italy would prevent a quick response. He may also have anticipated the devastating financial collapse that the Roman losses in Asia precipitated. He thought he had time to secure Greece and take Rhodes, so that war with Rome could be fought far from his Pontic homeland and would be confined to crushing Sulla's legions on Greek soil.[6]

The ruthlessness and scale of the massacre—among other dark incidents—raises questions about Mithradates' psychology, for moderns anyway (notably, no ancient writers thought him mad). Danish scholar Tønnes Bekker-Neilsen recently considered whether Mithradates possessed a "borderline" or "psychotic" personality disorder, based on a checklist of modern psychiatric characteristics. Some traits exhibited by Mithradates—a grandiose sense of self-worth; a charismatic, manipulative personality; theatricality; impulsive and callous behavior; criminal versatility—appear to match the patterns of some psychopaths. Other traits, however, such as promiscuous sexual behavior, paranoia, and seeking opportunities to exert power, even political murders, were normal in the cutthroat world of Hellenistic kings. Some psychopathological traits do not apply, since Mithradates reportedly experienced deep emotions including love, anxiety, remorse, and depression; he took responsibilty for his own actions; maintained long-term relationships; and planned long-term goals. The recently created category, "successful psychopath," might best describe Mithradates: one who exhibits ruthless, exploitative, grandiose behavior, but whose mitigating social traits and intelligence allow that person to achieve success and acclaim. Today such people succeed in politics, law, medicine, and sports, areas that Mithradates also excelled in (see appendix 1).[7]

According to Memnon, Mithradates "killed 80,000 Romans scattered throughout the cities of Anatolia because he received word that they were hindering his designs." Rose Mary Sheldon, a historian of ancient espionage, suggests that Mithradates may have learned that the Roman community was forwarding intelligence to Rome to sabotage his plans. Memnon's claim and Mithradates' drastic order suggest that a resistance or saboteur movement had already arisen, led by Romans and their supporters. This notion is also supported by Mithradates' "Wanted" posters for Chaeremon.[8]

Mithradates may have ordered the massacre to show solidarity with the Italian rebels, in response to their requests for aid in defeating the Romans. Some have suggested that besides removing opponents and potential troublemakers, confiscations of Roman property brought much wealth to Mithradates. Certainly the resulting collapse of credit in Rome, which had been based on exorbitant taxation and profits in Asia, was a boon to Mithradates. The satraps of the murderous cities promised to divide the confiscated Roman property with Mithradates. But it seems safe to say that money was not his main object—he was already richer than the legendary kings Midas and Croesus combined. When Mithradates later accused Chios of not sharing the confiscated property with him, it was a matter of punishing traitors, rather than a concern for lost profit.[9]

Mithradates' plans were subtle and carefully laid. In previous chapters, we saw how Mithradates employed oblique control, alliances, bribery, assassinations, military maneuvers, rhetoric, propaganda, and cunning diplomacy in the first two decades of his reign, to persuade the Romans that they should withdraw from Anatolia and Greece. Now it was outright war. It would seem that two pressing motives led Mithradates to order the elimination of the Roman people remaining in Anatolia. Although his victories sent many Romans—including thousands of legionaries—into flight, many remained, especially in the cosmopolitan ports. These cities were notorious for switching sides; as commercial centers they depended on business. Mithradates knew they could not be trusted to remain loyal should the war with Rome begin to go badly. He could not afford to allow a resistance movement to coalesce around resident Romans and their sympathizers in the lands he now occupied, while he was engaged in Greece and Rhodes.

Second, the killing ensured and publicized the widespread credible commitment to his cause. All the cities and territories whose diverse but well-integrated citizenry—Greeks, Jews, and Anatolians—had agreed to murder Romans were now irrevocably bound to Mithradates. Another benefit of the "ethnic cleansing" included freeing numerous slaves and debtors who would join his forces, bolstering the king's reputation for generosity toward non-Romans, rich and poor alike.[10]

Mithradates may have issued the order from Ephesus, but his location on the day itself is unknown. Scholars of ancient intelligence wonder how the clandestine order was delivered—orally? in writing? in code? Numerous ancient accounts describe top-secret missives inscribed on wax tablets or hidden in the soles of sandals, inside dead rabbits, under horse blankets, braided into women's hair or horses' tails, or even tattooed on the shaved scalps of messengers. Mithradates' "intelligence coup" is still a great puzzle, remarks Sheldon. "We do not know, to this day, how Mithridates coordinated this feat, how he communicated with his agents, or how he kept such a deadly plan secret" for a month, especially in places like Tralles, where the order was discussed in the assembly.[11]

The year 88 BC was crammed with gripping events. It is impossible to determine the exact sequence of the execution of Aquillius, the massacre of Romans, the battle for Rhodes, and the Greek campaign. But one thing is certain: the massacre plot was set in motion at least thirty days in advance, allowing Mithradates to concentrate on his two-pronged operation: the all-important liberation of Greece and the conquest of Rhodes.

ATHENION, MITHRADATES' ENVOY IN ATHENS

Greeks in Anatolia, the Aegean islands, and mainland Greece saw Mithradates Eupator as a heroic freedom fighter who could restore democracy to democracy's homeland. In the months before the massacre, the citizens of Athens voted to send the philosopher Athenion to Pergamon for an audience with Mithradates, requesting him to free Greece from Rome's grasp. It was traditional for philosophers to act as ambassadors, but this must have happened over the objections of Romans in Athens or perhaps in secret.

Mithradates warmly welcomed Athenion and presented him with typically sumptuous gifts—a gold and agate ring carved with the king's likeness and a fine purple robe. The men became good friends. Athenion wrote many letters home assuring the Athenians that Mithradates would restore their democratic constitution and cultural life, promising peace and great benefits, including relief from debts.

Athenion's story is recounted, in a negative light, by the supercilious, imperial-era author Athenaeus, who lived in Egypt in the late second century AD. In his *Learned Banquet*, a miscellany of Roman gossip and popular culture, Athenaeus wrote that "after all Asia had revolted to join the King," the philosopher Athenion sailed back to Athens. All Athens— men, women, and children, citizens and foreigners—turned out in the parklike setting of the Kerameikos, the cemetery along the Sacred Way, to welcome Athenion as he entered the great Dipylon Gate. Athenaeus's description, written two hundred years later during the height of the Roman Empire, is filled with sarcasm directed at all those who had once placed their hope in Mithradates' "revolution." But Athenaeus's sources did have access to contemporary, possibly eyewitness reports of Athenion's return. Keeping in mind that Athenaeus certainly twisted the story for the amusement of his smug, elite imperial audience, we must read between the lines to imagine the emotions of the Roman Athenians of Mithradates' day.[12]

Athenaeus berates Athenion as a "preposterous freak of fortune," a demagogue who traded his "ragged philosopher's cloak for a purple robe" to be "conducted with obnoxious pomp into Athens in a silver-footed litter." Athenaeus portrays the Athenians as credulous fools to hope that Mithradates could bring them a "glorious" future. He ridicules the adoring crowds who gathered outside the philosopher's new "mansion adorned with costly couches, paintings, statues, and displays of silver plate." Athenaeus depicts the procession by litter, the rich garments, and the flashy gold ring as signs of Athenion's arrogance, hypocrisy, and greed. Obviously, however, all these things had been traditional gifts from King Mithradates, intended to show the Athenians that Athenion was his true envoy.

The Kerameikos and the Sacred Way were filled with throngs of excited citizens converging on the Agora, the public square where Athenion was to speak. Along the way, speeches, sacrifices, and libations were offered in his honor. In the Agora, Athenion climbed onto a large wooden platform in front of the Portico of Attalus, the grand covered marketplace. On the stage where the Roman generals who controlled Greece held tribunals, Athenion delivered his dramatic message from King Mithradates to the assembled people of Athens. Athenion began with a self-effacing comment, traditional in democratic Greek oratory. "O

Athenians, the state of affairs of my country compels me to tell you what I know. But the situation and the magnitude of the news to be discussed overwhelm me!" At this, a great cheer went up from the audience, urging him to continue.

I tell you, then, of things which could never have been hoped for, nor imagined in a dream. King Mithradates is now master of Bithynia and of Cappadocia, and he is master of all Asia, as far as Pamphylia and Cilicia. The kings of the Armenians and Persians are his guards, he is lord of all nations around the Black Sea and Pontus. Mithradates' dominions now encompass a vast territory. The Roman commander, Oppius, has surrendered and is in the king's retinue as a prisoner. Manius Aquillius, the consul who once celebrated a Triumph in Rome for his victory over Sicilian slaves, is now dragged around behind a horse ridden by the giant ogre Bastarna. The Romans living in Asia are bowing down before the gods, others are donning Greek clothing, and many recent Roman citizens are reverting to their original nationalities.

Every city in Asia is honoring Mithradates with divine honors and calling him a god! Oracles everywhere promise him dominion over the whole world. He is sending armies to Thrace and Macedonia and even Europe is coming over to his side. Not only are the Italian rebels sending ambassadors to Mithradates, but the Carthaginians too, all begging to ally with him for the destruction of the Romans.

Here Athenion paused and wiped his face, giving the multitude time to absorb and exclaim over this news.

Athenians! We must not bear this state of anarchy any longer, imposed by the Roman Senate while it controls our government. The Romans have closed our temples and let our schools fall to dust. Our theaters are off limits and our courts of justice and schools of philosophy are silenced. They have even taken the Pnyx, our sacred place of Assembly, away from the people!

After this rousing speech, the crowd rushed to the Theater of Dionysus and voted to elect Athenion general of the citizen army. Athenion accepted the generalship, a one-year post. "Now, Athenians," he declared, "you yourselves are your own generals, and I am commander-in-chief. If each of you exert everything in your power to cooperate, I shall be able to do as much as all of you put together!" Nine *archons*, high officials, were selected, following ancient democratic practice. Archaeologists have discovered an inscription with their names, showing that the men were all from prominent Athenian families.

Athenaeus (like other Roman-era writers) characterized the philosopher as a dictator seizing power: "Athenion thus appointed himself tyrant." Yet as Athenaeus himself describes, Athenion was democratically elected by the majority of citizens in Athens, according to the traditional process set out in the ancient Athenian constitution. Other contradictions in Athenaeus's account reveal his antidemocratic biases and his resort to stock insults. For example, he calls Athenion's mother a "lowly Egyptian slave" and accuses him of growing fabulously wealthy as a philosophy teacher, even while he reviles him as impoverished. The historian Strabo, writing in the generation after the Mithradatic Wars, also asserted that Mithradates "placed tyrants in Athens who violently oppressed the city." In fact, as modern historians agree, these leaders were elected by majority vote, by an electorate that included all classes.[13]

The restoration of democracy in Athens gave Athenion a mandate in a city previously controlled by Roman conquerors and elite sympathizers among the citizenry. Athenaeus's report of what happened next in Athens is elaborately detailed, portrayed as a "reign of terror" by the democratic majority. The events he describes were probably based on the experiences of Romans and pro-Roman Greek aristocrats who escaped prosecution and death after Athenion's election. Athenion placed guards at the city's gates, but many Romans and their sympathizers fled over the walls by night. Athenion sent out soldiers in pursuit, killing some and imprisoning others. Citizen assemblies and people's courts were convened. Athenians who collaborated with Romans were tried for treason. The convicted were beaten or executed, their property confiscated. Later that year, because of disruptions in trade, food and supplies became scarce in the city. Athenion had to order strict rations on barley and wheat. In Athenaeus's snide words, the "ignorant Athenians were forced to subsist on grain that was barely enough to keep a chicken alive."[14]

Had Mithradates informed Athenion of his secret plans to wipe out Romans in Anatolia? Did Athenion order similar actions in Athens? The violence against Romans and their supporters in Athens after Athenion's election does parallel what was occurring in the cities of Anatolia in 88 BC. Mithradates appealed to both rich and poor, but any opposition that arose always came from aristocratic quarters. As in Athens, Roman collaborators among Anatolian oligarchic families lost their lives. For example, in Adramyttion, one of the towns where Romans were massacred, the local philosopher-statesman Diodorus, a partisan of Mithradates, was elected general. Diodorus had some members of the city council killed—undoubtedly these were aristocratic supporters of Rome.[15]

The restored democracy in Athens, with Athenion and his successor Aristion elected on anti-Roman platforms, prepared the way for the co-ordinated arrival of Mithradates' liberation forces in Greece. A host of barbarian allies, led by his son Arcathius, marched out from Pontus across Bithynia and Thrace to northern Greece. At the same time, a large Pontic fleet and army, commanded by Metrophanes, occupied Euboea and Thessaly. Meanwhile, Archelaus's troops took Delos by force. The sacred island served as the treasure house of the Aegean, controlled by Rome. Traditionally allied with Athens, the Greek residents of Delos had welcomed Mithradates early in his reign and honored him with the monument decorated with statues of the king and a dozen of his friends. But now Delos was pledged to aid Rome. After the massacre in 88 BC, the Italian residents who dominated the island took up hammers and smashed the fine marble portraits in the Mithradates Monument on Delos, obliterating the faces of Mithradates and his friends.

All the while, Mithradates' shipbuilders had been expanding his navy for the attack on Rhodes, still loyal to Rome. Now, bidding farewell to Queen Monime, Mithradates boarded his flagship as supreme naval commander of the fleet bound for Rhodes. The Rhodians hurried to "strengthen their walls and harbors and erect engines of war everywhere," recruiting reinforcements from the mainland.[16]

THE BATTLE FOR RHODES

Rhodes, as Mithradates was well aware, had defended itself forcefully against Demetrius Poliorcetes, "Besieger of Cities," back in 305/304 BC. That grueling siege went down in history as one of the greatest battles in antiquity. Demetrius's engineers had erected the tallest, most powerful mechanized siege tower ever built. The "City Taker" was 130 feet high, weighed 160 tons, and was equipped with 16 heavy catapults. It required relays of more than 3,000 men to activate it. Iron plates fireproofed the wooden tower, and curtains of soaking wet wool and seaweed protected the windows from the Rhodians' fusillades of fiery arrows and flaming oil grenades. Demetrius had also deployed a 180-foot-long battering ram manned by 1,000 soldiers, and he constructed huge drills for boring through walls. Despite all this technology, however, Rhodes had repelled the invader after a year of fierce fighting. Both sides won everlasting fame. Demetrius's glorious failure was materialized for all to see. The Rhodians melted the metal from his abandoned siege equipment to create the massive Colossus of Rhodes.[17]

Mithradates intended to outdo Demetrius. Planning his attack by sea and land, Mithradates' engineers constructed a *sambuca*, an immense tower mounted on two ships. It had a movable wicker bridge, for scaling city walls from the sea. Meanwhile, Mithradates' land forces massed at Caunus; from there they would sail to join the Pontic navy at Rhodes.

Appian and other historians described the battle for Rhodes. As Mithradates' grand navy, decked out with magnificent carved figureheads and fancy equipment, hove into view, the people of Rhodes took drastic, "scorched earth" measures, destroying and burning the outskirts of the city to deny Mithradates shelter and food. The Rhodian navy, commanded by the experienced and bold Greek admiral Damagoras, advanced, ready to attack the Pontic ships head-on. Mithradates, sailing ahead in his quinquereme (the largest warship of the day), saw that he greatly outnumbered the Rhodians and ordered his vessels to encircle the enemy. But Damogoras quickly withdrew within Rhodes' walled harbor, and the Rhodians prepared to fight from their city walls. Mithradates camped in the burned-over suburbs outside the city, while his ships continually probed the harbor.[18]

But the Rhodians maintained their defensive advantage. Damagoras sent a bireme (a small, fast ship with two decks of rowers) to engage one of Mithradates' merchant vessels. Mithradates sent a multitude of warships into the fray, fighting with zeal, but his sailors were inexperienced and undisciplined compared to the expert Rhodians. Damogoras skillfully rammed Mithradates' vessels. The Rhodians came away with a great many costly figureheads and rich spoils, as well as a Pontic trireme and crew.

The next day, Damogoras took six swift ships out to search for a lost ship. Mithradates' royal quinquereme and twenty-five of his fastest ships set off in pursuit. Damogoras cleverly evaded Mithradates all day, drawing him far out to sea. At sunset, as Damogoras expected, Mithradates ordered his ships to turn back. At that point, Damogoras plowed into them, ramming the enemy ships in the dark. During the confusion, while Mithradates was yelling orders at his sailors, one of his allied triremes—from Chios—rammed hard into Mithradates' own ship. The king's quinquereme somehow survived the jarring impact. In the thick of battle, Mithradates continued fighting. But Damogoras sank two Pontic ships and drove two others all the way to the Lycian coast.

FIG. 8.2. During the naval battle for Rhodes in 88 BC, Mithradates' ship was rammed by an allied Chian ship (center). (Foreground) archers aim fire missiles. Rise and Fall: Civilizations at War video game screenshot, courtesy of Midway Games, Inc.

Rattled by the surprising successes of the outnumbered Rhodians, Mithradates brooded suspiciously on the collision with the Chian ship during the night battle. Was it deliberate? He had the Chian pilot and the lookout sailor flogged. From that day on, says Appian, Mithradates "conceived a hatred for all Chians." Someday he would find a way to get even.

Ominous prodigies began to undermine Mithradates' morale. In the burned-over countryside, where Mithradates was camped, a gang of crows suddenly attacked a vulture. Then that night, a "huge star" (a meteorite?) fell on the very spot where the vulture had been pecked to death. The king's Magi and soothsayers muttered grimly.

The campaign for Rhodes was not going well. Where were his land forces? Mithradates' troops were supposed to board merchant vessels and triremes in Caunus and join him. In fact, they had set sail, but a massive storm drove the battered fleet toward Rhodes in no condition to fight. Damagoras's navy sailed out and "fell upon the ships while they were still scattered and suffering the effects of the tempest. Damagoras captured some ships, rammed and sank others, and burned still more." The Rhodians took four hundred prisoners that day.

Some Rhodian deserters appeared in camp requesting a meeting with Mithradates. Perhaps things were looking up. The men led the king to the highest mountain on the island, a two-hour climb up to the walled Temple of Zeus. Here Mithradates decided to station some soldiers, with instructions to create a fire signal later that night. Then he sent half of his army under cover onto his ships, directing the other half to sneak into positions with scaling ladders. At the fire signal from the mountain, all would attack Rhodes by land and sea simultaneously. But some Rhodian sentries posted on another hill detected the sneaky movements and lit a fire. Mithradates' army and the naval contingent, thinking this was the fire signal from Zeus's temple, were tricked into attacking too early. The Rhodians rushed to their walls and beat off Mithradates' men. Somehow, it seemed that the Rhodians had been prepared for his surprise attack. Had those "deserters" been double agents?

It was time to bring up the *sambuca*. The enormous contraption, astride two ships, drew up alongside the outer seawall of the Temple of Isis, great mother goddess of Asia. The back wall of her temple formed part of the harbor fortifications. Mithradates' men labored to operate the pulleys of the *sambuca* to raise the bridge to the top of the wall, so that the soldiers, massed in small ships below with ladders, could swarm into the city.

The Rhodians were struck with fear at the sight of the colossal siege machine. Its approach must have aroused anxiety for Cassius and the little group of Roman refugees inside the walls too. Mithradates' troops began to clamber up the *sambuca*. Suddenly a great cheer went up among the Rhodians. Mithradates' grand structure was collapsing under the weight of all the men. And just at that moment, a glowing apparition of the goddess Isis appeared atop her temple! The goddess hurled a great fireball down onto the *sambuca* and the men clinging to it. The huge contraption fell burning into the sea.

The Rhodians had long been masters of fire power. During the fight against Demetrius in 305 BC, the entire night sky was lit up by spectacular fire missiles dipped in burning pitch and sulphur. Demetrius had been stunned: Rhodians fired more than eight hundred flaming projectiles in a single night! Now Mithradates was beginning to appreciate Demetrius's decision to sue for peace with Rhodes. Was the vision of the goddess throwing masses of fire an illusion caused by a burst of awesome

Rhodian incendiary power? Another meteor? A case of freak lightning? It didn't matter: for Mithradates' dispirited army, Isis's anger was a very bad omen.

Mithradates despaired of taking Rhodes. Undefeated but displeased, he sailed away to the coast of Lycia, leaving the charred remains of his *sambuca* floating in the sea below the temple walls. Damagoras, itching to finish off Mithradates, would have another chance, but that duel lay years ahead.[19]

THE FURIES

On the coast of Lycia, Mithradates and his general Pelopidas decided to lay siege to Patara (Lycian *Pttara*), an ally of Rhodes and Rome. Nearby, the Temple of Apollo boasted an oracle nearly as famous as Delphi. If Mithradates consulted this oracle, he and his soothsayers observed a school of sacred fish summoned by a flute, as Apollo's priests scattered bits of meat on the water. If the fish devoured the scraps, all was well; if they flipped the offering away with their tails, things looked bad. Given the trajectory of Mithradatic omens in this campaign, the fish probably turned tail.

Lycia was also the center of worship of the Anatolian and Greek mother goddesses Eni, Cybele, and Leto, the mother of Apollo and Artemis. Leto's sanctuary has been uncovered by archaeologists in the lush Xanthus valley near Patara's shore. Mithradates ordered his men to cut down the old trees along the beautiful white sand beach. He knew this grove was sacred to Leto, but he desperately needed wood to rebuild his siege machines. That night, however, the king tossed and turned in his tent. The goddess Leto appeared in a dream and warned Mithradates to spare her sacred trees. Mithradates and his Magi took dreams very seriously—they analyzed and recorded not just the king's dreams but those of his concubines as well.[20]

More bad news came in the morning. Some other Greek islands had defected, joining Delos, pledging to help Rome. They must be punished. Resourceful enemies, angry gods, evil omens, bad weather, stubborn fish, now even his once-loyal allies—everything seemed to be turning against him. Suspicion coiled in Mithradates' guts; paranoia raised its Hydra heads. First Isis, now Leto. Mother goddesses in particular seemed upset with him. How to placate them? The dour seers in his entourage began murmuring the names of the Furies, she-demons of justice who

Fig. 8.3. Mithradates portrait, marble, life-size. Photograph © The State Hermitage Museum, St. Petersburg.

haunted murderers, especially those who had killed their own mothers
and families. These horrid hags, carrying scorpion whips, hair writhing
with poisonous serpents and eyes dripping blood, were relentless avengers, hounding a murderer till he or she went insane with guilt and terror.
The Furies had sent famous Greek heroes over the brink of madness, and
mortals—even emperors—feared them. Mithradates, steeped in Greek
myth and drama, may well have believed he was being pursued by the
Furies for his murders, particularly of his mother and siblings.

Could this be the explanation for the sensational story that Mithradates sacrificed a virgin to the Furies after the failure to take Rhodes?
The incident appears in a list of omens by the Roman historian Livy, now
lost but preserved in the *Book of Prodigies* by A. Julius Obsequens. For
the year 88 BC, several prodigies were reported in Rome associated with
"Mithradates' preparations for war with Rome's allies." Some, like the apparition of Isis at the battle for Rhodes, are confirmed by other sources.

Mithradates and his Magi went to a sacred Grove of the Furies, a forest of dark yew trees. Pregnant sheep and turtledoves were the usual
sacrificial animals for the Daughters of the Night. Just as Mithradates
began to kindle the fire for his sacrifice of the ewe and dove, the sound
of supernatural laughter filled the grove. According to Livy and Obsequens, this terrified everyone present, interrupting the ritual. Mithradates' Magi conferred and instructed the king that he needed to sacrifice
a virgin on the altar of the Furies. A young girl was procured. The next
evening Mithradates began the incantations again, the knife poised over
the victim's neck. But all of a sudden, the girl herself began laughing in a
frightening, mirthless way. Her hysterical laughter, echoing the horrible
laughter of the Furies, completely disrupted the sacrifice.

Is it plausible that Mithradates really intended to sacrifice a human
being? It seems shocking, but the practice was not unknown in his or
in the Roman world. According to Herodotus, the Magi took pleasure
in killing living things with their bare hands: animals, snakes, birds,
butterflies, and ants. We know that the Magi sometimes ordered human
sacrifice, ritually killing young boys and girls to ensure victory in battle.
For example, when Xerxes invaded Greece in 480 BC, his Magi buried
alive nine children abducted from Greek families. For their part, Athens
and Sparta had killed Persian ambassadors as ritual sacrifices, and some
Greek generals made vows to the Furies before battle—either to excuse
the slaughter of innocents or to ask the Sacred Avengers to support their
cause. Mithradates knew the Greek plays of Aeschylus, Sophocles, and
Euripides, describing how King Agamemnon sacrificed his own virgin

daughter Iphigenia to ensure good sailing winds at the beginning of the Trojan War.

But human sacrifice was not just something from old myths or deep antiquity. Surprisingly, in 97 BC, just a decade before Mithradates lost Rhodes, the Roman Senate found it necessary to pass a decree outlawing human sacrifice. The Druids in Gaul and cults in Spain and Carthage practiced human sacrifice, but the Senate's decree was directed at preventing such "barbarian" practices in the city of Rome itself. Indeed, the Romans had sacrificed humans in recent memory. During the Hannibalic Wars, the Romans buried alive two Greeks and two Gauls, as ordered by the soothsayers who interpreted the Sibylline Books. The Romans had carried out a similar sacrifice as recently as 114 BC, just before the Jugurthine War, again burying alive two Greeks and two Gauls.[21]

These recent precedents, combined with Mithradates' knowledge of Persian and Greek kings who sacrificed virgins at the beginning of their great wars, lend plausibility to the ancient reports that Mithradates attempted to sacrifice a young girl. It is impossible to know whether the murders of his mother, brother, and sister—not to mention the murder of eighty thousand Roman residents—weighed on Mithradates' conscience. But a sacrifice to the Furies could appease angry divinities, absolve bloodguilt, and ensure victory in what Mithradates saw as a just war. The ritual could also be a useful propaganda move to demonstrate his religious commitment. What is so fascinating about the Roman account of Mithradates' human sacrifice is that it was reported in Rome without any sense of surprise or outrage. The fact that the sacrifice of the maiden was not actually carried out only adds to the credibility of the account.

After these untoward events, Mithradates abandoned the siege of Patara. He could use the excuse that trying to take Rhodes and Patara at this time was forbidden by the gods. Leaving Pelopidas to continue the war in Lycia, Mithradates ordered Archelaus to "gain allies by persuasion or by force" in the Aegean en route to Greece. Delegating the war to his generals, the king returned to Pergamon to concentrate on manufacturing more weapons and siege machines, building more ships, and raising more reinforcements for Greece. He celebrated his forty-sixth birthday in grand trencherman style. Appian tells us that Mithradates also spent a good deal of time enjoying himself in the arms of his new wife, Monime. While the king had been away at war, the lovers had exchanged many billets-doux filled with longing and lust.[22]

The setbacks—possibly exacerbated by misgivings about his own murderous tactics—triggered paranoid behavior in Mithradates. The near
miss with the Chian trireme at Rhodes led him to distrust his allies. The
king resorted to harsh retributions, establishing tribunals to try those
who were conspiring against him, much like the trials already going on
in Athens and Adramyttion. People accused of inciting revolution against
the king or supporting the Romans were brought before Mithradates
and his judges. Many were convicted, but these courts do not appear to
have been simply rubber stamps for juridical murder. As we saw, Mithradates had appointed the orator Metrodorus as an expressly independent
judge. Perhaps Metrodorus was to thank for the acquittal of a fellow orator, Diodorus Zonas of Sardis, who had frequently pleaded Mithradates'
cause in Rome. Falsely accused by some sycophants in Mithradates' court
of urging cities to revolt, Diodorus was able to prove his innocence and
survived the king's wrath.[23]

Despite the stalemate in Rhodes, Mithradates' rule extended from the
Black Sea and most of western Asia to Greece, and his navy ruled the
Aegean Sea. The extermination of Romans in Asia had gone like clock-
work. Mithradates' vast stores of money were multiplying, he enjoyed
his new love and basked in popular adulation, and his armies and navies
were undefeated. His generals were advancing on Greece by land and
sea, to complete the capstone in Mithradates' new version of Alexander's
great Greco-Persian Empire. Now everything depended on the Greek
campaign.

9

Battle for Greece

WHILE he eagerly awaited the news from Greece, Mithradates was also following developments in Italy. His takeover of Provincia Asia appeared to be the least of Rome's problems now. Roman legions were battling the Italian insurgents in the countryside, and civil war had broken out in Rome. Sulla, Marius's rival, had been elected to a consulship. Gangs of Sulla's Oligarch faction were at war with Popular party mobs loyal to Marius. Sulla was driven out of the city by the Populars; he took command of a Roman legion fighting Marsi rebels. Encouraged by a dream in which Cybele, the great mother goddess, gave him a divine thunderbolt, Sulla stormed Rome and occupied the city, with murderous street fighting. Sulla posted a reward for the head of Marius, who fled into hiding, but many Romans remained loyal to the old warrior.

Now master of Rome, Sulla was nevertheless in a precarious situation. Sacred treasures from Rome's temples had already been sold to finance Sulla's war chest for the Mithradatic War. After Mithradates' victories in Anatolia and Greece, his influence was gaining momentum; he had promised to aid the Italian insurgents. Rome's power in the East would be lost forever if Sulla failed to defeat Mithradates. A decisive triumph over the Republic's deadliest threat since Hannibal would elevate Sulla's status from civil warrior to heroic conqueror. But would Sulla dare to leave Italy? How could he fight Mithradates and still maintain control in Rome?

In 87 BC, the horns of Sulla's dilemma sharpened when Cinna, loyal to Marius, won a consul seat. That summer, Halley's Comet appeared, a portent of disaster for Rome. Cinna swore an oath to keep peace with Sulla's aristocratic party, but his promise rang hollow. Marius's gangs were poised to fall on Sulla's supporters, and the lives of Sulla's wife and children were in grave danger.[1]

What course would Sulla take? Mithradates assumed that Sulla, the Senate, and the Roman People intended to try to avenge his killing of Italians in Anatolia. But he believed the chaos in Italy would tie their hands for some time. After his liberation of the Greek world became a fait accompli, he could hope that Rome would have to accept the new division of power, and respect Mithradates the Great, King of Kings, as the new Alexander at the helm of a reborn Greco-Persian empire.[2]

THE LIBERATION OF GREECE

While war ravaged Rome, Mithradates gloried in the victories of the Greek campaign. Halley's Comet was taken as a good omen by Mithradates' Magi and by his allies. In Athens, the philosopher Aristion succeeded Athenion, elected on a pro-Mithradates platform; Aristion's name appeared with Mithradates' on Athenian coins of 87–86 BC.

Mithradates' own handsome coins featured his idealized portrait— looking very much like his hero Alexander, with parted lips and luxuriant hair. Imagery evoking Mithradates' Persian connections appeared on the reverse, such as winged Pegasus and the star and crescent. Other

Fig. 9.1. (Left) Mithradates' portrait, silver tetradrachm, 86/85 BC, idealized profile, similar to Alexander's coin (right), with tousled hair and parted lips. Mithradates' coins are distinctive for artistic excellence and sense of dynamic movement. 1980.109.66, bequest of A. J. Fecht, and 1944.100.45726, bequest of E. T. Newell, courtesy of the American Numismatic Society.

coins displayed Dionysus the Liberator (associating him with opposition to Rome by slaves and rebels in Italy). Mithradates made sure his portrait was known to everyone. He employed the best Greek artisans, and he understood the propaganda value of aesthetically pleasing currency. His coinage conveyed the message that Mithradates was the great unifier—and protector—of Greek and Persian civilizations. Knowing that his unsurpassed coins would be admired, collected, and selected for hoards of buried treasure, Mithradates also designed them for posterity. Indeed, Mithradates' portrait coins are considered by numismatic experts to be the most beautiful of all ancient coins. Mithradates also commissioned numerous seal rings bearing his portrait, which he presented to friends and allies. Such rings bestowed political authority on the wearer. They also carried propaganda messages, as we saw with Sulla's signet ring depicting his victory over Jugurtha, and the ring with Mithradates' likeness flaunted by Athenion in Athens.

In 87 BC, Mithradates' generals Archelaus and Metrophanes stormed Roman-controlled Delos. The destruction was devastating: the city was sacked and burned to the ground. Thousands of able-bodied slaves, suddenly freed from Roman chains, joined the Greek liberation army. Mithradates' generals killed virtually all the unarmed Italian merchants of Delos and sold their wives and children into slavery. The estimated number killed on Delos was 20,000, bringing the death toll of noncombatant Roman citizens in 88–87 BC to at least 100,000, perhaps more.

Metrophanes and Archelaus took possession of the island's valuables and seized the coffers inside the great Temple of Apollo. They stored most of the plunder on the little wooded island of Skiathos, Metrophanes' naval base and hospital. But what should be the fate of Apollo's sacred hoard, stored over the centuries in his temple? Traditionally, Apollo's treasure on Delos had been safeguarded by Athens. Mithradates decided that the treasure would be delivered to Aristion in Athens by a contingent of 2,000 handpicked soldiers. This grand gesture sealed Mithradates' promise to liberate all Hellas from Rome.[3]

Aristion used the treasure to finance the revolution begun by Athenion. The 2,000 Pontic soldiers sent by Archelaus probably completed the purge of Romans and pro-Romans remaining in Attica. They also trained the mainland Greeks, whose armies had long ago been disbanded by the Roman overseers. Then, in the words of one modern historian, "with absurd and sublime devotion" to its old ideals, Athens declared war on Rome and announced its alliance with the savior-king Mithradates the Great. Athens still enjoyed prestige throughout Greece and the non-

Roman world. The once great, now ghostly city-states of Sparta and Thebes set aside their ancient rivalry with Athens and joined the Pontic Alliance, anticipating the arrival of Mithradates' liberation army. General Archelaus's troops, mostly Gauls from Galatia, were welcomed with joy in the Peloponnese, Attica, and Boeotia. As they marched north, bands of eager but ill-trained and poorly armed citizen-soldiers from Sparta, Athens, and other Greek towns joined the liberated slave auxiliaries in Archelaus's ranks.[4]

Mithradates divided his forces into a three-pronged operation. One prong moved across Thrace to Macedonia, led by his favorite son Arcathius (who had proved himself in the battles against Aquillius and Nicomedes) and General Taxiles (named for an Indian prince who had welcomed Alexander the Great). They commanded about 100,000 barbarian foot soldiers (called the Bronze-shields) and 10,000 horsemen from Thrace, Sarmatia, Scythia, and Armenia. Once Arcathius and Tax-

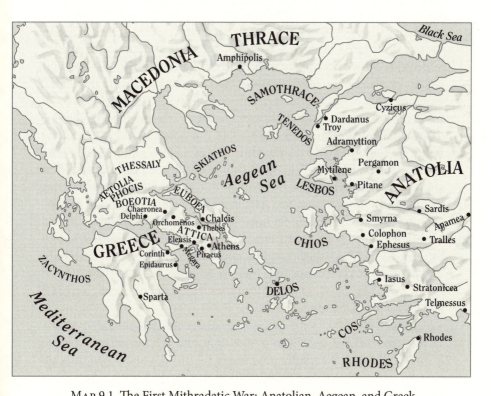

MAP 9.1. The First Mithradatic War: Anatolian, Aegean, and Greek campaigns. Map by Michele Angel.

iles took control of Amphipolis on the border, Macedonia came to Mithradates' side. This victory meant they could ship plentiful food supplies to Archelaus in Piraeus, Athens' port.[5]

Archelaus had secured southern and central Greece; now he and Aristion occupied Attica, the territory of Athens and Piraeus, making up the second prong. The third prong was led by Metrophanes, who took Euboea, establishing headquarters at Chalcis. His fleet was advancing up the coast of Thessaly. (Meanwhile Neoptolemus and Dromichaetes were sailing with more men from Anatolia to Chalcis, and Dorylaus stood ready with another highly trained army of 80,000 reinforcements in Pontus.) Mithradates' three armies were to converge on Macedonia. If all went according to plan, the small, isolated Roman garrison there would be pinned beneath the trident by the summer of 87 BC.

But the commander of the Roman outpost in Macedonia decided on a bold preemptive strategy to blunt Mithradates' three-pronged assault. He sent troops out to meet Arcathius's barbarian horde and ordered his legate Bruttius to engage Metrophanes at sea. Bruttius's small fleet was successful—Metrophanes had to watch helplessly as his sailors flailed in the waves, begging for mercy. Bruttius's men killed them one by one.

Bruttius chased Metrophanes back to Euboea, forcing him to leave his hospital and depot on Skiathos unprotected. Bruttius overran the island, grabbing up loot and capturing thousands of soldiers. The prisoners of war—many of them wounded or sick—might have hoped for humane treatment at the hands of the Romans. In the campaign for Rhodes, Admiral Damogoras had treated Mithradates' captives honorably. Even Mithradates had famously granted amnesty to Roman soldiers and their allies in earlier battles. But the Roman Bruttius meted out revenge for the Italian victims in Provincia Asia and Delos. He separated the prisoners into two groups: freeborn men and Roman slaves who had joined Mithradates. Bruttius's centurions announced that the free men would be released. But first, they methodically lopped off the prisoners' hands. The maimed soldiers were free, but would never lift a sword or shield again. And the runaway slaves? All were crucified, nailed to rough crosses and left to die on Skiathos.

Although elated with his success, Bruttius could not follow up with a direct attack on Euboea. Even with a thousand reinforcements drafted from Macedonia he was still outnumbered. Instead, he marched through Boeotia to try to stop the middle prong, led by Archelaus. The armies met at Chaeronea, the broad plain surrounded by rocky hills that controlled the route between northern and southern Greece. So many battles had been fought at Chaeronea that the plain was known as the "dancing ground of Ares," god of war. This was the same battleground where Alexander's father, Philip, had defeated the Greeks in 338 BC.

Bruttius and Archelaus clashed here for three days. As Alfred Duggan commented, Bruttius was actually holding his own until a "typically Roman piece of red tape compelled him to break off the campaign." A communiqué arrived from Sulla's young lieutenant, Lucius Lucullus, informing Bruttius that Sulla alone was commissioned by the Roman People to conduct the war on Mithradates. Bruttius was ordered to return to Macedonia. Bruttius obeyed. That allowed Archelaus to occupy Boeotia and set up winter quarters in Piraeus. Meanwhile Aristion's citizen army battened down in Athens. They felt secure inside the great walls and fortifications protecting the city and its port.[6]

Meanwhile in Pergamon

Mithradates must have been annoyed by the losses at Skiathos, but he could glory in his spectacular successes so far. He was popular, prosperous, victorious. The grand future foretold by the oracles and comets was coming true at last. He had wrested Asia from Rome's grip, and he ruled Bithynia, Cappadocia, Paphlagonia, and Anatolia. The Romans were driven out of Asia. His general Archelaus was master of the Aegean and mainland Greece. Mithradates' son Machares was viceroy of Pontus and Bosporus, including the Scythian lands beyond the Sea of Asov. His beloved son Arcathius, steamrolling south, overcame Bruttius's small garrison in Macedonia. Arcathius had subdued northern Greece and was already appointing satraps to govern what was to become his kingdom.

As ambassadors from rebel cities in Italy, North Africa, Egypt, Parthia, and Syria sang Mithradates' praises, the savior-king amassed more gold and dispensed riches, principalities, and satrapies to his friends. Cities allied with Mithradates issued grateful decrees, minted coins with his name and image, and dedicated portrait statues to him in their agoras. The king commissioned impressive statues of himself. Large silver and gilded images of the Mithradatic ancestors decorated the palace in Sinope, but those of Mithradates were even more grandiose. We know of at least two statues cast in solid gold, one life-sized, the other ten feet tall. Not only was gold impressively expensive; its color was sacred to fire, the Sun, and Mithra.[7]

In Pergamon, a splendid festival was planned to celebrate Mithradates' successes. In the Theater of Dionysus, where Aquillius's gruesome last supper had been served, the royal engineers put the finishing touches on an immense mechanized statue of Nike, the goddess of victory, suspended on cables behind curtains high above the royal box.

On the day of the celebration, King Mithradates and Queen Monime, dressed in lavish finery, nodded and beamed at the audience from their silk-canopied, cushioned thrones as choirs sang, officials orated, and actors representing various lands thanked the liberator-king for his benevolence. The pageant was to climax with the appearance of Winged Victory bearing a real crown in her outstretched hands. By means of pulleys and levers, the goddess would majestically descend to place this crown on Mithradates' brow and then magically rise up to the heavens again. If there were any witnesses of the awful collapse of the colossal *sambuca* at Rhodes in the audience, they must have collectively held their breath, trying to suppress premonitions of disaster.

Their fears were justified. Just as the stagehands were lowering the heavy statue in front of the royal box, the cables broke. Winged Victory crashed to the ground, the victor's crown dashed to pieces. Shocked silence, then pandemonium. Crowd and king shuddered in horror. The royals were hustled away from the scene of the terrible omen.

Mithradates, naturally, fell into a depression. But not for long. The king emerged from seclusion a few days later, summoning his seers, the Magi, his advisers, and spies. He pored over all the dispatches from the front, questioned everyone closely, demanded the freshest intelligence. He was certain that some disaster must have befallen one of his armies in Greece or Asia at the very moment that Victory had come crashing down in Pergamon. His inquiries revealed nothing but sunny reports from his command posts. But he did hear a scrap of ominous news. On that very day, Lucius Cornelius Sulla had set sail from Italy, bringing five Roman legions to Greece.[8]

SULLA

This report must have sent an icy sliver of anxiety into Mithradates' already troubled mind. Far from the action, he could not personally supervise his armies in Greece. But he had great confidence in his excellent generals. And after all, how could Sulla's mere thirty thousand troops prevail against Mithradates' myriads?

But Sulla's men were battle-hardened, disciplined professionals. These tough veterans would fight ferociously for Sulla—as long as they were

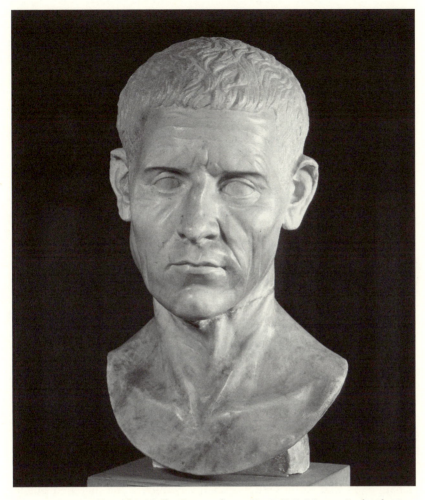

Fig. 9.2. Lucius Cornelius Sulla, Roman bust, 80–75 BC, Museo Archeologico, Venice. Scala/Art Resource, NY.

paid handsomely in plunder. What sort of man was their commander? The Roman biographer Plutarch paints a portrait of an arrogant, repellent character, with a hypnotically commanding presence and fathomless hunger for power. From an obscure patrician family without wealth, Sulla (b. 138 BC) spent his youth carousing in the company of theatrical lowlifes. A rich courtesan financed his political career. At age fifty, Sulla retained his louche habits, but cultivated a love of art and literature and won a reputation as a hard-driving, brave military leader. Shrewd and calculating, Sulla could also be rash and unpredictable. As Sulla and many other leaders well understood, capricious behavior made one seem god-like, and it kept friends and foes off balance. Alternating clemency with sudden brutality was a tried-and-true power trip, practiced by autocrats of all eras, including Mithradates.

Sulla was distinguished by red-blond hair, pale gray eyes, and very fair skin. According to Plutarch, the name Sulla ("Pimples") was an insulting reference to his unfortunate complexion. Perhaps because of some der-matological affliction, his skin was spotty with coarse, bright red patches. Jesters joked that Sulla's face resembled a purplish-red mulberry mash sprinkled with white flour; today the cruel expression might be "pizza-face." Yet Sulla's imperious personality and his piercing gray eyes gave him a fearsome expression.

Years before, when Sulla had bested Tigranes' army in Cappadocia, to reinstate Ariobarzanes, a Babylonian seer had cast Sulla's fortune. Star-ing into the Roman's cold, pinpoint pupils, taking account of his haughty bearing, his striking red hair and odd skin markings, the holy man pre-dicted that Sulla was bound to rise to great power. In his own memoirs (lost, but quoted by Plutarch and others), Sulla proudly recounted how a chasm had opened up in the earth, belching forth huge gouts of flames to the sky. Interpreting this omen, the soothsayers predicted that "a brave man of rare valor and surpassing appearance would take charge of Rome." Sulla identified himself as that man, because of his "golden hair and his great and noble deeds."

As soon as Sulla's ships set sail across the Adriatic Sea, his political rival Cinna broke his promise of peace. Cinna issued a People's Decree nullify-ing Sulla's command and proclaiming Sulla Public Enemy of Rome. Thus it happened that Rome's Public Enemy Number One marched out to battle Rome's Most Dangerous Enemy.[9]

Cut loose from Rome, Sulla now had to provision his five legions in a hostile land, with no supply lines or money from Italy. The year's delay since the massacre meant that instead of sailing directly to Anatolia to crush Mithradates and retake the Province of Asia, Sulla had to defeat the vast and victorious Pontic army occupying Greece. Upon landing in Greece, Sulla demanded money, reinforcements, horses, mules, and food from Aetolia, Thessaly, and Boeotia. At Sulla's approach, the city of Thebes got cold feet about its alliance with Mithradates and promised to supply iron, catapults, and weapons to the Romans. Dispatching half of his legions to attack Aristion in Athens, Sulla marched to Piraeus. He could have simply laid siege and waited for starvation and thirst to wear down Piraeus and Athens. But he was too worried about the events out of his control in Rome, impatient to return to Italy as supreme war hero.

THE BATTLE FOR PIRAEUS

Like the great walls surrounding Athens, Piraeus's walls were constructed of limestone blocks with upper courses of brick and wood. Sulla immediately sent his men to try to scale the high walls, but Archelaus's defenders inflicted heavy casualties. Sulla's legions dragged themselves to safety, taking over the nearby towns of Eleusis and Megara.

As hardware and materiel began to arrive from Thebes, Sulla scoured the countryside for mules. He needed at least ten thousand draft animals to operate his huge siege engines and towers. To build those machines, he ordered his men to hack down all the beautiful olive trees in the vicinity, ancient groves sacred to Athena. A bolt of lightning killed one of Sulla's soldiers cutting trees—but his soothsayers insisted it was a good omen because the man had fallen with his head pointing toward Piraeus. Next, Sulla's soldiers set about demolishing Piraeus's Long Walls connecting the harbor to Athens. They piled stones, timber, and dirt into a great mound for his catapults and siege machines.[10]

Inside Piraeus, two men conspired to betray Archelaus and help Sulla. Ironically, despite Mithradates' well-publicized liberation of the enslaved, these plotters were Athenian slaves. Were they, as Plutarch speculated, "simply looking out for their own safety in the emergency"? Perhaps the men suffered under cruel masters. At any rate, the pair secretly inscribed messages about Archelaus's plans onto lead sling balls and hurled them to land harmlessly near the Roman workers. After many volleys of these oddly aimed balls, Sulla noticed and picked one up. It read: "Tomorrow Archelaus's soldiers will sally out to attack your workers, while his cavalry attacks both flanks of your army." Thus warned, Sulla ambushed and killed Archelaus's assault force.

As Sulla's mound rose, Archelaus erected numerous catapult towers on Piraeus's ramparts, and sent for Dromichaetes' reinforcements (Neoptolemus's army remained in Chalcis). In this tense period before the battle, Archelaus armed all his oarsmen and distributed bowmen and slingers to defend his fire-archers and catapults on the walls. Other men massed inside the gates with torches, ready to dash out and burn the enemy's machines.

Appian and Plutarch recount how the first battle for Piraeus raged for many days. Archelaus led an all-out attack that sent the Roman legions reeling. Sulla's lieutenant, Murena, desperately screaming out orders, managed to drive the Romans forward, although the odds were against them. But just then, another Roman legion returned from a wood-gathering detail. Dropping the logs, these legionnaires barreled into the battle. The Romans managed to kill more than two thousand of Archelaus's men and forced the rest back inside the walls. Archelaus, hoarse and possessed, urged his men to keep fighting. Appian reports that Mithradates' valiant commander stood his ground so long—even after the city gates slammed shut behind him—that he barely escaped. At the last moment, he was hoisted over the wall by ropes.

Archelaus could inform his king in Pergamon that Piraeus stood fast against Sulla. Up in Athens, however, starvation loomed. Piraeus had abundant grain supplies, because Sulla could not stop ships in the fortified harbor. Archelaus attempted to deliver wheat to Athens under cover of night. But the two informers in Piraeus alerted Sulla by lobbing more messages on lead balls. Sulla ambushed several supply trains. Just as Archelaus realized that there were traitors in his city, he received miserable news from Neoptolemus in Chalcis. One of Sulla's officers had attacked there, killing fifteen hundred soldiers and capturing twice as many prisoners.

Work on Sulla's siege mound continued outside Piraeus. All winter, Archelaus kept up constant pressure, slamming the Roman workers with catapult boulders, lead balls, stones, javelins, and fire arrows. Unseen, Archelaus's sappers secretly tunneled under the mound, carrying away tubs of earth. Suddenly the mound collapsed, killing Romans and toppling war machines. The Romans rebuilt the mound and dug a counter-tunnel. The tunnelers met underground. Swords and spears clashed in the dark passage; above, Sulla pounded Piraeus's walls with battering rams until a section fell away. He directed volleys of fire bolts at Archelaus's catapult towers.

But Piraeus's towers were oddly impervious to fire. Archelaus knew a secret method. He had coated his walls and towers with alum, an opaque crystal formed by the vapors of volcanoes, imported from Smyrna, Syria, and Egypt. Alum was used in tanning, dyeing, and medicine; mixed with water it hardened plaster and strengthened rope. Painted on wood it is an effective fire retardant. Sulla's men, unfamiliar with alum, were sty-mied. Finally, the Romans lit an enormous bonfire of pine logs under the wooden beams of the damaged wall. Copying a tactic invented by the Spartans in the Peloponnesian War, Sulla tossed sulphur and pine resin onto the flames, which burst into a raging conflagration, spewing toxic gases. The burning wall crashed down, killing many defenders.[11]

Pressing his advantage, Sulla sent men to scale the walls in the middle of the night. They snuffed the sleeping guards, but Archelaus's soldiers hurled the attackers over the wall and ran out to set fire to Sulla's towers. A full-scale battle raged in the dark, lit by fires and flaming missiles. A great many defenders of Piraeus died, killed by fire from Sulla's siege towers, each of which could catapult twenty heavy lead balls and bolts at once, at a range of four hundred yards. In 2004, an exceptional archaeo-logical discovery in Greece—the skeleton of a soldier killed instantly by a catapult bolt—graphically illustrates the kind of massive damage that was inflicted by Sulla's machines.[12]

The demoralized and jittery troops on the walls "could only offer fee-ble resistance to Sulla's relentless assault." Sensing weakness, Sulla pushed harder, continually sending in fresh divisions and cheering them on: *This is our main chance!* But Archelaus met Sulla's challenge, bringing up fresh troops to replace the discouraged ones, and imploring his men to fight on. Casualties were extremely high on both sides. Appian's sources agreed that it was again Mithradates' general Archelaus who "surpassed all oth-ers in endurance and valor." Relief flooded his men when they heard Sulla sound the retreat. They labored several nights to repair their walls. Sulla tried one last attack, with his entire army. But the Romans fell back under a heavy rain of missiles from the restored walls.[13]

Archelaus honored his men with tokens for their bravery. A remark-able discovery of one of these tokens brings the battle for Piraeus alive for us more than two thousand years later—and it indicates the ethnic diversity of Mithradates' liberation army in Greece. The silver bracelet, presented to a soldier in 86 BC, is inscribed with the words "In Piraeus, the General Archelaus gives this to Apollonius . . . a Syrian, as a reward for his courage."[14]

Forced to abandon any idea of taking Piraeus by assault, Sulla had to settle in for a very long siege. But he still had no way to blockade the harbor and deny Archelaus food and reinforcements arriving by sea. Mithradates' strategy of occupying Euboea and Macedonia and domi-nating the Aegean Sea was paying off.

SHIPS AND TREASURE

Seething with hatred for the Greeks, anxious to win this damnable war and return to Rome, Sulla knew he needed a lot of money and a navy to destroy Mithradates' forces in Greece. But as Rome's Public Outlaw, he could expect nothing from the Senate. Sulla got a message through to Rhodes demanding ships, but to no avail. Rhodes had the ships, but pointed out that Mithradates' navy and pirate fleets controlled the entire Aegean. So Sulla sent his aide Lucullus on a daring secret mission. Sail to Rhodes and Alexandria to procure ships and sailors. Then somehow escort these fleets, evading Mithradates' navy, back to Sulla.

Lucullus embarked at night on a swift vessel. Taking evasive action, changing ships frequently, Lucullus managed to slip past Mithradates' blockade and roving pirates. He spent the winter in Rhodes, and in early 85 BC he arrived in Alexandria. But his success so far was unknown to Sulla.

Sulla, in the meantime, solved his financial problem. He seized the sacred treasures of Greece, plundering the temples of Zeus at Olympia and Asclepius in Epidaurus. Selecting the most beautiful, precious art objects for himself, he melted down massive amounts of silver to pay his men and buy supplies.

Delphi was the most ancient and richest treasury of antiquity, its integrity traditionally guarded by distinguished citizens from around the Greek world. Wealthy monarchs had dedicated magnificent riches and artworks to Apollo's Delphic Oracle over the centuries. In the sixth century BC, for example, King Croesus of Lydia had donated 117 enormous ingots of gold, many solid gold statues including a lion weighing more than five hundred pounds, immense silver urns and golden bowls, and other fabulous artifacts, jewels, and weaponry. The guardians at Delphi were horrified to receive Sulla's blunt command: Apollo's treasures were to be transferred to him for "safekeeping." If he found it necessary to melt down the god's property, Sulla assured them the "loan" would be repaid.

Sulla sent a Greek, Caphis, to take possession, with orders to record the weight of each valuable object. But once inside the temple, Caphis burst out crying. He could not bring himself to touch Apollo's treasure, which had escaped even Xerxes' Persian looters in 480 BC and marauding Gauls two centuries later. He sent a desperate message to Sulla, swearing that the god could be heard playing his lyre in the inner sanctum.

Sulla's reply: "Don't you understand? The music signals Apollo's approval! Bring me the treasure immediately."

Delphi's treasures were packed onto mules. Only one item remained, one of the Royal Gifts of King Croesus described by the historian Herodotus: a huge, repoussé silver jar with a capacity of five thousand gallons. The tearful guardians were forced to cut the beautiful jar into pieces to be loaded on the mules. Plutarch, who later served as a priest at Apollo's Delphic Oracle, felt their anguish. In the past, he exclaimed, more honorable, disciplined Roman commanders had not only spared Greece's sanctuaries; they had bestowed important gifts to the gods themselves. "But those generals were lawful, self-restrained, incorruptible Romans from olden days," wrote Plutarch, nothing like the grasping and brutal Sulla "who paved the way for horrors" in Greece and Italy.

From the treasures of Delphi, Sulla again picked out choice artifacts for himself. One of the dedications became his personal amulet, an exquisite little golden figure of the god Apollo. From that day on, says Plutarch, Sulla always wore this image around his neck. Before battles, it was his habit to ostentatiously pull out the little statuette and kiss it, admonishing the god to bring a speedy victory.[15]

The Fall of Athens

While Lucullus negotiated for ships in Egypt, Sulla set up camp outside Athens. From the Dipylon Gate, the Athenians watched aghast as Roman soldiers hacked down the venerable groves of Plato's Academy and Aristotle's Lyceum. The logs were hammered into enormous siege engines on the very spot where an unbroken line of philosophers had taught since Socrates. Sulla took personal possession of the precious library of works by Aristotle and Theophrastus, which had been rescued from a moldy cellar in Scepsis (near Troy) and stored in Athens. A gifted Athenian student named Lenaeus may have been taken as Sulla's slave at this time—many years later he would find himself translating Mithradates' toxicological notes into Latin.[16]

The citizens of Athens, delirious with starvation, defiantly took to the ramparts, deriding the Romans, mocking Sulla's ugly mulberry face, and belting out obscene songs about his wife. Their leader, the philosopher Aristion, put on his bronze helmet and breastplate and danced about on the walls with them, shouting out insults. Against Aristion's orders, a party of councilmen ventured out to beg Sulla for mercy. They began by reminding the Roman warlord of Athens' heroic ancient history, from the mythic Theseus to the great panhellenic victory in the Persian Wars. Sulla interrupted, "Stop rambling!" He sent them away: "I'm not here for a history lesson. Rome sent me to subdue you Athenian rebels!"

Roman intelligence, probably wrung from famished Greeks attempting to forage herbs outside the walls, had informed Sulla that the Athenians were starving. All the sheep, goats, cattle, rabbits, chickens, tortoises, and other animals had disappeared long ago. There was no oil; even Athena's sacred lamp was extinguished in the Parthenon. A shower of black ashes the year before had been a very bad omen, and still no rain fell to fill the cisterns. There was no wheat or barley, no fruit or olives. The people devoured weeds that grew on the Acropolis. Sulla's sources revealed that the trapped citizens were boiling down cow hides and leather sandals in cauldrons, "licking up whatever sustenance they could." There were even rumors of cannibalism.

With wolfish pleasure, Sulla directed his men to strangle the city by digging a deep trench around the walls. Plutarch wondered, Why was Sulla "possessed by such a dreadful and inexorable passion to punish Athens?" Was Sulla so resentful of Athens' former glory? Was he "provoked by the scurrilous abuse showered on him and his wife by Aristion and the Athenians on the walls?" Appian, writing centuries later, believed that Sulla's wrath stemmed from Greece's brazen loyalty to Mithradates and the "Athenians' violent animosity toward himself." Every day the Athenians held out was a day wasted, while Sulla's enemies grew strong in Rome and Mithradates gloated in Pergamon.[17]

Plutarch's description of Sulla's destruction of Athens is vivid. A native of Chaeronea, Plutarch (b. AD 46) interviewed some elderly Athenians whose grandparents had survived Sulla's siege; his other details came from Sulla's own journals and soldiers serving with him. Appian and Pausanias add further information. Sulla commanded his army to raze Athens' walls. He had learned that the weakest area, between the Agora and the Kerameikos cemetery, was not well guarded. Evidence of Sulla's attack is still visible today; several of his stone catapult balls can be seen in the ruins of the Kerameikos cemetery.

The citizen-soldiers defending the walls were courageous, fully committed to Mithradates and freedom, but they were no match for five Roman legions. The starving people wandering or dying inside were too frail to fight. At midnight, Sulla himself led the charge. Screaming war cries, the Roman soldiers vaulted over the walls and rammed through the gates. They ran through the dark streets swords drawn, lusting to

FIG. 9.3. Catapult balls, from Sulla's siege of Athens, still visible in the Kerameikos cemetery outside the Dipylon Gate. Deutsches Archaologisches Institut, photograph, Hedwig Brueckner.

carry out their leader's explicit orders to pillage, rape, and massacre. No one, not even women and children, was to be spared. One exception was slaves—they counted as loot, at least as profitable as the hidden Athenian valuables the Romans dragged up from the wells.

"A great and pitiless slaughter" swept through Athens, gem of ancient Greek civilization. The city of Athens, which had survived burning by Xerxes nearly five hundred years earlier, the Peloponnesian War, and the Macedonian conquest, was utterly destroyed. Amid terrifying trumpet blasts and bloodcurdling cries, many of the hopeless mustered their last wisp of energy to rush onto the enemy swords. Others, "expecting no humanity from Sulla," killed their families and themselves. As the Roman soldiers went about their bloody business, they found evidence of human flesh prepared as food in the houses. "In this way," laments Appian, "did Athens have her fill of horrors." Plutarch's sources described blood coursing from the Agora to the Kerameikos cemetery. The only way to gauge how many died that night was to measure how much ground was soaked in blood, wrote Plutarch.

FIG. 9.4. Athens pillaged by Sulla's invading Romans, by Leutemann. Media Storehouse.

When the attack came, Aristion and company "made their feeble way up to the Acropolis," the citadel where the last Athenians would make their last stand. On the way, Aristion stopped to set fire to the timbers of Pericles' famous concert hall, the Odeon, to deny Sulla wood for storming the sacred hill.[18]

The next day, Sulla was busy auctioning off captive slaves, while his officers laid siege to Athens' last garrison on the Acropolis. Thirst compelled Aristion and his companions to surrender some days later. Sulla seized the Acropolis treasure, six hundred pounds of silver and forty pounds of gold. He gave a curt speech praising the Athens of antiquity, boasting that he had spared the city from burning, and pardoned some citizens who had survived on the Acropolis. Then, as the skies opened up and poured down rain, too late to save the holdouts, Sulla executed Aristion, the last elected leader of democratic Athens.

Nearly three centuries later, the Greek historian Pausanias decried the merciless destruction inflicted in 86 BC on Athens by Sulla, whose "cruelty surpassed even what you might expect from a Roman." Athens did not begin to flourish again until two hundred years later.[19]

Unable to wait any longer for besieged Piraeus to surrender, Sulla now brought all his troops, catapults, battering rams, and siege towers to strike

Archelaus with savage force. Sulla led the attack himself, riding his large white warhorse among the troops, shouting encouragement, promising lavish rewards. His men, "spurred to their work by love of glory and pride in the idea that it would be a splendid thing to conquer such impressive walls as Pericles' fort at Piraeus, pressed on like madmen."

The Romans' frenzied surge astounded Archelaus. A wise tactician, and eager to fight another day, he ordered his men to abandon the walls and run for their ships in the fortified harbor. Behind them, the enraged Sulla ravaged the city of Piraeus, setting fire to Philo's magnificent Arsenal, the navy yard, and all the other buildings admired since antiquity. Victory was finally his, yet Sulla had nothing to show for it but loot, ashes, and ruins. He had no ships to pursue Archelaus. Burning with frustration, Sulla watched as Mithradates' intrepid general escaped with his army of ten thousand.[20]

CHAERONEA

When Archelaus joined Mithradates' other forces in Thessaly, he learned tragic news from Arcathius's cocommander Taxiles, news that would deal a grievous blow to Mithradates in Pergamon. The king's beloved son Arcathius had fallen ill in Macedonia and died near Mount Tisaion, Thessaly. Despite his untimely death, I think Arcathius was the happiest of Mithradates' many sons. His father placed absolute confidence in him. He died a victorious war hero who knew nothing but pride and love from Mithradates—unlike his brothers, who would end up enmeshed in betrayal and suspicion.

The combined Mithradatic army was now 120,000 strong, with 90 scythed chariots. Each nationality in this polyglot mass had its own general, with Archelaus as supreme commander. This horde marched south as Sulla advanced north. In late summer of 86 BC, the two armies converged in Phocis. Archelaus led out his multitudes again and again, trying to provoke a battle. But Sulla held back. According to Appian, Sulla's troops numbered only about 30,000 or 40,000.

As Archelaus anticipated—and Sulla understood—the sight of Mithradates' milling throngs of warriors from so many unfamiliar lands presented a fearsome spectacle for the Roman soldiers. The sheer opulence of the barbarians' equipment awed the Romans. "Huddled in their trenches," the soldiers eyed the fine swords inlaid with precious gems, flashing armor "embellished with silver and gold, the rich colors of the Median and Scythian corselets and mail, all intermingled with gleaming bronze and glinting steel."[21]

The clamor of dozens of different languages filled the air. Mithradates had gathered recruits from a vast area: joining the former Roman slaves, Greeks, and pirates were Thracians, Macedonians, Bastarnae, Sarmatians, Scythians, Taurians, Maeotians; from the Caucasus came Colchians, Heniochoi, Albanoi, Iberi; there were Pontians, Bithynians, Phrygians, Paphlagonians, Cappadocians, Chaldeans, Cilicians, Galatians, Turret-Folk, Chalybians, Tibarnae, Armenians, Medes, and Syrians. Some of the Eastern groups brought camels, presenting the Romans and their horses with strange sights and stranger smells. Many of the barbarians wore their hair long and adorned themselves with golden, copper, and silver earrings, wristlets, and necklaces. Warriors from Thrace, Sarmatia, Scythia, Trapezus, and Colchis proudly sported extensive tattoos as signs of manhood and battle prowess—a confusing concept for the Romans, who inflicted tattoos to brand slaves and punish runaway soldiers. Swaggering about and shouting out insults and boasts, the barbarian multitude intimidated the Roman soldiers—even though no one could understand their speech.[22]

Indeed, so many language and culture differences posed problems for Mithradates' generals. The unruly barbarians often ignored the chain of command and even raided towns and villages in Boeotia while they waited for the battle to commence.

Sulla hunkered down and set onerous tasks to distract his nervous soldiers: digging ditches and taking over forts in the area. He reasoned that they would soon tire of the drudgery and be eager to fight. Meanwhile he sent out spies, communicating with them secretly. One of Sulla's methods was to inflate a pig bladder like a balloon and dry it out. A message was written on the inflated bladder, dried out, and stuffed into an oil jar. Oil carefully poured into the neck of the bladder caused it fill and adhere to the inside of the jar. The recipient broke open the jar and replied by the same method.[23]

Sulla's spies informed him that Archelaus's army had moved southeast and camped in the rocky hills above Chaeronea. It seemed a clever choice—defensible high ground with a good view of the plain below. Obviously Archelaus did not expect to fight here. Two pro-Roman Greeks from Chaeronea, Anaxidamos and Homoloichos, approached Sulla with a plan. They knew a hidden path high above Archelaus's encampment. They proposed to sneak up this trail and rain down stones on the enemy tents, forcing the army out onto the plain in disorder. Sulla agreed. While the raiders set off, Sulla moved to occupy a broad meadow with an advantageous slope facing the cramped enemy encampment. If he could force Archelaus to muster his army in haste on uneven ground, they would be hedged in by boulders and outcrops, unable to maneuver or retreat.

The sneak attack worked! Suddenly boulders crashed down on the unsuspecting barbarians. Crowded together, they stumbled in confusion down the steep cliffs, some falling on their own spears. The attackers leaped down and finished off at least three thousand men. The survivors rushed down to the lower main camp, causing a domino effect of terror and chaos. This was Sulla's chance—he immediately charged Archelaus's snarled army.

Archelaus's advantage of higher numbers was lost. There was a cacophony of shouted commands in many languages, as Archelaus sent out cavalry to meet Sulla's attack. But his horsemen were driven back onto the rocks. Desperate now, Archelaus launched sixty scythed chariots to rip through Sulla's legions. The goal was to replay the shock charge that had routed Nicomedes in 89 BC. But the situation was far from ideal. War chariots require a very long start on smooth ground, a target in disarray, *and* the element of surprise. The chariots failed to get up enough speed in the confined, rocky space and everyone saw them coming. Plutarch says the Romans burst out in guffaws and simply stepped aside, mimicking the evasion used by Alexander's army in 331 BC. Scythes whirling impotently in the empty air, the chariots passed through the openings. All the chariot drivers were cut down by the javelins of Sulla's rear guard. Applauding uproariously, the Romans shouted for more chariots, as if they were at the races in the circus at Rome.

As Sulla's forces steadily advanced, Archelaus organized his remaining men in the craggy cliffs. The barbarians resolutely locked their shields together and held their spears out before them. As the Romans marched forward, they were astonished to see that Archelaus's front lines consisted of fifteen thousand Roman slaves! These men, freed by Mithradates' proclamations since 88 BC, were probably identified by their slave tattoos and a special standard. Jeering in rage, the Roman soldiers dropped their javelins and drew their short swords, ready to slash through the wall of lowly slaves to get to the "real" soldiers. But Plutarch reported that the dense ranks of former slaves, boiling with hatred of everything Roman, demonstrated tremendous courage and grace under pressure.

They held steadfast for a very long time. At last they fell back under the storm of fire bolts and javelins unleashed by Sulla's rear guard.

Now Archelaus himself led a cavalry charge. It was a wild success, cutting the Roman formation in half. Slashing at the surrounded Romans, inspired by their commander at their side, the barbarians fought "at the highest pitch of valor." Mithradates' general Taxiles led his Bronze-shield barbarians into the fray. In the din of men, horses, and weapons echoing off the hillsides, Sulla plunged into the maelstrom, yelling out directions. His cavalry struck with an impetuous charge, joined by Murena's cohorts.

Both wings of Archelaus's army gave way. In the constricted space, blinded by swirling dust and fear, many of his men ran headlong into the Roman lines; others scattered into the hills. Archelaus desperately tried to rally, but there was no room to regroup. The cheering Romans crushed the fleeing troops against the rocks. Hacking and stabbing, Sulla's men demolished the enemy. Mithradates' Greek liberation army was shredded. The Romans took thousands of prisoners, and only 10,000 men of the original 120,000 escaped. The survivors straggled to Archelaus's ships and retired to Chalcis, their haven in Euboea.

Few believed Sulla's preposterous claim to have lost fewer than twenty men at Chaeronea. But he still commanded a sizable body of troops. His men piled up a mountain of barbarian weapons, scythed war chariots, and spoils. After selecting the best things for his Triumph in Rome, Sulla "burned the heaps of spoils as a sacrifice to the gods of war." He planned his victory festival in Thebes—but to punish the city for its earlier support of Mithradates, he seized half its territory and dedicated it to the gods. With this cynical act, Sulla claimed to have paid back the treasures he had "borrowed" from the gods at Delphi, Epidaurus, and Olympia.[24]

Sulla erected two victory monuments at Chaeronea, one of the greatest battles in ancient history. To celebrate the two decisive moments in the battle, Sulla's monument followed the archaic Greek style of a battle trophy (Greek *tropaion*, from *trophe*, "turning point"), a branching tree festooned with the armor, shields, and weapons of the vanquished. The exotic arms and armor of Mithradates' colorful barbarian warriors, carved in marble, made an especially striking display.

Plutarch, who lived his whole life overlooking the "dancing ground of Ares," saw the Roman victory monuments himself (and they were still standing in the time of Pausanias, in AD 180). Sulla placed his first trophy on the precipice where the rolling stones had routed the barbarians. The base was inscribed with the names of Mars, Zeus, and Aphrodite,

Fig. 9.5. Sulla's marble victory monuments at Chaeronea and Orchomenus took the form of a typical Roman trophy, a tree draped with barbarian armor and weapons, in this case of the Dacians. Cast of Trajan's Column, Victoria and Albert Museum, London.

and those of the two Chaeroneans who masterminded that exploit. The other monument stood on the battlefield by the brook where Archelaus's troops first gave way.

Sulla's first monument was discovered in 1990, by archaeologist John

Camp and students of the American School of Classical Studies in Athens. Their discovery allowed modern historians to pinpoint for the first time the precise location of the ambush with stones. The Greek inscription matches Plutarch's account. Just below the monument, Camp found a crude rubble wall, the remains of the barbarians' crushed encampment, still known in Plutarch's day as "Archelaus."[25]

Sulla featured his two trophies on coins issued in Greece (and later in Rome). After his triumph at Chaeronea, Sulla began to refer to himself as Felix ("Lucky") and bragged in his memoirs that Greek oracles predicted another great victory soon in the same neighborhood. But Mithradates' wily general Archelaus was still free, with a substantial army and navy. Sulla, still lacking a fleet, was helpless to pursue him. Archelaus sailed here and there among the Greek islands—venturing as far west as Zacynthos across from Italy—requisitioning and raiding more supplies and money at will. Appian remarked that Archelaus and his men returned to their headquarters in Chalcis "more like pirates than soldiers."[26]

Orchomenus

Meanwhile, bad news from Rome overshadowed Sulla's battlefield victory. Under Cinna and Marius, there was a mass slaughter of Sulla's supporters in 86 BC. Cinna's newly elected coconsul, Flaccus, was officially named as Sulla's replacement in the war against Mithradates. Flaccus, inexperienced and unpopular with his troops, was accompanied by a young officer named Fimbria. They were hurrying to Greece with two legions to take over Sulla's command—and they had orders to make war on Sulla if he resisted. Compelled to turn his back on Mithradates, Sulla had to prepare to fight his Roman rivals. The fortunes of Sulla the "Lucky" were seesawing wildly. As he marched west to meet Flaccus and Fimbria, Sulla received equally alarming news from the Greek front he'd just left behind. Somehow, Mithradates' forces had regained Boeotia.

In Pergamon, by all ancient reports, Mithradates was appalled to hear the bad tidings from Chaeronea. The disaster took him by surprise and struck fear into the heart of a father already grieving over the death of his son Arcathius. Some in his court suggested that only treachery could account for such lopsided losses. But Mithradates reacted quickly and forcefully. For the first time, he collected taxes in Anatolia. Gathering another enormous army from all his subject lands, he sent his most trustworthy friend from Pontus, Dorylaus, to the rescue.

Dorylaus sailed to Chalcis with a large fleet and 80,000 fresh, highly trained, disciplined soldiers, eager to take back Greece and get even with Sulla for the humiliating losses at Chaeronea. Behind Sulla's back, Dorylaus and Archelaus, with a combined army of about 90,000 soldiers, secured Boeotia. The two generals decided to camp at Orchomenus, east of Chaeronea. For an army like theirs, with a superior cavalry of 10,000 horsemen, the sweeping, treeless plain along the River Melas was the best battleground in Boeotia. But they made notes to avoid the reedy swamps at the margins of the plain.[27]

Sulla was forced to turn away from Flaccus and Fimbria and rush back to Orchomenus. Observing the landscape's advantages and disadvantages, Sulla immediately dug wide trenches that would funnel the enemy into the treacherous marshes. But Archelaus and Dorylaus responded with a bold cavalry charge that sent the edgy Romans into flight. Sulla rode back and forth in the mad dash, but his soldiers were terrified of Mithradates' fearsome nomad horsemen. Finally, Sulla leaped off his horse, grabbed up a standard, and pushed past his soldiers, bellowing: "Romans, I'll win an honorable death here without you! When they ask where you betrayed your commander, you'll have to tell them about Orchomenus!"

His words spurred his men to surge back. In the ferocious fight, both sides struggled bravely. Archelaus's son Diogenes, a cavalryman, was cut down. The barbarian archers were so hard-pressed by the Romans at close quarters that they couldn't draw their bows. Grabbing handfuls of arrows, they wielded them like swords to hold off the Roman soldiers. But Archelaus and Dorylaus passed a dismal night collecting their dead. Incredibly, they had lost fifteen thousand men.

Tasting blood, Sulla fell upon the decimated enemy camp the next morning, exhorting his men to finish the job once and for all. He had to make certain that Archelaus could not escape yet again and raise yet another army. Archelaus roused his men and the terrible last battle began. His defenders leaped down from a wooden parapet and stood with their swords drawn against a cohort of Romans, advancing behind their shields. For an excruciatingly long moment no one moved.

The standoff seemed to last forever. Suddenly the spell was broken—a daring Roman soldier dashed out and chopped down the man in front of him. Then all hell broke loose. "There was a great rush and shouting on each side, followed by many valiant deeds," wrote Appian. Mithradates' second grand army was driven into the marshes that Archelaus strove to avoid. Many barbarians fell into deep pools and drowned. Others perished as they pleaded for mercy in their strange tongues, mocked by their slayers. The corpses of Mithradates' warriors choked the stagnant ponds where the Boeotians used to gather reeds for their famous flutes. Their commander, Archelaus, was presumed dead.

Two hundred years after the battle, Plutarch and his fellow Chaeroneans often dragged up from the mud bows and arrows, embossed helmets, bronze shields, fragments of fine armor, and decorated spears and swords, all of barbarian manufacture. Even today, metal remnants emerge from the soggy ground, the only memorial to Mithradates' Greek liberation warriors from distant lands.

Sulla's tactical skills and amazing personal power over his troops were factors in the spectacular upsets in Boeotia; his battle-hardened legions' loyalty and courage constituted another. Mithradates' infantry was just as valiant and determined, but they suffered from significant disadvantages. The ancient historian Memnon reported that the barbarians did not understand how to manage supply lines; Sulla ambushed them when they carelessly foraged for food. Each barbarian group had its own dialect and distinctive style of fighting. Managing such diverse cultures, groups that had never fought together before, presented problems of coordination and discipline. Dorylaus's units trained in old-fashioned Greek hoplite combat proved cumbersome and slow in the face of the efficient, fast, and flexible new Roman formations, part of Marius's military legacy.

Sulla erected another monument to mark this victory at Orchomenus, won against daunting odds. He also minted coins depicting his three victory monuments. And on his meaty, freckled fingers, the signet ring commemorating Sulla's triumph over Jugurtha was joined by another large agate ring carved with a design depicting his three trophies.[28]

In 2004, a Greek farmer plowing his cotton field at Orchomenus uncovered Sulla's victory monument of 86 BC. The farmer scooped up the marble column and broken pieces with a bulldozer and deposited them anonymously at the local archaeological institute. Eventually the farmer was located, and Greek archaeologist Eleni Koundouri unearthed the rest of the trophy. This monument from another of the most spectacular battles in Greek history was more extravagant and much more complete than the one found at Chaeronea in 1990. Standing twenty-three feet high, it also took the form of a branching tree draped with the defeated enemy's arms and armor. The marble fragments represent a pair of greaves, a breastplate, spears, and other weapons and equipment, including a chariot wheel to commemorate Mithradates' scythed chariots.

The inscription celebrates Sulla's victory over King Mithradates and his allies, and thanks Aphrodite for the victory.[29]

After his victory, Sulla spitefully ordered his men to ravage Boeotia, cutting down olive groves and burning vineyards and crops. He did this to take further revenge on the Greek population for supporting Mithradates. But the war was far from over. Sulla still had no idea whether Lucullus had succeeded on his dangerous mission to get a fleet. He also needed to monitor Flaccus and Fimbria's two legions, coming to take over his command. Sulla's plan was to set up winter quarters in northern Greece and spend the season building his own ships.

As Sulla had retired exhausted but exultant from the battlefield at Orchomenus, his greatest victory, he was unaware of furtive movement at the edge of the swamp still red with blood of the defeated army. In the waning light of dusk, a shadowy form emerged from the muddy stand of reeds. It was Archelaus. The crafty general had survived the slaughter, hiding for two days in the marshes. Now he headed for the seashore, found a small boat, and rowed alone to Chalcis, his headquarters. Archelaus summoned all the detachments of Mithradates' army stationed around the Aegean and Anatolia.[30]

Killers' Kiss

HOW LONG could Mithradates' "honeymoon of absolute power and freedom" last? That question was answered by the gods of war in 86/85 BC. The heartbreaking loss of Mithradates' favorite son Arcathius was followed by inexplicable losses in Greece. How on earth could Sulla's five legions have destroyed so many multitudes?

Mithradates' friends encouraged the king to suspect treachery. Dorylaus had voiced his own suspicions after the defeats in Greece. Traitors were a genuine threat—betrayals were involved in the Greek losses, and there were others who conspired with the Romans. Mithradates feared that his Anatolian allies would withdraw their support, perhaps abet his enemies—even plot assassination. Before disaffection could spread throughout his realm, he sent out agents to arrest turncoats. There was a new urgency for the royal toxicologists to perfect an antidote to all forms of poison.[1]

Mithradates still held the strategic island of Euboea, and he trusted his generals in the Aegean. But Archelaus's army contained many Galatian soldiers. Had some of them aided Sulla? Galatians had a reputation for treachery. If Sulla advanced to Anatolia, Mithradates felt certain that Galatia would aid him. Something had to be done.

GALATIA

Mithradates invited sixty princes from Galatia's ruling families to reside in Pergamon as his "guests." They were really hostages, under surveillance. One chieftain named Poredorix, a very large, robust man, plotted to kill Mithradates. The assassination was to take place during a tribunal in a small pavilion perched on a ravine. In a Superman-like feat, Poredorix and his friends intended to tip the structure into the gorge. But informers overheard and Mithradates canceled his court appearance.

Poredorix devised a new plan. The Galatian "guests" would attack Mithradates at the next banquet. But this plot also reached the king's ears. He seized Poredorix and his coconspirators, and summoned the other chiefs, along with their families, to a feast. Enough arsenic was on the Poison King's menu to murder all the guests. Somehow, however, three princes survived and managed to escape to Galatia, where they raised an army. They drove out Mithradates' satrap Eumachus. Despite his careful planning, this outcome was just what Mithradates had feared. He no longer controlled Galatia.

Now an example had to be set. In Pergamon, Poredorix and his friends were sentenced to death by the sword. Their bodies were to be denied burial, left to rot on the outskirts of the city.[2]

As the Galatians were marched away to the execution ground, Mithradates reflected on his affection for one of them, a handsome youth named Bepolitanus. They'd enjoyed such friendly conversations. Surely this innocent young man did not deserve to die for the older men's conspiracy! Plutarch says Mithradates became extremely distressed imagining the death of this youth. Did Bepolitanus remind Mithradates of his lost son Arcathius? The king sent an emergency order to spare the youth's life. Poredorix and the others had already been thrown out for the crows. But, as Plutarch relates, by a stroke of luck Bepolitanus was wearing beautiful, costly clothing when he was seized. His executioner wanted this fine outfit for himself. To keep the garments from being bloodstained, the soldier was "stripping them off in a leisurely way when he saw Mithradates' messengers running towards him and shouting the youth's name."

So Bepolitanus lived, while his friends lay unburied. The next day, Mithradates' guards discovered a young woman weeping by the naked corpse of Poredorix. For the crime of trying to cover him with dirt, she was brought before the king. The girl's lovely appearance, her touching grief and innocence stirred pity in Mithradates. Why had she dared to disobey his orders? When he discovered that she was Poredorix's lover, Mithradates relented. He allowed her to give the would-be assassin a proper burial. Mithradates knew the famous tragedy *Antigone* by Sophocles, in which a tyrant executes a young girl for this very same crime. By giving this widely known story a happy ending, Mithradates enhanced his reputation for mercy.

According to Plutarch, these two realistic and detailed stories of Mithradates' empathy for innocent lives circulated by word of mouth more than a century after his death, as counterpoints to other tales of his cruelty and hard heart. Leavening harsh behavior with chivalrous gestures made one's power seem godlike; it commanded the respect of enemies and friends, and might salve a bad conscience too. Mithradates was familiar with the stories of the great Alexander's gallantry toward courageous men and women, and mercy was an important virtue of the ancient Persian kings.

Mithradates still trusted his Galatian general Konnakorix and he loved a Galatian princess named Adobogiona, the sister of a prince distrusted by Mithradates. Part of a portrait bust of Adobogiona has been discovered by archaeologists in the ruins of Pergamon. Perhaps she captured Mithradates' heart during his purge of the Galatian royal families. We might guess that the king saved her from succumbing to the poison he served at the deadly banquet.[3]

CHIOS

Mithradates' paranoid thoughts kept returning to Chios, that prosperous island whose sailors had rammed his royal warship during the battle for Rhodes. Chios had allied with Rome in the past: was it another nest of traitors? Some Chian aristocrats had joined Sulla after the massacre of 88 BC. When Mithradates sent spies to Chios, their reports doomed the island.

Master of malicious punishments on a theatrical scale, Mithradates wrote detailed instructions to his generals Dorylaus and Zenobius. Mithradates' revenge began with a surprise attack on Chios. Zenobius's army took over the city and delivered a proclamation: The citizens of Chios were to come to the Assembly to hear a message from Mithradates. In happier times, he had won chariot races in Chios. One of the island's prized possessions was a letter from Alexander the Great, written after he captured Chios in 333 BC (now displayed in the island's museum). Alexander had exiled all Chians who aided his enemies. Now Mithradates the Great wrote his own letter to Chios. He accused them of aiding his enemies, noting that his suspicions were first aroused when the Chian trireme tried to sink his boat.

Why, he demanded, "have you refused to confiscate the Romans' property, as agreed? Why have you allowed Romans to flee to Sulla? For cooperating with Sulla and conspiring against me, all my friends say I should condemn you to death! But I am merciful," wrote Mithradates. "I will be satisfied if you turn in your weapons and send the children from the leading families of Chios to me as hostages." The Chians gave over their arms and the young men and women of aristocratic families to Zenobius and Dorylaus, who sent them to Pergamon.

But Mithradates was not finished with Chios. Zenobius read out another royal letter. "I know that you still favor the Romans! But instead of the death you deserve, I sentence you to pay a penalty of 2,000 talents." One talent was equal to 6,000 drachmas; 2,000 talents was a very large amount of silver. The total yearly income of Athens at the height of its empire was 1,000 talents. In Mithradates' day, 2,000 talents was equal to 12 million drachmas. A mercenary soldier's pay averaged about 1 drachma per day of active service, so 2,000 talents would provide a year's pay for an army of about 35,000 soldiers.

Crying out lamentations, the Chians gathered ornaments from their temples and women's jewelry to pay the fine. Following Mithradates' secret orders, Zenobius summoned everyone—men, women, children, and slaves, but no foreigners—to the theater to weigh out the goods. Fear shot through the crowd as Zenobius thundered: "You have short-changed the king!"

His soldiers had surrounded the theater and lined the street to the harbor. Inside the theater, Zenobius singled out the slaves owned by the Chians and declared them free. This act by Mithradates carried a powerful propaganda message. Chios was notorious in antiquity for introducing the slave trade to the Greek world, a commerce that later became so profitable on Delos under the Romans. Chios was a wealthy society with an inordinate number of slaves—as early as the fifth century BC, the island possessed more domestic slaves than any other Greek state except Sparta.[4]

Next, the soldiers roughly separated the men from the women and children. They marched the two groups down the gauntlet of soldiers to the sea. The entire population of Chios was loaded onto Mithradates' ships. While their former household slaves watched from shore, the ships full of wretched, wailing Chians sailed away. They were destined for the Black Sea, where they were to spend the rest of their lives as slaves in Mithradates' mines in remote Colchis. Again, in devising this theatrical punishment for Chios, it appears that Mithradates may have been replaying yet another famous Greek tragedy, Euripides' *Trojan Women*.[5]

For their payment of 2,000 talents, the Chians had purchased slavery! The calamity inspired an ironic proverb in antiquity: "The Chian has finally bought himself a master." The Roman writer Athenaeus blamed the slave-trading Chians for their fate, and the "ancient villainy of Chios" was often recalled in the nineteenth century by antislavery groups. For example, the abolitionist-poet John Greenleaf Whittier penned his famous poem "Mithridates at Chios" in 1864, during the American Civil War. Whittier praised Mithradates for his "just punishment of that slave-cursed land."

> Chained and scourged, the slaves of slaves
> The lords of Chios into exile went.
> The fisher in his net is caught
> The Chian hath his master bought.[6]

From Chios, Mithradates plucked another prize for his harem, a captivating young woman named Berenice. She must have been very young, since her mother accompanied her to the royal harem. Berenice was probably selected from among the aristocratic children sent to Pergamon. Like the Galatian princess Adobogiona, Berenice was saved from her people's fate by the all-powerful, compassionate—and lustful—king.

Another honeymoon was now over: Mithradates had grown dissatisfied with Queen Monime. Plutarch says that their marriage became unhappy—she complained that her beauty had "won a master instead of a husband." Maybe the king superstitiously believed that his strong-willed Greek wife had brought him bad luck in the Greek campaign. At any rate, at some point after the terrible omen of the crashing statue of Victory and the defeats in Greece that this event seemed to foretell, Monime was sent away. She traveled in opulent fashion, probably in a Persian-style *harmamaxa*, a private four-wheeled golden chariot with purple awnings, attended by royal eunuchs, to live the rest of her days in luxury in Pontus.[7]

Mithradates found comfort with his recently acquired lovers. He savored the sound of Berenice's name on his tongue. She was his new lucky charm. A Macedonian name, *Berenice* means "bringer of victory."

Rebellion and Repression

His tasks completed in Chios, Zenobius approached Ephesus with his army. Unnerved by Mithradates' setbacks in Greece and the fate of Chios, the Ephesians insisted that Zenobius enter the city alone and unarmed. He agreed and visited Philopoemen, Monime's father, Mithradates' overseer in Ephesus—perhaps to reassure him that Monime was well cared

FIG. 10.1. Monime and Mithradates, a tense scene. Illustration for Racine's
play *Mithridate*, engraving by Girardet.

for in Pontus. Ephesus had been an early supporter of Mithradates, com-
plying with his orders to murder Romans just two years ago. We don't
know what Mithradates had in mind for Ephesus, but the citizens of the
wealthy commercial city were nervous enough to disobey Zenobius's
ominous summons to the theater the next day. That night the Ephesians

murdered Zenobius. Nothing personal, just business—the city depended on stable trade and gambled that Rome would prevail. After the murder, Ephesus went on red alert, hoarding food supplies and preparing to defend the city.

Other towns now had two violent models to follow, Chios or Ephesus. Tralles, Hypaepa, Mesopolis, Smyrna, Colophon, Sardis, and other towns previously allied with Mithradates followed the example of Ephesus and revolted. Mithradates reacted with rage, dispatching armies to inflict terrible vengeance on these rebels (was this when Mithradates poisoned his rival in chariot racing, Alcaeus of Sardis?). To preempt further defections, Mithradates sent proclamations to many Anatolian cities freeing slaves, canceling debts, and bestowing citizenship rights on resident foreigners. These privileges irritated the local aristocracy but won strong popular support among former slaves, debtors, and new citizens in each town.[8]

Some of the king's closest associates, alarmed by the events in Greece and western Anatolia, began to hold secret meetings. Prominent Greeks began to reconsider their devotion to Mithradates. Two men of Smyrna invited two men of Lesbos to join a cabal against Mithradates. But one of them, a personal friend of the king, informed on the others. He arranged for Mithradates himself to hide under his couch to hear the plot from their own mouths. The three men were tortured to death.

Mithradates' paranoia emerged in full force now. His fears were justified: betrayals and revolts were not imaginary. But his draconian reactions cut his support among the upper classes, and many people took advantage of the climate of fear to turn in their personal enemies. Mithradates rewarded informers lavishly. Plots continued, very close to home. One night in Pergamon, eighty citizens were discovered planning to murder the king. Mithradates executed them. According to Appian's sources, about sixteen hundred men suspected of treason lost their lives in this purge.[9] We don't have the details of how they died. But many of these men must have been involuntary guinea pigs for Mithradates' poison experiments. The king was known to test toxins and antidotes on prisoners condemned to death.

In 85 BC, Mithradates' spies reported more bad news. Sulla's aide, Lucullus, had done the impossible! Despite pirates and winter storms, he had assembled a navy. Ptolemy of Egypt welcomed Lucullus, inviting him to visit the Pyramids in luxurious style. But Lucullus declined, worried about his commander in chief Sulla enduring hardships at the siege of Athens. Lucullus accepted an emerald-and-gold ring engraved with

Ptolemy's likeness, and enough cash to hire ships and sailors from Syria, Cyprus, Phoenicia, Pamphylia, and Rhodes. He sailed on the Rhodian flagship, commanded by Mithradates' old enemy Admiral Damagoras, who had chased the Pontic navy away from Rhodes in 88 BC. Moving north, they took possession of Cos, Samos, and Chios. But Mithradates' admiral Neoptolemus (Archelaus's brother) was lying in wait near the small island of Tenedos. In the naval battle that followed, Damagoras put Neoptolemus to flight.

Is this the moment when Mithradates finally began to realize that he would not be victorious in the war against Rome, as suggested by the historian Reinach? Sulla had the upper hand. Yet there were some positive signs for the king. His defeats in mainland Greece had not been due to disloyalty or disillusionment on the Greeks' part; his armies fought courageously but were overwhelmed by professional, technologically advanced Roman legions. Even so, Sulla had struggled for nearly two years to take Greece, and Archelaus held Euboea, a key position. Flaccus, Sulla's rival, lost most of his ships in a tempest in the Adriatic. Through intelligence sources, Mithradates learned that Flaccus was detested by his soldiers; many deserted to join Sulla. Meanwhile in Rome, Marius was dead, but Sulla's supporters were murdered on a daily basis, exerting a strong pull on Sulla to return as soon as possible.

Flaccus had bypassed Sulla, marching across Thrace. It appeared that he intended to invade Mithradates' territory by himself! Sulla was tracking this rival Roman army with his own legions, and Lucullus was bringing up a vast navy. Mithradates still commanded two hundred ships and an army of eighty thousand men in Anatolia, under the command of Dorylaus. It was time to make contingency plans. Perhaps diplomacy—a truce—could buy time. Reflecting on the enormity of his losses in Greece and calculating that Sulla must be itching to get home, Mithradates sent word to Archelaus to make peace on the best terms possible.[10]

The Peace of Dardanus

Sulla and Archelaus met at the Roman camp near Delion, Boeotia. Both men were practical soldiers of fortune looking to make the best bargain. Their first volleys over the peace table were tests of the other's commitments. As Archelaus well knew, Sulla was in a great hurry to conclude the war so he could take his army back to Italy, kill his foes there, celebrate a Triumph, and become the absolute dictator of Rome. Archelaus proposed that Sulla should be satisfied with recovering Greece and leave Asia to Mithradates. "If you promise to return to Italy now, my king Mithradates promises to give you a very generous war chest, many ships, and as many soldiers as you need. With these, you can destroy Marius's Populars and take over Rome!

Sulla's counteroffer was equally audacious. "Why don't you desert Mithradates and bring me all his mercenary armies? Together we can crush Mithradates and I'll crown you king of Pontus!" Each general professed to be insulted by the other's treasonous proposal. With their cards on the table, they began the negotiations.[11]

Sulla summarized Mithradates' crimes, deploring his takeover of vast territories; his confiscations of public and sacred funds of cities allied with Rome; his seizures of Roman property, land, and slaves; his murder of Roman allies; and the great massacre of Italian men, women, and children and even slaves of Italian blood in 88 BC. "Such hatred did Mithradates bear towards Italy! And now he professes to want our friendship and mercy—but only after I destroyed 160,000 of his troops in Greece!"

Archelaus responded coolly: "It was the greed of other Roman generals that caused this war. My king will agree to fair terms." These were the conditions the generals hammered out:

- Return to territorial status quo of 89 BC: Greece belongs to Rome. Mithradates keeps his possessions as of 89 BC, but withdraws from Paphlagonia, Bithynia, and Cappadocia, allowing Nicomedes and Ariobarzanes to recover their thrones.
- Sulla promises that Mithradates will be declared a Friend and Ally of Rome, upon Mithradates' payment of a fine equal to the cost of the war.
- Mithradates must give Sulla seventy fully equipped bronze-armored war ships.
- Mithradates must release all Roman prisoners of war, including captive ambassadors and officers.
- All Roman deserters and runaway Roman slaves who had joined Mithradates' armies must be surrendered to Sulla.
- A general amnesty would be declared; no reprisals against partisans.

Archelaus had been fighting as a mercenary general for Mithradates for several hard years. The war to liberate Greece was lost, with sobering casualties. As Sulla enjoyed pointing out, Boeotia was left "impassable for the multitude of dead bodies," the remains of Mithradates' grand army. Archelaus negotiated an armistice remarkably favorable to Mithradates, by playing to Sulla's impatience. One of the terms of their agreement was personal: Sulla gave Archelaus an estate of ten thousand acres in Euboea. Archelaus withdrew his troops from Euboea and agreed to accompany Sulla to Dardanus to finalize the treaty with Mithradates.

On the way, Archelaus fell ill. Sulla tended Archelaus as if he were one of his own officers. Sulla's favors and concern for Archelaus made some in Mithradates' court suspicious that there had been collusion, that Archelaus had somehow "thrown" the battles at Chaeronea and Orchomenus, a dubious notion. Sulla defended his treatment of Archelaus in his memoirs, now lost. It seems likely that Sulla respected the commander as a noble adversary and realized that he needed his cooperation in convincing Mithradates to accept the treaty quickly.

Mithradates sent envoys to Sulla and Archelaus, to contest two of the conditions. Mithradates wanted to keep Paphlagonia, which he had always maintained was his by inheritance. And he refused to turn over seventy ships. The ambassadors slyly hinted that Mithradates might obtain a better deal if he were to negotiate with "your other general, Fimbria." Sulla flew into a rage. "What! Mithradates has been sitting in Pergamon all this time, directing a disastrous war from afar! He should humbly thank me for not chopping off his right hand, with which he signed the death warrant for thousands of innocent Romans. He'll sing a different tune when I march into Asia!"

Archelaus intervened. According to Sulla's memoirs, the general tearfully begged for a chance to personally persuade Mithradates to accept the treaty. "If I fail," Archelaus vowed, "I'll kill myself!" That emotional scene may have been concocted by Sulla, but he did send Archelaus to confer with Mithradates.[12]

FIMBRIA AND LUCULLUS INTERVENE

Mithradates held a stronger hand than it might seem, but it had to be played carefully. Civil war was raging in Italy. Sulla was desperate to return, but suddenly he found himself caught in new emergencies. And Mithradates himself was in the same boat. An incredible situation was developing. Before their peace treaty could be ratified, a strange parallel war loomed on the horizon.

Sulla's rival, Flaccus, had now reached Bithynia with his army. But, taking advantage of his superior's ineptitude, Flaccus's young officer

Fimbria led a mutiny against the older man. Flaccus ("Rabbit Ears") fled to Bithynia's capital, Nicomedia. But Fimbria and his men hunted him down and discovered Flaccus cowering in a well. Fimbria chopped off Flaccus's head and flung it into the sea, leaving the body on the beach for the gulls.

The Roman Senate angrily withdrew support for Fimbria, who was now an outlaw but in control of two legions. Mithradates now faced *two* rogue Roman armies in his territory, commanded by outlawed generals who were bitter enemies, each lusting to win credit for Mithradates' downfall. Sulla feared that the ruthless, hotheaded Fimbria, a Marius loyalist, would steal his hard-won victory over Mithradates. These unforeseen developments meant that Fimbria was now the common enemy of both Mithradates and Sulla!

Cut off from Rome, Fimbria desperately needed to reward his troops with rich booty. He fixed his sights on Pergamon. He would sack Mithradates' palace and take all the credit for concluding the war on Mithradates. Along the way, Fimbria devastated the land "like a hurricane," destroying towns that refused to open their gates to his army. At Ilium, ancient Troy, the citizens reminded Fimbria that, according to the Roman foundation myth, Troy was Rome's sacred mother city. Fimbria sardonically thanked the citizens and demanded entry. Once inside, he slaughtered the men, women, and children. Many fled into the Temple of Athena; Fimbria ordered the temple burned down along with the entire town, and unleashed his men to pillage. Witnesses described the awesome sight of the marble statue of Athena left standing in the ashes of her temple. Plutarch remarked that Troy had not experienced such utter destruction since Agamemnon had sacked Priam's city in the legendary Trojan War. Indeed, Fimbria crowed that it took him only ten days to raze Troy, while it took Agamemnon ten years.[13]

While Sulla sped to intercept the rival outlaw general, Mithradates sent out a contingent led by his oldest son, Mithradates the Younger. But Fimbria set a trap and killed six thousand of Mithradates' cavalry. Fimbria continued toward Pergamon. Pergamon's walls were strong, but after the recently discovered plots, Mithradates could no longer trust the citizens. Fearing they might sell him out to Fimbria before he could make peace with Sulla on advantageous terms, Mithradates was compelled to flee for his life. From Pergamon, he rushed to Pitane on the coast. Fimbria pursued and laid siege to Pitane.

As if on cue, Lucullus suddenly arrived on the scene with his armada. Fimbria ordered Lucullus to block Pitane's harbor, trapping Mithradates,

Rome's dire enemy, inside the city. "Together you and I will win all the glory in this war," promised Fimbria, "and Sulla's exploits in Greece will be forgotten!" What would happen now?

Lucullus was loyal to Sulla; he loathed Fimbria, an ally of the hated Marius. Lucullus announced that his navy belonged to Sulla. He refused to block Mithradates' escape route, so that the king could approve the treaty worked out between Sulla and Archelaus. It was an extremely close call. Had Lucullus thrown in with Fimbria, Mithradates would have been finished. Instead, Lucullus allowed Mithradates to take a boat from Pitane to Lesbos. There Mithradates joined Neoptolemus's navy and arrived in Dardanus.[14]

Here on a plain, not far from Troy, in view of both their armies, in late 85 BC, Sulla and Mithradates met face-to-face. Both were wary, but extremely eager to declare peace.

Sealed with a Kiss

Each man was a master showman, skilled in the art of self-presentation. Each man scored propaganda points with oratory and body language, witnessed by thousands on the plain at Dardanus and recorded for history by Appian and Plutarch. Mithradates, defeated but still not beaten, wanted to make a strong impression. He was accompanied by Neoptolemus's 200 ships, Dorylaus's 20,000 infantry and 6,000 cavalry, and "a throng of scythe-bearing chariots." The victor's party was more modest: Sulla brought 1,000 men and 200 cavalry.

Mithradates, in his old-fashioned Persian finery, walked forward, hand outstretched. Sulla, standing at attention in Roman army attire, stiffly asked whether Mithradates accepted the terms agreed to by his general Archelaus. Mithradates did not reply immediately. "Surely," spat out Sulla, "it is the victor who has the right of silence, while a suppliant should ask forgiveness!"

Mithradates broke his dramatic silence, pointing out that he and his father had been good friends of Rome. "But Roman ambassadors, governors, and generals started this war out of pure greed—the vice of most Romans. They wronged me by taking away Phrygia and Cappadocia, and they urged Nicomedes to attack my kingdom. Everything I've done since then was in self-defense and out of necessity."

"I know you are a clever orator," Sulla cut in, "always justifying your wrongdoing. You should have sent an embassy to Rome long ago if you thought you were the victim of injustice. You had no right to Cappadocia and Phrygia. Nicomedes attacked you because you sent the assassin named Alexander to kill him and you armed his rival Socrates the Good. You have been planning this war a long time, thinking you could rule the whole world—why else have you allied with Thracians, Sarmatians, and Scythians? That's why you built up such a huge army and navy—and that's why you timed your takeover of our Asian Province while we were subduing revolts in Italy! You freed our slaves and canceled debts! You killed sixteen hundred men on false accusations; you poisoned the princes of Galatia! You butchered or drowned all the residents of Italian blood in Provincia Asia, including mothers and babies, not even sparing victims who fled into temples! What cruelty, what impiety, what boundless hatred you showed toward us!"

Playing to the audience of officers, soldiers, and officials, Sulla continued to castigate Mithradates for war crimes, even declaring himself the "liberator" of Greece from the "slavery" of Mithradates. "You invaded Greece and deprived the Greeks of their freedom!"

Mithradates' final card was unspoken: *Deal with me or I deal with Fimbria.* Knowing he had the upper hand, he calmly broke in on Sulla's vehement discourse. "I consent to the terms agreed by my general Archelaus."

Before the crowd, Sulla and Mithradates embraced and sealed the Peace of Dardanus with a kiss. What were the sentiments of each man during this intimate, traditional ritual? It's interesting to consider the cultural differences. Romans sealed treaties with the *osculum pacis*, a mutual kiss on the cheek. Persians kissed equals on the mouth, but superiors accepted a kiss from inferiors on the cheek. Did Mithradates fake his kiss and accept Sulla's lips on his cheek as that of an inferior? What passed through Sulla's mind as he kissed the man who had snuffed out the lives of tens of thousands of Romans?

Mithradates promised to withdraw from Bithynia, Cappadocia, and Paphlagonia. He hated to give up the title "King of Kings." It was galling to go through the motions of a formal reconciliation with the loathsome puppet kings. Mithradates had agreed to hand over Roman deserters and former Roman slaves in his armies, but he had no intention of following through. He did release Oppius, the captive Roman general who had served as the king's personal servant since his defeat in 89 BC (Oppius went to the temple of healing on Cos, to recover from his ordeal).

Mithradates paid the fine demanded by Sulla—2,000 talents. As we saw above, Mithradates had recently imposed a fine of 2,000 talents on

Chios, as a penalty for their revolt. Considering the king's present circumstances and wealth, the fine requested by Sulla was a piddling sum—Mithradates could simply transfer the Chian payoff to Sulla. He turned over 70 ships to Sulla, along with 500 archers, but he still commanded more than 100 ships and an army of 80,000.[15]

Mithradates the Great sailed away to Pontus, his original stronghold, leaving Sulla to deal with the loose cannon Fimbria. The war between Mithradates and Rome was over. All parties had given their word to abide by the truce—with one exception. The Roman Senate, controlled by Marius's Populars, never recognized Sulla's Peace of Dardanus. Yet who—besides the irrepressible king of Pontus—could imagine in 85 BC that this was only the first round in a conflict that would last a lifetime?

SULLA MOPS UP

Sulla's soldiers were not impressed with the Peace of Dardanus. In fact, they were enraged. They had witnessed Sulla's eloquent speech, reminding everyone of the crimes of Rome's most hostile enemy. Mithradates had killed 150,000 innocent Romans in a single day! Now they saw Sulla kiss this vicious murderer and allow him to simply sail off, loaded with fabulous wealth, to his kingdom by the sea. Where was justice?

Sulla's mild conditions were due to his haste to return to Rome, after regaining Greece and punishing Anatolia, and his belief that Aquillius, an ally of Marius, bore responsibility for starting the war.[16] But Sulla perceived his soldiers' anger and deflected it, explaining that Fimbria was the clear and present danger now. What if Mithradates had joined Fimbria? How could they carry on a war against those combined forces? After we defeat Fimbria, Sulla promised, there'll be riches galore and victory will be ours in Italy.

Sulla marched to Fimbria's camp and demanded that he surrender the two legions, which he held illegally. Fimbria refused, pointing out that Sulla had been voted Rome's Public Enemy. War between Roman legions on foreign soil seemed inevitable. While Sulla's soldiers fortified their camp and dug trenches around Fimbria's camp, a wondrous thing occurred. Fimbria's men came out and pitched in to help their fellow Romans. In despair, Fimbria fled to Pergamon and entered the great Temple of Asclepius, where so many Romans had lost their lives in 88 BC. There Fimbria fell on his sword and died. In the words of the contemporary

Greek historian Diodorus, "Fimbria should have died a thousand deaths" for the terror he had spread.[17]

Issuing proclamations praising Lycia, Rhodes, Stratonicea, Magnesia, Patara, and other places that had cooperated with Rome, Sulla dispatched troops to punish all the towns that had allied with Mithradates. Blatantly ignoring the treaty's amnesty terms, banning reprisals against partisans, he proceeded to take savage revenge on Anatolia for supporting Mithradates. Sulla imposed a penalty on the entire Province of Asia in the extraordinary amount of twenty thousand talents, *ten times* what he had demanded of Mithradates.

He assigned his mild-mannered and efficient officer Lucullus to collect this money. Sulla billeted his unruly troops in private homes and forced the Anatolians to pay outrageous sums for the "privilege" of feeding and clothing their insolent "guests." All freed slaves were ordered back into slavery. In Ephesus and other cities, Sulla compelled citizen assemblies to borrow money at exorbitant interest rates, "mortgaging their theaters, gymnasiums, harbors, city walls, statues, and every other scrap of public property." Sulla also plundered artworks and treasures on a massive scale. All this money and property went into Sulla's personal war chest.

Many towns resisted. In retaliation, massacres were carried out by Sulla's soldiers, despite his many speeches claiming that "Romans would never dream of indiscriminate slaughter or other acts of barbarism." In this chaotic period of Mithradates' withdrawal and Sulla's vindictive rampage, swarms of pirate ships plagued the Aegean coast, attacking harbors and castles in coastal cities and islands from Miletus to Samothrace. Sulla callously allowed the brigands access to sack and burn towns, such as Iasus, that had supported Mithradates. The economic devastation was deep and long-lasting. Many of these cities would not recover the prosperity they had enjoyed under Mithradates until the reign of Constantine four hundred years later.[18]

In 84 BC, Sulla declared his mission accomplished. He left his eager young officer Murena to occupy Phrygia with the two legions that had served Fimbria. On his way back to Italy, Sulla stopped briefly in Greece. He visited a hot spring to treat a mysterious illness and arranged for the shipment of thousands of objets d'art, famous paintings, precious manuscripts, fine sculptures, and other antiquities, including colossal columns from the unfinished Temple of Olympian Zeus in Athens. Several ships laden with Sulla's loot sank in a storm on the way to Italy; archaeologists have identified the contents of at least one shipwreck as part of his plunder. From the bottom of the sea, modern divers hauled up a great number of marble columns, bronze statues of Eros and Dionysus, and marble sculptures of Aphrodite, Pan, Satyrs, and other figures.[19]

Sulla returned to Italy with forty thousand men, many of them recruits from Macedonia and Thrace. Historian Barry Strauss speculates that one of these auxiliaries may have been Spartacus, a Thracian who, in ten years' time, would become the gladiator who led the great slave revolt in Italy.[20]

The horrors visited upon Asia and Greece were now repeated in Italy. In 83 BC, Sulla's ruthless confiscations of land, proscriptions, and murders culminated in a partisan bloodbath of such horrendous proportions that, in the view of the Roman historian Cassius Dio, Sulla's cruel tortures and killings of his fellow Romans surpassed even Mithradates' massacre of 88 BC. "Husbands were butchered with their wives, mothers and babies were slain," wrote Plutarch, "homes and even temples were soaked in blood." "What a sea of Roman blood was shed," wrote Saint Augustine, the scale of death "beyond computation." Sulla's men annihilated 18,000 of Marius's men at Fidentia; at Capua, 7,000 enemies were slaughtered; at Signia, 20,000; one day Sulla ordered a massacre of 6,000 innocent people locked inside the Circus of Rome; on yet another day, Sulla executed 12,000 men accused of favoring Marius. Sulla became dictator in 81 BC. At his Triumph, Pliny the Elder says Sulla paraded 115,000 pounds of silver and 15,000 pounds of gold, the combined loot from all his victories.[21]

THE SECOND MITHRADATIC WAR, 83–81 BC

What was Mithradates' state of mind as he retired to his drastically reduced corner of the world after a grueling Round One with Rome? Among the conflicting emotions of chagrin, resentment, relief, despair, hope, determination, suspicion, and calculation, one conviction stood out. He was King Mithradates VI Eupator Dionysus *Vazraka* ("The Great"), proud descendant of Persian and Macedonian monarchs, emperor of the Black Sea Empire, the divinely chosen champion of liberty, Light, and Truth, the enemy of Darkness and Deceit, the one true alternative to Roman imperialism in the East.[22]

He was aware that the Roman Senate had failed to ratify the Peace of Dardanus, which he and Sulla had sealed with a kiss. In fact, there had been no written, signed document setting out the terms of the truce. Just exactly how binding was a verbal agreement with a renegade Roman bent on ravaging Italy? The same idea occurred to Murena, the commander in charge of the twelve thousand "Fimbrians" that Sulla left in Anatolia. Murena (the "Eel"), who had rallied Sulla's men at the battle for Piraeus, was among those disgusted by the lenient terms of the treaty. He decided to take matters into his own hands. Murena's ill-considered, self-serving decision to resume the war played right into the hands of Mithradates.

But first Mithradates had to do some housecleaning. He decided not to restore all of Cappadocia to Ariobarzanes—the populace favored Mithradates, and he had always considered Cappadocia part of his kingdom. Disturbances brewing in Colchis and among some of the tribes around the Cimmerian Bosporus demanded immediate attention. To convince the tribes of the northern Black Sea of his power, Mithradates enlarged his navy and recruited another huge army. Learning from his defeats in Greece, Mithradates gave up the old-fashioned, lockstep hoplite formation and drilled his foot soldiers in smaller, more flexible units dispersed in thin lines, better able to fight Roman legions. He increased the number of lightly armed skirmishers and archers. He made a personal decision to fight in the front ranks when necessary. A large cavalry, made up of courageous, highly skilled Persian and Armenian knights, was the centerpiece of his new army. These forces were dispatched to quell the restive north, where his son Machares was viceroy of the Bosporan Kingdom.[23]

The Colchians requested that the king's eldest son, Mithradates the Younger, be their ruler. As soon as Mithradates agreed, they renewed their allegiance. Without any evidence, Mithradates instinctively suspected that his son harbored ambitions to supersede his father. Mithradates sent for his son and heir, who had served faithfully in the war against Fimbria. But after all, this son was the offspring of Queen Laodice the Younger, the king's sister, his first wife, who had to be executed for plotting against him. Had Laodice's oldest son inherited the treachery inbred in his maternal lineage? Perhaps he held a grudge for the murder of his mother. In sorrow, Mithradates bound his son in golden fetters and put him to death. We can imagine that for this regrettable necessity, he administered the most gentle and rapid poison in his apothecary, perhaps hemlock mixed with opium (the deadly cocktail drunk by the philosopher Socrates), or the microscopic toxin from India, *dikairon*. A trusted Persian, Moaphernes from Amasia (great-uncle of the historian Strabo) became Mithradates' viceroy in Colchis.

Paranoid thoughts continued to assail the king. The question of Archelaus's loyalty preyed on his mind. The more Mithradates mulled it over, the more convinced he became that his star general had yielded far too much to Sulla in the peace negotiations. Word of the king's suspicions reached Archelaus. Was Archelaus was really planning to jump ship? That is unknown, but the veteran soldier of fortune understood that it was time to look out for himself. Archelaus defected to the Romans. (His brother Neoptolemus remained loyal, as commander of Mithradates' navy in the Aegean.) It seems likely that Archelaus was the source of much of the information available to Roman historians about Mithradates' personality, strategies, troop numbers, and other facts.

Archelaus requested a meeting with Murena. He convinced the Roman commander that Mithradates was creating the large fleet in the Black Sea and training another grand army with the secret intention of renewing hostilities against Rome. Murena, eager for plunder and a triumph of his own—and seeking "trifling pretexts for war"—was persuaded to launch a preemptive strike before Mithradates could make the first move.[24]

In the summer of 83 BC, without any declaration of war, Murena marched deep into western Cappadocia and made a lightning strike on Mithradates' garrison at Cappadocian Comana. In this large sacred city, said to have been founded by Agamemnon's descendants after the Trojan War, was a fabulously rich Temple of Love, similar to the sanctuary at Comana in Pontus. In the temple was an archaic statue of Artemis. It was said that Agamemnon had sacrificed his daughter Iphigenia to Artemis—Iphigenia's sword was one of the precious relics displayed in Comana.[25]

Many of Mithradates' cavalry were killed in Murena's attack. Taken by surprise, and angry over Archelaus's treason, Mithradates nevertheless scrupulously refrained from escalating the war. He sent ambassadors to Murena, protesting that he had broken the treaty. Murena's sarcastic reply: "Treaty? What treaty? I've never seen a treaty document!" Murena proceeded to rob all the money and ornaments in the Temple of Love and set up winter quarters in Cappadocia.

Still Mithradates held back, following a strategy of restraint and statesmanship. He sent an embassy to Rome to appeal to the Senate and Sulla, registering a formal complaint that Murena had broken the terms of the Peace of Dardanus. He would await their reply before reacting to Murena's unauthorized aggression. Meanwhile, his old Cappadocian friend Gordius replaced the traitor Archelaus as general.

In the spring of 82 BC, Murena crossed the Halys, flooded with melted snow, into Mithradates' home territory. That summer and fall, Murena's legions raided four hundred villages in Pontus, amassing wagonloads of plunder. He departed with his haul across Roman-controlled Galatia. Still Mithradates did nothing but sent spies to track Murena.

Sulla and the Senate dispatched a commissioner to investigate Mithradates' complaint about Murena in 81 BC. The official met Murena and announced that the Senate ordered him to cease attacking Mithradates, who had made peace with Rome. But, as Mithradates' spies reported, the commissioner also admitted that the Senate had not issued a written decree to that effect. Then the spies observed the official whispering privately with Murena. Murena invaded Mithradates' home territory again! Mithradates was now perfectly justified in assuming that the commissioner had conveyed a secret message from Rome to Murena, authorizing him to attack Mithradates in an all-out war. This was even more bald-faced than the unauthorized war begun by Aquillius and Nicomedes back in 89 BC.

Mithradates gave Gordius the order to retaliate. Gordius quickly collected a local citizen army eager to fight for Mithradates. They took up a position across the Halys River from Murena's two legions. Mithradates himself arrived, riding a fine horse at the head of his very large new army. With little personal combat experience, Mithradates vigorously threw himself into battle against Murena, a determined young veteran of Roman victories under Sulla. Well aware that his royal Persian ancestors never took part in actual combat, Mithradates—at age fifty-one—was now emulating young Alexander in his decision to rush into the thick of battle.

The opposing armies exploded into fierce fighting at the riverbank. Mithradates prevailed, pushing across the river and sending Murena and his men running up a hillside. Commanding his smaller, flexible units, Mithradates decisively routed the Romans. In the hail of arrows from Mithradates' Armenian archers, the jackal Murena and his men fled west over the mountains "by a pathless route." Mithradates and Gordius drove the rest of Murena's garrisons out of Cappadocia. The entire country welcomed Mithradates as liberator. The brilliant victory over Murena was a much-needed jolt of good news. Ebbing popular devotion surged back, and Mithradates Eupator was again hailed as the people's savior-king against rampaging Romans. He was still the "Good Father" who drove off the ravening wolves.[26]

At some point in this period, a young patrician in the Marius faction named Julius Caesar (b. 100 BC) enlisted in the Roman army. Sailing

to Anatolia, he was captured by Cilician pirates and held for ransom—
Caesar escaped by a clever ruse involving poison wine. He earned his
first battle honors at Lesbos, where Romans killed five hundred soldiers
allied with Mithradates and enslaved six thousand people. Caesar was
sent to Bithynia to request ships from Nicomedes IV. It seems that Caesar's sojourn in the Bithynian court took much longer than necessary.
For the rest of his life, Caesar's enemies taunted him with the nickname
"Queen of Bithynia," claiming that he had become Nicomedes' lover.[27]

In Rome, meanwhile, Sulla had been urgently scrambling to try to stop
Murena, before his foolish war obliterated Sulla's victory over Mithradates. Sulla sent a stern tribune, Gabinius, to threaten Murena with severe
punishment. As Sulla's peacemaker, Gabinius also arranged a conference
between Mithradates and Ariobarzanes, whose throne in Cappadocia
was wobbling again. Mithradates, arguing from a position of righteous
indignation and military strength, had his conditions ready. He betrothed his little daughter Athenais, age four, to Ariobarzanes to seal
their new friendship under Mithradates' terms. As part of the alliance,
Mithradates stipulated that he not only retain western Cappadocia but
receive another large chunk of central Cappadocia. Desperate to ensure
stability in the region where Mithradates suddenly held all the cards,
Gabinius and Ariobarzanes had to agree.

Then everybody attended a lively Persian-Macedonian-style banquet
hosted by an expansive and jubilant Mithradates. As in the old days before the wars, Mithradates was the master of ceremonies, surrounded by
happy friends and beautiful consorts. He bestowed lavish rewards on the
best singers and cithara players, the most amusing jesters, and the most
amazing jugglers. He doled out prizes of gold to those who excelled in
boisterous drinking and eating contests. According to Appian, everyone
at the party—Ariobarzanes, Gordius, Dorylaus, even Monime—joined
in the jolly excess, everyone except for the glum Roman at the foot of the
table, Gabinius.[28]

FIRE ON THE MOUNTAIN

Mithradates also celebrated his victory over Murena with a solemn ritual, a mountaintop fire ceremony to thank Zeus and Mithra. Appian described this ceremony, which he says Mithradates performed according
to the ancient traditions of his ancestors, Cyrus and Darius. He had
learned the ceremony at his father's side as a boy in Sinope.

FIG. 10.2. Persian Magus-king performing fire ritual. Mithradates' fire
ceremony was carried out in the traditional manner of his Persian ancestors.
Detail, red figure vase 3297, side A, Underworld Painter, 4th c BC. Staatliche
Antikensammlungen und Glyptothek, Munich.

Mithradates and his entourage ascended Buyuk Evliya Dag, to the
sanctuary of Zeus the Warrior. Archaeologists have discovered many
inscriptions in this important site of native Anatolian and Iranian-
influenced worship. At this and many other similar shrines in Cappadocia, Zoroastrian priests, called "Fire-keepers," tended an eternal flame

(the source was petroleum) on the altar. Mithradates' Magi, wearing high felt turbans, murmuring incantations, and waving their *barsoms* (myrtle wands), sacrificed white animals to fire, earth, wind, and water. Then, following old Persian custom, the chief Magus Mithradates himself dragged logs to the hilltop, creating an immense woodpile. Around the altar, he arranged trestles made of logs and branches and laid out a feast of meat and bread for the celebrants.

Mithradates donned a purple headdress studded with silver stars and the pure white cape of the Magus over his purple robe of kingship. He climbed to the top of the woodpile to pour the sacred libations: milk, honey, wine, and oil. Throwing handfuls of sweet-smelling frankincense and myrrh over the offerings, Mithradates recited a heartfelt prayer to the gods. His prayer was not recorded, but it was probably something like the prayer offered by Cyrus, according to Xenophon: "O ancestral Zeus and Helios and all of the gods, accept these offerings as tokens of gratitude for help in achieving many glorious enterprises." After the king descended, the Magi knelt at the bottom of the high woodpile and kindled a fire with laurel fans, taking care not to pollute the sacred flames with their breath.

The spectacular bonfire to the gods burned for many days, lighting up the night sky. The heat was so intense that no one could approach the altar. The towering flames could be seen for a distance of 1,000 stades, about 115 miles, visible to Mithradates' ships at sea. Gazing up at the fire on the mountain, Mithradates and his followers could still fervently believe in his grand destiny.[29]

11

Living Like a King

"Like a wrestler ready for another bout," marveled Plutarch, Mithradates "had risen to his feet, despite the blow Sulla had dealt him." And now, wrote Appian, after his resounding victory over Murena, Mithradates "was at leisure."

The war for Greece had ended in disaster, with terrible casualties and the destruction of Athens. Yet in a way, the result was an ancient forerunner of what modern military strategists call the "Tet Offensive effect." The phenomenon was named after a massive assault by the North Vietnamese in 1968 during the Vietnam War. The offensive failed on a grand scale—but the nominally victorious U.S. and South Vietnamese forces were demoralized by the strength and determination of the enemy. The North Vietnamese gained international support and eventually won the war. The "Tet effect" describes a disastrous major military campaign against a more powerful enemy, which nevertheless becomes a public relations victory, with renewed support for what is seen as a righteous cause. The concept of glorious failure, noble defeat, was well known in antiquity: the Spartans at Thermopylae, Hannibal, Aristonicus, and Spartacus are some famous examples. Justin described a Tet-like effect for Mithradates, who "went down in defeat before the greatest generals . . . only to rise again all the more redoubtable for his losses." In Rome, Cicero sought to account for Mithradates' remarkable ability to draw reinforcements after so many losses. Somehow, exclaimed Cicero, Mithradates "has done more by being defeated, than if he had been victorious!"[1]

Sulla's reign of terror continued in Rome. A great many of Marius's Populars fled Italy. These exiles—veterans and statesmen who had held high offices under Popular rule—regrouped on the eastern and western frontiers of the empire and raised banners of revolt. Some went to Spain to join Sertorius, the Roman commander leading an insurgent army of native Spaniards. Others joined Mithradates in Pontus. These experienced Roman officers brought six thousand soldiers—a full legion—and trained Mithradates' new armies in Roman discipline and tactics.

From now on, Mithradates' war chest no longer paid for ostentatious equipment—which had simply provided rich booty for the enemy. No more lavishly decorated ships with silk canopies and luxurious pools on the decks for entertaining concubines; no more armor, shields, and weapons inlaid with gold tracery and precious stones.

Mithradates maintained peaceful coexistence under the Peace of Dardanus, which he knew he had been lucky to win from a very distracted Sulla. But he was determined to keep his Black Sea Kingdom secure. According to Appian, Mithradates took an army to subdue the Achaeans of northern Colchis. A fierce tribe that claimed descent from Greek heroes of the Trojan War, the Achaeans were notorious for luring ships to wreck on their rocky shores and then sacrificing the sailors to their gods. Fighting in their mountainous terrain was harsh. Mithradates lost a great many men to ambushes and freezing snow. The Achaeans were never defeated; their allegiance could not be counted upon, although some Achaeans later joined Mithradates' army, and the experience of mountain warfare was valuable.[2]

Mithradates remained ever vigilant for both opportunity and threat. But for nearly a decade, he ruled in relative peace.

AGATES FOR MY MEAT, STRYCHNINE IN MY CUP

Mithradates loved spectacle and theatricality—he often staged dramatic performances to demonstrate his remarkable ability to dine on poison-laced meat and wine. Such evenings not only provided entertainment but enhanced the Poison King's carefully crafted reputation of invincibility. And, of course, the morbid proceedings also furthered his experimental research.

Let us imagine one of these banquets. The evening might feature the poisoning of someone condemned to die for a heinous crime—Mithradates followed the "ethical" approach of Attalus III of Pergamon, experimenting only on criminals. In the Greek world, capital punishment was usually carried out with poison hemlock. But Mithradates was systematically studying the effects of known and rare *pharmaka*, and men on death row were his scientific subjects. In at least one instance, we know that Mithradates received a messenger carrying a letter and package from his friend Zopyrus, the royal physician in Alexandria. Zopyrus's letter informed Mithradates that the messenger was sentenced to death, and invited the king to test the accompanying antidote on him.[3]

So, as the guests take their places on couches, turbaned Hindus might charm cobras with sinuous flute music, and Psylli serpent handlers allow themselves to be bitten by Libyan adders. Scythian shamans milk venom from the fangs of a steppe viper. Dipping an arrowhead in the poison, a Scythian archer shoots the criminal, the arrow zipping over the heads of the guests. On another evening, the old root-cutter Krateuas might measure out some dread plant poison. With a flourish, he sprinkles it atop a tasty dish and serves it to another condemned man. Mithradates provides learned commentary as everyone observes the result of the poison. Suspense builds as servants proffer the same dish to the guests—minus the poison, of course. Meanwhile, the dying victims were quickly carried out of sight for secret experiments with antidotes (see plate 1).

With grand gestures and banter, Mithradates awes the guests by swallowing a drop of snake venom. For the climax of the evening, the Poison King invites the guests to salt his own plate of roast lamb or his winecup with arsenic or belladonna. Mithradates was not only a toxicologist; he was a Magus, a magician. Both skills came into play in creating his image of invincibility. With a debonair smile, the Poison King raises his goblet in a toast.[4]

The reactions of the courtiers and foreign dignitaries to Mithradates' sensational demonstrations of immunity fascinated the poet and classical scholar A. E. Housman. This verse from his 1896 poem about Mithradates became famous:

> There was a king reigned in the East:
> . . . .
> With poisoned meat and poisoned drink
> He gathered all the springs to birth
> From the many-venomed earth;
> First a little, thence to more,
> He sampled all her killing store;
> And easy, smiling, seasoned sound,
> Sate the king when healths went round.
> They put arsenic in his meat
> And stared aghast to watch him eat;
> They poured strychnine in his cup
> And shook to see him drink it up:
> They shook, they stared as white's their shirt:

Them it was their poison hurt.
—I tell the tale that I heard told.
Mithridates, he died old.

It was his mastery of poisons and his long life that made Mithradates a household word in Western literature and popular culture. His name is memorialized in the term *mithridatism*, the practice of systematically ingesting small doses of deadly substances to make oneself immune to them. With some toxins, the process is effective. It is possible to acquire tolerance for levels of arsenic that would kill others, for example, and it was observed in antiquity that some people in Libya, Armenia, or Egypt were unaffected by local venomous insects, scorpions, and vipers. Mithradates also grasped the little-known fact that snake venom can be safely digested if swallowed—it is deadly only if it enters the bloodstream.[5]

The rising popularity of poisoning in the Roman Empire inspired the Roman satirist Juvenal to joke that murder weapons of "cold steel might make a comeback if people would take a hint from old Mithradates and sample the pharmacopia till they are invulnerable to every drug." Nearly two millennia later, in "Mithridates," the poet-philosopher Ralph Waldo Emerson (1803–82) visualized the Poison King calling for more and more poisons to test on himself, from blister beetles (cantharids) to cyanide (prussic acid):

Give me agates for my meat,
Give me cantharids to eat,
. . . bring me foods,
From all zones and altitudes.

From all natures, sharp and slimy,
. . . wild and tame,
Tree, and lichen, . . .
Bird and reptile be my game.
. . . .
Hemlock for my sherbet cull me,
And the prussic juice to lull me.[6]

MITHRADATES' SECRET ANTIDOTE

In antiquity, every natural poison—animal, plant, or mineral—was believed to have a natural antidote. Mithradates combined both toxic and beneficial *pharmaka* into his personal *theriac* (later called *Mithridatium*).

Traditionally, theriacs combined substances thought to counter poisons. Some common ingredients were cinnamon, myrrh, cassia, honey, castor musk from beaver testicles, frankincense, rue, tannin, garlic, Lemnian earth, Chian wine, charcoal, curdled milk, centaury, aristolochia (birthwort), ginger, iris (orris root), rue, *Eupatorium*, rhubarb from the Volga, *Hypericum* (Saint-John's-wort), saffron, walnuts, figs, parsley, acacia, carrot, cardamom, anise, opium, and other ingredients from the Mediterranean and Black Sea, Arabia, North Africa, Eurasia, and India. Modern science reveals that some of these substances can counteract illness and toxins. For example, the sulfur in garlic neutralizes arsenic in the bloodstream. Charcoal absorbs and filters many different toxins. The chemical composition of Lemnian earth was recently analyzed and shown to contain toxin-absorbing and antibacterial minerals. Garlic, myrrh, cinnamon, and Saint-John's-wort are antibacterial. Recent scientific studies of many common *Mithridatium* ingredients reveal alexipharmic bioactivities in the immune system. Certain plants traditionally used by folk healers in Africa and India can actually neutralize cobra, adder, and viper venoms.[7]

Building on the work begun by Attalus III, Nicander of Colophon, and others, Mithradates recorded the properties of hundreds of poisons and antidotes in experiments on prisoners, associates, and himself. "Through tireless research and every possible experiment," says Pliny, he sought ways to "compel poisons to be helpful remedies." We can imagine Mithradates and his team (Krateuas, Papias, the Magi and Agari healers, and Timotheus, a specialist in war wounds) wearing protective masks made from pig bladders (used by ancient alchemists) and testing, say, the colorless "fiery poison" of Egypt, created by fusing natron (sodium carbonate, common in Egypt) with realgar or orpiment (arsenic). Health-giving essences were compounded with minute amounts of poisons into an *electuary*, a paste held together with honey. The paste was molded into a pill the size of an almond. The king began each day by chewing his secret theriac tablet with cold spring water. Apparently the concoction caused no serious physical problems and promoted his immune system, since ancient sources agree that Mithradates enjoyed excellent health and sexual vigor throughout his long life.[8]

After his death, Mithradates' personal library and papers were taken to Rome, and translated into Latin by Pompey's secretary Lenaeus (95–25 BC). Pliny, who studied Mithradates' own handwritten notes, praised his erudition. "We know from direct evidence and by report," wrote Pliny, that Mithradates "was a more accomplished researcher into biology than any man before him. In order to become immune to poison by making his body accustomed to it, he alone devised the plan to drink poison every day, after first taking remedies." At the height of his reign, Mithradates "amassed detailed knowledge from all his subjects, who covered a substantial part of the world." His international library of ethnobotanical and toxicological treatises may have described drugs used by the Druids of Gaul, Mesopotamian doctors, and the works of Hindu ayurvedic ("long-life") practitioners. The theriac of Sushruta (ca. 550 BC) boasted eighty-five ingredients, and the *Mahagandhahasti* of Charaka (300 BC) had sixty.[9]

Mithradates could have studied the alchemical writings of Democritus of Egypt, drawing on King Menes who cultivated poisonous and medicinal plants in 3000 BC, and we know Mithradates corresponded with Zopyrus in Egypt, who shared his "universal remedy" of twenty ingredients. Another scientific colleague was Asclepiades of Bithynia, who founded an influential medical school in Rome. He declined Mithradates' invitation to work in Sinope but dedicated treatises to the king and sent him antidote formulas.

Perhaps Mithradates sought out the last living members of the Ophiogenes ("Snake people") near Troy, to learn the secrets of venoms. The Marsi of Italy, whose envoys met with Mithradates in 88 BC, were also known for venom-based *pharmaka*. We know that the king's Agari doctors milked the venom of steppe (Caucasian) vipers to make antidotes and medicines. Recently, scientists studying traditional healing practices using Caucasian vipers in Azerbaijan (ancient Baku) discovered that tiny doses can stop life-threatening hemorrhage (as we shall see, this fact, known to the Agari more than two thousand years ago, would save Mithradates' life). Crystallized Caucasian viper venom is now a valuable medical export.[10]

The key principle of Mithradates' theriac was the combination of beneficial drugs and antitoxins with tiny amounts of poisons, the approach followed by Attalus and Hindu doctors. Myriad poisons were known in antiquity, from vipers, scorpions, and jellyfish venoms to the deadly sap of yew trees and crimson crystals of cinnabar. Pliny described about seven thousand venific substances in his encyclopedia of natural history and listed scores of plants (some toxic themselves) said to counter them, such as scordion, agaric mushrooms, artemesia, centaury, polemonia, and aristolochia.[11]

Arsenic—the notorious "powder of succession"—would have been the first poison Mithradates sought to defend against. Arsenic interferes with essential proteins for metabolism. In small doses, however, enzymes produced by the liver bind to and inactivate arsenic. Taking minuscule amounts over time causes the liver to produce more enzymes, allowing one to survive a normally lethal dose. Might a similar process work with plant poisons? Mithradates had observed tolerances to poison plants in rats, insects, birds, and other creatures. Pliny and Aulus Gellius stated that the poison blood of Pontic ducks was included in his *Mithridatium*. It is now known that some species of ducks, larks, and quails eat poison hemlock without harm. Because they do not excrete the toxic alkaloids, their blood and flesh are poisonous.[12]

What other poisons were included in the original *Mithridatium*? Perhaps toxic honey from Pontus—bees were immune to the poison nectar, and in tiny amounts it was considered a tonic. Reptiles—toxic skink, salamander, or viper—were said to be part of Mithradates' recipe, based on the ancient belief that all poisonous creatures produce antidotes to their own toxins in their bodies. Recent scientific experiments show that nonfatal doses of snake venom can stimulate the immune response and allow humans to withstand up to ten times the amount of venom that would be fatal without inoculation. A similar process works with some insect stings and a variety of toxins. Surprising new studies of a "counterintuitive" process called *hormesis* show that very low doses of certain toxins activate a protective mechanism, so that when a larger dose is encountered, it is not as damaging. As the scientists describe this new concept—remarkably akin to Mithradates' own hypothesis—minute doses of poison substances can be beneficial, analogous to a vaccine.[13]

Saint-John's-wort, *Hypericum*, listed in many *Mithridatium* recipes, might help solve the ancient riddle of Mithradates' immunity to poisons. Molecular scientists have recently discovered *Hypericum*'s astounding antidote effect. This herb activates the liver to produce a potent enzyme that can neutralize literally *thousands* of potentially dangerous chemicals. The scientists suggest that if Saint-John's-wort was included in Mithradates' antidote, it would have stimulated a powerful "chemical surveillance system" on "high alert," able to sense and break down "otherwise deadly doses" of many different toxins.[14]

After Mithradates' death, imperial doctors in Rome claimed to possess the top-secret *Mithridatium* formula. Poisonings and fears of poisoning had become rife in Rome—as dictator, Sulla had enacted strict laws against poison sellers. "If you want to survive to gather rosebuds for another day," commented Juvenal, "find a doctor to prescribe some of the drug that Mithradates invented. Before every meal take a dose of the stuff that saves kings."[15]

How might Mithradates' recipe have come into the hands of the Roman emperors? One possibility is that Mithradates entrusted the secret to his friend Asclepiades, the most famous doctor in Rome. A doctor named Aelius prescribed *Mithridatium* for Julius Caesar, who was in Pontus only sixteen years after Mithradates' death. Aelius was a colleague of Asclepiades and perhaps knew Mithradates himself.[16]

An intriguing inscription from the time of Augustus, Rome's first emperor (b. 63 BC), was discovered near the Appian Way. It describes one L. Lutatius Paccius (a non-Roman name) as an "incense-seller, from the family of King Mithradates." Reinach assumed that L. Paccius was a liberated slave or relative of Mithradates who was the king's "chief perfumer." But there is little doubt that Paccius, like other ancient apothecaries, sold more than aromatics; why else might an "incense" purveyor advertise his relationship to the legendary Poison King? (Poisons had been strictly regulated since Sulla's legislation, which explains why an apothecary might advertise only aromatics for sale.) Many of Mithradates' family and friends ended up in Italy. The inscription suggests that Paccius might have known (or claimed to know) the original *Mithridatium* recipe and produced this famous "trademark" antidote in Rome. In fact, another Paccius, probably this man's son, later made a fortune selling a very special medicine in Rome. This Paccius family formula was a profound secret, and Paccius the Younger bequeathed it to the Emperor Tiberius, Augustus's successor in AD 14.[17]

Was the Paccius family formula the basis for the later imperial Roman recipe, said to improve on Mithradates' original, compounded by the imperial doctor Andromachus for Nero? Andromachus's *Mithridatium* had 64 ingredients; he replaced minced lizards with venomous snakes and added opium poppy seeds. Italian archaeologists made an exciting discovery at a villa near Pompeii (AD 79) in 2000. Analysis of the residue inside a large vat consisted of reptile remains and several medicinal plants, including opium poppy seeds. The archaeologists concluded that the vat might have been used to prepare Andromachus's *Mithridatium*.[18]

After Nero (d. AD 68), every Roman emperor religiously ingested what his doctor claimed was a version of the Poison King's own personal antidote. Recipes multiplied—more and more costly and rare ingredients were added along the way. A century after Mithradates' death, Celsus in Gaul listed 36 ingredients mixed into a concoction weighing nearly three pounds, good for about six months' worth of pills, to be taken with wine. In AD 170, Galen of Pergamon, who prescribed a liquid *Mithridatium* for the emperor Marcus Aurelius, added more opium and fine vintage wine, improving the flavor and ensuring that his patient drank his medicine every day. Later medieval recipes contained as many as 184 ingredients.[19]

Arabic (*tiryaq-i-faruq, mithruditus*) and Persian (*daryaq*) theriac recipes in ancient and medieval Islamic toxicology manuscripts followed Mithradates' concept of combining poisons with antidotes. In his treatise on *tiryaq*, Averroes, the learned Spanish-Arabic philosopher-physician (b. 1126), cautioned against the prolonged use of theriac by a healthy person, warning that it "could actually transform human nature into a kind of poison," an allusion to paranoid despots of his day who were obsessed with poisoning. In AD 667, Islamic ambassadors from Rum (or Rumieh, the Byzantine Roman Empire) presented the Tang emperor of China with a gift of the *Mithridatium* theriac (Chinese *tayeqie, diyejia*). It was described as a dark red lump the size and shape of a pig's gall bladder. Chinese manuscript illustrations show foreigners wearing Persian-style clothing offering these *Mithridatium* pills as tribute to the emperor.[20]

In Europe, from the Middle Ages on, *Mithridatium* was eagerly ingested. European laws required apothecaries to openly display all the precious, expensive ingredients and to concoct *Mithridatium* in the public squares. For more than two millennia after the death of Mithradates, aristocrats and royalty, from Charlemagne and Alfred the Great to Henry VIII and Queen Elizabeth I, swallowed some version of the *Mithridatium* faithfully every day of their lives. The royal mixture was kept in ornate apothecary jars illustrating scenes from the life of Mithradates (see fig. 15.3, plate 4). There were also cheaper versions of *Mithridatium* for the poor. The Poison King's universal antidote became the most popular and longest-lived prescription in history, available in Rome as recently as 1984.[21]

Most of the surviving recipes for theriacs in Latin, Greek, Hebrew, Indian, Arabic, and early Islamic medical writings include an array of plant, animal, and mineral *pharmaka* to counteract toxins and disease. Aside from Andromachus's addition of chopped vipers for Nero's antidote, however, most of these theriac recipes did not deliberately include poisons. Yet the ancient writers agreed with Pliny that Mithradates achieved immunity to poisons by ingesting deadly substances *along with* a cocktail of specific or general antidotes. In Pliny's words, he "thought

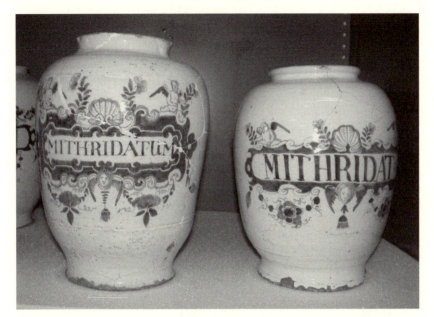

FIG. 11.1. *Mithridatium* jars, sixteenth–seventeenth century.
Wellcome History of Medicine Museum collections, London,
photo courtesy of Christopher Duffin.

out the plan of drinking poisons daily, after taking remedies, in order that sheer habit might render the poisons harmless."[22]

Although we can guess some of the counteracting drugs that Mithradates is likely to have put in his formula, his method of calibrating minuscule doses of poisons and exactly what they were remain a mystery. Mithradates worked in secrecy. The original lost recipe was believed to contain more than fifty ingredients, many of them expensive substances from faraway lands. Oddly, however, the notes translated after his death revealed only a few commonplace ingredients, with the exception of the blood of Pontic ducks. Even the learned naturalist Pliny expressed surprise at the lack of arcane or toxic substances in the Mithradatic notes he studied. He ridiculed a scrap of paper in the king's handwriting: "Pound together two dried walnuts, two figs, and twenty leaves of rue with a pinch of salt: he who takes this while fasting will be immune to all poison for that day." As Pliny remarked, this mundane recipe cannot be taken seriously; some modern scholars suggest it was a forgery or hoax.[23]

So what happened to Mithradates' formula? Several possible explanations come to mind. The archives taken to Rome may have recorded only Mithradates' earliest experiments, superseded by successful tests whose records we do not have. The genuine records could have been lost or hidden during the chaos of the Mithradatic Wars. The documents may have been encrypted. Ancient alchemists wrote in codes or obscure languages; Mithradates possessed the linguistic skills to facilitate this. Perhaps the real formula was kept secret by the imperial Roman doctors who inherited Mithradates' papers or Paccius's recipe, but was later forgotten or lost. Maybe written versions of the perfected formula were destroyed on Mithradates' orders, or entrusted only to closest friends and allies, such as Tigranes, who, like Mithradates, enjoyed robust health and an extremely long life. Perhaps it was destroyed when Callistratus, Mithradates' personal secretary, was murdered by Roman soldiers. Pompey might have burned some of Mithradates' archives, as he did with Sertorius's papers. Or—as suggested by historian Alain Touwaide—maybe Pompey obtained the recipe but kept it secret within his circle.[24] Finally, the instructions for the *Mithridatium* may never have been written down; perhaps they were recorded only in Mithradates' prodigious memory.

Unless new evidence emerges—say, a verifiable recipe on papyrus or stone, or sealed jars of the king's own *Mithridatium* containing residue, or Mithradates' mummified corpse sufficiently preserved to allow an autopsy and hair and bone sampling—the Poison King's universal antidote is irretrievable. Yet Mithradates' ambitious goal of creating a "universal antidote" lives on. Serguei Popov, a top scientist in the ultrasecret Soviet bioweapons program (based in the homeland of the Agari), defected to the United States in 1992. Popov now seeks to perfect a broad-spectrum biodefense, a "universal" antidote to promote immunity to a wide range of biotoxins and "weapons-grade" pathogens. Like the Janus-faced *pharmaka* of the *Mithridatium*, the materials Popov works with carry the potential for great harm or great good.[25]

Mithradates took further precautions against assassination by poison, employing guards in his kitchens and royal tasters. Some metals and certain other crystals and stones were said to detect—even neutralize—poison in wine or food. Mithradates and his best friends surely owned "poison cups," chalices of electrum, a gold and silver alloy. A goblet of electrum revealed the presence of poison when iridescent colors rippled across the metallic surface with a crackling sound, apparently the result of a chemical reaction. Red coral, amber, "adamas," and *glossopetra* ("tongue stones") were thought to have magical properties against poison. Tongue stones (fossilized giant shark teeth from limestone deposits) would "sweat" or change color on contact with poison; ground into power, they deactivated poison. In fact, the calcium carbonate in fossils does react with arsenic. In a chemical process called *chelation*, the arsenic molecules are mopped up by the calcium carbonate.[26]

Mithradates tested the nature of poisons for many reasons besides immunity. Which poisons were best for efficient, undetectable assassination? What if one found oneself in the situation of Hannibal or Jugurtha, with enemies closing in and no escape route? Which poison was ideal for suicide? We know that Mithradates carried suicide capsules and distributed them to Dorylaus, his generals, and close friends. Those capsules, concealed in rings, bracelets, amulets, or sword hilts, obviously contained an extremely fast-acting, relatively gentle, lethal poison with no known antidote.[27]

AGATES AND ART

Mithradates' dominions were rich in mineral resources. Perhaps toxic pigments such as red cinnabar, yellow orpiment, blue azurite, and green malachite led to his fascination with gemology, the magical properties of precious metals and gems. Mithradates himself wrote a treatise on the powers of amber, sacred to the Sun. He corresponded with the leading gemologist of the day, Zachalias, a Jew in Babylon who dedicated his treatises to the king. Mithradates was especially fond of agates, beautiful translucent forms of chalcedony. Gazing on agates' colored bands and speckled, swirling patterns was thought to bring pleasant dreams; agates from Sicily were said to repel scorpions; and the Magi advised athletes to wear red agates ro become invincible. Zachalias recommended wearing a ring of heliotrope ("sun reflecting," a green jasper agate flecked with red iron oxide) to make one a convincing speaker. Mithradates often gave agate rings with his likeness to his ambassadors, to help them argue his case before the Romans and others.[28]

Mithradates' vast *dactylotheke*—collection of agate rings—was renowned. In his love of carved gemstones, Mithradates followed Alexander, the first to inspire the popularity of glyptics, the intricate art of engraving animals, mythic scenes, and other images on intaglio seals and cameos (reliefs on sardonyx, a multilayered agate). The only artist permitted to create gem portraits of Alexander was his personal engraver,

Pyrgoteles. Like Alexander, Mithradates patronized his own highly skilled engravers and artisans.

A connoisseur of precious objets d'art, Mithradates owned thousands of cups, pitchers, plates, and bowls of polished agate from the Rhodopi Mountains, Crimea, and Colchis, and onyx and rock crystal from Cappadocia. His treasury at Talaura alone held two thousand onyx and gold drinking cups, wine kraters, and drinking horns. A precious burnished agate pitcher now in the Louvre was believed to have belonged to Mithradates. Artisans achieved its unique dark brown coloring by slowly heating Rhodopian agate in honey.

The rare beauty of Mithradates' collection inspired a fashion for agates among the Roman aristocracy. Mithradates' *dactylotheke* ended up

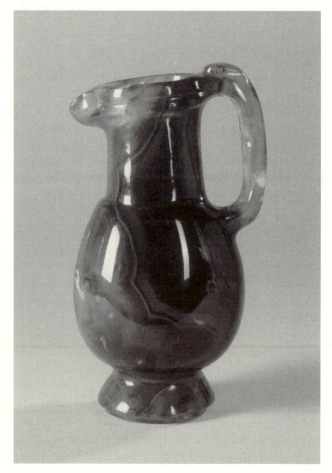

FIG. 11.2. The Mithradates vase. Polished and carved sardonyx (Rhodopian agate), 7 inches high. The burnt-caramel coloring was achieved by heating with honey. Louvre. Réunion des Musées Nationaux/Art Resource, NY.

in Roman hands after his death in 63 BC. Pompey dedicated several large chests of his carved gems to Rome's Temple of Jupiter; Julius Caesar placed six of Mithradates' agate rings in the Temple of Venus; and other rings were dedicated to the Temple of Apollo. Some of Mithradates' agates and miniature gem portraits have survived. During the Crusades, the Venetians plundered Constantinople, dispersing many fine Mithradatic agates among European royalty. Agates from rich hoards and royal tombs of Mithradates' friends, envoys, and concubines, and some belonging to Mithradates himself, found their way into Catherine the Great's personal *dactylotheke* of ten thousand ancient cameos. The Hermitage Museum in St. Petersburg now stores a large collection of exquisite cameos, many taken from wealthy Mithradatic-era tombs around the Crimea.[29]

Mithradates also amassed bejeweled caskets, golden horse trappings, curios and ornaments, armor and weapons set with precious stones, jewelry, vintage robes, carpets and tapestries, and unique scientific instruments. He inherited antique couches and chairs from Darius I, and Mithradates himself enjoyed making furniture of maple and nut woods. On state occasions, the king sat on a fancy throne under a silk canopy, carried an ornate scepter, and rode in a chariot studded with gems. The opening of the Silk Road from India and China (120 BC) to the Black Sea meant that he could acquire silks, brocades, jade, cinnabar, rare spices, exotic drugs, and hardy camels from Bactria and Margiana (Afghanistan and Turkmenistan). An admirer of fine art, Mithradates could afford the highest quality and the best artists (Reinach believed that Mithradates himself had the "soul of an artist"). His coin portraits are remarkable for their clarity and beauty, vigor and kinetic energy. Their superb artistic quality advertised Mithradates as a discerning patron of high culture. Some coin profiles, with windswept hair, evoke a futuristic illusion of speed and progress, hinting at Mithradates' ability to escape danger (see figs. 9.1, 12.1, 13.2).[30]

A handsome bronze krater, over two feet high, shows off the skills of Mithradates' craftsmen—and reveals the complex destinies of his treasures. Part of his largesse to supporters in Greece, this inscribed krater was given to a *gymnasion* (college, probably in Athens) early in his reign. The members called themselves the *Eupatoristai* after their patron Eupator, who promised to liberate Greece. During the First Mithradatic War, this krater was apparently plundered by Sulla and taken to Rome. Two hundred years later, the krater belonged to the emperor Nero, who kept it in his luxurious seaside villa at Antium (Anzio). Unearthed from the

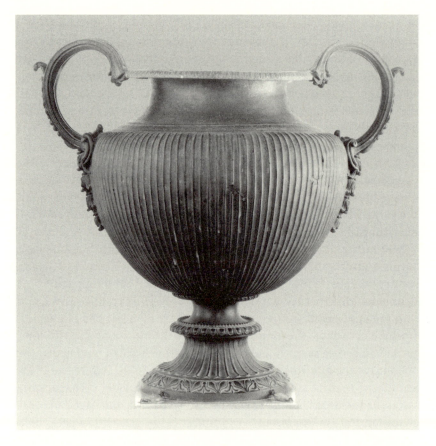

FIG. 11.3. Bronze krater of Mithradates, 27 inches high, 120–63 BC, discovered in Nero's Villa, Anzio, eighteenth century, Benedict XIV donation MC1068. Capitoline Collection, Rome.

villa's ruins by Pope Benedict XIV in the eighteenth century, the krater is now a centerpiece in Rome's Capitoline Museum.[31]

During Mithradates' reign, cosmopolitian Pontus on the Black Sea became the intellectual and cultural capital of the ancient world, drawing sophisticated artists and scholars from many lands. A lover of Greek poetry, literature, music, and theater, Mithradates sponsored plays, dramatic readings, and musical contests. Tyrannio the Grammarian, a leading poetic orator, was one of many stars in Mithradates' court. The modern Greek poet Constantine Cavafy (b. 1863) imagined the private thoughts of a Cappadocian poet in Mithradates' retinue. In Cavafy's poem, this poet is penning an epic about Darius I, commissioned by Mithradates. Suddenly he is interrupted by a servant shouting that the Roman army is coming. The terrified poet realizes that Mithradates' interest in poetry will be set aside in favor of war. Before taking cover, the poet searches for the perfect phrase to describe the Persian king and, by implication, Mithradates. The final words on the page: "arrogance and exultation."[32]

A MUSICAL INTERLUDE

As we've seen, an evening with the king might feature any manner of entertainments, from rowdy drinking contests and shocking poison pageants to elegant cultural events. At one of the royal banquets, a musician brought along his pretty daughter. She played the cithara for Mithra-

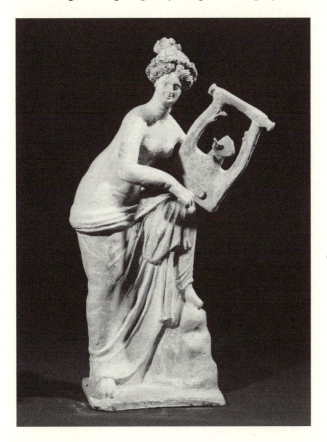

FIG. 11.4. Stratonice may have resembled this flirtatious cithara player, Greek terracotta, ca. 200 BC. Erich Lessing/Art Resource, NY.

dates while he was savoring a mellow old wine. Female harpists were unusual. Mithradates was charmed, perhaps recalling that Aristonicus's mother had played the cithara. The girl's Macedonian name, Stratonice, was a good omen ("Victory in War"). Plutarch says that Stratonice made "such a swift conquest that Mithradates immediately took her away to his bed," without a word to her father.

The next morning the distraught father awoke to find his tables laden with silver beakers and golden dishes. Servants and smiling eunuchs held out beautiful garments. Outside his humble house stood a fine horse caparisoned like those of the king's knights. Assuming the fairy-tale trappings were a mean practical joke, the man tried to run away. The retainers explained the situation. Stratonice was now Mithradates' favorite concubine, held in such high esteem that the king was bestowing the estate of a rich, recently deceased friend upon her father. The dubious musician was finally convinced. To the good-natured amusement of Mithradates and the townspeople, Stratonice's father donned his new purple robe and rode through the streets on his handsome horse, shouting "All this mine! *Mine!* I'm mad with joy!"[33]

KABEIRA

Doctors, pharmacologists, botanists joined the artists who flocked to Pontus, along with architects, scientists, and military engineers, such as Niconides of Thessaly and Callimachus, who designed fortifications, catapults, siege machines, and other innovative projects. Not all of these scientists' bold technological experiments were successful—remember the collapsing *sambuca* at Rhodes and the catastrophic Nike deus ex machina at Pergamon. But the ambitious construction projects at Kabeira were striking examples of Mithradates' scientific interests and unlimited wealth.

Young Mithradates had been struck by the natural beauty and defensibility of Kabeira, surrounded by steep mountains and forests of beech, maple, walnut, pine, and spruce, on the Lycos River. There were important cinnabar mines (toxic mercury ore used for pigments). Perhaps the Poison King knew a useful toxicological fact that modern scientists have only recently discovered, that mercury in the soil here taints the local wild mushrooms. On a remote rocky peak, Mithradates constructed Kainon Chorion ("New Castle"), a fortified treasury for precious valuables. The vaults contained not only gold and silver and priceless artworks, but also Mithradates' private papers, court archives, and personal correspondence. Strabo, who traveled there, said it was about 200 stades (about 25 miles) north of Kabeira. In 1912, the ruins of this citadel were discovered, complete with underground stone staircases.[34]

At Kabeira, Mithradates built towers to confine his younger sisters Nyssa, Roxana, and Statira, sentenced to lifelong spinsterhood. The king's new lover, the cithara player Stratonice, became the lady of Kabeira: perhaps their son Xiphares was born here. Mithradates loved to relax at this luxurious, secure residence. The well-watered grounds, with willows, poplars, grape arbors, and apple trees, were surrounded by extensive gardens where the royal botanists tended plants and ducks nibbled hellebore and hemlock. Mithradates maintained a large zoological garden and game park at Kabeira, for rare creatures from far-flung allies and trading partners: ostriches, cobras and scorpions, crocodiles, pheasants from Colchis, Bactrian camels, perhaps an Indian elephant and tigers. Mithradates and Dorylaus and their friends stayed at the hunting lodge and chased rabbit, partridge, quail, fox, lynx, bear, and boar. The king modeled these lavish features on the Persian gardens, zoos, and hunting parks created by Cyrus, Xerxes, and Darius. He was also following the example of Alexander, who kept an exotic menagerie of lions, bears, mongooses, and ostriches.

One of the most striking features of Kabeira was a very high waterfall. The prodigious force and volume of the waterfall inspired Mithradates and his engineers to harness the rushing water. They constructed the first water-powered mill. It was described by Strabo, who observed the mill or its ruins after the Mithradatic Wars. Until this invention of the water mill, humans and oxen had laboriously turned heavy grindstones to mill grain. After Strabo wrote his description of Mithradates' mill at Kabeira, water-mill technology spread to Italy and Europe.[35]

MASTER OF LANGUAGES

Mithradates' dazzling memory and facility with languages were legendary in his own time (and a book in several languages is still called a "mithridates"). The king was naturally endowed with these gifts from childhood. But he may also have benefited from special memory techniques taught by the leading philosopher in his court, Metrodorus the Roman Hater. Metrodorus invented a memory device based on the Zodiac and mythological stories. The twelve constellations were subdivided into 360 storage compartments, each "box" a category of information. This technique could be invaluable for toxicological experiments and languages.

Mithradates far excelled Cyrus the Great, who knew the names of all his officers and satraps. Only one other individual in antiquity had linguistic abilities that even approached those of Mithradates. According to Plutarch, Queen Cleopatra of Egypt "spoke many languages and gave audiences to most foreign ambassadors without the help of interpreters." She knew Greek and Latin, and some Ethiopian, Coptic, Hebrew, Median, Arabic, Syrian, and Persian. Mithradates was reportedly so fluent in the languages of his subjects and soldiers that he never required interpreters. Aulus Gellius remarked that "he was thoroughly conversant in the dialects of the 25 nations that he ruled, and spoke each language as if it were his native tongue." Pliny, who personally studied Mithradates' library and letters, declared, "Mithridates spoke or read the languages of 22 nations; he could address and listen to the petitions of all of his subject peoples without interpreters." Valerius Maximus cited Mithradates' linguistic proficiency as a shining example of "industrious study." [36]

Mithradates' international court, allies, and armies presented unique opportunities. Consider Colchis: this region was said to have more than 100 tribes, each with a different dialect—Roman traders in Colchis required the services of 130 interpreters, according to Pliny. In the lands south of Colchis, 26 different tongues were spoken. It is unlikely that Mithradates learned every single dialect of these remote places, but he could make himself understood by most of his subjects.

Which languages did Mithradates speak or read with ease? These are certain: Greek, Macedonian, Persian, Latin, Aramaic/Hebrew, Parthian, Armenian, Old and New Phrygian, Cappadocian, and the Gaulish dialect of his Galatian lover Adobogiona. Other languages may have included Avestan (Old Iranian, used in Zoroastrian prayers); Sanskrit (Hindu medical texts); Egyptian and Punic; Celtic/Gallic (perhaps Allobrogesean, the language of his bodyguard Bituitus). He knew some Anatolian tongues, such as Carian, Mysian, Isaurian, Lydian, Lycian (and Pisidian), and maybe had a smattering of Syriac, Elamite, and Sumerian (used in religious texts of the Seleucid era). He could have learned Italian dialects, Marsic, Oscan, and Umbrian; Thracian (spoken by many of his cavalry regiments; and Getic (spoken in Tomis on the Danube). Other possibilities include vestigal forms of Assyrian or Hittite and dialects of Colchis, Sarmatia, and Scythia.

Mithradates' ease with languages meant that he could receive and send messages in private, without risking wide knowledge of his dealings. In the peaceful interlude after the treaty of Dardanus, the king reigned uneventfully, shoring up his Black Sea Empire, building new strongholds, training armies, seeking new allies, and considering strategies vis-à-vis Rome.[37] Meanwhile, what were his friends and foes up to?

TIGRANES THE GREAT, KING OF KINGS

The Romans now controlled Bithynia and western Anatolia. To collect the massive fine of 20,000 talents imposed by Sulla, tax collectors returned to prey on Anatolia. Plutarch compared them to "harpies, stealing the food of the people," causing "unspeakable and incredible misfortune." In fact, Sulla's fine had been paid off. Roman creditors had already made a profit of 20,000 talents—their exorbitant interest rates had inflated the total public debt to an astronomical 120,000 talents. Anatolian families were forced to sell their young sons and virgin daughters into prostitution and slavery; towns sold sacred statues and temple dedications. The Roman creditors were vicious, torturing debtors before selling them into bondage. The land was also oppressed by the greed and violence of the two occupying Roman legions who had run wild under Fimbria and Murena.[38]

Just as Mithradates had anticipated, Galatia, the buffer zone between Pontus and Bithynia, allied with Rome. Cappadocia remained uneasily divided between Mithradates and Ariobarzanes, who owed his crown to Sulla. Mithradates' ally and son-in-law Tigranes of Armenia had taken over Syria. After violent intrigues among the Syrian king Grypos and his murderous relatives, the Syrians looked abroad for a stable monarch. They wanted to invite Mithradates to rule Syria, but others (perhaps Mithradates himself) worried that this might attract the attention of Rome. In 83 BC, the Syrians chose Tigranes of Armenia to be their king.

Tigranes was powerful and imperious. After the Peace of Dardanus, the title "King of Kings" was up for grabs. Tigranes took it. He now ruled a kingdom that stretched from Syria to the Caspian Sea, from Artaxata to Mesopotamia. Tigranes' armies swelled with divisions from Arabia, Caucasia, and central Asia, but Rome had paid little attention since Sulla turned Tigranes out of Cappadocia in 95 BC. The new King of Kings was building a magnificent fortified city for himself on the Tigris River, Tigranocerta, "City of Tigranes."[39]

In about 80 BC, Mithradates sent ambassadors to Rome, hoping to sign the peace agreement of five years earlier. But Ariobarzanes had complained to Sulla that Mithradates still held part of Cappadocia. Sulla ordered Mithradates to give it up, as agreed at Dardanus. Mithradates complied and withdrew his army. He dispatched his ambassadors back to Rome, ready to formalize the treaty.

But in the meantime Sulla had unexpectedly resigned his dictatorship. The man so feared as a monstrous tyrant resumed his old lifestyle, drinking and carousing with musicians and prostitutes. At age sixty, Sulla succumbed to a mysterious, gruesome disease (78 BC). According to Plutarch, Sulla's bowels rotted, corrupting his entire body into a mass of worms. Relays of servants worked to scrub away the teeming maggots. Sulla spent hours in the baths, "but the vermin defied all purification." Upon Sulla's death, his young associate Pompey took the body to Rome for cremation. To mask the stench, Sulla's female friends contributed vast quantities of spices and perfumes: these alone required 210 litters in the funeral cortege. A large figure of Sulla himself was molded out of frankincense and cinnamon and placed next to the corpse on the pyre. On the day of the funeral, glowering clouds dumped heavy rains. According to Plutarch, everyone heaved a sigh of relief when the rain lifted long enough for the flames to consume the repulsive remains.[40]

Mithradates' reaction to the news of Sulla's dreadful affliction and death is unknown, but his feelings must have swung between schadenfreude and apprehension. Mithradates' envoys came home again with no official agreement with Rome. The Senate was too preoccupied to meet Mithradates' ambassadors—or were they hostile? In fact, many in Rome considered the Mithradatic Wars unfinished. Mithradates may have compared his uncomfortable situation to the tragedy of Jugurtha in North Africa. Jugurtha had struggled in vain to reach a viable peace with Rome, but the Senate repeatedly refused to sign the terms of his surrender, and in the end he was betrayed to Sulla and murdered.

By all accounts, Mithradates had lived up to the terms of the Peace of Dardanus. He had made good-faith efforts to formalize the treaty with the Senate in Rome.[41] He complied with Sulla's last demand to leave

FIG. 11.5. This Roman portrait of Sulla seems to express cruelty and corruption. Staatliche Antikensammlungen und Glyptothek, Munich

FIG. 11.6. Perfuming the corpse of Sulla. Caricature by John Leech, in *The Comic History of Rome* by Gilbert Abbott A Beckett, 1852.

Cappadocia. His actions certainly appear to have been those of a man desirous of peaceful equilibrium. Trying to deal with the Republic as it was thrashing about in its death throes was frustrating, nerve-wracking. But the situation also presented interesting possibilities for a man as ambitious, resourceful, and opportunistic as Mithradates.

CAPPADOCIA

Mithradates conferred with his old ally Tigranes. With Sulla dead, Rome was in no position to enforce the still-unsigned treaty. The two monarchs agreed that Tigranes should invade Cappadocia. This time, they intended to succeed.

The Armenian army was massive. Tigranes drew up 120,000 foot soldiers and many ranks of war chariots. His general Mithrobarzanes led a hard-core cavalry, 12,000 strong. Tigranes' *Ayrudzi* ("horsemen" in Armenian) were mostly Parthian-style *cataphracts*, knights in chain mail riding large, heavily armored Nisaean horses. The historian Sallust praised Armenia's cavalry as "remarkable for the beauty of its steeds and armor." Tigranes also commanded 12,000 mounted archers, deadly accurate at more than two hundred yards—and their arrows were tipped with poison for good measure.

Jewish historian Josephus gave the figure of 500,000 for Tigranes' entire army, which included all the camp followers: men who tended the camels and mules loaded with baggage, weapons, provisions, and chests of gold and silver; trailing families and servants; shepherds with herds of cattle, sheep, and goats to feed the thousands. Tigranes' multitudes were likened to a "swarm of locusts or the dust of the earth."

Tigranes marched into Cappadocia: he met no resistance. According to the terms of Tigranes' agreement of 95 BC with Mithradates, the land of Cappadocia fell to Pontus, while Tigranes seized all the spoils and captives. Tigranes' army rounded up 300,000 Cappadocian men, women, and children. They were not harmed and families were kept intact; they were even allowed to keep a few possessions and animals. This great mass of uprooted people was herded south to populate Tigranes' fabulous new city on the Tigris. Tigranes also moved captive populations of Greeks from Cilicia, Jews from Palestine, and nomadic Arabs to Tigranocerta. This forced transfer of whole populations was a very large-scale example of an age-old practice of powerful conquerors.[42]

Sertorius and the White Fawn

The disintegration of Rome's foreign policy during the civil wars had allowed the pirate fleets to "multiply by tens of thousands" in the Mediterranean Sea. The pirates—always seeking loot and now a great military force—were allied with Mithradates and with Sertorius in Spain. No Roman ships were safe, a significant advantage for both men. In one of his orations in Rome, Cicero described how Mithradates and Sertorius corresponded through intelligence couriers aboard pirate corsairs.[43]

Sertorius sent two military strategists to Pontus, Lucius Magius and Lucius Fannius. They encouraged Mithradates to imagine a scenario in which the rebellions in Spain and Anatolia could succeed. They painted a rosy future of a reasonable Roman empire, led by Marius's moderate

Populars, an empire that would be content to rule the western Mediterranean while Mithradates ruled his Black Sea Empire.

The last hope of the Populars, Sertorius was a master of ambush, disguise, and guerrilla warfare. He had won military honors (and lost an eye) in Gaul and helped put down the Marsi revolt in Italy. As rebel governor of Spain, Sertorius established a Senate-in-exile for fugitive Marius supporters. Even though he dreamed of retiring to the idyllic Canary Islands, "far from tyranny and endless wars," he agreed to head the Spanish resistance movement and was winning battles against legions sent from Rome. Good at languages, Sertorius was a courageous revolutionary leader beloved by his soldiers and the Spaniards.

One day, a Spanish hunter presented Sertorius with a pure white fawn. Wearing a garland of blossoms, the fawn followed the stern general around camp, to the delight of his men. This little albino doe was sent by the goddess of war, Diana (Artemis), declared Sertorius. She slept in his tent and whispered to him, warning him of dangers. Whenever his spies reported a victory, Sertorius kept it secret. He brought out his white doe, assuring his soldiers that she had predicted success. The next day, he would publicly announce the victory to his men, thereby fulfilling her forecast.[44]

THE THIRD MITHRADATIC WAR BEGINS

Sertorius was in many ways a Roman counterpart to Mithradates. The civil wars had "filled Sertorius with venom" against oligarchic Rome. As governor of Spain, Sertorious had become disillusioned with the greed and harshness of Roman tax officials. Like Rutilius Rufus in Anatolia, Sertorius sympathized with the native peoples embittered and oppressed by Rome's administration of the province. Because he reduced taxes and governed mildly, the Spaniards invited him to lead their revolt against Sulla. As Plutarch described Sertorius, his charismatic personality mirrored that of Mithradates. Sertorius "inspired his followers with fresh hopes, offered them new adventures, and kept them united in spite of hardships."

Sertorius's prestige had spread throughout the Mediterranean world. Traders, pirates, and envoys from Spain regaled Mithradates with tales of Sertorius's victories. Mithradates' Roman advisers compared Sertorius to Hannibal and convinced Mithradates to ally with him. "If you, the most powerful king in the world, were to combine your strength with the world's most successful general," they promised, then Rome, destabilized by civil wars and slave uprisings in Italy, would be paralyzed by an unstoppable attack on two fronts.[45]

In 76 BC a severe earthquake shook Italy. That year Sertorius won great victories over Roman armies. The next year, 75 BC, Sertorius and Mithradates began negotiating in earnest. Mithradates promised to supply ships and money for a joint war on Rome. In return, Mithradates asked Sertorius to confirm him as sovereign over the former Province of Asia, restoring the land he had given up under the treaty with Sulla. Sertorius told Mithradates that he was welcome to Bithynia, Cappadocia, Galatia, and Paphlagonia, but insisted that western Anatolia should remain a Roman province. Sertorius's audacity surprised Mithradates. Plutarch records the king's response: "This Sertorius was driven to the shores of the Atlantic Ocean, and yet he dares to mark out the frontiers of our kingdom! Can you imagine what he will demand when he is master of Rome?"[46]

Despite some arm wrestling over Anatolia, Sertorius and Mithradates drew up a treaty and swore oaths to uphold it. Sertorius agreed that Mithradates should resume possession of eastern Anatolia, and sent his general, Marcus Varius, with an army to Pontus. Mithradates sent Sertorius forty ships bearing 3,000 talents of silver—half again the penalty of 2,000 talents he had paid Sulla in 85 BC. In 76–74 BC, Mithradates' mints issued gold and silver coins at a great rate, in anticipation of war.

Sertorius's general M. Varius and Mithradates together "captured certain cities in Asia." Plutarch does not name the towns, but presumably they were places that had been harshly punished by Sulla for supporting Mithradates, yet without Roman garrisons. Mithradates graciously—wisely—allowed Sertorius's general to enter these Anatolian cities as their liberator. The towns were declared free and exempt from taxation, on the authority of Sertorius, Mithradates' new, compassionate Roman ally. Suddenly, wrote Plutarch, the downtrodden people of Anatolia "were inspired anew by the prospect of better days to come," and they longed for the benign rule of Mithradates and Sertorius to begin.[47]

In Bithynia, Rome's "miserable puppet" Nicomedes IV died childless in 75/74 BC. In a suspicious déjà vu move—calling to mind the last testament of Attalus III willing Phrygia to Rome—Nicomedes bequeathed his kingdom to Rome. The Senate sent a governor, Cotta, to organize the new province. This was the spark that kindled the Third Mithradatic War. Mithradates immediately declared the will phony. The alliance with

Sertorius had given Mithradates new capacities and new hope. The unilateral Roman takeover of Bithynia was, as Reinach commented, "tantamount to a declaration of war—it ruptured the equilibrium established by the Peace of Dardanus."[48]

The king of Pontus threw himself into feverish preparations to recover his empire. He stored a huge amount of grain from the steppes in granaries all around the Black Sea. Scythia normally sent 180,000 medimni of grain and 200 talents of silver a year as tribute. But this year, according to records cited by Appian, Mithradates received an astonishing 2 million medimni of grain, enough to feed about 300,000 people for a year. All summer, fall, and winter, Mithradates cut great swathes of timber to build ships and purchased well-trained, strong horses. His arms-makers forged Roman-style spears, swords, and shields; his engineers constructed siege engines; his recruiters gathered up mobs of new soldiers to be trained by Roman officers.[49]

Mithradates called up armies from Cappadocia, Colchis, Armenia, and Scythia and beyond. From the remote territories of the Amazons, along the Thermodon and Don rivers to the Caspian Sea, mounted women warriors joined their male counterparts, the iron-mining Chalybes and Heniochi, Taurians of the Crimea, and Leucosyrians of eastern Cappadocia. Sarmatian men and women warriors joined the warlike tribes of the Basilidae, Dandarians, and the Iazyges around the Sea of Azov, the Coralli and hordes of Thracians of the Danube and Rhodopi and Haemus mountains. The ancient sources agree that the bravest of Mithradates' barbarians were the Bastarnae of Carpathia.

Altogether, says Appian, Mithradates recruited a fighting force of 140,000 infantry and 16,000 cavalry, attended by milling crowds of beasts of burden, baggage carriers, road makers, supply agents, and other camp followers. He had doubled his navy to 400 ships. Archelaus, Mithradates' former mercenary general, had gone over to Rome. But Mithradates' lineup of commanders was impressive: the Romans M. Varius, L. Magius, and L. Fannius joined Dorylaus, Gordius, Neoptolemus, Diophantus, Taxiles, Hermocrates, Alexander of Paphlagonia, Dionysius the Eunuch, Eumachus (former satrap of Galatia), Konnakorix (a Galatian), Metrophanes, and Aristonicus.[50]

Sertorius was about fifty years old and Mithradates was about sixty in 74 BC. Without ever meeting in person, they had recognized their similar spirits and common interests. Despite their personal longing for peace and security, the two leaders swore to make war on the mighty Roman juggernaut. A very great deal was at stake for each man.

Falling Star

FOUR snow-white horses pulled the golden chariot, encrusted with gems flashing in the sun's first rays. There was no driver. The beautiful horses galloped at full speed across the windswept cliff and plunged into the sparkling sea below.

It was dawn, the first day of spring, 74 BC. Mithradates' magnificent sacrifice, reported by Appian, to the Sun gods Mithra and Helios, and to Poseidon god of sea and earthquakes, was performed to ensure success in the new war on Rome. The vivid image of the majestic white horses plunging into the sea persisted in the later Roman, Byzantine, medieval, and modern imagination. Some five hundred years later, for example, the early Christian writer Sidonis Apollinaris described a splendid castle in Gaul adorned by a dramatic painting of Mithradates' sacrifice. In 1678, the English playwright Nathaniel Lee pictured Mithradates sending "a chariot, all with emeralds set, and filled with coral tridents, [and] a hundred horses, wild as wind" over the precipice.[1]

The grandiose ritual is ignored by modern historians, but its multicultural significance was not lost on Mithradates' followers. Horse sacrifices to the Sun were practiced by the ancient Greeks, Trojans, Scythians, and Persians. Ancient kings of Persia sacrificed horses to honor the Sun; the Magi traditionally killed fine white horses at the Euphrates River; and when Xerxes invaded Greece, they sacrificed horses at the River Strymon in Thrace. Mithradates must also have been influenced by—and perhaps even witnessed—the great horse sacrifice of Rhodes. Each spring the Rhodians—those brilliant seafarers who had bested Mithradates' fleet—drove a chariot and four horses into the sea to honor Helios, who guided his sun-chariot across the skies.[2]

For good measure, Mithradates also performed the great fire sacrifice, as he had done after his victory over Murena. After the rituals to appease

Fig. 12.1. Portrait of Mithradates, silver tetradrachm, 75/74 BC. His open mouth and manelike hair, even more windblown than previous coin images, evoke a kinetic sense of forward movement at great speed. 1944.100.41480, bequest of E. T. Newell, courtesy of the American Numismatic Society.

these powerful male deities, Mithradates marched into Paphlagonia at the head of his army. There he delivered a rousing speech to his soldiers.

GROUNDS FOR WAR

Mithradates expounded on his illustrious ancestry and described with pride how his small kingdom had grown great under his rule. Pointing out that his armies had never been defeated by Romans when he was present to lead them, Mithradates extolled his vast resources and strong

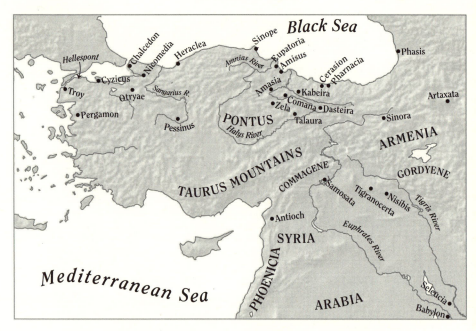

MAP 12.1. The Second and Third Mithradatic Wars: campaigns in Anatolia,
Armenia, and Mesopotamia. Map by Michele Angel

defenses. The Romans, he declared, were driven by "boundless greed" to
enslave everyone. "Why did the Senate refuse to sign the Peace of Dardanus? Because Rome never intended to give us peace! They intended to
break the treaty all along! Now this phony will of Nicomedes of Bithynia
reveals their lust to dominate us."

Mithradates emphasized Rome's troubles at home and abroad. "The
Romans are losing the war with our new ally Sertorius in Spain. Italy is
ravaged by civil strife and slave uprisings. Because of their wickedness,
the Romans have not a single ally and not one of their subjects obeys
them willingly!" Gesturing to his three Roman generals, Varius, Fannius,
and Magius, Mithradates shouted, "Look! Some of Rome's noblest citizens are at war with their own country and allied with us!"

After this stirring speech, Mithradates marched into Bithynia. The
Roman governor Cotta fled to Chalcedon. Cyzicus sent 3,000 hoplites to
Cotta, but the people of Bithynia overwhelmingly welcomed Mithradates as their liberator—they had been crushed under the heel of Sulla's
tax collectors. At Mithradates' approach, fearful Romans rushed to Chalcedon, crowding around the city's gates. But the gates were bolted shut

by Cotta, huddling inside. When Mithradates' army arrived, there was a pitiless slaughter. The Roman civilians and Cyzicene soldiers stranded outside the gates "perished, caught between their friends and their foes, beseeching both for mercy."[3]

Meanwhile, Mithradates' Bastarnae smashed through the massive bronze chain protecting the harbor of Chalcedon, burning 40 boats and capturing 60. Only 30 Bastarnae died in the naval battle, but more than 3,000 Roman, Chaceldonian, and Cyzicene sailors lost their lives. On land, Mithradates lost 700 men, but more than 5,000 Romans were killed and 4,500 were taken prisoner in this first battle of the Third Mithradatic War. The Roman general Lucius Licinius Lucullus, encamped on the Sangarius River, struggled to encourage his legions after this great disaster.[4]

Mithradates, reveling in victory, looking forward to regaining his Anatolian empire, marched on the fortified port of Cyzicus, gateway to Asia. The army of 120,000 infantrymen, 16,000 horsemen, and 100 scythed chariots trailed a horde of camp followers and road and bridge builders; Mithradates' total forces were said to approach 300,000.[5]

MEANWHILE IN ROME

Lucullus, Sulla's protégé, had become consul in Rome in 74 BC. His co-consul Cotta was sent to govern the new Province of Bithynia. Lucullus was envious of his rival Pompey (a younger and more ruthless protégé of Sulla), who was winning honors fighting Mithradates' new ally Sertorius in Spain. Determined to be the general who would triumph over Mithradates once and for all, Lucullus schemed to keep Pompey occupied in Spain.

Sure enough, Lucullus was chosen to fight Mithradates in 74 BC. The Senate, fearing that Mithradates planned to attack Italy itself with his armada, pledged three thousand talents to raise a fleet. But Lucullus bragged that he would not need a navy to overcome Mithradates. He raised three legions himself and took command of the two "Fimbrian" legions still stationed in Anatolia, for a total of about 30,000 infantry and 2,500 cavalry.

Not only was Lucullus seriously outnumbered, but the Fimbrian legions would prove to be a problem. They had been complicit in mutinies and the deaths of their two previous generals, Flaccus and Fimbria. Tough fighters, but insolent and unmanageable, the soldiers were, in Plutarch's words, "spoiled by habits of greed and luxury" and Murena's

FIG. 12.2. Lucullus, marble bust. Photograph © The State Hermitage Museum,
St. Petersburg.

undisciplined leadership. Like rotten apples, these Fimbrian legionnaires
would insidiously infect Lucullus's army with demands for booty and
with outright insubordination.

Rome's renewed war, to destroy the enemy Lucullus called the "new
Hannibal," was marked by ripsawing loyalties, devastating mayhem, and

shocking reversals. This conflict—which has been described as a struggle between Roman oligarchic hegemony and democratic ideals of suffrage, freedom, and nationalization of land—drew participants from all corners of the classical world, from Spain to the Caspian Sea, from the River Don to the Persian Gulf. Treacherous terrain, cataclysmic weather—even celestial marvels, strange prodigies, and the gods themselves—would be players in this epic contest between Lucullus and Mithradates.[6]

THE FALLING STAR

Lucullus's advisers urged him to take over Pontus, undefended while Mithradates was in Bithynia. The chief proponent was Archelaus—Mithradates' turncoat star general. Perhaps Archelaus recalled Sulla's earlier offer to crown him king of Mithradates' rich Kingdom of Pontus during the negotiations at Dardanus. But Lucullus scoffed: "Why would I hunt for a wild beast in his empty lair?" Then Lucullus caught sight of the massive army drawn up by Mithradates. Stunned, he hung back—he needed a cunning strategy to overcome such an immense force.

Mithradates immediately provoked a battle, sending out an army led by the Roman M. Varius, Sertorius's one-eyed general. At Otryae, Lucullus marched out to meet the challenge. The two armies faced each other on the plain under a clear blue sky and were just on the verge of combat.

Suddenly, the sky burst asunder. A huge, flaming object of molten silver ripped through the heavens and slammed into the ground between the two armies. The stunned armies "separated," in Plutarch's words, but the retreat must have been frantic. Fiction writer Michael Curtis Ford, in his adventure novel about the Mithradatic Wars, imagines the two armies pelted with a shower of clods of dirt and searing metal shrapnel as the burning celestial object plowed into the earth. Ford creates a scene in which Lucullus and Mithradates peer into the mysterious crater across from each other. The two generals lock eyes, each attempting to read the divine message that the other has taken from this event. In Ford's fantasy, the commanders wordlessly agree to fight another day.[7]

What was the extraterrestrial object? Richard Stothers, a NASA meteorologist who studies ancient observations of astronomical events, analyzed this incident using the scientific categories of Unidentified Flying Objects. Because there were thousands of eyewitnesses at close range,

Stothers considers Plutarch's account credible. The blinding flash in day-light indicates a high scale of magnitude. To be clearly observed over-head by armies standing just out of bowshot distance, the flaming object, Stothers estimates, must have measured more than four feet across.

A fresh meteorite (a meteor that lands and survives impact) is usually black, leading Stothers to suggest that the bright silvery color recorded was that of an incandescent fireball or bolide—an extremely bright meteor—while it streaked across the sky, before impact. Meteorites were revered in antiquity in shrines at Pessinus, Troy, Cyzicus, Abydus, and Ephesus. No surviving ancient sources indicate that the object at Otryae was recovered and placed in a shrine. Although Stothers believes that the evidence points to a meteorite, in strict scientific terms this event must be classified as a "Close Encounter of the First Kind," an observa-tion at close range of a large unidentified space object that leaves no apparent physical evidence. Since Plutarch's original Greek terminology indicates that witnesses did examine the object on the ground, it seems safe to say that the battle was interrupted by a spectacular meteorite—perhaps the meteor crater will be identified at Ortryae someday. After the impact, the witnesses compared the meteorite's size and shape to those of a *pithos*, a very large earthenware storage jar with a pointed end. Notably, as meteors hurtle through the earth's atmosphere, they can take on a tapered "nose-cone" shape, similar to a Hellenistic storage jar.

Modern historians pay little attention to this incident, except to as-sume that both sides saw it as an evil omen. Reinach, for example, says only that Lucullus used the ill-omened "chute d'un bolide" as an excuse to avoid fighting when outnumbered. No record survives to tell us how Mithradates' Magi or Lucullus's seers really did interpret this extraordi-nary prodigy. But we can make some educated guesses. It is true that Romans in this period feared comets, falling stars, and meteors. Both armies were alarmed and ran away. But afterward, I think it is likely that both Mithradates and Lucullus and their respective omen readers could find *positive* meaning in the event.

Meteors were associated with the Anatolian mother goddess Cybele, who was represented as a stone that fell to earth. Lucullus—as well as Mithradates and his circle—knew that Cybele's sacred black stone was worshipped at Pessinus—Marius made a pilgrimage there in 98 BC, hoping for victory against Sulla. Lucullus had been present when Sulla himself was encouraged by a dream of Cybele handing him a thunder-bolt. Cybele worship became popular in Rome after the Second Punic War. The Sibylline Books had declared that Rome could defeat Hannibal

Fig. 12.3. Witnesses described the meteorite that slammed onto the battlefield between the armies of Lucullus and Mithradates as a large, flaming object that resembled a giant *pithos* (storage jar) of molten silver. This artist's impression illustrates the scale and shape of the meteorite. Image by Michele Angel.

only if Cybele's "sky-stone" was brought to Italy. With great pomp, her sacred meteorite was transported from Pessinus to Rome in 204 BC. So, in 73 BC, when a meteorite at Otryae saved him from a battle against vastly superior forces, Lucullus may well have considered the prodigy as a sign of Cybele's protection.

Mithradates, aware that Cybele was a goddess of victory and protector of Anatolian cities, could have seen the meteor as a positive sign too. Because the meteorite halted the battle, his seers could take it to mean that he would be victorious against Lucullus without bloodshed, or that the gods forbade a battle at that time. Mithradates and his priests usually considered a blazing light in the sky to be a good omen, recalling the awesome comets that had attended his birth, his coronation, and his massacre of Romans in 88 BC.[8]

After the silvery fireball from heaven aborted the battle at Otryae, Mithradates took advantage of a dark, rainy night to march to Cyzicus, undetected by Lucullus. Mithradates captured about three thousand inhabitants of Cyzicus's *chora* and established what he assumed would be a brief siege to take the city.

SIEGE OF CYZICUS, 73–72 BC

Mithradates sent Metrophanes to blockade the harbor while his army camped on the slopes of the mountains. Cyzicus was losing hope—there had been no word from Lucullus since the ignominius defeat at Chalcedon. Menacing siege towers began to encircle the city walls, the work of Mithradates' engineer Niconides. Finally, Lucullus advanced. But Mithradates' soldiers terrified the Cyzicenes by pointing to the army far in the distance. "See those campfires? Those are Tigranes' great armies of Armenians and Medes, come to help Mithradates!"[9]

Lucullus's intelligence reported that Mithradates depended on foraging and supplies delivered by sea to feed his vast army. "All we have to do is stomp on Mithradates' belly," remarked Lucullus to his officers, "and simply wait for him to surrender without a fight." But Mithradates, on the advice of Taxiles, held the mountain pass to the territory Lucullus needed to occupy, to block Mithradates' foragers and feed his own legions. Lucullus's men were unhappy with the idea of camping idly all winter. No chance for plunder!

Mithradates, meanwhile, received dispiriting news from Spain. His ally Sertorius had been murdered. The hero of Marius's Populars was stabbed while at dinner with "friends." Pompey's legions had easily overcome what remained of the Spanish rebellion. The assassination of Sertorius was a severe blow to the Populars who had joined Mithradates. One of these was Lucius Magius, the general sent by Sertorius to advise Mithradates.

Magius told Mithradates that the two Fimbrian legions—once loyal to Marius—wanted to desert Lucullus. "So, let Lucullus camp wherever he likes," reasoned Magius. "With those Fimbrian legions on our side, we'll be victorious with no need for battle." Mithradates trusted Magius and pulled his guards from the mountain pass. Crucial details are missing to explain this apparently irrational move. Was Magius a traitor? Maybe, but a different possibility was suggested by the biographer of Lucullus. Magius may have acted in good faith, based on secret communications with the unreliable Fimbrians. After all, they had betrayed two previous commanders, and they chafed at Lucullus's restraint. The ancient historian Memnon alluded to a deal initiated by the Fimbrians that went terribly wrong.[10]

Whatever Magius's true motives, to give up the pass was a grave blunder. The Fimbrians did not defect, and Lucullus now occupied the heights above Mithradates. Hemmed in by Romans and mountains, Mithradates could receive supplies only by sea. But winter would halt shipping. Lucullus could hardly believe his good luck.

Speed was key now. Mithradates attacked Cyzicus with everything he had. His men brought up battering rams and catapult towers. One stupendous tower, more than 100 cubits high (about 140 feet), supported a superstructure for raining catapult bolts, stones, and fire missiles into the city. Another immense contraption, straddling two large ships lashed together, moved into position against the city's seawalls. This was a new version of the huge *sambuca* at Rhodes, with a drawbridge to allow men to swarm over the walls.[11]

Mithradates, like Lucullus, hoped to win without risk: both men wanted to avoid a bloody battle or long siege. Accordingly, Mithradates' first move was to herd three thousand prisoners of war from Cyzicus onto his ships. He directed his captains to row into the harbor, in full view of the Cyzicenes defending their seawall. As Mithradates expected, the captives shouted to their fellow citizens, begging them to spare them in their perilous position.[12] But the Cyzicene general was unmoved: "You are in Mithradates' hands now—we cannot save you! Meet your fate like men!"

When he saw that the Cyzicenes would not surrender even to save their compatriots, Mithradates let down the *sambuca* drawbridge. The Cyzicenes were dumbfounded to see enemy soldiers running across the skyway to their walls. But the rest of Mithradates' men hesitated to follow the first sortie, and the Cyzicenes quickly recovered from their shock. They poured burning pitch onto the ships, forcing the whole contraption to back away from the wall.

Next Mithradates deployed all his siege engines on land. Again, the city manned an amazing defense, hurling boulders to break the battering rams and wrecking the machines with gigantic grappling hooks. The defenders had draped their wooden parapets with wet hides and doused the stone walls with vinegar to fireproof them against Mithradates' hail of fiery missiles. In Appian's words, the Cyzicenes "left nothing untried within the compass of human energy" to repulse the attack. But, as

Mithradates knew (and as modern scientists have proven), if vinegar-soaked limestone is heated enough, it crumbles. The intense heat of his fire bolts collapsed a section of wall.[13]

The Cyzicenes toiled all night to repair the breach. Then, "as if in admiration for their resolve and bravery," Plutarch claims that Cyzicus was aided by female deities, who appeared to oppose Mithradates in all his wars. A tremendous winter gale suddenly toppled all Mithradates' siege towers. Inside the city, it was time for the annual sacrifice to Persephone, protector of Cyzicus. Her ritual called for a black heifer, but the herds were in pastures across the water. Miraculously, a black heifer swam over to the city. Then Persephone herself appeared, urging her people to be resolute against the "Pontic trumpeter." Spirits soared in Cyzicus.[14]

Spirits plunged in the camp of Mithradates. Was he always fated to incur the wrath of goddesses? His friends and advisers strongly counseled a retreat from Cyzicus, obviously under the protection of very powerful deities—or magicians.

But the king had received some good news. In Italy, a gladiator named Spartacus had gathered an army of six hundred slaves, which eventually swelled to seventy thousand and defeated a series of Roman legions. Spartacus was said to be Thracian; he may have belonged to a tribe allied with Mithradates. Spartacus sympathized with and apparently planned to join Sertorius's rebellion; he may have seen military action in Greece when Sulla defeated Mithradates there. In the pantheon of Rome's three most dangerous enemies, Spartacus stood alongside Hannibal and Mithradates. Notably, both Plutarch and Appian wrote admiringly of Spartacus's military skill and his humane ideals. The news of Spartacus's victories against Rome encouraged Mithradates. He had lost his ally Sertorius in Spain, but now the Romans faced a formidable foe on Italian soil.[15]

In another piece of cheering news, Mithradates learned that his general Eumachus (former satrap of Galatia) was victorious in southern Anatolia, killing a great many Romans there, along with their families. Yet Mithradates desperately needed to succeed here in Bithynia, before supplies ran out. He stubbornly devised an ambitious strategy. All winter, his sappers dug tunnels under the city walls, and his soldiers constructed an enormous ramp out from Mount Dindymus (ominously for Mithradates, a mountain sacred to Cybele). New siege towers were built all along this mound.

Provisions dwindled. Winter storms prevented ships from bringing Mithradates' great stores of grain around the Black Sea. Some of his famished soldiers looking for food were captured by Lucullus, who slyly asked each man how much food was left in his cohort's tents. From their replies, Lucullus calculated that Mithradates would run out very soon. Exulting that his strategy of "kicking Mithradates in the stomach" was working, Lucullus promised his impatient troops, whining for loot, that they would be victorious without bloodshed.

Mithradates' generals tried to keep him in the dark about the specter of starvation. But the king soon learned the truth. He was appalled to discover his soldiers eating weeds, pack camels and mules, and even dead comrades. Plague had arisen from hundreds of unburied corpses, killing as many as the famine. There was no grass for the starving horses. Mithradates decided to send his entire cavalry on a roundabout route over the mountains for the winter. The horses, pack mules, and shaggy Bactrian camels were accompanied by a large contingent of wounded and sick soldiers. In freezing weather, the weak men and animals struggled through ice and snow.[16]

Lucullus pursued them with 5,000 men and cavalry. A blizzard struck; many Romans fell behind with frostbite. But Lucullus forged on and attacked Mithradates' limping cavalry at the River Rhyndacus. Many were slain in the snow, and Lucullus captured 15,000 of Mithradates' men, 6,000 horses, and the beasts of burden. For many of the Roman soldiers, this was their first sight of two-humped camels, imported from distant Bactria to the snows of Bithynia. Lucullus deliberately marched this long train of feeble prisoners and animals before the eyes of Mithradates' demoralized men.[17]

That humiliating spectacle was compounded by more bad tidings. Galatia hated Mithradates for murdering their leading families, and now the Galatian army, allied with Rome, had driven Mithradates' general Eumachus out of southern Anatolia.

The Cyzicenes still had plenty of grain, which they had cleverly preserved from spoilage by mixing it with Chalcidic earth (lime carbonate). Lucullus sent some Roman soldiers into the city to dig a countertunnel. They managed to trick Mithradates himself into entering his own tunnel. A Roman centurion inside Cyzicus sent a message to the king promising to betray the city. That Mithradates actually agreed to meet this man in the tunnel reveals his desperation at this point, as well as his personal courage. Mithradates went down alone into the subterranean passage. As he cautiously approached the shadowy figure, the Roman suddenly rushed forward with his sword. Mithradates turned and dove behind the tunnel's door, slamming it shut in the nick of time!

The Cyzicenes rejoiced when yet another winter storm struck. The wind tossed up immense waves, and Mithradates' new siege towers began to creak and sway. Suddenly a gust of wind burst forth "with incredible fury," shattering the towers. In nearby Ilium (ancient Troy)—where the statue of Athena still stood after Fimbria's sacking—it was reported that an apparition of Athena had appeared. The goddess, panting and disheveled, had just come from saving Cyzicus. Centuries later, Plutarch read all about the goddess's marvelous manifestation on a marble inscription in Ilium.

Vengeful goddesses, treacherous weather, awful reversals of fortune, the irritating fortitude of Cyzicus, dreadful plague, and famine combined with Lucullus's constant pressure convinced Mithradates that he had no choice but to withdraw. Ironically, he had a fantastic amount of gold in his camp, but no food. As a last resort, Mithradates directed his admiral Aristonicus to sail with a shipload of ten thousand pieces of gold. The idea was to bribe loot-hungry Romans with the gold while distracting Lucullus, so Mithradates and his army could escape. But someone betrayed the plan to Lucullus. The Romans captured all the gold before the ship even set sail. Mithradates' situation was dire indeed.[18]

POISON PILLS

Mithradates abandoned the siege of Cyzicus. He sneaked out to his ships at night and sailed with his navy to the Hellespont, while his infantry marched overland by night. Many drowned trying to cross a river flooded with heavy snows. Lucullus set out in pursuit and slaughtered about twenty thousand men and took a great many prisoners. The survivors plodded on and took refuge in Lampsacus.

Lucullus set up a siege there. But Mithradates sent a pirate fleet to rescue his soldiers and the entire population of Lampsacus. Lucullus was left besieging a ghost town. Mithradates sailed for Nicomedia, leaving fifty ships in the Hellespont with ten thousand of his best soldiers, under the command of three generals: the one-eyed Roman M. Varius, Alexander of Paphlagonia, and Dionysus the Eunuch. Yet another winter storm swept across Bithynia; many of Mithradates' naval divisions perished at sea.

Lucullus hurried back to Cyzicus to accept the victor's laurel wreath, then returned to the Hellespont to raise a fleet. To mop up his victory, he divided his forces among several officers. One, Voconius, was directed to

sail east to Nicomedia to defeat Mithradates. The others subdued Bithynian cities. In these places, Appian and Memnon report that the Roman
armies not only fought each other over booty, but they butchered a great
many people inside temples where they had sought refuge, replaying the
dreadful scenes of the massacre of Roman civilians in 88 BC. Ships full
of plunder, including a golden statue of Hercules, set sail for Rome, but
many, massively overloaded, sank in the Black Sea winter storms.[19]

Near Troy, Lucullus decided to pitch his tent inside the sanctuary of
Aphrodite. Goddesses had been good to him. One night, Aphrodite appeared in a dream, shaking him awake: "Why are you sleeping, Great
Lion? The deer are in reach!" Lucullus hopped out of bed and discovered
that messengers had arrived in the night. Thirteen of Mithradates' warships had been sighted in the Aegean, going to join the rest of Mithradates' fleet commanded by Varius, Alexander the Paphlagonian, and
Dionysus the Eunuch at Lesbos. The Romans believed that Mithradates'
navy was poised to sail across the Mediterranean to attack Italy.[20]

Lucullus's fleet pursued the three generals. But the latter drew their
bronze-prowed warships up onto the beach of a small island off Lesbos.
Frustrated, Lucullus sailed behind the island and sent soldiers ashore.
They hiked across the island to attack the entrenched enemy from the
rear. With this clever pincer movement, Lucullus trapped Mithradates'
men. Some remained ashore inside their beached ships to fight the Romans on both fronts; others tried to set sail. They were surrounded and
slaughtered; the survivors fled inland.

Lucullus ordered his troops, "Spare any soldier missing an eye." According to Plutarch, Lucullus wanted to capture Varius alive so that he
could personally inflict a degrading death upon the Roman senator
who had supported Marius and served Sertorius and then Mithradates.
Lucullus's men discovered Varius hiding with Dionysus the Eunuch and
Alexander the Paphlagonian in a cave. Mithradates always supplied his
commanders with poison for this kind of emergency. At the approach of
the Romans, the eunuch broke open his capsule, gulped down the bitter
poison, and died immediately.

Alexander and Varius were taken prisoner. Lucullus kept Alexander
alive to be paraded as a trophy in his Triumph. The Senate awarded a
formal Triumph if a commander had killed at least five thousand enemies
in a single action in a foreign war. Hundreds of thousands of Romans
would come to gawk at the defeated barbarians and their families, wearing their native dress and in chains, trudging behind elaborate tableaux
illustrating major battles and events in the campaign, and cartloads of

weapons, armor, and other spoils. At the end of the parade, captives could be imprisoned, sold as slaves, freed, or strangled before the statue of Mars, god of war. According to Appian, Lucullus immediately tortured and killed Varius on the island, claiming that it would be "unseemly" to parade a Roman senator in a Triumph.[21]

According to Plutarch's sources, Mithradates' losses were devastating. In this first campaign against Lucullus, nearly all 300,000 of Mithradates' land forces and camp followers were killed or taken prisoner (Memnon says 13,000 were captured). Lucullus sent an official communiqué wreathed in laurel leaves, signifying a great victory, to the Senate in Rome. His letter brought great relief, since it was feared that Mithradates had intended to invade Italy by sea. Lucullus set sail for Nicomedia, where he expected to find the "wild beast" of Pontus cornered by his officer Voconius. Lucullus looked forward to personally capturing Mithradates alive for his Triumph.

But his confidence was misplaced. His man Voconius had taken a detour for personal reasons. Instead of going after Mithradates at Nicomedia, Voconius had sailed off to Samothrace, where he was busy celebrating his initiation into a sailors' mystery cult.[22] Gnashing his teeth, Lucullus discovered that his prey had already departed Nicomedia, sailing for Pontus with his surviving ships. The war Lucullus had declared over was still on.

PIRATES TO THE RESCUE

Weather and goddesses turned against Mithradates yet again. Another severe storm raged across the Black Sea. Everyone said this tempest was sent by the goddess Artemis. She was enraged because some of Mithradates' pirates had plundered her shrine at Priapus, a place renowned for excellent wine and all manner of lewd and lascivious activities. The pirates had partied there on their way to rescue the soldiers and people of Lampsacus, described above. Now high winds and towering waves destroyed about sixty of Mithradates' ships. For many days afterward, the sea tossed up wreckage and nearly ten thousand bloated, battered corpses onto the shore.

At the height of this storm, Mithradates' own ship, weighed down with royal equipment and treasure, was damaged, swamped by cresting waves. It began to sink. A light brigantine drew alongside. It was manned by pirates; Admiral Seleucus of Cilicia had come to rescue the king. Mithradates' companions, fearing the buccaneer's motives, urged the king not to abandon ship. But Mithradates and Seleucus were old friends; he respected the pirates' seamanship. Their craft were fast and seaworthy.[23]

Mithradates daringly leaped overboard onto the heaving deck of the small cruiser, entrusting his life to the pirates. They disappeared into the teeth of the howling storm. His companions expected never to see Mithradates alive again.

Against all odds, Mithradates and his pirate rescuers made it to Heraclea. Some friends there distracted the citizens with a sumputous feast outside the city, while Mithradates, Seleucus, and his pirates sneaked in. The next morning, the king assembled the populace, greeted them cheerfully as their liberator, and distributed gold and silver coins to everyone. Leaving a garrison of four thousand men with his Galatian commander Konnakorix at Heraclea, Mithradates and his pirates sailed away through rough seas and foul weather, home to Sinope.[24]

From Sinope, Mithradates sailed on to Amisus. Taking stock there, reflecting on his miraculous multiple narrow escapes from the jaws of death, Mithradates remained optimistic. The situation was certainly perilous, but his subjects in Pontus were steadfast and willing to fight bravely against the Romans. What would Lucullus do now? Would he withdraw, assuming he had neutralized Mithradates, or would he pursue and invade Pontus? As usual, Mithradates intended to cover all contingencies.

Mithradates could not allow his extended family and harem to fall into Roman hands. It was intolerable to think of the terror, rape, and torture they would suffer before being dragged to Rome and killed in the wolves' den. Several of his children were already safe in the Bosporan Kingdom. Other members of the royal family, including his sister Nyssa, were confined in the towers of Kabeira. His lover Stratonice and son Xiphares were also in Kabeira. Drypetina, Mithradates' doting daughter with double teeth, was the Lady of Laodicea—she now moved for safety to the fort at Sinora, accompanied by Menophilus, a trusted eunuch-doctor.[25]

Mithradates decided to send the rest of his royal household to a fortress in Pharnacia, on the rugged east coast of Pontus, the land of his old allies the Turret-Folk. Eunuchs accompanied this caravan, which included the two spinster sisters Roxana and Statira, Queen Monime, and the Chian concubine Berenice and her mother.

Descending into his secret vaults at Sinope, Mithradates filled a chest with a large quantity of gold and precious gifts. He ordered a courtier to deliver this treasure to his allies in Scythia, in exchange for more aid. But unbeknownst to the king, this man was more of an opportunist than an optimist. He defected and delivered the treasure to Lucullus. Undeterred, the king sent messengers to his son Machares, viceroy of the Bosporus, and to his son-in-law Tigranes, requesting assistance. Mithradates placed the city of Amisus under the command of his master of siegecraft, Callimachus. With his friend Dorylaus, the Magus Hermaeus (a Greek-Bactrian name), and the rest of his inner circle, Mithradates traveled to his stronghold at Kabeira for the winter of 72/71 BC.

From this secure base, he and Dorylaus raised a new army, bringing together about forty thousand foot soldiers and four thousand cavalry. Most modern historians assume that neither Machares nor Tigranes replied to Mithradates' urgent messages. But these new reinforcements surely came from Scythia and Armenia. According to Memnon, Machares did intend to send grain and supplies to Sinope, and Mithradates' daughter Cleopatra convinced Tigranes to help her father.[26] Some reinforcements went to defend Amisus and Sinope. Mithradates also stationed garrisons and scouts along the routes to Kabeira to watch for Lucullus's approach in spring. He placed Phoenix, his son by a Phoenician concubine, in command, with orders to relay fire beacons from the borders to Kabeira, to signal Roman troop movements.

Lucullus was in a jam. He had officially—and prematurely—declared victory over Rome's most feared enemy, and then let Mithradates slip away. Meanwhile, the detestable Pompey not only had smashed the insurgency in Spain but took (many said unfairly) all the credit for putting down the great slave uprising in Italy. Spartacus was killed and six thousand of his followers were crucified on the Appian Way. For very different reasons, this dramatic news dismayed both Mithradates and Lucullus. Mithradates had lost an important political ally in Italy; Lucullus's rival Pompey was now ascendant in power.

Lucullus's own supplies were running very low. Morale in his legions was rocky, the soldiers carped at the lack of looting opportunities. Many in Lucullus's command urged him to abandon the war. Lucullus ignored their advice. Realizing that the only way to stop Mithradates was to kill him, Lucullus ordered his army to invade Pontus—just as Mithradates had anticipated. To do this, Lucullus had to hire thirty thousand Galatians. Each of these human beasts of burden lugged a bushel of wheat on his shoulders, slogging along behind the Roman legions.[27]

INVASION OF PONTUS

As the Romans crossed into western Pontus, they found untold wealth and abundance. Lucullus's soldiers seized so much booty and so many prisoners that the glut drastically devalued everything. The price of a male slave dropped to four drachmas and an ox sold for one drachma (a soldier's daily wage). As they marched across Mithradates' land of plenty, the soldiers who had howled for booty now abandoned or destroyed their worthless loot and captives.

Lucullus left troops to besiege Amisus and Eupatoria and sent another legion to besiege Themiscrya, a remote castle on the River Thermodon, one of the fabled lands of Amazon horsewomen. Mithradates had sent men and weapons to these cities. At Amisus, the defenders constantly raided the Roman camp, and even provoked the legionnaires into single combat, as if they were reenacting the glorious duels of Homer's champions on the fields of Troy. At Themiscrya, named for an Amazon queen, the Romans toiled underground digging "tunnels so large that great subterranean battles were fought in them." But Lucullus's men abandoned the siege after the defenders resorted to wildly unconventional tactics. They tossed hives of furious bees into the tunnels. Then, while the frantic Romans flailed at the stinging swarms, the ingenious Themiscryans released wild beasts—weasels, foxes, wolves, boars, and bears—into the underground passages.[28]

While these Romans contended with Mithradates' stalwart, resourceful subjects, Lucullus himself led most of his legions on a wandering course around the Pontic countryside that fall and winter. Leaving rich and sophisticated western Pontus far behind, they entered the territory of rustic tribes like the Chalybes and Tibareni. Ironically, Lucullus had no idea that this wild landscape hid more than seventy secret fortresses and secret treasuries built by Mithradates.

Lucullus busied his men raiding tiny villages and ravaging orchards. A gourmand, Lucullus was enchanted by the luscious red fruits of Cerasion ("city of cherries"). Cherries were unknown in Italy. Carefully stashing away the pits from his repasts, Lucullus also dug up several cherry saplings to bring back to Rome. Perhaps he was emulating Alexander the Great, who had introduced the Armenian apricot tree to Greece. In the opinion of his impatient men and officers, however, Lucullus seemed to have completely lost focus, coddling trees and ordering useless raids. They agitated anew for battle and loot.

"We haven't taken a single city by storm! Why are we wasting time raiding these worthless villages of poor tribes? When will we enrich ourselves with plunder? Why are we leaving Mithradates' wealthy city of Amisus behind? Why should we follow our feckless general into the wilderness, while our greatest enemy rebuilds his army?"

"That's exactly why we are lingering here!" Lucullus retorted in a speech to his army, justifying his strategy of delay. "I am waiting for Mithradates to become powerful again! I want him to gather up a force that will be worth our while to fight and so that he will stand his ground at Kabeira instead of fleeing again. Don't you see that he has a vast and trackless wilderness to fall back on? The Caucasus Mountains could hide ten thousand wily enemy kings like Mithradates!"

Lucullus remembered the advantages enjoyed by Jugurtha and his son-in-law Bocchus, who repeatedly vanished into the North African hinterlands and surged back with new forces. His warning about Mithradates' ability to disappear into the Caucasus was more prescient than he knew.

Lucullus also raised the daunting image of Tigranes' vast hordes. "Only a few days' ride from Kabeira lies Armenia, ruled by Tigranes, King of Kings, Mithradates' son-in-law. Tigranes rules such armies that he levels cities and transplants entire populations, subduing Parthia, Syria, Media, Palestine, murdering the rightful rulers and ravishing their wives and daughters! Tigranes is eager to make war on Rome—if we drive Mithradates into his arms, then we'll have to fight Tigranes the Great and his Medes and Armenians! No," declared Lucullus, "we'll give Mithradates the time to gather up his own motley forces and muster up fresh courage. Then we'll crush him forever at Kabeira."

Lucullus was an able and fair commander, trying to stave off a strike by his men—most of them landless, homesick legionnaires seeking riches and glory, exhausted by years of duty in Anatolia since the First Mithradatic War. As Plutarch foreshadowed, Lucullus, a Roman aristocrat who lacked rapport with the common soldier, underestimated his men's grievances, "never dreaming that their resentment and insubordination would later send them to commit acts of madness and mutiny."[29]

The Battle for Kabeira

In spring, Lucullus finally marched on Kabeira. Warned by the fire signals sent by his son Phoenix from the watchtowers, Mithradates himself led four thousand cavalry to meet Lucullus. His fierce horsemen—Scythian nomads—sent the Romans fleeing in terror. Lucullus's bravest cavalry officer was captured. He was taken to Mithradates' tent, grimacing in pain from several arrow wounds. "Will you be my friend if I spare your life?" asked Mithradates, smiling encouragingly. "Only if you surrender to Rome," the soldier shot back, "otherwise I remain your foe!" The king admired the Roman's spirit and spared his life.[30]

Phoenix, Mithradates' son by a courtesan, was torn between filial loyalty and fear of defeat. Phoenix dutifully relayed signals to warn his father of Lucullus's approach, but then deserted to the Romans, bringing along his scouts. Lucullus was stymied, however. How to avoid Mithradates' superior cavalry? There was no way to sneak up on impregnable Kabeira, defended by mountains and thick forests. Luck was with Lucullus. His men happened to capture two Greek huntsmen. They agreed to guide the Romans up a mountain trail to a stronghold overlooking Kabeira. At nightfall, Lucullus lit all his campfires as a ruse. Then he and his army followed the hunters up switchbacks and over a deep ravine by an arched stone bridge (its foundations still exist). Lucullus set up camp by dawn, with a view of Mithradates' camp at Kabeira, just out of reach. Stalemate—neither commander dared to risk outright battle.[31]

One day Mithradates' men went hunting. Chasing a stag, they were cut off by some Roman horsemen. Watching from their camp high above the skirmish, Lucullus's men cheered. But Mithradates' reinforcements arrived and routed the outnumbered Romans. Lucullus bravely rode down to the plain alone and ordered his fleeing cavalrymen to wheel around and attack Mithradates' force. His disciplined audacity won the day.

In another battle at Kabeira, Lucullus's men were winning. This time it was Mithradates in gleaming armor who leaped on his white horse, galloped out alone, and rallied his men. The king—remarkably fit and courageous for a man over sixty—led a formidable cavalry charge, sending the terrified Roman army crashing though the trees up the mountainside.

Mithradates sent messengers throughout the land proudly announcing this impressive victory over the Romans. His spies reported that Lucullus, low on supplies, had sent out ten cohorts (about five thousand men) to Cappadocia to get grain. Here was a chance for Mithradates to stomp on the Roman belly, as Lucullus had done to him at Cyzicus.[32]

Mithradates dispatched Menander to intercept Lucullus's convoys returning from Cappadocia. Constant battle stress and inconclusive outcomes were beginning to fray nerves, interfering with judgment.

Menander's advance cavalry caught the Roman supply train, marching single file down a steep trail into Pontus. But Menander was too impatient to wait until they reached the open plain. His cavalry horses slipped on the rocky trail, and the Roman foot soldiers were able to force the men and horses over the cliff. A few cavalry reached Mithradates' camp before the others. They exaggerated the calamity into a disaster of great magnitude, claiming they were the sole survivors. As Appian remarked, the losses were large but not overwhelming, yet the rumors whipped up fear in Mithradates' camp.

Mithradates remained steady. He sent out another large force to cut off another of Lucullus's returning convoys led by Adrian. But Mithradates' forces really were annihilated his time. According to Plutarch, only two survivors returned to Kabeira. Mithradates tried to hide the extent of this true catastrophe. Plutarch says he blamed "this slight setback" on the inexperience of his generals. But when Adrian "marched back pompously past Mithradates' camp," showing off hundreds of wagons groaning with grain and the armor and weapons of Mithradates' dead cavalrymen, everyone in Kabeira—already tense—learned the terrible truth.

Finally, after this string of disasters, including the loss of his navy, Mithradates' optimism deserted him. A "great despair fell upon the king," reported Plutarch, and his soldiers were seized by "confusion and helpless fear." As soon as Lucullus received the news of Adrian's victory, he would attack Kabeira. That night, Mithradates called his close companions—Dorylaus, the Magus Hermaeus, eunuch-advisers Bacchides and Ptolemaeus, and his generals—to his tent. All agreed that flight was the only option. The plan was to meet at Comana, the rich, fortified town of the Temple of Love, and then seek refuge in Armenia with Tigranes. Before dawn, each man hastily packed his own baggage on horses outside the gates, and helped to load a mule train with bag upon bag of gold, royal regalia, and treasure.[33]

I imagine that Mithradates followed the practical advice of his old friend King Parisades of the Bosporus: "Always wear your finest costume to address your soldiers. But when it is necessary to flee, put on commoners' clothing to conceal your identity from the enemy as well as your subjects."[34] Changing from royal garb into nondescript apparel for the flight, Mithradates concealed his daggers and essential drugs under his clothes. He had one final task before daylight. As Appian tells us, in "utter despair for his kingdom," Mithradates assigned the eunuch Bacchides to carry out a terrible mission. The eunuch was to ride to the castle at Pharnacia. There he was to put to death the royal harem before the Romans could find them.

Mithradates planned to give the general order for retreat at daybreak. But his frightened soldiers heard the commotion in the night and jumped to the conclusion that their high command was abandoning them. Panic raced through the camp. Fear mingled with rage scattered soldiers helter-skelter in the dark. In the chaos, the men attacked their own baggage trains. Mithradates dashed out of his tent and ran among his soldiers, shouting and pleading for calm in every dialect he knew. His second in command, Dorylaus, throwing on his purple robe, rushed out to join the king in the tumult. They tried to reassure the crowd that they were not abandoning them, that all would depart together at daylight.

But no one could hear the king's words in the mad crush. He and Do-rylaus were separated. Hermaeus, the royal seer, was one of those trampled to death by the mob at the gates. And Mithradates? The king was swept up—alone and on foot—in the torrent, borne along by the crowd surging out onto the dark road to Comana.

Without his diadem and finery, Mithradates was an anonymous figure in the fleeing throng. Far behind, at the gates of Kabeira, desperate soldiers were still pillaging the baggage train of the king's friends. Some seized fine horses, while others murdered for an officer's fancy dagger, another man's glittering rings, or someone's money belt of gold. It was in this frenzy that Dorylaus—Mithradates' steadfast companion since their childhood and years in exile—met his end. Dorylaus was stabbed to death by one of his own men for the possession of his purple cloak.[35]

When Lucullus received the news of Mithradates' flight, he sent his cavalry to pursue the fugitives. Strict orders: the king was to be captured alive, along with his private papers. Lucullus himself led his infantry to take Kabeira. As they surrounded the city, still a scene of confusion and hysteria, Lucullus ordered the legionnaires to refrain from killing anyone and to hold off looting, until they could impose order. But the men, extremely resentful at having been starved of loot for two years and contemptuous of their leader's restraint, refused to listen. Dazzled by the eye-popping riches of Kabeira—silver vessels, jewelry and gems, royal ornaments, and exquisite purple and gilt-embroidered garments—the Romans snatched up whatever spoils they could carry. They set about killing indiscriminately. Lucullus stood by powerless to stop them.

At last, while his exhausted legionnaires slept cradling their treasures, Lucullus investigated the desolate palace, castles, and towers of Kabeira. He found even more treasure stored in vaults. He also found dungeons;

Fig. 12.4. Lucullus's soldiers sacked Mithradates' fortress and residence at
Kabeira. Artist unknown.

breaking the locks, he discovered many relatives of Mithradates, long
given up for dead. Plutarch described their release as "more of a resur-
rection than a rescue." Among these wretched souls was Nyssa, Mithradates' younger sister. For nearly forty years, since she was a little girl,
Nyssa had been hidden away so that she could never marry. Nyssa joined
Mithradates' captive general Alexander, to be paraded later in Lucullus's
Triumph. No records explain exactly how Stratonice and her son Xiphares escaped—but somehow they reached the secret stronghold of
Kainon Chorion, undetected by Lucullus.

While Lucullus took possession of Kabeira, Bacchides arrived in Pharnacia to carry out his grim duty. He was the perfect choice. Strabo described this eunuch as a ruthless paranoid, always suspecting treachery.
Bacchides enlisted the help of the other eunuchs to execute Mithradates'
family in the most expedient ways at hand, to prevent their capture by a
mob of Roman soldiers.

Detailed descriptions of that harrowing night were related by Plutarch,
who had access to the accounts of witnesses who were later captured or
deserted to the Romans. The scene in all its poignant horror has inspired
artists, composers, poets, and playwrights to imagine the tragedy. Among
the women at Pharnacia were young Berenice and her mother, rescued

FIG. 12.5. Mithradates' queen Monime tried to hang herself with her diadem,
a tragic scene popular in early modern Europe. Drawing, Claude Vignon the
Elder (1593–1670), Louvre, Réunion des Musées Nationaux/Art Resource, NY.

FIG. 12.6. Mithradates' sisters Statira and Roxana take poison. Illustration for Racine's play *Mithridate*, engraving by P. J. Simon.

from their enslaved island of Chios, only to die now on the stormy shores of the Black Sea. Monime, the intelligent Greek beauty who had resisted Mithradates' gold, holding out for the diadem and title of queen, was also in Pharnacia. Plutarch wrote, "Bacchides ordered them all to die, in what ever manner each woman deemed easiest and most painless." The eunuch's inner thoughts are unknowable, as he stood there with his dagger in one hand and a chalice of poison in the other. But the last words of some of the women were recorded for posterity.[36]

Monime bewailed her unhappy marriage. Tearing off the purple ribbon that decorated her hair, she twisted it in her hands, sobbing. "I traded my freedom and beauty for captivity, surrounded by barbarian eunuchs!" Mithradates, she claimed, had once promised to take her to Greece, where she had hoped to find happiness. "All the blessings I yearned for are nothing but dreams!" Monime knotted the diadem around her neck and hanged herself from the rafters. But the ribbon snapped. Clutching the frayed ends in her fist, she screamed, "You cursed bauble! You have never been any use to me, not even for hanging!" She spit on the diadem, hurling it away. Monime bared her throat to Bacchides' knife.

Berenice took the cup of poison. As she lifted it to her lips, her mother cried out, begging to share the same cup. Together they drank the poison, the daughter making certain that her mother drank more. The dose killed the older woman immediately, but Berenice was young and strong. "As Berenice was long in dying, and Bacchides was in a hurry," writes Plutarch, the eunuch strangled her.

Mithradates' two unmarried sisters, Roxana and Statira, in their forties, were next. Both chose poison. Like Monime, Roxana was embittered, heaping curses upon her brother. But Statira drank calmly from her cup, without uttering a single reproach. Instead, Statira asked Bacchides to convey her thanks to her brother. For even when his own life was in danger, she declared, he had not neglected his sisters and concubines. She praised Mithradates for ensuring that they would not suffer at the hands of the Romans but would die in *eleutheria*, freedom.[37]

Renegade Kings

WHEN we last saw Mithradates, he was swept away by a desperate mob, fleeing Kabeira. The ancient sources tell us what happened next, but we can only imagine the king's emotions. No doubt his mind was replaying an anguished panorama of his disasters on land and sea. Anxiety for his companions and kingdom mingled with images of the deaths he himself had ordered for his family, queen, lovers, children. But there can be no doubt that Mithradates also forced himself to think ahead, to calculate options for survival. If only he had a horse. . . . Suddenly he hears a familiar voice shouting his name, addressing him as king. Across the sea of fugitives he spies Ptolemaeus, one of his eunuch-advisers, with other friends on horseback, leading mules loaded with the royal treasure. The eunuch offers his mount to the king. After hurried words, Mithradates and his companions spur their horses toward Comana. The Roman cavalry is in hot pursuit.

An advance party of Lucullus's Galatians catches up with them. It looks like curtains for Rome's elusive foe. But Mithradates whips out his dagger and leans down to slash open the bags on the back of the nearest mule. A cascade of golden coins pours out. While the squabbling Galatians gather up the trail of gold in the road, Mithradates escapes.

These greedy soldiers cheated Lucullus out of capturing his prize quarry, the great adversary whom the Romans had chased for nearly twenty years of hardship and danger. The story of how Mithradates finessed his narrow escape by dazzling his pursuers with gold was retold often in Rome. The incident seemed to confirm the sense that Lucullus's campaign was more about robbing Mithradates' riches than crushing the mortal enemy of Rome. In the Senate, Cicero compared the king's ploy of scattering gold to the famous escape of the witch Medea, who scattered the severed limbs of her victims to distract her pursuers.

Yet another group of soldiers disobeyed Lucullus's orders to bring Mithradates' personal secretary back alive. Callistratus was carrying Mithradates' private papers, a highly desirable prize. Roman soldiers did capture Callistratus—but then killed him in a melee over his money belt stuffed with five hundred gold coins. The king's bloodstained private papers were carelessly flung away, never to be recovered (was the secret formula for the *Mithridatium* among them?).[1]

Meanwhile, the fugitives from Kabeira reached Comana, the Temple of Love where Mithradates had tarried with Dorylaus and his friends so long ago. They were joined by about two thousand cavalry. Mithradates' little party included key players: General Taxiles and other officers, field medic Timotheus, and the Agari shamans. Taking on supplies, the fugitives rode to Talaura, where Mithradates had stashed heirlooms and gold. Then they made their way over mountain passes toward Armenia.[2]

With the Pontic navy no longer supreme in the Black Sea and his army destroyed amid mounting defections, Mithradates had to expect his son Machares to make a deal with the Romans. His only hope for personal survival lay with Tigranes, who would surely shelter his father-in-law. But could Mithradates somehow also convince Tigranes—now the most formidable bulwark against Roman rule in the East—to help him regain his kingdom?

Lucullus and his army arrived four days later at Talaura. Too late! The Roman commander absorbed the dismal news. His prey had escaped yet again. Mithradates and two thousand horsemen had already slipped over the frontier into Armenia, ruled by the all-powerful Tigranes and his barbarian hordes.

PLENTY OF PLUNDER, NO PREY

In 70 BC, Lucullus completely lost track of his quarry. When he learned that Mithradates had also deprived him of capturing the royal family alive, Lucullus expressed sorrow for the loss of innocent lives. Historians portray Lucullus as humane, but he also regretted the loss of trophies to show off in Rome. Now, capturing or killing Mithradates was the missing capstone of his mission. Lucullus dispatched a stolid young officer named Appius to demand that King Tigranes turn over the fugitive war criminal.

Lucullus continued taking over Pontic strongholds and besieging cities faithful to Mithradates. The historian Strabo's grandfather was a local

Pontic leader, overseeing fifteen forts. But because Mithradates had executed some kinfolk for treason, Strabo's grandfather decided to surrender the forts to Lucullus. That was a mistake, Strabo reported: not only did the Romans renege on the promised rewards, but after Lucullus returned to Rome, his successor Pompey actually arrested Strabo's grandfather and other relatives as enemy combatants.

Thanks to Callimachus's countersiege machines, Amisus fought off the Romans for a long time. In the end, Callimachus set fire to the city before escaping by sea. As the flames enveloped the walls, Lucullus desperately begged his troops to save the beautiful city before looting it. But the soldiers shouted him down, clashing their shields and banging their spears, baying for booty. They rushed in to pillage and slaughter all night, setting more fires with torches. Just before dawn, a cold rain doused the fires. But the destruction was total. At daybreak Lucullus viewed the ruins and burst into tears. Callimachus had deprived him of an opportunity to make a grand gesture of mercy. Luculus devoted himself to rebuilding Amisus. Alexander the Great had restored the town's democracy when he liberated it from Persia, and Mithradates was not the only leader in this era who strove to emulate Alexander. Lucullus, a philhellene, deliberately invoked Alexander's gesture, claiming he had "liberated" the destroyed city from Mithradates.[3]

In Sinope, Mithradates had left a eunuch and a pirate in command. They were an unlikely pair: Bacchides had saved the royal consorts from fates worse than death, and Seleucus of Cilicia had rescued Mithradates in the storm. They vigorously resisted the Romans (although at one point Seleucus considered killing the citizens and handing the city over to Lucullus for a reward). When it became obvious that Sinope would fall, Bacchides and Seleucus burned all their warships, crammed treasure into a few pirate biremes, and sailed to Colchis.

Lucullus was able to save Sinope from total destruction by his loot-crazed men, but they killed more than eight thousand Sinopeans. Lucullus personally plundered Mithradates' most valuable possessions, including his great library, masterpieces of art, and scientific instruments. Two outstanding trophies were singled out by Strabo. One was the statue of the city's founder, Autolycus the Argonaut (the Sinopeans had tried to protect it by swathing it in linen, but the Romans found the bundle abandoned on the seashore). The other prize was an object taken from Mithradates' palace, the "Globe of Billarus." This astronomical "globe" or "sphere" (terms used for mechanized planetariums) was not described by Strabo, but there is reason to believe that it was an invention of renown.

Mithradates had a keen interest in technology and collected precious things.[4]

Italian historian Attilio Mastrocinque proposes an intriguing theory. Could the Globe of Billarus be the mysterious Antikythera device, the oldest complex scientific instrument ever discovered? This intricate, gear-driven bronze mechanism—the world's first computer—was recovered in 1901 by sponge divers from a Roman shipwreck near Antikythera, an island north of Crete. The three-hundred-ton ship sank between 70 and 60 BC on the way to Italy, crammed with plunder from the Third Mithradatic War. The divers also brought up superb marble and bronze statues, jewelry, datable coins, and an ornate bronze throne—all treasures looted from defeated Anatolian cities allied with Mithradates, perhaps including Sinope. The strange bronze instrument apparently belonged to Mithradates or someone in his circle.

In 2008, advanced technology deciphered the Antikythera device's complex workings and revealed inscriptions. The device's sophistication is astounding: it calculated the precise movements of celestial bodies (a particular concern for the Magi and Mithradates). The newfound inscription suggests that the device was created in 150–100 BC, in (or by a scientist associated with) Syracuse or Alexandria, places linked to the famous scientist Archimedes. A similar but older "celestial globe," in-

FIG. 13.1. Antikythera mechanism, Athens National Museum. Replica, American Computer Museum, Bozeman, Montana, photo by Michelle Maskiell.

vented by Archimedes himself, was looted from Syracuse by the Romans in 212 BC.

Scholars who study the Antikythera device are puzzled: how did this amazing instrument in the Archimedian tradition come to be among Mithradatic treasures seized by Romans? They assume that the device must have belonged to a pro-Roman Greek living in Rhodes. But Mastrocinque's idea that the Antikythera device could be the lost Globe of Billarus, taken by Lucullus from Sinope, is persuasive. As we know, Mithradates befriended leading scientists and had an interest in technology. Mastrocinque argues convincingly that the Billarus sphere was an astronomical instrument, and he notes that it was never mentioned again after Strabo. It would be quite a coincidence if two rare and important "celestial globes" were lost in this same time period. It is not unreasonable to suppose that the Billarus sphere from Sinope was on the Roman treasure ship lost at sea near Antikythera. If Mastrocinque is right, Mithradates' passion for technology, Lucullus's cultivated eye for fabulous plunder, and a sponge diver's lucky find combined to give us a unique glimpse into a high point of ancient science.[5]

After the fall of Sinope, Mithradates' son Machares, viceroy of Bosporus and Scythia, sent Lucullus a golden crown worth one thousand gold pieces—a crystal-clear message that he wanted to be an official "Friend of Rome." According to Plutarch, this was the moment that convinced Lucullus that he had decisively completed the war with Mithradates.[6]

Yet Lucullus remained awkwardly at loose ends until his man Appius returned with Mithradates in tow. Lucullus set about reorganizing Pontus as a new Roman province of Asia. As we saw, Sulla's war penalty of 20,000 talents had resulted in "unspeakable and incredible misfortunes" perpetrated by tax collectors, who tortured and enslaved debtors. Even though the Anatolians had already paid more than 40,000 talents to the moneylenders, because of sky-high interest rates the outstanding public debt now totaled 120,000 talents, a staggering amount of silver. All the Roman sources praise Lucullus for his honest efforts to alleviate the tax burden and establish order in Anatolia.[7]

In 69 BC, still no word from Appius. Nevertheless, Lucullus celebrated his defeat of Mithradates with festivals, gladiator contests, and sacrifices. The only thing lacking was a humbled Mithradates in chains, the perpetrator of so many crimes against Rome and its allies. More than a year and a half had passed since Mithradates—and Appius's search party—had vanished into Armenia. Where could they be?

Tigranes the Great

Tigranes' devious guides had promised to conduct Appius to Antioch, Syria. For many months they led the Romans on a circuitous route. Finally, a former Syrian slave in Appius's party pointed out the direct route to Antioch. There Appius was commanded to await the pleasure of the King of Kings, busy subduing Phoenicia. While he waited—for a whole year!—Appius met many vassals of Tigranes. They regaled him with tales of the breathtaking riches and haughty omnipotence of the monarch who conquered great nations and moved diverse peoples around the chessboard of the Middle East.

At last, *Shahanshah* Tigranes appeared in all his glory, clad in a red-and-white tunic, a purple mantle with gilt stars, and his comet-studded tiara, riding a white horse, with four vassals running alongside. As his bodyguards took their places on the dais, arms folded across their chests, the monarch arranged himself on his magnificent throne. Appius was summoned to the great hall. It was Tigranes' first audience with a Roman legate. Unimpressed by the grandeur and the majestic personage, Appius brusquely handed over the letter from Lucullus and stated his mission in plain—and tactless—language (probably Greek). "Hail Tigranes. Lucullus, Imperator of the Roman Army and Governor of the Province of Asia, has sent me to take charge of Mithradates, who is to be brought to Rome as our prisoner and as an ornament in our Triumph. Surrender Mithradates now. If you do not, Rome will declare war on you."

Plutarch's description is amusing: "It must have been five and twenty years since His Majesty had heard such rude speech in his court. Tigranes made every effort to listen to Appius with a pleasant expression and forced smile." But all in attendance winced at the arrogant Roman who did not even address Tigranes as "King of Kings." Everyone could sense Tigranes' rage. But Tigranes replied evenly: "I will not surrender Mithradates. If the Romans begin a war, the King of Kings will defend himself. You are dismissed."

Appius prepared to depart. He was interrupted by Tigranes' servants bearing heaps of splendid farewell gifts. Appius refused them. More arrived. Appius selected one simple silver bowl and "marched off with all speed to join the Imperator Lucullus."

Upon Appius's return with nothing but an empty silver bowl, Lucullus felt compelled to follow up on his own rash ultimatum. The war on Mithradates of Pontus that had begun back in 88 BC—the war Lucullus had *twice* declared over and won—suddenly expanded into a "reckless attack on a boundless region," in Plutarch's words. Driven by pride and seeking glory, Lucullus was now committing to an unlimited war over an unknown land, stretching from the Caucasus to the Red Sea, from Antioch to Seleucia, a wilderness of deep rivers and nameless deserts and impassable mountains covered in perpetual snow, defended by "untold thousands of nomad-warriors from countless warlike tribes." Lucullus's soldiers, unruly in the best of times, were near rebellion when they heard the orders to advance into Tigranes' empire. Earlier, Lucullus had played on his men's terror of Tigranes' barbarian armies. Moreover—as Tigranes and Mithradates knew—Lucullus had no authority to expand his campaign beyond the Euphrates. Back in Rome, there was a great outcry in the Senate, with the Populars accusing Lucullus of deliberately perpetuating a needless war in order to accrue personal power and profit. Lucullus was clearly the aggressor in this new campaign.

Leaving his two least reliable legions (the defiant Fimbrians) to occupy Pontus, Lucullus marched into Armenia with twelve thousand infantrymen and about three thousand cavalry, to confront Tigranes and arrest Mithradates—whereabouts unknown.[8]

FORTRESS OF SOLITUDE

We left Mithradates riding into Armenia with two thousand horsemen. Tigranes had arranged for Mithradates to stay on one of his hunting estates, ordering retainers to provide necessities and entertainments, cooks, thespians, musicians, fine Armenian wine, and dancing girls. With Mithradates' well-known love of history and literature, it is likely that a library of Greek classics was at hand. This long interlude—a year and eight months to be exact—in Armenia was an important respite.[9]

Here in safety, Mithradates could mourn his devastating losses. But, from what we know of his character, it would not take him long to regain equilibrium. Hiding out in the mountain fastness might have evoked bittersweet memories of roaming Pontus with his friends, in the anxious years after his father's assassination. As in the tales of his Greek and Persian ancestors and myths in which heroes overcome incredible odds, adversity seemed to invigorate Mithradates. Lucullus appeared to be crashing and burning, but the danger remained—sooner or later, the Romans would renew the war. How should he prepare? After the flight from Kabeira in 70 BC, Mithradates returned to basic survival, essentially following a mature version of his youthful exile, taking on a no-madic life, striking obliquely, eluding direct conflict. Come defeat or victory, Mithradates would remain on the move for the rest of his days, a decision that was both personal and militarily strategic.

During nearly two years in Armenia, Mithradates and his advisers devised new tactics that would define the rest of his epic struggle with Rome. The new approach appears to have been partly inspired by classi-cal history—Herodotus's and Xenophon's accounts of the conflicts be-tween the Persian Empire and Scythia and later accounts of Alexander's cavalry innovations in Afghanistan. Jugurtha and Aristonicus had also practiced "asymmetrical" warfare against Romans. In the past, Mithra-dates had depended on set battles, sending his numerically superior, formally arrayed hoplite armies marching out onto a plain for pitched combat. In battles to come, light, flexible cavalry attacks would be the key. From now on, his military strategy would mirror his diplomatic strategies: he would probe for weakness, feint, jab, and withdraw, keep-ing the Romans confused, exhausted, impotent to strike back.

Besides studying past mistakes and planning strategies, how did the fugitives from Pontus spend their days? We would expect Mithradates and his men to maintain top physical condition, with military exercises and athletic contests. Another pastime may have been visits to Armenia's temples of love, similar to those in Pontus and Cappadocia. Scattered throughout Armenia, these idyllic sanctuaries were temporary dormito-ries for maidens consecrated to the goddess Anaitis/Anahit for a year before marriage. Many of the young women came from wealthy families. According to Strabo, they selected sexual partners of equal rank and en-joyed giving the men valuable gifts. The dashing King Mithradates would have been warmly welcomed. Beavers abound in Armenia's lakes and streams—perhaps their testicles contributed to Mithradates' celebrated vigor.

Armenia's pastures provided grazing for horses, and Mithradates and his men could hunt stags, boars, lions, lynxes, bears, snow leopards, and fowl. The high plateaus held a profusion of herbs and wild flowers. In the short summers, the mountain air was perfumed by sage, juniper, and honeysuckle-scented thistles called "flowers of the sun," sacred to Zoro-astrians. Brilliant yellow irises dotted the mountain slopes, along with poisonous blue monkshood, the mysterious narcotic *silphium*, and a strange wormwood parasite, a lilylike blossom of velvet crimson. An-other curious, highly toxic plant bore drooping bunches of dark-red berries on a tall stalk. About 10 percent of Armenia's thousands of plant species are now recognized by modern science as medicinal. Mithradates and his doctors would have been familiar with all these and more. Rich veins of gold ore and purple sandyx (Armenian arsenic) lay in the mountains. As the seasons turned, we can imagine Mithradates and his Agari gathering and testing novel ingredients for theriac.[10]

Plutarch claimed that Tigranes insulted Mithradates by shunting him off to a remote, inhospitable landscape. But the evidence indicates that the two kings enjoyed mutual esteem and rapport.[11] They had been friends since their alliance in 94 BC. True, their political styles certainly differed: King Tigranes, about seventy, was an absolute autocrat with little understanding of the Roman threat, while King Mithradates, about sixty-five, accommodated democratic traditions and had dealt with Rome for decades. Both men enjoyed extraordinary physical stamina and intellectual vitality all their long lives (did Tigranes, as one of the king's friends, benefit from a daily dose of *Mithridatium*?). Both rulers had been raised to carry out Persian fire rituals, and each believed that divine Mithraic comets had blessed their reigns. While Mithradates' appreciation for Greek culture ran deeper than Tigranes', they shared Persian culture, love of hunting, erudition, and grandiose ambitions. Moreover, their goals were compatible, and each man hated Rome as the dark force that opposed righteousness. Another strong link was Mithradates' daughter, Cleopatra—she was Tigranes' chosen queen and adviser, favored above all his concubines.

A dependable military ally when called on, Tigranes was never enthusiastic about Mithradates' Roman wars, preferring to carve out his own empire beyond Rome's notice. Mithradates' empire was a useful buffer. Instead of snubbing Mithradates, Tigranes arranged for Mithradates' safety and comfort from afar, without arousing Roman ire. Then he simply went about his own pressing business—until Appius delivered Lucullus's insolent demand.

Lucullus's ultimatum spurred Tigranes to meet personally with his father-in-law. Tigranes warmly welcomed Mithradates to his palace. The reunion with Queen Cleopatra carried special meaning given the fates of so many of Mithradates' other children. The two monarchs spent three days together in private. No translators. No witnesses. Based on papers discovered after Mithradates' death, Plutarch speculated that their conversation revolved around casting blame on others. He pointed to the case of Metrodorus (the Rome-Hater), long a favorite of Mithradates, who had been sent to request aid from Tigranes. Tigranes revealed that Metrodorus had urged him to honor the request, but then honestly acknowledged that it might not be in Armenia's best interest. The philosopher died mysteriously. Plutarch implies that Metrodorus may have been killed by Mithradates, whose unerring instinct for detecting betrayal had kept him alive for more than half a century.[12]

KILL THE MESSENGER

The two monarchs surely did compare notes about who could be trusted, but they also conversed about practical, urgent matters. Tigranes generously gave his old friend ten thousand expert Armenian cavalrymen. With renewed hope, Mithradates prepared to set off from his hunting lodge base camp for Pontus with his new army. Case closed, thought Tigranes.

But then a messenger arrived, shouting that the Romans were coming. Before the man could catch his breath, the King of Kings had him beheaded for disturbing the peace. As McGing pointed out, Tigranes reasonably thought such a report was false; he was confident that Lucullus was not authorized to invade Armenia. That was a logical assumption, but Lucullus was following his own irrational agenda, aggressively attacking Armenia because of Tigranes' refusal to surrender Mithradates. After Tigranes' execution of the messenger, no one else dared to inform him of Lucullus's approach. It is safe to assume that no one spoke, either, of the great earthquake that had recently destroyed several cities in Syria. The quake killed 170,000 people; soothsayers were interpreting this as a sign that Tigranes would no longer rule Syria. Unlike Mithradates, who always sought out the freshest intelligence however dire, the King of Kings, commented Plutarch, sat in a cocoon of "ignorance while the fires of war blazed around him."[13]

While Tigranes was camped with his army in the Taurus Mountains, Lucullus coaxed his grumbling army of 15,000–20,000 men across the Euphrates into Armenia. His target was Tigranocerta, where Tigranes kept his concubines and other treasures. An attack there would compel Tigranes to fight, reckoned Lucullus, and after his defeat he would surrender Mithradates. And there would be plenty of booty for the soldiers. Although the city was still under construction, Tigranocerta's walls rose seventy feet high. A contingent of Romans dug in for a siege, while Lucullus camped on the plain across the Tigris.

Finally Tigranes' brave general Mithrobarzanes dared to inform His Majesty about the Roman invasion and threat to Tigranocerta. Mithradates, at the hunting lodge, also received the startling news from his own spies. Mithradates immediately canceled plans to recover his kingdom and turned back with his cavalry to help Tigranes. This was a thrilling if daunting new development—here was a chance to crush the Romans using Tigranes' great resources. Mithradates sent letters and messengers ahead to Tigranes, offering excellent advice, based on his own failures and his new ideas for resisting legions. "Do not fight the Romans head-on," he warned. "Harass and surround them with your cavalry. Devastate the countryside to reduce them by exhaustion and famine." Mithradates sent General Taxiles ahead with the same advice: "Stay defensive! Avoid clashing directly with the invincible Romans."

But Tigranes decided to attack head-on. It was not an insane decision, given his vastly superior numbers, but he would have done better to follow Mithradates' wise counsel and knowledge of the Romans' battle prowess even when they were outnumbered. According to Plutarch and Appian, Tigranes called up an army of about 250,000, including 20,000 nomadic archers and slingers and 55,000 cavalry (17,000 were *cataphracts*, knights in heavy chain mail wielding long lances, riding large armored Nisaean horses). Trailing behind came a horde of carpenters, road and bridge builders, baggage handlers, grooms, cooks, supply agents, and families, totaling 35,000. This immense barbarian force, some trained as traditional hoplites and others in tribal warfare (like the fierce headhunters from the Taurus range), each division in native armor, carrying traditional weapons and speaking hundreds of dialects, came from Armenia, Media, Syria, Commagene, Gordyene, Sophene, Mesopotamia, Atropatene, Mardia, Adiabene, Arabia, Parthia, and Bactria.[14]

Inside the city-in-progress, Tigranocerta's population was another great melting pot, made up of Cappadocians, Jews, Greeks, Arabs, Assyrians, Adiabeni, Gordyeni, and other nameless displaced peoples—including a large contingent of professional actors—all transplanted by Tigranes and now besieged by the Romans.

Tigranes led his massive army down from the Taurus. Queen Cleopatra was safe in Artaxata, Armenia's old fortified capital. But—as Lucullus expected—Tigranes worried about the Romans' capturing his concubine Zosimé and the rest of his harem in Tigranocerta. Mithradates had been unable to defend his own harem during the defeat of Pontus. Perhaps he or Taxiles helped plan the daring rescue of Tigranes' harem, which featured his new hit-and-run strategy. Suddenly six thousand nomad horsemen burst through the Roman besiegers surrounding the city. The riders dashed to the tower and roughly scooped up Tigranes' concubines, children, and valuables, and galloped back behind the lines.

From a hill high above the Tigris River, Tigranes and his eldest son (Tigranes, by Cleopatra) looked down on the antlike Roman army across the river. They seemed so insignificant. His men made witty jokes about the doomed Romans, while his Armenian, Median, and Adiabeni generals lazily cast lots to divide up the anticipated spoils. Tigranes' famous quip has come down in history as ironic last words: "If those Romans have come as ambassadors, there are far too many of them. If they have come as an invading army, there are far too few!"

Only Taxiles, Mithradates' experienced general, was worried as he watched the Romans don their gleaming helmets and armor, raise their polished shields and standards, and begin to form ranks. Where was Mithradates? He was on the way but saw no need to hurry, because he expected Lucullus to continue with the cautious approach he had followed in Bithynia and Pontus. No one imagined that Lucullus would provoke a battle.[15]

But Lucullus's strategy was the opposite of what Mithradates anticipated. Seriously outnumbered, the Roman used a lightning strike against Tigranes' cumbersome masses. Riding out at the head of his army, in a red cloak with golden tassels, his steel breastplate flashing in the October sun, Lucullus had his finest hour. For once, his men were impressed. Dismounting, Lucullus raised his sword, shouting "This day is ours, my fellow soldiers!" He gave the signal for attack before Tigranes' archers could let fly, and directed his Thracian and Galatian cavalry to slash the enemy's mail-clad horses from behind, giving them no time to maneuver.

Incredulous that such a piddling force would actually initiate the attack, Tigranes could only choke out the same words over and over again: "What!? Are *they* really attacking *us*?" It was a tremendous rout. Tigranes' wall of *cataphracts* reared up and bolted, running down their own infantry, trampling tens of thousands. The heavily armored horses collided with Tigranes' baggage train. Confusion and terror clotted the multitudes. The Romans closed in for the slaughter and pursued the fleeing enemy till nightfall. For once, Lucullus's legionnaires followed orders and did not stop for plunder, bypassing mile after mile of glittering armor, weapons, and ornaments lying in the road.

Shocked out of his fantasy of easy vistory, aghast at the disaster, Tigranes rushed with his son and attendants into the foothills. With great emotion, the King of Kings removed his tiara and handed it to his son, urging him to save himself. Not wanting to stand out as royalty, the prince entrusted the crown to his slave for safekeeping. Father and son fled by different routes into the mountains.

Lucullus tallied only 100 men wounded and 5 killed, while he claimed that more than 100,000 of Tigranes' infantry and most of the cavalry perished. Many escaped; many were taken captive. Among the prisoners was the slave carrying Tigranes' tiara: his capture might explain how we know of Tigranes' personal reactions to the battle. Ancient and modern historians marvel at this spectacular upset, a battle like no other. Never had the Romans been so outnumbered, and never had they won so decisively against overwhelming odds. Alfred Duggan, writing in the 1950s, described the battle in racist-colonialist terms, comparing the Syrian and Mesopotamian soldiers to "feeble cattle" and commenting that the "Arabs of the desert think only of joining the winning side." Duggan even stated that the outcome was a striking example of Westerners ascendant over "cringing Asiatics."[16]

Yet Tigranes' diverse, sprawling army—reminiscent of Xerxes' great multinational army in 480 BC—had been spectacularly successful in all his conquests so far. Obviously, however, Tigranes' massive, polyglot forces also suffered problems of logistics and command and control similar to those faced by Xerxes. Tigranes' armies were ill-prepared and immobilized by Lucullus's blitzkrieg strategy and experienced legions. Indeed, historians praise Lucullus's military accomplishments: with delay and caution he had worn down the lightning-fast Mithradates, and now with speed and surprise he defeated Tigranes' ponderous juggernaut. Yet despite all his successes in battles, Lucullus failed to lay his hands on Mithradates or Tigranes, nor could he prevent them from surging back with renewed forces.

RISING FROM THE ASHES

Riding down from the mountains toward the Tigris Valley with his twelve thousand cavalrymen, Mithradates was unaware that the battle had already been lost. His heart sank when he met the first of Tigranes' soldiers fleeing in panic. As he encountered thousands of wounded fugitives streaming up from the plain, Mithradates learned the extent of the catastrophe. At this extremely bleak moment, after surviving a barrage of personal calamities and cutting short his own hope of recovering at

FIG. 13.2. (Left) Mithradates' coin portrait, 75/74 BC. As crises accumulated, Mithradates' image on coins seems to be more Dionysian than Alexandrian, with wild, disheveled hair; and the coins appear to be hastily produced. Silver tetradrachm, 1944.100.41479, bequest of E. T. Newell, courtesy of the American Numismatic Society. (Right) Tigranes the Great, Getty Images.

least his Kingdom of Pontus, one might expect Mithradates to criticize Tigranes' foolish arrogance and think only of saving himself. But, as Plutarch pointed out, it is praiseworthy and revealing of Mithradates' character that instead of abandoning Tigranes, Mithradates continued down the mountain in search of his old friend.

Mithradates found the king crying alone by the side of the road, forlorn and humiliated, without his crown or attendants. Leaping down from his horse, Mithradates embraced Tigranes. The two men wept together over their misfortunes. Mithradates quickly regained composure and inner fortitude. Placing his cloak over Tigranes' shoulders, Mithradates offered his own horse. He spoke encouragingly as they turned and hurried up into the mountains toward Artaxata. Mithradates must have persuaded Tigranes that they could still fulfill their grand—and now intertwined—destinies. The battle's outcome would have convinced Mithradates that his new indirect strategy was the only way to resist the Romans.[17]

In the face of overwhelming losses, the battered pair of kings began to forge plans to assemble yet another army. Tigranes graciously appointed

Mithradates as the commander and strategist of their new combined forces, citing his old friend's wisdom and experiences with the Romans.

MISSION IMPOSSIBLE

While Mithradates and Tigranes disappeared into northern Armenia, Lucullus remained on the plain to besiege Tigranocerta. For the first time, a Roman army experienced an extraordinary secret weapon, a flaming substance that burned everything, wood, metal, leather, horses, and human flesh. "This strange chemical," marveled the historian Cassius Dio, "is so fiery that it consumes whatever it touches and cannot be extinguished with any kind of liquid."[18]

Many men and machines were burned, but Lucullus finally took the imperial city after Tigranes' mercenaries opened the gates. He seized the royal coffers, containing eight thousand talents of silver, unimaginably costly raiment, jewels, and other valuables. Each legionnaire received eight hundred drachmas (the equivalent of more than two years' pay) and all the plunder he could carry. When Lucullus discovered the company of dramatic actors cowering in the theater, he ordered them to perform plays to celebrate his victory. Then, commanding his men to raze Tigranocerta to rubble, the Roman imperator saved the wives of prominent men from rape and arranged for the displaced people from Cappadocia and elsewhere to return to their native lands. All traces of Tigranocerta were erased. Its location is unknown, although in 2006 Armenian archaeologists announced the exciting discovery of the walls of a large, fortified Hellenistic city near the Tigris.[19]

Elated by his success, Lucullus decided to ignore the fact that Mithradates and Tigranes were still free in the north. Turning west, he stormed Samosata, the wealthy capital of Commagene, a small kingdom on the Euphrates. Allied with Mithradates and Tigranes, Samosata controlled the strategic trade routes from Asia north to Pontus. But the Samosatans wielded the same horrendous weapon used by the Tigranocertans: a "flammable mud called *maltha* that oozes up from pools in the desert," wrote Pliny. The defenders on the wall poured *maltha* over the Romans below. It clings like burning honey to anyone who tries to flee, said Pliny, and water only causes it to burn more furiously. *Maltha* destroyed Lucullus's siege machines and melted his soldiers' armor and flesh. The incendiary was well known in the Middle East to the worshippers of

Ahuramazda and Mithra, but unknown in Rome at this time. *Maltha* was viscous, highly combustible naphtha, skimmed from petroleum lakes in the deserts of northern Iraq, Syria, and eastern Turkey.

The terror of the burning *maltha* forced Lucullus to withdraw from Samosata. Venturing into Gordyene, his army suffered another biochemical attack. Archers on horseback suddenly bore down, shooting arrows even as they galloped away and vanished into the hills. Lucullus lost a great many men in these ambushes. Their wounds were "dangerous and incurable," wrote Cassius Dio. Not only did the nomads dip their iron arrows in deadly viper venom, but the tips were designed to break off inside the wound.[20] Lucullus retreated to the Tigris, with his soldiers vehemently protesting the hardships and lack of fresh loot. After the first flush of victory and plunder, the campaign now seemed endless, pointless. Why were they continuing to battle new barbarian enemies in these godforsaken lands, while the renegade kings Mithradates and Tigranes escaped to Artaxata?

According to Plutarch, Lucullus had convinced himself that he had already neutralized Mithradates and Tigranes. They were old men, Lucullus told himself, no longer worthy of notice. Like an athlete in a triathlon, wrote Plutarch, Lucullus now dreamed of vanquishing the Big Three, the greatest empires in the known world. First Mithradates, then Tigranes, and now—Parthia! Parthia's military power had been steadily growing in what is now Iran and Pakistan. Loosely allied with Mithradates and Tigranes, the king of Parthia refused to promise neutrality. Using this refusal to justify an invasion of Parthia, Lucullus dispatched a messenger back to Pontus with new orders for the two legions—the Fimbrian bad apples—left behind in Mithradates' kingdom. They were to join him in Mesopotamia, to help conquer Parthia.

But the two Fimbrian legions refused to obey—they even threatened to abandon Pontus. Word of their mutiny spread to Lucullus's soldiers on the Tigris. They berated Lucullus for leading them on a such a dangerous wild-goose chase. Suddenly, Lucullus, despite his strategic brilliance, was no longer the imperator of the Roman army in the East. His authority evaporated. Lucullus—who for all his courage and intellect had never connected with the common soldier—was now a virtual nonentity in the midst of a disobedient, battle-weary mob.[21]

MEANWHILE IN ARMENIA

Mithradates and Tigranes, from their base in Artaxata, energetically crisscrossed the countryside in 69 BC, raising fresh armies. They recruited fighters from Armenia and the warlike tribes of Colchis, Caucasia, and the steppes beyond the Caspian Sea. Mithradates, as supreme commander, personally selected seventy thousand Armenians to be trained as infantry. The rest were set to manufacturing armor and weapons. Taxiles divided the new army into Roman-style cohorts and drilled them in Roman battle tactics, which would be needed to drive the Romans out of Pontus.

But Mithradates also dipped into his Greco-Persian heritage, the experiences of Darius and Alexander. He counted on the maneuverability of smaller, flexible formations to fight the Romans in Armenia and eastern Pontus, where Lucullus's cavalry would be hobbled by rugged terrain. Mithradates recruited an unusually large cavalry force, about thirty-five thousand horsemen and -women from Caucasia (between the Black and Caspian seas) and the lands beyond. Among the nomads of Caucasia and the steppes, each man and woman was a potential warrior, since both genders were raised to ride and shoot the bow and arrow (thus influencing Greek and Roman tales of Amazons). Mounted on shaggy ponies, this light-armed, nimble cavalry would be the heart of Mithradates' new army.

It might have been during this recruiting drive that Mithradates met the nomadic horsewoman named Hypsicratea ("Mountain Strength"). Her age is unknown, but she could have been thirty or forty years younger than Mithradates. Her name suggests that that she came from the Caucasus region. Hypsicratea first served as the king's groom, caring for his horses; then she became his personal attendant and lover. They enjoyed riding and hunting together. The Amazon's endurance and courage rivaled the king's, and given Mithradates' love of literature, history, art, and intelligent women, we can guess that she was also his intellectual equal. Praising her "manly spirit and extravagant daring," he called her by the masculine form of her name, "Hypsicrates." Mithradates' relationship with Hypsicratea recalls famous mythic pairs—Theseus and Antiope, Achilles and Penthesilea, Hercules and Hippolyte—and he knew the story of Alexander and the Amazon queen from Caucasia. As we shall see, Hypsicratea's companionship would sustain Mithradates in future adventures.[22]

Mithradates and Tigranes stockpiled large supplies of grain, and sent envoys to Parthia to solicit money and troops. Mithradates' personal letter to the Parthian king was preserved by the Roman historian Sallust. Whether or not it is the actual wording of Mithradates' message is debated by historians, but the content and tone match his other letters and speeches. Mithradates did keep copies of his correspondence, discovered after his death, and early in his reign he enjoyed friendly relations with Parthian royalty (included among his friends in the Delos monument). Here is the essence of the letter of 69 BC, showcasing Mithradates' animosity toward Rome and persuasive diplomacy (so different from the approach of Lucullus and Appius).[23]

> King Mithradates to the King of Parthia, greeting [the letter begins]. As one who is enjoying prosperity and glory, you may wonder why you should listen to my request for a military alliance. You may ask whether such an alliance is honorable, wise, or risky. If I did not believe that you too were exposed to the same wicked enemies and that to crush Roman aggression would bring you glorious fame, I would not venture to ask for an alliance and I would never hope to try to unite my misfortunes with your glorious success.
>
> Rome has always had the same motive for making war upon all nations and kings. That motive is a deep-seated desire for domination and riches. These Romans turned to the East only because the Atlantic Ocean ended their westward expansion. From their very origins, Romans have possessed only what they could steal from others—their homes, their wives, their lands, their empire—all stolen! Nothing prevents them from attacking and destroying allies and friends alike, weak and powerful, near and far. Rome is viciously hostile to every government not subject to Rome—especially monarchies.

Mithradates lambastes Rome's hypocrisy and betrayals of those they pretend to befriend. "The Romans stripped Anatolia of 10,000 talents when they betrayed Antiochus the Great; they enslaved King Eumenes of Pergamon; they forged the wills of Attalus III and Nicomedes IV so that they could take over all Anatolia." Here Mithradates describes the Roman murder of the tragic hero Aristonicus, the true son of King Attalus. That he brings up Aristonicus's rebellion now, more than fifty years after the fact, indicates that the Sun Citizens' uprising still resonated in the anti-Roman East, as far away as Parthia, the birthplace of Persian Sunworship.

You have great resources of men, weapons, and gold [writes Mithradates]. It is inevitable that Rome will make war on you to obtain those resources. Ask yourself, if Tigranes and I are defeated, would you really be better able to resist the Romans? There is no end to war with the Romans. They must be crushed.

Here Mithradates makes his pitch: "Ally with us, while Tigranes' kingdom is intact and while I have an army of soldiers trained in warfare with Romans. If you send us help now, Tigranes and I can win this war at the expense of *our* armies, far from *your* borders, and with no effort, losses, or risk on *your* part." He concludes,

The Romans hate us as the avengers of all those they subjugate. You possess all the riches and grandeur of Persia, but you can expect nothing but deceit and war from Rome. Romans want power over all, but they always aim their deadliest weapons against those with the richest spoils. It is through arrogance, treachery, and never-ending warfare that Rome has grown great. Believe me, they will blot out everything or perish in the attempt.

Mithradates had lost his strong ally in the West, Sertorius. Spartacus was dead. Now he endeavored to convince Parthia that Rome was a real threat, and that helping Mithradates and Tigranes was in Parthia's best interests. Ultimately, however, the king of Parthia negotiated with Mithradates and with Lucullus, but aided neither side.

LUCULLUS CHASES SHADOWS

Mutiny by his army forced Lucullus to abandon the dream of subduing the Parthian Empire. In summer of 68 BC, Lucullus took up his old goal, to wrest Mithradates away from Tigranes' protection (indeed, as long as Mithradates was alive, he was a threat to Rome). Lucullus's soldiers agreed to march to Tigranes' headquarters in Artaxata, designed by Hannibal. Lucullus liked to refer to Artaxata as the "Armenian Carthage."[24]

Marching up into Armenia, the Romans were surprised to find no food even though it was midsummer. Armenia's high plateau of 4,000 to 7,000 feet is surrounded by 10,000-foot, snowy mountain ranges. At such high altitudes, the grain and fruit had not yet ripened. The soldiers were continually harassed by mounted archers. To the great consternation of the legionnaires, these male and female warriors skirmished in typical nomadic fashion, swooping in and then scattering. To the Romans, it seemed a cowardly way to fight. But it was effective: the legions were constantly under fire without being able to land a blow.

Finally, a vast cloud of dust announced the approach of Tigranes and Mithradates. The two enemy commanders appeared, flanked by cavalry units from Atropatene (Azerbaijan), leading an army of such splendor and might that Lucullus was suddenly struck with fear. He turned to attack the Atropateni flanks, but they melted away into the hillsides instead of meeting him head-on. It may have been in this battle that Lucullus's Macedonian cavalrymen decided to desert en masse to Mithradates.[25]

Lucullus found it impossible to engage with Tigranes or Mithradates. They had become shadows, constantly withdrawing. Lucullus doggedly pursued. He took a lot of captives and amassed a great deal of exotic booty. Yet skirmish after skirmish proved indecisive. Lucullus and his army seemed to be chasing an illusion. Fleeting engagements were followed by unnerving silence. They never really lost, but they could not win either. By autumn, Lucullus had been drawn onto Armenia's highlands of golden-brown parched grass and alkaline lakes. Plutarch says he was still hoping for a decisive battle that would "subdue the barbarian realm utterly."

Plutarch, Appian, and other ancient (and modern) historians have criticized the "poor" battle performance of Mithradates and Tigranes and their army of barbarians, accusing them of "shamefully" running away over and over again. Appian, for example, remarked that all that summer and fall, Lucullus could not "draw Mithradates out to fight." Plutarch even claimed that Mithradates "fled disgracefully" because he "could not endure the shouting" and clamor of battle. The barbarian warriors "did not shine in action," continued Plutarch. "Even in a slight skirmish with the Roman cavalry, they would give way before the advancing infantry, scattering to the right and left." Maddeningly, the Gordyeni and Atropateni kept galloping off instead of "engaging at close quarters with the Romans." The "pursuit was long and exhausting. The Romans," concluded Plutarch, "were worn out."[26]

Exactly. The historians—and Lucullus—failed to understand the new guerrilla tactics that Mithradates had put in place, adopting the asymmetrical style of fighting that his barbarian warriors excelled in. Mithradates and Tigranes gave way in close quarters, avoiding direct conflict and turning the enemies' own momentum against them. While the Romans grew more frustrated and baffled, the barbarians and their tough little ponies were at home in the harsh landscape as fall turned to winter. They knew exactly where to find food, water, shelter, and hideouts. They monitored the movements of Lucullus and his men, while Lucullus had no idea where he himself was, where the enemy was hiding, or when they would strike next.

Mithradates, astute student of history, appears to have studied Xenophon's discussions of his Greek hoplite army's difficulties fighting the mounted archers native to this same region where Lucullus now found himself. As noted above, Mithradates was also aware of Alexander's creation of new, mountain-trained, light-armed, highly mobile cavalry to match the mounted resistance fighters he faced after his invasion of Afghanistan (330 BC). The tactics were similar to those used by Jugurtha, and by Mithradates' allies, the Scordisci horsemen from the Danube, against Lucullus in Pontus.

Mithradates could also recall how the nomads of Scythia had outwitted Darius and his Persian army in 512 BC. As the Greek historian Herodotus commented, the nomads "understood self-preservation better than anyone on earth. . . . if they wish to avoid engaging with an enemy, that enemy can never come to grips with them." Luring Darius to penetrate deep into Scythian territory, the nomads melted away whenever Darius attempted to attack. Darius sent an exasperated message to the Scythian chief: "Why on earth do you keep running away? Why are you wandering all over the place trying to escape? If you are so weak, surrender! If you think you are strong enough to oppose me, stand and fight!" But as Herodotus pointed out, the Scythian strategy was not employed out of fear or cowardice; it was psychologically and militarily sound. As a result of their falling back whenever the Persians had the upper hand, and then unpredictably striking and fading away, Darius was kept off balance, and his supply lines were stretched to the breaking point. "Again and again," wrote Herodotus, "Darius's momentary success gave way to acute embarrassment." In this way the nomads led Darius to march across the entire Scythian territory, all the way to the Danube, without ever engaging with the enemy.[27]

In 68/67 BC, Mithradates ensured that Lucullus was in the same predicament as Darius had been. The Roman army, unused to high-altitude weather, trudged on, wary, hungry, complaining. Where was the enemy hiding? How could the air be so frigid when the sun shone brightly in an azure sky? Suddenly, long before the Romans expected it, winter arrived.

Snow blanketed the ground; icicles crusted the pine boughs; streams froze solid. The sun's rays gave no heat, and the glare on the snow blinded the men. The freezing temperature gnawed at toes and fingers and caused the breath to "congeal upon mustaches and beards, speedily forming icicles, which hurt horribly." Ice on the dark rivers shattered when the horses tried to cross, and the jagged shards cut their legs. Wrapped in skimpy cloaks, legionnaires marched single file through narrow canyons and over frozen marshes. They were always shivering now, huddling in frosty tents and melting ice to drink.[28]

The soldiers' complaints escalated into "tumultuous assemblies" in their tents at night and threats of desertion. Trying to avert another mutiny, Lucullus urged them to persevere—they would soon destroy the city built by Hannibal and seize Mithradates, triumphing over "Rome's two most hated foes." But Plutarch reports that the soldiers forced Lucullus to abandon his pursuit of the renegade kings. He accompanied his army back down from the mountains, to the mild winter of the Tigris.

There Lucullus roused his men to storm Nisibis, held by Tigranes' brother Gouras. Defending this city was none other than Mithradates' engineer Callimachus, Lucullus's nemesis at Amisus, as we have seen. Gouras surrendered; he was saved for the Triumph. Callimachus was brought before Lucullus. He promised to reveal Mithradates' secret stores of fabulous treasures, but Lucullus tortured Callimachus to death for burning Amisus, denying him the chance to spare the Greek city. When Callimachus died, the knowledge of many of Mithradates' most cleverly hidden caches of gold and valuables was lost, hoards overlooked by the Romans and perhaps still awaiting discovery today.[29]

Lucullus and his army were burned out. The officers and men castigated him as arrogant and distant, thinking only of enriching himself. Comparing their leader unfavorably to Pompey, who triumphed in Spain and Italy and looked after the welfare of his soldiers, they ignored Lucullus's pleas to resume the pursuit of Mithradates. In 67 BC, Lucullus's army camped at Nisibis and refused to budge.

MITHRADATES' SURGE IN PONTUS

Mithradates was free to recover his Kingdom of Pontus. Tigranes would arrive later to retake Cappadocia. Accompanied by the Agari, Timotheus, Hypsicratea, his bodyguard Bituitus, Roman deserters, and a highly trained army of about eight thousand infantrymen and cavalry, Mithradates received a joyful welcome from his people. Many eagerly joined his new army, as he visited old strongholds to establish garrisons.[30]

Filled with optimism, in spring of 67 BC, the old warrior, now about sixty-seven years old, led his army against the two Fimbrian legions (about twelve thousand men) still occupying Pontus. These were the soldiers who had refused to leave their lax tour of duty to join Lucullus in Mesopotamia. As the historian Eutropius remarked, it was their negligence and greed that gave Mithradates the chance to recover Pontus. Taken by surprise, the Roman legate desperately sought to increase his forces by arming the slaves kept by the Fimbrians. Could he be the one finally to stop Mithradates the Great? He led his crew of slaves and legionnaires onto the field, where the battle lasted all day. The Romans retreated, leaving behind five hundred dead.[31]

Although the Roman threat still loomed, this was a rousing victory. Rising phoenixlike from the ashes, Mithradates was surging back. But fighting in the front lines, the king was wounded, his first war injury. An arrow pierced his cheek, just missing his eye. He had to be carried from the battlefield. For several days, his worried troops feared for his life, as he hovered in critical condition. The Agari shamans successfully treated the arrow wound, using their secret knowledge of serpent venom as a coagulant to stop hemorrhage. Mithradates was back in the saddle in time to repulse a renewed Roman assault a few days later.

Now Nature intervened, once again sending extraordinary meteorological events. Before the battle began, wrote Appian, a freak tornado struck with howling winds "the likes of which were unknown in living memory." The cyclone blew away the canvas tents in both camps, sweeping men and pack animals over precipices. Both sides regrouped. The next battle would prove decisive.

The Romans attacked Mithradates at night, at Zela. Throwing on his helmet and armor, Mithradates rallied his men. They drove the legionnaires into trenches filled with rainwater and mud, soon clogged with dead Romans. But in the heat of the battle, a brave centurion came running up alongside Mithradates' horse. The centurion stabbed his sword into Mithradates' thigh with all his might. Those nearby—maybe Bituitus and Hypsicratea—immediately chopped the Roman to pieces, but Mithradates was felled, bleeding profusely. Again, the king was carried off the field. The high spirits of victory descended into alarm and despair. Would their intrepid commander survive such a grave wound?

The soldiers crowded together on the plain, trying to catch a glimpse of Mithradates lying on the muddy ground, attended by the field medic Timotheus and the Agari wizards. For the second time in this campaign, medical history was made. Again the Agari staunched the flow of blood, using snake venom. Mithradates regained consciousness. Everyone knew that Alexander had suffered a similar grievous thigh wound, and they recalled how his doctors had raised him high up above the Macedonian army to reassure the men that their beloved leader still lived. Now Mithradates' doctor Timotheus lifted Mithradates up so that he could be seen by his cheering soldiers.[32]

By late afternoon, Mithradates the invincible was back on his horse, storming the Roman camp. But the camp was empty: the survivors had fled in terror, leaving behind 7,000 dead. As Mithradates and his men viewed the carnage, they counted 24 tribunes and 150 centurions, the largest number of officers ever killed in a single ancient battle. Mithradates' recovery of Pontus in this great battle at Zela in 67 BC was one of the most unexpected, remarkable feats in his long career. He erected a large victory trophy on the battlefield, thanking Zeus Stratios.

Lucullus arrived in Pontus after the devastating defeat at the muddy trenches. He took command of the shattered Fimbrian units but did not arrange for burial of the 7,000 Roman corpses strewn over the battleground. This neglect, according to Plutarch, was the last straw for his demoralized soldiers.

And Mithradates was long gone. True to his new strategy, Mithradates had withdrawn out of reach in western Armenia. Tigranes was coming to help secure his kingdom. Lucullus gave the order to march to the point where the two grand armies would meet, hoping to defeat the two rogue kings once and for all. But the battered Fimbrians deserted their posts. The mutiny spread throughout Lucullus's legions. At this point, says Plutarch, Fortune completely abandoned Lucullus. "So ill-starred and wandering had his course become, that Lucullus nearly lost all that he had accomplished, through no fault but his own." Lucullus went from tent to tent in tears, begging the men to obey. The soldiers mocked their commander, hurling their empty purses at his feet, telling him to fight the enemies alone since he alone knew how to get rich from them.[33]

Lucullus sat by helplessly as Tigranes the Great rolled through Cappadocia, taking it over for the third time since the Mithradatic Wars first began. One wonders whether Lucullus gave any thought to the masses of wandering Cappadocian refugees, who had been transplanted to Ti-

granocerta by Tigranes, and now had been liberated by Lucullus and
sent back to their homeland—just in time to meet Tigranes' reinvasion.

In Rome, the Populars denounced Lucullus for prolonging the war
and stripping the palaces of Mithradates and Tigranes for his own profit.
He had wasted years, money, and lives, railed his critics, "compelling his
soldiers to conduct caravans of camels and carts laden with golden beakers set with gems" when he should have annihilated Rome's great enemy.
Lucullus had assured the Senate that he had completely subdued Mithradates. Now officials arrived from Rome and observed the utter anarchy
and collapse of the mission—the mission Sulla had failed to accomplish,
the mission that Lucullus had claimed to achieve. Lucullus, fifty-two
years old, was relieved of his command, his soldiers released from military service.

In 66 BC, Gnaeus Pompey—dubbed "the Great" by his patron Sulla
who admired his ruthlessness—was appointed to take over the war on
Mithradates. At age forty, Pompey had already celebrated two Triumphs;
he claimed credit (many said unfairly) for defeating both Sertorius and

FIG. 13.3. Pompey (left) takes over the command of the Mithradatic Wars
from Lucullus (right). Engraving, Augustyn Mirys, ca. 1750.

FIG. 13.4. Lucullus introduces the cherry tree to Rome. *Journal des gourmands*, Paris 1806–07. Courtesy of the Boston Athenaeum.

Spartacus. Pompey and his older rival Lucullus met at a village in Galatia. Through gritted teeth they congratulated each other, then proceeded to snipe. Pompey belittled Lucullus, and Lucullus likened Pompey to a lazy vulture alighting on the kills of others. He warned that Mithradates was an illusory shadow-enemy. Pompey assigned a mere sixteen hundred soldiers to accompany the disgraced commander to Rome. The rest of the legionnaires eagerly reenlisted under Pompey.[34]

Returning to Italy with shiploads of plunder, captives, and his precious cherry tree saplings, Lucullus was allowed to celebrate a Triumph. His parade began with mail-clad Parthian knights, followed by ten of Mithradates' scythed chariots. Tigranes' hapless brother Gouras carried the tiara of Tigranes: these had to stand in for Tigranes himself. Mithradates, of course, was also conspicuous by his absence. He was represented by a life-sized golden statue and a huge bronze shield adorned with precious stones. Trudging behind the statue came Mithradates' downcast sister Nyssa captured in Kabeira, and about 60 of Mithradates' generals and advisers. Next, 110 bronze prows from Mithradates' warships trundled by. There were 50 litters heaped with Mithradates' gold, and 56 mules loaded with more than 2.5 million silver coins, all looted by Lucullus from Pontus and Tigranocerta.[35]

Lucullus used his war profits to take up a life of such excess that he went down in history as Rome's most notorious libertine and gastronome, lolling in luxurious villas and staging lavish banquets featuring exotic delicacies (the adjective "lucullan" now describes an extravagant feast). Anecdotes were told about Lucullus's outrageous lifestyle, while gourmands praised him for introducing the cherry to Italy. Within a few years of handing over his command to Pompey, however, Lucullus began to lose his mind. He died insane in 57 BC, poisoned, some whispered, by an overdose of a love potion.[36]

But those events were far in the future. For Mithradates, buoyed by his success in regaining his kingdom, battered though it was, the future looked bright again. Tenacity and his new tactics had paid off. He knew that Pompey could not afford to take up a new war against him right now. Rome—and Pompey—faced a crisis on the high seas that could not be ignored. During the wars, the pirates—more than a thousand ships equipped with silver oars, gilded sails, and awnings of purple silk—had infested the entire Mediterranean, from Cilicia to Gibraltar, plundering, raiding, and kidnapping to their hearts' content.[37] While Pompey took on the task of destroying the pirate nests across the Mediterranean, Mithradates rebuilt power and wealth from his headquarters in Pontus.

14

End Game

FROM their tree houses in the rhododendron forests, the Turret-Folk observed Pompey's army on the march across Mithradates' kingdom. As a young prince, Mithradates had befriended this fierce tribe. They knew the secrets of the local wild honey, the powerful neurotoxin that had felled Xenophon's Greek army in 401 BC. After tasting the honey, his soldiers had collapsed, open to attack in hostile territory. To Xenophon's great relief, his men eventually recovered.

In 66 BC, however, the poison honey would be deployed as a deliberate biological weapon against the Roman invaders, ignorant of Xenophon's experience. The Turret-Folk placed tempting honeycombs along Pompey's route. Mithradates had recently passed through their territory, ahead of Pompey. Were the Turret-Folk following Mithradates' suggestion? That is unknown, but the ploy certainly would have pleased the Poison King, and it was a great success. Pompey's advance cohorts stopped to enjoy the treat. Struck dumb and blind, wracked by violent vomiting and diarrhea, they lay paralyzed along the roadside. The Turret-Folk descended with their iron battle-axes. When Pompey arrived on the scene, a black cloud of flies buzzed over a thousand legionnaires sprawled on the road, sticky with honey and blood.[1]

And Mithradates? He was far away, a desperado on the run again from the long arm of Roman rule.

POMPEY

A year earlier, in 67 BC, Pompey had received a budget of 6,000 talents, an army of 120,000 soldiers, 4,000 cavalry, and 270 ships to quash the pirates, whose armadas of "odious extravagance" dominated the Mediterranean. Other Roman campaigns against the pirates had failed, but by skillfully marshaling his resources, Pompey caught or killed about 10,000 of the Mithra-worshipping buccaneers. Rome's massive response to the piracy emergency persuaded most of the remaining pirates to relocate on land grants in Rome's provinces.[2]

Pompey's success gained him unlimited war powers to take over the command of Lucullus's failed war on Mithradates. Cicero urged Pompey to "wipe out that stain . . . which has now fixed itself deeply and eaten its way into the Roman name." Cicero was referring to the unavenged atrocity of 88 BC, when Mithradates had ordered "all the Roman citizens in all Asia, scattered as they were over so many cities, to be slaughtered and butchered." Yet Mithradates "has never yet suffered any chastisement worthy of his wickedness," continued Cicero. "Now, twenty-three years later, he is still a king, and a king not content to hide himself in Pontus, or in the recesses of Cappadocia, but a king who seeks to emerge from his hereditary kingdom, and ravage Rome's revenues, in the broad light of Asia."[3]

While Pompey was pounding the pirates, Mithradates had a year to secure his kingdom, raise armies, and ensure the safety of his remaining family members. Concubines were assigned to various strongholds; Stratonice and Xiphares held Kainon Chorion; his daughter Drypetina held Sinora; other children were with Mithradates' sons Machares and Pharnaces in the Bosporan Kingdom. In Pontus, Mithradates stationed about thirty thousand infantry and three thousand cavalry to guard the frontiers. After the Roman depredations, provisions were scarce. This would hinder any new Roman invaders, but starvation also led to desertions. Mithradates harshly punished those caught abandoning the frontier outposts.

Many Roman officers and soldiers had defected from Lucullus to join Mithradates. In 66 BC, their connections reported that Pompey the Great was en route from Rhodes to Pontus with a large army and navy, authorized to make war on both Mithradates and Tigranes. Pompey had even forged an alliance with the king of Parthia.

Seeking an honorable way to avoid this new war and determined to retain his ancestral homeland—the kingdom he had just rescued from the grip of Roman occupation—Mithradates immediately sent envoys to Pompey. What terms would he demand for peace? Pompey's blunt reply: "Unconditional surrender—and deliver up our Roman traitors." Mithradates relayed this response to the Romans in his ranks. They urged the king to resist. The rest of his soldiers agreed with their Roman comrades.

FIG. 14.1. Marble statue discovered near Pompey's house, in Rome, identified as an idealized portrait of Pompey. Palazzo Spada, Rome, Alinari/Art Resource, NY.

Their reaction impressed Mithradates; Pompey's intransigence enraged him. Confident of the loyalty of his supporters, Mithradates vowed that this would be a united struggle to the end: "No! I'll never make peace with the rapacious Romans! I'll never surrender anyone to them! I refuse to do anything that is not for the common advantage to all!"[4]

The Last Campaign

Pompey provoked an attack on the border outposts. Mithradates sent out his full infantry and the Romans retired. After ascertaining the extent of Pompey's formidable forces, Mithradates withdrew to a mountain stronghold in southeastern Pontus that Pompey did not dare attack. Indeed, a large number of Pompey's men deserted to Mithradates.

Mithradates created the impression that he was digging in. But one night, after lighting their campfires as usual, Mithradates' army sneaked away from the stronghold—catching the Romans by surprise. Plutarch and Appian both claimed that Mithradates departed because he was ignorant of water and food in the region. That seems highly unlikely given his intimate knowledge of his homeland. Appian was puzzled: why did Mithradates "allow Pompey to enter his territory without opposition?"

Mithradates expected that Pompey would be unable to find food. But Pompey maintained his supply lines, dug deep wells for water, and set up a siege of Mithradates' new position. After forty-five days, Mithradates killed his pack animals, keeping his cavalry horses and fifty days' worth of provisions. According to Plutarch, his wounded men unable to march were killed by their comrades, to spare them from ignoble death at Roman hands. Again, Mithradates and his army "stole away silently by night over bad roads" to yet another stonghold.

Cassius Dio thought Mithradates had "become frightened [and] kept fleeing, because his forces were inferior." Appian assumed these actions meant Mithradates must have been "suffering from fear and mental paralysis at the approach of calamity." But these notions are dubious, given Mithradates' history, character, and recent vow to resist. Instead, Mithradates' evasive actions were in keeping with his new guerrilla tactics, modeled on nomadic warfare and on Alexander's innovations in Afghanistan—and already tested successfully against Lucullus. Mithradates' actions appear to have been calculated to lure Pompey deeper into the unfamiliar, rugged terrain between Pontus and Armenia. Indeed, in the next century, Frontinus, a Roman military strategist, would present these incidents as examples of Mithradates' overall strategy to deceive Pompey.

Mithradates' next movements confirm this explanation. Pompey followed Mithradates over the rough mountain paths with great difficulty, reported Appian. When Pompey caught up, Mithradates refused to fight directly. Instead, he "merely drove back the assailants with his cavalry—

and then disappeared into the thick forest in the evening." These new tactics perplexed the Romans—including the Roman friends who served in Mithradates' own army. They tried in vain to convince the king to fight Pompey head-on. But Mithradates took up a strong position in the mountains, near Dasteira. The place was naturally defended by boulders and steep cliffs, accessible by only one path up the slope, guarded by about two thousand of Mithradates' troops. Again, Mithradates counted on the scarcity of provisions to force Pompey to turn back.[5]

Nightmare by Moonlight

At this place, during a full moon, Mithradates had a dream. It was written down by his soothsayers and discovered by Pompey among his papers after his death. The dream began happily. Mithradates was sailing with a good wind north across the Black Sea, enjoying the salt breeze, his face warmed by the sun's rays. His mood was exuberant; he and his companions on the deck were all conversing pleasantly. Soon the green pastures and towers of Pantikapaion came into sight. Mithradates felt a glow of supreme confidence, joy, and security. He and his Amazon companion, Hypsicratea, would find peace in the Kingdom of the Bosporus on the northern shore of the Black Sea, with the freedom of the vast steppes at their backs. Suddenly the idyllic dream flipped into a nightmare. Mithradates found himself "bereft of all his companions, and tossed about in a rough sea, clinging to a bit of wreckage." As the king thrashed in his sleep, his friends shook him awake. It was the middle of the night, but they were shouting: "Pompey is attacking!"[6]

Grabbing weapons and armor, Mithradates, Hypsicratea, and his generals rushed out to confront Pompey. Under the bright moon, Pompey observed their rapid deployment and called off his surprise attack. But his officers, eager to exterminate Mithradates once and for all, came up with a cunning plan. The full moon would be Pompey's ally tonight. As it was setting behind the Roman position, the moonlight would shine forth behind their backs, illuminating the way as they advanced. But even more crucial, as the moon neared the horizon, it would cast extremely long shadows. As his officers sketched diagrams, Pompey suddenly saw that the elongated shadows would disorient the enemy, preventing them from correctly estimating the distance between the two armies (see plate 6).

In a lifetime of war and strife remarkable for extraordinary meteorological and astronomical events—comets, tempests at sea, cyclones, meteors—perhaps it was not surprising that yet another powerful force of Nature would be Mithradates' undoing. Certainly it is ironic that the Moon, Queen of the Night, would bring about the downfall of Mithradates, champion of Sun and Light, in his epic struggle against the forces of Darkness represented by Rome. That Pompey would chose to attack at night was in keeping with Rome's image in the Iranian-influenced East. Notably, Sulla had also attacked in the middle of the night. In contrast, Mithradates' hero Alexander had famously rebuffed his generals' advice to attack Darius at night, refusing to "steal victory like a thief."[7]

The Romans advanced by the pale white light of the moon. The long blue shadows thrown far ahead gave the impression that the Romans were much closer than they really were. Mithradates' archers, tricked by the optical illusion, let loose their arrows too soon. The missiles clattered harmlessly on the ground, far short of the mark. The Romans charged.

Many of Mithradates' troops up the slope were still arming, rushing back to mount their chargers, in the rear with the pack camels. As the front ranks panicked and fell back in the Roman onslaught, terror coursed through Mithradates' army, trapped in the rocky canyon. In the Moonlight Battle in the late summer of 66 BC, Pompey's men cut down and captured nearly ten thousand of Mithradates' warriors, many of them unarmed. Pompey seized his camp and supplies.[8]

But Pompey was disappointed. King Mithradates was not among the dead, the wounded, or the captured.

Mithradates and Hypsicratea

At the outset of the battle, Mithradates, with Hypsicratea riding at his side, had led eight hundred of his riders to slice through the Roman advance. The fighting was ferocious—Pompey had ordered his infantrymen to stab Mithradates' horses, to destroy his faith in his cavalry. Mithradates, Hypsicratea, and two other companions were cut off from the rest. These four finally broke out at the Roman rear and galloped up into the cliffs behind the battleground.[9]

Hypsicratea, in Persian-Amazonian garb—short tunic, cloak, pointed wool cap with earflaps, leather boots, and leggings with zigzag patterns— never tired of rough riding or combat. She wielded javelin, battle-axe, and bow with such "manly" expertise that it is not surprising that Mithradates called her "Hypsicrates." And she was devoted to him. This "heroic amazon would accompany her lover to the very end of his long odyssey,"

FIG. 14.2. Amazons, nomadic women warriors adept with javelin and bow, as portrayed in classical Greek art. They wear leopard skins, tunics, leggings, and Persian-Phrygian "liberty" caps. Drawings from vase paintings in Bulfinch, *Age of Fable*, 1897 and Smith 1873.

wrote Théodore Reinach. Mithradates had discovered the last, best love of his life, a stouthearted female companion for the desperate times ahead.[10]

After the Mithradatic Wars, as anecdotes from the last stage of the seemingly endless conflict circulated in Italy, even the Romans thrilled to the story of Mithradates and Hypsicratea. Within a generation or so, their companionship had become a romantic tale of noble courage, adventure, and abiding love. In the imagination of Valerius Maximus, writing in the early first century AD, Hypsicratea was "a queen who loved Mithradates so deeply that for his sake she lived like a warrior, cutting her hair and taking up arms to share his toils and dangers." When Mithradates was "cruelly defeated by Pompey" and fleeing among "wild peoples, she followed him with body and soul indefatigable."[11]

In later tales of chivalry, Hypsicratea's renown blossomed. She was the first in a long line of female pages, heroines in male disguise, featured in fairy tales, ballads, and Shakespearean plays. Medieval chroniclers depicted the king and the Amazon as friends and equals, and their love exemplified an ideal conjugal relationship. Boccaccio (1374) imagined Hypsicratea "choosing to make herself as tough and rugged as any man,

FIG. 14.3. Mithradates flanked by Hypsicratea (and Bituitus?). *Des dames de renom, De mulierbus claris/Hypsicratea,* Français 598, folio 116, Bibliothèque National de France.

journeying over hill and dale, traveling by day and night, bedding down in deserts and forests on the hard ground, in perpetual fear of the enemy and surrounded on all sides by wild beasts and serpents." Mithradates' comrade, wrote Boccaccio suggestively, "soothed him with the pleasures she knew he longed for."

Hypsicratea was included in the *City of Ladies*, a celebration by Christine de Pizan (b. 1364) of women who were the equals of men in war strength, intellect, and ingenuity. Like Boccaccio, Christine sympathized with Mithradates' struggle, reflecting the negative European image of the Roman Republic's avarice and antagonism toward popular monarchs. "The Romans waged a terrible war on Mithradates," wrote Christine. "The fate of the kingdom was at stake and the threat of death at the hands of the Romans ever present," yet Hypsicratea "travelled everywhere with him to far-off places and strange lands." Christine pictured her as a courtly lady "made for softer living," cutting off her "long, golden hair to disguise herself as a man," giving "no thought to protecting her complexion from sweat and dust." For love of Mithradates, Hypsicratea transformed her "graceful body" into that of a "powerfully built knight-in-arms" clad in helmet and "weighed down with a coat of chain mail" (see plate 2).[13]

In reality, of course, Hypsicratea was a robust horsewoman-warrior from a Eurasian nomadic culture in which girls and boys learned to ride, hunt, and make war together.

TAKE THE MONEY AND RUN

In the hills above the battlefield, Mithradates, Hypsicratea, and their two comrades caught their breath. The others were not named by Plutarch. Perhaps one was Bituitus, a cavalry officer from Gaul, praised for fighting valiantly by the king's side. Maybe the other was Gaius son of Hermaeus, a childhood friend, or General Metrophanes. The band of four walked their horses on rough trails away from the battlefield. Other survivors of the Moonlight Battle joined them, a few cavalry and about three thousand on foot. Mithradates had lost nearly ten thousand in Pompey's night attack, yet he and his most faithful followers had emerged from the ordeal.

Mithradates led this ragtag group to Sinora (*Synorion*, "Borderland"), his fortified treasury on the border of Armenia. Near a Turkish village still known as Sunur or Sinuri ("Border"), archaeologists have discovered the ruins of Sinora's strong tower. Here, the fugitives were welcomed by Drypetina and the eunuch Meniphilus. In the Middle Ages, Drypetina's devotion became an icon of filial love. "The girl was extremely ugly," wrote Christine de Pizan, but "she loved her father so much that she never left his side." As queen of Laodicea, Drypetina "could have lived a safe and comfortable life. . . . but she preferred to share her father's sufferings and hardships when he went to war. Even when he was defeated by the mighty Pompey, she did not abandon him but looked after him with great care and dedication."[14]

FIG. 14.4.
Drypetina
serves Mithra-
dates a meal at
Sinora. *Des
dames de
renom, De
mulieribus
claris/Drypetin*,
Français 598,
folio 113v,
Bibliothèque
Nationale de
France.

The atmosphere at Sinora was fraught with anxiety and foreboding, but Mithradates had already devised a plan. He sent a messenger to Tigranes to request refuge again in Armenia. Mithradates needed to move fast: Pompey would soon pick up their trail. Sinora's great treasure was essential. But how to transport the heavy load of money and goods? Mithradates' wealth was useless—unless it could somehow be made portable. He had no pack animals, only some cavalry horses and a few thousand loyalists.

For Mithradates, as he had vowed, it was all for one, one for all. His solution was ingenious and generous. The king gave all that remained of his riches to his followers, thereby distributing the burden—and possession —among the many. Cedar chests filled with sumptuous raiment and jewelry were flung open. The king handed out robes, bracelets, neck-laces, and rings to his soldiers. He then pried open bronze caskets filled with 6,000 talents' worth of gold and silver coins (equal to a year's pay for about 100,000 soldiers). He divided the coins, giving much more than a year's pay to each follower and generous rewards to senior vet-erans. The rest was stuffed in leather saddlebags. In efficiently and equi-tably dispersing his treasure, Mithradates' solution recalled Alexander, who had shared his possessions with his loyal troops. It was also a re-markable testament to the mutual trust and loyalty of Mithradates and his followers—his kingdom was lost, yet they would follow their leader into danger and exile for the rest of their lives.

Next, Mithradates and the eunuch Meniphilus went to the citadel's apothecary and prepared poison pills. Plutarch reported that before de-parting Sinora the king gave Hypsicratea and "each of his friends a deadly poison to carry with them, so that none of them would fall into the hands of the Romans against their will."[15]

The fugitive army must have been a bizarre sight: Mithradates' bat-tered armor topped with a purple cape, the Amazon draped in unaccus-tomed finery, and each foot soldier and rider decked out like royalty in fancy cloaks, gold and silver bangles, and bulging money belts. There had been a slight change in plans. Tigranes, worried about Roman ret-ribution (and against the advice of his queen Cleopatra, Mithradates' daughter), refused to shelter Mithradates in Armenia again. In fact, Ti-granes had put a price on his old friend's head. Mithradates couldn't decide whether to be insulted or amused by the stingy reward Tigranes was offering for his capture: a mere one hundred talents. This was less than what Mithradates had offered for his enemies Chaeremon and his two sons back in 89 BC.[16]

Mithradates revised his escape plan. The outlaw army marched day and night north, beyond the headwaters of the Euphrates River. Some of Mithradates' troops, natives of these mountains, served as guides. The region was teeming with snakes deadly to strangers (locals were not bothered by the venom). By hidden forest paths they passed through the land of the king's allies the Heniochoi and the Turret-Folk. Three days later the group reached Colchis. At Phasis, they might have been re-united with the eunuch Bacchides and the pirate Seleucus, who had sailed to Colchis after the fall of Sinope in 70 BC. Here, Appian tells us, Mithra-dates halted to "organize and arm his forces and those who joined him," Turret-Folk, Heniochoi, Iberi, Albanoi, and perhaps the Soanes of the noxious arrow poison, and the strange tribe known as the Lice-Eaters.[17]

IN THE LAND OF THE GOLDEN FLEECE

Mithradates' army crossed the Phasis River. In the grassy meadows strutted beautiful golden-red birds with iridescent blue-green heads and long tail feathers. The "Phasian" bird, known today as *pheasant*, was prized for its succulent dark meat. Mithradates led his army further north: the road ended where the Caucasus range met the Black Sea. Here they camped for the winter of 66/65 BC, at Dioscurias, a market town with a mild climate.

Early in his reign, Mithradates' army had tried to subdue the "wild" Achaeans in the mountains here, but he lost many men to ambushes and freezing cold. Since boyhood, Mithradates had been steeped in the mythology of this land. Somewhere in the alpine meadows above his camp Medea had once gathered magical plants and liquid fire. On a snowy crag in the Caucasus, Hercules freed Prometheus from his iron chains. The quest for the Golden Fleece ended here—ancient authors explained how the Colchians used lambskins to collect fine gold dust carried by streams flowing down from the Caucasus.[18]

During this strategic retreat, says Appian, Mithradates "conceived of a vast plan—a strange one for a fugitive on the run!" Pompey was closing in on Colchis, intending to trap Mithradates between the sea and the impassable mountains. Yet, marvels Appian, the irrepressible Mithradates pursued his "chimerical project" with supreme confidence and energy. The plan was indeed remarkable. Pantikapaion in the Crimea would become the new center of his Black Sea Kingdom. The Bosporus was presently in the hands of Machares, Mithradates' last living son by Laodice, his sister and first wife. Sadly, Machares had inherited her treacherous ways, making peace with Lucullus while his father fought for his life and realm. So Mithradates "planned to take back the kingdom he had given his ungrateful son and confront the Romans once more." The Black Sea itself was no longer in Mithradates' control, but most of the lands around it were allies. So the first step of his master plan was to trek overland counterclockwise around the Black Sea. Rounding the Sea of Azov, Mithradates would march across Scythia and Sarmatia, down to the Crimea. All along the way, of course, he would gather more followers and allies.[19]

It sounds feasible on paper, but a glance at a topographic map reveals the plan's breathtaking audacity (see map 5.1). Mithradates intended to cross over the Greater Caucasus Mountains, the monolithic barrier between Europe and Asia, stretching nearly a thousand miles from the Black Sea to the Caspian Sea. The highest peaks are eighteen thousand feet. Mithradates and his little army would attempt the crossing in early 65 BC, braving snow and ice, precipitous trails, and the danger of avalanche (see plate 7).

The final phase of this grand scheme, declared Appian, was even more audacious. After reclaiming the Bosporan Kingdom, Mithradates planned to take Rome by surprise. He would wage war on them from Europe while Pompey was still stuck in Asia. With his multitudes, he would march west, across the lands of the friendly Roxolani and Bastarnae, around the Carpathians to the Danube. His ever-growing army would push northwest across Pannonia, and then, repeating the feat of Hannibal, Mithradates would cross the Alps and invade Italy from the north.

CAT AND MOUSE IN COLCHIS

While Mithradates contemplated his grand strategy, where was Pompey? After the Moonlight Battle, Pompey's movements in 66/65 BC are confusing in the ancient sources, but one can reconstruct a rough chronology. Appian and Plutarch say that Pompey pursued Mithradates with major difficulties. In the land of the Turret-Folk, he lost a thousand men to poison honey, as we have seen. Reaching Colchis in fall of 66 BC, Pompey heard rumors of Mithradates' intention to escape over the Caucasus.

In Pompey's mind he had already won the war. Mithradates, he reasoned, had been driven out of his kingdom for good, his son Machares was now Rome's friend, and the Roman fleet owned the Black Sea. Pompey could not imagine that anyone, especially an old man of seventy, recovering from recent war wounds, could survive a journey over the mountain barrier. Assuming that Rome's mortal enemy was doomed to an ice coffin, Pompey decided to indulge in some military tourism at the edge of the "civilized" world. He prided himself on being the first Roman to claim this fabled territory. He was eager to see for himself the haunts of Hercules, Prometheus, and the Argonauts, and to retrace Alexander's route south of the Caspian Sea.[20]

Unsure of Mithradates' whereabouts, Pompey's expeditionary force marched east along the Phasis and Cyrus rivers. Skirting the foothills of the Caucasus, they encountered warlike bands, proud to have resisted the Medes, Persians, and Alexander. Now they were highly motivated allies of Mithradates. Iranian-influenced, they worshipped the Sun and Selene (Moon), and, noted Strabo, they "assembled by the tens of thousands whenever anything alarming occurs." Halfway between the Black and Caspian seas, at Armazi, the ancient fort overlooking the confluence of the Aragus ("fast water") and Cyrus rivers (near Tbilisi, Georgia), Pompey made winter camp, surrounded by the hostile Iberi and Albanoi.

While the Romans were celebrating Saturnalia, a jolly winter holiday of role reversals and heavy drinking, the Iberi, Albanoi, and allied bands ambushed the camp. The skirmishes were described by Appian, Plutarch, Strabo, and Cassius Dio. The barbarians numbered sixty thousand on foot and twelve thousand mounted. To the Romans, these tall, handsome people appeared "wretchedly armed, wearing the skins of wild beasts." They were formidable guerrilla fighters who attacked, then took cover in the forest.[21]

Pompey methodically set the forest on fire, to drive them out. After the battle, stripping the nearly nine thousand dead bodies, the Romans discovered many women warriors with typical Amazon weapons and clothing, just like what was depicted in Greek vase paintings (see fig. 14.2). Their wounds showed that their bravery matched that of the men. Female fighters were also found among the thousands of captives. According to Strabo, Amazons dressed in wild animal skins inhabited these mountains and the steppes beyond. In detailing the Amazon lifestyle, Strabo stated that his information came from the writings (now lost) of Mithradates' old friend the philosopher Metrodorus and from someone by the name of Hypsicrates (the masculine version of Hypsicratea) who was quite "familiar with this region."

As noted earlier, "Amazons" referred to Eurasian groups in which both women and men hunted and made war. Since the nineteenth century, archaeologists have discovered numerous graves containing the skeletons of women warriors buried with their weapons in the same regions where the ancients located Amazons. It was said that Alexander the Great had met the Amazon queen Thalestris and her three hundred women warriors here, between the Phasis and the Caspian Sea, the very region now traversed by Pompey. According to the tale, Alexander had devoted thirteen nights to gratifying the queen's desires. Now the Amazons were fighting on Mithradates' side! Pompey was eager to show off these captive women warriors in his Triumph.[22]

Pompey's winter camp was selected for its strategic location. Cassius Dio says Pompey occupied the citadel of Armazi (built in the third century BC) in order to "secure the nearly inpenetrable pass" over the mid-Caucasus, the main route between Scythia and Armenia. Armazi also blocked the way to the eastern end of the Caucasus. The citadel's massive blocks can be seen today; the ancient bridge is still called "Pompey's bridge." In spring of 65 BC, assuming he was "master of the pass," Pompey left a garrison there and ordered the Roman fleet to patrol the eastern Black Sea coast on the lookout for Mithradates. Then Pompey marched toward the Caspian, to explore and perhaps to assure himself that Mithradates had not somehow slipped around the eastern end of the mountains (through modern Azerbaijan and Dagestan). But Pompey was soon forced to turn back. The ground was crawling with deadly snakes, scorpions, and tarantulas.[23]

Filled with "wrath and resentment" (Plutarch's words), Pompey now had to retrace his route. Struggling across the flooded Cyrus, his army revisited hostile territory: the Albanoi, Iberi, and their friends had risen up again. After a series of frustrating skirmishes, Pompey decided to try to pick up Mithradates' trail. That summer, Pompey headed east again, fighting his way through "unknown and hostile tribes" along the Phasis to the Black Sea. Here, perceiving that Mithradates could not have escaped to the Crimea either by boat or by following the coast north, Pompey gave up the chase.[24]

Pompey's seemingly aimless wanderings are best seen as a game of cat and mouse. Mithradates seemed to have vanished into thin air. Pompey was trying to intercept or locate his prey's three likely escape routes out of Colchis: around the mountains by the Caspian Sea, along the Black Sea coast, or over the daunting pass at the highest point of the Caucasus—the pass Pompey thought he had blocked. But, as we shall see, the mouse enjoyed all the advantages and managed to slip away through a secret "mouse-hole," virtually under the cat's nose.

Tigranes Surrenders, Pontus Occupied

Pompey now crossed the Lesser Caucasus range into northern Armenia, to attack Tigranes' stronghold, Artaxata. His men suffered severe hardships, thirst, and ambush, because the guides—Albanoi, Iberi, and Amazon prisoners of war—deliberately misled him.[25]

In Artaxata, Tigranes, nearly seventy-five years old, had lost his will to fight. His son Tigranes (Mithradates' grandson) had revolted, and it looked as though his old friend Mithradates was beaten at last. Tigranes accepted Pompey's terms, prostrating himself on the ground and hand-ing over his tiara in ancient Persian fashion. In exchange for six thou-sand talents and the surrender of Mesopotamia, Syria, and Phoenicia, Tigranes was pardoned. He ruled Armenia as a Friend of Rome until his death at age eighty-five in 55 BC. "Mithradates, he died old" is the fa-miliar refrain, but Mithradates' friend Tigranes would die even older.[26]

Considering the Mithradatic War won at last, in late 65 BC Pompey returned to Pontus and founded Nicopolis ("Victory City") on the battle-field near Dasteira where he had defeated Mithradates by moonlight. He traversed Pontus seizing fortresses and treasures that "would add splen-dor to his triumph." The vaults at Talaura yielded cups of onyx and gold, splendid furniture, bejeweled armor and gilded horse bridles, Persian antiques, and the treasure from Cos—including the precious cloak of Al-exander the Great.[27]

When the Romans stormed Sinora Tower, the eunuch Meniphilus feared that his mistress Drypetina would be raped. He killed her and then himself with his sword. Several royal concubines were captured in other strongholds and brought to Pompey—Plutarch points out that he refrained from raping them. Stratonice, certain that she would never see her king alive again, surrendered Kainon Chorion to Pompey. In ex-change for a promise to spare her young son Xiphares, she revealed the underground vault filled with Mithradates' treasure and archives. Stra-tonice and Xiphares were allowed to sail to Phanagoria on the Taman Peninsula. They joined other members of Mithradates' family there, overseen by Machares.[28]

Pompey spent long hours poring over Mithradates' private papers, for they "shed much light on the king's character." Curiosity ran high about the man who had defied Rome for so many decades. Rumors and specu-lations arose later about what state and private secrets these documents revealed. Did Pompey discover the *Mithridatium* recipe? The papers were shipped to Rome to be translated into Latin verse by the freedman Cn. Pompeius Lenaeus, Pompey's learned Greek secretary. Lenaeus's life ex-emplifies the rapidly shifting fortunes of many in the Mithradatic Wars. Captured as a boy of twelve, during Sulla's siege of Athens in 87 BC, Lenaeus somehow escaped and returned to Greece to study. He was recaptured but freed by Pompey, whom he accompanied on all his campaigns. It would be fascinating to read Lenaeus's character sketch of Mithradates—but, sadly, that work and all of Lenaeus's writings are lost.[29]

None of Mithradates' archives, which passed through the hands of Pompey, Lenaeus, Plutarch, and Pliny, are extant. In the first century AD, Plutarch and Pliny consulted the original writings. The notes, according to Plutarch, named victims of Mithradates' poisons and included interpretations of the dreams of the king and his lovers. There were sheaves of royal and personal correspondence, including the racy love letters penned by Mithradates and Monime.

Plutarch says that Pompey shrugged off pursuing Mithradates beyond Colchis because—just as Lucullus had warned—the king was far more slippery in flight than in battle. Lucullus's premonition, that Mithradates' strength could multiply a thousandfold if he escaped to the Caucasus, was more accurate than Pompey realized. Remarking that "famine" would finish off Mithradates, should he somehow survive the mountain snows, Pompey established a blockade to cut off trade to the Bosporus (apparently forgetting that the Crimea had access to abundant fish and grain). Then Pompey set off to embellish his résumé of conquests, from the Atlantic Ocean to the Red Sea. Leaving Pontus far behind, Pompey marched south to subdue Commagene, Cilicia, Phoenicia, Syria, and the lands of the Arabs and Jews.[30]

The Trek over the Caucasus Mountains

While Pompey was traipsing around Colchis, Mithradates accomplished his most daring exploit, crossing the Caucasus Mountains in early 65 BC. To the great surprise of his son Machares, Mithradates and his army suddenly appeared in the capital of the Bosporan Kingdom that summer. Four ancient historians provide imprecise, contradictory information on Mithradates' route over the mountain barrier and around the Sea of Asov to Pantikapaion (unfortunately, Livy's account has not survived). Mithradates' stunning feat was a mystery in antiquity and remains a puzzle today. Drawing on the ancient evidence and topographical conditions, I propose a mountain trek that differs from the coastal route accepted by historians since Reinach in 1890.

Cassius Dio said Mithradates "outstripped Pompey's pursuit, fleeing by the Phasis River" to "reach the Sea of Azov and the Bosporus on foot." Plutarch says he traveled all the way around the Sea of Asov and down to Pantikapaion. Strabo states that Mithradates "despaired of the route north of Dioscurias [the Klukhor Pass] owing to the rugged mountains

MAP 14.1. Caucasia, between the Black and Caspian seas: Pontus, Armenia, Colchis, Scythia. (Top) Pursued by Pompey, Mithradates escaped from Pontus into Colchis, reaching Pantikapaion by way of Daryal Pass into Scythia, across the Don River and around the Sea of Azov. (Bottom) Detail of Mithradates' probable route over the Caucasus Mountains. Map by Michele Angel.

and ferocious inhabitants, the Zygi," and "embarked on another route, along the sea, traversed with great difficulty." Perhaps because he himself was uncertain, Strabo's passage is ambiguous: the Greek word for "embark" can mean "to set off marching" or "to set off in boats" (English has similar dual meanings for "embark," and "launch an attack"). Both translations appear in scholarly translations of Strabo's passage. A further difficulty is that Strabo claims the Achaeans were friendly to Mithradates; Appian says they were hostile.

It is Appian who offers the most specific details. In describing Machares' shock at his father's unexpected arrival, Appian states that Mithradates traveled over the pass known as the "Scythian Keyhole, which no [army] had ever done before," and then journeyed through the lands of strange Scythian tribes around the Sea of Asov and the River Don, arriving in Pantikapaion.[31]

Mithradates had several options to consider. He rejected the Klukhor Pass north of Dioscurias because of forbidding topography and fierce Zygi (rumored in antiquity to be cannibals). The Caspian Gates pass at the far eastern end of the Caucasus range was nearly nine hundred miles distant. And the Iberi, Albanoi, and other allies would have advised him that the way east was blocked by the Roman garrison at Armazi Citadel, and that Pompey's army was exploring near the Caspian. Armazi also controlled the main approach to the high pass over the central Caucasus, the Scythian Gates mentioned by Appian.

Believing that crossing the central Caucasus, as implied in the other three sources, was impossible for even a small army, Reinach interpreted Strabo to mean that Mithradates marched along the shore from Dioscurias, emerging at the Taman Peninsula (this raises the question of why Mithradates would then travel all around the Sea of Azov instead of going directly to Phanagoria and Pantakapaion). By Reinach's day a modern road had been dynamited above the sea coast. But in antiquity, there was only a narrow strip of beach obstructed by deep gorges, marshes, and sheer cliffs. Reinach imagined that Mithradates and his army bypassed these obstacles by taking *camarae* (dugout kayaks) provided by friendly "pirates" (the Achaeans).

Reinach's route entails several drawbacks. An army of three thousand, stretched out single file along the narrow beach, would be vulnerable to attack by Zygi and Achaean bandits. As Appian and others state, the Achaeans could not be counted on; this rugged coast had never been pacified as part of Mithradates' Black Sea Empire. Moreover, according to Strabo, each *camara* held only twenty-five people, requiring more than one hundred dugouts for Mithradates' army and equipment. And Pompey's navy was patrolling the coast, looking for Mithradates. If Reinach's theory is correct, this would have been an impressive feat. But I suggest that the route described by Appian, the pass over the mid-Caucasus known as the "Scythian Keyhole," is the more likely route. This would take Mithradates on foot through friendly tribes, to the heartland of the Scythian tribes around the Sea of Asov, matching the details preserved by Cassius Dio and Plutarch.[32]

The so-called Scythian Keyhole (or Gates) was only a faint rumor for Romans at the time, but in fact it was the most reliable way over the Caucasus, the major migration route for Eurasian nomads, traders, and invaders. The Persians had named this strategic pass Daryal, *Dar-e Alan*, "Gate of the Alans," one of the nomadic tribes of Scythia whose territory lay over the pass (Tigranes' mother was an Alan; the region is now Alania-North Ossetia). Fortification ruins dating from 150 BC or earlier, mentioned by Strabo, are still visible in the pass. The Daryal's narrow defile with vertical walls accounts for its ancient nickname "Scythian Keyhole." Famed for its wild grandeur, the Daryal Pass is featured in romantic Russian art and literature. The Georgian Military Road (begun in 1799) follows (and obliterates) the ancient route. Today, this region is violently contested by Georgia, Russia, Chechnya, Ossetia, Ingushetia, and others.[33]

The main route to the Scythian Keyhole/Daryal followed the Aragus River up from its confluence with the Cyrus to the Daryal Gorge. Pompey had secured this approach, guarded by Armazi Citadel. But he was unaware that there was an alternate route, a "back way," to the Daryal Pass.

From Dioscurias, a march of less than 150 miles would take Mithradates to a lesser-known trail (near modern Kutaisi), separated from Pompey's garrison at Armazi by 100 miles of rugged foothills. Described by Strabo, this steep, winding path followed the Phasis River to its source in the Caucasus. The route crossed 120 footbridges over rushing torrents and yawning gorges to the Mamisson (Mamisoni) Pass, at an elevation of nearly 10,000 feet (the Ossetian Military Road, built in 1854–89, followed this ancient route). After crossing another pass (Roki, 9,800 feet, in South Ossetia, ancient Iberia), this path joined the main route to the Daryal Pass (about 8,000 feet). I propose that this daunting route, avoiding hostile tribes and the Roman navy, and bypassing Pompey's garrison at Armazi, was Mithradates' only hope of escape.[34]

Pompey and the Romans believed it was certain death to attempt to cross the massive wall of eternal snows at the edge of the known world. But Mithradates' plan—though extremely dangerous—was not as unrealistic as it seemed. Many of his warriors—including Hypsicratea—were recruited from Caucasia. They were already familiar with this traditional migration route, and they were used to cold weather at high altitude. Indeed, it may have been their local knowledge that led Mithradates to camp at Dioscurias and to cross at Daryal, taking the lesser-known route up the Phasis River. Mithradates could also have learned of this important pass from his Scythian allies and his study of Cyrus the Great, who was the first to fortify Daryal.

The Caucasus is one of the most linguistically and ethnically diverse regions in the world. According to Strabo, seventy tribes—speaking seventy dialects—dwelled in the high Caucasus, living on milk, wild fruit, and game. In the winter, says Strabo, these peoples came down from the mountains to camp at Dioscurias and barter for salt and other goods (the northern branch of the Silk Route linked the Caspian and Black seas).[35] We know that in the winter of 66/65 BC, Mithradates was camped at Dioscurias. It follows that he learned the logistics of the Daryal and other passes from these mountaineers, benefiting from their survival tips and scouts.

Mithradates' experiences with winter battles in Achaea and Cyzicus, and the battles on ice fought by his general Neoptolemus in the Bosporus, as well as details in Xenophon's *March of the Ten Thousand*, could have helped him to anticipate the dangers of crossing the high snowfields. Xenophon had trekked forty-five miles over snowbound mountains from Armenia to Pontus, a shorter journey at a lower elevation but with a much larger army. He was harassed by hostile tribes, something Mithradates could avoid. The freezing north wind cut Xenophon's men's faces like a knife; many animals and soldiers were lost in snowdrifts. The men suffered frostbite and snowblindness. Remove your boots at night and shade your eyes with dark cloth, advised Xenophon.[36]

In planning his mountaineering expedition, Mithradates enjoyed three crucial advantages over Pompey. His small army was lightly armed, mountain trained, and locally supplied; the Iranian-influenced tribes in the central Caucasus were his allies; and he possessed local information and friendly guides.

According to Strabo, the strenuous passage through the Daryal Pass was a journey of about 130 miles, perhaps a week in good weather. But 2,000 or 3,000 people traveling single file would stretch out at least 5 miles. Mithradates' crossing may have taken a month. Although the elevation of this route is consistently higher than the highest passes of the Alps, Strabo remarked that this pass could be traversable by early spring—but only with the right equipment. In Dioscurias, Mithradates could provide his army with winter clothing and boots, dried food, and hardy pack animals, all paid for with gold coins from the Sinora hoard.

Snow gear could be obtained from the mountain people wintering in Dioscurias. For ascending the summits, Strabo described their snow-shoelike footwear: "The people fasten to their feet broad 'shoes' made of rawhide, like drum covers, furnished with spikes to grip the snow and ice." Others "tie large spiked wooden disks" to their boots. For transporting loads, they made sleds of animal hides. On this route, continued Strabo, "whole caravans are often swallowed up in the snow by extremely violent blizzards" and avalanches. For this reason, says Strabo, travelers carry long, hollow sticks, which they can push to the surface of snow drifts to breathe and signal their location so they can be dug out. He also told how to find drinking water trapped in large air bubbles under the ice and even mentioned the clouds of tiny, high-altitude insects that hatch in the snow.[37]

Mithradates' allies would have kept him informed about Pompey's movements in the winter and spring of 65 BC. Pompey's early spring expedition to the Caspian provided Mithradates the opportunity to sneak up to the Daryal Pass, avoiding the garrison at Armazi.

The adventure of setting off once again into the unknown was reminiscent of Mithradates' previous daring journeys with loyal entourages. Now he was about sixty-nine years old, vigorous and optimistic, this time accompanied by the love of his life, Hypsicratea. Let us follow them as they ascend the trail north along the Phasis torrent. The oak, almond, and maple trees give way to beech, spruce, and pine. Golden finches flit through the forest. The band crosses alpine meadows dotted with the first purple primroses and cobalt gentians of spring. The path begins to climb, crossing stone bridges over tremendous waterfalls and gaping gorges, up steep switchbacks. Each night, the long line of soldiers make campfires; they sleep wrapped in furs wherever they have halted on the narrow trail.[38] There is game to hunt (ibex, mountain goats, hares), but there are dangers too: bears, Persian leopards, wolves, and frostbite, blizzards, and avalanches.

Here and there, the travelers glimpse Caucasian wallcreepers, tiny crimson birds often mistaken for butterflies clinging to the sheer granite walls. Turning east, the guides lead Mithradates' band across the dangerous ice fields of the high Mamisson Pass, then the Roki Pass. As they

FIG. 14.5. The approach to the Daryal Gorge from the south, with Mount
Kazbek looming ahead. Photo courtesy of Hans Heiner Buhr, Tbilisi, Georgia,
www.hansheinerbuhr.com.

approach the snow line at 9,000 feet, trees disappear, the temperature
drops, oxygen thins. The desolate call of the Caucasian snowcock echoes
in the bare rocks. Then, as the army turns north to join the main Daryal
footpath, ahead looms the 16,500-foot peak of Mount Kazbek, mantled

in perpetual snows. Large Eurasian griffon-vultures soar over the black basalt crags, the fabled site of Prometheus's ordeal. Single file, Mithradates' army threads through the narrow "keyhole" of Daryal, two perpendicular walls of rock (the "gates") less than 30 feet apart, surrounded by glacier-capped peaks.[39]

Mithradates' trek over the highest passes of the snowbound Caucasus Mountains in early spring, with an army, was an epic journey in a long career distinguished by daring exploits. The exhilaration of accomplishing this astonishing feat, while Pompey searched in vain for his quarry on the other side of the mountains, must have restored Mithradates' sense of invincibility and destiny.

Across Scythia to the Crimea

The descent through alpine pastures was relatively easy, onto the steppes of what is now south Russia. Here the enormity of the land and sky stuns the senses, with monotony so vast that it achieves majestic proportions. The sight of unbroken horizons in every direction overwhelms some travelers, but I imagine that for someone like Mithradates (and Hypsicratea), who loved to ride and hated to be boxed in, the sea of grass represented freedom. The only features on the flat prairie were *kurgans*, tomb mounds, some ancient, others recent. It has been said that the steppes seem incomplete without a horse and rider, and these soon appeared to meet Mithradates' army. In the territories of "strange and warlike Scythian tribes," says Appian, they traveled "partly by permission and partly by force, so respected and feared was Mithradates still, even though he was a fugitive" (see plate 10).[40]

Around the Azov and across the Don, nomadic chieftains and their bands rode out to greet Mithradates, bestowing gifts and horses and escorting him to the next territory. His reception was very different from that of Darius—it must have thrilled Mithradates to be welcomed in these immense, fertile lands of his fellow nomads. Appian points out that he was a celebrity here: his deeds were legendary, his great empire renowned, and most of all, his courage and perseverance in defying Rome deeply admired. An exuberant Mithradates renewed alliances, heartily promising to send his beautiful daughters to marry the chieftains and engaging them in his grand design to march across Europe and over the Alps to destroy the Roman wolves in their den.

Fig. 14.6. The Kerch Straits between the Crimea (Pantikapaion) (left) and Phanagorea on the Taman Peninsula (right), looking toward the Sea of Azov. Steel engraving by W. H. Bartlett, 1838, courtesy of F. Dechow.

Meanwhile, in Pantikapaion (Kerch), Machares was stunned to hear that his father had crossed the Caucasus by way of the Scythian Gates. Knowing his father's fearsome temper, Machares killed himself. His brother Pharnaces welcomed his father—Mithradates was often heard to say Pharnaces would be his successor. Taking charge of his Kingdom of the Bosporus and Scythia, Mithradates put to death several disloyal former friends there, including some Romans who had plotted against him. Mithradates' eunuch Gauros was said to be the instigator of many cruel tortures and executions. True to his ideals, Mithradates spared inferiors who acted out of loyalty to corrupt superiors. There were two shocking exceptions, however. Mithradates killed a son named Exipodras for conspiracy. And he was enraged by Stratonice's bargain with Pompey. Betrayal by sons or women he loved was unendurable to Mithradates, and his revenge was particularly spiteful. He seized their son Xiphares and killed him on the deck of a ship in view of Phanagoria's castle. He threw the body overboard while Stratonice in her tower watched in anguish.[41]

In this descent into suspicion and cruelty, Mithradates resembled Alexander, who near the end of his life became violently suspicious, seeing plots and conspiracies everywhere, spying on companions and torturing friends. But perhaps Mithradates' paranoia and fury were exacerbated at this time by a serious illness. According to Appian, the king withdrew from public view because of an outbreak of nasty ulcers on his face. For some time, he remained inside his palace on the acropolis (Mount Mithradates) overlooking Pantikapaion. Only three eunuch-doctors were allowed in his presence. Had the king been poisoned?

This intriguing ancient medical mystery has not been seriously investigated by modern historians. Duggan supposed Mithradates suffered a rash caused by "strange food eaten during his terrible journey." It seems more likely that the lesions resulted from a severe case of frostbite, from the trek over the Caucasus. Frostbite causes the skin to blister and redden, resulting in hard, purple-black areas of necrosis and gangrene.[42]

Another strong possibility is that the facial ulcerations—as well as the episode of acute paranoia—were the result of long-term ingestion of arsenic, part of Mithradates' antipoisoning regimen. Prolonged exposure to arsenic can cause bouts of mental imbalance, hallucinations, and paranoia. Arsenic also causes keratoses, which progress after ten to twenty years to skin cancers. Notably, frostbite causes arsenic-related skin cancers to putrify. Frostbite, combined with a lifetime of tiny doses of arsenic and other photosensitizing toxins such as rue and Saint-John's-wort, appears to be the best explanation of Mithradates' skin ailment.[43] Appian says the ulcers were "healed" (or perhaps covered up) by the eunuch-doctors. It is unknown how long Mithradates remained out of the public eye—apparently some months—curtailing crucial face-to-face contact with his followers.

PETITION FOR PEACE

Mithradates usually went to war as a last resort after what he saw as rejection of his attempts to negotiate with the Romans. Now that he had regained the Bosporan Kingdom and in light of recent events (including Tigranes' humiliating surrender to Pompey), Mithradates first considered options for avoiding further wars with Rome. He felt optimistic that he could make a deal similar to that given to Tigranes. So it came to pass that while Pompey was busy annexing Syria in 64 BC, he received a message from Mithradates. Not only was the indestructible renegade king alive in the Crimea, but he had kept track of Pompey's movements.

Mithradates promised that if Rome would restore his paternal Kingdom of Pontus, he would pay tribute to Rome. His request asked for nothing more than what Tigranes had received. But Pompey rejected the petition—demanding that Mithradates pay obeisance in person as Tigranes had done. Understandably wary and characteristically proud, Mithradates refused. But he offered to send an adult son (probably Pharnaces, his designated heir) to petition Pompey.

DENIED

Pompey rejected this offer too. Ignoring Mithradates, he pushed further south, seeking adventure and glory. He made war on the Jews in Palestine, capturing their king and the holy city of Jerusalem. In late summer of 64 BC, Pompey attacked the Nabataean Arabs in Petra (Jordan). Some of his soldiers began to murmur that their general was evading his patriotic duty to destroy Rome's real enemy, Mithradates. They had heard rumors that the "new Hannibal" was preparing to march a new army across the Alps to invade their fatherland.[44]

Indeed, Mithradates always had contingency plans and usually found the means to carry them out. He had "fought the Romans over a period of 46 years with intermittent successes," wrote the historian Justin. He had suffered "defeat before Rome's greatest generals—only to rise again greater and more glorious than before in renewing his struggle." As Cassius Dio remarked, "relying more on his willpower now than on his actual power, Mithradates did not falter." Sustained by his dream of saving the East from Roman rule and by his own astonishing resilience, Mithradates prepared to make war for what would prove to be the last time.

His illustrious ancestors must have been much on his mind at this point in his life. Darius had sent spies to Italy and contemplated an invasion of Carthage, Persia's great rival empire across the Mediterranean. Alexander, who dreamed of conquering all India, had persevered despite great dangers and obstacles. Like his hero, Mithradates had suffered grievous wounds and shared hardships and treasures with his soldiers, "drinking from rivers fouled with blood, crossing streams bridged by corpses, surviving on grass and seeds, digging through snowbound mountains," sailing rough seas, and traversing parched lands. Yet, in spite of all the setbacks dealt by Fortune, all the "sieges, pursuits, revolts, desertions, riots of subject peoples, and defections of kings," Mithradates, like Alexander, set his mind on "high enterprise," clung to his "high hopes [and] refused to submit to defeat."[45]

Believing that his request to rule peacefully in his homeland of Pontus was unfairly denied, Mithradates had three options: surrender, flee, or attack. Accept Pompey's unconditional terms, groveling like Tigranes? Out of the question. Mithradates rejected flight, too, but if he stayed, war with Rome was inevitable. He chose a bold offensive strategy. The king resumed his Hannibalistic plan to invade Italy.

Appian called this scheme "chimerical." Modern historians debate whether it was a rational strategy or the sign of a desperate, even deranged mind. McGing, analyzing Mithradates' foreign policy, wondered whether the "wildly unrealistic" plan was invented by the Romans or Pharnaces to paint Mithradates as a would-be world conquerer. But, notably, in 74 BC, when the Senate financed Lucullus's campaign, Rome had believed that Mithradates intended to invade Italy by sea. It is telling that Roman historians of this era argued over whether or not Alexander the Great could have successfully invaded Italy, as Hannibal had done. As we saw, Mithradates had promised the Italian rebels that he would come to help them when the time was right. Some Romans thought his invasion plan was feasible. In the Senate, Cicero declared that Mithradates, despite "having lost his army and having been driven from his kingdom, is even now planning something against us in the most distant corners of the earth."[46]

Adaptability, surprise, and creativity were strong features of Mithradates' character. Duggan saw the plan as the "stupendous fantasy of a solitary mind," yet he appreciated the logic of it. From the Crimea, it was an easy march across friendly lands to the mouth of the Danube. Following the Danube to the Alps was a journey of about six hundred miles— half the distance Mithradates' beleaguered band had traveled from Pontus to Colchis and on to Pantikapaion. After the first obstacle, the Iron Gates gorge in the Carpathians, the Alps crossing (over Brennus Mons, Brenner Pass, 4,500-foot elevation) would be easy compared to that of the Scythian Keyhole in the Caucasus. One would emerge in the lands of the Gauls and Etrurians, chafing under Rome's rule. Reinach also recognized the feasibility of the plan. Who could predict what would happen, he asked, if suddenly a vast army of 100,000 barbarians, led by an invincible and brilliant king, appeared on the plains of northern Italy?[47]

"By nature attracted to grand projects," wrote Cassius Dio, Mithradates considered his many victories and failures and decided, "nothing ventured nothing gained." Should he fail, "he preferred to perish along with his kingdom, with pride, honor, and liberty intact." Mithradates directed his commanders, Roman officers, and Pharnaces to prepare for war on Italy. They levied heavy tributes and taxes to make up for the loss of his wealth in Pontus, began a massive fort-building program, and drafted workers and soldiers. By 64 BC, his new army numbered six thousand crack troops trained in Roman-style fighting and "a great multitude of others"—steppe nomads, mountain fighters, archers, lancers, and slingers. Mithradates minted coins at a high rate; stored grain and other supplies; cut timber for ships and seige machines; set up factories to make armor, spears, swords, and projectiles; and killed many plowoxen, whose tough sinews were needed for catapults.[48]

These war preparations dismayed and burdened many in the peaceable Kingdom of the Bosporus, so far untouched by Rome's Mithradatic Wars. Then, in 64/63 BC, a frightening natural calamity—a strong earthquake—seemed to portend a regime change. Some recalled the devastating quake that had foretold Tigranes' loss of Syria. The earthquake was described by Cassius Dio, Livy, and Orosius: it occurred while Mithradates was celebrating the festival of the goddess Demeter. The epicenter is unknown, but the tremor was severe at Pantikapaion, according to evidence discovered by Russian archaeologists in the ruins of the fortress and other structures. According to Cassius Dio, the quake was felt even in Rome. Several cities allied with Mithradates suffered destruction, which fueled anxiety about the old king's future.[49]

REVOLT IN THE BOSPORUS

In order to secure both sides of the Bosporus, Mithrdates dispatched his eunuch Trypho (a Hebrew name) to take charge of Phanagoria.[50] Inside the citadel, under the care of other eunuchs, were Stratonice (mourning her murdered son Xiphares) and Mithradates' children Artaphernes, Eupatra, Orsabaris, Cleopatra the Younger, and their little brothers Darius, Xerxes, Cyrus, and Oxathres.

Things seemed to be proceeding according to plan, until an act of revenge and terror intervened. A citizen of Phanagoria rushed up and stabbed the eunuch Trypho. The killer, a Greek named Castor, incited Phanagoria to revolt. Inflamed by Mithradates' unpopular war preparations, a mob set fire to the citadel to smoke out the royal family. Artaphernes and the children were taken prisoner. One courageous daughter—Cleopatra the Younger—resisted and escaped on a ship sent by Mithradates to rescue her.

The rebellion at Phanagoria sparked a domino effect in the Bosporan Kingdom. Mithradates distrusted his army—compulsory service under a commander perceived to be unlucky was a formula for mutiny. He quickly gathered his daughters in Pantikapaion's harem. Guarded by palace eunuchs with an escort of five hundred soldiers, these girls were sent to the Scythian chieftains to whom they had been promised, with an urgent request that they send reinforcements to Pantikapaion. The two youngest girls, Nyssa and Mithradatis, betrothed to the kings of Egypt and Cyprus, remained with Mithradates.

Mithradates' overbearing eunuch advisers were despised by the soldiers, because they isolated the king from his subjects and carried out purges. The caravan to Scythia was not long on the road before the soldiers killed the eunuchs and kidnapped the young princesses, intending to deliver them to Pompey for a reward. Appian expresses wonder at Mithradates' energetic and resourceful response to these new calamities. "Although bereft of so many of his children and castles—and of his whole kingdom—and too old for war and and unable to expect any immediate help from the Scythians, there was still no trace of humility befitting his present circumstances!"[51]

Mithradates stubbornly pursued his idea of invading Italy by land. After all, his feat of crossing the Caucasus surpassed Hannibal's crossing of the Alps. He knew that Hannibal's ability to attract insurgent Italians to join him had terrified Rome. Similar opportunities for an invader of Italy existed now. As Appian points out, Mithradates knew that "almost all of Italy had recently revolted because of hatred of Rome," and that tens of thousands had joined the Thracian gladiator Spartacus. Mithradates had long cultivated the friendship of the Gauls of Europe, who resisted Rome, and he could count on the Scythians and other northern allies. In Mithradates' grand vision, he and an enormous army of Rome-hating warriors from the Caspian Sea to Gaul would smash the empire once and for all.

It was, acknowledged Appian, a very bold plan. If he could succeed, Mithradates would cover himself with spectacular glory. His mind filled with these ideas, Mithradates hastened to contact the Gauls.[52]

But his officers and soldiers, even the Roman exiles, were taken aback by the sweeping design. They began to get cold feet. The awesome scale of Mithradates' vision was intimidating. Many shrank from the idea of waging war in a distant foreign land, says Appian, against an enemy they had not been able to overcome in their own countries. His Bosporan subjects had enjoyed autonomy for the past twenty-five years; now heavy taxes and mandatory army service seemed to contradict Mithradates' core values and former promises. Some soldiers who had served him for years were becoming disillusioned; they had hoped to retire in the wealthy Bosporan Kingdom. The two or three thousand who had come over the Caucasus with their king each had a full year's pay; they had hoped to make a new life. And it is worth noting that half a century separated the septuagenarian Mithradates from his rawest recruits.

Some older followers perceived the king's grandiose plan as a suicidal exit strategy. Not unreasonably, they believed it was a sign of despair. It offered a way for Mithradates to end his life honorably, fighting for a noble lost cause rather than surrendering. How much better to die on the battlefield than to be strangled at the end of Pompey's Triumph! Yet Mithradates was still so deeply respected and beloved for his courage, his generosity, and his unbowed perseverance that the majority of his followers remained loyal and silent about their doubts. For even in his dire misfortunes, marveled Appian, "there was nothing petty or contemptible" about King Mithradates. He was the last independent monarch left standing in the new Roman world.[53]

But one key figure dared to act decisively on his fears and doubts. Pharnaces, Mithradates' favorite son and successor, was alarmed and motivated. The kingdom he was to inherit would be ruined if his father really attempted to invade Italy. Pharnaces (in his thirties) believed he could bargain with Pompey, but he had to prevent his father from carrying out his crazy plan. Pharnaces began secret talks with friends about usurping his father's crown.

PHARNACES' REBELLION

Pharnaces' treachery was discovered by the omniscient Mithradates, of course. The conspirators were tortured and killed. Except for Pharnaces. According to Appian, Pharnaces was spared thanks to Mithradates' old friend General Metrophanes. He persuaded Mithradates that it would be wrong and inauspicious to put to death the son he loved most, his designated heir. Disagreements were common in wartime, counseled the old general, but they healed once the wars were over. Perhaps Metrophanes spoke of the sorrow such an act would bring to Mithradates' grandchildren, Pharnaces' children Darius and Dynamis ("Power").[54] It seems that affection for Pharnaces and concern for the future of his kingdom overcame Mithradates' instinct for self-preservation. Mithradates, who had lost so many and so much, pardoned his son. It was the first time he had ever forgiven a traitor. As the king retired to his bedchamber, did he have second thoughts? Or was he already reconciled to the reality that Pharnaces would become king either now or in the near future?

Pharnaces, perhaps thinking of the fate of so many of his brothers, most recently the murders of Xiphares and Exipodras, and Machares' suicide, could not believe his father could ever truly forgive him. He sneaked to the camp of the Roman exiles and "magnified the dangers—which they well knew—of invading Italy." Promising great rewards, Pharnaces convinced them to desert Mithradates. Then he sent emissaries to other camps and ships in the harbor and won them over too. All agreed that the next morning they would rise up and demand that the king abdicate in favor of Pharnaces.

In his castle, Mithradates was awakened by angry voices. Many citizens joined the army's revolt because, in Appian's view, they were fickle and worried about the king's string of bad luck, or because they feared being the only outsiders in an overwhelming rebellion. Mithradates sent retainers to find out what the commotion was about. The mob surrounded the castle. Soon he could hear for himself the people shouting out their grievances and demands:

> We don't want a king ruled by eunuchs!
> We don't want a king who kills his own sons, his generals, and his friends!
> We want a young king instead of an old one!
> We want Pharnaces to be king!

Mithradates went down to the square to reason with the people. At the same time, some fearful guards from the palace ran to join the mob. But rabble-rousers in the crowd pointed at the king, refusing to welcome the guards until they proved their commitment by "doing something irreparable." Some of the mob ran to the royal stables and killed Mithradates' horses. Mithradates quickly returned to his castle. He climbed the spiral stone stairs to the highest tower.[55]

From the tower window, Mithradates saw Pharnaces appear in the square below. He heard the people hail his son as their new king. Someone rushed up with a sacred papyrus leaf from the temple garden and offered Pharnaces this makeshift crown. A great roar of approval went up from the crowd.

15

In the Tower

WHAT happened in the tower after Pharnaces was acclaimed king? There was apparently only one witness, Mithradates' bodyguard Bituitus, and it is not clear that he lived to tell the story. What we do know comes from Roman historians who pieced together the scene from the contradictory reports of people in Pantikapaion at the time, interpretations of the evidence found in the tower, and hearsay and popular traditions about Mithradates' last hours. Let us look first at what the ancient writers tell us, and then consider how to read between the lines to reconstruct events and make sense of incomplete evidence.

The Most Deadly of All Poisons

Mithradates' worst fear was that he would be turned over to Pompey for a degrading public display and death in Rome. He understood that he had lost the goodwill of his people; he acknowledged that his son was the new king. His only hope was to go into exile. He sent several messages to Pharnaces, requesting safe passage out of Pantikapaion. Not one of his messengers returned. Next Mithradates sent old friends to petition his son, but either they were killed by Pharnaces' followers (according to Appian), or they were convinced to turn against the king (Cassius Dio's report).[1]

His entreaties for safe passage unanswered, Mithradates found himself in the same straits as Hannibal had been in 182 BC, trapped in his palace in Bithynia. Like Hannibal, Mithradates had prepared for this situation. Mithradates thanked his bodyguard and other companions who had remained faithful. As in previous catastrophes, Mithradates directed his eunuchs to distribute poison to the courtesans and children in the

FIG. 15.1. Mithradates poisons his young daughters (right) and requests his bodyguard Bituitus (left) to stab him. Illustration by Adrien Marie, in Church 1885.

FIG. 15.2. *Mithridates, His Rash Act.* An unsympathetic caricature by Punch artist John Leech, depicting the suicide pact of Mithradates and his daughters as a drawing room comedy. *The Comic History of Rome* by Gilbert Abbott A Beckett, 1852

seraglio. The two youngest princesses, Mithradatis and Nyssa, were being raised in the palace with their father, which explains how they came to be in the tower with him. (They were betrothed but had not yet reached the age of marriage, so they were perhaps between nine and thirteen.) According to the literary traditions, the king and his daughters took poison, while Bituitus stood guard.

Mithradates uncapped the secret compartment in the hilt of his dagger and tipped out the little golden vial, beautifully crafted by Scythian artists. The two girls entreated their father to share his poison with them, begging him to stay alive until they died. He held them in his arms while they sipped from the vial. The drug took immediate effect.[2]

When the girls were dead, Mithradates drank the rest. But the poison did not kill him. He paced energetically, to propel the toxin through his body. He became very weak, but death did not come. In the oft-repeated legend—heavy with irony and recounted in nearly every ancient version of Mithradates' death—the king who had made himself invulnerable to poisoning by ingesting infinitesimal doses of poisons all his life, was in the end unable to poison himself. Mithradates' last words were widely reported: "I—the absolute monarch of so great a kingdom—am now unable to die by poison because I foolishly used other drugs as antidotes. Although I have kept watch and guarded against all poisons, I neglected to take precautions against that most deadly of all poisons, which lurks in every king's household, the faithlessness of army, friends, and children."[3]

This pithy parable was taken up by medieval chroniclers and repeated by modern historians, because the moral seemed so poetically apt for the Poison King.

But logic raises objections. If the *Mithridatium* regimen was effective through what is now known as the process of *hormesis*—as Mithradates certainly believed—what would be the point of his lifelong precaution of carrying poison for suicide, unless it was a carefully calculated lethal dose of some special, fast-acting poison that was not included in his daily antidote? Over his lifetime, Mithradates had tested numerous poisons on human subjects and knew exactly how much he would require for a quick, private, dignified death.[4] On the other hand, if the *Mithridatium* did not actually shield against poison, then why was the precisely measured dose ineffective?

There is a natural explanation that addresses both questions, overlooked by modern scholars but evident in the ancient reports. The king had shared his single dose with two others, at least halving the amount.

There was not enough left to kill a man of Mithradates' size and constitution. Like his unexpected mercy for his traitorous son Pharnaces, Mithradates' compassion for his innocent daughters brought harm to

FIG. 15.3. Bituitus stabbing Mithradates, who was unable to poison himself because of his lifelong ingestion of antidotes. The illustration on this ornate sixteenth-century *Mithridatium* vessel was meant to advertise the potency of the theriac within—so strong that even self-poisoning fails. Annibale Fontana, 1570. Paul Getty Museum, Los Angeles.

FIG. 15.4. Tragic neoclassical view of Mithradates' death, showing Pharnaces' soldiers bursting into the tower, as described by Cassius Dio. The artist, Augustyn Mirys (1700–1790) depicts three dead daughters.

himself. The true irony is that his sacrifice was repaid with his own suffering. Perhaps this was a fitting mythic ending after all, for one who had been hailed as a savior.

When it became obvious that the poison was inadequate, Mithradates drew his sword and attempted to stab himself, but physical weakness and mental distress interfered with his ability to drive the sword home. At that point, he called upon his faithful guard, Bituitus, who faltered before his king's "majestic countenance." According to Appian's version of the tradition, Mithradates encouraged Bituitus: "Your strong right arm has kept me safe from my enemies many times in the past. Now, I shall benefit most of all if you will kill me, to save me—for so many years the ruler of so great a kingdom—from being a captive led in a Roman triumph." Deeply moved, Bituitus "rendered the king the service he desired." Cassius Dio gives an alternate version: Pharnaces' soldiers "hastened his end with their swords and spears." But Reinach reasonably suggested that Pharnaces' soldiers burst into the tower too late to capture the king alive and in frustration mutilated his body.[5]

The ancient historians agree that after the bodies were discovered in the tower, Pharnaces sent a message to Pompey, now far away in Petra (Jordan), requesting permission to rule his father's kingdom as a Friend of Rome. Pharnaces embalmed his father's corpse, clothed it in Mithradates' kingly raiment and armor, and sent it, along with the royal weapons, scepter, and other treasures, across the Black Sea to Pontus. Other triremes carried the dead bodies of the royal family (including Nyssa and Mithradatis) and the surviving children (Artaphernes, Eupatra, Orsabaris, and little Darius, Oxathres, Xerxes, and Cyrus). Pharnaces also turned over numerous Greeks and barbarians who had served Mithradates—including the men responsible for capturing Manius Aquillius, executed by molten gold for starting the Mithradatic Wars twenty-five years earlier. The presence of these men with their king, after such a tumultuous quarter century, is a testament to the remarkable loyalty of some of Mithradates' followers.[6]

POMPEY'S VICTORY

Months later, Pompey received the news in camp somewhere between Petra and Jericho. Messengers flourishing javelins wrapped in victory laurels arrived, exulting that Mithradates had been forced by his son Pharnaces to commit suicide in Pantikapaion. Pompey clambered to the top of a hastily constructed mound of packsaddles to announce the tidings to his troops. Great feasts and sacrifices followed—just as though they had won a great battle and killed huge numbers of the enemy.

Pompey's biographer Plutarch hints at a whiff of resentment and annoyance in Pompey's awkward situation. Indeed, what in the world was Pompey doing nearly a thousand miles *south* of the Black Sea? He had been sent to kill or capture Mithradates in 66 BC—yet Mithradates not only had escaped but had ruled the Bosporan Kingdom in peace for the past three years, and had been preparing to invade Italy. Now, the elimination of Mithradates terminated Pompey's legal justification for continuing to win personal glory in the Near East. Pompey sent an official letter to the Senate in Rome. The news was greeted with great relief and joy, and Cicero, as consul, proclaimed ten days of thanksgiving. Meanwhile, Pompey took his time traveling to Pontus to receive the remains of his adversary.[7]

But when Pompey's soldiers opened the royal coffin on the beach, the dead man's face was totally unrecognizable! Everyone knew, from widely publicized portraits on coins and statues, what Mithradates looked like—

but decomposition made identification of the corpse impossible. According to Plutarch, the embalming was poorly done: the face had rotted because the brain had not been removed. But the long, damp sea voyage and exposure at Amisus in summertime, the effects of poison, the ravages of Mithradates' recent facial ulcerations, and any mutilations by Pharnaces' soldiers would also have done their work.[8]

The obliterated face immediately raised suspicion: was this really the body of Mithradates the Great? Had Mithradates' brilliant halo of *xvarnah* (spirit or luck) truly been extinguished at last?

"For superstitious reasons," Pompey averted his eyes (or perhaps did not care to look on the corpse after hearing that the face was not worth seeing). Those who did examine the corpse claimed to recognize it "by the scars." Modern scholars have accepted this claim without careful analysis. Mithradates' most distinguishing scar, of course, was the mark on his forehead from the lightning strike in infancy, but that would not have been visible on the decomposed face. For the same reason, the scar from his cheek wound in the battle of 67 BC could not be seen. That leaves the scar from the sword gash on his thigh, from the same battle, and the recent fatal stabbing wound dealt by Bituitus (with no witnesses). If the body had been mutilated by soldiers, as Cassius Dio reported, old scars would be difficult to read. A former friend of Mithradates, Gaius, was part of Pharnaces' delegation, according to Plutarch. Perhaps he was one of those who identified the body by the thigh scar. But thigh wounds were commonplace for anyone who rode a horse in battle, and Mithradates' distinctive facial scars were obliterated. This means that the royal paraphernalia in the coffin was the only physical evidence that the dead man was King Mithradates (see plate 9).

The armor, cuirass, and greaves matched Mithradates' reputedly large proportions; the helmet was ornate (perhaps with a hyacinth-dyed plume like that of Cyrus the Great). There were other rich trappings of royalty: the purple cloak, Mithradates' opulent sword—the scabbard alone worth four hundred talents—his gem-encrusted scepter, a golden crown. Plutarch says Pompey admired these marvelously wrought things and was "amazed at the size and splendor of the arms and raiment that Mithradates used to wear." After Pompey left the scene, the Roman officers and some men who had once served Mithradates circled the loot like jackals—grabbing up the scabbard, haggling over the crown and other treasures.[9]

Pompey's true feelings are unknown. Foremost must have been awe at this momentous occasion, the end of an era, the passing of a charismatic,

grandly ambitious and independent monarch who had been Rome's relentless, elusive enemy for as long as Pompey had been alive. But Plutarch also suggested there was a sense of anticlimax at the "unexpectedly
easy completion" of Pompey's campaign, which he had been prolonging
to great advantage. Frustration, too: Mithradates had slipped away yet
again, ever defiant and now forever immune to revenge, denying Pompey the glory of personally delivering to the Roman People and Senate
the perpetrator of so many outrages and decades of warfare. Suicide, in
antiquity as in modern times, could be a noble escape from tyranny or
capture by the enemy. It also robs the victor of the satisfaction of killing
his enemy or bringing him to justice.[10]

The historian Cassius Dio stressed that Pompey did not subject the
body of Mithradates to any indignities or desecration. Instead, Pompey
consciously copied Alexander's chivalrous treatment of the remains of
his Persian enemy King Darius. Treating the corpse with respect, Pompey commended Mithradates' bold exploits and declared him the greatest king of his time. He paid for a royal funeral and ordered that the body
be placed with Mithradates' forefathers. No other enemy of Rome had
ever been accorded such honors. As historian Jakob Munk Høtje points
out, by treating Mithradates as Darius had been treated, Pompey con-
trived to demote "the philhellene king to an oriental despot" while he
himself appeared as the new Roman Alexander.[11]

More Questions

Where was the body buried? According to Cassius Dio, Mithradates was
placed "in the tombs of his ancestors." Plutarch and Appian believed that
he was laid to rest "in the tombs of the kings at Sinope," because that had
become the royal residence of Pontus. In 1890, Reinach assumed that
a new royal necropolis must have existed in Sinope. But the traditional
mausoleum of Mithradates' forefathers was the set of rock-cut tombs at
Amasia, above the Iris River (see fig. 4.4). Extensive modern archaeology in Sinope has failed to turn up any tombs that would qualify as those
of Mithradates or his royal ancestors. So the ambiguity surrounding
the identity of Mithradates' body is further compounded by uncertainty
about his gravesite. Ambiguity over a venerated figure's final resting
place is one of the hallmarks of a mythic hero, a sure sign that Mithradates had passed into the realm of legend (see appendix 1).[12]

The legendary aura and mystery surrounding Mithradates' demise

Fig. 15.5. Mithradates and Hypsicratea take poison together, with
Mithradates' daughters and Bituitus. Boccaccio, *Des cleres et nobles
femmes*, ca. 1450. Spencer Collection, New York Public Library,
Astor, Lenox and Tilden Foundations.

raises other questions unanswered in the ancient histories. What, for
example, became of his devoted Amazon companion Hypsicratea?

If it was known or even rumored that Hypsicratea had been poisoned,
killed, or captured, one would expect this to be included in the accounts

of the fates of other members of Mithradates' family and entourage. The disappearance from the historical record of this appealing figure, the brave horsewoman who was so intimately involved with Mithradates in his last years, leaves a blank page too tempting to ignore. "Queen Hypsi-cratea's love for Mithradates knew no bounds," declared Valerius Maxi-mus; she was devoted to him "body and soul." Her "extraordinary fidel-ity was Mithradates' greatest solace and comfort in the most bitter and difficult conditions, for he considered that he was 'at home' even when wandering in defeat, because she was in exile with him." Even Théodore Reinach fell under the spell of this romantic "*passion sincère.*" Reinach pictured Hypsicratea, "the last living embodiment of his lost kingdom," tenderly comforting Mithradates in defeat.[13]

The novelist Michael Curtis Ford accounted for Hypsicratea's dis-appearance by imagining that she had been swallowed by a crevasse in the ice during the Caucasus crossing, leaving Mithradates in true mourn-ing for the first time in his life. Medieval and Renaissance authors also speculated about Hypsicratea's fate. In an illustrated manuscript (ca. 1450) of Boccaccio's *Famous Women*, the artist depicted Mithradates and Hypsicratea drinking chalices of poison together with the king's two daughters and their retainer Bituitus. Some French dramas of the 1600s about Mithradates also placed Hypsicratea in the tower, succumbing to poison with the king and princesses.

Hypsicratea did possess the poison that Mithradates had given her after the defeat in the Moonlight Battle, and she could have committed suicide. But she was young, strong, resourceful, and free, not compelled to accept death like a courtesan trapped in the harem. An alternative story, in which Hypsicratea survived, is just as plausible.

No ancient account speaks of Hypsicratea after the winter of 63 BC. But an exciting recent discovery by Russian archaeologists in Phanagoria proves that Hypsicratea did survive the Caucasus crossing and was with Mithradates after he regained the Kingdom of the Bosporus. An inscrip-tion, on the base for a statue of Hypsicratea, honors her as the wife of King Mithradates Eupator Dionysus. Unfortunately, the statue itself is missing, but the inscription tells us that Hypsicratea was commemo-rated as Mithradates' queen in the Bosporan Kingdom. The inscription holds another extraordinary surprise, as we will see.[14]

So Hypsicratea was in the Bosporus before Pharnaces' revolt. But an idle life at Mithradates' court in Pantikapaion might not have suited the independent horsewoman-warrior. It would not be unreasonable for Mithradates to assign her military duties associated with his war preparations. Perhaps she was away during Pharnaces' revolt, carrying out some mission on his majesty's service. Mithradates often employed close friends as envoys. Hypsicratea could have been dispatched to visit the nomads of the north or west, to prepare for the invasion of Italy. She and Mithradates might have expected to be reunited on the march.

If Hypsicratea was in Pantikapaion in 63 BC, one would suppose that Mithradates arranged for her safety at the first signs of Pharnaces' revolt. Was she among the soldiers escorting the princesses to Scythia? The only escape route would have been into Scythia; she and Mithradates might have hoped to meet there in triumph—or in exile if he received safe passage.

Could Hypsicratea have been captured by Pharnaces and delivered to Pompey? If so, such a prize would have been displayed prominently in Pompey's Triumph. But that is implausible, since her name is not included in the very detailed records of that celebration.

Remember You Are Mortal

Pompey's Triumph took place in 61 BC, two years after his victory. For two days, all Rome marveled at a spectacle of such magnitude and extravagance that it surpassed all previous triumphs. As Appian pointed out, no Roman had ever vanquished so powerful an enemy as Mithradates the Great nor conquered so many nations, extending Roman rule to the Euphrates and the Black Sea.

There were 700 captured ships on view in the harbor and countless wagons loaded with barbarian armor and weaponry and bronze ship prows. Banners and inscriptions lauded Pompey's capture of 1,000 castles and 900 cities. There were carts laden with an astounding 20,000 talents' worth of silver and gold coins, vessels, and jewelry. Litters heaped with millions of coins, chests of carved gems—truly, the official records of Pompey's incredible plunder were exhaustive and too exhausting to catalog in full here. It had taken Pompey's secretaries 30 days just to make an inventory of the 2,000 onyx and gold chalices from Mithradates' hoard at Talaura; and only a fraction of the loot was actually included in the procession. Not to be outdone by Lucullus's lone cherry tree, Pompey even paraded two exotic trees from Judea, ebony and balsam.

A host of 324 captives marched in the parade, among them Mithradates' grandson Tigranes, the son of Tigranes the Great, with his wife and daughters; and Zosimé, Tigranes' courtesan. Poor Nyssa, Mithradates' sister, was trotted out again to walk in shame beside five of Mithradates' sons, Artaphernes, Cyrus, Oxathres, Darius, Xerxes, and Princesses Eupatra and Orsabaris. There were various kings and royal families of Mithradates' allies, followed by Aristobulus, king of the Jews. A troop of Amazons captured by Pompey in the Caucasus was led past the crowd. Only Aristobulus and Tigranes the Younger were strangled after the parade.

As in Lucullus's Triumph, King Mithradates himself was conspicuously absent. In his place, his throne and scepter were carried aloft, followed by litters of antique Persian divans and old silver and gold chariots, treasures passed down to Mithradates from Darius I. Next came a large silver statue of Mithradates' grandfather, Pharnaces I, and the marble statue of Hercules holding his little son Telephus, modeled on Mithradates (fig. 3.7). Surpassing Lucullus's life-sized golden statue of Mithradates, a colossal ten-foot-tall solid gold statue of the king was displayed by Pompey.

Pompey also commissioned large painted portraits of Mithradates and his family. Another series of giant paintings illustrated key scenes from the Mithradatic Wars. For a spectator, this narrative sequence of images would have produced the effect of the frames of a stop-motion animation film or the panels of a graphic novel (for a medieval version of a similar narrative effect, see plate 3). Here were Mithradates and his barbarian multitudes attacking; here was Mithradates losing ground, and Mithradates besieged. There were Tigranes and Mithradates leading their magnificent hordes, followed by images of these great armies in defeat, and finally Mithradates' "secret flight by night." Next came a series of emotionally gripping paintings showing how Mithradates had died in his tower, drinking poison with "the daughters who chose to perish with him." These, of course, were scenes that no Roman had witnessed. They were based on artistic license and second- and thirdhand reports.

Taking credit for Pharnaces' revolt, Pompey boasted that he had accomplished what Sulla and Lucullus had failed to do, bring about the death of "the untamed king" of Pontus. The inscription on his dedication of war spoils announced, "Pompey the Great [had] completed a thirty years' war [and] routed, scattered, slew, or received the surrender of 12,183,000 people; sank or captured 846 ships [and] subdued the lands from the Sea of Azov to the Red Sea" to the Atlantic Ocean. Pompey "restored to the Roman People the command of the seas [and] triumphed over Asia, Pontus, Armenia, Paphlagonia, Cappadocia, Cilicia, Syria, the

Scythians, Jews, Albanoi, Iberi, Arabs, Cretans, Bastarnae, and, in addition to these, over Kings Mithradates and Tigranes."[15]

For Rome, commented Plutarch, the death of Mithradates was like the destruction of ten thousand enemies in one fell swoop. Emphasizing the greatness of Mithradates and his ultimate defeat served to aggrandize Pompey's own accomplishments. And after four decades of conflict, a certain admiration and awe surrounded this king who eclipsed all other kings, a noble ruler who had reigned fifty-seven years, who had subdued the barbarians, who took over Asia and Greece, and who resisted Rome's greatest commanders and shrugged off what should have been crushing defeats; a warrior who never gave up but renewed his struggle again and again, and then—against all odds—had died an old man by his own choice, in the kingdom of his fathers.

Mithradates' life had been a roller-coaster of sublime victories and harrowing losses, loyalties corrupted into betrayals, moments of divine happiness and terrible revenge, as players both East and West jockeyed to choose the winning side, to make the best investment in a volatile market of alliances. The risks Mithradates took were never for mere riches or fame—though those stakes could be high—but for the very survival of his Greco-Persian-Anatolian ideals and for freedom from Roman domination. Indomitable even in defeat, marveled Appian, Mithradates "left no avenue of attack untried." Pliny praised him as "The greatest king of his era." Velleius eulogized Mithradates as "ever eager for war," a man of "exceptional courage, always great in spirit . . . in strategy a general, in bodily prowess a soldier, in hatred to the Romans a Hannibal." He was the greatest king since Alexander, declared Cicero—a compliment that would have thrilled Mithradates.[16]

Pompey identified with Alexander too. Now he assumed Alexander's mantle, in a symbolic and literal sense. Pompey the Great was borne along the triumphal route in a golden chariot studded with glittering gems of every hue. Across his shoulders lay the fragile, faded purple cloak of Alexander the Great, once the cherished possession of Mithradates the Great, the "Hellenized Iranian Alexander." Appian was dubious about that cloak, but belief had imbued the ancient garment with reverence whatever its true provenance. As Pompey lovingly arranged the fabled robe for maximum visibility, the slave standing behind him began to murmur the traditional caution in the victor's ear: "Remember you are mortal."[17]

Did this memento mori send a ripple through Pompey's mood? Did it revive a lingering doubt, suppressed ever since he had declined to examine that ravaged body in the magnificent armor? It had been two years since the corpse had been laid in the tomb of the Pontic kings. Yet Mithradates had made fools of both Sulla and Lucullus by popping back after everyone assumed he was demolished. One can imagine Pompey's fleeting thought, *Yes, I am surely mortal. . . . but is Mithradates?*

WHAT IF?

Mithradates' life story is incomplete in many crucial details, and much is suspended in the amber glow of legend, inviting the imagination to fill in what we long to know. In the introduction, I discussed how narrative history and historical reconstruction help make sense of imperfect evidence and flesh out missing details and dead ends in the sketchy ancient record, without violating known facts, probabilities, and possible outcomes. A related approach, counterfactual or "what if" scenario building, allows us to reasonably suggest what might have happened under given conditions.

The mysterious circumstances surrounding the demise of a larger-than-life individual like Mithradates beckon historians to imagine what happened behind the scenes presented in the fragmentary sources. As we saw, the ancient historians themselves sometimes disagreed over facts and presented alternative versions of the same events, such as Mithradates' Caucasus crossing and his last hours. From the Middle Ages on, the uncertainty in the ancient record is reflected in the numerous artistic illustrations of alternative scenarios for Mithradates' death. Just as Hypsicratea's disappearance encouraged medieval and modern writers to write the rest of her story, there is ample justification to try to reconstruct a plausible alternative scenario for Mithradates.[18]

By all ancient accounts, Mithradates' died in his palace in Pantikapaion in 63 BC, owing to a combination of self-administered poison and the sword of his bodyguard or the weapons of Pharnaces' men. The body retrieved from the tower should have provided incontrovertible evidence of this event. But, in fact, the decomposed body identified as that of Mithradates—after the passage of some months and far removed from the scene of death—was unrecognizable except for a commonplace scar and the royal insignia. Everyone involved—from Mithradates' son Pharnaces and his old friends, to Pompey and the Romans—agreed to assume that the dead man was Mithradates.

But the extraordinary situation raises a host of questions. Was Mithradates really dead? Was this really his body? Others have posed these questions. Notably, the great French playwright Jean Racine began his famous tragedy *Mithridate* (1673) with Mithradates' faked death. Mozart's opera of 1770 also opens with Mithradates' reappearance after rumors of his death. Historian Brian McGing suggested in 1998 that the story of Mithradates' suicide in the tower might have been invented by Pharnaces, perhaps to divert accusations of parricide (a strong taboo among Persian-influenced cultures). But other deceptions and motivations were also possible. What if Mithradates was still alive?[19]

If anyone was capable of orchestrating a ruse to deceive the Romans into believing he was dead, it was Mithradates. He once substituted his son for the real king Ariathes. A brilliant escape artist, he had frequently eluded capture by stealth and trickery, and more than once he traveled incognito among his own subjects. Mithradates had cheated death repeatedly—and on at least four occasions he had disappeared and was presumed dead.

Moreover, Mithradates was a connoisseur of Greek myths, and theatricality and dramatic allusions were his trademarks. Ancient tragedy as well as comedy often turned on mistaken identities, distinctive scars, birthmarks, gestures, favorite possessions. Mithradates—and Pompey—knew the story of how Alexander's corpse had been faked. Alexander's best friend, Ptolemy, had stolen the body from Babylon and transported it in secret to Alexandria, Egypt. To throw his rivals off his track, Ptolemy had sculptors fabricate a realistic wax model of Alexander and clothed it in his royal robes. This double was placed on a sumptuous bier of silver, gold, and ivory inside one of Alexander's own elaborate Persian carriages. Surrounded by Alexander's royal belongings, the replica fooled the pursuers, while the real corpse was taken in a nondescript wagon by an obscure route to Egypt.[20]

Pharnaces could have sent Pompey a double, a corpse of a man of Mithradates' age and physique and displaying a cavalryman's scarred thigh, recent sword wounds, and a decomposed face. Such a deception would prevent the Romans from desecrating Mithradates' true remains if he had really died in the tower (no one expected Pompey to inter his enemy's corpse with honors in the Pontic royal tombs). According to the ancient historians, Mithradates had requested safe passage from Pantikapaion, to take refuge among his allies. A deception involving another's corpse could have been devised to cover Mithradates' last great escape.

What follows is a plausible—admittedly romantic—alternative scenario, drawing on the ancient sources and curious medieval and Gothic legends, and turning on logical "decision forks," but without venturing beyond the limits of the possible.[21]

THE GREAT ESCAPE

In his long life, "no conspiracy ever escaped Mithradates' notice," wrote Appian, "not even the last one," plotted by Pharnaces, "which he voluntarily overlooked and perished in consequence of—so ungrateful is wickedness once it is pardoned." But what if Pharnaces actually had been "grateful"? If a deception about Mithradates' death and remains were to be perpetuated, it would have begun at this point, upon Mithradates' discovery of Pharnaces' conspiracy. Pharnaces knew that his betrayal warranted death—Mithradates had never spared a proven traitor's life. He was especially harsh in punishing treachery within his family. His surprising pardon of Pharnaces was the opposite of what was expected, totally out of character for the practical, ruthless, unsentimental Mithradates.[22] The pardon guaranteed that Pharnaces would be king, if not now, then soon. What was Mithradates' true motivation?

When pressed to the wall, when all seemed lost, Mithradates had a long history of successfully slipping away and eluding pursuit. It is not difficult to imagine that, with the help of the old general Metrophanes, father and son might have negotiated a bargain. When the plot was first discovered, Mithradates still held the upper hand. The stakes were high for both men. For Pharnaces, it was life or death. Only by agreeing to Mithradates' conditions could he survive to inherit his father's kingdom. Mithradates, after a half century of dealing with Romans, knew Rome would never allow him to rule in peace. His plan to invade Italy lacked crucial support, and Pharnaces was his chosen successor. If he forgave his son, Mithradates could pass the crown to his designated heir and promise to disappear completely in exchange for safe passage and a ruse to convince Pompey that he was dead.

Pharnaces carried his great-grandfather's Persian name and had been raised within Persian culture. He named his son Darius, and the mother of his daughter Dynamis was probably a Sarmatian (later, as queen of the Bosporus, Dynamis wore an Amazon-Persian-style headdress decorated with Zoroastrian Sun symbols). Perhaps Mithradates discerned a strong strain of his own independent spirit in this son. Indeed, as king Pharnaces would retrace his father's path: after a peaceful early reign as a Friend of Rome, he would take advantage of the Roman civil war to suddenly rebel, marching a large army, with scythed chariots and a strong cavalry, across Colchis and into Pontus in a quixotic quest to recover his father's old kingdom.[23]

Fig. 15.6. Queen Dynamis, bronze bust. As ruler of the Bosporan Kingdom, Mithradates' granddaughter wears a star-studded Persian-Phrygian cap like those of Amazons and Zoroastrians. The Hermitage, St. Petersburg. Photo, M. Rostovtzeff 1919.

So let us imagine that at the crisis of Pharnaces' attempted coup in 63 BC, father and son acknowledged each other as equals at the bargaining table, facilitated by Metrophanes. They would have sworn a sacred oath by the gods Men and Mithra that allowed them both to survive with honor. Then they could work out the details of the grand illusion.

Now let's replay the events according to the script that might have been composed by Pharnaces and Mithradates. A large, robust corpse that could pass as Mithradates had to be discovered in the tower and shipped to Pompey. Any veteran cavalryman was likely to have the requisite battle scar on the thigh; the face could be easily obliterated beyond recognition with corrosive lime or acid. One cannot help wondering whether the faithful cavalry officer Bituitus volunteered for this supreme sacrifice. Mithradates' armor, scepter, crown, and other regalia would complete the illusion. Old retainers, perhaps Gaius or Metrophanes, could confirm the identification of the body for Pompey.

Keeping his part of the bargain, Mithradates dons ordinary traveling clothes and steals away by night, something he had done many times in the past (perhaps his castle had secret exits, like Hannibal's in Bithynia). The king takes his weapons and what treasures he can carry: gold coins, favorite agate rings, some valuable papers. Where would he go? Escape by sea was impossible. The only safe route was north.

Mithradates could ride out and join any one of the Scythian or Sarmatian tribes on the steppes. Their ideals and physical prowess were compatible with his, and he could speak their languages. Mithradates had experienced a nomadic lifestyle in his youth and early reign, and during his evasions of Lucullus and Pompey. He had recently renewed his friendships with the nomad chieftains. Pharnaces had maintained good relations with these tribes. Two intriguing facts lend support to the idea of an escape into Scythia. Mithradates' son by Adobogiona, Mithradates of Pergamon, was ruler of the Bosporan Kingdom after Pharnaces. During an uprising, this Mithradates really did take refuge among the Scythians. Mithradates' granddaughter Dynamis, queen of the Bosporan Kingdom during the time of Augustus, also went into exile for a time—she was sheltered by a Sarmatian tribe, perhaps that of her mother.[24]

Who would have accompanied Mithradates into secret exile? Perhaps Bituitus, if he survived (his fate is not recorded). And surely Hypsicratea—or perhaps she and the king had already arranged a rendezvous (see plate 8). There are ancient precedents for imagining a "posthistorical" second life for Mithradates and Hypsicratea in the lands beyond the Black Sea. In romances about heroes and heroines of Greek myth, for example, Achilles and Helen of Troy were paired in an idyllic afterlife. They never met in the Troy of Homer's *Iliad*, but in popular lore the couple enjoyed "an extraordinary post mortem existence" as lovers in a mythical Black Sea paradise. Notably, the 1707 opera *Mitridate* by Scarlatti offers an alternate history in which Mithradates and Hypsicratea disguise themselves as Egyptian envoys.[25]

An obscure will-o'-the-wisp legend, mentioned by Edward Gibbon in *Decline and Fall of the Roman Empire* (1776–88), even gives Mithradates his final revenge. I have traced this tradition back to medieval Norse saga, in which a barbarian tribe from the Sea of Azov, allied with Mithradates, carried on his dream of one day invading Italy. Led by their chieftain Odin, this tribe was said to have escaped Roman rule after Pompey's victory, by migrating to northern Europe and Scandinavia. They became the Goths, who, still inspired by Mithradates' old struggle, avenged his defeat by overwhelming the Roman Empire. In the vision of the poet William Wordsworth, this old tale tells

> How vanquished Mithridates, northward passed,
> And, hidden in the cloud of years, became
> Odin, the Father of a Race by whom
> Perished the Roman Empire. . . .[26]

And so let us suppose that on a May morning in 63 BC, riding across the vast expanse of green grass carpeted with wild red peonies, Mithradates sheds his royal skin and chooses a nomad's life for the rest of his natural days. In this story, he and Hypsicratea would live among the "untamed" men and women who loved to roam the boundless plains. In the vision limned by the Roman historian Ammianus Marcellinus, the steppe nomads were "tall, handsome, and robust people with piercing eyes," who "wandered like happy fugitives from place to place," dressed in furs and wool leggings, with blue tattoos, "living on the milk of their herds, wild cherries, and meat, never spending a night under a roof . . . eating and drinking, buying and selling, holding assemblies, and even sleeping on their steeds or in their wagons." They were "no one's subjects, none can even tell you where they are from, since they are conceived, born, and raised in faraway places." Skilled warriors, "they delight in danger and warfare and do not know the meaning of slavery, since all are born of noble blood, and they choose as their chiefs those who are conspicuous for long experience as warriors."[27]

In this new life, our companions would have the leisure to share their life stories, Mithradates recounting the history of his kingdom, Hypsicratea telling of her free and equal people of Caucasia. Thanks to his Persian heredity and theriac, Mithradates could have lived another five, ten, or even twenty years had he not died in the tower in 63 BC.[28] In time, death might have come to Mithradates in battle, on a hunting expedition, or quietly in sleep. He would die in *eleutheria*, freedom, confident of his exalted place in history and myth. Mithradates' friends would have buried him in the nomads' traditional way, with his horse and a modest cache of golden treasures and cameo rings, in an anonymous *kurgan* on the steppes.[29]

Mithradates' passing—whether it occurred in the tower as reported in 63 BC or later in secret exile—would have been mourned by the strong woman he liked to call by the masculine form of her name, Hypsicrates. Younger than Mithradates, perhaps in her forties, Hypsicratea still had good years ahead. How did she spend the rest of her life?

What follows is a further speculation, based on the conditions of possibility set out in the ancient sources—and on new archaeological evidence. Let us begin with the name Hypsicrat*ea/es*. Only two instances of this name are known in the latter part of the first century BC. One is Mithradates' Amazon friend Hypsicrat*ea*. The other is a mysterious historian named Hypsicrat*es*, who was also associated with Pontus and the

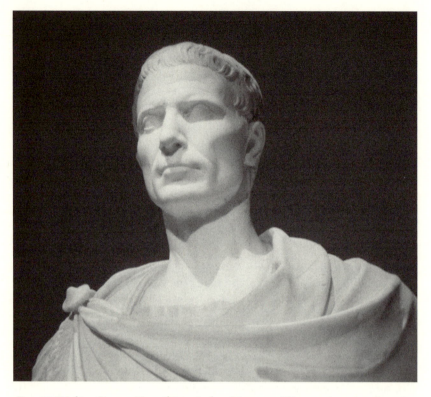

FIG. 15.7 Julius Caesar. Kunsthistorisches Museum, Vienna, Austria, photo by
Andrew Bossi, Wikipedia Commons, cc-by-sa-2.5.

Black Sea Kingdom. Coincidence? Or is there a more interesting explanation for this doubling of a very rare name?

Little is known about the shadowy figure called Hypsicrates. The historian turns up after 47 BC, some sixteen years after Mithradates' death
in 63 BC, when Julius Caesar crushed Pharnaces' attempt to regain his
father's lost kingdom. Taking over Pontus, Caesar freed a prisoner of war
named Hypsicrates at Amisus. This Hypsicrates accompanied Caesar as
his historian on campaigns and wrote treatises on the history, geography,
and military affairs of Pontus and the Bosporan Kingdom.

Hypsicrates' works have not survived, but they were quoted by other
historians. Strabo of Pontus cited Hypsicrates as an authority on two
highly significant topics: the military fortifications of the Bosporan Kingdom, and the lifestyle and customs of the Amazons of the Caucasus region. Notably, Strabo mentioned Hypsicrates along with another close

friend of Mithradates, the philosopher Metrodorus. Josephus quoted Hypsicrates on the campaigns of Julius Caesar and on Mithradates of Pergamon. Lucian, a Syrian from Samosata (second century AD), described Hypsicrates as a "historian from Amisus who mastered many sciences." There is one more salient detail. Hypsicrates, he died old. According to Lucian's list of remarkably long lives, Hypsicrates lived to be ninety-two.[30]

This set of striking coincidences linking Hypsicrat*ea* and Hypsicrat*es* has been overlooked by modern scholars, apparently because of the gender difference. But we recall that Mithradates called Hypsicratea by the male form of her name. Mithradates' intellectual and athletic equal, she lived a manly life, riding, hunting, and making war. The name "Hypsicratea" disappeared from the historical record after 63 BC, the year Mithradates' death was reported. Everything we know about the person known as Hypsicrates, especially the topics of expertise attributed to him—Amazons and Mithradates' kingdom—points to someone very close to Mithradates (and the notably long life could even hint at access to *Mithridatium*).

I suggest that the historian writing under the name Hypsicrates was none other than Mithradates' beloved companion, Hypsicratea.

The newfound inscription for the statue honoring Hypsicratea, described earlier, lends support to this idea. The statue was probably erected

Fɪɢ. 15.8. Inscription honoring Hypsicratea, discovered in Phanagoria. Her name is given in the masculine form: "Hypsikrates wife of Mithradates." Photo courtesy of Jakob Munk Højte, after V. Kuznetzov, "Novye nadpisi iz Fanagorii," 2007.

Fig. 15.9. Portrait of Mithradates, seventeenth-century marble copy of ancient original. Racine's tragedy, *Mithridate* (1673) was a favorite of Louis XIV, the Sun King (1638–1715). Amphitheater of the Grand Trianon garden, Grand Canal, Versailles, MR 2488, 85 cm/33 in high. Réunion des Musées Nationaux/Art Resource, NY.

during the reign of Mithradates' granddaughter, Queen Dynamis, who knew Hypsicratea. Amazingly, the text of the inscription spells her name with *es*, *Hypsicrates*, the masculine form of Hypsicratea. We now know that this was not just a private nickname, but that Mithradates' companion was in fact publicly known as Hypsicrates.

So let us suppose that at some point after 63 BC, Hypsicratea returned to Pontus. Perhaps disguised as a man she took up a scholarly life at Amisus, and was captured by Caesar after the battle at Zela in 47 BC. Another possibility is that she was fighting on Pharnaces' side and was taken prisoner by Caesar's soldiers. The lot of a female captive was not enviable. A permanent male persona as Hypsicrates would be advantageous. Caesar, impressed by this person's unique knowledge of Mithradates' kingdom and recent history—and possibly even aware of the gender switch and true identity—made Hypsicrates his personal historian. Even the politics of this association are fitting. Mithradates and his circle were pro-Marius, foes of Sulla and Pompey. Caesar was pro-Marius, and an enemy of Sulla and Pompey.

Who was more qualified than Hypsicratea to preserve the story of Mithradates and his kingdom? She had loved Mithradates and fought by his side. She knew the king's store of personal anecdotes, desires, and accomplishments. If Hypsicratea later wrote as the historian Hypsicrates, she may well have been the source of many of the details about Mithradates' character and reign that were preserved by other ancient historians. Mithradates, from the beginning, was the self-conscious author of his own life. Through Hypsicrat*ea/es*, he could also have been responsible for his own legend.

I have sketched a continuation of Mithradates' story as a historical thought experiment, but in reality Mithradates enjoyed a vital afterlife in history, science, and popular legend for more than two thousand years after his death (appendix 2). In his relentless resistance to Rome, Mithradates, the savior born under an Eastern star, represented a genuine alternative to Roman imperialism in the turbulent last days of the Republic. Some sixty years after Mithradates' death, another savior and champion of Truth and Light was born under a different Eastern star. In the turn of the millennium, in the new world that emerged from Mithradates' armed resistance and the Republic's military response, that new King of Kings would challenge and eventually win over the mighty Roman Empire, but not by force of arms.

Mithradates battled against the tide of history. This intrepid, complex, ideological leader ultimately failed to conquer Rome by violence and war.

Yet, if we let Rome stand for tyranny, the grandeur of Racine's vision of
Mithradates' legacy still rings true:

> Take charge. Let us, following your name,
> Live up to being your sons everywhere we go.
> Set dusk and dawn on fire by your hands;
> Fill the universe without ever leaving the Bosporus;
> May the Romans, hard pressed from one end of the world
>   to the other,
> Be unsure where you will be, and find you everywhere.[31]

Mythic Hero or Deviant Personality?

T HE FOLLOWING sections discuss Mithradates' scores on two, very different, "diagnostic" tools: first, the traits of traditional mythic heroes and, second, the characteristics of personality disorders. Both measures should be taken with generous grains of salt; both lists are susceptible to misuse and necessarily entail anachronistic assumptions based on incomplete knowledge.

THE MYTHIC HERO SCRIPT

Mithradates' extraordinary life story fulfills the expectations for mythic heroes, first identified by Otto Rank in 1914 and elaborated by Lord Fitzroy Raglan in 1936. Rank's basic model is summarized in six steps: (1) Prophecy surrounds birth; (2) Divine, aristocratic, or royal parents; (3) Abandoned, given or sent away, separated; (4) Rescued or reared by foster parents or surrogates; (5) Return to the land of father, proves his worthiness; (6) Claims royal birthright and wins honors.

Raglan's twenty-two heroic attributes overlap with Rank's, except for "prophecies," number 23 in the following composite list, adapted from Rank, Raglan, and Dundes 1990. Here is my scoring rationale for Mithradates' perfect score of 23. His very high ranking is overdetermined: several traits receive multiple points.

1. *Mother is a princess.* Queen Laodice was a Seleucid princess.
2. *Father is a king.* King Mithradates V Euergetes.
3. *Parents are related or have complex relationship.* They may have been remote kin; both had entangled Macedonian and Persian family trees. Relationship complicated: Laodice was suspected of complicity in the murder of her husband.
4. *Unusual circumstances before birth.* The rare, spectacular comet of 135 BC coincided with Mithradates' conception.
5. *Reputed to be son of or sent by gods.* Mithradates' name means "sent by Mithra"; his authority to rule was bestowed by Mithra. In ancient Iranian

belief, the king was sacred, descended from the Sun god. Mithradates' birth fulfilled oracles predicting a savior-king rising in the East. He was compared to the god Dionysus and the demigod Hercules, and he claimed both as ancestors. He also claimed descent from Alexander the Great, a revered cult figure by the first century BC. Mithradates himself was hailed as a god by followers.

6. *Attempts to kill the hero during childhood, often by relatives.* Young Mithradates' enemies within the palace attempted to murder him; his mother was suspected of trying to poison him.

7. *Abandonment, exile, separation; escapes premature death.* Mithradates survived a lightning strike as a baby. His father was murdered when Mithradates was a boy, abandoning him to a treacherous mother. Teenage Mithradates disappeared into the countryside for seven years, again escaping premature death. Another long sojourn, during which he was presumed dead, occurred early in his reign. As a young man, he escaped another poisoning plot by his sister-wife.

8. *Grows up in a faraway land, among peasants and wild animals.* Mithradates survived and grew strong in the countryside, hunting and living off the land for seven years, encountering remote mountain folk. In his second long expedition incognito, he visited his future dominions.

9. *Little is known of childhood.* Very few details exist about Mithradates' childhood; his teen years are shrouded in mystery.

10. *Upon reaching adulthood, returns to kingdom.* After seven years, Mithradates returned to his Pontic Kingdom. After losing his kingdom in adulthood, he regained it again; he lost it once more but recovered his Bosporan Kingdom.

11. *Victory over powerful enemies.* Mithradates overcame dangerous enemies at court, got rid of his mother and other rivals. He also won sweeping victories over the Romans.

12. *Marries a princess, daughter of his enemy or predecessor.* Mithradates married his own sister, Princess Laodice—not only the daughter of his predecessor (his father) but also the daughter of his enemy (his mother).

13. *Acknowledged as king.* Mithradates was hailed as king of Pontus, called "King of Kings."

14. *Rules peacefully for a time.* The first decade of Mithradates' reign was peaceful.

15. *Prescribes new laws, promotes a new world order.* Mithradates established new laws (freeing slaves, canceling debt, expanding citizenship) and promoted a "new world order": his alternative to Roman rule in his new Black Sea Empire.

16. *Later loses favor with gods and/or subjects.* During the wars against Rome, omens indicated gods' disfavor; heavy losses caused allies to abandon Mithradates. His subjects turned against his increasingly draconian

rule; he was beset by defections, desertions, betrayals. In the end, he lost his power in a revolt.

17. *Driven from throne and city.* Lucullus and Pompey both drove Mithradates from his throne in Pergamon and Pontus, forcing him to abandon his kingdom and flee for his life, first to Armenia, and then to his Kingdom of the Bosporus in the Crimea. His son Pharnaces revolted, driving Mithradates from his throne.

18. *Unusual or mysterious death.* The circumstances of Mithradates' death were extraordinary, mysterious, and violent. Barricaded in a tower, he attempted to commit suicide with poison. He died by the sword of his bodyguard; some sources say he was killed by his son's soldiers. His body was never indentified with certainty; his death was not "simple" but in effect "double" (Cassius Dio 37.13).

19. *Dies in an elevated place.* Mithradates died in the high tower of his fortress, on Mount Mithradates, above the town of Pantikapaion.

20. *Children do not succeed him.* Mithradates himself ensured that his sons could not succeed him, murdering or getting rid of all but one viable heir, Pharnaces, who betrayed him to the Romans and usurped the crown. Pharnaces did not independently inherit Mithradates' original Kingdom of Pontus; his status was that of a client of Rome. Crushed by Julius Caesar, Pharnaces died in 47 BC.

21. *Corpse buried unconventionally, or somehow hidden or obscured.* Mithradates' corpse was poorly embalmed and shipped across the Black Sea to Pompey. The face was unrecognizable, raising doubts that he was really dead. Even though Pompey could not be certain it was Mithradates' body, he gave it a grand burial, yet the location is unclear.

22. *More than one revered tomb.* Pompey placed the body in Mithradates' family tomb. But the sources conflict, and scholars still debate whether Mithradates' body was interred in Sinope or in Amasis.

23. *Prophecies predicted future greatness.* Numerous prophecies and oracles predicted Mithradates' birth, his rise to power, and his grand destiny.

PERSONALITY DISORDERS

Does Mithradates fit the typical personality profile of "the poisoner"? In Rome and Greece, poison was considered the weapon of women and "unmanly" Persian-influenced barbarians; today it is often seen as the weapon of the greedy, weak, oppressed, or cowardly (Stuart 2004, 114–15), or the murder method of psychopaths, "controlling, sneaky people with no conscience" or remorse. Some call the poisoners of family members "custodial killers" (Newman 2005, 18–19). Perhaps this label best

APPENDIX ONE

fits Mithradates as poisoner of his harem, since he felt he was protecting his family and acting as guardian of his and their honor. In other cases, however, Mithradates mastered what was the traditional weapon of succession and assassination in his world.

Is it possible or useful to apply current psychiatric diagnostic tools to historical figures, based on reported behavior and character? In the case of Mithradates, the temptation is great. Among the many drawbacks is the fact that all the evidence was presented by his enemies. Yet "the question deserves to be asked," declares Danish historian Tønnes Bekker-Neilsen, who initiated the analysis of Mithradates' mental health in 2004. The king's known activities, "crimes," emotions, and contradictions have been thoroughly detailed in the preceding chapters. Based on the available evidence of Mithradates' psychiatric history, what might be measured by modern diagnostic rating scales for personality disorders?

In modern psychiatry, psychopaths are usually highly intelligent, superficially charming individuals who do not experience deep emotions or empathy and habitually lie and manipulate others. Some, but not all, psychopaths are violent criminals. Other conditions are often confused with psychopathy. For example, a "borderline personality" suffers severe mood swings, fragile emotional defenses, and fluctuating self-image, among other traits (Bekker-Neilsen equates borderline personality with psychopathy). Antisocial personality disorder is applied to those who commit aggressive, criminal acts. Mithradates could be considered a sociopath: someone who may commit crimes but has a strong sense of right and wrong based on the values of his or her particular social group.

The standard Psychopathy Checklist-Revised (PCL-R), devised and refined by psychologist Robert Hare in the 1980s, has twenty traits. The highest possible score is 40; the score of the general population falls under 5. The following list condenses the traits into fourteen characteristics and considers whether or not they apply to Mithradates, as he was known to his contemporaries and ancient historians.

1. *Superficial, glib charm, intelligent, articulate.* Mithradates was a highly intelligent, charismatic leader and a brilliant, persuasive orator. Yet by all reports, his appeal was not superficial but reflected a genuinely likable personality and deeply held principles.

2. *Grandiose sense of self-worth, narcissism.* Mithradates had a penchant for theatrical gestures and a grandiose sense of self-worth. But these traits could be seen as an occupational hazard for an ambitious, popular Helle-

nistic monarch with a dazzling family tree, revered as divine and surrounded by prophecies of grandeur. Unlike his friend King Tigranes, Mithradates was flexible and realistic, responsive to adversity, and able to func-
tion as an ordinary individual, and as an equal of his soldiers when
necessary.

3. *Early behavior problems.* Boyhood experiments with poisons and running away from home were rational reactions to Mithradates' dysfunctional
family situation and genuine plots on his life by his mother and guardians.

4. *Lack of conscience, lack of guilt or remorse.* Documented incidents indicate that Mithradates did not lack a conscience. He had a strong sense of
right and wrong and suffered guilt and remorse, which in some cases led
him to pardon those who wronged him.

5. *Lack of empathy, callousness, cold-blooded violence.* As a leader determined to wipe out enemy Romans in Anatolia, Mithradates certainly exhibited extreme ruthlessness in 88 BC and callous, cold-blooded behavior
in other instances. Some of his murderous acts were policy decisions under
duress; others were planned revenge. Yet, as noted above, several episodes
show that Mithradates was also capable of compassion and forgiveness,
even against his own interest.

6. *Manipulative, deceitful, habitual lying.* Mithradates could manipulate
and intimidate others, an asset in diplomacy and politics. As one educated
to respect Truth as opposed to Deceit, he was generally honest; he did not
have a reputation as a liar, even among his enemies. He was a master of
deception in warfare, a positive attribute in his day.

7. *Refusal to accept responsibility for actions, unreliable.* Although during
bouts of paranoia Mithradates was quick to suspect treachery and blame
others, this was often a rational response to real threats. In general, he
prized loyalty and was a reliable friend and ally; he took responsibility for
his own decisions, an important tenet of his Persian upbringing.

8. *Promiscuous sexual behavior.* Mithradates was sexually vigorous, with
numerous partners, fathering many children. But harems and multiple offspring were the norm for Macedonian-Persian royalty in the Hellenistic era.
He was not reputed to be sexually dissolute, as some contemporaries were.

9. *Parasitic, dependent lifestyle.* Mithradates was wealthy but generous.
He was never lazy or parasitic, but was universally admired as extremely
hardworking and resourceful.

10. *Impulsive behavior, easily bored, requires stimulation.* Remarkably intelligent and creative, Mithradates probably required constant stimulation;
his interests were wide-ranging, from botany, toxicology, gemology and art,
literature, and music to engineering technology and furniture making.
There is evidence for violence and a hot temper, but Mithradates was usually shrewd and calculating, capable of great patience and restraint. He was
also a defiant and daring risk-taker, once again an asset in his day.

11. *Incapable of realistic, long-term planning.* Mithradates' reign was distinguished by long-term planning, which he and others deemed realistic. He was quick to revise strategies to meet new challenges. As Bekker-Neilsen points out, Mithradates did have a tendency to underestimate obstacles and adversaries, but this is a common trait among successful leaders in any era.

12. *Shallow emotions, fearlessness, lack of anxiety or depression.* Mithradates was courageous but not without fear. He experienced strong negative and positive emotions: love, hate, compassion, humor, generosity, revenge, anxiety, fear, grief, loyalty, and depression.

13. *Lack of appreciation for art and music.* By all reports, Mithradates had a passionate appreciation for art, literature, theater, and music.

14. *Failure to form long-term relationships and loyalties, many short-term relationships.* Mithradates faced "difficulty in creating durable alliances," remarked Bekker-Neilsen, "even with rulers who were his relatives." But in the cutthroat, violent world of his reign of more than fifty years, Mithradates was the target of numerous conspiracies and betrayals by his enemies and those closest to him. Yet he maintained many remarkably long-term relationships, with Dorylaus and other boyhood friends, his military companions, allies including Tigranes, his daughters, and the women he loved.

Mithradates scores highly on measures of grandiose self-assessment, and his behavior was at times cruel and vengeful. Yet he cannot be labeled a psychopath. As Bekker-Neilsen remarks, "being charismatic is no vice, and ruthlessness, fratricide . . . grandiosity and promiscuity" were necessary for survival in his milieu. Of course, a low score on the PCL-R is not a certificate of moral integrity: one can do very bad things without being a psychopath.

Recently it has been suggested that some social traits associated with psychopaths and sociopaths—superficial charm, ruthless aggression, manipulation, and callousness—reflect behavioral options that are highly valued in modern business, sports, the armed forces, and politics, leading to the new concept of "successful" sociopaths or psychopaths. This label might fit Mithradates, whose antisocial and sociopathic traits were assets ensuring his survival and memorable achievements. Mithradates also exhibited traits common among successful modern entrepreneurs: bold gambles, high tolerance for risk, resilience in the face of defeat, and unwavering confidence against all odds.

Mithradates' Afterlife in the Arts and Popular Culture

M ITHRADATES' legendary status began during his own lifetime and continued for more than two millennia, inspiring literature, art, music, popular culture, and scientific investigations. This brief compilation is not comprehensive: a full accounting of his legacy would fill a book. See Summerer 2009 for a survey of representations of Mithradates in scholarship and the arts, from the fifteenth to the twentieth century.

VISUAL ARTS

Mithradates, sometimes with his companion Hypsicratea, appears in numerous medieval illuminated manuscripts; e.g., Plutarch's lives of Pompey, Sulla, and Lucullus; Boccaccio; and Christine de Pizan (figs. 6.2, 7.3, 14.3, 14.4, 15.5; plates 2, 3, 6, 8, 9); see Summerer 2009 for more images of the deaths of Mithradates and his family

Monime, Mithradates' tragic queen, was a popular subject of European paintings, for example, by Bartolomeo Pinelli (1816); Genovesio, Nord-Pas-de-Calais, Hotel de Ville, France (sixteenth century); and fig. 12.5

Mithradates bust, Versailles (fig. 15.9)

Mithradates bust, by Verchaffen, ca. 1760 (N. Penny, "Lord Rockingham's Sculpture Garden," *J. Paul Getty Journal* 19 [1991]: 15 and fig. 11)

Mithradates bust, marble, Palais Justiniani, Rome, engraving by Monnier

Mithradates' life story illustrated on two ornate sixteenth-century drug jars, J. Paul Getty Museum (fig. 15.3; plate 4)

Illustrations of Racine's *Mithridate* (1673), e.g., figs. 7.4, 10.1, 12.6

Paintings illustrating the history of pharmacy, e.g., plate 1; Mithradates' herbalist Krateuas appears in medieval medical manuscripts, e.g., Codex Vindobonensis Medicus, Munich

Illustrations of Mithradates' death in Roman history books, e.g., figs. 15.1, 15.2, 15.4

Drama

Pageau, *Monime* (1600), based on Plutarch, Florus, and Appian
Behourt, *Hypsicratée* (1604) dramatized Plutarch's description in *Life of Pompey*
Gautier de Costes de La Calprenède, *La Morte de Mitridate* (1635) highly esteemed by Cardinal Richelieu and Anne of Austria, mother of Louis XIV (Brèque 1983 and Snaith 2007)
Jean Racine, *Mithridate* (1673), Louis XIV's favorite play (Goodkin 1986; Brèque 1983)
Nathaniel Lee, *Mithridates, King of Pontus, a Tragedy,* London, 1678

Opera

There are eighteen librettos based on Mithradates, including Aldrovandini, *Mithridate in Sebastia*, 1701; Scarlatti, *Mitridate Eupatore*, 1707; Capello, 1723; Vittorio Cigna-Santi and Gasparini, 1767. Mozart's first serious opera, written at age fourteen, was *Mitridate, re di Ponto*, Milan, 1770 (Sadie 1972; Brèque 1983; for illustrations and photos of productions, see *L'Avant Scene Opera*, special issue, 1983). Recent performances: Santa Fe Opera, 2001; Convent Garden, London, 2005.

Literature

Because of Mithradates' linguistic brilliance, his name came to denote a book written in several languages, a *mithridates*. For example, the *Mithridates* by Konrad Gesner (b. 1516) was a study of 130 languages. Mithradates' life story or, in particular, his special regime of ingesting poisons in small doses has been featured in many literary genres in Europe and the United States, for example:

William Wordsworth, *Prelude*, 1798–1850
Nathaniel Hawthorne, "Rappaccini's Daughter," story, 1844
Alexandre Dumas, *The Count of Monte Cristo*, novel, 1845
"The Modern Mithidates," illustrated satirical poem, *Vanity Fair* (December 31, 1859), 5, lists poisons readily available on "every grocer's shelves"
John Greenleaf Whittier, "Mithridates in Chios," poem, 1865
Ralph Waldo Emerson, "Mithridates," poem, ca. 1847
A. E. Housman, "Terence, this is stupid stuff," poem, 1896

Agatha Christie, *The Mysterious Affair at Styles*, mystery, 1920
Constantine Cavafy, "Darius," poem about a poet in Mithradates' court, 1920
Dorothy Sayers, *Strong Poison*, mystery, 1931
Poul Anderson, *The Golden Slave*, novel, 1960
William Goldman, *The Princess Bride*, novel 1973; movie, 1987
Colleen McCullough, *The Grass Crown*, novel, 1991
E. E. Smith, *Triplanetary*, novel, 1997
Michael Curtis Ford, *The Last King*, novel, 2004

POPULAR CULTURE

Mithradates appears in the "Total War: Rome" video game, 2008
History Channel game, Anachronism (2008), "Mithradates VI the Great" set of four cards: "Use the King of Pontus, Rome's most feared adversary, to outwit, out-think, and outmaneuver your opponents." www.TriKing Games.com
SPARTACVS: Crisis in the Roman Republic 80-71 BC (2009), board game pits the Roman Republic against the allies Mithradates, Spartacus, and Sertorius www.compassgames.com/spartacus.htm

⊰ NOTES ⊱

INTRODUCTION

1. "Fairy tale" aspects: McGing 1986, 44–46; Holland 2003, 43; Goodkin 1986, 205; cf Champlin 2003, 92–96, 237, for folkloristic features of Nero's story. Were some European folk motifs inspired by Mithradates' story? For example, M's love affair with his female page disguised as a male may be the origin of that stock figure in medieval tales and Shakespearean drama. M's imprisonment of his sisters in towers so they could never marry is another fairy tale-motif. M in Norse mythology: *Younger Edda* 1879 and Ch 15.

2. Both spellings found on ancient coins, inscriptions, and historical manuscripts: Welles 1974, 296 n2; Ward 1749–50, 490–92; Reinach 1890, 49 n2. Justin 37.1 says M fought Rome for 46 years; Appian *Mithradatic Wars* 118 and *Syrian Wars* 48 say the wars lasted 42 years; Florus 1.40 and Eutropius 6.12 say 40; Pliny 7.26.98 says 30. It depends on when the conflict is said to have begun. M's active resistance to Roman rule began in about 103 BC; war with Rome broke out in 88 BC.

3. See Baley 1585 for typical medieval view, praising M's nobility and "gifts to the whole world," far surpassing Rome's "victory and profit" in the Mithradatic Wars. Machiavelli *Art of War* (1519), 2.84–99. Summerer 2009: M was the subject of scientific works and a source of inspiration in popular literature and opera over centuries; facts were used, distorted, overlooked to construct positive and negative images. In the 1500s to 1700s, M was a tragic figure, a victim of betrayal and defeat by conspiracy.

4. Corner 1915, 222.

5. Rostovtzeff 1921, 220 (R left Russia for the United States in 1918). Reinach 1890, xiv. Gozalishvili 1965. Russian novels: Polupudnev 1993 and Samulev 2004. Recent Russian scholarship, eg Saprykin 2004, Kesmedzhi 2008, Tsetskhladze 2001, Zin'ko 2004, and see Højte 2009a, Bowersock 2008. Suspected political poisonings of Russia's opponents reported in the media include a Bulgarian defector's murder by ricin-tipped umbrella in 1978 and former Russian spy A. Litvinenko's death in 2006 by radioactive polonium-210 in his sushi; in 2003 and 2004 two journalists critical of Vladimir Putin died mysteriously; and in 2004 Ukrainian presidential candidate V. Yushchenko was deliberately poisoned by Soviet-made "Yellow Rain" dioxin, which hideously disfigured his face (Ch 14, similar malady suffered by M before his death). Gutterman 2004. Newman 2005.

6. Thanks to discussions with Gevork Nazaryan, www.ArmenianHighland .com; Vahe Gurzadyan; and Rubik Kocharian; also see Kurkjian 1958, ch 13. Armenians revere Tigran Mets (Tigranes the Great) and M, "the glorious King of Pontus," Tigranes' "true ally." They "struggled together . . . against Roman dominance," writes Yuri Babayan in 2002, www.armenianhistory.info, fulfilling the ancient Zoroastrian-influenced Armenian folk belief that a "great hero would wield a magic sword of lightning at the most critical time—when the world was in the grip of evil tyrants and people were yearning for liberation" (Nazaryan 2005). Mirdad/Mrhtat is a popular first name in Armenia. For

an Iranian point of view, see Badi' 1991, ch 5, "Mithridate Eupator ou la révolt de l'Asie." Kurdish historian Mehrdad Izady considers M of Kurdish ancestry, and Pontus, Cappadocia, and Commagene as ancient Kurdish states: Izady 1992, 36–38, 86.

7. Thanks to Deniz Erciyas and Mehmet Tezcan for insights about the long-standing neglect of M in Turkey. A popular book of 1973 by Mahmut Gologlu portrayed Mithradates as a local hero and his Pontic Kingdom as "Turkey's First National State." Thanks to Murat Arslan for summarizing his book and the introduction by Dr. Sencer Sahin. Comparison of M's and Alexander's protection of Asia, Arslan 2007, 529. Turkey's silence on M may be associated with accusations of Turkish genocide against Greeks living in Pontus and Armenians after World War 1.

8. Reinach 1890, 418–7; McGing 1986, 176–79. Erciyas 2006, 4–8, for sources and evidence for M's reign. Mastrocinque 1999, 59–75, 119–22, ancient sources and inscriptions. Højte 2009a.

9. Diodorus's hostility to Rome, Sacks 1990, 134–37. Cicero: Balsdon 1979, 170–76; Sanford 1937. Lands outside Rome's sphere, see Sitwell 1986.

10. Sir Arthur Conan Doyle, "Hound of the Baskervilles."

11. "Broken shards," Holland 2003, xx. Cf Lee 2007, 280. Goodkin 1986, 204, 216 n3. M unique: McGing 2009; Erciyas 2006, 121.

12. Euripides' *Helen* (412 BC) was based on a version of an alternative legend about Helen recounted in Herodotus 2.113–20. Livy 9.17–19.

13. Gaddis 2002, 100–109, principles and rules for counterfactual reasoning.

14. Ferguson 2000, introduction. Notable examples of narrative ancient histories: Holland 2003, Reinach 1890, Champlin 2003, Strauss 2004 and 2009, Lee 2007.

15. Summerer 2009. Bengston 1975, Matyszak 2008, vi, 152.

16. Alcock 2007. Tezcan 2003 and 2007, 91–102. Black Sea Trade Project, www.museum.upenn.edu/Sinop. Centre for Black Sea Studies, Aarhus, Denmark: www.pontos.dk. Højte 2009a. Chinese Eurasian studies: www.eurasianhistory.com/english.htm.

17. Mayor 2009; Maskiell and Mayor 2001; Mayor, "Dirty Tricks in Ancient Warfare," *MHQ: Quarterly Journal of Military History* 2 (Autumn 1997): 32–37; Mayor, "Amazons," *Reader's Companion to Military History* (Boston: Houghton Mifflin, 1996).

18. Summerer 2009. Kopff 2007, director, conservative Center for Western Civilization, Univ. Colorado, Boulder, was arguing in favor of defending the American "empire" against terrorists.

19. Merry 2005, 217–21, ch 12, "Ghosts of Mithridates."

20. In November 2006, for example, Abu Ayyub al-Masri, leader of al-Qaeda in Mesopotamia, vowed that the Islamic jihad would destroy "Rumieh" (Arabic for the Roman Byzantine Empire). K. Gajendra Singh, ambassador to Jordan during 1990–91 Gulf War; to Turkey and Azerbaijan 1992–96. Singh's editorials against the Iraq War appear in Islamic news service Al-Jazeerah and in *Asia Times*. Singh 2003 and 2006, per cor Dec 2006.

21. Kay 2008, notes that Cicero's *Pro lege Manilia* is "remarkable in its contemporary tone. If we substitute 'US sub-prime loans' for 'Asian monies' and the UK banking system for 'the system of monies which operates in the Roman Forum,' Cicero's speech could have been written about the current credit crisis." Piracy: Harris 2006.

22. Champlin 2003, 34–35, 236–37, esp 46–47 on handling legendary and contradictory ancient biographical reports.

23. Balsdon 1979, 60–64.Challenges to the Eurocentric historical view of the divides East/West, Greece and Rome/Persia, barbarian/civilized, evil/good are gaining momentum. See Summerer 2009 and Alain Gresh, Jan 7, 2009, http://mondediplo. com/2009/01/07west, citing Touraj Daryaee, "Go Tell the Spartans," March 14, 2007, Iranian.com and Tzvetlan Todorov's *La peur des barbares* (Paris: Laffont, 2008).

· 1 ·

KILL THEM ALL, AND LET THE GODS SORT THEM OUT

1. Unless otherwise noted, all references to Appian are from *Mithradatic Wars.* Massacre: Appian 22–23, 54, and 61–63. Appian's sources, Mastrocinque 1999, ch 4; McGing 1986, 176–79; massacre, 106, 111, 113–18. Intelligence mystery: Sheldon 2003, 85, and 2005, 74–77. The chapter title comes from a Latin phrase first used during the Inquisition, ca 1210: *Neca eos omnes. Deos suos agnoset.*

2. Valerius Maximus 9.2 and Memnon 22.9 reported 80,000 dead; Plutarch *Sulla* 24 puts the death toll at 150,000. Others, Appian 61–63; Cicero *Pro Flacco* 25 and *Pro lege Manilia* 5.11; and Velleius 2.18, say that "all Italians" in Anatolia were wiped out. Sarikakis 1976, 255. Some, eg Brunt 1971, 38, and McGing 1986, 111–18, who are skeptical about the high death toll assumed a lower Italian population overall. Ñaco del Hoyo et al. 2009, 6–8. The lower estimate of 80,000 is now generally accepted as at least plausible. As Badian pointed out (1981, 66 and n22), "The extent of the massacre is, in general terms, not in doubt." Population is very difficult to assess for this period. Rome's census of 114 BC recorded 394,000 Roman citizens (men only? or including women?) in Italy and elsewhere. In 70 BC, Romans in Italy and the empire were said to number about 910,000. The figure of about 4 million was recorded for 28 BC: that census probably included men, women, and children over age 1. It has been estimated that the total population of the Roman Empire in AD 14 was about 54 million people. See Matthew White's useful "Body Count of the Roman Empire" (2002). Thanks to Walter Schiedel and Bruce Hitchner for discussions of the death toll and population figures. Roman settlers "swarmed" to Asia Minor: Warmington 1969, 77. Magie 1950, 2:1103 n37, the higher number may have been inflated by Sulla in battlefield speeches to motivate Roman troops. Reinach gave the massacre the name "Ephesian Vespers" (after the Sicilian Vespers of 1282, when native Sicilians killed French colonists); it is also known as Asian or Roman Vespers. Reinach 1890, 129–32; Duggan 1959, 61–62. Ballesteros Pastor 1996, chs 8 and 10.

3. Pergamon, first capital of Roman Asia: Rigsby 1988, 137–41; mixed demographics of Hellenistic cities in Asia, 130–37. Greek cities under Roman rule, Gleason 2006.

4. Adramyttion: McGing 1986, 117. Ephesus: Rigsby 1996, 385–90. Pliny 36.21; Paul, Acts 19.27; cf Pausanias 4.31.8. "Barbarians" was used by the Greeks to denote non-Greeks; the Romans used the term for non-Greeks and non-Italians, even for very civilized cultures.

5. Rigsby 1996, 1–31, 110, 173, 177, 184, 362, 366, 385–90, 400–420, 427, 582–83. Cos spared Romans who fled to Temple of Asclepius: Tacitus *Annals* 4.14.3. Extending asylum at Ephesus: Strabo 14.1.23. Alexander abided by *asylia* for runaway slaves in Babylonia: Plutarch *Alexander* 42.1–2.

6. Caunus, Tralles: Bean 1989, 139–51, 177–79. Smith 1890. Cassius Dio fragment 101.1; McGing 1986, 116.

7. Rigsby 1996, 402–3.

8. Appian 23. Augustine *City of God* 3.22, written in AD 413; other pre-Christian disasters for Rome, see 2.24, 3.7, and 3.23.

9. Sarikakis 1976, 262–64, compared the killing to nineteenth-century massacres of Armenians and Greeks by Turks in Anatolia, and suggested the killing of Romans was carried out by urban mobs of debtors and slaves, rather than by Asian Greeks. Amiotti 1980 claims the killing was done by Greek lower classes and merchants, rather by than indigenous Anatolians. McGing 1986, 113–17, 122, discusses M's initial appeal to both upper and lower classes in Asia and rebels in Italy, noting, "It has usually been assumed that the massacre was carried out by the 'rabble' and it has been argued that [M] represented the 'lower' classes in a great war against their Roman and 'upper' class repressors" (113). Jewish communities were well integrated, generally wealthy citizens of the Anatolian cities of Ephesus, Pergamon, Adramyttion, Aphrodisias, Apamea, Laodicea, Sardis: Mitchell 1995, 2:32–37. Cassius Dio, fragment 109, declares the later massacres of Greeks by Sulla far exceeded the terror of 88 BC. Roman historian Tacitus was also very critical of Roman brutality. Greco-Western Asian hatred of Roman avarice, and Roman self-criticism, Sanford 1937 and 1950; Buitenwerf 2003, 222–23. Arslan 2007, 159–74, sees the killings in 88 BC as a "common, voluntary revolt" by all ethnic groups against harsh Roman administration. Cicero: Balsdon 1979, 168 and n42.

10. Alcock 20047. Roman differences stood out in Anatolia, Balsdon 1979, 220. Mastrocinque 1999, 54–59. Mitchell 1995, 1:30.

11. "Enlightened" kingship traditions of ancient Persia, Widengren 1959, 244. Slaves, Strabo 14.5.2. Thanks to Walter Scheidel for demographic information about slaves; see Scheidel 2005. Galen of Pergamon (b. AD 130) on Roman slaves in Anatolia, *De Propr. Anim.* 9. Brunt 1971, 40.

12. Classic study of Roman slavery: Hopkins 1978. See also Balsdon 1979, 77–81. Tattoos: Mayor 1999; punitive tattooing of slaves and criminals, Jones 1987. The Monumentum Ephesinum, legal inscription at Ephesus, dates to 1st century BC. This long Roman customs law decrees that slaves imported to and from Asia must be tattooed "tax paid" by the tax-farming company; see *Epigraphica Anatolia* 14 (1989), sec 51, p 151 (thanks to Christopher Jones).

13. Ephesians descended from slaves, Athenaeus 6.267. Runaway slave at Ephesus: Rigsby 1988, 138. Cures at Temple of Asclepius, Pergamon: Bean 1979, 60–61. Slaves and Mithradates: McGing 1986, 114–16, 128–29. Duggan 1959, 62: number of freed slaves, 6,000, lends support to the death toll of 80,000.

14. "Credible commitments" and "precommitments": economic game theory applied to conflicts among nation-states by 2005 Nobel Prize winner Thomas C. Schelling. Credit collapse, described by Cicero: Kay 2008.Trumpet: Plutarch *Sulla* 7; Diodorus of Sicily (hereafter Diodorus) frag 38–39.5. Halley's Comet appears about every 76 years; it was visible summer 87 BC. Gurzadyan and Vardanyan 2004. Comets sinister omens for Rome, see Ch 2.

15. For some, M's coordinated strike against noncombatant citizens of an enemy empire in 88 BC, intended to drive Rome out of the Near East, evokes resemblances to modern terror attacks on Western targets, especially Islamic jihadist Osama bin Laden's synchronized attack on three US targets, September 11, 2001 (four commercial air-

planes hijacked in different cities deliberately crashed into the World Trade Center, New York City, and the Pentagon in Washington, DC). Merry 2005; Kopff 2007. Osama bin Laden's intended victims were noncombatants; the motive was to force the United States to alter its foreign policy. Unlike M's plan, bin Laden's reportedly entailed selecting targets for symbolic value, and the death toll was higher than he expected.

16. Boudicca's insurgency: Tacitus *Annals* 14.29–39 says 70,000 perished; Cassius Dio 62.1–12 says 80,000 and gives ghastly details. Warmington 1969, 77. King Herod's order to kill all Jewish male infants in Bethlehem (Matthew 2.16–18) could be classified as genocidal, since it was intended to stifle reproduction.

17. Definition of genocide: the attempt to annihilate an ethnic, religious, national, or political group. In a comparative study of genocide in history, Jonassohn and Bjornson 1998, 190–91, include the massacre of 88 BC as a case study of historical examples of genocide. Holt 2006 and Eliot 1972 discuss the difficulties of quantifying man-made death tolls with precision and moral response to the vast "nation of the dead," countless victims of mass violence in human history. Genocide as an "exercise in community-building": Alcock 2007.

18. US Federal Bureau of Investigation defines terrorism as the "unlawful use of force against persons or property to intimidate or coerce a government, the civilian population, or any segment thereof, in the furtherance of political or social objectives." Bolich 2006.

19. Terrorists or freedom fighters: "Consensus on Terror" 2005. In 2005, the UN General Assembly attempted to formulate a political definition of terrorism for a comprehensive international treaty against terrorism, genocide, ethnic cleansing, war crimes, and crimes against humanity.

20. I am grateful for conversations with R. Bruce Hitchner on inhumanity in the Roman world. I have also benefited from discussions with international relations scholar Robert Keohane, Princeton, who sees the massacre of 88 BC as a clear case of ancient terrorism and genocide. Roman terrorism: Bolich 2006, Ñaco del Hoyo et al. 2009.

21. Alcock 2007, "archaeology of memory." Many Greek and Latin authors also avoided detailed discussions of the massacre, according to Sarikakis 1976, 256. Appian quotes three speeches by Sulla harping on the bloody details of the slaughter, 54, 58, and 62. For another example of very high death tolls exacted by a single leader, Pliny 7.25.92 stated that Julius Caesar killed more than one million people in his conquests, a "prodigious even if unavoidable wrong inflicted on the human race." See also Plutarch *Caesar*, one million Gauls killed, one million captured. Turkish scholar Murat Arslan (2007) surmises that the total killings by M were equal in scale to the total number of people killed by the Romans in Asia. For estimates, see White 2002.

22. Erciyas 2006, 23–24. From Erciyas's "scientific point of view," M was "brave" yet "overzealous" in his struggle against Rome. Erciyas per cor Sept 3, 2008.

23. Figures for armies and battlefield casualties in the Mithradatic Wars given by the ancient writers generally agree; they had access to official records and eyewitness memoirs, now lost. Most modern historians consider many of the numbers to be exaggerated. I state the figures given by the ancient sources and cite recent scholarly opinions in notes; Callataÿ 2000 and Pillonel 2005. It is worth keeping in mind that this period was marked by the largest armies and biggest battles in Western history, until the early modern period in Europe. Even if the figures are halved, historians agree that the magnitude of armies and of casualties was staggering in the Mithradatic Wars.

24. Cicero *Pro Flacco* 25; *Academica Priora* 2.1. Velleius 2.18. Roman attitudes toward Greeks and vice versa, Gleason 2006, 228–29, 240–42; antipathy between Romans and "barbarians," Balsdon 1979, 66–67, 161–92; "great rift between East and West," 60. Mommsen was responsible for establishing the East-West divide in the 1850s, casting M as an "oriental sultan" acting out of blind cruelty. Summerer 2009.

·2·

A SAVIOR IS BORN IN A CASTLE BY THE SEA

1. Justin 37.2. Justin's summary of Pompeius Trogus is unique for descriptions of events and perspectives outside and even hostile to the Roman Empire; Justin may have lived in the 2nd century AD. Writing in the late 1st century BC, Trogus drew on sources including lost biographies of Hellenistic kings and firsthand accounts of his relatives. Comet of 135 BC, Seneca *Natural Questions* 7.15: "There appeared a comet which was small at first [then] spread . . . its vast extent equaled the size of the Milky Way." As noted earlier, in this period, "Asia" referred to lands from the eastern Mediterranean to India. The Near and Middle East, including the lands around the Black Sea, Anatolia (called *Asia Minor* by the Romans), Armenia, Syria, Persia, Babylonia, Parthia, and Scythia, constitute Eurasia or Western Asia. Sanford 1937, 453. Ramsey 1999, 230. Athenaeus 5.213.

2. "Luster": Ramsey 1999, 198–99. Fotheringham 1919, 166: European astronomers as early as 1783 had assigned M's comets to 135 and 119 BC. Two authoritative classical encyclopedias, Pauly-Wissowa *RE* 1932, and the *Oxford Classical Dictionary*, 3rd ed, 1996, ignore the comets, as does Højte 2009a. Reinach 1890, 51 n2, offered a symbolic interpretation of the comet "fable"; 52, he dated M's birth to 132 BC. Various dates and lifespans of M given by ancient sources, see McGing 1986, 43 and n1, who accepts the year 133 for M's birth and 120 for accession at age 13; 45–46, story of the comets is "Iranian legend." The comets were "myths": Ballesteros Pastor 1996, ch 2. Comets in M's coins and propaganda, Arslan 2007, 73–76.

3. Fotheringham 1919. Han Dynasty (206 BC to AD 220) comet records and drawings: Loewe 1980, 12–14; diagram of "war banner" comet, no 639, pl 4, p 32. The comet of 135 is mentioned by Justin, Pliny 2.24.95, and Seneca; for these and other Greco-Roman and Chinese records of comets 500 BC to AD 400, see Ramsey 2007, esp years 135, 134, 119, 88, and 87 BC.

4. Ramsey 1999, esp 200 and n9, 206 and n30. Eutropius 6.12 and Orosius 6.5 (probably following Livy) give M's birthdate as 135 BC. Appian 112, M lived to be 68–69 and ruled 57 years. Strabo 10.4.10 and Memnon 22.2

5. Greco-Roman dread of comets, eg Seneca *Natural Questions*, "On Comets"; Pliny, *Natural History* 2.23. Ramsey 1999, 201 and n11; on 228–30, Ramsey speculates that M's followers reinterpreted the comets in a favorable light by referring to ancient Iranian prophecies; comet coins, minted 110–80 BC, found around the Black Sea, 216 and n71; photos of comet coins, see 245–46, figs 1–2. The crescent moon and eight-rayed star (sun) symbolized the Anatolian god Men and the Persian god Ahuramazda/Mithra, respectively, according to Rostovtzeff 1919, 91–93; Erciyas 2006, 131–32.

6. Gurzadyan and Vardanyan 2004. Halley's Comet reappeared in 87 and 12 BC and

AD 66. Tigranes' comet coins, probably issued before 69 BC, show a younger man than his other coins. Some associate Halley's appearance in 12 BC with the birth of Jesus. Augustus issued a coin with a comet in 17 BC, but by that time Romans had begun to accept Persian-influenced interpretations of comets as marking the birth or death of great leaders. Ramsey 2007, "Caesar's Comet" of 44 BC, 180, 183 (ancient sources), 196, nn21 and 23.

7. Thanks to John Ramsey for insightful discussions on comets in this era. Ramsey points out that the tiny coins issued by young M were anonymous, while Tigranes placed the comet on his tiara with his name on larger coins, perhaps signaling more confidence about the comet symbolism. Tigranes may have intended to appropriate the comets to his own reign. Ramsey 2007 notes that Tigranes' comet tail resembles the comets of 135 and 119, which had long curved dust trails; Halley's gaseous tail is never curved.

8. The comet's position in the constellation Pegasus was first proposed by Ramsey 1999, 218–28. Horse omen: Widengren 1959, 244. Pegasus coins: McGing 1986, 85, 94–95.

9. Comets shaped like swords, Pliny 2.22.89; Josephus *Jewish War* 6.5.3; 1 Chronicles 21.16; Revelation 1.16. The *harpe* was also the signature weapon of Perseus, Iranian-influenced Greek hero who beheaded the Gorgon, releasing Pegasus. Xenophon *Cyrus* 1.2.9. Perseus with *harpe* is featured on Pontic coins, Højte 2009c; McGing 1986, 35, 94.

10. Prophecies about Rome, Sanford 1937, 437–39, on messianic hopes in provinces of Rome, 446; Holland 2003, 31–58; Buitenwerf 2003. See Gruen 1984.

11. Strabo 6.4.2, Roman expansion. Brutal Roman warfare: Polybius 10.15; Livy 31.34.4; Walbank 1984, 2:215–16; Holland 2003, 3–6, 10–11; Ñaco del Hoyo et al. 2009, 12. Hatred of Rome, Appian 23; self-criticism by Romans: Cicero *Pro lege Manilia* 65, *Pro Flacco* 8.19; Tacitas *Agricola* for barbarians' grievances against Romans. Sanford 1937 and 1950; Balsdon 1979, 161–92.

12. Persian and Egyptian oracles: Widengren 1959, 248–49; Zoroastrian Bahman Yasht 3.13–15. Rome later banned the Oracle of Hystaspes under penalty of death. Sanford 1937 and 1950, 35. Star and comet omens, Lewis 1976, 68, 144–47. Oracles about Rome, Balsdon 1979, 188–89. The name Anatolia comes from *Anatolo*, ancient Greek for "rising sun or heavenly body," see Lewis 2001, preface. Lewis discusses the history of the problematic nomenclature for Asia Minor, Anatolia, the Orient, and the Near and Middle East. Prophetic texts expressing anti-Roman sentiments, Lewis and Reinhold 1990, 1:403–9. Balsdon 1979, 188–92.

13. Here I have condensed Publius's long, rambling prophecy into a single sentence in italics: full utterance in Phlegon of Tralles' *Book of Marvels*, in Hansen 1996, 32–37, 101–12. Sanford 1950, 29–30 on the story and its source; cf McGing 1986, 102–4.

14. The original Sibylline Books are probably lost; surviving versions may date from the 2nd century BC. Parke 1988; Sanford 1937, 438, 448–49. Third Book of the Sibylline Oracles and pro-Mithradates Jews in Asia, Buitenwerf 2003, 220–35, 302–10. See also Holland 2003, 31–35.

15. Athenaeus 5.211–15. McGing 1986, 84, 102, 118–21, 123. M hailed as a god: Widengren 1959, 245, 248–49, in Iranian royal traditions, M would be seen as a divine savior, proven by his birth legends, similar to those of Cyrus, Mithra, and Zarathustra.

16. McGing 1986, 170 and 107 (quotes), 102–8, 122, 149–50.

17. Dionysus associated with rebellion against Rome, Strauss 2009, 33–35. Neverov 1973. One of M's maternal ancestors was called Dionysus, Appian 10. Dionysus in inscriptions and coinage of 105–80 BC, Erciyas 2006, 117, 119, 133, 135, 165.

18. M's lightning story, reported by Plutarch *Moralia* 624 B and *Quaestiones Convivales* 1.6.2, is unsensational and naturalistic: "While Mithradates was an infant, lightning burnt his cradle but did not harm him, only leaving a little mark on his brow, which was covered by his hair when he grew up." Plutarch remarked that the nickname "Dionysus" was deemed fitting because of M's capacity for wine. Lightning and Alexander, Plutarch *Alexander* 2.1–5, 6.3. Lightning plus horse omen designated Darius king of Persia: Herodotus 3.86–93. Savior-king identified by special marks, Widengren 1959, 249, 256. Sibylline Books allude to lightning marking great rulers, Buitenwerf 2003, 228, and see eg Artemidorus, *Interpretation of Dreams* in Lewis 1976, 68–69. Lightning predicted birth of Emperor Augustus, Suetonius *Augustus* 94. See Ramsey 1999, 199 and nn4 and 118; and Widengren 1959, 248–49.

19. According to Appian 112, 115–16, M was sixteenth in descent from Darius I and inherited his treasures. Pontic rulers, Eder and Renger 2007, 110–12. See also Polybius 5.43.2; Sallust *Histories* 2.73–85; Justin 38.7.1; Tacitus *Annals* 12.18. Since Reinach 1890, 3–5, M's Persian and Macedonian ancestry was dismissed as pretentious propaganda. The "ancestry [was] fictitious," "all propaganda invented . . . in the time of Mithradates Eupator, to give added respectability and nobility," according to McGing 1986, 13, 14–15, 35–38, 95. "Later propaganda": B. McGing, "Mithradates" in *Oxford Classical Dictionary*, 3rd rev. ed, 1996. But M's claims are supported by ancient sources: see the painstaking study of evidence by Bosworth and Wheatley 1998, now accepted by McGing 2009, 2–3, and 2003, 84. M's descent from Cyrus, Darius, Seleucus Nikator, and perhaps Alexander, accepted by Arslan 2007 and Saprykin and Maslennikov 1995, among others. On M's Macedonian bloodline, see Ballesteros Pastor 1996, ch 1. Macedonian-Persian relationships: Plutarch *Alexander* 70–71. Barsiné and son murdered by Cassander, Pausanias 9.6.1.

20. After the massacre of 88, Cos welcomed M, turning over Cleopatra III's young grandson and treasure; M raised the boy in royal style. Appian 23 and 117. M associated with Alexander, Glew 1977, 254–55; McGing 1986, 44–46, 99, 101–2, 107, 141–42. Ptolemy hijacks Alexander's body, Aelian *Historical Miscellany* 12.64.

21. Maskiell and Mayor 2001, 24–26, symbolic and literal meanings of donning another's robe or royal khilat in Greece, Persia, India, and Old Testament. In Plutarch *Alexander* 18.6–8, Darius dreams that Alexander wears his royal robe. In Xenophon, *Cyrus* 1.4.26, future king of Persia presents his magnificent robe to most beloved friend. Persian king's gift of a robe, *dorophorike*: Aelian *Historical Miscellany* 1.22, also 1.32. In the Sibylline Books, a purple cloak confers high status: Buitenwerf 2003, 228. Jerome, *Life of Paul*, Bishop St. Athanasius's robe, and Paul's tunic inherited by St. Anthony. According to John 19.23, a Roman soldier obtained the mantle worn by Jesus after the Crucifixion. Today that relic is claimed by two cities: "Holy Coat," *Catholic Encyclopedia*. Elvis Presley's comet-design cape sold for $24,000 at Dick Clark's Rock and Roll Memorabilia auction, Dec 1, 2006. Hassan Nasrallah's robe displayed to Hezbollah followers across Lebanon, *Time* magazine, Dec 11, 2006.

22. Comparisons of M and Alexander, Arslan 2007 nn114, 122–23, 137, 140–41, 150.

23. Reinach 1890, 49–56, devoted a chapter to imagining M's "joyful" youth. Modern historians, including McGing 1986 and Ballesteros Pastor 1996, decline to speculate on M's youth, commenting on the legendary quality of the ancient reports. Holland 2003, 43, dismisses M's early biography as "florid propaganda, read[ing] like a fairytale." Memnon 22.2 says only that M was a "serial poisoner in childhood." Appian (112) says only that M was an "orphan" when crowned king. Strabo 10.4.10 mentions M's birth in Sinope. Duggan, the popular historical novelist who wrote M's biography in 1958, spent only a few pages on M's youth. Novelist Michael Curtis Ford 2004, 23–30, imagines a few scenes from M's boyhood memories.

24. Rank, Raglan, and Dundes 1990 reprints Rank and Raglan's original works. See appendix 1 for the heroic traits and scoring. Joseph Campbell's *Hero with a Thousand Faces* (1949) focused on the milestones of the hero's quest or journey, see Rank, Raglan, and Dundes 1990, introduction. Scores for ancient and modern heroes, from diverse cultures such as Java, Ireland, Egypt, and the United States, are widely available. Thanks to Dr. Thomas J. Sienkewicz and students, Monmouth College, for several scores cited here; to Sage Adrienne Smith for Harry Potter's score; and to Barry Strauss for Spartacus's score. For a satire of Raglan's mythic hero system, see Utley 1965 (thanks to Ted Champlin). Matyszak 2008, vi, rejects "hero" status for M.

25. Snowball Effect: Barber and Barber 2004, 146, "possibility may be restructured as probability and then as fact, which may entrain yet other probabilities which come in turn to be told as fact." Propaganda is a modern concept; perhaps it is anachronistic to apply this concept to antiquity.

26. Cyrus's life story, Herodotus 1.108–30. Cf Champlin forthcoming for evidence that Roman Emperor Tiberius consciously "channeled" the life of Homer's Odysseus. See Champlin's 2006 working paper: www.princeton.edu/~pswpc/pdfs/champlin/090602.pdf. Cyrus the Great was the original example of mythic hero model: Rank, Raglan, and Dundes 1990, 22–31. See Arslan 2007 on M's conscious emulation of Alexander as a "savior" who liberated Anatolia from Persian tyranny.

27. "Ostension" coined by semiotician Umberto Eco to describe actions that substitute for words; the concept is applied by folklorists to actions in real life guided by legends and myths. Definitions, examples, and publications, see John Lundberg, www.ostension.org; and see Kvideland 2006.

28. Herodotus 1.136–39. Eunuchs: Xenophon, *Cyrus* 7.5.58–69; Strauss 2004, 53–54, 58–59. Balsdon 1979, 227–29; Guyot 1980; Reinach 1890, 405; McGing 2009.

· 3 ·

EDUCATION OF A YOUNG HERO

1. I elaborate on Justin 37.2. Ghosts of charioteers panic racehorses, Pausanias 6.20.15–19. Alexander's horsemanship, Plutarch *Alexander* 6. McGing 1986, 44, suggests that Justin misunderstood royal Persian education, and that the horse story was invented by M's supporters to foster comparisons with Alexander. Xenophon *Cyrus* 1.4.5–9 described young Cyrus's risk taking and skills in riding and hunting.

2. M's personality, Bekker-Neilsen 2004, Olbrycht 2009, McGing 2009.

3. Poisoning in antiquity, Cilliers and Retief 2000.

4. Strabo 10.4.10, 12.3.11. Plutarch *Pompey* 42, M also considered Gaius son of Hermaeus a "foster brother."

5. Strabo 10.4.10, 11.2.18. See H. L. Jones, introduction, Loeb ed of Strabo's *Geography*, 1:xiii–xvii. Strabo's life and Theophilus: Richards 1941, 81. Strabo also wrote a history, now lost. See Bowersock 2008 on Strabo and M.

6. Rostovtzeff 1921, 223. Iranian culture in Pontus, McGing 1998; Mitchell 1995, 2:14–30. Greek cities under Roman rule, Gleason 2006.

7. Anatolian history after Alexander, see Mitchell 1995, 1:29–31, 81–85. History of Pontus through reign of Euergetes, Hind 1994, 130–37; Højte 2009a. Bosworth and Wheatley 1998; Reinach 1890, 1–47; McGing 1986, 1–42, 93 and n27. Black Sea: West 2003. Strabo 10.4.10; 11.2.18; 12.2.13; 12.3.15, 33, 39; 14.1.48; Justin 37–38; Valerius Maximus 1.8; Plutarch *Lucullus* 18.

8. Religion in Pontus, Saprykin 2009. Persian religion and customs, Herodotus 1.130–42, see 1.138, Persian hatred of lying and debt; also Xenophon *Cyrus*. Strabo 15.3.13–14, Persians worship "the Sun whom they call Mithra." Magi and Zoroastrianism, Ammianus Marcellinus 23.6.32–8. Fire, Widengren 1959, 251; Champlin 2003, 227–29. Royal name *Mithradates* indicates that authority to rule was "given by Mithra," endowing kings with divine light, Wynne-Tyson 1972, 21–26. Greek, indigenous, Persian, Jewish religions in Anatolia, Mitchell 1995, 1:11–35; exploitation by taxation, 1:30; ancient Iranian influences in Anatolia, 2:29–30. Roman tribute, taxation, extortion, moneylending: Balsdon 1979, 167–70.

9. Reinach 1890, 52–53. Gleason 2006, 243–47. Herodotus 1.136–39.

10. Pliny 25.14.33 (*pharnaceon*); for other medicinal plants discovered by another king of Pontus (Polemon) and M, see 25.7.22–25.20.46; many antidotes and poisons known to the Magi are discussed in Pliny bk 25. Paradox of poisons, Newman 2005, 7–9. Scientific survey of poisons known in antiquity, Cilliers and Retief 2000, 91–95; antidotes 96.

11. Memnon 22.2 (Jacoby fragment, FGrH 434).

12. Xenophon *March* 5; see Lee 2007, 36–37, 169–71.

13. Xenophon *Cyrus* 1.1.3–5 (secrets of power); 8.1.1, 8.2.9, 8.8.2 (good father).

14. Xenophon *Cyrus* 6.1.27–30, 50–53; 6.2.7–8; 7.1.31 and 47; 8.3.33; Xenophon *Hellenica* 4.1.17–19.

15. Equestrian victory inscriptions, McGing 1986, 92. M drove sixteen horses abreast: Appian 112. Suetonius *Nero* 24; Champlin 2003, 59.

16. Xenophon *Cyrus* 1.2.8–13; Strabo 15.3.17–19.

17. A bronze statuette in the British Museum has been identified as M dressed as a wrestler or a charioteer, barefoot, wearing wide belt, short tunic, and lionskin cap like Hercules, holding a wreath: Oikonomides 1962; McGing 1986, 100; Erciyas 2006, 156–58; but Jakob Munk Højte is dubious, per cor Feb 4, 2009.

18. History of Mithradatid dynasty and lands, Bosworth and Wheatley 1998. Scythians and other nomads, West 2003, 154, 156–57; Batty 2007; Sitwell 1986.

19. Appian 10. Rome's client-kings, Eich and Eich 2005.

20. Strabo 11.2.12 describes pirates' ships and methods. Appian 92–96. See Charachidzé 1998 for design of Black Sea pirate ships for carrying slaves and booty from antiquity on. Extraordinary wealth of Pontus in grave goods: Erciyas 2006, esp ch 3.

21. Road system of Pontus: Munro 1901. Pliny 8.47.109. Black Sea fishery, King 2004, 32–33. Castoreum was also used in perfumes.

22. Crimea, Taman, northern Black Sea during M's reign, Saprykin and Maslennikov 1995. Erciyas 2006, 76, 163–66. Black Sea history and geography, Ascherson 1995; King 2004.

23. Fossils of Taman, Mayor 2000, Phlegon of Tralles in Hansen 1996, 45. Strabo 11.2.10. Logan 1994.

24. Persian-style luxuries: Plutarch *Alexander* 36–37, 40; Justin 38; Athenaeus 5 and 12; Valerius Maximus 9.

25. Plutarch *Lucullus* 31. For detailed digital topographical maps of entire Black Sea region, based on American National Geospatial Intelligence Agency data, see Centre for Black Sea Studies http://www.pontos.dk/e-resources/terrain-models. For chronological royal records of Pontus and its neighbors, Eder and Renger 2007.

26. *Oxford Clasical Dictionary* sv "Hannibal." Hannibal's influence on M: Sonnabend 1998. Hannibal's ruses, Mayor 2009, 154–55, 188–89.

27. Justin 36.4; Plutarch *Demetrius* 20.2; Diodorus 34–35.3; Rigsby 1988, 123–27. On Galen *Antidotes* 1.1 and Attalus, see Scarborough 2007, proposing that Nicander of Colophon, a contemporary compiler of antidotes, worked with Attalus III. Attalus: Totelin 2004, 3 n10. Portrait of Attalus, Holland 2003, fig 4. M world's first "experimental toxicologist": Griffin 1995.

28. Lewis and Reinhold 1990, 1:344–45. Attalus's will, Mitchell 1995, 1:29–30, 62. Aristonicus and M claimed the will a forgery, McGing 1986, 157–58; see Ussher 2007, 486, 133 BC, for ancient sources on Attalus's will. Delphic Oracle predicting Aristonicus's rebellion, Diodorus 34–35.13. Leucae, Tralles, and Phocaea: Bean 1979, 97–98, and Bean 1989, 177–78. Blossius: Scullard 1970, 25, 31, 40. Deep causes of Mithradatic Wars and M's early expansions, Mastrocinque 1999, 18–28. Romans underestimated local loyalty to Aristonicus, Sanford 1950, 31–32.

29. Desperation: *Oxford Classical Dictionary* sv "Aristonicus." Strabo 13.4.2–3; 14.1.38–39 (resourceless people).

30. Details of Aristonicus's revolt: Eutropius 4.20 (Crassus); Orosius 5. Appian 2 and 9; Florus 1.35, 2.7.7–8; Justin 36.4, 37; Livy 59.14; Valerius Maximus 3. Sallust *Catiline War* 55. Children of the Sun, Arewordik' or Arevordik, Robert Bedrosian, "Soma among the Armenians, Ethnobotany . . ." www.rbedrosian.com; Gevork Nazaryan, www.Armenianhighland.com, 2006; and Raffi 1959. Apollo wept, Obsequens in Lewis 1976, 120.

31. Statue of Aristonicus, Alexander's friend, in Delos, Plutarch *Fortune of Alexander* 334. Hellebore in sieges: Mayor 2009, 100–103, Aristonicus, 109–10.

32. West 2003, 158–61.

33. Strabo 12.3.11. Ancient knowledge of petroleum incendiaries: Mayor 2009, 207–8, 228–31. This image of Medea is from Apollonius of Rhodes *Voyage of the Argo* 3.844–62; Euripides *Medea* (the plant is unknown). Argonauts: King 2004, 40–42.

34. Baby's resemblance to adult M: Andreae 1994–95 and 1977; Højte 2009c. After defeat of M in 63 BC, Pompey installed this Hercules statue in his Theater on the Field of Mars, Rome; the statue was discovered in 1507 in Campo dei Fiori, near ruins of Pompey's Theater, and now in Museo Chiaramonti, Vatican. Prometheus group, McGing 1986, 100.

35. See McGing 2009 for insights on M's relationship with Alexander.

36. Plutarch *Fortune of Alexander* 335, *Alexander* 4; Pliny 35.10.92. For M portraits with left-inclined head, Høtje 2009c. M's imitation of Alexander, McGing 1986, 101–2.

37. Xenophon *Cyrus* 1.3. Fox 2004. Plutarch *Alexander* 32 and 45, and *Fortunes of Alexander* 330. Strabo 11.13.9–10.

38. Persian birthday banquets, Herotodus 1.130–35.

39. I've imagined M's father's death scene, based on reports that he was poisoned at a banquet. Various historians give M's age at his coronation as 11–13; the evidence of the comets, supported by Chinese sources, suggests he was about 14 in 120 BC (see Ch 2). McGing 1986, 41–43 and Ramsey 1999. Strabo 10.4.10; Justin 37; Appian 112. See Peck 1898, sv "Mithradates" for disputed dates; eg according to Memnon, Mithradates was 13 when his father died, while Appian says he reigned 57 years and died at age 68–69, and Cassius Dio gives his age at death in 63 BC as 75. See Ussher 2007, 495, 124 BC, for ancient sources on date of Euergetes' death.

40. Justin 9.6–7; Plutarch *Alexander* 2.1–5, 77.5, Pausanias 8.7.5.

41. Reinach 1890, 50–51, 53. The motives for murdering Euergetes are unknown.

42. We know that M kept his weapons close at all times; I suggest that he emulated Alexander's habit. Plutarch *Alexander* 19.

43. The Styx waterfall near Nonacris in Arcadia is the highest in Greece. Plutarch *Alexander* 77.1–5, Pausanias 8.17.6. Herodotus 6.74.Today locals avoid drinking from Mavro Nero (Black Water) River and say no vessel can hold it. I thank Antoinette Hayes, exploratory toxicologist at Wyeth Pharmaceuticals, for suggesting the extremely toxic bacteria calicheamicin (discovered by scientists in caliche clay in the 1980s and now used as an anticancer drug) as a possible basis of this myth, per cor March 9, 2007.

44. Justin 37.2.4–6. Plutarch *Alexander* 8, 19.4–10, and 41.5–10. Harmatelia snake antidote, Mayor 2009, 89–90 and references.

45. Mayor 2009, 145–48. Xenophon *March* 4.8; Lee 2007, 29–30, 229–30. Ducks, quail, and goats thrive on toxic hellebore, Lucretius 4. Venomous fish, Aelian *On Animals* 17.31.

46. Strabo 12.3.40–41; see also 11.14.9, arsenic mines in Armenia.

47. Toxic minerals: Pliny 33.31.98, 33.32.99–100, 33.36–41, 35.13–15, 34.55–56.178. Theophrastus *On Stones* 8.48–60, toxic minerals and mining. Healy 1999, 215–19, 235–36, 258–62. Mitchell 1995, 1:82 n23. Smith 1890, sv "Arsenikon," "Sandaracha." Aggrawal 1997. Poisonous minerals, Cilliers and Retief 2000, 95.

48. Juvenal *Satire* 6.630–34.

· 4 ·

THE LOST BOYS

1. Justin 37. Reinach 1890, 53–54.

2. Mithradates I, founder of Pontus, went into exile to escape danger and build power, Bosworth and Wheatley 1998, 161–64. Xenophon *Cyrus* 1.4.13–15 and *On Hunting*. Plutarch *Alexander* 8–14, 23, 40–41. McGing 1986, 45–47, rejected the story of M's voluntary exile as an example of propaganda deriving from Iranian legend and the desire to emulate Alexander.

3. Justin 37.2.

4. Statues and inscriptions of M on Delos, dating to 116 or 115 BC: Erciyas 2006, 122–23; McGing 1986, 88. Justin 37 relates two episodes in which M disappeared for several years, once as a youth and a second time as the true king of Pontus, traveling

incognito with friends in the lands he planned to conquer. Ballesteros Pastor 1996, ch 2, suggests that M's second expedition was a safety precaution, undertaken to enable him to escape intrigues in the court, paralleling the voluntary exile of Mithradates I.

5. From a folklorist's perspective, M's two absences from Sinope fulfill two events of the mythic hero pattern: 7, abandoned or exiled, separated from home, escapes premature death; and 8, grows up in a faraway country (see appendix 1). It is not surprising to find doublets of events with a folkloric aura in later retellings (heroic episodes are doubled for Cyrus and Alexander too). Peck 1898: "whatever truth there is" in Justin's accounts, "it is certain that when [M] attained manhood . . . he was not only endowed with consummate skill in all martial exercises, and possessed of a bodily frame inured to all hardships, as well as a spirit to brave every danger, but his naturally vigorous intellect had been improved by careful culture."

6. Justin 37.2.7. Xenophon *Cyrus* 6.2.25–32, Cyrus's detailed list of provisions for an expedition.

7. Representations of geography had been developed by Persians and Romans by this time, so we can guess M had access to a map or diagram of the road system, towns, and rivers of Pontus; Harley and Woodward 1987. Forts: McNicoll and Milner 1997.

8. Landscape and roads of Pontus, Strabo 12.3; Munro 1901; Stoneman 1987, 207–20. Erciyas 2006, 37–52. Zeus as Ahuramazda, McGing 1986, 10. Sacrifices to Zeus Stratios, Appian 66, 70; M's sacrifice on the summit of Buyuk Evliya Dag, Mitchell 1995, 2:22; Erciyas 2006, 41–43.

9. Amasia castle on the summit of Harsena Dag, Fleischer 2009.

10. Strabo 12.3.38–42. Topography, history, and archaeology of Pontus, Erciyas 2006, 37–120; Amasia fortress ruins, 41.

11. Strabo 12.3.38. Munro 1901, 60–61. Geography, forts, tribes of Pontus: Strabo 12. Reinach 1890, 54 and n4, 55. Cohen 2007, 386–87.

12. Duggan 1959, 29.

13. Justin 38.5.3. According to Arslan 2007, 72–113, M's distrust of Rome began in 116 BC, when Rome took back Phrygia.

14. Archaeology of the tombs, Fleischer 2009. Kings Mithradates I, II, and III, Ariobarzanes, and Pharnaces I were buried here; probably Mithradates IV and Euergetes too. The tomb chambers contained more than one body, Høtje 2009b. *Xvarnah*, Persian burials, Widengren 1959, 254.

15. Strabo 11.8.5, 12. 3.37; Erciyas 2006, Zela, 51; coin hoards, 162–73. Munro 1901, 58–59 for Talaura.

16. Kabeira, geography, roads, archaeology: Erciyas 2006, 43–45; Men, 131–32.

17. "Poisons and witchcraft," Hind 1994, 129.

18. People and geography of the eastern Black Sea, Strabo 12.3; Soanes, 11.2.19; Turret-Folk or Mosynoeci, also called Heptacometae or Byzeres: Xenophon *March* 5.4.

19. Foraging, Aelian *Historical Miscellany* 13.24. The mysterious cherry tree (*ponticon*) and fermented drink (*aschy*) first described by Herodotus 4.21–25. Cherries, Athenaeus 2.50–51. Idyllic scene of boys fishing in antiquity, Church 1885, 10–13.

20. Boar hunting as male rite of passage in Greek myth and history: Homer *Odyssey* 19.430–58; Xenophon *Cyrus* and *On Hunting* 10. Anderson 1985.

21. Xenophon *March* 4.8.

22. M "yielded only to the pleasures of women," with no interest in male sex partners, Appian 112.

23. Quotations in italics here and below integrate several passages on love and sex from Lucretius 4.1018–1140.

24. Herodotus 1.199; Strabo 4, 11.14.16, 12.2.3 (Comana Cappadocia); Diodorus 4.83.6; Justin 18.5.4. Archaeological remains at Comana Pontica: Erciyas 2006, 48–50.

25. Mayor 2009, 221, 237. Cilliers and Retief 2000, 94.

26. Vinegar, alum: Appian 74; Mayor 2009, 220–22. Vellum, Duggan 1959, 13.

27. Alexander's *Iliad*: Strabo 13.1.27; Plutarch *Alexander* 8 and 26.

28. Alexander at Troy: Plutarch *Alexander* 15. Priam's tower, Herodotus 7.43. Homer *Iliad* 2.800–865.

29. Cyrus and warrior-queen, Herodotus 1.205; Justin 1.8, 2.4, 12.3.5–7, 42.3.7. Strabo 11.5.4, 11.11.8; Herodotus 4.105–20.

30. Herodotus 7.60–99.

·5·

RETURN OF THE KING

1. Classicist-novelist Church 1885, 286, 294, imagined M's complexion deathly pale from arsenic. Novelist Anderson 1960, 202, gave M blue fingernails.

2. Justin 37.3. Sallust *Histories* 2.87–88. Memnon 22.2. "Impossibly compressed," McGing 1986, 74, 67–108. M's early reign, Scullard 1970, 74–79, Reinach 1890, 55–56: "At age 20, when he reclaimed his crown, Mithridates radiated vigor and beauty." His mother Laodice deserved death "a thousand times over," but M showed clemency in putting her in prison, where she later died. Duggan 1959, 31–32, imagines that M first claimed Sinope, then marched on Laodicea with his "mob." In Duggan's scenario, Laodice surrendered, and the merciful M put her in prison, where she died of natural causes, while Mithradates the Good was tried for treason and executed. Duggan claimed that no one ever accused M of matricide, but Memnon 22 said M murdered his mother and brother, and Appian 112 stated, "He was bloodthirsty and cruel . . . the slayer of his mother, his brother, three sons, and three daughters."

3. Examples of incest in tangled family relations of Syria and Egypt during M's time, Justin 39. Herodotus 3.31, *hvaetvodatha*, cited by Reinach 1890, 295 n4. Duggan 1959, 33–34; McGing 1986, 35. Statues identified as M and Laodice, his sister/wife, in Delos, Erciyas 2006, 155. Hero script, Ch 2 and appendix 1. M's sisters: Plutarch *Lucullus* 18.

4. Krateuas's books influenced the famous physician Dioscorides. Copies of Krateuas's drawings survive in medieval manuscripts. Pliny 25.26–28.

5. For recent scientific literature on snake venom's medicinal uses, see www.medicalnewstoday.com, Hopkins 1995, and Ch 11. Agari: Appian 88; Strabo 11.2.11. Agaric mushrooms (Armenian *T'nipi* and *K'ujulay/K'tuch'ula*) were sacred to Mithra, and common in Pontus and Armenia: Bedrosian, "Soma among the Armenians, Ethnobotany," www.rbedrosian.com. See also Cilliers and Retief 2000, 93.

6. Stuart 2004, 114. Pliny 25.1.1–3.

7. *Dikairon* poison: Mayor 2009, 73–74, 86–88, with notes; Aelian *On Animals* 4.36, 4.41.

8. Mayor 2009, 91–92, 148–51 and nn.

9. Louvre Museum Collections text for fig 5.1 by Charlotte Lepetoukha. Balsdon

1979, 215-16, 214-59 on differences of appearance and customs among Romans and other peoples. Coin portraits: McGing, 1986, 97-100; Erciyas 2006; and Højte 2009c.

10. Persian dagger: Xenophon *Cyrus* 1.2.9; Josephus *Jewish Antiquities* 20.186, describes the weapons of *sicarii*, "a type of bandit whose numbers were rising in this era, and who used small swords, which were like the Persian *acinaces* in size and curved like the *sica*, which gave these bandits their name." Plutarch *Alexander*. Appian 111, M's poison was kept in the scabbard.

11. Aelian *On Animals* 7.46.

12. Plutarch *Quaestiones Conviviales* 6.

13. Inopus statue, Delos, Erciyas 2006, 122-25, 134-43, 155; Højte 2009c. Charbonneaux 1951 identified the statue as M, noting similarity to Venus de Milo of the same era. Louvre Collection description by Lepetoukha; McGing 1986, 100 and n70.

14. McGing 1986, 89-93 and nn. Kreuz 2009. The unidentified portraits may have been the Greek philosopher Athenion, Dionysus son of Boethius, or Metrodorus of Scepsis, listed elsewhere as special Friends of the King. Grypos, Justin 39.2.

15. Eleven other similar headless legionnaire statues in Rhodes, Pergamon, and other sites, Erciyas 2006, 158; Højte 2009c.

16. Roman history up to and during the Mithradatic Wars: Strabo 6.4.2; Eutropius 6.12.3; Florus 1.40.2; Appian 62, 112, 118-19. Festus *Brevarium* 11.3, Augustine *City of God* 5.22, Orosius 6.1.30. Sallust *Jugurthine War*; Plutarch *Sulla, Marius*. Crook, Lintot, and Rawson. 1994; Sherwin-White 1994, 229-55; Mitchell 1995, 1:29-31; Brunt 1971; Scullard 1970, 13-40 for wealth, slavery, rebellions, and reforms. Slave uprisings, rebellions, and civil conflicts in Italy, and M's envoys, at this time: Diodorus 36-37 fragments. M's "formidable" intelligence methods, Sheldon 2005, 74-77.

17. Balsdon 1979, 161, 180, and 182-92 on Rome's "bad press" and oracles of doom for Rome. Scullard 1970, 67 (coin), 66-70. Sending wolves to guard flocks is an ancient proverbial folk motif (*Motif Index* K206.1), see Cassius Dio 56.16.3. On the wars between Rome and the Italians (Social Wars), see Brunt 1971 and Scullard 1970. Coins, Erciyas 2006, 133.

18. Strabo 6.4.2, 13.1.55. Strabo often cites Metrodorus, but his writings are lost. Plutarch *Lucullus* 22. Roman conquest of Italy, Eich and Eich 2005, 4-20.

19. Balsdon 1979, ch 14, "A Generally Good Press for Rome."

20. Rome as wolf, Eich and Eich 2005. Rome's "predatory interest" in Anatolia, Hind 1994, 142.

21. Corinth, Florus 2.16.

22. Eich and Eich 2005 analyze the links between expanding hegemony and profits from taxes, tributes, and plunder, 26-29.

23. Psylli and others' immunity and antidotes to venom: Pliny 7.2.13-15.

24. Sallust *Jugurthine War*. Scullard 1970, 48-53.

25. Plutarch *Sulla* 3, and *Marius*.

26. Roman armies, Goldsworthy 2003. M's army, Matyszak 2008, 9-12.

27. Honeymoon custom, Strabo 15.3.17. McGing 2009 includes Laodice's bastard Ariathes as M's son. Duggan 1959, 42, 8 (Duggan names only 13 children of M). The name Orsabaris appears on a contemporary coin issued in Bithynia; some suggest she married Socrates the pretender, supported by M against Nicomedes IV (Ch 6). Orsabaris comes from the same Persian root, *berez*, as Barsiné, Alexander's Persian concubine. Reinach 1890, 297-98, names 20 children of M. Mithradates of Pergamon's name

strongly suggests that he was Adobogiona's son by M; she had been married to Menodotus of Pergamon (Ch 10): Strabo 13.4.3. Adobogiona's tangled family tree, see Mitchell 1995, 1:28–29, and 35 n102; Reinach 1890, 297 and n5. Phoenix "member of the royal family," see Appian 79; the name is Phoenician, Duggan 1959, 123. M killed Exipodras in 65 BC in Pantikapaion, Orosius 6.5. Orsabaris: Appian 117; for Pharnaces' birthdate, 17. M's son with Adobogiona was well educated by his father; by 64 BC he was in charge of Pergamon; he served under Julius Caesar, who gave him the Bosporan Kingdom: Peck 1898. Archelaus's son claimed to be the son of M: Strabo 12.3.34, 17.1.11. Drypetina, see Valerius Maximus 1.8.13. Drypetina's baby teeth may have been retained or wisdom teeth erupted alongside molars, doubling some teeth (thanks to Dr. Robert Hickman, DDS).

28. Appian 107. Strabo 12.3.28, names several of these strongholds, Sinora, Hydara, Basgoidariza. Names and locations of M's castles, Mitchell 1995, 1:84–85.

29. *Kurgans*, Ascherson 1996, 126–27. *Kurgan* looting in antiquity, Logan 1994.

30. Duggan 1959, 37. Silk Route north from Iran to Colchis and Pontus by land and over the Caspian Sea, Tezcan 2003. Silk and spice routes, Sitwell 1986.

31. Cicero *Pro lege Manilia* 31ff; Omerod in *Piracy in the Ancient World* (1924), cited by McGing 1986, 139, describes close relationship between M and pirates. Holland 2003, 164–71; Arslan 2007.

32. Memnon 22.3–4, M ruled Colchis and "regions beyond the Caucasus" and allied with the Parthians, Medes, Armenia, Phrygia, and Iberia (in Caucasia).

33. Scythian bow image: West 2003, 156; Ammianus Marcellinus 22.8.9–13 and 37. Black Sea Empire: Strabo 12.3.2; McGing 1986, 47–64, 169. King 2004, 47, 49. Højte 2009a.

34. On the peoples of Eurasia, Sitwell 1986, ch 3 and maps.

35. Chronology of M's conquest of Scythia and the Bosporus unknown. Reinach 1890, 57–80; Rostovtzeff 1921, 220; Erciyas 2006, 124; McGing 1986, 50–65; inscriptions, 50–52.

36. Rostovtzeff 1919, 95–96.

37. Appian 112, Justin 2.3, 37.3, and 12. 2.16. Memnon 22.4. Diophantus's brilliant campaign in Scythia, McGing 1986, 47–65, 50–51 (inscriptions thanking M in the northern Black Sea region), and 122. Pliny 16.59.137–38. On numismatic evidence for M's Black Sea Empire, Saprykin 2004.

38. McGing 1986, 57, 61, on cities at mouth of Danube. Bastarnae bravest of M's allies (Appian 69); specific Sarmatian tribes, McGing 1986, 61–63. Nomadic tribes around the north and west Black Sea region and relations with Rome and M, Batty 2007.

39. Benefits, tributes, and "enormous power" from M's Black Sea Empire, McGing 1986, 59–65; it was M "who developed the full potential of the Black Sea," 169. Hind 1994, 137–43. Saprykin 2004.

40. Justin 37.

41. Justin 37.3. McGing 1986, 66, dates this journey to 109/108.

42. Justin 37.3. Reinach 1890, 81.

43. Aelian *Historical Miscellany* 10.2. Appian 112.

44. Strabo 12.3.41, 12.5.2; Appian 9–10.

45. Herodotus 7.31; Aelian *Historical Miscellany* 2.13; Plutarch *Alexander* 9.2–3.

46. *Blue Guide to Greece* 1995, 616–17, McGing 1986, 90–92. Kreuz 2009.

47. Justin 37.3.6–7.

·6·

STORM CLOUDS

1. Justin 37.3.6–8.

2. M cultivated the Danube Gauls, and a Gaul chieftain from the Danube region, Bituitus (Bisthocus, Bituikos, Bistokos, an Allobrogesean or Arveri name), was M's bodyguard. Valerius Maximus 9.6; Florus 3.2; Galen *de Theriaca, ad Pisonem*, see Reinach 1890, 410 n2.

3. We do not know the boy's name. Reinach 1890, 86 n1, 208, supposed that Artaphernes was Laodice's bastard son. McGing 1986, 75, n37.

4. Justin 37.4. Chios inscription, published in 1932; similar inscription in Rhodes, McGing 1986, 92. See Oikonomides 1962 for a bronze statuette of M wearing Hercules' lionskin, dressed as a wrestler or charioteer, holding a victory wreath.

5. "Inconveniences of greatness" comes from the French philosopher Montaigne. Sosipater: Athenaeus 6.252. Plutarch *Moralia*, "How to Tell a Flatterer from a Friend" 14. Greek meaning of *sycophant* is "false accuser."

6. M's gargantuan appetite, Aelian *Historical Miscellany* 2.41, 12.25, and 1.27, "They say the following were gluttons"; of the 11 men named, 6 were from Anatolia. Athenaeus 10.9.

7. Justin 37.4.2. Events in this chapter, see McGing 1986, 66–88; Duggan 1959, 41–47. Scullard 1970, 40–75. M's intelligence about Roman activities, Sheldon 2005, 74–77.

8. Justin 37.4. Sallust *Jugurthine War* 37. Diodorus 36.3. Scullard 1970, 48–53. McGing 1986, 37, 68–71. Mithradates I had forts in Paphlagonia. Mithradateion fort, see Mitchell 1995, 1:33 and n74.

9. Appian 10. Justin 38.1. McGing 1986, 73–74 believes Justin's account. Reinach 1890, 90. Ballesteros Pastor 1996, ch 2, thinks Gordius acted on his own.

10. Justin 38.1.5–10; I have inserted the sounds and mood of the army, M's words, and Gordius leading the young king away. For Cappadocian chronology, Eder and Renger 2007, 105–6.

11. Justin 38.2.2. Memnon 22 gives a slightly different version. Sherwin-White 1977. McGing 1986, 72–77. It appears that M consciously copied Nicomedes' trick of renaming his son and placing him on the Paphlagonian throne. Strabo 12.2.11. So far, the body counts suggest that M was responsible for several murders: his mother, brother, and their accomplices; his sister Laodice and her accomplices, Ariathes VI, Ariathes VII, probably Ariathes VIII and Socrates the Good (below).

12. Diodorus 36.15.

13. Pliny 2.58.148; Plutarch *Marius* 17.4. See Obsequens 43 in Lewis 1976; Valerius Maximus 1.2.3; Frontinus *Stratagems* 1.11. I guess Martha's slaves were Syrians, preferred by Romans for carrying litters.

14. McCullough 1991, 112–18, imagined the meeting of Marius and M in her novel; she depicted M as a childish, dangerous "barbarian."

15. The meeting: Plutarch *Marius* 31.2–3. Valerius Maximus 2.2.4. McGing 1986, 76. Scullard 1970, 58–60. Ballesteros Pastor 1996, ch 2. On political events in Rome at this time, see Ballesteros Pastor 1999, who suggests that Marius referred specifically to the Cappadocian situation.

16. These events: Justin 38.2; Appian 9–11. McGing 1986, 83–88. According to Frontinus *Stratagems* 1.5.18, Sulla's legion fought troops commanded by M's Cappadocian general Archelaus. Events in Cappadocia, Sherwin-White 1977; Mastrocinque 1999, 29–46.

17. Tezcan 2003.

18. Armenia, Eder and Renger 2007, 94–98. Olbrycht 2009. Strabo 11.14–16; Justin 38.3. According to Duggan 1959, 44, Cleopatra was 13, Tigranes 40. I have added the detail of a gift of horses.

19. "King of Kings," Persian royal and religious title available to only one ruler at a time, Widengren 1959, 244. Tigranes' dress (he wore his tiara "even when hunting"): Kurkjian 1958, ch 13.

20. Justin 38.3.5. Coin minting, Erciyas 2006, 128–31; McGing 1986, 101, idealized portrait coins intended to portray M as the new Alexander who would liberate Asia.

21. Strabo 11.14.15; Justin 38.3; Plutarch *Lucullus* 14, 15. McGing 1986, 77–79.

22. Appian 57. Nothing is known of the assassin Alexander. Could he have been the Alexander who was later M's general in the Third Mithradatic War?

23. Alliances, Justin 38; Appian 13; Strabo 12.3.1–2. Memnon 22. Aulus Gellius 17.17 says 25 nations paid homage to M; the number was 22 according to Pliny 7.24.

24. Choice of Aquillius a mistake, even a provocation, according to Reinach 1890, 116–17.

25. Appian 11. Mastrocinque 1999, 47–58. Badian 1981, 56–58. Bithynia's kings, Eder and Renger 2007, 99–100.

26. Appian 12. Roman Senate alarmed by M's rise, but Aquillius "seriously underestimated" his military power and influence, McGing 1986, 81–88.

27. McGing 1986, 87–88. McGing 2009 (quote) reassesses M's motives, arguing that he was not a compliant Hellenistic king, but his policy was cautious, "steady escalation" to achieve his great ambitions. Strabo 13.1.66.

28. Appian 12–14. Rutilius Rufus, Livy 70; Valerius Maximus 6.4; Cassius Dio 28; see Ussher 2007 for other ancient references. Appian's sources, Ballesteros Pastor 2009. Mastrocinque 1999, 59–76; Rutilius Rufus, 54–58, 62–63; Sisenna as source for speech and dialogue, 69–79.

29. Although Appian's account of the run-up to the war is "doubtless a literary expansion . . . it contains no basic improbabilities," McGing 1986, 80, n53, citing Sherwin-White. Mastrocinque 1999, 59–72, suggests Appian's main sources, Sisenna and Sulla, recorded the speeches. See Olbrycht 2009.

30. On M's options before the first Mithradatic War, see Arslan 2007, 72–126, and Matyszak 2008, 29–33.

31. The foregoing: Appian 15–16; Memnon 22; Reinach 1890, 116–19. "Rickety throne," Duggan 1959, 45. Aquillius as first example of developing Roman policy in the last years of the Republic, and the Senate's waning power, McGing 1986, 81. Mastrocinque 1999, ch 2 and 3, portrays Aquillius in a positive light and believes the Senate was responsible for the ultimatum that caused the war; see ch 4 for these events.

32. Appian 17; Memnon 22.6.

·7·

VICTORY

1. Appian 17–18 had access to official archives, memoirs, and other documents. Memnon 22.6. The figures seem high to some scholars, but the relative strength is accepted. McGing 1986, 85 n72. Duggan 1959, 48, Appian gave "ration-strengths," including porters, muleteers, grooms, servants, and so on. Ballesteros Pastor 1996, the figures reflect M's extensive networks of alliances. According to the statistical-historical analysis by Swiss historian Pillonel (2005), Appian's troop proportions were probably accurate, but the totals were exaggerated. Pillonel's calculation suggests that, realistically, M commanded between 90,000 and 112,500 soldiers, against 36,000 to 45,000 Roman allied forces, with 16,800 to 21,000 recruits from Bithynia. Matyszak 2008, 34, points out that Romans often magnified enemy numbers; battle and maps, 35–38.

2. Duggan 1959, 48–56, for details of troops, weapons, and formations in this battle; and McGing 1986, 108–10. Fancy armaments, Plutarch *Lucullus* 7; cf Thucydides' description (6.30–31) of the magnificent Athenian navy's psychological impact in 415 BC. Later M stripped down to plain weaponry and warships, McGing 1986, 140; First Mithradatic War, 108–31.

3. Diodorus 16.86. Memnon 22.6–7 and see Munro 1901, 56.

4. Scythed chariots and ancient sources, Smith 1890, sv "falx," 429. Antiochus the Great of Syria had some scythed chariots, but they were useless at his defeat at Magnesia in 189 BC because archers quickly took out the drivers.

5. The passage that follows integrates Lucretius's descriptions in 3.656–700 and 5.1321.

6. The foregoing battle: Appian 17–18; Memnon 22. Leonardo da Vinci was fascinated by scythed chariots; drawings in Codex Arundel, folio 1030, 1487, British Museum, London.

7. Appian 18: M "treated the prisoners kindly and sent them to their homes with supplies for the journey, thus gaining a reputation for clemency." I have guessed what M said to the prisoners, based on Appian 18–19 and M's other speeches. Cf Diodorus 37.26. Plutarch *Alexander* 21, 30.6, Alexander's humane treatment of prisoners of war. Glew 1977, 254–55. Cyrus the Great also released captives: Xenophon *Cyrus* 4.4.

8. "God and savior": Diodorus 37.26; divine titles: Athenaeus 5; Cicero *Pro Flacco* 25 says M was addressed as Lord, Good Father, Savior of Asia, and Liberator. Anatolian gods "made manifest": Mitchell 1995, 2:11 and ch 16. McGing 1986, 109, see 108–25 for beginning of Mithradatic Wars. Glew 1977 discusses the propaganda benefits of M's reputation for "liberality" toward the enemy and imitation of Alexander, including mercy to enemies, and appeal of canceling debts.

9. These events, Appian 19. First Mithradatic War, Hind 1994, 144–49.

10. Cassius's letter to Nysa, McGing 1986, 109 and n100; Welles 1974, 297–98. Mithradatic inscriptions at Nysa, Rigsby 1988, 149–52, and 1996, 400–403.

11. Apamea and Nysa: Strabo 12.8.18, 13.4.14. Mitchell 1995, 2:33.

12. Strabo 13.4.14. Bean 1989, 177–87, 203–4.

13. Welles 1974, 294–99. Mithradatic inscriptions in Nysa: Rigsby 1988, 149–53. M's spies, Sheldon 2005, 74–77.

14. Welles 1974, 298.

15. McGing 1986, 110 and nn102 and 103.

16. Justin 38.3.7–9. Appian 20. Glew 1977, 254, M's tent-site intended to win over Macedonians in Anatolia, and recalled Aristonicus.

17. Appian 20. Erciyas 2006, 23.

18. Bean 1989, 189.

19. McGing 1986, M's allied cities, 94, 109–12. M's coins circulated widely in Mediterranean and East: hoards discovered in Piraeus, Athens, Italy, Anatolian coast, Delos, Macedonia, mouth of Danube, Armenia, Ukraine, Taman Peninsula, Crimea, Albania, and Caucasia (Georgia and Azerbaijan). Hoards of M's coins were buried around the Black Sea in about 85 BC, 75 BC, and 65 BC, dates reflecting crises of the three Mithradatic Wars. Erciyas 2006, 162–73; Saprykin 2004; Saprykin and Maslennikov 1995, 267, 271, 279; Callataÿ 2000; Levy 1994.

20. Italian appeal to M and his response: Diodorus 37.2.8–11. Erciyas 2006, 132–33.

21. Ballesteros Pastor 1996; McGing 1986, 114–18, 128–29, 131.

22. McGing 1986, 89, sees M using philhellenism as a "weapon to help him expand his kingdom" and a source of support for opposition to Rome; see also 107–8.

23. M's huge armor at Nemea and Delphi, Appian 112. Quintilian 8.3.82, quoting fragment of Sallust *Histories* 2.77: M "being of huge stature, carried weapons of a proportionate size." Cf Florus 1.7.4. Plutarch *Alexander* 62. La Penna 2003.

24. Justin 38.3–7 says Trogus preserved M's speech as "indirect discourse," because he believed this was more honest and objective than Sallust and Livy, who inserted what they labeled "direct quotations" in their histories but which were really reworded in their own writing styles. See McGing 1986, 106–8.

25. "Only by having agents in Rome or in the provinces, can we explain how [M] was always so well-informed about the political situation" in Rome: Sheldon 2005, 74, and see 75 for an example of his intelligence methods.

26. Cos treasures, Appian 23 and *Civil Wars* 1.11; Josephus *Jewish Antiquities* 14.111–13.

27. Monime, Plutarch *Lucullus* 18; Appian 21 and 48. Reinach 1890, 128, 147, 296.

28. Appian 22. Kallet-Marx 1995, chs 9–11, argues that Rome's expansionist policies in the East were in reaction to M's challenges.

29. Appian 21. Diodorus 37.27. Display on a donkey was a traditional ancient ritual of public humiliation.

30. On taxes, Brunt 1971, 39–40. The Greco-Latin word for treasure, *gaza*, comes from Old Persian, Balsdon 1979, 61. Appian 21.

· 8 ·

TERROR

1. Pergamon's theater seated 10,000, a logical setting for Aquillius's public execution. See Chaniotis 1997 on M's theatricality; cf Nero, who often devised punishments and enacted scenes from tragedy, Champlin 2003, 236–37. This execution scene is based on details in Appian 21; Pliny 33.14.48–49; Athenaeus 5.50, Diodorus 37.26–27 confused Aquillius with another Roman who committed suicide, cf Velleius 2.18, Aquillius "should have committed suicide." Cicero *Pro lege Manilia* 11 and *Tuscan Disputations* 5.5, Aquil-

lius beaten. Ballesteros Pastor 2009, 11, punishment by gold a traditional "Persian ordeal."

2. Roman avarice, death of Aquillius, and Orodes II's execution of Crassus in Parthia: Sanford 1950, esp 32–34; Cassius Dio 40.27; cf Plutarch *Crassus*. Death by molten gold byword for cruelty, eg Cicero *Tuscan Disputations* 5.14. In 1500s, Europeans claimed that the Aztec king avenged Spanish conquistadors' lust for gold by M's means: Theodor De Bry's painting *Great Voyages*, 1594, graphically illustrates "death by gold."

3. Mastrocinque 1999, ch 3, citing Plutarch *Pompey* 37. Balsdon 1979, 51, 220 and n42; Holland 2003, 42–43.

4. Rigsby 1988, 149–52; Rigsby 1996, 173, 177. Cities allied with M: Reinach 1890, 130; McGing 1986, 109–20.

5. Participation of governing classes and lower classes in massacre, McGing 1986, 116; Arslan 2007, 159–74. See also Introduction. Balsdon 1979, 66–71, 78–79, 170–81, 194–200, with ancient sources including Fronto. Views of Romans, Sanford 1937. Diodorus 37.3. "Mutual suspicion": Gleason 2006, 241.

6. Balsdon 1979, 73–74, for other massacres of Romans, traders, colonists, and noncombatants in Jugurtha's Numidia. Sallust *Jugurthine War* 66–68. Financial crisis in Rome, Kay 2008.

7. Champlin 2003, 236, assumes the sanity of Nero, often portrayed as mad. Bekker-Neilsen 2004 citing Gordon Banks, 1990, www.gordonbanks.com/gordon/pubs/kubricks.html.

8. Memnon 22.9; Memnon places massacre after battle for Rhodes. Sheldon 2005, 75–76 and nn. M's motives, McGing 1986, 115–16; Scullard 1970, 76–77. Mommsen declared that the massacre was a "meaningless act of brutally blind revenge." Summerer 2009.

9. Ñaco del Hoyo et al. 209, 6–8. Solidarity with Italians, Erciyas 2006, 23. See Arslan 2007 for another Turkish perspective. Kay 2008: massacre and M's invasion of Anatolia caused massive credit collapse in Rome, described by Cicero in *Pro lege Manilia*. Chios: Appian 47.

10. Jewish populations in Anatolia: Mitchell 1995, 2:32–37. Ballesteros Pastor 1996, ch 3: Roman soldiers remaining in Anatolia would be an obstacle.

11. McGing 1986, 113. Leo the Emperor, Polyaenus *Stratagems* 1, in Krentz and Wheeler 1994, 2:1011–15. Sheldon 2003, 85, 60, 63; Sheldon 2005, 74–77. Frontinus *Stratagems* 13.

12. Athenaeus 5.211–15, based on lost work by Posidonius. Other sources for Athenion and Aristion in Athens: Appian 28, 38. Posidonius FGrH 87 F 36. Strabo 9.1.20. Plutarch *Sulla* 12–13; Pausanias 1.20. See also Ballesteros Pastor 1996, ch 3; Glew 1977, 255; McGing 1986, 118–21; Mastrocinque 1999, ch 5.

13. Archons inscription, McGing 1986, 119–20. Strabo 9.1.20. Mastrocinque 1999, ch 5, proposes that a Roman soldier with Sulla was the source for Athenion and his successor, Aristion, in 88/87 BC (conflated by later historians).

14. Athenaeus 5.213–15. Ballesteros Pastor 1996, ch 3, fleeing Romans were pro-Sulla partisans.

15. Strabo 13.1.66. Scullard 1970, 77.

16. Appian 24.

17. Demetrius vs Rhodes, Mayor 2009, 212.

18. Following description of battle for Rhodes is based on Appian 24–27; Diodorus

37.28; Memnon 22.8. Hind 1994, 149–50. *Sambuca*: Polybius 8.4. Reinach 1890, 144–47. See Strauss 2005 for details of naval battles in trireme's heyday.

19. History, descriptions, and illustrations of siege equipment, Campbell 2006, esp 134–43. Crows, meteor, and Isis hurling fire recorded by Obsequens, *Book of Prodigies* for the year 88 BC, see Lewis 1976. Notably, Rhodes never removed M's statue or buildings, Cicero *Verr.* 2.2.159.

20. Appian 27. Rigsby 1996, 339. Patara, "city in the sand," is excavated by Akdeniz University, Antalya.

21. Obsequens 56, see Lewis 1976, 126. Aeschylus *Agamemnon*; Sophocles *Iphigenia* (fragments); Euripides *Iphigenia* (two plays). Magi: Herodotus 1.140, 7.114; Pliny 30.3.12. Diodorus 13.102.2, on vows to Furies. Nero, who murdered his mother, was haunted by the Furies; he requested Persian Magi to placate her ghost, Champlin 2003, 91, 98. Human sacrifice in Roman period, see Balsdon 1979, 246–48; Scullard 1970, 48. Surprisingly, there is little discussion of this interrupted sacrifice by modern historians of the Mithradatic Wars. Reinach 1890, 148, puts it in a footnote about "superstition" without commentary; see McGing 1986, 149–50, on the propaganda value of omens.

22. Appian 21, 27. Racy love letters, Plutarch *Pompey* 37.

23. Strabo 13.4.9.

·9·

Battle for Greece

1. Events in Rome and Sulla: Keaveney 2005 and Santangelo 2007. Halley's Comet of 87 BC: Ramsey 2007, 179. Rome's Eastern foreign policy: Gruen 2004.

2. McGing 1986, 123, points out that the invasion of Greece "was an excellent move"; even if M lost Greece, he had a strong bargaining position.

3. Appian 28. Appian 110; Memnon 22.7; and Pausanias 3.23.2–6 refer to Metrophanes as "Menophanes." Campaign for Delos and Greece, Hind 1994, 150–59.

4. Greek campaign, Plutarch *Sulla*; Appian 28–45; Velleius 2.18; Machiavelli *Art of War* 4.50–52, 4.68. Duggan 1959, 67–82, quote 64. Thebes, Pausanias 1.7. Reinach 1890, ch 3; McGing 1986, 121–27. Matyszak 2008, 59–72.

5. Memnon 22.10–13. First Mithradatic War and Sulla's troops, Scullard 1970, 76–79.

6. These events: Appian 29; Plutarch *Sulla*; Duggan 1959, 68.

7. Plutarch *Lucullus* 37; Justin 38.7; Erciyas 2006, 146–62. Gold, Strabo 15.3.18.

8. This scene was described in Plutarch *Sulla* 11; Duggan 1959, 69. M's theatrical gestures, Chaniotis 1997.

9. Preceding events: Valerius Maximus 6.9.6, Plutarch *Sulla* 1.2–7 and *Fortunes of the Romans* 318. Appian 28–37. Keaveney 2005. Scullard 1970, 63–87; Balsdon 1979, 168–69.

10. Greek battles remarkably detailed in ancient sources, unlike battles of later Mithradatic Wars. Piraeus: Appian 30–37, 40; Plutarch *Sulla*. Lightning, Obsequens in Lewis 1976, 127.

11. Alum, Aulus Gellius 15.1. Pliny 35.52.

12. Photos of catapult victim, 2nd century BC, Macedonia: Antikas et al. 2004.

13. Appian 37.

14. Inscribed silver bracelet published by J.-Y. Empereur in *Bulletin de Correspondance Hellenique* 105 (1981): 566–68, no 7 and fig 48. For photograph and discussion, see Habicht 1998, 15–16, fig 1. Thanks to John Ma for bringing this artifact to my attention.

15. Delphi: Herodotus 1.51. Pausanias 9.7. Diodorus frag 39–39.7. These actions are from Plutarch *Sulla* 12, 19, and 29 (amulet); Frontinus *Stratagems* 1.11; Valerius Maximus 1.2.3.

16. Appian 30; Strabo 13.1.54. Lenaeus, captured as a boy in Athens, was later freed by Pompey and accompanied him on campaigns; after 63 BC Lenaeus translated M's antidote notes (Ch 14). Suetonius *Grammarians* 15.

17. These events and quotes, Appian 30, 38. Ashes, Pausanias 9.6.2.

18. Plutarch *Sulla* and Appian 38–39. Pausanias 1.20.

19. Pausanias 1.20.4 and 9.40.4. Habicht 1998, 121–22.

20. Appian 39–40. Sulla forced Aristion to drink poison (probably hemlock). Plutarch *Sulla* 23. Aristion killed inside the sacred Parthenon, Athena's temple, Pausanias 1.20.

21. For realistic estimates of the troop numbers at Chaeronea, see Pillonel 2005, who concludes that the number of men mobilized by M in Greece was extremely impressive. According to ancient sources, Sulla received 6,000 reinforcements; Appian 41 says M had 120,000 troops; Memnon 22.13 estimates 60,000. Plutarch *Sulla* 16.1 says the Romans numbered only 15,000 infantry and 1,500 cavalry, but his source was Sulla himself, who had an interest in claiming that he won with a small army. Sulla came with 30,000 and received another 6,000. See also McGing 1986, 126 n173.

22. Tattoos, Mayor 1999. Camels, Plutarch *Lucullus* 11.4. Pillonel 2005.

23. Leo the Emperor, Polyaenus *Stratagems* 1, in Krentz and Wheeler 1994, 2:1011. Sheldon 2005 on sending clandestine messages in the Roman era. A popular pro-M uprising in Chaeronea: Ñaco del Hoyo et al. 2009, 5.

24. Plutarch *Sulla*; Appian 41–45. Pausanias 9.7. Duggan 1959, 77–78.

25. Camp et al. 1992.

26. Appian 45.

27. Orchomenus: Appian 46, 49–53. Matyszak 2008, 78–81. For estimates of troop numbers at Orchomenus, see Pillonel 2005. M had promised no taxes for five years in 88 BC.

28. Plutarch *Sulla*. The battle relics are in the National Museum: thanks to John Ma for this information. Memnon 22.10–13. Camp et al. 1992, 449–50.

29. Gatopoulos 2004; "Stopping Mithridates" 2005. Thanks to Ron Stroud, UC Berkeley.

30. Appian 50. Plutarch *Sulla* 22. Dorylaus also survived, but his movements were not recorded.

· 10 ·

KILLERS' KISS

1. "Honeymoon," Reinach 1890, 148. Dorylaus suggested treachery was involved in Archelaus's devastating losses in Greece, Plutarch *Sulla* 20. M's propaganda and strategy in this period, McGing 1986, 121–36. Events in 85–81 BC, Duggan 1959, 82–96.

2. Appian 46. Galatia crucial ally of Rome, Mitchell 1995, 1:31. Galatian rulers, Eder and Renger 2007, 102–5.

3. Plutarch *Bravery of Women* 23. M consciously replayed scenes from Greek tragedy, Chaniotis 1997. Plutarch *Alexander* 41, compassion toward lovers. Adobogiona, Strabo 13.4.3; Mitchell 1995, 2:35. Reinach 1890, 297.

4. Athenaeus 6.266, gods were angry with Chios for inventing slavery "while most other nations provided for themselves by their own industry."

5. Events in Chios and aftermath of Greek defeat, Appian 46–47; Hind 1994, 159–64. Duggan 1959, 79. According to Memnon 23, Dorylaus attacked Chios. Memnon's native city, Heraclea, allied with Rome, attacked M's ships and rescued the Chians.

6. M's theatricality and orchestration of dramatic events, Chaniotis 1997. Whittier, "Mithridates at Chios." Quotes from Whittier's note, in *War Time*, 1864.

7. Plutarch *Lucullus* 28. Deluxe transport for harems, Casson 1974, 54.

8. A Roman inscription of 86/85 BC found in Ephesus accuses M of "breaking the treaty and gathering his forces [and] attempting to snatch territory he had no claim over." Mastrocinque 1999, ch 3. Alcaeus of Sardis, Plutarch *Pompey* 37.

9. On these repressive acts, Appian 48. Duggan 1959, 80–81. McGing 1986, 128–31.

10. Peace at Dardanus, Reinach 1890, ch 4, esp 204. On the preceding events, Ballesteros Pastor 1996, ch 4; Duggan 1959, 80–81; McGing 1986, 130–32.

11. Dialogue in quotation marks in the pages that follow represents a condensation of quotations in Plutarch *Sulla* 22, based on Sulla's own account, and on Appian 54–55. Memnon 25. Duggan 1959, 83. Situation in Italy: Diodorus 37.

12. Plutarch Sulla 22. Appian 54. Theme of Roman greed, Sanford 1950, 32.

13. Plutarch *Sulla* 22–24; Appian 52–53. "Hurricane," Diodorus frag 38–39.8. Cassius Dio frag 30–35.104.7. Lewis 1976, 127. Strabo 13.1.27. See Ballesteros Pastor 2009.

14. Fimbria's trap, Frontinus *Stratagems* 3.17.5. Plutarch *Lucullus* 3.4–7. Matyszak 2008, 86, suggests M made a deal with Lucullus.

15. Treaty negotiations and Fimbria's actions: Appian 54–58, Memnon 25, and Plutarch *Sulla* 22–24. See Reinach 1890, 200–209. McGing 1986, 131–38. Erciyas 2006, 25–26, 124. Roman treaties traditionally sealed with *osculum pacis*, kiss of peace, an embrace and ritual kiss on cheek. Ancient Persians kissed equals on lips, superiors on cheek, Herodotus 1.35; Strabo 15.3.20.

16. Sulla's motives, Mastrocinque 1999, ch 4; McGing 1986, 130–31.

17. Sulla's haste and soldiers' disgust, Holland 2003, 151–52; Plutarch *Sulla* 24.4; Diodorus 38–39.8.

18. Contrary to his promise not to punish M's supporters, Memnon 25 says Sulla "forced many cities into slavery." Many cities ruined and impoverished, Reinach 1890, 209–11; Buitenwerf 2003, 308–9. Pausanias, Greek native of Anatolia, 2nd century AD, emphasized the brutality of Sulla and other Romans—he did not regard them as "liberators" of Greece or Anatolia, see Habicht 1998, 120–22. Sulla's punishment of Ephesus, Lewis and Reinhold 1990, 1:200–211. Appian 63. Duggan 1959, 85–86. Iasus, Bean 1989, 53.

19. Sulla's exorbitant taxations, penalties, and plunder help explain his success in the Civil War, Mastrocinque 1999, 91–93. Sulla's plunder: Pausanias 9.7; Habicht 1998, 121–22; Mastrocinque 2009.

20. Strauss 2009, 18, 21.

21. "The deed of Mithridates, deemed so terrible, in slaughtering all the Romans in Asia in one day, was regarded as of slight importance in comparison with the numbers now massacred and their manner of death" at the hands of Sulla. Cassius Dio frag 30–35, quote 109.8. Plutarch *Sulla* 27–34. Augustine *City of God* 3.28. Triumph, Pliny 33.5.16. Beard 2007.

22. See McGing 2009, reassessing M's pride in Persian heritage, long-term goals, and policy of "steady escalation" and "raising the stakes," instead of compliance with Rome.

23. Duggan 1959, 87–89, 94. Bosporan Kingdom, Logan 1994; Saprykin and Maslennikov 1995.

24. The preceding events involving Mithradates the Younger and Archelaus are from Appian 64. Effects of hemlock and opium, Stuart 2004, 111–12.

25. Iphigenia used her sword to sacrifice animals to Athena: Cassius Dio 36.11.

26. "That jackal" Murena, Ford 2004, 178; Murena's war, see 161–86. "Pathless route," Appian 64–65. Memnon 26 says M's envoys to Murena were traitors, McGing 1986, 133–35.

27. Suetonius *Julius Caesar* 4; Plutarch *Caesar* 2.6–7. Caesar's clever escape, 80–75 BC, Mayor 2009, 162 and nn.

28. Murena's war, see McGing 1986, 133–36; Mastrocinque 1999, 94–98; Appian's reliance on Strabo, 103–8. Appian 66. Athenais's mother unknown: Sullivan 1980, 1137, 1139. Reinach 1890, 298, Athenais's mother was Monime, and she was betrothed to Ariobarzanes' son.

29. Appian 66 and Strabo 14–15 provide details; also see Ammianus Marcellinus 23.6.32–37; Xenophon *Cyrus* 8.5.25–26 and (prayer) 8.7.3; Mitchell 1995, 2:22; Widengren 1959, 250–51; Champlin 2003, 225–29.

· 11 ·

LIVING LIKE A KING

1. Plutarch *Sertorius* 23; Appian 67. North Vietnam's massive Tet Offensive of 1968 elicited a groundswell of international support, turned the US public against the war, and led the United States to withdraw from Vietnam. In 2004, during the US Iraq War, Secretary of Defense Donald Rumsfeld expected Islamic insurgents to deliberately copy the Tet Offensive to win "psychological victory." Oberdorfer 2004. In an AP news story (2007) the US commander in Iraq predicted a sensational "mini-Tet" offensive by "Islamic extremists" to destroy US support. Justin 37.1.6–9; Cicero *Pro lege Manilia*. Goodkin 1986, 207, "Losing the battle [was] another source of glory" for M.

2. Plain equipment, Plutarch *Lucullus* 6. M's restraint, Duggan 1959, 96–100. Achaeans: Appian 67, 69; Reinach 1890, 76–77, 305, 396. Achaea is modern Abkhazia.

3. Aulus Gellius 16: M publicly ingested poisons "to show his immunity." M tested drugs on himself, on friends, and on criminals, Scarborough 2007. Galen *De compositione medicamentorum per genera* 13.416 K; *De antidotis* 14.150 K. Zopyrus: Totelin 2004, 5.

4. Illusions of immunity, magic, and sleight of hand with poisons, Corner 1915, 225–26; Magi and magic, Widengren 1959, 252. Bierman 1994, 8, snakebite trickery.

5. Housman, "Terence, this is stupid stuff," in *A Shropshire Lad*. Tolerance of local venoms, Aelian *On Animals* 9.29. Mayor 2009, 92–96 and 272 nn23–24; Majno 1991, 381; Cilliers and Retief 2000.

6. Juvenal *Satire* 6.659–61, written ca AD 80. Emerson, "Mithridates."

7. Bioactives in *Mithridatium*, Norton 2006; ingredients, Totelin 2004. Plants counteract venom, Raloff 2005; Alam and Gomes 2003. See Pliny's bks 24–26 for plant *pharmaka* and antidotes, theriacs, and *Mithridatium;* see 25.3.5–7 for M's toxicology; 25.32.69 for centaury plant, discovered by Pharnaces I of Pontus; betony seeds; *aristolochia* to reverse effects of poisons. Smith 1890, sv "Theriac." Watson 1966. Illustrations of medicinal and lethal plants, Stuart 2004, 74–75, 109–31. Lemnian earth: Hall and Photos-Jones 2008.

8. Pliny 25.6, 25.26, 25.29. Corner 1915, 223. History of *Mithridatium* and details of compounding, Bierman 1994, Griffin 1995, Baley 1585.

9. Pliny 25.3.5–8; and see bk 25 on antidote plants. Cilliers and Retief 2000, 88–89; 91–95 (known poisons in antiquity). Hindu and Chinese versions, Majno 1991, 415–17. Islamic, Hindu, Chinese theriacs, *Mithridatium*, and longevity elixirs, Nappi 2009.

10. Cilliers and Retief 2000, 89. Zopyrus, Norton 2006, 2. Oscan, McGing 1986, 85 and n70. Pliny 25.2.5–6; Galen *De antidotis* 14.2 K: 14.150K. Asclepiades was extremely long-lived, Pliny 7.37.124. Ophiogenes and Marsi: Pliny 7.2.13–15. Caucasian vipers: Hopkins 1995.

11. Poison plants, Pliny bk 25; see 29.8.24–26: some individual *Mithridatium* ingredients weighed "one-sixtieth of one denarius," and "cinnabar, red lead," used in many theriacs, is "poisonous."

12. Arsenic, Newman 2005, 8–9; ducks and rats, Stuart 2004, 113–14. Aulus Gellius 16: M mixed duck blood with "drugs that expel poisons" to create "the most celebrated antidote, the *Mithridatios*."

13. Pontic honey both toxic and healthful, Aelian *On Animals* 5.4. See Totelin 2004 for full discussion of Pliny on *Mithridatium*. Skinks and salamanders exude toxins, included in M's recipe, Bierman 1994, 5–6. Venoms, Metz et al. 2006. Hormesis, thanks to Dr. Stephen Galli, Pathology Department, Stanford, per cor March 5, 2008. Raloff 2005 and 2007, 40.

14. Vogel 2001; Moore et al. 2000. It is still unknown exactly how the process wards off so many toxins.

15. Juvenal 14.251–55. Sulla and Juvenal, Cilliers and Retief 2000, 89–90. Poisoning in Rome, Stuart 2004, 113–15.

16. Asclepiades, Totelin 2004, 3–4. Caesar's doctor Aelius: Norton 2006, citing Galen *Opera Omnia* vol 14, *De Antidotus*, bk 2; Scarborough 2008.

17. Impossible to recover original *Mithridatium*, Totelin 2004, 13 and nn for Paccius inscription. Baley 1585 chastises the ancient "historyographers" for neglecting to preserve M's recipe. Ancient Chinese apothecaries sold incense, medicines, and antidotes, Nappi 2009. Reinach 1890, 293. Celsius, Galen, Paul of Aegina, and Scribonius Largus cited Paccius, who left his formula to Tiberius.

18. Andromachus's recipe, Griffin 1995; Bierman 1994, 5; Pain 2008; Baley 1585. Vat, Ciaraldi 2000.

19. Celsus *On Medicine* 5.23.3. Griffin 1995; Corner 1915; Swann 1985; Norton 2006.

20. Islamic and Arabic treatises on chemistry of plant, mineral, and animal toxins and royal obsession with poison: Stuart 2004, 116. Arab physicians Rhazes (d. AD 854) and Avicenna (d. AD 1037) praised M's antidote: Griffin 1995; Corner 1915. Averroes: J. Ricordel, "Le traité sur la thériaque d'Ibn Rushd (Averroes)," *Revue d'Histoire de la Pharmacie* 48 (2000): 81–90. *Mithridatium* in China, Nappi 2009.

21. By the 1st century AD, production of *Mithridatium* had already become a "showy parade of art and science," Pliny 29.8.24–26. M's theriac stimulated the earliest concepts of "regulated medicine": Griffin 1995, 3, for European royalty who took *Mithridatium*; Bierman 1994, 8, for *Mithridatium* in Rome in 1984. Baley 1585. See Duffin 2003 and Swann 1985 for longevity of M's trademark antidote.

22. Cassius Dio 37.13, M built resistance to poison by taking "precautionary antidotes"; Appian 111, M accustomed himself to poisons by taking "Mithridatic drugs." Celsius *On Medicine* 5.23.3 attributes M's immunity to antidotes only, not poison intake. Pliny 25.3.5–7.

23. Pliny 29.8.24–26, 23.77.149, and Totelin 2004, 7 and table 1, 18–19. Critics of *Mithridatium*, Corner 1915, Swann 1985, Bierman 1994, Griffin 1995.

24. Pompey burned Sertorius's papers, Plutarch *Sertorius* 27. Touwaide's theory cited in Totelin 2004, 9 and nn39–40.

25. Residue of *Mithridatium*, Ciaraldi 2000. Touwaide (2008) analyzes residues in medicine containers from 1st century BC/AD shipwrecks and studies ancient "recycled" botanical texts retrieved from bindings of Byzantine books. Residue labeled "Mitridatio" in deluxe 1500s medicine chest from Chios: Burnett 1982, 333 no 36. Black Sea's anaerobic deep waters result in remarkable preservation of organic material in ancient shipwrecks, King 2004, 18–19; West 2003, 166–67; Markey 2003. Thanks to Dr. Serguei Popov for discussion of current "antidote" research. Popov's Mithradates-like work on poisons and antidotes, see "Biowarriors" Interview, *Nova*, PBS, www.pbs.org/wgbh/nova/bioterror/biow_popov.html.

26. Royal tasters, Xenophon *Cyrus* 1.3.9–10; Newman 2005, 31. Electrum, Pliny 33.1 and 33.23. Q. Serenus Sammonicus *Liber Medicinalis* 60.5. Chelation, Zammit-Maempel 1978, 218.

27. Pliny 33.5.15, 33.6.25–26, poison rings. Poison pills for friends, Plutarch *Pompey* 32.

28. Sources of agates included Phrygia, Crete, Lesbos, Rhodes, Egypt, Cyprus, and Persia. Zachalias (Hellenized Hebrew for Zacharias), Pliny 37.60.139–43 and 169; M's work on amber, 37.11.39, and cf Champlin 2003, 135, Nero's love of amber, "tears of the daughters of the Sun." Heliotrope also called bloodstone. Healy 1999, 264–65, 269.

29. Pliny 37.5–6, 33.6.22–28. Appian 115. M's gem portraits, esp those resembling Alexander, Vollenweider 1995, no 218; and Neverov 1973; Erciyas 2006, 148–51, 160–62, figs 73, 74, and 85. Højte 2009c on M's gem portraits. Thanks to Robert Proctor for discussions of M's agates and their provenance.

30. Alexander used Darius III's luxurious tent, ornaments, and furniture; wore vintage Persian finery and armor; and used frankincense, myrrh, and other exotic perfumes. Reinach 1890, 278–93, quote 285; Plutarch *Alexander* 32. Balsdon 1979, 144–45. Bactrian camels and trade routes, Casson 1974, 55, 123–24; Stuart 2004, 92.

31. Mithradates krater first published in 1745, for inscription, Ward 1749–50; Erciyas 2006, 125.

32. Patron of arts and sciences, Appian 112; Orosius 6.4.6. McGing 1986, 92. Reinach 1890, devoted a chapter, 276–300, to the character of M, the "Hellenistic sultan," the "soul" of the Pontic-Bosporan Empire. Cavafy, "Darius," 1920, "exultation" sometimes translated as "intoxication" or "exhilaration."

33. Stratonice: Plutarch *Pompey* 36. Reinach 1890, 296–97.

34. Kabeira and Kainon Chorion (Caenum) near Niksar, Turkey: Strabo 12.3.30–40. Plutarch *Pompey* 36–37. Kainon Chorion and M's strongholds, Munro 1901, 60–61. Talbert 2000, map 87, 2:1233, 1241. Cramer 1832.

35. Erciyas 2006, 43–46. Strabo 12.3.30–40.

36. Xenophon *Cyrus* 5. Plutarch *Antony* 27.3–4 (Cleopatra). Aulus Gellius 17.17; Pliny 7.24.88–90, 25.3.6–7; Valerius Maximus 8.7; Quintilian 11.2. Aurelius Victor (AD 360) claimed M spoke 50 tongues. See Balsdon 1979, 116–45; Gleason 2006, 229; Summerer 2009. Thanks to Josh Katz for help with M's languages.

37. Pontic-Bosporan Empire, Reinach 1890, 213–75.

38. Plutarch *Lucullus* 20. McGing 1986, 141.

39. Justin 40; and see Olbrycht 2009 and Reinach 1890, 311–13, and ancient sources for Tigranes.

40. Plutarch *Sulla* 36–38; Strabo 10.1.9; Valerius Maximus 9.3.8; Appian *Civil Wars* 1.105; Keaveney 2005, 175; McGing 1986, 136; Reinach 1890, 305–6; Scullard 1970, 86. Novelist Ford 2004, 157, was Sulla's disease caused by M's poisons?

41. McGing 1986, 137; cf McGing 2009.

42. Justin 40.1–2; Sallust *Catiline War*, Book of Judith, Josephus cited in Nazaryan 2005. Plutarch *Lucullus* 21.3–5. Strabo 12.2.9.

43. Appian 92–93. Sertorius and M's secret messages carried by pirates and traders, Sheldon 2005, 75, citing Cicero. Strauss 2009, 132–34.

44. Sertorius was "seized with an overwhelming desire to settle in the islands and live in peace," but pirate friends thwarted his plan. Plutarch *Sertorius* 9 and 11 (fawn); Pliny 8.50.117; Frontinus *Stratagems* 1.11 (fawn).

45. Appian 68. Plutarch *Sertorius* 9 (quotes); McGing 1986, 137–39, 142.

46. Obsequens in Lewis 1976, 128. For these events, see Appian 68. Plutarch *Sertorius* 23–24 (calls Marcus Varius "Marius").

47. Minting, Erciyas 2006, 130; Saprykin 2004; Levy 1994; Callataÿ 2000. Plutarch *Sertorius* 24. Balsdon 1979, 75, 122.

48. Eutropius 6.6. "Miserable puppet," Duggan 1959, 99. Reinach 1890, 319–20. McGing 1986, 144. Nicomedes IV's will: Mitchell 1995, 1:62.

49. Strabo 7.4.6; Appian 68–69.

50. Appian 69. Tribes: Ammianus Marcellinus 22.8.18–30; Ovid *Pontus* 4 and *Trist.* 2.198; Strabo 7; Livy 40.58; Amazons, Justin 2.4.

· 12 ·

FALLING STAR

1. Appian 70. Sidonis Apollinaris's poem 22, about the castle of Pontius Leontius (ca AD 460); Reinach 1890, 321 n2. This villa also had a painting of the siege of Cyzicus, below. Lee 1797.

2. The king as chief Magus carried out the horse sacrifice, Widengren 1959, 251–52, horse sacrifice in Rhodes, citing Festus 181, ed. Muller. Trojans: Homer *Iliad* 21.132. Herodotus 7.113 and 1.215–16, Scythians sacrificed horses to the Sun, "offering the swiftest animal to the swiftest god." Xenophon *Cyrus* 8.3.24 and *March* 4.5; Pausanias 3.20.4; Philostratus, *Apollonius of Tyana* 1.31; Tacitus *Annals* 6.37. Strabo 11.8.5. Alexander sacrificed bulls and golden cups to Poseidon in the Indian Ocean, Arrian *Anabasis* 6. 19.5. Helios and Poseidon worship in Anatolia, Mitchell 1995, 2:26.

3. The speech and these events: Appian 70–71. Erciyas 2006, 26–27, M's speeches and letters in various sources display the same style and complementary content, reflecting M's format and tone. Reinach 1890, 321; Munro 1901, 56, on M's invasion route. Some high-ranking Romans supported M, see McGing 1986, 145.

4. Appian 70–71. Memnon 27 says M had 150,000 infantry, 12,000 cavalry, and 120 scythed chariots, and an equal number of workers, and that the Romans lost 8,000 at sea.

5. Battles for Chalcedon and Cyzicus described in Appian 72–78 and Plutarch *Lucullus* 8–12; Strabo 12.8.11; Memnon 27–29. Reinach 1890, 318–42; McGing 1986, 146–53; Holland 2003, 154–64; Duggan 1959, 100–129. Matyszak 2008, 108–13. Lucullus and Third Mithradatic War, Keaveney 1992, ch 5; complicated chronology and ancient sources, 183–205. See also Hind 1994, 129–38, and Mastrocinque 1999, 103–5. The figure 300,000 is supported by the separately reported fact that M's grain stores would feed that many for a year, see Ch 11.

6. Plutarch *Lucullus* 5.5, 7 (Fimbrians). Rome feared that M intended to invade Italy by sea, Keaveney 1992, 85–86. Duggan 1959, 103. On Rome's self-perpetuating search for profit by continuous warfare in booty-rich lands, Eich and Eich 2005, 14–15, 23–24.

7. Plutarch *Lucullus* 8.5–7. Ford 2004, 203–4. It is not clear from the sources whether M was actually present.

8. Stothers 2007, 87. This and other meteors in antiquity, D'Orazio 2007. Keaveney 1992, 77, "Both sides, recognizing an evil omen, withdrew." Reinach 1890, 324. Cybele's meteorite, Strabo 12.5.3; Mitchell 1995, 2:20. A "star" fell near M's camp just before he withdrew from Rhodes, Ch 8. Meteorites could signal that a battle should not take place.

9. Appian 72–78. Lucullus's ruses at Cyzicus, Frontinus *Stratagems* 3.13.6.

10. Plutarch *Sertorius* 26; Keaveney 1992, 79–80. Memnon 28.2.

11. Campbell 2006, 139–43, M's shipborne tower illustrated on 141. See Ford 2004, 215–18, for realistic description of the *sambuca*.

12. This tactic described in Appian 73 and Frontinus *Stratagems* 4.5.22.

13. Appian 73–78. Vinegar, Ch 4; Mayor 2009, 220–22.

14. Appian 75; Plutarch *Lucullus* 10; Rigsby 1996, 341–42. McGing 1986, 148–50, omens and prodigies were examples of anti-M propaganda by the Romans. Notably, M's rituals entreated male gods.

15. Plutarch *Crassus* 8–11; Appian *Civil Wars* 116–20. Strauss 2009.

16. Appian 75–76. Plague at Cyzicus, Mayor 2009, 120–22. Siege: Eutropius 6.6.

17. Plutarch *Lucullus* 11. Mithradates' camels, Ammianus Marcellinus 23.6.56.

18. Strabo 12.8.11; Diodorus 37.22b; Plutarch *Lucullus* 11; Keaveney 1992, 83.

19. Appian 75–76; Plutarch *Lucullus* 12; Memnon 35–36. Mastrocinque 2009.

20. Plutarch *Lucullus* 12; Cicero *Pro lege Manilia* 1.8.

21. Appian 77–78. Triumph laws in effect since 143 BC: Valerius Maximus 2.8.1. Enemy leaders executed at Triumph, Josephus *Jewish War* 6.423. Smith 1890, sv "Triumph"; Champlin 2003, 210–15; Beard 2007.

22. Plutarch *Lucullus* 13.

23. Aftermath of ancient sea battles, Strauss 2005. In this scene, I follow McGing 1986, 139, who suggests that M's pirate rescuer was his good friend Seleucus. Black Sea notoriously dangerous in winter, West 2003, 166. Sailing speeds, Lee 2007, 169–70. Casson 1974, 149–62.

24. Memnon 29.3–4. A plague struck Heraclea later, Konnakorix made a deal with the Romans, and the citizens were slaughtered, Memnon 35.

25. Valerius Maximus 1.8.13; Ammianus Marcellinus 16.7.9.

26. Memnon 29.6, 37.5. Was Metrodorus M's messenger to Tigranes? see Ch 13.

27. Plutarch *Lucullus* 14; Memnon 30. Strauss 2009, 181–94.

28. Appian 78–79, 115. Detailed information on roads, terrain, and Pontic campaign, Munro 1901, esp 56–59. Themiscryans prepared zoological attacks in advance; I list wild beasts of the region. Insects and animals in ancient warfare, Mayor 2009, ch 6.

29. Plutarch *Lucullus* 14; 15–20, on invasion of Pontus; see also Appian 78–83 and Keaveney 1992. Cherries, Pliny 15.30; Athenaeus 2.35. Lucullus's army, Holland 2003, 160–61.

30. Plutarch *Lucullus* 15. Scythian chiefs of these nomads: Frontinus *Stratagems* 2.5.30; Appian 79.

31. Duggan 1959, 125, suggests the "hunters" were bandits on the run from M. Lucullus's route to the stronghold and battles for Kabeira, Munro 1901, 57–58.

32. M master of intelligence, often using advance scouts and fire signals, Sheldon 2005, 75.

33. Appian 79–82; Plutarch *Lucullus* 15–17.

34. King Parisades of the Bosporus (Ch 5) died in a Scythian-led uprising in 110 BC. Polyaenus *Stratagems* 7.37, Krentz and Wheeler 1994, 2:693.

35. Route of M's flight, Munro 1901, 52, 58; Talbert 2000, map 87, 2:1226–42. Plutarch *Lucullus* 17. Strabo 12.3.33 suggests that his distant relative Dorylaus was later suspected of treachery against M, but Plutarch's account of Dorylaus's end seems credible. Romans bribed a cousin of Dorylaus, Lagetus, to lead a revolt. M seized Lagetus's property but did not kill him, and the family fell into poverty.

36. Plutarch compiled his detailed account from descriptions of defectors and captives who ended up in Lucullus's hands. Of course, some accounts may have been elaborated over time. Plutarch *Lucullus* 18. Appian 82. Memnon 30.1. Strabo 12.3.11. Appendix 2 for these tragic deaths in art, music, and literature. See Summerer 2009, fig 6, death of Monime (1816).

37. Suicide to preserve freedom, liberty, independence versus survival under tyranny, Balsdon 1979, 162–67. Suicide or killing of one's family practiced in many ancient and modern cultures, to prevent falling into enemy hands. One of many examples is Hannibal's sister Sophonisba, who drank poison to escape capture by Romans in 203 BC.

·13·

RENEGADE KINGS

1. Plutarch *Lucullus* 17.4–7; Appian 81–82; Orosius 6.4. Cf Memnon 30.1. Polyaenus *Stratagems* 7.29.2 described a similar ruse by M in Paphlagonia, distracting pursuers by setting his fine furniture and golden dishes on the road. Final phase of Lucullus's campaign against M and Tigranes, 70–66 BC: Appian 82–90; Plutarch *Lucullus* 19–37; Memnon 30–39; Cassius Dio 36; Keaveney 1992, 91–128; Duggan 1959, 133–67, 343–76; Sherwin-White 1994, 229–47; McGing 1986, 152–63. Cicero, *Pro lege Manilia* 127.

2. I base this list of companions on Plutarch's and Appian's reports of who was with M later in Armenia and Pontus. Location of Talaura, route into Armenia, Munro 1901, 58–59; Appian 82, 115; Plutarch *Lucullus* 19; Cassius Dio 36.14–16.

3. Strabo 12.3.33. Tyrannio the Grammarian, a member of M's circle, was captured in Amisus and taken to Rome, where he worked on books of Aristotle and Theophrastus plundered by Sulla from Athens. He later taught Strabo (12.3.16, 13.1.54). Plutarch *Lucullus* 19. Memnon 30 says that "many citizens of Amisus were slaughtered immediately" although Lucullus tried to stop the killing, and "Eupatoria was immediately destroyed." Keaveney 1992, 93. Heraclea was destroyed after it was betrayed by M's Galatian general Konnakorax, Memnon 34–36.

4. Ancient sources are contradictory about what actually happened in Sinope. Memnon 37; Strabo 12.3.11; Appian 83; Plutarch *Lucullus* 23.

5. Globe of Billarus, Strabo 12.3.11. Mastrocinque 2009. The statues and Antikythera device are in the Archaeological Museum of Athens. Recent scientific studies of gears, purpose, dating and inscriptions: Marchant 2008; Freeth et al. 2008.

6. Plutarch *Lucullus* 24; Memnon 37.

7. Plutarch *Lucullus* 20 (quote). Appian 83; Keaveney 1992, 95–98.

8. The dialogue of Appius and Tigranes is based on Plutarch *Lucullus* 19 and 21; Memnon 31. Reinach 1890, 351; Keaveney 1992, 99–104; McGing 1986, 152–53, Ballesteros Pastor 1996, ch 7. Armenia and Tigranes: Reinach 1890, 453–55; Ussher 2007, 4041, 4085–86, 4199, 4217, 4228–29, 4264, 4282–83, 4308. Armenian view: Kurkjian 1958, ch 13. Turkish view: Tezcan 2007, 100–101.

9. Memnon 31, Tigranes gave M "bodyguards and all other marks of hospitality"; 38, M stayed at the lodge for a year and eight months. Tigranes as philhellene, Kurkjian 1958. See also Raffi 1959.

10. Strabo 11.14.8–9 and 16, 11.13.7. Flora and terrain of Armenia described by early travelers, Stoneman 1987, 186–207; *Ravanea coccinea* (wormwood parasite), *Morena orientalis* (flower of the sun); sacred to Zorastrians, www.rbedrosian.com/soma.htm.

11. Plutarch *Lucullus* 22; Appian 82; Memnon 38. Keaveney 1992, 99–104. Kurkjian 1958 and other Armenian historians deny that Tigranes was "cold and unconcerned" about M.

12. Plutarch *Lucullus* 22; Strabo 13.1.55; Memnon 38. Scullard 1970, 102–5.

13. Memon 38. Appian 82–84. Justin 40.2. Plutarch *Lucullus* 22–24. McGing 1986, 153 n67. Kurkjian 1958.

14. Plutarch *Lucullus* 26 and Appian 85 say Tigranes had 250,000–300,000; cf 150,000 in Plutarch, *Sayings of Romans* 203. Eutropius 6.9: Tigranes 600,000 and Lucullus 18,000. Phlegon of Tralles frag 12, in Hansen 1996, 62, gives Tigranes 40,000 infantry and 30,000

412 NOTES TO PAGES 299–305

cavalry. Certainly Tigranes' army was vast and probably more than twice the size of Lucullus's 30,000 (and the Roman strength of 15,000–20,000 was probably minimized by Roman writers). See Matyszak 2008, 128–29; maps, 132–35. In 1916, an Ottoman army of 60,000 retraced Tigranes' route over the Taurus range and lost 30,000 men to cold and starvation. Kurkjian 1958, ch 13, estimates Tigranes' army at 70,000–100,000.

15. Battle for Tigranocerta described by Plutarch *Lucullus* 25–29; Appian 84–86; Memnon 38. Cassius Dio 36.1–3. Machiavelli *Art of War* 2.76. In fiction: Church 1885, 233–79; Ford 2004, 259–74. Plutarch *Sayings of Romans* 203.1–2. Keaveney 1992, 106–11; Sherwin-White 1994, 239–47. Tribes and Tigranocerta, Strabo 11.14.14–15.

16. Plutarch *Lucullus* 28; Appian 85. Duggan 1959, 147. Tigranes' women were transported to Artaxata, but some were captured later by Lucullus and others by Pompey—that would explain how we know of the earlier rescue.

17. This scene is detailed in Plutarch *Lucullus* 29; Memnon 38. Appian 87. Cassius Dio 36.1–2. Kurkjian 1958, ch 13, gives the modern Armenian view of the disaster dealt by Lucullus.

18. Cassius Dio 36.1–2.

19. Keaveney 1992, 111. Kurkjian 1958, ch 13 n2, placed Tigranocerta northwest of Nisibis below a spur of the Taurus chain, among other suggested sites. Based on ancient roads, in 1997 T. A. Sinclair suggested Tigranocerta lay near Arzan, Turkey, cited in Talbert 2000, map 89, and 1280, 1290. In 2006, the Armenian Institute of Archaeology and Ethnology of the Academy of Sciences and Yerevan State University, led by Dr. Hamlet Petrosyan, announced the excavation of Tigranocerta, near modern Martakert (Miyafarkin, Martyropolis, modern Silvan), constructed with advanced Hellenistic techniques and an estimated population of about 50,000; see www.armeniadiaspora.net/ADC/news.asp?id=1341.

20. *Maltha* and poison arrows: Mayor 2009, 234, 245–47; Cassius Dio 36.5–8; Pliny 2.108–9; Healy 1999, 255. Samosata, Munro 1901, 62. Ammianus Marcellinus 23.4.15, 23.6.16, and 37. Naphtha wells near a fortress in this region, Stoneman 1987, 205.

21. Plutarch *Lucullus* 30–31. Keaveney 1992, 112–17. Badian 1981. Duggan 1959, 153–55.

22. Appian 87. Plutarch *Pompey* 32.8. Eutropius 6.12. Xenophon's Greeks were accompanied by fighting women, Lee 2007, 272–73. Alexander and Amazon, Lane Fox 2004, 276, 432 and 531. Reinach 1890, 297, 387, Hypsicratea, "*intrepide amazone.*" Autonomous barbarian women and equal status with men in this period, see Konstan 2002. See Izady 1992, 194, on ancient and modern women warriors of Kurdistan. Women in M's army, Cassius Dio 36.49.3.

23. Letter to Arsaces, Sallust *Histories* 4.69 Maurenbrecher, abridged, see Lewis and Reinhold 1990, 235–36. Cassius Dio 36.1–3 and Plutarch *Lucullus* 30.1–2. Ahlheid 1988 gives a detailed analysis of the rhetorical strategies in M's letter. Many modern historians have wrangled over whether Sallust's letter is genuine or composed to represent what M communicated, see eg Erciyas 2006, 27–28; Sanford 1937, 439–40. An entire PhD dissertation is devoted to the letter, L. Raditsa, Columbia University, 1969, cited in McGing's extensive discussion, 1986, 84, 105, 154–62. There is no doubt that M communicated with Parthia; Parthian royalty was represented in the early monument on Delos. The message is plausible, the language in M's style; the letter appears to be either genuine or based on M's other authentic letters and speeches. McGing 1986, 155–62. Olbrycht 2009: "The letter reflects a genuine document found by the Romans" in M's personal archives.

24. Plutarch *Lucullus* 31.

25. Ammianus Marcellinus 31.2.8: nomad warriors, lightly armed and swift, "purposely divide suddenly into scattered bands and attack, riding about in disorder here and there, dealing terrific slaughter." Cf Justin 41, "alternate charge and retreat" of nomads, they "quit in the very heat of the fight," then surge back "just when one thinks he has won!" The Macedonian cavalry's desertion was foiled, Frontinus *Stratagems* 1.7.8.

26. Plutarch *Lucullus* 31.5–8. Appian 88: Lucullus could not draw M into a fight. According to Keaveney 1992, 118–20, 123, M was brave vs "lesser men" but "would not face his superior" enemy, Lucullus.

27. Scordisci: Frontinus *Stratagems* 3.7. Xenophon *March* 3.4; Lee 2007. Herodotus 4.46–48, 4.120–40.

28. Strabo 11.13–14. Early travelers' descriptions of Armenian winter, Stoneman 1987, 197. Cf Lee 2007, 202, 228, for Xenophon's travails in Armenia's rough terrain and snow.

29. Plutarch *Lucullus* 32.3–5; Cassius Dio 36.6–8.

30. M's route from Armenia to Pontus, Munro 1901, 58.

31. Campaign to recover Pontus: Cassius Dio 36.9–17; Plutarch *Lucullus* 35; Appian 88–90; Eutropius 6.9.

32. Use of snake venom to stop hemorrhage, Hopkins 1995. Appian 88–89; Cassius Dio 36.9. Alexander suffered a gash on the thigh fighting Darius at Issus. The incident of showing Alexander to his troops took place in India. Plutarch *Fortune of Alexander* 341.

33. M's trophy at Zela, Cassius Dio 42.48. Plutarch *Pompey* 39; *Lucullus* 33–35. Keaveney 1992, 124–26; Holland 2003, 172–73.

34. Plutarch *Lucullus* 35–36 and *Pompey* 31; Strabo 12.5.2. Keaveney 1992, 125–28. Cicero *Pro lege Manilia*, in favor of giving Pompey the authority in 66 BC, to destroy the menace of M who had escaped punishment for 22 years after the atrocities of 88 BC. As long as M lives, said Cicero, Rome's economic and political status was in peril.

35. Plutarch *Lucullus* 37; Keaveney 1992, 135.

36. Plutarch *Lucullus* 39–43; Athenaeus 2.50–51, 5.274, and 12; Appian 90–91. Love potion, Pliny 25.7.25. Keaveney 1992, 164–65. Poison love potions, Cilliers and Retief 2000, 89.

37. Piracy crisis, Plutarch *Pompey* 24–25; Appian 91–97; Cicero *Pro lege Manilia*; Holland 2003, 164–65.

·14·

END GAME

1. Strabo 12.3.18; Diodorus 14.30. Lee 2007, 229. Toxic honey as weapon, Mayor 2009, 146–48, 153–54. Root-Bernstein 1991, 44–45 suggested Krateuas devised the plan, based on Xenophon's experience.

2. Pirates, Appian 91–96. "Odious," Plutarch *Pompey* 24–30. Pompey's war on M, Appian 97–117; Plutarch *Pompey* 30–45; Scullard 1970, 88–108. Cilician pirates worshipped Mithra; pirates and veterans helped spread militaristic Zoroastrian-influenced cults of Mithra/Mithras in the Roman world after Mithradatic Wars. Champlin 2003, 227–29 and n30; Wynne-Tyson 1972, 46–47; Plutarch *Pompey* 24.5; Balsdon 1979, 238; Holland 2003, 167–68; Tezcan 2003.

3. Cicero, *Pro lege Manilia* 121.

4. Exchange reported by Appian 97–98, based on accounts of veterans and Romans later captured by Pompey. Cassius Dio 36.45.3–4.

5. Preceding events described by Plutarch *Pompey* 32; Cassius Dio 36.47–50 (deserters); Frontinus *Stratagems* 1.1.7; Eutropius 6.12–14; Appian 97–101. Strabo 12.3.28–41.

6. Plutarch *Pompey* 32. I added Hypsicratea to M's dream; she was with M at this time.

7. Appian 100–101. Plutarch *Alexander* 31. M's night attack on Rhodes failed, Ch 8.

8. Moonlight Battle detailed in Plutarch *Pompey* 32; Appian 99–100; Livy *Epit.* 101, and see Florus 3.5.22–24, 1.40.23; Orosius 6.4.4–5. Cassius Dio 36.48–49, both men and women were in M's forces. According to Frontinus *Stratagems* 2.1.12, Pompey attacked that night to force M to come out and fight. Turkish view of Pompey's campaign in Pontus and Colchis, Tezcan 2007, 101–4.

9. Orders to stab horses, Frontinus *Stratagems* 2.33.

10. Plutarch *Pompey*, 32.8; Eutropius 6.12; Orosius *5.3–5, 6.4.6;* Reinach 1890, 387. Duggan 1959, like Christine de Pizan, below, assumed Hypsicratea was a courtesan forced to throw on Persian men's clothing for the first time during Pompey's attack.

11. Valerius Maximus 4.6.2, 6.6. Orosius 6.5.3–5.

12. Boccaccio, *Famous Women* 6.323–27, inspired by V. Maximus. Cf Petrarch *Triumphus cupidinis* 3.28.30. Hypsicratea in 17th- and 18th-century French dramas, such as Behourt's *Hypsicratée*, 1604, see Snaith 2007, 16–17.

13. Typical criticism of Roman avarice in this 12th-century poem: "the treacherous Roman people . . . worshipped silver and went mad in pursuit of gain . . . . they worship the gold of Arabia, the brocaded robes of Greece, the ivory and gems of India, . . . silver and gold of England." Sanford 1950, 36. Machiavelli *Art of War* 2.84–99, calls M a "valiant" hero. See Baley 1585, for blistering attack on Rome and praise of M's gifts to the world. Christine de Pizan 1999, 110–12.

14. Bituitus fought at M's side in battle, traveled with M to Bosporan Kingdom, was present at M's death in 63 BC. Walked horses, Orosius 6.4. Sagona and Sagona 2005, 67, for location and archaeological discoveries at Sinora. Talbert 2000, map 87, "Sinoria" 1256, 1241. Drypetina: Ammianus Marcellinus 16.7.9; Christine de Pizan 1999, 103–4.

15. Appian 100–101 makes it clear that this small army fled with M to Colchis. Plutarch *Pompey* 32; Plutarch *Fortune of Alexander* 41–42 and *Alexander* 15 for sharing wealth. A soldier's pay was about 1 drachma/day; 6,000 talents was about 36 million drachmas. Reinach 1890, 387–89. Mutual trust, Duggan 1959, 175. Cf Romans' reliance on loot for pay, Ñaco del Hoyo et al. 2009, 3.

16. Tigranes' reward, Plutarch *Pompey* 32.9; Cassius Dio 36.50. Arslan 2007, 392–405, 463–70.

17. Appian 101. Euphrates snakes, Aelian *On Animals* 9.29; probably Levantine vipers. Strabo 11.2.13–19, describes M's journey of 4,000 stades (about 500 miles) from Pontus to Colchis. Ancient Colchis, Braund 1994.

18. M and Hercules, Erciyas 2006, 148–53. Dioscurias: Appian 67 and 101–2; Strabo 11.2.19; Pliny 6.5. King 2004, 32; Ascherson 1995, 244–56.

19. Appian 101–2; Plutarch *Pompey* 35.

20. Pompey's movements 66/65 BC: Appian 103–5; Plutarch *Pompey* 33–38; Cassius Dio 36–37. Strabo 11.1.6, Pompey crisscrossed the region between the Caspian and Black seas. Sherwin-White 1994.

21. Appian 103. Strabo 11.4–8 says 22,000 cavalry; Plutarch *Pompey* 35 says 12,000 cavalry. Cassius Dio 37.

22. Appian 103. Strabo 11.3.3, 11.5.1–4. Ammianus Marcellinus 22.8.26, writing in AD 350, claimed Amazons still lived between the Don and the Caspian Sea. Aelian *Historical Miscellany* 12.38. Plutarch *Alexander* 46.1–2; Curtius 6.5.24–25 and 29; Lane Fox 2004, 276. "Amazon" tombs, Ascherson 1995, 111–24. M's allies around the Phasis, Caucasus, and beyond: Memnon 22.3–4.

23. Cassius Dio 37.1–7. Armazi is Armozicon (Harmozica) in Strabo 11.3.5. Archaeological excavation at Armazi began 1890, ended 1940s, resumed 1985. Daryal Pass and Armazi Citadel (Armaziskhevi), Talbert 2000, map 88 and 2:1255–67; Braund 1994. Snakes, Plutarch *Pompey* 36; scorpions and spiders, Strabo 11.4.6.

24. Plutarch *Pompey* 35. Cassius Dio 37.3.

25. Cassius Dio 37.3.

26. Appian 104–5; Cassius Dio 37.51–53; Plutarch *Pompey* 33 and *Fortune of Alexander* 336.3; Holland 2003, 173–74. A. E. Houseman's poem, see Ch 11. Tigranes' surrender, Kurkjian 1958, who laments Tigranes' empire doomed to be "a mere flash of lightning in history because of Roman ruthlessness and the mad audacity" of M.

27. Appian 115.

28. Drypetina's fate, Valerius Maximus 18.13; Ammianus Marcellinus 16.7.9; Appian 107; Pompey 36. Cassius Dio 37.7, gives a different version: Stratonice, angry at being left behind, surrendered the fort to Pompey.

29. Aulus Gellius 17.16, cited by Totelin 2004, 5. Suetonius *Grammarians* 15; Balsdon 1979, 56. Baley 1585.

30. Appian 104–6; Plutarch *Pompey* 33, 36–41. Cilicia and Taurus Mountains, Mitchell 1995, 1:70–79.

31. Cassius Dio 36.50. Plutarch *Pompey* 35.1. Strabo 11.2.13. Appian 101–3. Livy *Epit.* 101. Klukhor Pass, Talbert 2000, map 87. Strabo's *embainon* can mean "to set off, march out, or embark." Jones, Loeb, 1928, translates: "only with difficulty could he go along the coast, most of the way marching on the edge of the sea." Cf translation by Hamilton/Falconer, 1856: "embarking in vessels." For help with translations, thanks to Henryk Jaronowski, John Ma, and Josh Ober.

32. Reinach 1890, 396–97 and map. Covered boats, *camarae*, Charachidzé 1998 and Strabo 11.2.5; 11.2.11–13, on Achaea's harborless shore with sheer cliffs. Strabo says that after M "despaired of going through the land of the Zygi, because of the rugged terrain and the ferocity of the people," he changed his mind and "completed his journey from the Phasis, traveling about 4,000 stades" (500 miles). Appian 67, 69: M fought Achaeans in 84 BC; they sent warriors in 74 BC, but could not be relied on as allies. M never subdued the Zygi; they "were the serious obstacle to his march," McGing 1986, 58, 164, on the "remarkable journey." Unpredictable Achaeans: Saprykin and Maslennikov 1995, 276; map 262–63 for impassable coast and rugged western route. Reinach's route accepted by McGing 1986, 164; 179; Gozalishvili 1965; Matyzsak 2008, 154 (quoting the 1856 translation, n31 above). Ford's novel (2004, 324–28) describes an attempt at a coastal route, abandoned for the Klukhor route. King 2004, 49, M avoided the coast "because it was patrolled by Roman ships." Duggan 1959, 179, follows Appian 102.

33. *Encyclopedia Britannica* 11th ed. Forts, Strabo 11.3.5. Maps of the passes: Talbert 2000, maps 87–88. Daryal Pass was sometimes called Caspian Gates and confused with two other fortified passes by same name, one between eastern spur of the Caucasus and

the Caspian (Diodorus 2.2.3) and the other on Silk Route south of the Caspian. Scythian Keyhole or Gates, Daryal, Dariel, Darial, Darioly, Caucasiae Pylae, Sarmatian Gates. Tacitus *Annals* 6.33.3: Iberi controlled strongholds and passes over the mid-Caucasus, and the Caspian Gates pass on the Caspian Sea was sometimes closed due to gale-driven floods. Pliny 5.27, "unbroken continuity" of the Caucasus, except for the "Armenian and Caspian Gates."

34. Routes and passes: Strabo 11.3.4–5. Bryce 1878, 43–48, 69–87. Roki Pass now a tunnel on the Transcaucasian Highway (1971–81). War broke out in August 2008 among Russia, Georgia, North and South Ossetia, and Abkhazia (ancient Achaea and Zygi); Russian tanks invaded Georgia by way of Roki Pass. Thanks to Hans Heiner Buhr, adventurer and mountain guide in Tbilisi, Georgia, who often traverses these passes. His knowledge of the history and terrain of this region was immensely helpful in enabling me to reconstruct M's route.

35. Tezcan 2003. Strabo 11.2.15–16.

36. Xenophon *March* 4.5; Lee 2007, 165–67. M's general Neoptolemus fought Scythians on frozen Bosporus Strait, Strabo 2.1.16, 7.3.18.

37. Strabo 11.2.16–19, 11.5.6, 11.14.4.

38. Cf Xenophon *March* 4.5.19–21; Lee 2007, 166.

39. Descriptions draw on memoirs of early European travelers who retraced M's route in 1837 and 1876: Wilbraham 1839, 140–42; Bryce 1878, 42–87; descriptions of Caucasus, 88–156. Complex logistics of large army traveling single file over constricted, snowbound mountain passes, progressing in peristaltic movements, cf Xenophon's winter crossing of Armenian passes in Lee 2007, 163–67.

40. Appian 102. *Kurgans*, Ascherson 1995, 126–35.

41. M's trip around Sea of Azov and arrival in Crimea; Machares and Xiphares: Appian 102 and 107. Cassius Dio 37.12, M killed some remaining sons who incurred his suspicion. Exipodras: Orosius 6.5. The eunuch Gauros: Reinach 1890, 405; Valerius Maximus 9.2.3. On Pantikapaion, Crimea, and "Little Scythia," Strabo 7.4 and 11.2; Ascherson 1995, 220–26.

42. Plutarch *Alexander* 49, Appian 107–8. The facial ulcers that caused M to withdraw bear similarity to the disfigured popular Ukrainian leader Viktor Yushchenko, poisoned by political enemies in 2004. Like M, Yushchenko's charisma relied on face-to-face contact. This and other poisonings in the region, Gutterman 2004. Duggan 1959, 181. In his novel, Ford 2004, 337, attributed the facial ulcers to stress and delayed effects of a cheek wound four years earlier.

43. Hair samples of King George III (1760–1820), who suffered mental derangement, showed a high arsenic concentration of 17 ppm, from a lifetime of prescribed arsenic. Cox et al. 2005. Rue and Saint-John's-wort (*Hypericum*), included in *Mithridatium* recipes, have toxic photosensitive compounds that can cause severe blistering. Vogel 2001. Arsenic poisoning, www.toxipedia.org.

44. Plutarch *Pompey* 41; Josephus *Jewish War* 1.122–55.

45. Justin 37.1.7. Darius: Herodotus 3.136. Plutarch *Fortune of Alexander* 340–42.

46. Debate about Alexander, Livy 9.17–19; Sacks 1990, 135 and n75. McGing 1986, 122–23; see 165 and n95, "wildly unrealistic" plan anti-Mithradatic propaganda. Sherwin-White 1994 also dismisses the plan as rumor. Cf Ballesteros Pastor 1996, ch 13. Cicero's speech, 63 BC, *De lege agraria contra Rullum* 437.

47. Duggan 1959, 186–87. Ford 2004, 344–46. Maps of overland route to Alps, Tal-

bert 2000, maps 11–12, 19–23. Reinach 1890, 403–4. M's invasion plan figures in Norse oral traditions written down ca AD 1250: *Younger Edda* 1879, 229–30. See Mallet and Scott 1847, 51: in Scythia, M "sought refuge, and a new means of vengeance. He hoped to arm against the ambition of Rome, all the barbarous nations, his neighbors, whose liberty [Rome] threatened. He succeeded in this at first, but all those peoples, ill-united as allies, ill-armed as soldiers, and still worse disciplined, were forced to yield to . . . Pompey." But one tribe, led by a chief named Odin, migrated to northern Europe and kept Mithradates' dream alive. This legend is featured in Anderson 1960.

48. Cassius Dio 37.11 marveled that M's mind, at age 71, grew more steadfast even as his body was weakened by age, war wounds, and the mountain crossing. Appian 102, 107–8; Plutarch *Pompey* 41; Florus 1.40.15. On the economics, war preparations, and archaeology of Bosporan Kingdom, Saprykin and Maslennikov 1995; Logan 1994.

49. The region sustained nomadic attacks and Diophantus's conquests, Ch 5, but was not involved in the Mithradatic Wars except to supply tributes of grain and recruits; Saprykin and Maslennikov 1995. Cassius Dio 37.11 synchronizes this earthquake with the capture of M's children at Phanagoria. Orosius 6.5.1, during grain harvest (or spring?) festival of the Greek mother goddess Demeter (the only recorded ritual by Mithradates directed to a goddess). Archaeological evidence of the quake of 63 BC, Blavatskij 1977; Logan 1994, 72; Saprykin and Maslennikov 1995, 267, 269, 273; but cf Traina 1995. This was not the same quake reported by Justin 40.2.1 in Syria, predicting Lucullus's defeat of Tigranes, Ch 13. Cassius Dio 37.25, a "mighty" earthquake occurred in Rome in 63 BC, with lightning in a clear sky, flashes of fire, and apparitions; cf Obsequens in Lewis 1976, 128.

50. Rostovtzeff 1921, 221, on Iranian, Jewish, Greek, and indigenous populations of Bosporan Kingdom; he suggests that the large Jewish presence was directly related to their support of M vs Rome. Artaphernes, age 40, apparently never a viable heir.

51. M's military men hated M's "all powerful" eunuchs. This and other events of the revolt, Appian 108–14, Castor of Phanagoria was later designated Friend of Rome by Pompey. Sherwin-White 1994. The final fates of Cleopatra the Younger and Stratonice are unknown.

52. Appian 109. Some of Appian's speculation may be his own interpretation, but he also had access to memoirs of Romans and others with M. Grievances in Bosporan Kingdom, Saprykin and Maslennikov 1995, esp 281. Rostovtzeff 1921, 220, on the threat these northern tribes organized by M posed to Rome.

53. Appian 109. "Last autonomous monarch," Velleius 2.40.1; McGing 1986, 171.

54. Appian 110 calls Metrophanes "Menophanes"; cf Appian 28 and Pausanias 3.23.2–5. Pharnaces' children, M's grandchildren: Dynamis later became queen of Bosporan Kingdom; Darius, Pharnaces' son, grandson of Mithradates, was appointed king of Pontus by Mark Anthony in 39 BC. Eder and Renger 2007, 112–13. Mitchell 1995, 1:38–39; Rostovtzeff 1919.

55. Appian 110–11.

·15·

IN THE TOWER

1. The details that follow are from M's death scenes reported by Livy *Periochae* 102; Appian 110–12; Plutarch *Pompey* 41; Cassius Dio 37.12–14; Valerius Maximus 9.2.3;

Justin 37.1–2, 6; Aulus Gellius 17.16; Aurelius Victor 1.76; Orosius 6.5; Florus 1.40; and Galen *De theriaca, ad Pisonem* 14.283–84, cited in Totelin 2004, 5–6 and n22. Medieval version, Baley 1585. Ramsey 1999, 203 n16: M was thought to be alive in January 63 BC, but by November word of his death reached Rome. Reinach 1890, 406–13. His suicide appears to have been late spring or early summer of 63.

2. I added the detail of a golden vial, based on Herodotus's description of the small golden vials of poison that Scythian archers attached to their belts, Mayor 2009, 78–79. I also assume M comforted his daughters as they died. According to late Roman tradition, Orosius 6.5, M uttered a bitter curse, wishing the same ill treatment on Pharnaces by his own children. Did M pray? If so, it may have been similar to Cyrus the Great's last prayer, Xenophon *Cyrus* 8.7.3.

3. Appian 111–12. How old was M in 63 BC? About 71, based on birth date of 134 BC (Ch 2). Appian 116 calculated his age as 68 or 69; Eutropius 6 and Orosius 6.5 (following Livy) say he was 72, giving birth date of 135 BC. Average life expectancy for a man in the 1st century BC was about 50.

4. What was the suicide poison? A tiny amount of aconite (monkshood, a neurotoxin) is deadly and painless, with numbness and full consciousness until respiration ceases; aconite was used in antiquity by old people in Chios to commit suicide. Henbane's toxic ingredient is hyoscyamine, bringing hallucinations, euphoria, restlessless, dizziness, tachycardia, fever, coma, and death. Hemlock, used in ancient Greece and Rome for criminal executions and suicide, causes gradual paralysis and death by asphyxiation, like aconite. Hemlock could be combined with opium for a calm, dignified, painless death, like that of Socrates. Stuart 2004, 73–78 and 110–12; Cilliers and Retief 2000.

5. Cassius Dio 37.13; Reinach 1890, 410. Entreaty to Bituitus, Appian 111.

6. Appian 113 says the triremes went to Sinope; Plutarch *Pompey* 42 says Amisus. Cassius Dio 37.14. Was Metrophanes one of the men responsible for Aquillius's capture?

7. Plutarch *Pompey* 41; Josephus *Jewish War* 1.1.139. Høtje 2009b sums up the irritation and awkwardness in the situation. Thanksgiving to mark M's death: Cicero *Prov. cons.* 27. Pompey's campaigns in the Near East, Sherwin-White 1994.

8. Egyptian embalmers removed the brain in sophisticated mummification techniques; Persians traditionally covered royal corpse with wax and placed in rock-cut tombs; Scythians also had embalming procedures. Herodotus 1.137–41, and 4.84–86, on length of voyage across Black Sea.

9. Corpse delivered to Pompey: Cassius Dio 37.14; Appian 113. Quotes, Plutarch *Pompey* 42. *Xvarnah*, Widengren 1959, 246 and 251, 254. Reinach 1890, 412, suggested Gaius, an old schoolmate, identified the scars. Hyacinth plume, Xenophon *Cyrus* 6.4.2. Gaius gave the crown to Sulla's son; the scabbard was stolen by Publius and sold to grandson of Ariobarzanes I of Cappadocia. Reinach 1890, 412 n3 and 298.

10. Plutarch *Pompey* 42. Pausanias 3.23.3–5, Apollo caused M to kill himself as punishment for sacking Delos. Ancient attitudes toward suicide, see Seneca *Ep. Morales* 70. Balsdon 1979, 249–52: a calm, premeditated, dignified suicide, by poison or weapon, was approved to provide escape from incurable illness, disgrace, subjugation, or tyranny, oppressive political conditions that destroyed dignity and liberty. Suicide "an escape route from slavery," a way to achieve freedom, *eleutheria*, 250. Symbolism of suicide by poison as "deliverance," Goodkin 1986, 212. Many modern war criminals have used

suicide to cheat justice, eg Adolf Hitler and his officers in 1945 and Serb leader Slobodan Milošević in 2006. Notably, in the wars against Middle Eastern enemies in the early 21st century, the US military considered suicides of prisoners of war a hostile act of "asymmetrical warfare." Selsky and Loven 2006.

11. Cassius Dio 37.13. Alexander showed great chivalry toward Darius, laying out the body in state, paying for funeral at Persepolis and burial in royal Persian sepulcher: Arrian *Anabasis* 3.22.1; Plutarch *Fortune of Alexander.* Høtje 2009b.

12. Appian 113; Cassius Dio 37.14; Plutarch *Pompey* 42.2–3. Sinope became the new royal residence under Pharnaces I, but the tombs at Amasia were still used, according to Strabo 12.3.29 (a native of Amasia). Archaeological surveys at Sinope: Fleischer 2009. Arslan 2007 assumes Pompey oversaw burial at Sinope. Høtje 2009b reasonably concludes that Appian and Plutarch were wrong about Sinope, since the royal tombs of the Pontic kings were in Amasia, and Pompey and people of Pontus knew M's ancestors were in Amasia's rock-cut tombs.

13. Valerius Maximus 4.6.2 (source Cornelius Nepos?). Eutropius 6.12. Reinach 1890, 297, 387. On unique relationship of M and Hypsicratea, see Konstan 2002, 16–17.

14. Ford 2004, 332. Boccaccio, *Des cleres et nobles femmes,* ca 1450, f. 47v; and Jean Boccace, "Hipsicratee royne de ponce" illustration in *Hypsikrateia et Mithridate le grand.* Cavalli's *Pompeo Magno,* 1666. French views of M, Flinois 1983; Snaith 2007. Inscription at Phanagoria: Bowersock 2008, 600–601, citing Plutarch *Pompey* 32; Valerius Maximus called her "queen."

15. Preceding events from Appian 116–17; Josephus *Jewish War* 1.6.6 and *Jewish Antiquities* 14.3; Lucan 2; Plutarch *Pompey* 44–45; Pliny 7.26. Beard 2007.

16. Plutarch *Pompey* 42. Justin 37.1.6–9. Appian 112. Pliny 25.3.5. Velleius 2.18; Cicero *Academica Priora* 2.1. After the Mithradatic and Civil Wars, Rome's taxation policies were more enlightened, and Rome "grew more receptive to eastern ideas," Sacks 1990, 184.

17. Appian 117. Hellenized "Iranian Alexander," Rostovtzeff 1919, 95. Pompey was assassinated in Egypt by supporters of his enemy Julius Caesar, in 48 BC.

18. Gaddis 2002; Ferguson 2000. For artistic alternative histories, se Summerer 2009. I thank Michelle Maskiell for suggesting an alternative historical narrative in which M survives; and Deborah Gordon, Ian Morris, and Josh Ober for valuable conversations about the following scenario.

19. Racine 1965; see Goodkin 1986, 204–7; citing remarks of Roland Barthes, *Sur Racine* (1963) on M's "elusive" and "double death," the faked and the real. Mozart's *Mitridate* of 1770, Sadie 1972 and "Mozart Mithridate," *L'Avant Scene Opera,* special issue, July 1983, essays, photos, and libretto. Political, diplomatic, and emotional intrigues of M's Pontic Kingdom held strong appeal for Racine and Louis XIV, at a time when armies of the Ottoman Empire of Turkey had marched into Europe (they would besiege Vienna in 1683). See Brèque 1983. McGing 1986, 166 n98. According to Herodotus 1.137, Persians "hold it utterly improbable that a son would ever murder his true father."

20. See Ch 6 for substitution of M's son. M presumed dead while in youthful exile, while reconnoitering as king, when he leaped onto a pirate ship in a raging storm, and when he disappeared into the Caucasus. Ptolemy's ruse, Aelian *Historical Miscellany* 12.64. "Faked celebrity death" conspiracies have fascinated since antiquity; there were postmortem sightings of Nero in the 1st century AD and of Alexander the Great in AD 221: Champlin 2003, 20–24, 235–37, on heroes and antiheroes who "die but return any-

way," eg King Arthur, Adolf Hitler, John Kennedy, Elvis Presley, Marilyn Monroe, Saddam Hussein.

21. Some consider counterfactuals mere nostalgia for "what might have been" unless they test causation claims. In this alternative outcome, we can show that, despite Pompey's and Rome's anxiety, the specific place and time of M's death, whether in the tower or among the nomads a decade or so later, would not have changed the course of history (thanks to Ian Morris). See Bekker-Nielson 2004 on whether M's life or death "mattered" in the long run.

22. Appian 112. M pardoned, at the last minute, the Galatian Bepolitanus, believing he was innocent, Ch 10. M's personality, see Olbrycht 2009 and Bekker-Neilsen 2004.

23. Pharnaces' revolt and bid to take back his father's kingdom crushed at Zela, Pontus, 47 BC, by Julius Caesar. The victory was so overwhelming that Caesar reported the result with the celebrated phrase *Veni, Vidi, Vici* ("I came, I saw, I conquered"). Cassius Dio 37.12–14; 42.7–9 and 42.45–48. Dynamis: Rostovtzeff 1919, esp 98–105, Eder and Renger 2007, 112.

24. M's relatives who took refuge among the nomads, Rostovtzeff 1919, 104.

25. Achilles and Helen of Troy enjoyed a halcyon afterlife on the legendary White Isle, in the northern Black Sea. West 2003, 162–66.

26. For this Northern European-Scandinavian legend, based on the 9th-century Norse Saga, see *Younger Edda* 1879, 229–30 and sources cited, esp Paul Henri Mallet's influential *Northern Antiquities* (1756), which Gibbon read in 1770. Mallet and Scott 1847, 51. Henri de Tourville, in *Histoire de la formation particularise* (1903), proposed that the hero Odin was originally based on a historical Scythian chieftain allied with M, a far-traveling caravan leader and warrior, who brought Asian nomad culture to the north, from the city "Asgarda" on the Azov, after M's death. Thanks to William Hansen for help in tracing this legend's origins. For a novel based on this legend in the writings of Snorri Sturlason, see Anderson 1960, 275–82. Wordsworth, *Prelude* (1798–1850), lines 185–89.

27. Ammianus Marcellinus 31.2. King 2004, 33–37. History of Bosporus after M's and Pharnaces' deaths, Rostovtzeff 1919.

28. Long-lived Persian ancestors of M: Cyrus the Great said to have died at 100, Artaxerxes at 86 or 94, Mithradates I at 84, and Tigranes the Great at 85, according to Lucian *Macrobii* (Long Lives) 10–14.

29. Numerous *kurgans* have been looted and excavated around the Sea of Asov and steppes of south Russia; many more are undiscovered. There is no evidence to support the rumor that Brigadier-General Sir Harry Paget Flashman (1822–1915) discovered the "true grave" of Mithradates in the Crimea in 1854–55.

30. Hypsicrates: Strabo 7.4.6 and 11.5.1–4. Strabo coyly says Hypsicrates was "not unfamiliar" with Amazon customs of Caucasia—if my theory is correct, this was "the historian's" homeland. Hypsicrates mentioned in Josephus *Jewish Antiquities* 14.8.3 (as historian of Julius Caesar's campaigns); fragment in FGrH 190 F 3; Orosius 5.3.5; Lucian *Macrobii* (Long Lives) 22. Rostovtzeff 1919, 103 and n28. Stern, *Greek and Latin Authors* 1.220; and *Oxford Classical Dictionary* sv (freed by Caesar when he took Amisus); Pauly-Wissowa sv. Did Hypsicrates give M's antidote to Caesar's doctor Aelius?

31. Battling the tide of history: M "was an anachronism," McGing 1986, 171. Racine (1673) 1965, act 3, scene 1, lines 929–34, my translation. These words are spoken to M by his sons before his death.

⊰ BIBLIOGRAPHY ⊱

ANCIENT SOURCES

Greek and Latin texts are available in translation in the Loeb Classical
Library or online at www.perseus.tufts.edu, unless otherwise noted.

Aelian, *On Animals*; *Historical Miscellany*
Ammianus Marcellinus, *Roman History*
Appian, *Mithridatic Wars*, bk. 12 of *Roman History*; *Civil Wars*; *Syrian Wars*
Athenaeus, *Learned Banquet*
Augustine, *City of God*
Aulus Gellius, *Attic Nights*
Cassius Dio, *Roman History*
Celsus, *On Medicine*
Cicero, *Pro lege Manilia*; *Tuscan Disputations*; *De lege agraria contra Rullum*;
    Pro Flacco; *In Verrem*; *Academica Priora*
Diodorus of Sicily, *Library of History*
Eutropius, *Abridgement of Roman History*, trans. J. S. Watson. London, 1853.
Florus
Frontinus, *Stratagems*
Galen. C. G. Kühn, *Galeni Opera Omnia*. Leipzig: 1821–33, rpt. Hildesheim,
    1965. G. Fichtner, *Corpus Galenicum*. Tubingen,1990. *Selected works by
    Galen*, trans. P. N. Singer. Oxford: Oxford Univ. Press, 2006.
Herodotus, *Histories*
Josephus, *Jewish Antiquities*; *Jewish War*
Justin, *Epitome of the Philippic History of Pompeius Trogus*, trans. John Yardley.
    Scholars Press, 1994.
Juvenal
Livy, *History*; *Epitome*; *Periochae*. Budé edition, 1984.
Lucan, *Civil War*
Lucian, *Macrobii*
Lucretius
Memnon, *History of Heracleia Pontica*. FrGH 336.
Obsequens, *Book of Prodigies*. In Lewis 1976.
Orosius, *Histories against the Pagans*. Budé edition, 1990–91.

Pausanias, *Description of Greece*
Phlegon of Tralles, *Book of Marvels*. In Hansen 1996.
Pliny the Elder, *Natural History*
Plutarch, Lives of *Alexander, Lucullus, Pompey, Sertorius, Marius, Sulla; Moralia*
Polyaenus, *Stratagems of War*, 2 vols., trans. P. Krentz and E. Wheeler. Chicago: Ares, 1994.
Polybius, *Histories*
Quintilian
Sallust, *Histories; Jugurthine War; Catiline War;* and fragments
Strabo, *Geography*
Suetonius, *Nero; Grammarians*
Tacitus, *Annals; Agricola*
Valerius Maximus, *Memorable Deeds and Sayings*. Teubner, 1888.
Vegetius, *On Military Matters*
Velleius Paterculus, *Roman History*
Xenophon, *Education of Cyrus; March of the Ten Thousand; Hellenica; On Hunting*

MODERN REFERENCES

Aggrawal, Anil. 1997. "Arsenic—the Poison of Kings." *Science Reporter* (February).
Ahlheid, F. 1988. "Oratorical Strategy in Sallust's Letter of Mithridates Reconsidered." *Mnemosyne*, ser. 4, 41, fasc. 1–2:67–92.
Alam, M. I., and A. Gomes. 2003. "Snake Venom Neutralization by Indian Medicinal Plants (*Vitex negundo* and *Emblica officinalis*) Root Extracts." *J Ethnopharmacology* 86, 1:75–80.
Alcock, Susan. 2007. "Making Sure You Know Whom to Kill." Paper, German-American Frontiers of Humanities Symposium, American Philological Society/Humboldt Foundation, Philadelphia, 2004. *Millenium* 4:13–20.
Amiotti, Gabriella. 1980. "I Greci ed il massacro degli Italici nell'88 A.C." *Aevum* 54:132–39.
Anderson, J. K. 1985. *Hunting in the Ancient World*. Berkeley and Los Angeles: Univ. of California Press.
Anderson, Poul. 1960. *The Golden Slave*. New York: Kensington.
Andreae, Bernard. 1994–95. "Eracle, Telefo e il re Mitridate VI del Ponto." *Rend. Pont.* 67:111–22.
———. 1997. "Telephos-Mithridates im Museo Chiaramonti des Vatikan." *Rheinisches Museum fur Philologie* 104:395–416.
Antikas, T., L. Wynn-Antikas, J. Naylor, and L. Stefani. 2004. "Perimortem

Weapon Trauma to Thoracic Vertebrae of a 2nd Century BCE Adult Male Skeleton, Central Macedonia, Northern Greece." *J Paleopathology* 16, 2: 69–78.

Arslan, Murat. 2003. "Piracy on the Southern Coast of Asia Minor and Mithridates Eupator." *Olba* 8:195–212.

———. 2007. *Mithradates VI Eupator: Roma'nin Büyük Düsmani*. Istanbul: Odin.

Ascherson, Neal. 1995. *Black Sea*. New York: Hill and Wang.

Badi', Amir Mehdi. 1991. *Les Grecs et les Barbares*, vol. 6, *D'Alexandre à Mithridate*. Paris.

Badian, E. 1981 [1968]. *Roman Imperialism in the Late Republic*. 2nd ed. Ithaca: Cornell Univ. Press.

Baley, Walter. 1585. "A Discourse of the Medicine Called Mithridatium." London: n.p.

Ballesteros Pastor, Luis. 1996. *Mitridates Eupator, rey del Ponto*. Granada: Univ. of Granada.

———. 1999. "Marius' Words to Mithridates Eupator." *Historia* 48, 4:506–8.

———. 2009. "Troy, between Mithridates and Rome." In Højte 2009a.

Balsdon, J.P.V.D. 1979. *Romans and Aliens*. London: Duckworth.

Barber, E., and P. Barber. 2004. *When They Severed Earth from Sky: How the Human Mind Shapes Myth*. Princeton: Princeton Univ. Press.

Batty, Roger. 2007. *Rome and the Nomads: The Pontic-Danube Realm in Antiquity*. Oxford: Oxford Univ. Press.

Bean, George. 1979. *Aegean Turkey*. 2nd rev. ed. New York: Norton.

———. 1989. *Turkey beyond the Maenander*. 2nd ed. London: Murray.

Beard, Mary. 2007. *Roman Triumph*. Cambridge: Harvard Univ. Press.

Bekker-Nielsen, Tønnes. 2004. "Mithridate Eupator, a Historical Personality." Seminar paper, Danish National Research Foundation Centre for Black Sea Studies, Aarhus, Denmark, June 9. www.pontos.dk

Bengtson, Hermann. 1975 [1956]. "Mithradates." In *Herrschergestalten des Hellenismus*, 251–78. Munich: Beck.

Bierman, A. I. 1994. "Medical Fiction and Pharmaceutical Facts about Theriac." *Pharmaceutical Historian* 24, 3:5–8.

Blavatskij, V. D. 1977. "The Earthquake of 63 BC in the Peninsula of Kerch." [In Russian.] *Piroda* n.v., n.p.

Bolich, Gregory G. 2006. "Terrorism in the Ancient World." *MHQ: Military History Quarterly* (Spring): 52–58.

Bosworth, A. B., and P. V. Wheatley. 1998. "The Origins of the Pontic House." *J Hellenic Studies* 118:155–64.

Bowersock, G. W. 2008. "In Search of Strabo, with Some New Light on Mithridates Eupator and His Concubine." *J Roman Archaeology* 21:598–601.

Braund, David. 1994. *Georgia in Antiquity: A History of Colchis and Transcaucasian Iberia*. Oxford: Oxford Univ. Press.

Brèque, J.-M. 1983. "Mithridate, de Racine à Mozart." *Avant Scene Opera* 54, 8:8–13.

Brunt, P. A. 1971. *Social Conflicts in the Roman Republic.* New York: Norton.

Bryce, James. 1878. *Transcaucasia and Ararat: Being Notes of a Vacation Tour in the Autumn of 1876.* Adamant Facsimile ed. London: Macmillan.

Buitenwerf, Rieuwerd. 2003. *Book III of the Sibylline Oracles.* Leiden: Brill.

Burnett, J. 1982. "The Giustiniani Medicine Chest." *Medical History* 26:325–33.

Callataÿ, F. de. 2000. "Guerres et monnayages à l'époque hellénistique: essai de mise en perspective suivi d'une annexe sur le monnayage de Mithridate VI Eupator." In *Economie antique: la guerre dans les économies antiques,* ed. J. Andreau, P. Briant, and R. Descat, 337–64. Saint-Bertrand-de-Comminges: Musée archéologique départmental.

Camp, John, M. Ierardi, J. McInerney, K. Morgan, and G. Umholtz. 1992. "A Trophy from the Battle of Chaironeia of 86 BC." *American J Archaeology* 96, 3 (July): 443–55.

Campbell, Duncan. 2006. *Besieged: Siege Warfare in the Ancient World.* Oxford: Osprey.

Casson, L. 1974. *Travel in the Ancient World.* Toronto: Hakkert.

Champlin, Edward. 2003. *Nero.* Cambridge: Harvard Univ. Press.

———. Forthcoming. *Tiberius.* Princeton: Princeton Univ. Press.

Chaniotis, Angelos. 1997. "Theatricality beyond the Theater: Staging Public Life in the Hellenistic World." *Pallas* 47:219–59.

Charachidzé, Georges. 1998. "Les pirates de la Mer Noire (de Mithridate à Nicolas I)." *Comptes Rendus de L'Académie des Inscriptions,* fasc. 1 (January/March): 261–70.

Charbonneaux, J. 1951. "La Vénus de Milo et Mithridate le Grand." *Revue des Arts* 1:12–16.

Christine de Pizan. 1999. *The Book of the City of Ladies* (1405). London: Penguin.

Church, A. J. 1885. *Two Thousand Years Ago: The Adventures of a Roman Boy.* London: Blackie & Son.

Ciaraldi, Marina. 2000. "Drug Preparation in Evidence?" *Vegetation History and Archaeobotany* 9 (July): 91–98.

Cilliers, L., and F. P. Retief. 2000. "Poisons, Poisonings and the Drug Trade in Ancient Rome." *Akroterion* 45:88–100.

Cohen, Getzel. 2007 [1995]. *The Hellenistic Settlements in Europe, the Islands, and Asia Minor.* Berkeley and Los Angeles: Univ. of California Press.

"Consensus on Terror: New Blueprint for U.N. Reform Includes First Political Definition of Terrorism." 2005. Associated Press news story, July 24.

Corner, George W. 1915. "Mithridatium and Theriac." *Johns Hopkins Hospital Bulletin* 26, 292:222–26.

Cox, T., et al. 2005. "King George III and Porphyria: An Elemental Hypothesis and Investigation. *Lancet* 366:332–35.

Cramer, John A. 1832. *A Geographical and Historical Description of Asia Minor.*
N.p.: University Press.

Crook, J. A., A. Lintott, and E. Rawson, eds. 1994. *Cambridge Ancient History,*
vol. 9, *Last Age of the Roman Republic,* 146–43 BC. 2nd ed. Cambridge: Cambridge Univ. Press.

D'Orazio, Massimo. 2007. "Meteorite Records in the Ancient Greek and Latin
Literature: Between History and Myth." In *Myth and Geology,* ed. L. Piccardi
and W. B. Masse, 215–25. London: Geological Society.

Duffin, Rachael. 2003. "Why Was Theriac So Highly Esteemed during the Middle Ages?" Ph.D. diss., Royal Holloway Univ., London.

Duggan, Alfred. 1959. *King of Pontus: The Story of Mithradates Eupator.* New
York: Coward-McCann. *He Died Old: Mithradates Eupator, King of Pontus.*
1958. London: Faber & Faber.

Eder, W., and J. Renger, eds. 2007. *Brill's New Pauly: Chronologies of the Ancient
World.* Leiden: Brill.

Eich, Armin, and Peter Eich. 2005. "War and State-Building in Roman Republican Times." *Scripta Classica Israelica* 24:1–33.

Eliot, Gil. 1972. *The Twentieth Century Book of the Dead.* New York: Scribner.

Erciyas, Deniz Burcu. 2006. *Wealth, Aristocracy and Royal Propaganda under
the Hellenistic Kingdom of the Mithradatids in the Central Black Sea Region of
Turkey.* Colloquia Pontica 12. Leiden: Brill.

Ferguson, Niall, ed. 2000. *Virtual History: Alternatives and Counterfactuals.* New
York: Basic Books.

Fleischer, Robert. 2009. "The Rock-Tombs of the Pontian Kings in Amasya,
Turkey." In Højte 2009a.

Flinois, Pierre. 1983. "Mithridate, une haut figure historique." *Avant Scene Opera*
54, 8:4–7.

Ford, Michael Curtis. 2004. *The Last King.* New York: St. Martin's.

Fotheringham, J. K. 1919. "The New Star of Hipparchus and the Dates of Birth
and Accession of Mithridates." *Monthly Notices, Royal Astronomical Society*
79, 3:162–67.

Freeth, Tony, et al. 2008. "Calendars with Olympiad Display and Eclipse Prediction on the Antikythera Mechanism." *Nature* 454 (July 31): 614–17.

Gaddis, John Lewis. 2002. *The Landscape of History: How Historians Map the
Past.* Oxford: Oxford Univ. Press.

Gatopoulos, Derek. 2004. "Greek Farmer Finds 2,000 Year Old Monument." AP
News story. Greek Ministry of Culture report, August 12, www.ekathimerini
.com

Gleason, Maud. 2006. "Greek Cities under Roman Rule." In *Companion to the
Roman Empire,* ed. D. Potter, 228–49. Oxford: Blackwell.

Glew, Dennis. 1977. "The Selling of the King: A Note on Mithridates Eupator's
Propaganda in 88 BC." *Hermes* 105, 2:253–56.

Goldsworthy, Adrian. 2003. *The Complete Roman Army*. London: Thames and Hudson.

Gologlu, Mahmud. 1973. *Anadolu'nun Milli Devleti Pontus*. Ankara, Turkey.

Goodkin, Richard. 1986. "The Death(s) of Mithridate(s): Racine and the Double Play of History." *PMLA* 101, 2:203–17.

Gozalishvili, Giorgi V. 1965. *Mit'ridat Pontiisky* (Georgian, summary in Russian). Tbilisi, Georgia.

Griffin, J. P. 1995. "Mithridates VI of Pontus, the First Experimental Toxicologist." *Adverse Drug Reactions & Acute Poisoning Reviews* 14:1–6.

Gruen, Erich S. 1984. *The Hellenistic World and the Coming of Rome*. 2 vols. Berkeley and Los Angeles: Univ. of California Press.

———. 2004. "Rome and the Greek World." In *The Cambridge Companion to the Roman Republic*, ed. H. Flower, 242–67. Cambridge: Cambridge Univ. Press.

Gurzadyan, Vahe G., and Ruben Vardanyan. 2004. "Halley's Comet of 87 BC on the Coins of Armenian King Tigranes?" *Astronomy & Geophysics* 45 (August): 4.6.

Gutterman, Steve. 2004. "Poisoning Draws Attention to Post-Soviet Cases." Associated Press news story, December 14.

Guyot, P. 1980. *Eunuchen als Sklaven und Friegelassene in der griechisch-romischen Antike*. Stuttgart.

Habicht, Christian. 1998. *Pausanias' Guide to Ancient Greece*. 2nd ed. Berkeley and Los Angeles: Univ. of California Press.

Hall, A. J., and E. Photos-Jones. 2008. "Assessing Past Beliefs and Practices: The Case of Lemnian Earth." *Archaeometry* 50, 60:1034–49.

Hansen, William, trans. and comm. 1996. *Phlegon of Tralles' Book of Marvels*. Exeter: Univ. of Exeter Press.

Harley, J., and D. Woodward, eds. 1987. *The History of Cartography*, vol. 1. Chicago: Univ. of Chicago Press.

Harris, Robert. 2006. "Pirates of the Mediterranean: What a Terrorist Act in Ancient Rome Can Teach Us." *New York Times*, September 30.

Healy, J. 1999. *Pliny the Elder on Science and Technology*. Oxford: Oxford Univ. Press.

Hind, John. 1994. "Mithridates." In *Cambridge Ancient History*, ed. J. A. Crook, A. Lintott, and E. Rawson, vol. 9, *Last Age of the Roman Republic, 146–3 BC*, 129–64. 2nd ed. Cambridge: Cambridge Univ. Press.

Højte, Jakob Munk, ed. 2009a. *Mithridates VI and the Pontic Kingdom*. Black Sea Studies 9. Aarhus, Denmark: Univ. of Aarhus Press.

———. 2009b. "The Death and Burial of Mithridates VI." In Højte 2009a.

———. 2009c. "Portraits and Statues of Mithridates VI Eupator: Royal Propaganda." In Højte 2009a.

Holland, Tom. 2003. *Rubicon: The Last Years of the Roman Republic*. New York: Random House.

Holt, Jim. 2006. "Math Murders." *New York Times Magazine*, March 12, 11–12.

Hopkins, Keith. 1978. *Conquerors and Slaves*. Cambridge: Cambridge Univ. Press

Hopkins, Mark. 1995. "Droplets of Life or Death: The Venom of Caucasian Vipers." *Azerbaijan International* 3, 2:30–31, 73.

Izady, Mehrdad R. 1992. *The Kurds: A Concise Handbook*. London: Taylor & Francis.

Jonassohn, K., and K. Solveig Bjornson. 1998. *Genocide and Gross Human Rights Violations in Comparative Perspective*. New Brunswick NJ: Transaction Publishers.

Jones, Christopher. 1987. "Stigma: Tattooing and Branding in Graeco-Roman Antiquity." *J Roman Studies* 77:139–55.

Kallet-Marx, R. 1995. *Hegemony to Empire: The Development of the Roman Imperium in the East from 148 to 62 BC*. Berkeley and Los Angeles: Univ. of California Press.

Kay, Philip. 2008. "Financial Meltdown in Republican Rome." Lecture, Oxford Roman Economy Project, November 28, http://oxrep.classics.ox.ac.uk/index .php

Keaveney, Arthur. 1992. *Lucullus: A Life*. London: Routledge.

———. 2005. *Sulla, the Last Republican*. London: Routledge.

Kesmedzhi, P. A. 2008. *Mitridat Evpator: Istoricheskii ocherk*. [Biography.] Simferopol, Ukraine: Krymuchpedgiz.

King, Charles. 2004. *The Black Sea: A History*. Oxford: Oxford Univ. Press.

Konstan, David. 2002. "Women, Ethnicity and Power in the Roman Empire." *Ordia Prima* 1:11–23.

Kopff, E. Christian. 2007. "Cicero and Tacitus on Empire: Roman Tradition and American Conceptions of Foreign Policy." Paper, Foreign Policy Research Institute, Philadelphia, September 20.

Kreuz, Patric-Alexander. 2009. "Monuments for the King." In Højte 2009a.

Kurkjian, Vahan M. 1958. *A History of Armenia*. N.p.: Armenian General Benevolent Society of America.

Kvideland, Reimund. 2006. "Legends Translated into Behaviour." *Fabula* 47: 255–63.

Lane Fox, Robin. 2004 [1994]. *Alexander the Great*. London: Penguin.

La Penna, Antonio. 2003. "La grande armatura di Mithridate: Nota a Sallustio, *Hist*. II Fr. 77 Maurenbrecher." *Maia-Rivista de Letterature Classiche* 55, 1 (January–April): 1–3.

Lee, John W. I. 2007. *A Greek Army on the March: Soldiers and Survival in Xenophon's Anabasis*. Cambridge: Cambridge Univ. Press.

Lee, Nathaniel. 1797 [1687]. *Mithridates, King of Pontus: A Tragedy*. London: Cawthorn.

Levy, Brooks. 1994. "Money for Mithridates?" *American J Archaeology* 98, 2:311.

Lewis, Bernard. 2001. *A Middle East Mosaic: Fragments of Life, Letters and History*. Modern Library

Lewis, Naphtali. 1976. *The Interpretation of Dreams and Portents*. Toronto: Hakkert.

Lewis, Naphtali, and Meyer Reinhold, eds. 1990. *Roman Civilization*, vol. 1, *Selected Readings: The Republic and the Augustan Age*. New York: Columbia Univ. Press.

Loewe, Michael. 1980. "The Han View of Comets." *Bulletin of the Museum of Far Eastern Antiquities* 52:1–31.

Logan, Nicole Prevost. 1994. "The View from Mount Mithridates." *Archaeology* (November–December): 69–75.

Magie, David. 1950. *Roman Rule in Asia Minor to the End of the Third Century after Christ*. 2 vols. Princeton: Princeton Univ. Press.

Majno, Guido. 1991 [1975]. *The Healing Hand: Man and Wound in the Ancient World*. Cambridge: Harvard Univ. Press.

Mallet, Paul Henri, and Sir Walter Scott. 1847 [1770]. *Northern Antiquities*. Trans. Bishop Thomas Percy. London: Bohn.

Marchant, Jo. 2008. "Archimedes and the 2000 Year Old Computer." *New Scientist* 2686 (December 12): 36–40.

Markey, Sean. 2003. "Ancient Greek Wreck Found in the Black Sea." *National Geographic News*, January 16.

Maskiell, M., and A. Mayor. 2001. "Killer Khilats, Part 1: Legends of Poisoned 'Robes of Honour' in India." *Folklore* 112:23–45.

Mastrocinque, Attilio. 1999. *Studi sulle guerre Mitridatiche*. Historia 124. Stuttgart: F. Steiner Verlag.

———. 2009. "The Antikythera Shipwreck and Sinope's Culture during the Mithridatic Wars." In Højte 2009a.

Matyszak, Philip. 2008. *Mithridates the Great, Rome's Indomitable Enemy*. London: Pen and Sword.

Mayor, Adrienne. 1999. "People Illustrated." *Archaeology* 52 (March/April): 54–57.

———. 2000. *The First Fossil Hunters*. Princeton: Princeton Univ. Press.

———. 2009 [2003]. *Greek Fire, Poison Arrows & Scorpion Bombs: Biological and Chemical Warfare in the Ancient World*. 2nd rev ed. New York: Overlook.

McCullough, Colleen. 1991. *The Grass Crown*. New York: William Morrow.

McGing, Brian C. 1986. *The Foreign Policy of Mithridates VI Eupator, King of Pontus*. Leiden: Brill.

———. 1998. "On the Fringes: Culture, History, and the Kingdom of Pontus." English abstract. *Vestnik Drevnei Istorii* [*J Ancient History*, Moscow] 37:112.

———. 2003. "Subjection and Resistance: To the Death of Mithridates." In *A Companion to Hellenistic History*, ed. A. Erskine, 71–89. Oxford: Blackwell.

———. 2009. "Mithradates VI Eupator: Victim or Aggressor?" In Høtje 2009a.

McNicoll, A. W., and N. P. Milner. 1997. *Hellenistic Fortifications from the Aegean to the Euphrates.* Oxford: Clarendon Press.

Merry, Robert W. 2005. *Sands of Empire: Missionary Zeal, American Foreign Policy, and the Hazards of Global Ambition.* New York: Simon and Schuster.

Metz, Martin; A. M. Piliponsky; C.-C. Chen, et al. 2006. "Mast Cells Can Enhance Resistance to Snake and Honeybee Venoms." *Science* 28, 313 (July): 526–30.

Mitchell, Stephen. 1995 [1993]. *Anatolia: Land, Men, and Gods in Asia Minor.* 2 vols. Oxford: Oxford Univ. Press.

Moore, L., B. Goodwin, S. Jones, et al. 2000. "St. John's Wort Induces Hepatic Drug Metabolism." *Proceedings of National Academy of Sciences* 97:7500–7502.

Munro, J. Arthur R. 1901. "Roads in Pontus, Royal and Roman." *Journal of Hellenic Studies* 21:52–66.

Ñaco del Hoyo, T., et al. 2009. "The Impact of the Roman Intervention in Greece and Asia Minor upon Civilians (88–63 BC)." In *Transforming Historical Landscapes in the Ancient Empires*, ed. B. Antela-Bernardez and T. Ñaco del Hoyo. Oxford: British Archaeological Reports, International Series.

Nappi, Carla. 2009. "Bolatu's Pharmacy: Theriac in Early Modern China." *Early Science and Medicine* (May).

Nazaryan, G. 2005. Armenian History of Tigranes the Great. ArmenianHighland .com.

Neverov, O. J. 1973. "Mithridates as Dionysus." *Soobshcheniya Gosudarstvennogo Ermitazha* 37:41–45.

Newman, Cathy. 2005. "Twelve Toxic Tales." *National Geographic* 207 (May): 2–31.

Norton, Stata. 2006. "The Pharmacology of Mithradatium: A 2000-Year-Old Remedy." *Molecular Interventions* 6:60–66.

Oberdorfer, Don. 2004. "Tet: Who Won?" *Smithsonian* (November): 117–23.

Oikonomides, A. N. 1962. "A Statuette of Mithridates the Great." *Archaeology* 15:13–15.

Olbrycht, Mark. 2009. "Mithridates Eupator and Iran." In Højte 2009a.

Pain, Stephanie. 2008. "From Poison to Plague: Mithridates's Marvelous Medicine." *New Scientist* (January 26): 52–53.

Parke, H. W. 1988. *Sibyls and Sibylline Prophecy in Classical Antiquity.* London: Routledge.

Peck, Henry Thurston. 1898. "Mithridates VI King of Pontus." *Harper's Dictionary of Classical Antiquities.* New York: Harper.

Pillonel, Cédric. 2005. "Les guerres mithridatiques: essai de quantification des armées pontiques." Univ. of Lausanne, Switzerland. www.strabon.ch/ mithridate/quantification/article.html

Polupudnev, V. 1993. *Mitridat: Istoricheskii roman.* [Historical novel.] Moscow: Izd-vo Kvorum.

Racine, Jean. 1965 [1673]. *Mithridate*. Ed. and comm. G. Rudler. Oxford: Blackwell.

Raffi, Aram. 1959 [1916]. "Armenia, Its Epics, Folk-Songs, and Mediaeval Poetry." Concluding essay in *Armenian Legends and Poems*, ed. Z. C. Boyajian. 2nd ed. London: Dent.

Raloff, Janet. 2005. "Plants Take Bite Out of Deadly Snake Venoms." *Science News* 167 (March 26): 206.

———. 2007. "Counterintuitive Toxicity." *Science News* 171 (January 20): 40–42.

Ramsey, John T. 1999. "Mithridates, the Banner of Ch'ih-yu, and the Comet Coin." *Harvard Studies in Classical Philology* 99:197–253.

———. 2007. "A Catalogue of Greco-Roman Comets from 500 B.C. to A.D. 400." *J History of Astronomy* 38:175–97. Also published in *Syllecta Classica*, special issue 17.

Rank, Otto, F.R.S. Raglan, and Alan Dundes. 1990. *In Quest of the Hero*. Princeton: Princeton Univ. Press.

Reinach, Théodore. 1890. *Mithridate Eupator, roi de Pont*. Paris: Firmin-Didot. Facsimile ed., Elibron Classics.

Richards, G. C. 1941. "Strabo: The Anatolian Who Failed of Roman Recognition." *Greece & Rome* 10, 29:79–90

Rigsby, Kent J. 1988. "Provincia Asia." *Transactions of the American Philological Association* 118:123–53.

———. 1996. *Asylia: Territorial Inviolability in the Hellenistic World*. Berkeley and Los Angeles: Univ. of California Press.

Root-Bernstein, Robert S. 1991. "Infectious Terrorism." *Atlantic Monthly* 267, 5 (May): 44–50.

Rostovtzeff, M. 1919. "Queen Dynamis of Bosporus." *J Hellenic Studies* 39: 88–109.

———. 1921. "South Russia in the Prehistoric and Classical Period." *American Historical Review* 26, 2:203–24.

———. 1932. "Mithridates." *Cambridge Ancient History*, vol. 9, ch. 5. Cambridge: Cambridge Univ. Press.

Sacks, Kenneth. 1990. *Diodorus Siculus and the First Century*. Princeton: Princeton Univ. Press.

Sadie, Stanley. 1972. "Note on Mozart's First Serious Opera." *Musical Times* 113:41–42.

Sagona, Antonio, and Claudia Sagona. 2005. *Archaeology at the North-East Anatolian Frontier, I: An Historical Geography and a Field Survey of the Bayburt Province*. Ancient Near Eastern Studies. Oakville CT: David Brown.

Samulev, V. F. 2004. *Tsar' Mitridat VI Evpator: Povesti I rasskazy*. [Novel.] Ialta, Ukraine: El'ga.

Sanford, Eva M. 1937. "Contrasting Views of the Roman Empire. *American J Philology* 58, 4:437–56.

———. 1950. "Roman Avarice in Asia." *J Near Eastern Studies* 9, 1:28–36.

Santangelo, Federico. 2007. *Sulla, the Elites, and the Empire: A Study of Roman Policies in Italy and the Greek East*. Leiden: Brill.

Saprykin, Sergey. 2004. "Unification of Pontus: Bronze Coins of Mithridates Eupator as Evidence of Commerce in the Euxine." Paper, Conference, Black Sea in Antiquity: Regional and Interregional Economic Exchanges, Sonderborg, Denmark, May 28.

———. 2009. "Religion and Cults of the Pontic Kingdom." In Højte 2009a.

Saprykin, S. Y., and A. A. Maslennikov. 1995. "Bosporan Chora in the Reign of Mithridates VI Eupator and His Immediate Successors, Part I." *Ancient Civilizations* 2, 3:261–81.

Sarikakis, Theodore. 1976. "Les Vespres Ephesiennes de l'an 88 av. J.C." *Epistemonike Epeteris tes Philosophikes* (Thessaloniki) 76:253–64.

Scarborough, John. 2007. "Attalus III of Pergamon: Research Toxicologist." Paper, 27th Annual Meeting of the Classical Association of South Africa, Cape Town, July 2–5.

———. 2008. "L. Aelius Gallus." In *Encyclopedia of Ancient Natural Scientists*, ed. P. Keyser and G. Irby-Massie, 34–35. London: Routledge.

Scheidel, Walter. 2005. "Human Mobility in Roman Italy, II: The Slave Population." *J Roman Studies* 95:64–79.

Scullard, H. H. 1970. *From the Gracchi to Nero: A History of Rome from 133 BC to AD 68*. 3rd ed. London: Butler and Tanner.

Selsky, A., and H. Loven. 2006. "Three Detainees Hanged Themselves." Associated Press news story, June 11.

Sheldon, Rose Mary. 2003. *Espionage in the Ancient World: An Annotated Bibliography*. Jefferson NC: McFarland.

———. 2005. *Intelligence Activities in Ancient Rome*. New York: Frank Cass.

Sherwin-White, A. N. 1977. "Ariobarzanes, Mithridates, and Sulla." *Classical Quarterly*, new ser., 27, 1:173–83.

———. 1994. "Lucullus, Pompey and the East." In *Cambridge Ancient History*, ed. J. A. Crook, A. Lintott, and E. Rawson, 229–55, vol. 9, *Last Age of the Roman Republic*. 2nd ed. Cambridge: Cambridge Univ. Press.

Singh, K. Gajendra. 2003. "West vs East, at Daggers Drawn." *Asia Times* (April 3).

———. 2006. "The Great Western Demonology Circus." Editorial. *Al-Jazeerah*, April 10. www.aljazeerah.info/Opinion

Sitwell, Nigel. 1986. *Outside the Empire: The World the Romans Knew*. London: Paladin.

Smith, William, ed. 1890 [1843]. *A Dictionary of Greek and Roman Antiquities*. London: John Murray.

Snaith, Guy, ed. 2007. *La Morte de Mitridate, by La Calprenede*. Critical Edition. University of Liverpool Online Series, French Texts. www.liv.ac.uk/soclas/los/index.htm

Sonnabend, H. 1998. "Ein Hannibal aus den Osten?" In *Alte Geschichte: Wege-Einsichten-Horizonte: Festshrift fur Eckart Olshausen zum 60. Geburtstag*, ed. U. Fellmeth and H. Sonnabend, 191–206. Zurich: Hildesheim.

Stoneman, Richard. 1987. *Across the Hellespont*. London: Hutchinson.

"Stopping Mithridates." 2005. Field Notes. *Odyssey* (March–April): 12.

Stothers, Richard. 2007. "Unidentified Flying Objects in Classical Antiquity." *Classical Journal* 103:79–92.

Strauss, Barry. 2004. *The Battle of Salamis*. New York: Simon and Schuster.

———. 2005. "The Agony of War under Oars." *Naval History* (February): 39–42.

———. 2009. *The Spartacus War*. New York: Simon and Schuster.

Stuart, David. 2004. *Dangerous Garden*. Cambridge: Harvard Univ. Press.

Sullivan, Richard. 1980. "The Dynasty of Cappadocia." In *Aufstieg und Niedergang de romische Welt/Rise and Fall of the Roman World*, 2. Principat, Band 7, ed. E. Temporini and W. Haase. Berlin and New York: De Gruyter.

Summerer, Lâtife. 2009. "The Search for Mithridates: Reception of Mithridates between the 15th and 20th Centuries." In Højte 2009a.

Swann, John P. 1985. "The Universal Drug: Theriac through the Ages." *Medical Heritage* 1, 6:456–58.

Talbert, Richard. 2000. *The Barrington Atlas of the Greek and Roman World*, and *Map-by-Map Directory*. 2 vols. Princeton: Princeton Univ. Press.

Tezcan, Mehmet. 2003. "The Iranian-Georgian Branch of the Silk Road, 1st to 4th centuries." Paper, 1st International Silk Road Symposium, Tbilisi, Georgia, June 25–27.

———. 2007. "Pontos Kralligi" ("Pontus Kingdom, 3rd c BC to 4th c AD"). In *The Pontos Question from the Beginning to the Present* (in Turkish), ed. V. Usta, 77–108. Serander.

Totelin, Laurence. 2004. "Mithradates' Antidote—A Pharmacological Ghost." *Early Science and Medicine* 9, 1:1–19.

Touwaide, Alain. 2008. "More Than the Sex of Angels." *History of Science Society Newsletter* (April): 4–13.

Traina, Giusto. 1995. "From Crimea to Syria: Re-defining the Alleged Historical Earthquake of 63 BC." *Annali di Geofisica* 38, 5–6:479–89.

Tsetskhladze, Gocha. 2001. *North Pontic Archaeology: Recent Discoveries and Studies*. Leiden: Brill.

Ussher, James. 2007 [1658 English, 1654 Latin]. *The Annals of the World*. Ed., rev., and updated by L. Pierce and M. Pierce. Green Forest AR: Master Books.

Utley, Francis Lee. 1965. *Lincoln Wasn't There, or Lord Raglan's Hero*. Washington, DC: College English Association.

Vogel, Gretchen. 2001. "How the Body's 'Garbage Disposal' May Inactivate Drugs." *Science* 291 (5 January): 35–37.

Vollenweider, Marie-Louise. 1995. "218–Mithridates vi assimilé à Alexandre le Grand." *Camées et intailles,* vol. 1, *Le Portraits grecs du Cabinet des médailles, Catalogue Raisonné.* Paris: Bibliothèque nationale de France.

Walbank, F. W. 1984. *A Historical Commentary on Polybius.* Vol. 2. Oxford: Clarendon Press.

Ward, John. 1749–50. "An Attempt to Explain an Antient Greek Inscription, Ingraven on a Curious Bronze Cup." *Philosophical Transactions* 46:488–99.

Warmington, B. H. 1969. *Nero: Reality and Legend.* New York: Norton.

Watson, G. 1966. *Theriac and Mithridatium: A Study in Therapeutics.* London: Wellcome Historical Medical Library.

Welles, C. Bradford. 1974 [1934]. *Royal Correspondence in the Hellenistic Period.* Chicago: Ares.

West, Stephanie. 2003. "The Most Marvelous of All Seas: The Greek Encounter with the Euxine." *Greece & Rome* 50, 2:151–67.

White, Matthew. 2002. "Body Count of the Roman Empire." www.users.erols .com/mwhite28/romestat.htm

Widengren, Geo. 1959. "The Sacral Kingship of Iran." In *The Sacral Kingship,* Studies in the History of Religions, suppl. 4. Leiden: Brill.

Wilbraham, Richard. 1839. *Travels in the Trans-Caucasian Provinces of Russia . . . 1837.* London: Murray.

Wynne-Tyson, E. 1972. *Mithras.* New York: Barnes & Noble.

Younger Edda (Snorre's Edda, Prose Edda). 1879. Ed. and trans. Edda Snorra Sturlusonar, Snorri Sturluson, and Rasmus Björn Anderson. N.p.: Griggs and Co.

Zammit-Maempel, G. 1978. "Handbills Extolling the Virtues of Fossil Sharks' Teeth." *Journal of Maltese Studies* 7:211–24.

Zin'ko, V. N. 2004. *Iz sobranija Kerc(hat)enskogo gosudarstbnnogo istoriko-kul'turnogo zapobednika, tom. 1, Antic(hat)naja skul'tura.* Kiev: Mistetstvo.

INDEX

Note: "M" indicates Mithradates. Page numbers in italic type indicate illustrations.